An Introduction to Operations Management

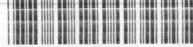

BUSINESS ADMINISTRATION SERIES

Consulting Editor: Gordon Anderson
                     University of Strathclyde

A Practical Introduction to Management Science   C.D.J. Waters

Published in association with the Strathclyde Business School

An Introduction to Operations Management

C.D.J. Waters
University of Calgary

 ADDISON-WESLEY PUBLISHING COMPANY

Wokingham, England · Reading, Massachusetts · Menlo Park, California
New York · Don Mills, Ontario · Amsterdam · Bonn · Sydney · Singapore
Tokyo · Madrid · San Juan · Milan · Paris · Mexico City · Seoul · Taipei

© 1991 Addison-Wesley Publishers Ltd.
© 1991 Addison-Wesley Publishing Company Inc.

Many of the designations used by manufacturers and sellers to distinguish their
products are claimed as trademarks. Addison-Wesley has made every attempt to
supply trademark information about manufacturers and their products mentioned in
this book.

Cover designed by Crayon Design of Henley-on-Thames and
printed by The Riverside Printing Co. (Reading) Ltd.
Typeset by V.A.P. Publishing Services, Kidlington, Oxford.
Printed in Great Britain by The Bath Press, Avon.

First printed 1991

British Library Cataloguing in Publication Data
Waters, C. D. J.
  An introduction to operations management.
  1. Production. Management
  I. Title II. Series
  658.5

  ISBN 0 – 201 – 41678 – 6

Library of Congress Cataloging in Publication Data
Waters, C. D. J. (C. Donald J.), 1949 –
  An introduction to operations management / C. D. J. Waters.
    p.   cm.
  Includes bibliographical references and index.
  ISBN 0 – 201 – 41678 – 6 :
  1. Production management. I. Title.
TS155.W395   1991
658.5—dc20

90 – 28254
CIP

To Lyn

Preface

Operations management

This book gives an introduction to operations management. To appreciate the scope of this subject we need to define the purpose of organizations. In essence, every organization takes a number of inputs and transforms these to outputs. Assembly plants transform components and raw materials into finished products, hospitals transform sick patients into healthy ones, power stations transform fuel into electricity, and so on. These transformations are achieved by operations. Then, operations management is concerned with the way operations are planned, organized and controlled.

At the core of every organization is a set of operations. This means that operations management is a broad subject that is important for all organizations. It gives the foundations on which all other decisions are based.

In recent years operations management has become increasingly important. There are several reasons for this, ranging from improvements in manufacturing processes to increasing competition and changing consumer expectations. Perhaps the key feature is the realization that an organization's continuing success depends almost entirely on its products.

Early books on operations management concentrated on manufacturing industry. It was soon realized, however, that industrialized countries get about 80% of their GNP from the service sector. This encouraged operations management to expand into new areas, and discuss all types of industry from primary to services.

There are a number of subjects related to operations management. Management science, for example, looks at the use of the scientific method in decision making. This is described in a companion book, *A Practical Introduction to Management Science* by C.D.J. Waters, published by Addison-Wesley. Production management concentrates on manufacturing industry, industrial engineering takes a technical view of the process used, and operational research is becoming increasingly mathematical.

Audience

Management education is a priority in many countries. In the United States a quarter of all graduates are in management or business subjects. Any reputable course in management must cover operations management, and the American Assembly of Collegiate Schools of Business requires it in all accredited schools.

This text gives a broad introduction to operations management. It is aimed at all students of management, business or related subjects who are doing a first level course. These students might be undergraduates taking either general courses or more specialized business ones. Undergraduates in other disciplines, such as engineering, may also need an introductory text for a minor course in operations management. The book could be used by many postgraduate courses in business studies, including general MBAs or specialized postgraduate/post-experience courses in management, engineering or other disciplines. Overall, the book would be useful to anyone wanting an introduction to operations management.

Content

Any introductory book on operations management must take a specific view-point or it would be unacceptably long. In this book we have concentrated on the development of a product and the rational analyses which help with this. We have taken a broad view of the subject, without concentrating on one area at the expense of others. A range of applications and industries is considered.

Some of the analyses described use quantitative arguments, but this certainly does not mean it is a branch of applied mathematics. All the analyses described are widely used in practice, and principles are illustrated by examples rather than theoretical argument. There is almost no mathematical prerequisite for the book, except the ability to manipulate algebraic equations. A passing knowledge of probabilities and the Normal distribution would be an advantage.

The contents of the book follow a logical path through the decisions faced when making a product. Chapter 1 starts by defining operations management and discussing its role in the decision making of an organization. The next few chapters look at some strategic decisions, answering questions about what product is made, how much of it is made, where it is made, and how it is made. Thus, Chapter 2 discusses product planning, which decides what product to supply. Chapter 3 considers how much to make by examining demand forecasting. The next question is where to make the product, which is considered in Chapter 4 which examines aspects of facility location.

Chapter 5 considers how a product is made by considering process planning and design. The process has an effect on facilities layout, which is described in Chapter 6. There must be enough capacity to meet demand, while utilization and productivity measure the efficiency with which this capacity is used. These related topics are discussed in Chapter 7. High productivity can be achieved by careful planning and scheduling of work. Methods for this are described in Chapter 8. Much planning is concerned with one-off projects and methods for this are outlined in Chapter 9.

Production plans can be used to determine the requirements for materials. In recent years, material requirements planning has become widely used, as described in Chapter 10. This is followed by a discussion of stockless production made possible by just-in-time systems. Most inventories are not suitable for these approaches to stock control, so alternative procedures are described in Chapter 11.

A key requirement in stockless production is total reliability of supplies. This, and increasing competition, has increased the emphasis on quality assurance, which is discussed in Chapter 12.

Finally, a brief review of topics is given in Chapter 13.

Format

Each chapter uses a consistent format. This starts with a list of contents. A synopsis outlines the material to be covered and then a set of objectives lists the specific things a reader should be able to do by the end of the chapter. This is followed by the main material of the chapter, divided into coherent sections. Summaries and self assessment questions ensure the material is being understood, while worked examples are used to illustrate the methods. Each chapter has a conclusion to summarize the main points, followed by a set of numerical problems. Most of the chapters have a case study to set the context in which decisions are made. These cases show how the principles described in the chapter can be applied to real problems. Solutions to self assessment questions and references for further reading are given at the ends of chapters.

Many people have access to computers. The book does not assume that everyone has a computer, but many of the calculations can be done most easily using standard packages. A variety of spreadsheet packages can also be used for some of the analyses.

It is worth mentioning the notation used for calculations. This is based on computer notation where arithmetic operators are given explicitly ($+$, $-$, $*$ and $/$) while variables are given upper case names. Sometimes there are standard names for variables, and where appropriate these have been used.

C.D.J. Waters
Calgary, February 1991

Contents

Contents

Contents

Contents

Chapter 1

Introduction to operations management

SYNOPSIS

This chapter gives an overview of operations management (OPMA). It starts by showing that the efficiency of an organization depends on the quality of its management. This observation, together with increasing competition, has encouraged the development of operations management.

All organizations can be viewed as transformers of various inputs to useful outputs. 'Operations' are the processes that achieve these transformations. Operations management tries to ensure that the transformations are organized as efficiently as possible.

Operations management is a broad subject, and we must take a specific viewpoint. This book emphasizes its role in the management of work (rather than people). Most of this occurs at an organizational level, but the accumulated effects have an impact nationally. Japan is an obvious example of a country that is prospering largely because individual companies have adopted good operations management practices.

All organizations can be described as having three central functions. Operations management is one of these, together with sales/marketing and accounting/finance. Other views of OPMA look at the jobs done by operations managers, the areas in which decisions are made and the approach to decision making.

Although there are some differences between manufacturing and service organizations, there are many similarities. These allow operations management to tackle problems in a range of organizations.

Decisions are made at several levels in an organization, and we differentiate strategic, tactical and operational ones. The context for all decisions is set by an organization's mission, which describes its overall beliefs and aims. This leads to other strategic decisions, which may be about the organization as a whole (defining corporate strategy) or within functional areas.

Operations management is concerned with decisions at all levels, and we illustrate its scope as ranging from long-term facility location to short-term production scheduling. Ultimately, all decisions lead to a product that satisfies customer demand.

OBJECTIVES

After reading this chapter and completing the exercises you should be able to:

- outline the way national economies develop;
- define 'operations' and 'operations management';
- say why operations management has been given more attention in recent years;
- appreciate the role of organizations as transformers of inputs to outputs, and the function of operations management in this transformation;
- describe operations management as a central function in an organization (along with sales/marketing and accounting/finance);
- describe operations management as a profession, by its approach to solving problems or by the type of problems it tackles;
- discuss the differences between manufacturing and service organizations;
- appreciate the different levels of decision making in an organization;
- understand how an organization's mission, corporate strategy and other decisions are related;
- describe some strategic, tactical and operational OPMA decisions;
- discuss competitive strategy and focus.

1.1 OPERATIONS MANAGEMENT

1.1.1 Background

In the eighteenth century Britain underwent a profound change that became known as the industrial revolution. During this period the country moved from an agricultural economy to an industrial one, with:

- the establishment of industry in factories; and
- the introduction of machines to do work.

Since this revolution, most manufacturing facilities have been organized into large units that are efficient at making a range of products.

The industrial revolution was made possible by a series of inventions and technological developments. Perhaps the best known of these is the improved steam engine of James Watt. About the same time Hargreaves invented the spinning jenny, Cartwright the power loom, Maudsley the screw-cutting lathe, and so on. For the next century manufacturers relied on continuously improving technology to increase productivity and output.

It was 100 years later, at the turn of the twentieth century, that people began to study the management and operations of factories. Frederick Taylor, for example, developed work measurement and 'scientific management' in the 1890s. Other work was done by Frank and Lillian Gilbreth (motion study, effects of fatigue, etc.), Gantt (Gantt chart) and Barth (wage incentive schemes). These studies clearly showed that the productivity of organizations depended both on the technology available and how this technology was managed. This recognition laid the foundation of operations management. In essence, operations management tries to ensure that organizations are run as efficiently as possible.

The industrial revolution spread to other countries, and manufacturing output soon became a measure of national wealth. 'Developed' economies were differentiated from 'developing' ones by the amount of goods they produced. This acceptance of manufacturing as the dominant sector in an economy is now seen as one step in economic development. Current opinion suggests three such stages.

(1) In the first stage, economic activity is concentrated in the primary industries of agriculture, mining, quarrying, forestry, and so on.

(2) As the economy develops it moves towards an industrial base with emphasis on the secondary industries of manufacturing and construction.

(3) As prosperity (measured in terms of goods available) increases, economic activity moves to the service sector of government, education, health, retailing, catering, and so on.

Most countries of the world still have economies that are based on primary industries and are 'developing' by encouraging secondary ones. Western Europe, North America, Japan and some other countries are in the 'post-industrial' tertiary stage. These have very few people employed in primary industries (perhaps 5% of the workforce) and a decreasing number in manufacturing (perhaps 20%): the remaining 75% work in service industries.

In recent years many industrialized countries have been concerned by their declining share of world trade. In one sense this is inevitable as developing countries take a larger share of markets and become relatively more prosperous. The United States, for example, currently has 5% of the world's population but produces a quarter of its goods and services. In the long run, it is inevitable that other countries will become relatively more prosperous, not at the expense of the United States but by reducing the differences between them.

What caused more concern was the observation that some industrialized countries were continuing to increase their share of world trade. An obvious example is Japan, whose GNP per capita has now grown to overtake all other manufacturing countries and shows no sign of slowing down. Although many reasons can be suggested for this economic success, it has become increasingly clear that the success of many companies in these countries is largely a result of better organization and management.

Some countries responded to increasing international competition by protectionism, where local manufacturers were given preferential treatment. In the longer term it was recognized that steps must be taken to improve domestic production, and management education is now widely seen as a priority. Up to a quarter of graduates in the United States, for example, are in management or business subjects. It is also recognized that improved management must extend beyond the traditional area of manufacturing, and must include the service sector. This obvious need for efficient management has encouraged the study of operations management.

In summary
The efficiency of an organization largely depends on the quality of its management. Developments in the past few years, particularly increasing international competition, have emphasized the need for good management. Operations management can play a key role in this.

SELF ASSESSMENT QUESTIONS

1.1 What stages do national economies go through as they develop?

1.2 Most people in the world work in manufacturing industry. Is this statement:

(a) true
(b) false
(c) cannot say?

1.3 Why has interest in operations management increased in recent years?

1.1.2 Definition of operations management

In the last section we said that operations management is concerned with the efficient running of an organization. We also implied that:

* the efficiency of an organization depends on the way it is managed;
* good management is based on a range of knowledge and skills, rather than intuition and guesswork.

We can now develop this theme, starting with a formal definition.

> Operations management is concerned with all activities involved in making a product or providing a service: it is responsible for the transformation of various kinds of inputs to useful outputs.

This definition is based on the principle that all organizations can be viewed as transformers of inputs to outputs. They take various inputs (raw materials, money, people, machine time, and so on) and perform operations (manufacturing, assembly, packing, etc.) that convert these into outputs (goods, services, etc.). To give specific examples:

- a car assembly plant takes inputs of components, energy, robots, people, and so on; it performs operations of welding, assembly, painting, finishing, etc.; the outputs are cars, spare parts, wages, etc.;

- a restaurant takes inputs of a kitchen, customers, waiters, food, drinks, tables, etc.; it does operations of food preparation, cooking, serving, etc.; outputs include prepared food and (hopefully) satisfied customers.

The operations in an organization answer the question: 'What does the organization do?' Operations in General Motors, for example, centre around making cars; IBM makes and sells computers; hospitals cure sick people; schools teach children; banks borrow and lend money. Some more examples of this are shown in Table 1.1.

Operations management (OPMA) is concerned with the planning, direction and control of these operations. The examples show how OPMA is concerned with all kinds of organization from primary industry (agriculture, mining, quarrying, etc.) through secondary (construction, manufacturing, etc.) to tertiary (the service sector). It is important to emphasize, therefore, that 'products' can be either goods or services, and 'operations' are the processes by which either of these is produced.

Now we can develop a schematic view of operations management, as shown in Figure 1.1. This shows managers making the decisions which keep an organization working effectively. These decisions affect inputs, operations and outputs, with feedback on performance and other relevant information used to update future decisions.

Three other elements can be added to this diagram:

- customers and clients who receive the outputs, give comments and opinions, stimulate demand, etc.

- an external environment in which the organization operates, including competitors, government, national priorities, etc.

- the separation of 'operations' into a series of connected processes rather than a single step.

Table 1.1 Some examples of inputs, operations and outputs.

Organization	Inputs	Operations	Outputs
Farm	Seeds, fertilizer, fields, animals, machinery	Planting, growing, harvesting, milking, shearing	Cereals, milk, wool, meat
Coal mine	Miners, coal seam, tools, explosives, transport	Extraction, removing waste, cleaning, delivery	Coal, waste, wages
Oil refinery	Crude oil, chemicals, energy	Refining, distribution, processing	Petrol, oil, plastics
Car assembly plant	Components, raw materials, energy, robots, people, money	Assembly, welding, painting, finishing	Cars, wages, spare parts
Brewery	Hops, water, cans, grain, bottles, skills, experience	Preparing, mixing, brewing, canning, bottling, selling	Bottled and canned beer
Restaurant	Kitchen, utensils, food, drinks, customers, waiters	Preparation, cooking, serving	Food, contented customers
Hospital	Patients, staff, beds, medicines, equipment	Surgical operations, treatment, monitoring	Healthy patients, information
Retail shop	Goods, customers, space, servers	Selling, marketing, advising, packing	Purchases, satisfied customers
Airline	Planes, terminals, passengers, agents	Booking tickets, flying, entertaining	Satisfied passengers, goods moved

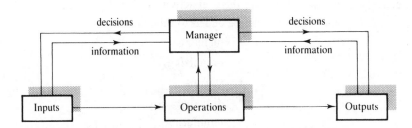

Figure 1.1 Schematic of operations management.

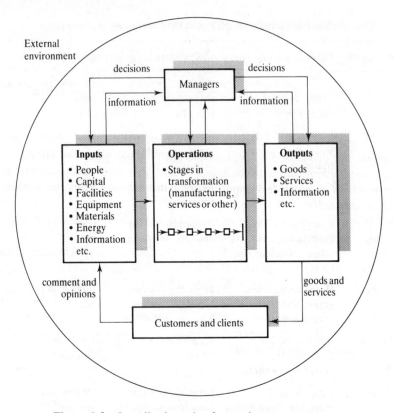

Figure 1.2 Overall schematic of operations management.

Adding these elements gives the overall picture of operations management shown in Figure 1.2.

We have now defined operations management as the function that is responsible for all decisions relating to the transformation of various inputs to useful outputs. The rest of this book looks at specific areas where decisions are made. Chapter 2 describes problems of product planning, Chapter 3 shows how demand can be forecast, Chapter 4 looks at location decisions, and so on. These are based on the general principle that managers are the decision makers in an organization. They ensure that the organization functions efficiently and effectively, and this will involve them in activities like:

- planning
- organizing
- staffing
- directing
- monitoring
- controlling

One useful distinction can be made between:

- management of people (personnel, rewards, grievances, industrial relations, etc.); and
- management of work (production schedules, planned maintenance, productivity, capacity, etc.).

Operations management is a broad subject and we must take a specific viewpoint. For this reason we will concentrate on those aspects of OPMA that are concerned with the management of work. This does not mean that the management of people is less important, only that we have deliberately taken a different approach.

We will also emphasize the role of operations management within individual organizations. All organizations have operations and should be concerned with their efficient management. We have already implied, though, that OPMA can have a much broader influence. If the majority of organizations in a country are run efficiently, they should produce attractive products that satisfy international demand. Such countries should expect their trade and prosperity to increase. Japan is an obvious example of a country that put considerable emphasis on operations management, and quickly moved to become a major centre of manufacturing and one of the world's dominant economies.

In summary

The operations within an organization transform inputs to outputs. Operations management is concerned with all the activities involved in such transformations. It is a wide subject that is relevant to all sectors of the economy. We will emphasize its role in the management of work at an organizational level.

SELF ASSESSMENT QUESTIONS

1.4 What is meant by 'operations'?

1.5 Define 'operations management'.

1.6 Look at an organization with which you are familiar and list the inputs, operations and outputs.

1.7 Is it true that operations management is only concerned with individual organizations?

1.1.3 Operations management as a central function

It is often said that the main purpose of an organization is to meet customer demand. The incentive for meeting demand is profit, and the method is through a product. Although this is a simplified view, it is useful for identifying the three

Table 1.2 Some examples of the central functions in organizations.

Organization	Sales and marketing	Operations	Accounting and finance
Brewery	Advertising, marketing, distribution	Brewing, packaging, delivery	Attracting investment, recording costs
Car assembly plant	Advertising, marketing, dealerships	Assemble cars, provide spares	Control investments, pay suppliers
Hospital	Publicity, public relations	Treatment, research, training	Pay staff, running costs, donations
Retail shop	Sales, advertising, purchasing	Selling, stockholding, delivering	Record costs, pay suppliers, collect cash
Airline	Sales, advertising, franchises	Flight ops., ground ops., engineering	Collect fares, pay expenses, buy planes
University	Marketing, publicity, recruitment	Teach, research, consulting	Pay staff, collect fees, plan changes

central functions of an organization:

- sales/marketing, which identifies demand, takes orders, and so on;
- operations management, which makes the required products by transforming a range of inputs;
- accounting/finance, which organizes and controls the flow of money.

These terms are used in a very broad sense, so the sales and marketing function is concerned with all aspects of identifying and creating demand, advertising, taking orders, ensuring products are passed to customers, follow-up, and so on; the accounting and finance function includes all aspects of raising funds, keeping track of transactions, collecting money, paying bills, maintaining accounts, and so on.

These central functions are *directly* concerned with the product. Many other functions are needed for the smooth running of an organization (personnel, catering, computer services, secretarial, etc.) but these either can be included in one of the central functions or are *not directly* concerned with the product. Table 1.2 shows some examples of the central functions in different organizations.

The three central functions exist in all organizations, but the emphasis put on each will vary. A manufacturing company, for example, might emphasize operations management, but must still market its products and control its finances. A brewery might emphasize sales and marketing, but must still have

Table 1.3 Percentage of chief executives in the United States with different backgrounds.

Operations	35%
Finance	25%
Marketing	20%
Research	10%
Law, etc.	10%

efficient operations and control its accounts. It would be fair to say that during the 1970s there was a tendency for companies to emphasize marketing, while the 1980s saw a move towards stronger financial management (including mergers and takeovers). More recently there has been a growing realization that the long-term survival of any organization depends on its ability to satisfy customer demand. In other words, the product is of paramount importance. One result of this realization is a growing emphasis on operations management. Some evidence for this comes from surveys of chief executives in the United States, which suggest that promotions are being made from the backgrounds shown in Table 1.3.

In summary

Operations management is a central function in organizations, along with sales/marketing and accounting/finance.

SELF ASSESSMENT QUESTIONS

1.8 What are the central functions within an organization?

1.9 Describe the central functions in an organization with which you are familiar.

1.10 Why is personnel management not considered a central function?

1.1.4 Other views of operations management

So far we have described operations management as a function within an organization. We could have taken other views, perhaps describing it as:

- a profession;
- using a specific approach to tackle management problems;
- looking at decisions in specific areas.

Most of this book describes how operations management looks at decision making in specific areas. We will examine decisions in product planning, process design, facility location, and so on. The remainder of this section briefly describes the alternative views.

Operations management as a profession

Most of the early studies in management looked for ways of improving the efficiency of manufacturing industries. These studies eventually became formalized in a number of related disciplines called 'manufacturing science', 'industrial engineering' and, most popularly, 'production management'. Typically, manufacturing companies would employ production managers to look after their operations. Later studies of management looked at the service sector, and the equivalent of a production manager became known as an operations manager. Then, the efficiency of a factory would depend on a production manager, while the efficiency of a transport fleet would depend on an operations manager. In recent years the obvious similarities between operations in manufacturing and service industries have led to the general title 'operations manager'.

Operations occur in so many diverse circumstances that we might be tempted to say, 'operations management is what operations managers do'. This seems an unhelpful remark, but it reinforces the wide range of jobs in OPMA. If someone tells us he or she is a solicitor or an editor, we have a good idea of what that entails, but would find it difficult to offer a precise definition of the job. Similarly, if someone tells us he or she is an operations manager we know that, in general terms, it involves managing a central function in his or her organization, ensuring its efficiency and effectiveness.

The diversity of jobs and organizations means that 'operations managers' are given a variety of titles including production manager, plant manager, site manager, materials controller, operations analyst, inventory controller, scheduler, shop manager, matron, postmaster, chef, supervisor, headmaster, transport manager, factory superintendent, maintenance manager, quality assurance engineer, production engineer, management scientist, and so on.

The OPMA approach to problems

Another view of operations management would be to consider the way it tackles problems. This typically consists of four stages:

(1) *Observation stage*, where it is realized that a problem exists and something must be done to improve matters; the problem is examined, data is collected, objectives are set, context is considered, various ideas are discussed, and so on.

(2) *Formulation stage*, where data is analysed, alternative courses of action are suggested and models built.

(3) *Analysis stage*, where alternative actions are analysed, solutions are

found and tested, values are given to parameters, additional data is collected and recommendations are made.

(4) *Implementation stage*, where final decisions about solutions are made, the solution is implemented, actual performance is monitored, feedback is given to management, models are kept up to date, etc.

This approach is not unique to OPMA, but is a widely used method of tackling problems. A more formal approach has been described in operational research methodology as:

- identify the problem
- formulate a model
- test the model
- obtain solutions to the model
- test and control the solutions
- implement the solution.

It is clear that an important part of the OPMA approach is its use of a model to describe the features of a problem. These models are simplified representations of reality and are often quantitative. A typical model could represent the number of units produced by a variable, N, and the price charged for each unit by another variable, P, so that the revenue generated is given by:

$$\text{Revenue} = N * P$$

If the average cost of making each unit is C, with other fixed costs of F, the model can be extended to give:

$$\text{Profit} = N * (P - C) - F$$

There are many benefits from using such models. The most important is that behaviour can be predicted without actually observing or interrupting the system. If, for example, the system outlined above has $N = 100$, $P = 8$, $C = 7$ and $F = 50$, we can predict the profit as:

$$\begin{aligned}\text{Profit} &= N * (P - C) - F \\ &= 100 * (8 - 7) - 50 \\ &= 50\end{aligned}$$

We can find this without having to change and observe the actual system, measure the results or disrupt it in any way. We can also perform experiments, to find say, the effects of changing P to 9:

$$\text{Profit} = 100 * (9 - 7) - 50 = 150$$

This is particularly beneficial when a proposed change would give a loss; the model can predict this, without actually changing the system and suffering the consequences.

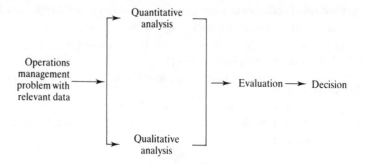

Figure 1.3 Use of both quantitative and qualitative analyses in OPMA.

Although many OPMA models are quantitative, they are not invariably so. There are many situations where numerical arguments are either inappropriate or impossible. When discussing restaurants, newspapers or cars, for example, we may feel that one has a higher quality than another, but it would be difficult to put a numerical value to this judgement. It is important to keep this principle in mind. Quantitative analyses do not give the whole answer but they give one view, which should be considered along with all other views. Managers should consider all available information when making decisions (see Figure 1.3).

Operations management decision areas

Another way we could look at operations management would be to list the type of problem tackled or the area where problems occur. This approach is developed in the following chapters.

In summary

There are many different views of operations management. We have now described it as a central function in an organization, as a profession and by the approach it uses, and will shortly describe the problem areas it tackles. The overall aim of OPMA is to find practical solutions to real problems. This usually involves a combination of quantitative and qualitative analyses.

SELF ASSESSMENT QUESTIONS

1.11 How could you define operations management in four different ways?

1.12 List ten different titles for 'operations managers' that you are familiar with.

1.13 Why does OPMA use models?

1.14 Operations management is only concerned with quantitative models. Is this:

(a) true
(b) false
(c) partly true?

1.2 OPERATIONS MANAGEMENT IN SERVICES

We have already emphasized the fact that operations management is concerned with all sectors of industry. As most people in developed countries work in the service sector, it is worth mentioning some ways in which organizations here differ from those in manufacturing. Some of the key distinctions include the following:

Characteristics of services
- The product is intangible.
- Services cannot be kept in stock.
- Products vary and cannot be mass produced.
- There is high customer contact.
- Customers participate in the service.
- Facilities are located near to customers.
- Services are labour intensive.
- Quality is difficult to measure.
- Quality depends largely on the server.

An assumption behind this list is that the service sector consists of fairly homogeneous organizations that are significantly different to manufacturing organizations. In practice this is not true. Service industries are certainly not homogeneous, and there is, for example, a range of size from national governments down to individuals. One classification of these would be the following:

- Public services provided by national and local government (such as defence, social services, health and education).
- Retail and wholesale shops.
- Distribution services for both goods and information (such as transport, mail, libraries and newspapers).
- Non-profit services (such as charities and churches).
- Other services for industry (including finance, legal and a variety of professional services).
- Other services for individuals (including leisure, banking and domestic services).

The other assumption, that service organizations are different to manufacturing ones, must also be questioned. A restaurant, for example, provides a service, but at the same time it 'manufactures' meals; a television company produces both products (programmes) and services (transmissions); a washing machine manufacturer provides an after-sales service. Almost all organizations supply products that are a combination of manufactured goods and services.

The conclusions we can draw is that many organizations contain basic similarities. Then, the problem of, say, locating facilities is fundamentally the same whether the organization is primarily making goods or providing a service. These similarities allow operations management to tackle a range of problems met in widely differing industries.

In summary

Although there are some differences between service and manufacturing organizations, there are many points in common. This allows operations management to tackle problems in a variety of organizations.

SELF ASSESSMENT QUESTIONS

1.15 In what way are service industries fundamentally different to manufacturing ones?

1.16 How can services be classified?

1.17 Operations management is another name for production management. Is this statement true or false?

1.3   DECISION MAKING IN ORGANIZATIONS

Earlier in this chapter we said that management was essentially concerned with the decision making within an organization. In this section we develop this idea by looking at the types of decisions made by managers, starting with a description of the different levels at which decisions are made.

1.3.1 Levels of decision in an organization

Some decisions are very important to an organization, with consequences felt for many years in the future: others are minor, with consequences felt over days or even hours. A standard classification reflects this importance by describing decisions as strategic, tactical or operational (see Table 1.4).

A useful analogy for the levels of decision shown in Table 1.4 considers a small boat. The captain (representing top management) examines charts and decides where the boat should go; the helmsman (representing middle management) is directed by the captain and steers the boat: a crewman (junior management) rows the boat to make sure it keeps moving.

Table 1.4 Levels of decisions in organizations.

- *Strategic decisions* are made by senior management; they are long term, use many resources and involve high risk.

- *Tactical decisions* are made by middle management; they are medium term, use fewer resources and involve less risk.

- *Operational decisions* are made by junior or supervisory management: they are short term, use few resources and involve low risk.

The different levels of decision can be illustrated by some examples:

- For a manufacturer, a decision to build a new factory five or ten years in the future is strategic; a decision to introduce a new product one or two years in the future is tactical; a decision about the number of units of a product to make next week is operational.

- In a university, a decision about whether to concentrate on post-graduate education in the next few years is strategic; whether to run a particular post-graduate course in one or two years is tactical; choosing someone to teach a course next week is operational.

- For a railway, a decision about whether to continue a passenger service to an area is strategic; whether to structure the fares to attract business or leisure passengers is tactical; finalizing short-term crew schedules is operational.

We must be somewhat vague about these terms because they vary so much between organizations. In electricity generation, for example, a strategic decision might concern the building of new power stations, look 20 years or more into the future and involve expenditure of hundreds of millions of pounds. A strategic decision for a small retail shop might look one or two years into the future and involve expenditure of a few thousand pounds. The important point is that decisions are needed at different levels, with some general features shown in Table 1.5.

Table 1.5 Summary of decision characteristics.

Decision	Strategic	Tactical	Operational
Level of manager	Senior	Middle	Junior
Importance	High	Medium	Low
Resources used	Many	Some	Few
Timescale	Long	Medium	Short
Risk	High	Medium	Low
Amount of detail	Very general	Moderate	Very detailed
Data	Uncertain	Some	Certain
Structure	Unstructured	Some	Structured
Focus	Whole organization	Parts	Individual units

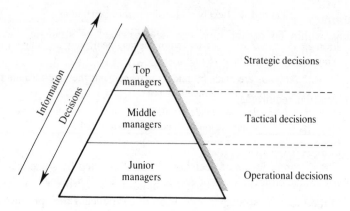

Figure 1.4 Levels of decision and information flow.

Senior managers make the strategic decisions that set an organization on its course. These decisions are not an end in themselves, but are the beginning of a planning process that filters down through the entire organization. Strategic decisions provide the environment in which lower level decisions are made; they are passed down to middle management and provide the constraints and objectives for their more detailed tactical decisions. These, in turn, are passed down to provide the constraints and objectives for the detailed operational decisions made by junior managers. The result is a hierarchy of decisions shown in Figure 1.4.

While decisions are passed downwards through the management hierarchy, information about actual performance and other feedback is passed upwards. This information must be filtered and summarized as it passes up the hierarchy, or top managers would be swamped by an excess of detailed, irrelevant information. This filtering is often difficult as it needs a compromise between passing too little information to be useful and too much to reveal overall patterns.

This exchange of information and decisions should allow consistent and achievable objectives to be set for each part of the organization. In particular there should be no conflicts between decisions at different levels. In practice, many organizations are so segmented that it is difficult to get all parts working towards the same strategic aims. Conversely, other organizations are so simple that the flows of information and decision need not be formalized, but occur naturally. A family is an example of a small organization that makes strategic, tactical and operational decisions, but there is seldom any need to set up a formal decision-making procedure.

Many organizations have adopted an overriding statement of their objectives which can be called a 'mission'. This sets the organization on its overall course, and allows a corporate strategy to be defined. This is discussed in the following section.

In summary
Decisions within an organization can be described as strategic, tactical or operational. Strategic decisions are made by senior management, involve more resources, more risk and a long timespan. By implication they are also less structured, look at the whole organization and have less well defined objectives and information requirements.

SELF ASSESSMENT QUESTIONS

1.18 What are the different levels of decision made in an organization?

1.19 Tactical decisions are most important to an organization because they concern its day-to-day running. Is this statement:

(a) true
(b) false
(c) partly true?

1.20 What kind of decision is:

(a) finding the best location for a new factory
(b) deciding how many hours of overtime are needed next week
(c) deciding whether to start making computers
(d) deciding whether to publish a proposed textbook?

1.21 Describe some decisions at different levels in an organization with which you are familiar.

1.3.2 Corporate strategy and the mission

In the last section we saw how decisions are made at various levels within an organization. In this section we will discuss some of the strategic decisions that determine the overall course of an organization, starting with the 'mission'.

Many organizations have some overriding statement of their purpose which, either explicitly or implicitly, defines their overall mission. Some examples are:

- a university might describe its mission as discovering and disseminating knowledge;
- a bank might safeguard and increase the value of its customers' investments;
- a manufacturer might supply high quality products to a wide market, while ensuring a satisfactory profit;
- a television network might entertain, inform and educate the widest possible audience.

These statements say something about the fundamental beliefs and aims of an organization, and look for answers to questions like, 'What is our purpose?', 'What business are we in?' and 'What are our overall objectives?'.

Sometimes the mission is a very formal statement, which includes the organization's responsibilities to its shareholders, employees, customers, community, and so on. Often, however, the mission is not formally stated, but is implicit from the actions of senior management.

The mission sets the context of all other decisions within an organization. Once it is defined, other strategic decisions can be made about the organization as a whole. These might include the structure of the organization, where it operates, what its relations are with other organizations, how it treats customers, and so on. These strategic decisions form the 'corporate strategy', and might include decisions about:

- competitive strategy
- level of technology used
- product or process focus
- geographical area of operation
- financial objectives
- marketing objectives.

We will return to some of these later, but this is a convenient point to discuss two of them, competitive strategy and focus.

Competitive strategy
An organization's mission effectively defines its competition, which consists of those who are currently supplying similar products and those who might start supplying similar ones in the future. An obvious step is to assess the strengths and weaknesses of competitors. If, for example, a company is good at providing a high quality product, while most of the competition is aiming for lower quality, its strategy is clear. It should produce the best product available, and this usually implies a low volume with high unit cost.

This illustrates the principle behind a competitive strategy, which searches for a favourable position in the industry. Such favourable positions can be found by cost leadership (providing the same products cheaper) or product differentiation (providing different products).

The characteristics of the industry in which an organization operates are, of course, important. A favourable position in a poor industry could give worse results than an unfavourable position in a good one. At the same time there are important considerations for competition, particularly as some industries have high entry barriers. A new company could not enter the mass-produced car market, for example, without spending hundreds of millions of pounds on equipment and research. Conversely, there are many kinds of consultant who can start operating in a very small way with almost no expenditure.

Other questions about competitive strategy are:

- What is our industry like?
- What are the future prospects?

- What are our strengths?
- Who are the competitors?
- What are the competitors' strengths?
- What flexibility do we have?

The answers to these suggest a range of more detailed questions like:

- What products should we concentrate on?
- What volumes should we produce?
- What quality should we provide?
- Do we supply low or high cost products?
- Are our products reliable?
- Do we give fast deliveries?
- Who are our biggest customers?
- Do we have adequate financing?

At this stage the decisions are becoming more directly related to functional areas. The next type of decisions, then, are still strategic, but they are made within the central functions (operations management, sales/marketing and accounting/finance), as illustrated in Figure 1.5.

These strategic decisions within the functional areas must, of course, still be made within the context of corporate strategy. As an example, a corporate strategy might be to supply large numbers of products at low cost. This might lead to a strategic decision within operations management to use an automated production line. This in turn will affect other strategic decisions about the product, customers, production process, costs, and so on.

Figure 1.5 Hierarchy of strategic decisions.

Product or process focus

The process is the precise means by which a product is made. Thus, 'baking' is the dominant process in making bread. An important question in some organizations is whether they have a product focus (that is, see themselves as making a product) or a process focus (that is, see themselves as using a process).

- A company that sees itself as running a bottling plant has a process focus; one that makes bottled lemonade has a product focus.

- Expensive restaurants have a process focus (they cook foods), while hamburger restaurants have a product focus (they supply hamburgers).

- A general store has a process focus (it sells things) but an ice-cream shop has a product focus (it supplies ice-cream).

This distinction is often unclear as all organizations use a process and supply a product. The question of focus asks if the organization sees itself *primarily* as making a product or using a process. This apparently simple question has significant effects on flexibility and operations. If, for example, the demand for bottled lemonade declines, a company with a process focus could change to bottling something else, but a company with a product focus would be more severely affected as it continued to make lemonade.

The layout of facilities and organization chart also depend on the focus. Figure 1.6 illustrates two different layouts. A process focus tends to cluster all similar equipment together and moves products as necessary to equipment; a product focus lays out all the equipment needed to make the product in an assembly line (this is discussed in more detail in Chapter 6).

The management structure of the organization may also differ. Figure 1.7 illustrates typical organization charts for a process focus (which has different divisions for each process) and a product focus (which has different divisions for each product).

In summary

The mission of an organization defines its fundamental views and aims. This sets the context in which other strategic decisions are made. These may be general decisions about the organization as a whole (defining corporate strategy) or within functional areas. Key issues are the organization's competitive strategy and whether it has a product or process focus.

SELF ASSESSMENT QUESTIONS

1.22 What is an organization's 'mission'?

1.23 What is 'corporate strategy'?

1.24 What questions are asked when determining competitive strategy?

1.25 What are the main characteristics of an organization with a product focus?

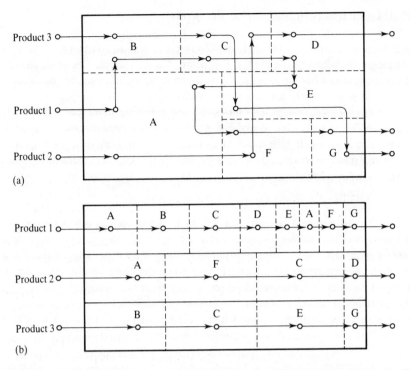

Figure 1.6 Layouts for different focus (for a factory with equipment of types A–G): (a) process layout with all similar equipment (A–G) clustered together; (b) process layout with equipment for each product laid out as an assembly line.

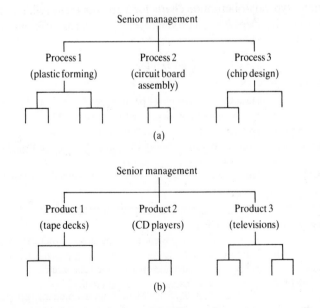

Figure 1.7 Organization charts for different focus: (a) process focus; (b) product focus.

1.3.3 Operations management decisions

We have now shown how strategic decisions in the organization as a whole lead to strategic decisions in the central functions. These strategic decisions in turn lead to tactical and operational decisions in the central functions. In this section we will list some of the decision areas tackled by operations management.

Operations management looks at strategic decisions concerning the product made, process used to make it, planned capacity and output, location of facilities, and so on. It also looks at tactical decisions such as layout, quality assurance, planned maintenance and replacement. On an operational level OPMA looks at scheduling, inventory control, reliability, expediting, and so on. Some illustrations of these decision areas are shown in Table 1.6, with more detailed discussions in later chapters.

The distinctions between strategic, tactical and operational decisions are not usually as clear as suggested in Table 1.6. Quality, for example, may be a strategic issue when the company is planning its products (perhaps aiming for a very high quality product), a tactical issue when deciding how quality can be measured and what targets should be set, or an operational decision when taking measurements to see if the current production is achieving the targets. Similarly, inventory may be a strategic issue when deciding whether to build a warehouse

Table 1.6 Illustrating some OPMA decision areas.

Decision area	Typical OPMA decisions
Strategic decisions	
Business	What business are we in?
Product	What products are supplied?
Process	How are products made?
Location	Where are products made?
Capacity	How large should facilities be?
Tactical decisions	
Layout	How should operations be arranged?
Planning	When should a new product be introduced?
Quality assurance	How well should products be made?
Distribution	How should distribution be organized: what transport should be used?
Maintenance	How often should equipment be maintained and replaced?
Operational decisions	
Scheduling	In what order should products be made?
Inventory	How much should be held in stock?
Reliability	How often is equipment breaking down: what can be done to improve this?
Maintenance	When can maintenance periods be scheduled?
Quality control	Are products reaching designed quality?

for finished goods or ship direct to customers, a tactical issue when deciding how much to invest in stock, or an operational issue when deciding how much of an item to order this week.

In all the decisions we have mentioned so far, the key element is the ultimate supply of a product (either goods or services) to satisfy customer demand. The long-term survival of any organization depends on its products. The organized supply of these products does not come by chance, but depends on effective planning of the type offered by operations management. This might start with product planning, which is described in the following chapter.

In summary
Operations management is concerned with a range of decisions at strategic, tactical and operational levels. Most decisions ultimately look towards a product that meets customer demand.

SUMMARY OF CHAPTER

This chapter gave an introduction to operations management. It described how 'operations' transform inputs to outputs, and a management function is needed to make associated decisions. The subject has been studied since the turn of the twentieth century, but its importance has become much clearer in recent years. This is largely because of international competition from companies that have organized their operations efficiently.

We emphasized the role of OPMA in the management of work at an organizational level. It can then be considered as a central function, along with sales/marketing and accounting/finance. We also described OPMA as a profession, by the approach it uses to tackle problems and by the problem areas it looks at. Although there are some differences between manufacturing and service industries, there are many similarities. These allow operations management to be relevant to all sectors of the economy.

Decisions within an organization can be described as strategic, tactical or operational. Strategic decisions are made by senior management, involve more resources, more risk and a long timespan; operational decisions are made by junior management, involve few resources, little risk and a short timespan. The fundamental views and aims of an organization are described by its mission. This sets the context in which other strategic decisions are made, either about the organization as a whole (defining its corporate strategy) or within functional areas.

Operations management is concerned with decisions at all levels. Most of these ultimately aim at supplying a product to satisfy customer demand.

SOLUTIONS TO SELF ASSESSMENT QUESTIONS

1.1 Development is usually considered in three stages where the main economic activity is in primary industry (agriculture, extraction, etc.), secondary industry (manufacturing, construction, etc.) and tertiary industry (services).

1.2 **(b)** False. Most people in the world still work in the primary industries.

1.3 Primarily because some companies (notably Japanese ones) are clearly organizing their operations more efficiently than others. International competition means that these companies are gaining considerable advantages over their competitors.

1.4 Operations are the processes that transform inputs to outputs.

1.5 The management function that is concerned with all operations involved in making a product or providing a service.

1.6 All organizations have operations so there are many to choose from, including universities, colleges, companies, shops, families, and so on.

1.7 Most operations management is done with individual organizations, but this has a cumulative effect on the economy as a whole. Some OPMA is done on a broader scale.

1.8 Those activities that are *directly* concerned with making a product, generally taken to be sales/marketing, operations management, accounting/finance.

1.9 Any organization can be described here. Some examples are given in Table 1.2.

1.10 Because it is not concerned *directly* with the product. This does not, of course, mean that it is not important.

1.11 By describing it as a central function in an organization, a profession, by the approach to problems or by the problems tackled.

1.12 There are many alternatives, including production manager, plant manager, operations analyst, shop manager, matron, postmaster, chef, supervisor, headmaster, transport manager, maintenance manager, management scientist, and so on.

1.13 Because it is easier, cheaper, more convenient and less risky than experimenting with the real system.

1.14 **(b)** False. OPMA is concerned with solving problems by the most appropriate means. This might involve quantitative models, but does not inevitably do so.

1.15 It can be argued that they are not *fundamentally* different in any way. Although they are primarily seen as providing services rather than goods (with consequent effects on stock, quality, size, etc.), all organizations share many common features.

1.16 One classification has: public services provided by national and local government; retail and wholesale shops; distribution services for both goods and information; non-profit services; other services for industry; other services for individuals.

1.17 False. Production management is primarily concerned with manufacturing while operations management is used in all sectors of industry.

1.18 Strategic, tactical and operational.

1.19 **(b)** False. Operational decisions concern day-to-day running. All decisions are important, but strategic ones are usually most important.

1.20 **(a)** strategic **(b)** operational **(c)** strategic **(d)** tactical.

1.21 Many alternatives are possible here: any reasonable description is acceptable.

1.22 A statement (either explicit or implicit) of the fundamental beliefs and aims.

1.23 The policies that result from strategic decisions about the organization as a whole.

1.24 These concern an organization's position in its industry, and include, 'What is our industry like?', 'What are the future prospects?', 'What are our strengths?', 'Who are the competitors?' and 'What are the competitors' strengths?'.

1.25 It considers itself as making a product, is organized by product, has a product-oriented layout, and so on.

REFERENCES FOR FURTHER READING

Early work on operations management includes:

Gilbreth F.B. (1912). *Primer of Scientific Management* New York: van Nostrand

Gilbreth F.B. and Gilbreth L.M. (1916). *Fatigue Studies* New York: Sturgis and Walton

Hoxie R.F. (1915). *Scientific Management and Labor* New York: Appleton

Taylor F.W. (1919). *Principles of Scientific Management* New York: Harper

There are many modern books on operations management available. Many of these are aimed at the American market and are similar in style, content and presentation. Other books emphasize production rather than operations management. Some useful introductory texts are listed below:

Adam E.E. and Ebert R.J. (1989). *Production and Operations Management* 4th edn. New Jersey: Prentice-Hall

Buffa E.S. and Sarin R.K. (1987). *Modern Production/Operations Management* 8th edn. New York: John Wiley

Chase R.B. and Aquilano N.J. (1989). *Production and Operations Management* Homewood: Irwin

Dillworth J.B. (1988). *Production and Operations Management* 4th edn. New York: Random House

Evans J.R., Anderson D.R., Sweeney D.J. and Williams T.A. (1990). *Applied Production and Operations Management* 3rd edn. St Paul: West Publishing

Gaither N. (1990). *Production and Operations Management* 4th edn. Chicago: The Dryden Press

Heizer J. and Render B. (1988). *Production and Operations Management* Boston: Allyn and Bacon

Hendrick T.E. and Moore F.G. (1985). *Production/Operations Management* 9th edn. Homewood: Irwin

Krajewski L.J. and Ritzman L.P. (1990). *Operations Management* 2nd edn. Reading: Addison-Wesley

Murdick R.G., Render B. and Russell R.S. (1990). *Service Operations Management* Boston: Allyn and Bacon

Nahmias S. (1989). *Production and Operations Analysis* Homewood: Irwin

Schmenner R.W. (1990). *Production/Operations Management* 4th edn. New York: Macmillan

Schroeder R.G. (1989). *Operations Management* 3rd edn. New York: McGraw-Hill

Stevenson W.J. (1990). *Production/Operations Management* 3rd edn. Homewood: Irwin

Vonderembse M.A. and White G.P. (1988). *Operations Management* St Paul: West Publishing

Weis H.J. and Gershon M.E. (1989). *Production and Operations Management* Boston: Allyn and Bacon

Chapter 2

Product planning

SYNOPSIS

In Chapter 1 we defined operations management and discussed the problems it tackles. Some of these problems are strategic and affect the working of organizations for a long time. In the next few chapters we will discuss some strategic issues that arise in all organizations. This chapter looks at aspects of product planning, where, as usual, the 'product' can be either goods or services.

The success of an organization depends on its ability to supply products that meet customer demand. The purpose of product planning is to ensure there is a continuous supply of suitable products.

Most organizations supply a range of products to meet differing requirements. Each product has a distinct life cycle, with each stage in the cycle having different characteristics in terms of operational requirements, cost, income and profit. Organizations with different strengths and objectives will start and stop making products at different points in the life cycle.

There are several stages in the development of a new product, with key factors being the technical and commercial evaluations. Most ideas are rejected at some point in this development process.

The rest of the chapter looks at ways of evaluating and comparing products. Such comparisons are often based on a number of factors, including both quantitative measures and qualitative opinions. Scoring models give a means of including these factors in decisions.

Break-even analyses determine the number of units which must be sold before all costs are recovered and a profit is made. A problem with this, and with all other financial analyses, is that the value of money varies over time. In particular, an amount of money has a higher value now than the same amount at some time in the future. Discounting factors allow such differences to be calculated, and lead to a discussion of net present value and internal rate of return.

OBJECTIVES

After reading this chapter and completing the exercises you should be able to:

- say why organizations need product planning;
- discuss the reasons why organizations offer a range of products;
- describe the stages in a typical product life cycle;
- appreciate the different emphasis of operations during a life cycle;
- describe typical costs and profits during a life cycle;
- outline different entry and exit strategies;
- describe stages in the development of a new product;
- appreciate the need to compare and evaluate products;
- use scoring models to compare products;
- calculate break-even points;
- appreciate the changing value of money over time and do related calculations;
- calculate net present values;
- define and use internal rates of return.

2.1 INTRODUCTION

2.1.1 Purpose of product planning

It is often said that the primary purpose of an organization is to meet customer demand. It does this by supplying a product, which may be physical goods (like a car or clothes) or services (like transport or insurance). In practice, most products are a combination of goods and services. Then, we can suggest that a product is supplied whenever a perceived customer demand is satisfied.

The success of an organization depends on its ability to supply products which are somehow 'better' than those from competitors. This judgement of how good a product is might depend on a number of factors, but the most common are:

- quality
- price
- availability.

There is now an increasing consensus that quality is the most important of these. This may appear an obvious statement, but many organizations are only just beginning to appreciate its significance. One illustration of this is the manufacture of consumer goods. In the past it was common to find manufacturers making goods with defect rates around 5%. When customers noticed these, they were corrected under a warranty. This approach is now becoming unacceptable and customers expect to buy goods that have almost no defects. If necessary, people seem willing to pay higher prices and wait for deliveries to get more reliable goods. Product quality is seen as the prime factor that determines demand, but sometimes a very broad definition of 'quality' is taken, which includes a packet of measures like price and availability. More details of this approach are given in Chapter 12.

In Chapter 1 we said that an organization's competitive strategy determines, in general terms, the types of product it will supply. Product planning is used to add some details to this strategy.

> The purpose of product planning is to ensure that an organization supplies the types of product that will satisfy perceived customer demand.

In summary

An organization's success depends on its ability to supply products to meet perceived customer demands. Product planning ensures that suitable products are available for this.

2.1.2 Range of products offered

Although some organizations supply a single product, most make a range of similar or related ones. Aggregate market demand is made up of a large number of individual demands, each of which is slightly different. We all buy clothes, for example, and the aggregate demand is made up of individual requirements which reflect different sizes, styles, purposes, and so on. Organizations can cater for this diversity by supplying a number of variations on a basic product. Colleges, for example, give different educational courses, bakers make different kinds of bread, restaurants supply different types of meals and car makers produce different models.

Decisions about the number of products an organization supplies must balance two competing factors:

(1) If it offers a narrow range, it can specialize, but potential custom will be lost to competitors who offer more or different products.

(2) If it offers too wide a range it may satisfy customers, but lose the efficiency that comes from specialization.

Current trends are, perhaps, towards more specialization. This has the advantages of:

- increasing experience and expertise in the product;
- allowing time to concentrate on perfecting the product;
- making production a routine activity;
- making associated purchasing, inspections, handling, etc., routine;
- reducing training time;
- allowing long production runs, perhaps with increased automation;
- reducing production set-up times;
- needing stocks of fewer parts and materials.

However wide the range of products, it is almost inevitable that changes are made over time. Demand for some products declines and they are withdrawn from the market, while new products are developed and introduced. This is described by a product life cycle, which is described in the following section.

In summary
Most organizations make a range of products, but there are some advantages in specialization.

SELF ASSESSMENT QUESTIONS

2.1 What is a product?

2.2 What is the purpose of product planning?

2.3 Why do most organizations supply a range of products?

2.2 PRODUCT LIFE CYCLE

2.2.1 Stages in the life cycle

Demand for some products inevitably declines over time and they are withdrawn from the market. To ensure its continued success an organization must develop new, replacement products. It may take several years to develop new products, so work must be well in hand some time before they are actually needed. This is a central function of product planning.

Experience suggests that, in the long term, demand for almost any product follows a standard life cycle. This life cycle can be considered in five

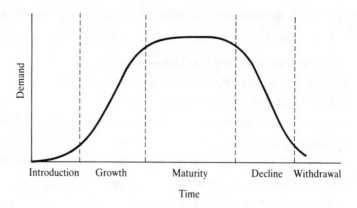

Figure 2.1 Life cycle of a product.

stages (as shown in Figure 2.1):

(1) *Introduction*: a new product is marketed, so demand is low while people learn about it, try it and see if they like it.

(2) *Growth*: as acceptance increases, more people use the product and demand rises.

(3) *Maturity*: when demand stabilizes at a more or less constant level.

(4) *Decline*: when alternative, new products become available and demand transfers to these.

(5) *Withdrawal*: when demand declines to the extent that it is no longer worth supplying the product.

This is a widely occurring pattern which relates to both specific products and whole ranges of product. Thus, it applies to a particular make of car, and to cars in general. The exact shape and duration of the life cycle will obviously depend on the product, but there are many common features.

We can illustrate this life cycle by looking at related products that are at different stages. There are, for example, several different kinds of printer available for microcomputers. Some of these are based on fairly new ideas, such as colour printers, which are at the introductory stage; laser printers are becoming established and as their price falls they are moving to a growth stage; ink-jet printers are in a later part of the growth stage; dot-matrix printers are the most widely used and are at the mature stage; printers based on typewriters are no longer selling well and are in the decline stage (see Figure 2.2).

There are some variations on the basic life cycle, but perhaps the most important variable is its length. Each edition of a newspaper has a life cycle of a few hours; fashions and fad games have a life cycle which lasts a few months or even weeks; consumer durables may have life cycles of five or ten years; some

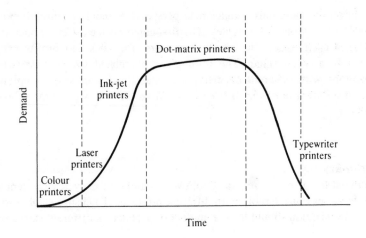

Figure 2.2 Example of products at different points in life cycle.

basic commodities like soap or cleaners remain in the mature stage for decades. Unfortunately, there are no real guidelines about the expected length of a life cycle other than experience. Some products have an unexpectedly short life and lead to commercial failure, while others have been at the mature stage for a long time and suddenly start to decline. Sugar and full cream milk, for example, have been at the mature stage for a very long time, and might now be in a decline (but are certainly a long way from withdrawal).

A key element of planning is that organizations should always have a range of products at different stages of their life cycle. This allows a stable aggregate demand, rather than having wide fluctuations in output. It also ensures long-term continuity, with new replacements available for older products that are declining or being withdrawn (see Figure 2.3).

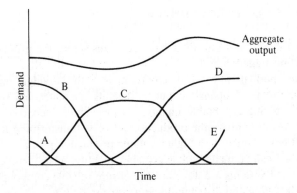

Figure 2.3 Introduction and withdrawal of products (A−E) to maintain more stable aggregate output.

From an operations management perspective, there are three important consequences of product life cycles. The first concerns the different operational emphasis at each stage. The second has costs, revenues and profits varying considerably at each stage. The third effect is related to the first two, as organizations with different expertise may start (and later stop) supplying a product at different points in its life cycle. These are discussed in the following sections.

In summary

The demand for products generally follows a standard life cycle. The length of this cycle varies considerably with different products. To ensure stable production, an organization should have a number of products at different stages in the cycle.

2.2.2 Emphasis of operations during the life cycle

We can illustrate the different operational emphases during a life cycle by following a typical manufactured product. The principles will be similar for services.

Before a new product can be marketed, work must be done on research and development (R & D). This is aimed at finding common ground between a proposed product and perceived customer demand. It answers questions like:

- What is the best design for the product?
- How can it be made efficiently?
- How can production costs be controlled?
- Can it be successfully marketed?

When these basic questions have been answered, the product moves to the introduction stage when it is offered to customers. Initially, small numbers may be made, perhaps in a 'craft' environment with individual units made to meet specific orders. Emphasis is put on meeting due dates and specifications and generally giving acceptable quality. As production increases, operational emphasis moves to improve the production process, transforming it from a low volume craft environment to a higher volume production process. This ensures that the product can be made with acceptable quantity, quality and cost. Supply and procurement systems are developed to ensure reliable components and raw materials. Marketing and distribution networks are built to meet and encourage customer demand.

If the introduction of the product is successful, it moves into the growth stage. Then demand is growing rapidly and emphasis is put on forecasting future demand and ensuring that there is enough capacity to meet it. Products are no longer made for specific orders, but are made for stock from which customer demand is met with short lead time. Production planning becomes important as resources are moved to match production and demand.

As the product matures its demand peaks. By this stage the production process might have changed several times, perhaps ending with a high volume process like an assembly line. This implies an increase in standardization and a reduction in the options offered. Competition may increase and emphasis is put on cost reduction and improved productivity. The production process may be highly automated and use very high technology.

During the decline stage, efforts may be made to enhance the product and prolong its useful life. Eventually, termination procedures are designed and implemented.

2.2.3 Costs and profits during the life cycle

When a new product is introduced, costs have already been incurred for research, development, design, planning, testing, tooling, setting up facilities, and so on. These are part of the 'fixed costs' that have to be recovered from later sales. In the early stages, when small numbers are made, the unit costs can be very high. This is primarily because the production process is expensive, but there may also be attempts to recover some of the fixed costs from early sales. At this stage the profit on each unit may also be high, as customers are willing to pay a bonus to get a new or novel product. Total revenue is, however, limited by small sales.

Income will only begin to rise substantially when the product moves from introduction to growth stage. At this point the fixed costs may be recovered to give an overall profit. This profit may be quite high, as the product is still perceived to be new and can attract a higher price, there may be little competition and new production equipment may be working efficiently. The profit per unit is high, and overall profit is rising with increasing sales volume (see Figure 2.4).

Increasing demand should allow profit to continue rising until some time into the mature stage. Continuously changing the production process to cater for higher volumes should reduce unit costs, but there will come a time when increasing competition or slackening demand may lead to price and profit reductions.

Beyond the mature stage, profits will decline as excess capacity leads to competition for the reducing demand. Sometimes, improved production methods, experience and higher productivity will offset the decline, but the opportunity for high profits is generally past. At some stage, demand and profit fall to an unacceptably low level and the product is withdrawn.

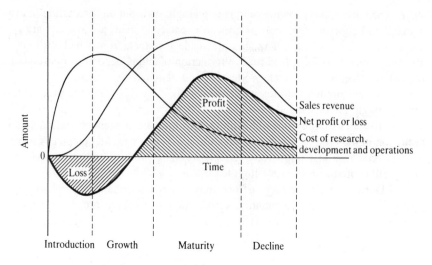

Figure 2.4 Revenue, cost, profit and loss during a typical life cycle.

The profits made by mature and growing products are, in part, needed to finance the development of new ones. One consideration, however, is that it is almost always cheaper to extend the life of an existing product than to introduce a new one. There are a number of ways of doing this, including:

- increasing advertising and market support;
- finding new uses for the product (and hence new markets);
- modifying the product to make it appear new or different (by redesign, additional features, etc.);
- changing the packaging (with new sizes, different emphasis, etc.);
- selling the product in new geographic areas.

The disadvantage of these methods is that they are usually short term and only really provide cover until a new product is available.

WORKED EXAMPLE 2.1

The revenue and cost of supplying a product over the past 13 months have been recorded as shown in Table 2.1 (values are in thousands of pounds). Where is the product in its life cycle and what plans would you expect the supplier to be making?

Table 2.1

Month	Revenue	Cost
1	12.3	4.2
2	13.0	3.4
3	13.3	2.7
4	13.2	2.4
5	12.9	2.0
6	12.7	1.8
7	12.4	1.6
8	12.0	1.4
9	11.4	1.1
10	10.8	1.0
11	9.7	0.8
12	9.0	0.6
13	8.3	0.5

SOLUTION

Subtracting the cost from the revenue gives the following profits in each month:

Month	1	2	3	4	5	6	7	8	9	10	11	12	13
Profit	8.1	9.6	10.6	10.8	10.9	10.9	10.8	10.6	10.3	9.8	8.9	8.4	7.8

A graph of these is shown in Figure 2.5. Although we do not know demand, the revenue and profit from the product have started to go down in recent months. This suggests that

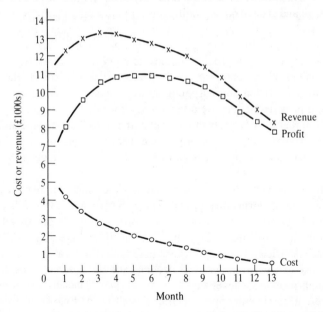

Figure 2.5 Graph of revenue, cost and profit for Worked Example 2.1.

the product has moved from maturity to decline. This decline is quite fast, and the product is clearly approaching the withdrawal stage. The company should have a replacement product either already introduced or very close to introduction.

In summary

Each stage in a product life cycle has different characteristics in terms of operational requirements, costs and profit.

2.2.4 Entry and exit strategies

Some companies spend a lot of money on research and development and aim at introducing brand new products to the market. Some pharmaceutical manufacturers, for example, develop entirely new products for illnesses. The introduction of video libraries a few years ago may also be seen as an entirely new product. It would be wrong, however, to suggest that all, or even most, companies start with basic research to develop an entirely new product and then continue supplying this until demand dies away. Most companies start their product planning by looking at products that are already being supplied by competitors. This allows them to identify any products that would fit into their existing range and start making modifications to create their own 'new' product. This effectively means that they start supplying an existing product that is already at some point in its life cycle. The timing when an organization starts (and later stops) making a product defines its entry and exit strategy.

Decisions about entry and exit strategies are based on the type of organization, its mission and corporate strategy. Some organizations do basic research and provide the ideas and technology for new developments, but they do not exploit them. They enter the market at the introduction stage and leave it before the growth stage. Typically, such organizations are very good at innovation, but lack the resources and production skills to manage a growing product.

Other organizations look for research which has commercial potential and then exploit it during the growth stage. These aim for the high prices available during growth, and exit when profit margins begin to fall. Other organizations are cost minimizers who enter at the mature stage and produce large quantities efficiently enough to compete with organizations already in the market. These exit when the product declines and the volume is insufficient to maintain high production levels.

These different entry and exit strategies allow the following classification of organizations:

Research driven

- good at research, design and development
- innovative with constant changes in product
- high quality and high cost
- low sales volumes
- slow delivery

Technology exploiters

- identify new products with wide appeal
- good at developing new processes for production
- strong in marketing to create demand
- high quality with reducing cost
- moving to high volume

Cost minimizers

- high volume, low cost production
- low innovation, concentrating on established products
- low price and fast delivery
- often automated with production or assembly lines

In summary

Organizations with different strengths and objectives adopt different entry and exit strategies.

SELF ASSESSMENT QUESTIONS

2.4 What are the stages in a typical product life cycle?

2.5 What would be typical lengths of life cycles for:

(a) a style of chair
(b) a model of car
(c) a style of ladies dress
(d) a newspaper?

2.6 As operations are performed throughout the life of a product, the main operational emphasis remains the same. Is this statement:

(a) true

(b) partly true
(c) false
(d) varies from product to product?

2.7 In general terms, how do costs and profits vary over a product's life?

2.8 Organizations usually do basic research for a product and then supply it throughout its life cycle until demand ceases. Is this statement generally true?

2.9 Suggest a classification for organizations based on their entry and exit strategies.

2.3   NEW PRODUCT DEVELOPMENT

We have said that organizations must continuously update their range of products, removing old ones and replacing them by new ones. New products do not appear spontaneously, but need careful planning. This section outlines some elements of the planning.

There are several stages between the initial idea for a new product and its development into a commercial success. One classification of these stages identifies:

> • Generation of ideas
> • Initial screening of ideas
> • Initial design, development and testing
> • Market and economic analysis
> • Final product development
> • Launch of product

This process starts with the generation of initial ideas. Typically, research departments may develop a new product, or a competitor's product would fit into the company's operations. Sometimes customers demand a product which is not currently available or new regulations make a new product essential. There are many sources for initial ideas, including:

- results from research and development;
- sales and marketing observations;
- other internal sources;
- competitor's products;
- customer's demands;
- changing government regulations;
- other external sources.

There used to be a well-worn saying, 'Build a better mousetrap and the world will beat a path to your door'. Unfortunately, the inventors of thousands of better mousetraps confirm that this is misleading. New ideas are usually easy to come by. The difficult part is transforming these ideas into viable products for which there is a demand.

All ideas must go through an initial screening to reject those which have obvious defects. This screening can quickly reject those which:

- are impossible to produce or technically difficult;
- have been tried before;

- duplicate an existing product;
- use expertise or skills which are not available;
- do not fit into current operations.

This screening might remove 80% of the original ideas. The remaining 20% have no obvious defects and can move to the next stages of development (see Figure 2.6).

Initial product design, development and testing take an extended look to see if the product is technically feasible. Typically, this stage takes an engineering perspective and looks at two questions. Firstly, the product is examined to see if it is entirely new, or a variation of an old idea (perhaps giving problems with patents), or if there are any current developments which will overtake it. Secondly, the product is examined to see if it is technically feasible, can be made with available technology, fits in with current operations, is compatible with available skills and experience, and so on. For some of these tests a prototype might be developed and tested. This stage might remove half the remaining ideas.

If the product passes the technical test it moves on to a commercial analysis. This looks at the market and financial aspects to see how it will sell, what competition there is, if it will make a profit, what investment is needed, what returns can be expected, and so on. Market surveys to gauge customer

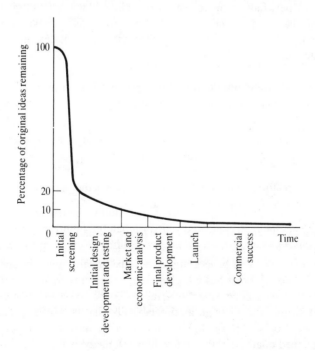

Figure 2.6 Proportion of ideas which are typically lost at each stage of development.

reaction are typically carried out at this stage. Unfortunately, the commercial evaluation rejects many apparently 'good' ideas. It is sometimes difficult to accept that an idea is technically feasible, but there is not enough demand to cover all costs and generate a profit. Some useful analyses for this stage are described later in the chapter, including break-even points, net present values and internal rates of return.

If it looks like the product will be a commercial success the product moves on to the stages of final design and tests. At this stage, lessons learnt from the technical and commercial evaluation are used and the production process is finalized. This is the point which allows production to start and a new product to be launched. Later, when actual revenues are compared with costs, a judgement can be made about whether the product is a success or not.

Very few ideas, perhaps 1% or 2%, complete this process and are launched on the market. Many of these are unsuccessful, so even fewer remain as successful products. The combination of a good idea that will give a profit, is technically feasible and will fit into existing operations is quite rare. There are many products that have not been successful despite apparently excellent decisions, ranging from the Ford Edsel to IBM's PC junior.

Organizations like to introduce new products, which are similar to those they already supply, so they have experience in the area, but are different enough to create new demand. Car makers, for example, will introduce a new model of car, but they will not start making perfume; ice-cream parlours will start selling a new flavour of ice-cream, but they will not start selling shirts. The success of the product then depends on how it is viewed in relation to competition. The organization's competitive strategy will determine whether it concentrates on:

- product differentiation (where the product is seen to be different from that of competitors, perhaps encouraging customers to pay a higher price); or
- cost leadership (where a similar product is supplied at lower cost, often achieved by removing all the frills).

Other features, which help to determine whether a product is likely to be a success, include quality, cost and availability.

(1) *Quality*. There are two central aspects to this. The first is designed quality, which shows how good a product is meant to be. A silk shirt, for example, will have a higher designed quality than a polyester one, and a luxury hotel has a higher designed quality than a boarding house. The second aspect of quality depends on actual achievement. An airline might design its timetables so that 98% of flights arrive on time. If only 30% of flights arrive on time during some period, the designed quality is high, but achieved quality is low. It is important for quality to be consistent so that customers have no uncertainty or doubt about what they will actually get.

(2) *Cost.* Usually, if more than one similar product is available the one with the lowest price will be most successful. This is, of course, not entirely true and there are many examples ranging from perfumes to limousines where it may be beneficial to charge higher prices.

(3) *Availability.* The most obvious aspect of availability is a fast delivery. A washing machine which can be delivered in two days will generally be more successful than an identical one which can only be delivered in six weeks. Similarly, more people will be attracted to a bus service if there are regular departures every few minutes than if there are only two or three departures a day. A second aspect of availability is on-time delivery. This relates to the availability actually achieved rather than planned. A relevant point to make here is that surveys find that customers prefer reliable deliveries at a later time to unreliable deliveries at an earlier time.

In summary

New products go through an extensive screening before they are marketed. This screening consists essentially of a technical evaluation of the product (Is it new? Is it feasible? Can it be made? Does it fit in with current operations?) and a commercial evaluation (What is the market? Will it sell? What competition is there? What are the financial implications? Will it be profitable? What initial investment is needed?). Even after this screening there is no guarantee that a product will be a commercial success. This depends on a number of factors like quality, cost and availability.

SELF-ASSESSMENT QUESTIONS

2.10 What are typical stages in the introduction of a new product?

2.11 What criteria are used to judge a new product?

2.12 The most difficult part of launching a new product is getting new ideas from the research team. Is this statement true?

2.4 EVALUATION OF PRODUCTS

We have already said that organizations are continually examining new products and evaluating them for both technical and commercial viability. It is difficult to make general statements about technical viability, but in this section we will describe some approaches to the commercial evaluation. These approaches are useful for:

- deciding whether a product should be developed;
- comparing alternative products.

Suppose an organization wants to develop a new product and has several alternatives which finish the initial screening at about the same time. Occasionally, the organization will have enough resources to develop and market all of these alternatives. More commonly, however, resources are limited and a decision must be made to proceed with one product in preference to the others. Some method of comparison is needed to identify the best. Ideally, this comparison should be done as early as possible, as the investment in a new product continues to rise throughout the development stages.

Market surveys are commonly used to assess a product's likely commercial success and to collect a range of customer reactions. Provided these are organized properly, they can collect a lot of useful information. They might, for example, find estimates of demand, reaction to various price, reactions to design, suggestions for improvement, comparisons with other products, and so on. Unfortunately, surveys are deceptively simple and many organizations have been misled by fundamental mistakes. A reasonable survey depends on:

- a clear understanding of the objectives of the survey;
- well designed questions;
- a suitable means of asking the questions;
- an appropriate sample of people answering;
- reliable analysis of data;
- informative and honest presentation of results.

If any of these is defective the survey results will be unreliable. Frequent mistakes include asking the wrong people to answer questions (perhaps those who are not potential customers), asking the wrong questions, asking questions in the wrong way (like sending a long questionnaire to busy people) or drawing too many conclusions from inconclusive data. There are several other ways of assessing potential demand which are discussed in the following chapter.

2.4.1 Scoring models

When a decision is needed between alternative products there is usually a range of factors which have to be considered. Some of these are quantifiable, in which case comparisons can be fairly straightforward. Many factors, however, will include a subjective or qualitative element. How, for example, could we quantify competitors' products, or the design of alternatives, or experience with similar products? A simple way of dealing with this is to list the important factors and decide whether or not a product gives satisfactory performance in each. With quantifiable factors it is fairly simple to see if a product is satisfactory or not, but with non-quantifiable factors this depends on opinions, discussion and agreement.

WORKED EXAMPLE 2.2

A company lists ten factors it considers important in a new product. There are currently four alternative proposals that may be developed, but the company only has enough resources to work on one of these. After intense discussions, agreement has been reached on whether each product reaches a satisfactory standard on these ten factors. In Table 2.2 a cross shows that the criterion has *not* been satisfied. Which product should the company develop? If product A is found to be infeasible, which product should the company develop?

Table 2.2

Factor	Product			
	A	B	C	D
Time to develop				
Expected useful life		X		
Cost of developing		X	X	
Fit with other products		X		
Equipment needed		X	X	
Initial demand				X
Stability of demand				X
Marketing required				X
Competition				X
Expected profit				

SOLUTION

The only product that satisfies all ten factors is A, so this one should be developed.

If product A is infeasible the company has several alternatives. It can say that no product satisfies all the factors, and therefore none of them will be developed but it will continue looking for alternatives. In practice, it is unusual to find an 'ideal' product which satisfies all criteria, so a compromise is needed and the best available product is selected. In this case the best is clearly not B. Product C satisfies all the conditions that B does, as well as some additional ones. The choice, then, is between C (which performs well in marketing) and D (which performs well in development). At this point, further discussions are needed. These may make the points that both products give satisfactory profits, C satisfies eight conditions while D only satisfies six, the company might have different strengths in marketing and development, and so on.

One problem with simple checklists is that different importance cannot be assigned to factors, except in discussion. Scoring models get around this difficulty by allocating different weights to each factor.

The first step in building a scoring model is again to list the important factors in a decision. This time their relative importance is noted by assigning a maximum possible score to each. Technical factors, for example, might be given a maximum score of 10; then marketing considerations are half as important and are given a maximum score of 5; return on investment is twice as important and is given a maximum score of 20, and so on. When maximum scores have been allocated, each product is examined to see how it performs. A score is given for each factor. Some quantifiable factors may have a score calculated from measured performance, but the scores are usually agreed after considerable discussion. The scores for each product are then added and the product with the highest score is, all other things being equal, the one that should be developed.

WORKED EXAMPLE 2.3

Four alternative products are judged by five criteria, as shown in Table 2.3. What is the relative importance of the criteria? On this evidence, which product is best?

Table 2.3

Factor	Maximum	Product			
		A	B	C	D
Technical	20	11	15	18	15
Finance	30	28	16	26	12
Market	15	9	13	12	8
Production	25	18	19	20	19
Competition	10	9	7	6	9

SOLUTION

The most important criterion is finance, which is given the highest maximum score. Production is considered to be slightly less important (25/30 times as important), then technical (20/30 times as important), market and competition.

Adding the scores for each product gives:

Total score of: A = 75
B = 70
C = 82
D = 63

On this evidence, product C is clearly the best.

WORKED EXAMPLE 2.4

A company is planning the introduction of a new product. There are three alternatives available and the company wants to select the best. A project team has been formed and has reported the most important factors, with maximum possible scores, as shown in Table 2.4. After considerable discussion the team also agreed scores for each product. Which product should be introduced?

Table 2.4

Factor	Maximum	Points		
		A	B	C
Product				
Time to develop product	7	7	3	5
Research and development needs	8	7	4	6
Experience with similar products	12	11	4	7
Similarity with existing products	5	4	1	3
Expected life	12	9	6	8
Ease of manufacture	18	16	9	14
Skills needed at various stages	8	8	3	5
New production equipment needed	4	4	2	3
Requirements of raw materials	6	4	4	2
Finance				
Research and development cost	12	11	9	10
Capital outlay	17	13	8	10
Return on investment	25	12	14	20
Net present value	18	10	14	18
Reduced profit from existing products	11	3	8	6
Market				
Initial demand	25	21	9	14
Marketing effort	8	6	3	8
Advertising needed	4	2	1	4
Current competition	15	5	12	10
Interactions with existing products	12	3	7	8
New competition likely	8	5	5	5
Stability of demand	5	3	2	4
Market trends	10	4	9	7
Totals	250	168	137	177

SOLUTION

The total number of points show product C to be best, but it is not far ahead of A. Product B is some way behind and should probably be discounted. An important observation is that A does well in the product section, while C does better in the finance and market areas. These factors should be looked at in detail, together with other relevant information, before a final decision is made.

This procedure for scoring models can be summarized as:

- decide the relevant factors in a decision and assign a maximum possible score to each;
- consider each product in turn and assign a score for each factor;
- add the total scores for each product;
- identify the best product as the one with the highest total score;
- discuss the result and make a final decision.

Scoring models provide a way of introducing some numerical foundation to qualitative decisions (harsher critics suggest that it is a way of building a defence for decisions which may turn out to be wrong).

In summary

Alternative products must be evaluated and compared. Choosing the best product from a number of alternatives may be a complex decision with both qualitative and quantitative factors. Scoring models allow direct comparisons of these.

SELF ASSESSMENT QUESTIONS

2.13 Why are scoring models used?

2.14 Can scoring models be used:

(a) only when financial data is available
(b) only when qualitative views are to be considered

(c) only for complex situations
(d) in any circumstances?

2.15 If a scoring model indicates that a particular product is the best of those available, would any further analysis be necessary?

2.4.2 Break-even analysis

When organizations are planning a new product, an important question is whether demand will be high enough to make a profit. The income generated must cover the cost of producing each unit, but it must also recover the money that was spent before the product was marketed. This includes any allowances for research, development, tooling, market surveys, trial runs, and so on.

The calculation of profit starts with a basic definition:

Profit = income − total costs

Suppose a company has run a market survey to find the price that people are willing to pay for a product and likely demand. The income generated is:

Income = price per unit * number of units sold

= $UP * N$

where:

UP = unit price

N = number of units sold

The total costs come from a number of sources and can be classified as:

- fixed, which are constant regardless of the number of units made; and
- variable, which depend on the number of units made.

Research and development costs, for example, are fixed regardless of the number of units made. Other fixed costs cover marketing, administration, lighting, heating, rent, debt and a range of overheads which are unaffected by the output. Conversely, the cost of raw materials, direct labour, maintenance and some other overheads are directly affected by output. A doubling of output will double raw material costs, and so on. An everyday example of this separation is the cost of running a car, which can be divided into a fixed cost (repayment of purchase loan, road tax, insurance, etc.) and a variable cost for each mile travelled (petrol, oil, tyres, depreciation, etc.).

Total costs = fixed cost + variable cost

= fixed cost + cost per unit * number of units made

= $FC + UC * N$

where:

FC = fixed cost

UC = variable unit cost

N = number of units made

We have now defined income and total cost which both rise linearly with the number of units made, as shown in Figure 2.7.

An important concept is the break-even point, which is the number of units which must be supplied before an organization starts to make a profit. We can illustrate this by a new product which had £150,000 spent on research and development, tooling and other preparations needed before production started. Other overheads cost £50,000, giving a total fixed cost of £200,000. During normal production, each unit has a variable cost of £30 and is sold for £40. The company will only start to make a profit on this product when the original £200,000 has been recovered. The point when this occurs is the break-even point. Here, each unit sold contributes £40 − £30 = £10 to the company, so

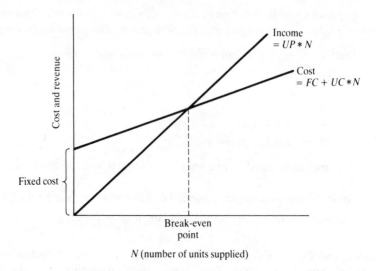

Figure 2.7 Income and total cost rising linearly with the number of units supplied.

£200,000/10 = 20,000 units must be sold to cover the fixed cost. Then:

- the break-even point is 20,000 units;
- if less than 20,000 units are sold the company will make a net loss on the product;
- if more than 20,000 units are sold the company will make a profit on the product.

In general the break-even point comes when:

Income = total cost   (see Figure 2.8)

$N * UP = FC + N * UC$

or:

$$\boxed{N = FC/(UP - UC)}$$

Each unit sold contributes $UP - UC$ towards costs or profits, so:

- if the number of units sold is greater than the break-even point the profit is:

$N * (UP - UC) - FC$

- if the number of units sold is less than the break-even point the net loss is:

$FC - N * (UP - UC)$

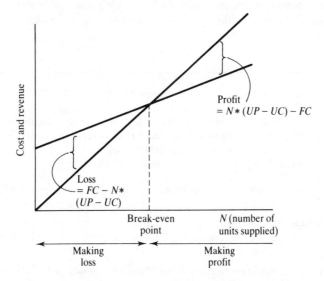

Figure 2.8 Profit or loss related to the break-even point.

The break-even analysis also shows why organizations can get 'economies of scale'. These allow the average unit cost to decline as the number of units sold increases. If an organization sells N units, the average cost per unit is:

$$(N * UC + FC)/N = UC + FC/N$$

If production is increased to the higher level N', average unit cost falls to:

$$UC + FC/N'$$

which is a reduction of:

$$FC * (N' - N)/(N * N')$$

In practice, it is often difficult to assign accurate fixed costs to products. If a factory is making a number of products, it may be difficult to calculate a reasonable proportion of overheads which should be assigned to each one. This problem is made worse if the product mix is constantly changing. Then the allocation of overheads to each product may also change. In other words, the costs, and therefore profits, made by each product may change, even though there has been no change in the product itself or the process used to make it. A consequence of this difficulty in allocating fixed costs is that 'profit maximization' may not be a reasonable objective for individual products. It would be more reasonable to replace this by 'maximizing contribution to fixed costs and profit'.

Break-even analyses are useful for the obvious purpose of seeing how many units must be made and sold to operate at a profit, but they also help with decisions about the choice between alternative products, whether to buy or lease equipment, ensuring adequate capacity when buying new equipment, whether to buy an item or make it within the company, choice of competitive tenders for services, and so on.

WORKED EXAMPLE 2.5

A manufacturing company makes 100 units of a product every month. Sales of this product are steady, and the revenue generated has to cover fixed costs for buildings, machines and employees amounting to £63,000 a month. Each unit of the product uses raw material and other variable costs amounting to £500.

(a) Does the company make a net profit if it fixes the selling price at £1200 a unit?

(b) It is suggested that sales might be improved if the selling price is reduced to £1000. If the price is reduced but sales do not change, would the company still make a profit?

(c) If the price reduction raised sales to 150 units a month, would the company make a profit?

SOLUTION

(a) The variables we know, using monthly values (in £), are:

$$\begin{aligned}
\text{Fixed cost } (FC) &= 63{,}000 \\
\text{Cost per unit } (UC) &= 500 \\
\text{Selling price per unit } (UP) &= 1200 \\
\text{Number of units sold } (N) &= 100
\end{aligned}$$

Substituting these values gives the break-even point from:

$$\begin{aligned}
N &= FC/(UP - UC) \\
&= 63{,}000/(1200 - 500) \\
&= 90
\end{aligned}$$

Actual sales are 100 so the product is making a profit of:

$$\begin{aligned}
N * (UP - UC) - FC &= 100 * (1200 - 500) - 63{,}000 \\
&= 70{,}000 - 63{,}000 \\
&= £7000 \text{ a month}
\end{aligned}$$

(b) With a selling price of £1000:

$$\begin{aligned}
\text{Total cost} &= 63{,}000 + 500 * 100 = £113{,}000 \text{ a month} \\
\text{Revenue} &= 1000 * 100 = £100{,}000 \text{ a month} \\
\text{Profit} &= \text{revenue} - \text{total cost} \\
&= 100{,}000 - 113{,}000 \\
&= -£13{,}000 \text{ a month}
\end{aligned}$$

If sales do not improve, the company is making a loss of £13,000 a month. In these circumstances, some thought should be given to reducing the costs of production, increasing the selling price or stopping production of the item.

(c) At the lower price the break-even point is:

$$N = FC/(UP - UC)$$
$$= 63,000/(1000 - 500)$$
$$= 126$$

If actual sales are 150, the product is making a profit of:

$$N * (UP - UC) - FC$$
$$= 150 * (1000 - 500) - 63,000$$
$$= 75,000 - 63,000$$
$$= £12,000 \text{ a month}$$

This shows that a profit can still be made with a low selling price provided production is high enough. The point where production is large enough to just cover total cost (126 a month) is the break-even point.

WORKED EXAMPLE 2.6

A company is planning to introduce a new product. It must select one product from three available and has estimated the data shown in Table 2.5.

Table 2.5

Factor	Product		
	A	B	C
Expected sales each year	600	900	1,200
Unit cost of production	£680	£900	£1,200
Unit selling price	£760	£1,000	£1,290
Fixed cost incurred before production	£200,000	£350,000	£500,000
Expected product life	3 years	5 years	8 years

Which product would you recommend?

SOLUTION

The break-even points for each product are calculated from:

$$N = FC/(UP - UC)$$

So for each product we have:

A: $N = 200,000/(760 - 680)$ $= 2500$

B: $N = 350,000/(1000 - 900)$ $= 3500$

C: $N = 500,000/(1290 - 1200) = 5556$

If the company wants the lowest break-even point it would select product A. It might, however, be more interested in the time taken to break even. This is given by:

Time to break even $=$ break-even point/demand

For each product this gives:

A: 2500/600 $= 4.2$ years

B: 3500/900 $= 3.9$ years

C: 5556/1200 $= 4.6$ years

In this case, product B would be best. Yet another objective might be to maximize long-term profit. Over the expected product lives:

Total profit $=$ revenue $-$ total cost

with:

Revenue $=$ lifetime $*$ annual demand $*$ unit profit

Total cost $=$ lifetime $*$ annual demand $*$ unit cost $+$ fixed cost

So:

Total profit $= L * D * (UP - UC) - FC$

where:

$L =$ lifetime

$D =$ annual demand

For each product the lifetime profit is:

A: $3 * 600 * (760 - 680) - 200,000$ $= -£56,000$

B: $5 * 900 * (1000 - 900) - 350,000$ $= £100,000$

C: $8 * 1200 * (1290 - 1200) - 500,000$ $= £364,000$

Product A would make a net loss over its expected life while product C would give the best total profit.

Overall, we can only say that the best decision would depend on the objectives of the company, but product B seems useful.

In summary

Costs can be classified as either fixed or variable, and revenue must cover both of these before a profit is made. The break-even point is the number of units which must be supplied to make revenue equal to total cost. Economies of scale may be achieved by spreading the fixed cost over a larger number of units.

SELF ASSESSMENT QUESTIONS

2.16 What does the 'variable cost' vary with?

2.17 What costs might be included in 'fixed cost'?

2.18 The break-even point for a product is calculated at 1000 units a week. If actual sales are 1200 units a week, does this mean:

(a) the product is making a profit
(b) the product is making a loss
(c) the product could be making a profit or a loss?

2.19 Why do economies of scale occur?

2.4.3 Net present value

Value of money over time

The break-even analyses described assume that the value of money does not change over time. In other words, £100 now has exactly the same value as £100 in ten years' time. In practice this is not true. Money which is sensibly invested earns interest and its value increases over time. Conversely, money which is kept under a mattress loses value as inflation raises prices. In this section we will analyse the changing value of money over time and show how this can be used to compare the net present value of alternative products.

Suppose an amount AP is put into a bank account and is left untouched for a year earning interest at a rate I. At the end of the year, interest will have been paid and the amount in the account will have risen to:

$$AP * (1 + I)$$

Here the interest rate, I, is a decimal fraction, or proportion, rather than a percentage, so an interest rate of 10% is represented by $I = 0.1$.

If the money is left untouched for a second year, it will earn interest not only on the initial amount deposited but also on the interest earned in the first year (see Figure 2.9). This amounts to:

$$\{AP * (1 + I)\} * (1 + I) \quad \text{or} \quad AP * (1 + I)^2$$

The amount of money will increase in this compound way, and at some time N years in the future the amount of money in the bank account, AF, will be:

$$\boxed{AF = AP * (1 + I)^N}$$

Provided consistent units are used the time period need not be years, but any convenient period. Turning this equation the other way around, we could

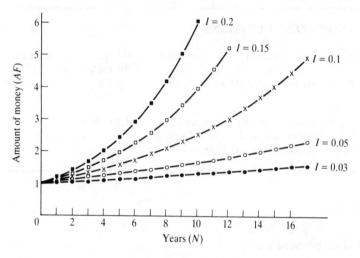

Figure 2.9 Increase of amount after earning interest with varying interest rates (initial investment = 1.0).

say that an amount, AF, N periods in the future has a present value of:

$$AP = AF/(1 + I)^N = AF * (1 + I)^{-N}$$

The process of calculating the present value of a specified future amount is called 'discounting to present value' or finding the discounted value.

We illustrated the principle of discounting using a simple interest rate, but this would usually be an over-simplification. It would, for example, ignore the effects of inflation, opportunity costs, taxes and other factors. A more general discounting rate should be defined which takes these into account. One step towards this would set I as a real interest rate, with:

Real interest rate = actual interest rate − inflation

If the rate of inflation is low, the real interest rate will be positive and the value of money invested will grow. If the rate of inflation is high, the real interest rate will be negative and any money invested will decrease in value (see Figure 2.10).

By discounting amounts to their values at some convenient time, we can directly compare profits that occur at different times. A frequently used convention is to discount all amounts to their present value. This principle is illustrated in the following worked example.

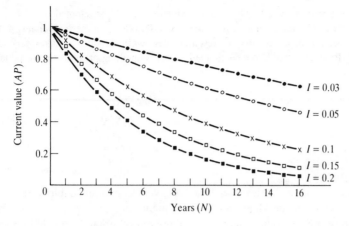

Figure 2.10 Decrease of present value of money N years in the future (present value = 1.0).

WORKED EXAMPLE 2.7

A company is considering the introduction of a new product. It has to choose one of two alternatives, both of which need an initial investment of £100,000. Although the returns are phased over many years, they can be summarized as:

- product 1 returns £300,000 in five years' time;
- product 2 returns £500,000 in ten years' time.

Which product should the company introduce if it uses a discounting rate of 20% a year for future revenues?

SOLUTION

This problem needs to compare amounts of money generated at different points in time. The way to make such comparisons is to find the values of both amounts at the same point. Any convenient time can be used, but the obvious one is to reduce amounts to their value at the present time.

Product 1 will return £300,000 in five years' time. To reduce this to its present value we divide by $(1 + 0.2)^5$:

$$\text{Present value} = 300,000/(1 + 0.2)^5$$
$$= 300,000/2.488$$
$$= £120,563$$

Product 2 will return £500,000 in ten years' time. To reduce this to its present value we divide by $(1 + 0.2)^{10}$:

$$\text{Present value} = 500,000/(1 + 0.2)^{10}$$
$$= 500,000/6.192$$
$$= £80,753$$

Product 1 clearly gives a higher present value and should be adopted.

If we subtract the initial investment of £100,000 from these revenues, product 1 makes a net profit of £20,563 at present values, while product 2 makes a net loss of £19,247. Product 2 should not be adopted even if something prevents the introduction of product 1.

In summary

The value of money varies over time. A given amount available at present will have a higher value than the same amount at some point in the future. Calculating present values allows a comparison of amounts which are available at different points in time.

SELF ASSESSMENT QUESTIONS

2.20 Which has the highest value?

(a) £5000 now
(b) £5000 in five years' time
(c) £5000 in ten years' time
(d) it does not matter as £5000 has the same value at any time
(e) cannot say without more information

2.21 How could you compare the net benefits from two products, one of which generates income for three years and the other for eight years?

2.22 What is a discounting rate?

Calculation of the net present value

Incomes which are generated at different times can be compared by discounting amounts to their value at the same point in time. The same discounting could be done for costs. The usual convention is to find the equivalent *present* values of all costs and incomes. Then, subtracting the present value of all costs from the present value of all incomes gives a 'net present value'.

$$\text{Net present value} = \text{Sum of discounted incomes} - \text{Sum of discounted costs}$$

If the net present value is negative a product will make a loss and we should not introduce it. If several alternative products have a positive net present value, the best is the one with the highest value.

WORKED EXAMPLE 2.8

Three alternative products have been proposed with initial development costs and projected incomes (each in thousands of pounds) for the next five years as shown below:

	Initial cost	Income generated in each year				
		1	2	3	4	5
A	2000	1000	800	600	400	200
Product B	1400	100	200	500	600	700
C	800	100	200	300	200	0

The company uses a discounting rate of 10% a year. If it only has enough resources to introduce one product, which should it adopt?

SOLUTION

Conventional accounting often uses an 'average rate of return'. This is found by taking the average annual income as a percentage of initial investment.

Product A generates a total income of £3000 over five years, or an average of £600 a year. This gives an average rate of return of 30% on the initial investment of £2000. Average rates of return for the other products are shown in Table 2.6.

Table 2.6

Factor	Product		
	A	B	C
Initial cost (£)	2000	1400	800
Total income (£)	3000	2100	1000
Average annual income (£)	600	420	200
Average rate of return	30%	30%	25%

Products A and B have the same average rate of return, but product C offers a lower rate and would only be considered if the company could not afford to develop the more expensive alternatives, if 25% was considered an acceptable rate of return, or if some other factor made products A and B less acceptable.

Looking in more detail at the money flows for products A and B, we see that incomes vary over time and in particular A offers more in early years while B offers more in later years. To give a valid comparison between these we can discount all amounts to present values and compare the net present value of each product.

Income for product A (see also Figure 2.11):

£1000 in year 1 has a present value of $1000/1.1 = £909.09$

£800 in year 2 has a present value of $800/1.1^2 = £661.16$

£600 in year 3 has a present value of $600/1.1^3 = £450.79$ and so on.

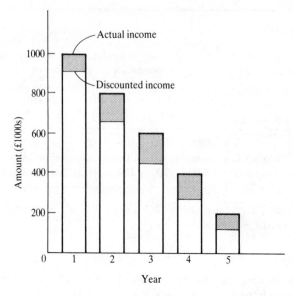

Figure 2.11 Actual and discounted income for product A (similar graphs could be drawn for the other products).

Details of these calculations are given in Table 2.7. Although such tables appear unwieldy, there are many commercial packages for this type of calculation, or it is easy to write a simple computer program. This is also the type of repetitive calculation which spreadsheet packages handle very well.

Table 2.7 Discounted values for incomes.

Year	Discounting factor	Product A Income (£)	Present value (£)	Product B Income (£)	Present value (£)	Product C Income (£)	Present value (£)
1	1.1	1000	909.09	100	90.91	100	90.91
2	1.21	800	661.16	200	165.29	200	165.29
3	1.331	600	450.79	500	375.66	300	225.39
4	1.4641	400	273.21	600	409.81	200	136.60
5	1.61051	200	124.18	700	434.64	0	0.0
Totals		2100	2418.43	2100	1476.31	1000	618.19

Subtracting the present value of costs (in this case the single initial project cost) from the present value of income gives the net present value, as shown in Table 2.8.

Table 2.8 Net present values.

	Product A	Product B	Product C
Present value of incomes (£)	2418.43	1476.31	618.19
Present value of costs (£)	2000.00	1400.00	800.00
Net present value (£)	418.43	76.31	− 181.81

Product A has the highest net present value and should, all other things being equal, be the one adopted. Product C has a negative net present value, indicating a loss, and this alternative should be avoided. One other consideration is that the incomes from A are declining (implying the product has a limited lifespan of around five years) while incomes from product B are rising (implying a longer potential lifespan). Factors like this should be taken into account before making any final decisions.

WORKED EXAMPLE 2.9

A company is about to expand its premises so it can offer a wider range of products. Building work is to be done by contractors, and two firms have submitted tenders. These allow projected cash flows as follows:

	Year 1 (£)	Year 2 (£)	Year 3 (£)
Firm A	− 50,000	20,000	60,000
Firm B	− 80,000	10,000	100,000

If inflation and opportunity costs suggest a discounting rate of 8% a year, which of the firms should get the contract?

SOLUTION

The two tenders can be compared by calculating the net present value of each. Using $(1 + I)^N$, with $I = 0.08$ gives the results shown in Table 2.9.

Table 2.9

Year	Discounting factor	Firm A Revenue (£)	Firm A Discounted revenue (£)	Firm B Revenue (£)	Firm B Discounted revenue (£)
1	1.080	− 50,000	− 46,296	− 80,000	− 74,074
2	1.166	20,000	17,153	10,000	8,576
3	1.260	60,000	47,619	100,000	79,365
Totals		30,000	18,476	30,000	13,867

These figures suggest using firm A which gives a net present value of £18,476.

In summary

The net present value is found by subtracting total discounted costs from total discounted income. This allows the profits from different products to be compared directly.

SELF ASSESSMENT QUESTIONS

2.23 What is meant by the 'net present value'?

2.24 If the net present value of a product is negative, does this mean:

(a) the product will make a profit
(b) the product will make a loss
(c) the product could make either a profit or a loss?

2.25 When the net present values of three products are calculated they are ranked in the order A, B, C. How would this ranking change if values were discounted to ten years in the future rather than the present?

2.4.4 Internal rate of return

In Worked Example 2.8 we assumed that the discounting rate was fixed and compared three products by calculating their net present values. We have also mentioned that it is frequently difficult to find a suitable discounting rate which takes into account interest rates, inflation, taxes, opportunity costs, exchange rates and everything else. An alternative means of comparison would be to find the discounting rate which would lead to a specified net present value. In other words, keep the same net present value for each product and calculate three

Table 2.10

Year	Discounting factor	Cost	Present value	Income	Present value
0	1	1400	1400	–	–
1	1.1	–	–	100	90.91
2	1.21	–	–	200	165.29
3	1.331	–	–	500	375.66
4	1.4641	–	–	600	409.81
5	1.61051	–	–	700	434.64
Totals		1400	1400	2100	1476.31

different discounting rates. The product with the highest discounting rate to achieve this would be the best. We could use any convenient target for the net present value calculations, but an obvious one is zero. Then the discounting rate which gives a net present value of zero is called the 'internal rate of return'.

> The internal rate of return is the discounting rate which gives a net present value of zero.

Unfortunately, there is no straightforward formula for calculating the internal rate of return, and an iterative approach must be used. In Worked Example 2.8 a discounting rate of 10% gave the values shown in Table 2.10 (in thousands of pounds) for product B.

With a discounting rate of 10% the net present value is £76,310. If the discounting rate is raised to 14% the figures in Table 2.11 are found (again in thousands of pounds).

Table 2.11

Year	Discounting factor	Cost	Present value	Revenue	Present value
0	1	1400	1400	–	–
1	1.14	–	–	100	87.72
2	1.2996	–	–	200	153.89
3	1.48154	–	–	500	337.49
4	1.68896	–	–	600	355.25
5	1.92541	–	–	700	363.56
Totals		1400	1400	2100	1297.91

The discounting rate of 14% reduced the net present value to − £102,090. In other words, a discounting rate of 10% gives a positive net present value while a discounting rate of 14% gives a negative value. The internal rate of return (which by definition gives a net present value of zero) must lie between these two, i.e. between 10% and 14%. By doing more calculations the range in which the internal rate of return lies can be found more accurately. Here, a discounting rate of 11.6% gives a net present value which is just positive, while 11.7% gives a value which is just negative, so the internal rate of return is between these two. Although this method of calculation seems haphazard, it can be done very easily using a spreadsheet.

WORKED EXAMPLE 2.10

What is the internal rate of return for a product which gives the following net cash flow?

Year	0	1	2	3	4	5	6	7	8
Net cash flow (£)	− 2000	− 500	− 200	800	1800	1600	1500	200	100

SOLUTION

To find the internal rate of return the net present value is calculated for a number of discounting rates until a result is found which is close to zero. Then the discounting rate is refined until a sufficiently accurate value is found. In this example the internal rate of return is 20%, as shown in Table 2.12 (the slightly negative value is caused by rounding).

Table 2.12

Year	Net cash flow (£)	Discounting factor	Discounted value
0	− 2000	1.0	− 2000
1	− 500	1.2	− 416.67
2	− 200	1.44	− 138.89
3	800	1.728	462.96
4	1800	2.074	868.06
5	1600	2.488	643.00
6	1500	2.986	502.35
7	200	3.583	55.82
8	100	4.300	23.26
Totals	3300		− 0.11

In summary
The internal rate of return is the discounting rate which gives a net present value of zero. The best products give high internal rates of return.

SELF ASSESSMENT QUESTIONS

2.26 How can the internal rate of return be used to compare products?

2.27 Three alternative products, A, B and C, are found to have internal rates of return of 10%, 15% and 20% respectively. Which product gives the best financial returns?

SUMMARY OF CHAPTER

This chapter has looked at some aspects of product planning. The purpose of this is to ensure that suitable products are available to meet perceived customer demand.

Most organizations supply a range of products so they can meet varied market demands and maintain a stable aggregate output. The life cycle for each product has a number of stages corresponding to introduction, growth, maturity, decline and withdrawal. These stages have different characteristics in terms of operational requirements, costs, revenue and profit.

Most organizations do not develop entirely new products, but adapt existing ones. The organizations' strengths and objectives will determine their entry and exit strategies.

The introduction of a new product involves several stages between the initial idea and launch on to the market. Important stages assess the technical feasibility of the product and its likely commercial success. Very few ideas go through this entire process and become successful products.

There are several circumstances in which an organization wants to evaluate products, including comparisons of alternative new developments. These evaluations are often based on a combination of quantitative measures and qualitative opinions. Scoring models give a way of adding a rational viewpoint to these comparisons.

Break-even analyses determine the number of units which must be sold before all costs are covered and a profit is made. One problem with the break-even analysis is that the value of money varies over time. In particular, an amount of money has a higher value now than the same amount at any time in the future. Discounting factors allow this to be taken into account, and are the basis of 'net present value' calculations. An alternative approach calculates the internal rate of return.

PROBLEMS

2.1   The revenue and costs of supplying a product over the past 11 months have
been recorded as shown in Table 2.13 (values are in thousands of pounds).
Where is the product in its life cycle and what plans would you expect the
supplier to be making?

Table 2.13

Month	Revenue	Cost
1	3.5	7.5
2	4.8	8.7
3	7.0	10.2
4	8.9	10.5
5	10.2	9.8
6	11.9	8.8
7	12.7	7.7
8	13.4	6.8
9	13.7	5.2
10	13.7	3.8
11	13.5	3.0

2.2   Four alternative products are judged by ten criteria, with points given to each
as shown in Table 2.14. What is the relative importance of the criteria? On
this evidence, which product is best?

Table 2.14

Factor	Maximum	Product A	B	C	D
Resources	10	8	10	8	7
Finance	30	28	27	24	17
Market	35	17	33	22	18
Production	25	18	19	20	19
Competition	20	12	11	16	19
Technical	15	10	9	5	12
Skills	10	9	4	3	9
Compatibility	5	3	3	1	5
Location	10	6	10	7	6
Experience	15	8	6	4	12

2.3   Each week a company makes 100 units of a product which it sells for £100
each. Unit variable costs are £50 and fixed costs amount to £150,000 a year.
What is the break-even point for the product, and what profit is the company

making? What is the average cost per unit? By how much would production
have to rise to reduce the average cost per unit by 25%?

2.4   An airline is considering a new service between Paris and Vancouver. Its
       existing airplanes, each of which has a capacity of 240 passengers, could be
       used for one flight a week with fixed costs of £30,000 and variable costs
       amounting to 50% of ticket price. If it is planned to sell tickets at £200 each,
       how many passengers will be needed for the airline to break even on the
       proposed route? Does this seem a reasonable number?

2.5   How much will an initial investment of £1000 earning interest of 8% a year
       be worth at the end of 20 years?

2.6   Several years ago a couple invested in an endowment insurance policy which
       is about to mature. They have the option of receiving £10,000 now or
       £20,000 in ten years' time. Because they are retired and pay no income tax,
       they could invest the money with a real interest rate expected to remain at
       10% a year for the foreseeable future. Which option should they take?

2.7   A product has projected costs and revenues (in thousands of pounds) as
       follows:

Year	1	2	3	4	5	6
Costs	100	–	–	50	–	–
Incomes	10	20	50	80	60	40

What is its net present value? What is the internal rate of return?

2.8   A company has to choose one of three alternative products to develop. The
       costs and incomes are shown in Table 2.15 (in thousands of pounds). What
       should the company do?

Table 2.15

Year	Product A Income	Costs	Product B Income	Costs	Product C Income	Costs
1	10	70	80	30	120	40
2	20	60	90	20	110	40
3	50	45	90	10	100	50
4	100	40	100	20	100	60
5	150	40	100	20	90	60
6	170	40	110	30	90	70
7	180	40	110	30	80	80

CASE STUDY – ESCENTIAL FRAGRANCES

Background

Escential Fragrances operate in the suburbs of Paris and make a number of well-known perfumes. They are a wholly owned subsidiary of a major French fashion house, but have considerable independence and are responsible for their own operations. All the production of Escential is transferred to the parent company where it is sold under its own name. This arrangement leaves Escential free to concentrate on production, while marketing and sales are done by the parent company.

Escential Fragrances make two types of perfume:

- a number of 'exclusive' brands, which are sold at high prices and in small numbers;
- a few 'mass' brands, which are less expensive and sell in larger quantities.

Production of exclusive brands causes few problems as they involve a small number of craftsmen making very low volumes. The mass products cause more concern.

One problem facing Escential is the limited lifespan of most brands of perfume. This means they are made for some period (sometimes as short as a few months but usually three or four years) and then are withdrawn from the market to be replaced by new brands. There is currently a range of nine mass perfumes designed to appeal to different types of people. Six of these are at different points in their life cycle and sell in different numbers. The remaining three are traditional perfumes that have been made for many years, and include a lavender perfume for women and an after-shave for men.

Financial arrangements

All marketing is done by the parent company. In one sense this is an advantage to Escential as they can concentrate on production and are not too worried by short-term variations in their financial state. Conversely, they are separate from the market and have to be guided by the specific requirements of the parent company. If, for example, Escential feel that perfumes based on spring flowers are growing in popularity, but the parent company is putting some effort into a new 'oriental look', pressure is put on Escential to produce perfumes with an oriental appeal rather than follow their own feelings. Such pressure is easy to exert as the parent company places orders with Escential (where it is the only customer) to create demand. These orders may reflect actual demand (with the parent company acting purely as a wholesaler) or potential demand (where the parent company tries to influence the market by promoting a certain style).

As their income is determined by internal transfer prices, which are set by the parent company, Escential are more interested in using their facilities to full capacity than in making a profit. Their performance is effectively judged by the number of bottles of perfume transferred to the parent company.

Production

A meeting was recently held to discuss medium-term production plans. In particular, the management of Escential wanted to discuss the possible withdrawal of perfumes which are no longer selling well and the introduction of replacements. Escential have enough capacity to make a total of around 5300 bottles of perfume a day. Of this, 500 bottles are exclusive brands and the remainder is available for mass brands. This capacity may be varied slightly in the short term by changing working hours or rescheduling, but in the longer term is fixed. The capacity has remained unchanged since the 1920s and there are no plans for alterations.

The design of a new perfume is straightforward, and a new brand could be available in a very short time. Before production starts, however, a series of market surveys is made and the parent company must be convinced that the new brand fits into its current requirements. Suitable bottles and associated artwork must be designed and manufactured. When this is complete, the parent company runs its marketing effort to launch the new brand. This process raises the time needed to introduce a brand to an average of nine months. Sometimes the process can be speeded up to a few months, but for others it can take up to two years.

Current demand

At their management meeting a lot of time was spent discussing expected sales of mass perfumes. Sales of three of the nine mass brands are relatively stable. Accurate records have been kept, which allow average daily sales to be found for the past 19 months, as shown in Table 2.16. (Within the company the perfumes are known by identifying codes.)

When these figures were presented to the meeting they caused some concern, particularly with Guy Mignard who is the Marketing Representative from the parent company. His problem was that perfume sales are known to be seasonal (with high peaks around Christmas) and yet the figures did not show this variation. The explanation from Marcel Gagnon, who is Escential's Materials Manager, is that the variation in sales is much more pronounced than the variation in production. Although perfume deteriorates over time it can be stored in refrigerators with variations in stock levels to allow a steady production. The figures he provided were movements from production to the refrigerated store. Long-term production plans are based on the rate of withdrawal from this store, so his figures were smoothed and removed seasonal variation.

Table 2.16

Month	Code number		
	LP1075	MA247	LT2240
1	320	724	403
2	286	693	519
3	307	751	622
4	310	660	540
5	324	703	490
6	301	691	603
7	279	673	397
8	292	711	501
9	314	741	488
10	288	687	561
11	292	729	473
12	301	700	502
13	314	691	450
14	306	673	423
15	285	659	607
16	299	712	555
17	305	736	487
18	289	705	491
19	310	603	497

Demand figures for the other six mass perfumes are slightly less reliable, but average daily sales over the past 19 months are estimated in Table 2.17.

Again Guy Mignard questioned the lack of variation in these figures. Marcel Gagnon explained that he was interested in the underlying pattern of demand rather than details of daily sales, so he had taken average values to smooth the figures, had used production numbers rather than sales, and had adjusted obvious short-term fluctuations.

There was much discussion about the figures and the consequences for changing brands. One suggestion from Guy Mignard was that to remain competitive in the perfume market the company needed to appeal to different type of people and should, therefore, expand their range as soon as possible. He suggested rushing an additional perfume on to the market in six months and adding another three brands within the next year.

The opposite view was taken by Marcel Gagnon who said that production was already stretched beyond capacity. Data showed the total production of mass perfumes averaged 5184 bottles a day in month 11, and this had risen to 5281 bottles in month 17. The company could not continue this rate for much longer, and was much more comfortable since average production had recently fallen. As it is easier to produce large batches of the same brand, he suggested removing the four brands with lowest sales and concentrating on the five remaining brands. Then new brands should only be considered when sales of existing brands fall considerably, or when they have expanded facilities.

Table 2.17

Month	Code number					
	LP4098	LP6032	LP6275	LT3127	LT4092	MA985
1	120	1170	–	1030	680	–
2	150	1180	–	1040	660	–
3	190	1170	–	1050	610	–
4	250	1170	–	1050	560	–
5	310	1150	–	1060	500	60
6	450	1130	–	1070	410	100
7	600	1080	–	1080	320	150
8	770	1050	–	1090	240	310
9	940	970	50	1200	150	370
10	1000	940	50	1210	110	390
11	1050	930	50	1190	90	380
12	1100	890	60	1200	80	380
13	1150	850	70	1210	70	390
14	1180	840	80	1200	60	370
15	1210	780	90	1210	60	380
16	1230	730	100	1210	60	370
17	1240	670	120	1090	50	360
18	1250	560	160	1000	50	320
19	1250	450	210	860	40	280

A middle view was taken by Jean Pouliot, who is the company secretary. He suggested that recent production levels had been too high for the company to manage and should be cut back to a reasonable level. The implication is that no extra brands should be considered immediately. However, sales of three current brands are clearly declining and the company will have to replace these. He had been holding discussions with the parent company (particularly the marketing area) and suggested Escential should consider introducing three new brands. He emphasized that he had only done a limited amount of work, but the introduction of these brands at some point would fit in well with the parent company's objectives over the next five years. There was, he emphasized, no pressure to introduce all three brands, or to introduce them at the same time.

Marcel Gagnon questioned the likely success of the three new brands. The only figures available are the estimates for quarterly costs and revenues given in Table 2.18 (values are in thousands of pounds).

The figures given by Jean Pouliot are not discounted (which would reduce future values by about 5% a quarter) and are based on an average transfer price of £5 a bottle. The costs are based on launch costs of comparable perfumes, while revenues are based on projected sales volumes.

Despite their differences the management of Escential Fragrances had to reach some decisions about their medium-term production plans.

Table 2.18

Quarter	LP6587 Costs	LP6587 Revenue	LP7045 Costs	LP7045 Revenue	LT4950 Costs	LT4950 Revenue
1	300	20	350	150	150	10
2	100	40	200	200	150	10
3	–	60	100	250	100	10
4	–	80	60	300	100	20
5	100	100	150	300	50	30
6	–	100	100	250	50	50
7	–	100	60	200	50	80
8	–	100	–	150	50	120
9	100	100	100	110	10	160
10	–	100	60	70	10	200
11	–	100	–	30	10	220
12	–	100	–	–	10	220

Code number spans the three code columns LP6587, LP7045, LT4950, each with *Costs* and *Revenue* sub-columns.

Suggested questions

- What is the main problem faced by Escential Fragrances?
- What alternatives are open to them?
- What are the company objectives and constraints?
- How useful is the data given and how accurate is it?
- At what stage in their life cycles are the nine mass perfumes?
- What are the likely sales of each perfume, and hence total demand over the next few months?
- What should Escential Fragrances do about withdrawing, replacing or extending their current brands?
- Which of the proposed new brands gives the best returns?

SOLUTIONS TO SELF ASSESSMENT QUESTIONS

2.1 Any goods or services that are used to satisfy customer demand.

2.2 To ensure that an organization has products available that will satisfy perceived customer demand.

2.3 To satisfy differing customer demands.

2.4 Introduction, growth, maturity, decline and withdrawal.

2.5 There is room for variation in these answers, but reasonable values might be: **(a)** 10 years **(b)** 5 years **(c)** 1 year **(d)** 1 day.

2.6 **(c)** False. In one sense it is difficult to draw

general conclusions about operations, so **(d)** may be justified.

2.7 Costs are higher near the beginning of the life cycle and decline over time, while revenue is highest around the maturity stage. High profits can be made in the growth stage, but these generally peak with maturity.

2.8 No. Few organizations follow a product throughout its life, but define their own entry and exit strategies.

2.9 Research driven, technology exploiters, cost minimizers.

2.10 Typical stages are: generation of ideas, initial screening of ideas, initial design, development and testing, market and economic analysis, final product development, launch of product.

2.11 The essential components are a technical evaluation (of the product) and a commercial one (of the product and finances).

2.12 No. Most ideas do not come from research teams, and the problem is not getting good ideas but getting ideas that will lead to a commercially successful product.

2.13 To allow comparisons of different alternatives when a combination of qualitative and quantitative information is available.

2.14 **(d)** In any circumstances.

2.15 Yes. A decision should be made on the basis of all available information and not just one analysis.

2.16 The number of units produced.

2.17 Research and development, administration, marketing, lighting, heating, rent, debt charges, marketing and any other overhead that does not vary with production.

2.18 **(a)** The product is making a profit.

2.19 Because the fixed cost is spread over a larger number of units.

2.20 **(a)** £5000 now.

2.21 By discounting all amounts to their equivalent values at some fixed point, the most convenient of which gives the discounted present value.

2.22 The fractional increase in value during one time period, used to calculate discounted values.

2.23 Net present value is the sum of discounted income minus the sum of discounted costs.

2.24 **(b)** The product will make a loss.

2.25 It would not change.

2.26 The internal rate of return is calculated for each product, with the best product selected as the one with the highest value.

2.27 C.

REFERENCES FOR FURTHER READING

Chang Y.L. (1989). *Quantitative Systems for Operations Management* Englewood: Prentice-Hall

Dennis T.L. and Dennis L.B. (1988). *Micro-computer Models for Management Decision Making* St Paul: West Publishing

Goslin L.N. (1967). *The Product Planning System* Homewood: Irwin

Hall O.P. (1989). *Computer Models for Operations Management* Reading: Addison-Wesley

Hudson R.G., Chambers J.C. and Johnson R.G. (1977). New product planning under uncertainty *Interfaces*, **8**, 82 − 96

Nathan J. and Cicilioni R.Y. (1987). *A Spreadsheet Approach to Production and Operations Management* St Paul: West Publishing

Pessemier E.A. (1966). *New Product Decisions* New York: McGraw-Hill

Sachs W.S. and Benson G. (1981). *Product Planning and Management* Tulsa: Penwell Publishing

Waters C.D.J. (1989). *A Practical Introduction*

to Management Science Wokingham: Addison-Wesley

Whitaker D. (1984). *OR on the Micro* Chichester: John Wiley

Wind Y.J. (1982). *Product Policy: Concepts, Methods and Strategy* Reading: Addison-Wesley

Zimmerman S.M. and Zimmerman S.M. (1988). *Structuring and Solving Operations Management Problems Using Lotus 1 − 2 − 3* St Paul: West Publishing

Chapter 3

Forecasting product demand

SYNOPSIS

Chapter 2 described how products might be evaluated. Expected future demand is often a central part of such evaluations. This chapter describes some methods of forecasting this future demand.

All decisions become effective at some point in the future. Managers should, therefore, make decisions that are not based on present circumstances, but on circumstances as they will be when the decisions become effective. These circumstances must be forecast.

Despite its importance, progress in many areas of forecasting has been limited. There are many different methods of forecasting, and it is not possible to identify the best method in all circumstances. When a forecast is made, there will almost certainly be a difference between the forecast and actual demand. If this were not true we could rely on weather forecasts, predict the winner of a horse race, become rich speculating on the price of shares, not buy too much food for a dinner party, and so on. There are, however, many situations in which good forecasts can be found and this chapter looks at some methods of getting these.

The chapter starts by discussing the role of forecasting in operations management. Then it classifies forecasting methods according to judgemental, causal and projective. Some judgemental methods are outlined, notably personal insight, panel consensus, market surveys, historic analogy and the Delphi method.

Most quantitative forecasts are concerned with time series, where demand is measured at regular intervals of time. This demand can usually be described by an underlying pattern with a superimposed random noise that cannot be forecast. This noise means that forecasts almost inevitably contain errors.

Quantitative forecasting is introduced by causal forecasts, where relationships are found between variables. These methods are discussed by reference to linear regression, which draws the line of best fit through a set of data. The quality of results is measured by the coefficients of determination and correlation.

Another way of getting quantitative forecasts is to look at the patterns in historic data and project these into the future. There are several ways of doing such projection, and this chapter considers simple averages, moving averages, exponential smoothing and models for seasonality and trend. The chapter ends with a case study which outlines an example of forecasting in practice.

OBJECTIVES

After reading this chapter and completing the exercises you should be able to:

- appreciate the importance of forecasting in operations management;
- list different types of forecasting;
- discuss the characteristics of judgemental forecasting;
- describe a variety of judgemental forecasting methods;
- define 'time series' and appreciate their importance;
- calculate forecast errors using mean error, mean absolute deviation and mean squared error;
- describe the characteristics of causal forecasts;
- find lines of best fit using linear regression and use these for forecasting;
- calculate coefficients of determination and correlation and appreciate their importance;
- describe the characteristics of projective forecasting;
- forecast using actual averages, moving averages and exponential smoothing;
- vary the sensitivity of projective forecasts by using appropriate parameters;
- make forecasts for time series with seasonality and trend.

3.1 FORECASTING IN OPERATIONS MANAGEMENT

One method of evaluating products suggested in Chapter 2 was a break-even analysis. This calculates the demand that allows a product to recover its fixed costs and begin contributing to profits. If a new product is proposed, but its sales are unlikely to reach the break-even point, the product should not be introduced. Such analyses are based on estimated future demand, and must use some method of forecasting.

This illustration shows one use of forecasts, but they are needed in many different circumstances. All decisions need a certain amount of information. The decisions actually become effective at some point in the future, so they should be based on circumstances not as they are at present, but as they will be when the decision becomes effective. The information required for decisions must, therefore, contain forecasts of future circumstances. This view shows that forecasting is of fundamental importance to an organization, with all plans and decisions based on forecasts of the future.

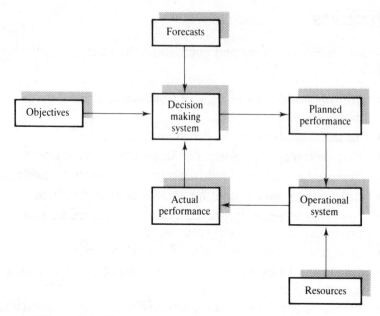

Figure 3.1 The position of forecasts in an operating system.

Demand forecasts, as well as helping with product planning, have implications for every aspect of operations. Forecast demand for a product may have regional variations, so will affect decisions about where to locate facilities (as discussed in Chapter 4). Demand affects the way a product is made with, for example, higher demand using automated assembly lines while lower demand uses less intensive methods (discussed in Chapter 5). Forecast demand will also affect the way facilities are laid out and their planned capacity (Chapters 6 and 7). If forecasts show wide variations in demand, these will affect planning, scheduling, and so on. The clear message is that forecasting demand is one of the most important functions in an organization.

Because of its importance, forecasting should be found throughout an organization and should not be perceived as the work of an isolated group of specialists. Similarly, forecasting should not be a job that is done once, and then left as finished. It is continuous, and there is no stage at which it is ever finished. As time progresses actual demand must be compared with forecasts, and updates made, plans modified, revised decisions made, and so on. This process is illustrated in Figure 3.1.

It would be convenient to say that 'much work has been done on forecasting and the best method is . . .'. Unfortunately this is not possible. Because of the diversity of things to be forecast and the different situations in which forecasts are needed, there is no single best method. This means that we should describe a variety of methods and indicate the circumstances in which each might be used.

Forecasting methods can be classified in several ways. One classification

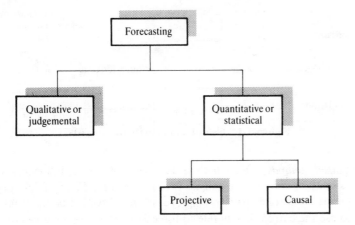

Figure 3.2 Qualitative and quantitative forecasting methods.

concerns the time in the future covered by forecasts. In particular:

- long-term forecasts look ahead several years (the time typically needed to build a new facility);
- medium-term forecasts look ahead between three months and two years (the time typically needed to replace an old product by a new one);
- short-term forecasts cover the next few weeks (describing the continuing demand for a product).

There is a clear link here with the different levels of decision making described in Chapter 1. In essence, long-term forecasts are concerned with strategic decisions, medium-term forecasts with tactical decisions, and short-term forecasts with operational decisions.

The time horizon affects the choice of forecasting method because of the availability and relevance of historic data, the time available to make the forecast, the cost involved, the severity of consequences if errors are made, the effort considered worth while, and so on.

Another classification of forecasting methods draws a distinction between qualitative and quantitative approaches (as shown in Figure 3.2).

If a company is already making a product, it will probably have records of past demand and know the factors which affect this. Then it could use a quantitative method for forecasting future demand. There are two alternatives for this:

(1) *Projective methods*, which examine the pattern of past demand and extend this into the future. If demand in the past four weeks has been 100, 120, 140 and 160, it would be reasonable to project this pattern and suggest that demand in the following week will be around 180.

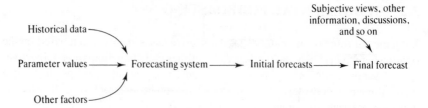

Figure 3.3   Use of subjectivity in forecasts.

(2)   *Causal methods*, which analyse the effects of outside influences and use these to produce forecasts. Productivity of a factory might depend on the bonus rates paid to employees. Then it would be more reliable to use the current bonus rate to forecast productivity than to project figures achieved in the past few months.

Both of these approaches rely on the availability of accurate, quantified data. Suppose, though, that a company is introducing an entirely new product. There are obviously no past demand figures that can be projected forward, and the factors that affect demand are unknown. In such circumstances there is no quantitative data and a qualitative forecasting method must be used. Such methods are generally referred to as judgemental, and they rely on subjective assessments and opinions.

This classification of methods does not mean that each must be used in isolation. Managers should look at all available information and then make the decision they feel most appropriate. This implies that forecasts will inevitably have some subjective review before they are adopted (see Figure 3.3).

The rest of this chapter looks at a number of different forecasting methods, starting with qualitative or judgemental methods.

In summary

Forecasting is an essential part of all planning and decision making. It is of fundamental importance to many areas of operations management. There are several ways of classifying forecasts, with two useful ones describing the time they look ahead, and the overall approach used.

SELF ASSESSMENT QUESTIONS

3.1   Why is forecasting used in operations management?

3.2   Forecasting is a specialized function which uses mathematical techniques to project historic data. Is this statement true?

3.3   List three fundamentally different approaches to forecasting.

3.4   What factors do you think should be considered when choosing a forecasting method?

3.2   JUDGEMENTAL FORECASTING

Judgemental forecasting methods are subjective assessments, often based on the opinions of experts. The methods are sometimes called qualitative or subjective.

Suppose a company is about to market an entirely new product, or a medical team is considering a new organ transplant, or a board of directors is considering plans for 25 years in the future. In these circumstances, there is no appropriate historic data on which to base a quantitative forecast. Sometimes there is a complete absence of data, and at other times the data available is unreliable or irrelevant to the future. As quantitative forecasts cannot be used, a judgemental method is the only alternative. These methods collect subjective opinions from various informed sources. Five widely used methods are:

- personal insight
- panel consensus
- market surveys
- historic analogy
- Delphi method.

Personal insight

A single expert who is familiar with the situation produces a forecast based on his or her own judgement. This is the most widely used forecasting method, and is the one which managers should try to avoid. It relies entirely on one person's judgement (opinions, prejudices and ignorance). It can give good forecasts, but often gives very bad ones and there are countless examples of experts being totally wrong. Perhaps the major weakness of the method is its unreliability. This may not matter for minor decisions, but when the consequences of errors are large some more reliable method should be used.

Comparisons of forecasting methods clearly show that someone who is familiar with a situation, using experience and subjective opinions to forecast, will consistently produce worse forecasts than someone who knows nothing about the situation but uses a more formal method.

Panel consensus

A single expert can easily make a mistake, but collecting together several experts and allowing them to talk freely to each other should lead to a consensus which is more reliable. If there is no secrecy and the panel are encouraged to talk openly, a genuine consensus may be found. Conversely, there may be difficulties in combining the views of different experts when a consensus cannot be found.

Although it is more reliable than one person's insight, panel consensus still has the major weakness that all experts can make mistakes. There are also problems of group working, where 'he who shouts loudest gets his way', everyone tries to please the boss, some people do not speak well in groups, and so on. Overall, panel consensus is an improvement on personal insight, but results from either method should be viewed with caution.

Market surveys

Sometimes, even groups of experts do not have enough knowledge to make a satisfactory forecast. This frequently happens with the proposed launch of a new product. Experts may give their views, but more useful information is found by talking to potential customers. Market surveys collect data from a representative sample of customers. Their views are analysed, with inferences drawn about the population at large.

Market surveys can give useful information but they tend to be expensive and time consuming. They are also prone to errors as they rely on:

- a sample of customers which is representative;
- useful, unbiased questions;
- reliable analyses of the replies;
- valid conclusions drawn from the analyses.

Historic analogy

Chapter 2 described how the life cycle of a product follows a characteristic pattern with introduction, growth, maturity, decline and withdrawal. If a new product is being introduced, it may be possible to find a similar product which was launched recently, and assume that demand for the new product will follow the same pattern. If, for example, a publisher is introducing a new book, it could forecast likely demand from the actual demand for the last, similar book it published.

Historical analogy relies on the availability of similar products which were introduced earlier. In practice, it is often difficult to find products which are similar enough, and which fit accurately the characteristic life-cycle curve.

Delphi method

This is the most formal of the judgemental methods and has a well defined procedure. A number of experts are contacted by post and each is given a questionnaire to complete. The replies from these questionnaires are analysed and summaries are passed back to the experts. Each expert is then asked to reconsider his or her original reply in the light of the summarized replies from others. Each reply is anonymous so that undue influences of status and the pressures of face-to-face discussions are avoided. This process of modifying responses in the light of replies made by the rest of the group is repeated several times (often between three and six). By this time, the range of opinions should have narrowed enough to help with decisions.

We can illustrate this process by an example from off-shore oil fields. A company may want to know when underwater inspections on platforms will be done entirely by robots rather than divers. A number of experts would be contacted to start the Delphi forecast. These experts would come from various backgrounds, including divers, technical staff from oil companies, ships' captains, maintenance engineers and robot designers. The overall problem would then be explained, and each expert would be asked when he or she

Table 3.1 Comparison of judgemental forecasting methods.

Method	Accuracy in term			Cost
	Short	Medium	Long	
Personal insight	Poor	Poor	Poor	Low
Panel consensus	Poor to fair	Poor to fair	Poor	Low
Market survey	Very good	Good	Fair	High
Historical analogy	Poor	Fair to good	Fair to good	Medium
Delphi method	Fair to very good	Fair to very good	Fair to very good	Medium to high

thought robots would replace divers. The initial returns would probably give a wide range of dates from, say, 1995 to 2050 and these would be summarized and passed back. Each person would then be asked to reassess his or her answer in the light of other replies. After repeating this several times, views might converge so that 80% of replies suggest a date between 2005 and 2015, and this would be enough to help planning.

Comparison of judgemental forecasts

Each of these judgemental methods is appropriate in different circumstances. If a quick reply is needed, personal insight is the fastest and cheapest method. Conversely, if reliable forecasts are needed it may be worth the time and effort needed to organize a market survey or Delphi method. A general comparison of methods is shown in Table 3.1.

In summary

Judgemental forecasts are typically used when there is no relevant historic data. They rely on subjective views and opinions, as demonstrated by personal insight, panel consensus, market surveys, historic analogy and the Delphi method.

SELF ASSESSMENT QUESTIONS

3.5 What are 'judgemental forecasts'?

3.6 List five types of judgemental forecast.

3.7 What are the main problems with judgemental forecasts?

3.3 MEASURES OF FORECAST ACCURACY

When a judgemental forecast is compared with actual performance there will usually be some error. As we will see later in the chapter, this is also true of quantitative forecasts. We need some measures of these forecast errors, and it is easiest to consider these in the context of time series.

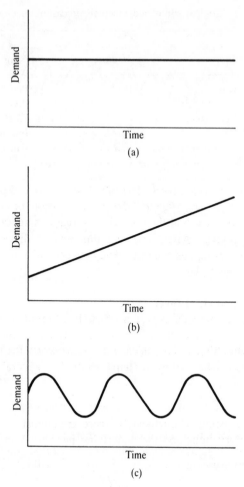

Figure 3.4   Common patterns in time series: (a) constant series; (b) series with trend; (c) seasonal series.

3.3.1 Time series

Most quantitative forecasting uses 'time series', which are series of observations taken at regular intervals of time. Thus, monthly unemployment figures, daily rainfall, weekly demand and annual population statistics are examples of time series.

If you have data for a time series, the most useful way of analysing it is to draw a graph. This will show clearly any underlying patterns. Three common patterns in time series are shown in Figure 3.4 as:

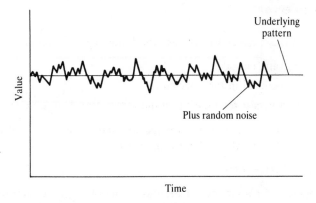

Figure 3.5   Random noise superimposed on an underlying pattern.

- constant series (where values take roughly the same value over time, such as annual rainfall);
- series with a trend (which either rise or fall steadily, such as the GNP per capita);
- seasonal series (which have a cyclical component such as the weekly sales of soft drinks).

If observations followed such simple patterns there would be no problems with forecasting. Unfortunately, there are almost always differences between actual observations and the underlying pattern. A random 'noise' is superimposed on the underlying pattern so that a constant series, for example, does not always take exactly the same value, but is somewhere close. Thus:

200 205 194 195 208 203 200 193 201 198

is a constant series of 200 with superimposed noise.

> Actual value = Underlying pattern + Random noise

It is the random noise which makes forecasting so difficult. If the noise is relatively small it is easy to get good forecasts, but if there is a lot of noise it obscures the underlying pattern and forecasting becomes more difficult (see Figure 3.5).

The random noise in a time series means that forecasts almost always contain errors. There are several ways of describing these errors, with three common measures outlined below.

3.3.2 Mean error

For the rest of this chapter we will use the following convention:

t = time period

$D(t)$ = demand in time period t

$F(t)$ = forecast for time t (*not* the forecast made at time t)

Suppose a forecast, $F(t)$, is made for the demand in period t, and the actual demand turns out to be $D(t)$. There is an error of:

$$E(t) = D(t) - F(t)$$

If this is repeated for a number of periods, n, an obvious measure of forecast error is the mean error per period.

$$\text{Mean error} = 1/n * \sum_{t=1}^{n} E(t) = 1/n * \sum_{t=1}^{n} [D(t) - F(t)]$$

WORKED EXAMPLE 3.1

Demand for a product was forecast for six periods as shown below. Later, actual demand was found. What was the mean forecast error?

t	1	2	3	4	5	6
$D(t)$	20	21	26	23	23	22
$F(t)$	22	24	23	27	25	23

SOLUTION

Calculating the errors for each period using $E(t) = D(t) - F(t)$ gives:

t	1	2	3	4	5	6
$D(t)$	20	21	26	23	23	22
$F(t)$	22	24	23	27	25	23
$E(t)$	-2	-3	3	-4	-2	-1

The mean error is $(-2 - 3 + 3 - 4 - 2 - 1)/6 = -1.5$. This means that on average the forecast for each period was 1.5 too high. This bias is also suggested by the fact that five forecasts are too high, but only one is too low.

The drawback with the mean error is that positive and negative errors cancel each other, and very poor forecasts can have zero mean error. Consider, for example, the following values:

t	1	2	3	4
$D(t)$	100	200	300	400
$F(t)$	0	0	0	1000

The demand pattern is clear and forecasting should be easy. The forecasts given are obviously very poor, but if we calculate the mean error this comes to zero. This shows that the mean error is not a reliable measure of accuracy, but measures bias. If the mean error has a positive value, the forecast is consistently too low; if the mean error has a negative value, the forecast is consistently too high.

3.3.3 Mean absolute deviation and mean squared error

The mean error allows positive and negative errors to cancel each other, so alternative measures are needed which avoid this. The two most common are to take the absolute values of errors (and calculate the mean absolute deviation), or square the errors (and calculate the mean squared error).

$$\text{Mean absolute deviation} = 1/n * \sum_{t=1}^{n} \text{ABS}[D(t) - F(t)]$$

$$= 1/n * \sum_{t=1}^{n} \text{ABS}[E(t)]$$

$$\text{Mean squared error} = 1/n * \sum_{t=1}^{n} [D(t) - F(t)]^2$$

$$= 1/n * \sum_{t=1}^{n} [E(t)]^2$$

The mean absolute deviation has an obvious meaning; when it takes a value of 1.5 the forecast is on average 1.5 away from actual demand. The mean squared error has a less clear meaning, but is useful for some statistical analyses (we will use it in the next section on linear regression). Whichever measure is used, smaller values mean better forecasts have been found.

WORKED EXAMPLE 3.2

Two forecasting methods have been used to give the following results for a time series. Which method is better?

t	1	2	3	4	5
$D(t)$	20	22	26	19	14
$F(t)$ method 1	17	23	24	22	17
$F(t)$ method 2	15	20	22	24	19

SOLUTION

It is clear that method 1 gives forecasts which are always nearer to actual demand than method 2, so in this case the decisions should be easy. This can be confirmed by calculating the errors.

Method 1

t	1	2	3	4	5
$D(t)$	20	22	26	19	14
$F(t)$ method 1	17	23	24	22	17
$E(t)$	3	−1	2	−3	−3
ABS$[E(t)]$	3	1	2	3	3
$[E(t)]^2$	9	1	4	9	9

Mean error = $(3 - 1 + 2 - 3 - 3)/5 = -0.4$ (so each forecast is slightly biased, being an average of 0.4 too high).
Mean absolute deviation = $(3 + 1 + 2 + 3 + 3)/5 = 2.4$ (so each forecast is, on average, 2.4 away from actual demand).
Mean squared error = $(9 + 1 + 4 + 9 + 9)/5 = 6.4$.

Method 2

t	1	2	3	4	5
$D(t)$	20	22	26	19	14
$F(t)$ method 2	15	20	22	24	19
$E(t)$	5	2	4	−5	−5
ABS$[E(t)]$	5	2	4	5	5
$[E(t)]^2$	25	4	16	25	25

Mean error = $(5 + 2 + 4 - 5 - 5)/5 = 0.2$ (so each forecast is slightly biased, being an average of 0.2 too low).

Mean absolute deviation = (5 + 2 + 4 + 5 + 5)/5 = 4.2 (so each forecast is, on average, 4.2 away from actual demand).

Mean squared error = (25 + 4 + 16 + 25 + 25)/5 = 19.0.

The first forecasting method has lower mean absolute deviation and mean squared error, and is the better choice. The second method has slightly less bias, measured by the mean error.

In summary

Many forecasts are concerned with time series, which are observations taken at regular intervals. Actual demand is usually a combination of random noise superimposed on an underlying pattern. This noise means that forecasts almost inevitably contain errors. The most common ways of measuring these errors are mean error, mean absolute deviation and mean squared error.

SELF ASSESSMENT QUESTIONS

3.8 Why do forecasts almost always contain errors?

3.9 What is the mean error of a forecast and why is it of limited value?

3.10 Define two other measures of error.

3.11 How would you compare different forecasting methods?

3.4 CAUSAL FORECASTING

We have already said that judgemental forecasting must be used if there is no historic data. Usually, however, there are some figures which can be used for quantitative forecasts, and we will look at two distinct approaches. The first of these is causal forecasting.

Causal forecasting looks for a cause or relationship which can be used to prepare forecasts. The sales of an item, for example, might depend on the price being charged. Then, we could find the relationship between price and sales, and use this to forecast future sales at any particular price. Similar relationships might be found between advertising expenditure and demand, bonus payments and productivity, interest rates and borrowing, amount of fertilizer and crop size, and so on. These are examples of true relationships where changes in the first (independent) variable will cause changes in the second (dependent) variable.

3.4.1 Linear regression

The principles of causal forecasting can be illustrated by linear regression. This assumes the dependent variable is linearly related to the independent one, as shown in Figure 3.6.

An introduction to operations management

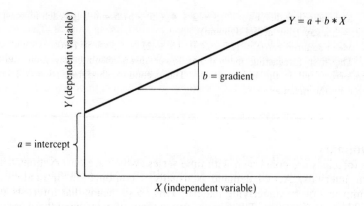

Figure 3.6 A linear relationship between variables.

WORKED EXAMPLE 3.3

A factory has recorded the number of shifts worked each month and the resulting output as shown in the following table. If 400 units are needed next month, how many shifts should be planned? How reliable is this result?

Month	1	2	3	4	5	6	7	8	9
Shifts worked	50	70	25	55	20	60	40	25	35
Units made	352	555	207	508	48	498	310	153	264

SOLUTION

As we said earlier, the best thing to do with a set of data like this is to draw a graph of it. A scatter diagram of shifts worked (the independent variable, X) and units made (the dependent variable, Y) shows a clear linear relationship (see Figure 3.7).

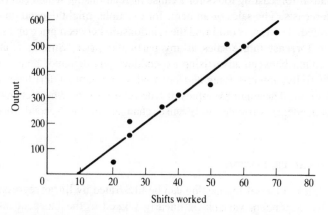

Figure 3.7 Scatter diagram for Worked Example 3.3.

A reasonable straight line can be drawn by eye through the data and the requirement of 400 units corresponds to about 50 shifts being worked. Thus we would arrange for 50 shifts and forecast an output of 400 units. Forecasts always contain errors, but in this case the error seems relatively small. We may already have definite orders for 400 units, so we should aim at making at least this number (as any unmet orders could be lost). We might finally arrange for something over 50 shifts to be worked.

In this worked example, we drew a scatter diagram, noticed a linear relationship and then drew a line of best fit by eye. Although this informal approach can work quite well, it would be useful to have a more reliable way of defining the relationship. In particular, we want to find the equation of the line of best fit. This involves finding values for the constants a and b in the equation:

$$Y = a + b * X$$

where X = independent variable

Y = dependent variable

a = point at which the line intersects the Y axis

b = gradient of the line.

The line of best fit through the data will not be a perfect fit, but there will be an error at each point, $E(i)$. In other words, at each point, i:

$$Y(i) = a + b * X(i) + E(i)$$

The line of best fit will minimize some measure of this error. We saw earlier that simply adding the errors and finding the mean allows positive and negative errors to cancel. Better alternatives would be to minimize the mean absolute deviation or the mean squared error. Because it allows other statistical analyses, the mean squared error is usually preferred for regression.

Deriving the equation for the line of best fit is quite straightforward, but we are more interested in the results than the derivation. (References given at the end of the chapter give the necessary details.) Using the abbreviations:

$$\Sigma X = \sum_{i=1}^{n} X(i)$$

MEAN(X) = mean value of X

N = number of observations

the line of best fit is given by:

$$Y = a + b * X$$
$$b = \frac{N * \Sigma(X * Y) - \Sigma X * \Sigma Y}{N * \Sigma X^2 - (\Sigma X)^2}$$
$$a = \text{MEAN}(Y) - b * \text{MEAN}(Y)$$

The use of this relationship is easiest to demonstrate by an example.

WORKED EXAMPLE 3.4

Calculate the line of best fit through the following data for an advertising budget (in thousands of pounds) and units sold. Hence forecast the number of units sold if the advertising budget is £30,000.

Month	i	1	2	3
Advertising budget	$X(i)$	20	40	60
Units sold	$Y(i)$	110	170	230

SOLUTION

There is a clear linear relationship here, as shown in Figure 3.8, with:

$$\text{Units sold } (Y) = a + b * \text{Advertising budget } (X)$$

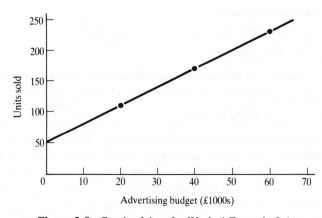

Figure 3.8   Graph of data for Worked Example 3.4.

The easiest way of doing these calculations is to use a table. Then, substituting the data and calculated values for $X * Y$ and X^2 gives the results shown in Table 3.2. (Actually, the easiest way to do this arithmetic is with a computer, either with special software or a spreadsheet.)

Table 3.2

i	X	Y	$X * Y$	X^2
1	20	110	2,200	400
2	40	170	6,800	1,600
3	60	230	13,800	3,600
Totals	120	510	22,800	5,600

The number of observations, N, is equal to 3, and substitution gives:

$$\text{MEAN}(X) = 120/3 = 40$$

$$\text{MEAN}(Y) = 510/3 = 170$$

$$b = \frac{N * \Sigma(X * Y) - \Sigma X * \Sigma Y}{N * \Sigma X^2 - (\Sigma X)^2}$$

$$= \frac{3 * 22{,}800 - 120 * 510}{3 * 5{,}600 - 120 * 120}$$

$$= 3$$

$$a = \text{MEAN}(Y) - b * \text{MEAN}(X)$$

$$= 170 - 3 * 40$$

$$= 50$$

The line of best fit is:

$$Y = a + b * X = 50 + 3 * X$$

With an advertising budget of £30,000, $X = 30$, so:

$$\text{Units sold} = 50 + 3 * 30$$

$$= 140$$

WORKED EXAMPLE 3.5

A company is planning on making changes to the way it inspects one of its products. Experiments were done with differing numbers of inspections, and figures are now available to show how the average number of defects varies with the number of inspections.

Inspections	0	1	2	3	4	5	6	7	8	9	10
Defects	92	86	81	72	67	59	53	43	32	24	12

If the company adopts six inspections, how many defects would it expect? What would be the effect of doing 20 inspections?

SOLUTION

The independent variable, X, is the number of inspections and the dependent variable, Y, is the consequent defects. There is a clear linear relationship between these as shown in the following table of data and calculations (see also Figure 3.9).

												Totals
X	0	1	2	3	4	5	6	7	8	9	10	55
Y	92	86	81	72	67	59	53	43	32	24	12	621
$X * Y$	0	86	162	216	268	295	318	301	256	216	120	2238
X^2	0	1	4	9	16	25	36	49	64	81	100	385

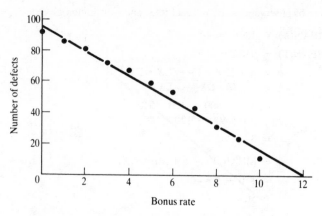

Figure 3.9 Graph of data for Worked Example 3.5.

With N = 11, substitution leads to:

$$b = (11 * 2238 - 55 * 621)/(11 * 385 - 55 * 55) = -7.88$$
$$a = 621/11 + 7.88 * 55/11 = 95.85$$

The line of best fit is:

$$Y = 95.85 - 7.88 * X$$

or:

Defects = 95.85 - 7.88 * Number of inspections

With six inspections the company could forecast 95.85 - 7.88 * 6 = 48.57 defects.

With 20 inspections we have to be a little more careful as substitution gives 95.85 - 7.88 * 20 = -61.75. It is clearly impossible to have a negative number of defects, so we would simply forecast zero defects (for any number of inspections above 95.85/7.88 = 12.16).

3.4.2 Coefficient of determination

We can now calculate the line of best fit through a set of data, but still need some way of measuring how good this line is. If the errors are small the line is a good fit, but if the errors are large even the best line is not very good. To measure the goodness of fit we will use a measure called the coefficient of determination.

We defined the line of best fit as the one that minimizes the sum of squared errors. If we look in more detail at these errors, we can separate this sum of squared errors (SSE) into different components. Suppose we take a number of observations of $Y(i)$ and calculate the mean, MEAN(Y). Actual values will vary around this mean, and we can define the total sum of squared

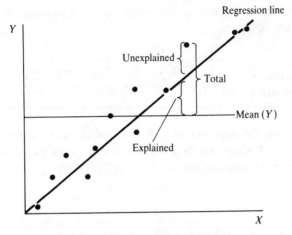

Figure 3.10 Total, explained and unexplained variation from the mean.

errors as:

$$\text{Total SSE} = \Sigma[Y(i) - \text{MEAN}(Y)]^2$$

When we build a regression model, we estimate values, $Y'(i)$, which show what the observations would be if all noise is eliminated. Thus, the regression model explains some of the variation from the mean.

$$\text{Explained SSE} = \Sigma[Y'(i) - \text{MEAN}(Y)]^2$$

Because of random noise, the regression model does not explain all the variation, and there is some residual left unexplained.

$$\text{Unexplained SSE} = \Sigma[Y(i) - Y'(i)]^2$$

With a little algebra it can be shown that:

$$\text{Total SSE} = \text{Explained SSE} + \text{Unexplained SSE}$$

as shown in Figure 3.10.

The coefficient of determination is defined as the proportion of total SSE explained by the regression model.

The greater the amount of the total variation explained, the more accurate is the linear relationship.

$$\text{Coefficient of determination} = \frac{\text{Explained SSE}}{\text{Total SSE}}$$

This measure has a value between 0 and 1. If it is near to 1, most of the variation is explained by the regression and the straight line is a good fit. Conversely, if the value is near to 0, most of the variation is unexplained and the line is not a good fit.

The easiest way of calculating the coefficient of determination is the rather messy looking equation:

$$\text{Coefficient of determination} = \left[\frac{N * \Sigma(X * Y) - \Sigma X * \Sigma Y}{\sqrt{[\{N * \Sigma X^2 - (\Sigma X)^2\} * \{N * \Sigma Y^2 - (\Sigma Y)^2\}]}} \right]^2$$

All values in this equation, except ΣY^2, have already been calculated to find the regression line. Perhaps we should say again that such calculations are well suited to computer spreadsheets or specialized programs.

WORKED EXAMPLE 3.6

Calculate the coefficient of determination for the data in Worked Example 3.5.

SOLUTION

Drawing the table of results as before, and adding the values for ΣY^2 gives Table 3.3.

Table 3.3

	X	Y	$X * Y$	X^2	Y^2
	0	92	0	0	8464
	1	86	86	1	7396
	2	81	162	4	6561
	3	72	216	9	5184
	4	67	268	16	4489
	5	59	295	25	3481
	6	53	318	36	2809
	7	43	301	49	1849
	8	32	256	64	1024
	9	24	216	81	576
	10	12	120	100	144
Total	55	621	2238	385	41,977

We already know the line of best fit through this data is $Y = 95.85 - 7.88 * X$, but are now checking to see how good this line is. The coefficient of determination is calculated as:

$$\text{Coefficient of determination} = \left[\frac{N * \Sigma(X * Y) - \Sigma X * \Sigma Y}{\sqrt{[\{N * \Sigma X^2 - (\Sigma X)^2\} * \{N * \Sigma Y^2 - (\Sigma Y)^2\}]}} \right]^2$$

$$= \left[\frac{11 * 2238 - 55 * 621}{\sqrt{[\{11 * 385 - 55 * 55\} * \{11 * 41977 - 621 * 621\}]}} \right]^2$$

$$= [-0.9938]^2$$

$$= 0.9877$$

This result shows that 99% of the variation can be explained by the regression model and only 1% is unexplained. This is evidence of a very good fit. Normally, any value for the coefficient of determination above about 0.5 is considered a good fit.

3.4.3 Coefficient of correlation

A second useful measure in regression is the coefficient of correlation which asks the question: 'Are X and Y linearly related?' The coefficients of correlation and determination answer very similar questions, and a straightforward calculation (which we need not describe) shows:

Coefficient of correlation = $\sqrt{\text{Coefficient of determination}}$

The coefficient of determination is usually referred to as r^2 and the coefficient of correlation as r.

The correlation coefficient has a value between $+1$ and -1.

- A value of $r = 0$ shows there is no correlation at all between the two variables and no linear relationship.
- A value of $r = 1$ shows the two variables have a perfect linear relationship with no noise at all, and as one increases so does the other.
- A value of $r = -1$ shows the two variables have a perfect linear relationship and as one increases the other decreases.

With correlation coefficients near to $+1$ or -1 there is a strong linear relationship between the two variables. When r is between 0.7 and -0.7 the coefficient of determination is less than 0.49 and less than half the sum of

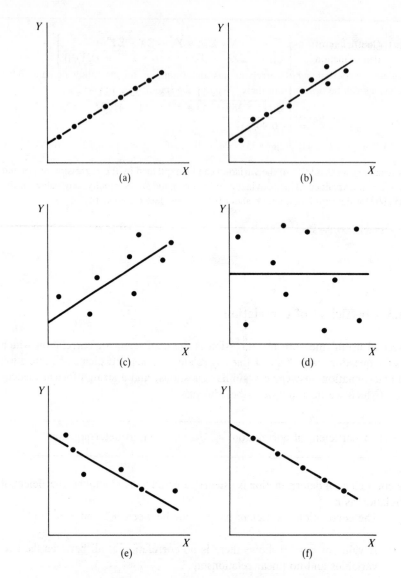

Figure 3.11 Coefficient of correlation: (a) $r = +1$ (perfect positive correlation); (b) r is close to $+1$ (line is a good fit); (c) r is getting smaller (line is getting worse fit); (d) $r = 0$ (random points); (e) r is close to -1 (line is a good fit); (f) $r = -1$ (perfect negative correlation).

squared errors is explained by the regression model. Thus, values of r between 0.7 and -0.7 suggest that a linear regression line is not very reliable (see Figure 3.11).

WORKED EXAMPLE 3.7

Calculate the coefficients of correlation and determination for the following data. What conclusions can be drawn from these? What is the line of best fit?

X	4	17	3	21	10	8	4	9	13	12	2	6	15	8	19
Y	13	47	24	41	29	33	28	38	46	32	14	22	26	21	50

SOLUTION

Using a table for the data (Table 3.4):

Table 3.4

X	Y	X * Y	X²	Y²
4	13	52	16	169
17	47	799	289	2,209
3	24	72	9	576
21	41	861	441	1,681
10	29	290	100	841
8	33	264	64	1,089
4	28	112	16	784
9	38	342	81	1,444
13	46	598	169	2,116
12	32	384	144	1,024
2	14	28	4	196
6	22	132	36	484
15	26	390	225	676
8	21	168	64	441
19	50	950	361	2,500
Total 151	464	5442	2019	16,230

Firstly, we can see if there is a linear relationship by calculating the coefficient of correlation.

$$r = \left[\frac{N * \Sigma(X * Y) - \Sigma X * \Sigma Y}{\sqrt{[\{N * \Sigma X^2 - (\Sigma X)^2\} * \{N * \Sigma Y^2 - (\Sigma Y)^2\}]}} \right]$$

$$= \left[\frac{15 * 5442 - 151 * 464}{\sqrt{[\{15 * 2019 - 151 * 151\} * \{15 * 16230 - 464 * 464\}]}} \right]$$

$$= 0.797$$

This indicates quite a strong linear relationship. If we square this we get the coefficient of determination:

$$r^2 = 0.635$$

This shows that 63.5% of the variation is explained by the linear relationship, and only 26.5% is unexplained.

As there is a fairly strong linear relationship, it is worth calculating the line of best fit.

$$\text{MEAN}(X) = 151/15 = 10.07$$
$$\text{MEAN}(Y) = 464/15 = 30.93$$
$$b = \frac{N * (X * Y) - \Sigma X * \Sigma Y}{N * \Sigma X^2 - (\Sigma X)^2}$$
$$= \frac{15 * 5442 - 151 * 464}{15 * 2019 - 151 * 151}$$
$$= 1.55$$
$$a = \text{MEAN}(Y) - b * \text{MEAN}(X)$$
$$= 30.93 - 1.55 * 10.07$$
$$= 15.32$$

Then:

$$Y = 15.32 + 1.55 * X$$

We can now answer questions about how good the line of best fit is, and the next step is to say how good an individual forecast is. In Worked Example 3.7, if we set X at 20 we could calculate $Y = 15.32 + 1.55 * 20 = 46.32$. But how good is this forecast? The easiest way of answering this is to assume there is a distribution of possible values. This has a mean (the value calculated from the regression equation) and standard deviation which can be calculated. If the regression line was drawn from more than 30 observations, the distribution can be assumed Normal. If the regression line was drawn from less than 30 observations, we can assume it follows a Student's t distribution with $N - 2$ degrees of freedom. In either case the standard deviation (or standard error as it is sometimes called) is calculated from:

$$\sigma = \sqrt{\frac{\Sigma Y^2 - a * \Sigma Y - b * \Sigma X * Y}{N - 2}}$$

Then we can look up standard tables to find the probability that an observation is within a particular range.

WORKED EXAMPLE 3.8

Using the data from Worked Example 3.7, find the range within which there is a 90% probability the forecast for Y will lie when X takes a value of 20.

SOLUTION

We know that when $X = 20$, $Y = 15.32 + 1.55 * 20 = 46.32$. Now this regression was drawn from 15 observations, so we assume the actual value follows a Student's t distribution with 13 degrees of freedom and mean 46.32. The standard deviation is:

$$\sigma = \sqrt{\frac{\Sigma Y^2 - a * \Sigma Y - b * \Sigma X * Y}{N - 2}} = \sqrt{\frac{16{,}230 - 15.32 * 464 - 1.55 * 5442}{15 - 2}}$$

$$= \sqrt{52.80}$$

$$= 7.27$$

We want to find the range within which 90% of values fall, so we look up Student's t probability tables and find the value with level of significance equal to 0.1 (signifying 5% of observations fall in each tail of the distribution) and 13 degrees of freedom. This value can be read (from Appendix B) as 1.771. Thus, 90% of observations are within 1.771 standard deviations of the mean. The range we want is:

mean $+ 1.771 * \sigma$ to mean $- 1.771 * \sigma$

$46.32 + 1.771 * 7.27$ to $46.32 - 1.771 * 7.27$

59.20 to 33.44

There are several extensions to the basic linear regression model. One would consider multiple linear regression, with a linear relationship between a dependent variable and several independent ones.

$$Y = a + b1 * X1 + b2 * X2 + b3 * X3 + b4 * X4 \ldots$$

The sales of a product, for example, might depend on its price, the advertising budget, number of suppliers, local unemployment rate, and so on. The arithmetic in multiple regression is very tedious to do by hand, and it should really only be tackled with a computer. There are many standard packages available for this.

Another extension would consider non-linear regression. In this a more complex curve is fitted to the data. Again this is simple with a computer, but is usually too complicated to do by hand.

In summary

Causal forecasts look for relationships between variables. This allows a dependent variable to be forecast by examining a related independent variable. Linear regression illustrates this approach, and draws the line of best fit (measured by the sum of squared errors) through available data. The proportion of the total variation explained by the regression line is given by the coefficient of determination, r^2, while the coefficient of correlation, r, shows how strong the linear relationship is.

SELF ASSESSMENT QUESTIONS

3.12 What is meant by 'linear regression'?

3.13 Define each of the terms in the linear regression equation $Y(i) = a + b * X(i) + E(i)$.

3.14 What is measured by the coefficient of determination?

3.15 What values can be taken by the coefficient of correlation and how is this related to the coefficient of determination?

3.16 What are the most common extensions to simple linear regression?

3.5 PROJECTIVE FORECASTING

Causal forecasting is extrinsic, in that it tries to forecast demand by looking at other variables. The last forecasting method we consider is intrinsic, in that it examines historic values for demand and uses these to forecast the future. Projective forecasting ignores any external influences and only looks at past values of demand to suggest future values. We will describe four general methods of this type:

- simple averages
- moving averages
- exponential smoothing
- models for seasonality and trend.

3.5.1 Simple averages

Suppose you are going away on holiday and want to know the expected temperature at your destination. The easiest way of finding this is to look up records for previous years and take an average. With a holiday due to start on 1 July you could find the average temperature on 1 July over, say, the past ten years.

This is an example of forecasting using simple averages, where in general:

$$F(t + 1) = 1/n * \sum_{t=1}^{n} D(t) \quad \text{Actual averages forecast}$$

where:

$$n = \text{number of periods of historic data}$$
$$t = \text{time period}$$
$$D(t) = \text{demand at time } t$$
$$F(t + 1) = \text{forecast for time } t + 1$$

WORKED EXAMPLE 3.9

Use simple averages to forecast demand for period 6 of the following time series. How accurate are the forecasts? What are the forecasts for period 24?

Period	t	1	2	3	4	5
Series 1	$D(t)$	98	100	98	104	100
Series 2	$D(t)$	140	66	152	58	84

SOLUTION

Series 1 $F(6) = 1/n * \sum_{t=1}^{n} D(t) = 1/5 * 500 = 100$

Series 2 $F(6) = 1/5 * 500 = 100$

Although the forecasts are the same, there is clearly less noise in the first series than the second. Consequently we would be more confident in the first forecast and expect the error to be less. This could be confirmed by calculating the errors.

Actual averages assume the demand to be constant. Therefore, the forecasts for period 24 are the same as the forecasts for period 6 (i.e. 100).

Using actual averages to forecast demand is easy and can work well for constant demands. Unfortunately, it does not work so well if the demand pattern changes. Older data tends to swamp the latest figures and the forecast is very unresponsive to the change. Suppose, for example, demand for an item has been constant at 100 units a week for the past two years. Actual averages would give a forecast demand for week 105 of 100 units. If the actual demand in week 105 suddenly rises to 200 units, actual averages would give a forecast for week 106 of:

$$F(106) = (104 * 100 + 200)/105 = 100.95$$

A rise in demand of 100 gives an increase of 0.95 in the forecast. If demand continued at 200 units a week subsequent forecasts are:

$$F(107) = 101.89 \qquad F(108) = 102.80 \qquad F(109) = 103.70$$

and so on. The forecasts are rising but the response is very slow.

Very few time series are stable over long periods and the restriction that actual averages can only be used for constant series makes this approach of limited value. The problem is that old data, which may be out of date, tends to swamp newer, more relevant data. One way around this is to ignore old data and only use a number of the most recent values. This is the principle of moving averages which is described in the following section.

In summary

Using actual averages can give reasonable results if the demand is constant. For any other pattern some alternative method should be used.

3.5.2 Moving averages

Demand often varies over time, and only a certain amount of historic data is relevant to future forecasts. The implication is that all observations older than some specified value can be ignored. This suggests an approach where, say, the average weekly demand over the past six weeks is used as a forecast, and any data older than this is ignored. This is the basis of moving averages, where instead of taking the average of all historic data, only the latest N periods of data are used. As new data becomes available the oldest data is ignored. Moving average forecasts are found from:

$$
\begin{aligned}
F(t + 1) &= \text{average of } N \text{ most recent pieces of data} \\
&= [\text{latest demand} + \text{next latest} + \ldots + N\text{th latest}]/N \\
&= [D(t) + D(t - 1) + \ldots + D(t - N + 1)]/N
\end{aligned}
$$

WORKED EXAMPLE 3.10

The demand for an item over the past eight months is as follows:

t	1	2	3	4	5	6	7	8
$D(t)$	135	130	125	135	115	80	105	100

The market for this item is unstable, and any data over three months old is no longer valid. Use a moving average to forecast demand for the item.

SOLUTION

Only data more recent than three months is valid, so we can use a three-month moving average for the forecast. If we consider the situation at the end of period 3, the forecast for period 4 is:

$$F(4) = [D(1) + D(2) + D(3)]/3 = (135 + 130 + 125)/3 = 130$$

At the end of period 4, when actual demand is known to be 135, this forecast can be updated to give:

$$F(5) = [D(2) + D(3) + D(4)]/3 = (130 + 125 + 135)/3 = 130$$

Similarly:

$$F(6) = [D(3) + D(4) + D(5)]/3 = (125 + 135 + 115)/3 = 125$$
$$F(7) = [D(4) + D(5) + D(6)]/3 = (135 + 115 + 80)/3 = 110$$
$$F(8) = [D(5) + D(6) + D(7)]/3 = (115 + 80 + 105)/3 = 100$$
$$F(9) = [D(6) + D(7) + D(8)]/3 = (80 + 105 + 100)/3 = 95$$

In this example, the error at each stage could be calculated to see how the forecast is performing. It is clearly responding to changes, with a high demand moving the forecast upwards and vice versa. At the same time the forecast is smoothing out variations, so that it would not blindly follow changes in the random noise.

The sensitivity of the forecast to changing demand can be adjusted by using an appropriate value of N. A large value for N takes the average of a large number of observations and the forecast will be unresponsive: the forecast will smooth out random variations, but may not follow genuine changes in demand. Conversely, a small value for N will give a responsive forecast which will follow genuine changes in demand, but may be too sensitive to random fluctuations. A compromise value of N is needed to give reasonable results and typically a value around six periods is used.

WORKED EXAMPLE 3.11

The following table shows monthly demand for a product over the past year. Use moving averages with $N = 3$, $N = 6$ and $N = 9$ to produce one period ahead forecasts.

Month	1	2	3	4	5	6	7	8	9	10	11	12
Demand	16	14	12	15	18	21	23	24	25	26	37	38

SOLUTION

The earliest forecast which can be made using a three-period moving average (i.e. $N = 3$) is $F(4) = [D(1) + D(2) + D(3)]/3$.

Similarly, the earliest forecasts for a six- and nine-period moving average are $F(7)$ and $F(10)$ respectively. Then the forecasts are as shown in Table 3.5.

Table 3.5

Month	Demand	Forecasts		
		N = 3	N = 6	N = 9
1	16	—	—	—
2	14	—	—	—
3	12	—	—	—
4	15	14	—	—
5	18	13.7	—	—
6	21	15	—	—
7	23	18	16	—
8	24	20.7	17.2	—
9	25	22.7	18.8	—
10	26	24	21	18.7
11	37	25	22.8	19.8
12	38	29.3	26	22.3
13		33.7	28.8	25.2

Plotting a graph of these forecasts shows how the three-month moving average is most responsive to change and the nine-month moving average is least responsive (see Figure 3.12).

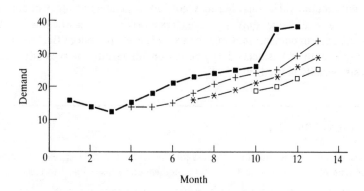

Figure 3.12   Forecasts for Worked Example 3.11: ■ demand; + forecast with N = 3; * forecast with N = 6; □ forecast with N = 9.

One particularly useful property of moving averages is seen when they are used to forecast demands which have strong seasonal variations. If N is chosen to equal the number of periods in a season, a moving average will completely deseasonalize the data. This is illustrated in the following example.

WORKED EXAMPLE 3.12

Use a moving average with two, four and six periods to calculate the one-month ahead forecasts for the following data:

Month	1	2	3	4	5	6	7	8	9	10	11	12
$D(t)$	100	50	20	150	110	55	25	140	95	45	30	145

SOLUTION

This data has a clear seasonal pattern, with a peak every fourth month. Calculating the moving averages gives the results in Table 3.6.

Table 3.6

Month	Demand	Forecast $N = 2$	$N = 4$	$N = 6$
1	100	—	—	—
2	50	—	—	—
3	20	75	—	—
4	150	35	—	—
5	110	85	80	—
6	55	130	82.5	—
7	25	82.5	83.75	80.8
8	140	40	85	68.3
9	95	82.5	82.5	83.3
10	45	117.5	78.75	95.8
11	30	70	76.25	78.3
12	145	37.5	77.5	65
13		87.5	78.75	80

The patterns can be seen clearly in a graph, shown in Figure 3.13.

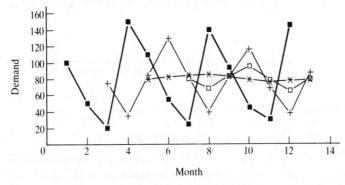

Figure 3.13 Forecasts for Worked Example 3.12: ■ demand; + forecast with $N = 2$; * forecast with $N = 4$; □ forecast with $N = 6$.

> The moving average with both $N = 2$ and $N = 6$ has responded to the peaks and troughs of demand, but neither has got the timing right: both forecasts lag behind demand. As expected, the two-period moving average is much more responsive than the six-period one. The most interesting result is the four-period moving average which has completely deseasonalized the data.

Although moving averages overcome some of the problems with actual averages, the method still has three major defects:

(1) All values used are given the same weight.

(2) The method only works well with constant demand (as we have seen it either removes seasonal factors or gets the timing wrong).

(3) A large amount of historic data must be stored to allow forecast updates.

The first of these defects can be overcome by assigning different weights to observations. A three-period moving average, for example, gives equal weight to the last three observations, so each is given a weight of 0.33. These weights could be changed to put more emphasis on later results, perhaps using:

$$F(4) = 0.2 * D(1) + 0.3 * D(2) + 0.5 * D(3)$$

In practice, a more convenient way of changing the weights is to use exponential smoothing, which is described in the following section.

In summary
Moving averages give forecasts based on the latest N demand figures and ignore all older values. The sensitivity can be changed by altering the value of N. Time series can be deseasonalized by setting N to the number of periods in the season.

SELF ASSESSMENT QUESTIONS

3.17 Why are actual averages of limited use for forecasting?

3.18 A moving average forecast can be made more responsive by:

(a) using a higher value of α

(b) using a higher value of N
(c) using a lower value of N
(d) changing initial values?

3.19 How can data be deseasonalized using moving averages?

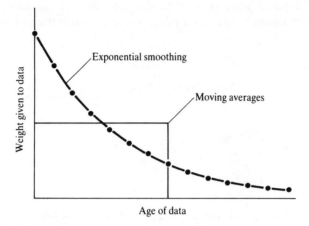

Figure 3.14   Weights given to data with exponential smoothing and moving
averages.

3.5.3 Exponential smoothing

Exponential smoothing is currently the most widely used forecasting method. It
is based on the idea that as data gets older it becomes less relevant and should be
given less weight. In particular, exponential smoothing gives a declining weight
to demand, as shown in Figure 3.14.

   This declining weight can be achieved using only the latest demand
figure and the previous forecast. In particular, a new forecast is calculated by
taking a proportion, α, of the latest demand and adding a proportion, $1 - \alpha$, of
the previous forecast.

   New forecast $= \alpha *$ latest demand $+ (1 - \alpha) *$ last forecast

or:

$$F(t + 1) = \alpha * D(t) + (1 - \alpha) * F(t)$$

In this equation, α is the smoothing constant which usually takes a value between
0.1 and 0.2.

   We can illustrate the way exponential smoothing adapts to changes in
demand with a simple example. Suppose a forecast was optimistic and suggested
a value of 200 for a demand which actually turns out to be 180. Taking a value of
$\alpha = 0.2$, the forecast for the next period is:

$$F(t + 1) = \alpha * D(t) + (1 - \alpha) * F(t)$$
$$= 0.2 * 180 + (1 - 0.2) * 200$$
$$= 196$$

The optimistic forecast is noted and the value for the next period is adjusted downwards. The reason for this adjustment is clear if we rearrange the exponential smoothing formula.

$$F(t + 1) = \alpha * D(t) + (1 - \alpha) * F(t)$$
$$= F(t) + \alpha * [D(t) - F(t)]$$

but

$$E(t) = D(t) - F(t)$$

so

$$F(t + 1) = F(t) + \alpha * E(t)$$

The error in each forecast is noted and a proportion is added to adjust the next forecast. The larger the error in the last forecast, the greater is the adjustment for the next forecast.

WORKED EXAMPLE 3.13

Use exponential smoothing with $\alpha = 0.2$ and an initial value of $F(1) = 170$ to produce one period ahead forecasts for the following time series:

Month	1	2	3	4	5	6	7	8
Demand	178	180	156	150	162	158	154	132

SOLUTION

We know that $F(1) = 170$ and $\alpha = 0.2$. Substitution then gives:

$$F(2) = \alpha * D(1) + (1 - \alpha) * F(1) = 0.2 * 178 + 0.8 * 170 = 171.6$$
$$F(3) = \alpha * D(2) + (1 - \alpha) * F(2) = 0.2 * 180 + 0.8 * 171.6 = 173.3$$
$$F(4) = \alpha * D(3) + (1 - \alpha) * F(3) = 0.2 * 156 + 0.8 * 173.3 = 84.2$$

and so on, as shown in the following table:

t	1	2	3	4	5	6	7	8	9
$D(t)$	178	180	156	150	162	158	154	132	
$F(t)$	170	171.6	173.3	169.8	165.8	165	163.6	161.7	155.8

Table 3.7 Weights given to data with $\alpha = 0.2$.

Age of data	Weight
0	0.2
1	0.16
2	0.128
3	0.1024
4	0.08192
5	0.065536
6	0.0524288
$\vdots$	$\vdots$

Although we have described how it works, it may not be obvious that exponential smoothing actually does give less weight to data as it gets older. We can demonstrate this by taking an arbitrary value for α, say 0.2. Then:

$$F(t + 1) = 0.2 * D(t) + 0.8 * F(t)$$

But substituting $t - 1$ for t gives:

$$F(t) = 0.2 * D(t - 1) + 0.8 * F(t - 1)$$

and using this in the equation above gives:

$$F(t + 1) = 0.2 * D(t) + 0.8 * [0.2 * D(t - 1) + 0.8 * F(t - 1)]$$
$$= 0.2 * D(t) + 0.16 * D(t - 1) + 0.64 * F(t - 1)$$

but

$$F(t - 1) = 0.2 * D(t - 2) + 0.8 * F(t - 2)$$

so

$$F(t + 1) = 0.2 * D(t) + 0.16 * D(t - 1) + 0.64 * [0.2 * D(t - 2) + 0.8 * F(t - 2)]$$
$$= 0.2 * D(t) + 0.16 * D(t - 1) + 0.128 * D(t - 2) + 0.512 * F(t - 2)$$

The weight put on older data is getting progressively less, and the above calculation could be continued to give the weights shown in Table 3.7.

In this calculation we took an arbitrary value of $\alpha = 0.2$, but repeating the calculations with other values would lead to similar results.

The value given to the smoothing constant, α, is important in setting the sensitivity of the forecasts: α determines the balance between the last forecast and the latest demand. To give responsive forecasts a high value of α is used (say 0.3 to 0.35); to give less responsive forecasts a lower value is used (say 0.1 to 0.15). Again, a compromise is needed between having a responsive forecast (which might follow random fluctuations) and an unresponsive one (which might not follow real patterns).

WORKED EXAMPLE 3.14

The following time series has a clear step upwards in demand in month 3. Use an initial forecast of 500 to compare exponential smoothing forecasts with varying values of α.

Period	1	2	3	4	5	6	7	8	9	10	11
Demand	480	500	1500	1450	1550	1500	1480	1520	1500	1490	1500

SOLUTION

Taking values of α = 0.1, 0.2, 0.3 and 0.4 gives the results in Table 3.8.

Table 3.8

Period	Demand	Forecast			
		$\alpha = 0.1$	$\alpha = 0.2$	$\alpha = 0.3$	$\alpha = 0.4$
1	480	500.00	500.00	500.00	500.00
2	500	498.00	496.00	494.00	492.00
3	1500	498.20	496.80	495.80	495.20
4	1450	598.38	697.44	797.06	897.12
5	1550	683.54	847.95	992.94	1118.27
6	1500	770.19	988.36	1160.06	1290.96
7	1480	843.17	1090.69	1262.04	1374.58
8	1520	906.85	1168.55	1327.43	1416.75
9	1500	968.17	1238.84	1385.20	1458.05
10	1490	1021.35	1291.07	1419.64	1474.83
11	1500	1068.22	1330.86	1440.75	1480.90
12		1111.39	1364.69	1458.52	1488.54

All these forecasts would eventually follow the sharp step and raise forecasts to around 1500. Higher values of α make this adjustment more quickly and give a more responsive forecast, as shown in Figure 3.15.

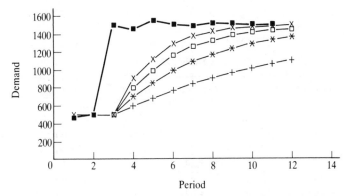

Figure 3.15 Forecasts for Worked Example 3.14: ■ demand; + forecast with $\alpha = 0.1$; * forecast with $\alpha = 0.2$; □ forecast with $\alpha = 0.3$; × forecast with $\alpha = 0.4$.

Although higher values of α give more responsive forecasts, they do not necessarily give more accurate ones. Demand always contains random noise, and very sensitive forecasts tend to follow these random fluctuations. One way of selecting an appropriate value for α is to test several values over a trial period, and select the one that gives smallest errors. This value is then used for all future forecasts.

An alternative to using this fixed value would be to change the value depending on circumstances. If, for example, errors begin to get larger, the forecast may be missing some real change in demand, and a more sensitive forecast may be needed. Thus, a check could be kept on errors, and if these get too big the value of α may be increased. This check on forecast performance can be done using a tracking signal. There are many possible tracking signals, but the simplest is defined as:

$$\text{Tracking signal} = \frac{\text{sum of forecast errors}}{\text{mean absolute deviation}}$$

If the forecast error remains small this tracking signal has a value close to zero. If, however, the error begins to grow the value of the tracking signal increases. When it reaches some subjectively defined limit around, say, 2.5, remedial action is needed. This might be a small adjustment like increasing the value of α by 0.1, or it may include major changes to the forecasting method.

WORKED EXAMPLE 3.15

Use a smoothing constant of 0.2 and an initial forecast of 15 to calculate the one-period ahead forecast for the following time series. Find the error in the forecast for each period. What conclusions can you draw from these results?

Period	1	2	3	4	5	6	7	8	9	10	11	12	13	14	15	16
Value	16	13	18	14	20	16	14	18	22	30	41	48	59	67	75	80

SOLUTION

Substitution gives the results in Table 3.9.

Table 3.9

Period	Demand	Forecast	Forecast error	Sum of errors	Mean absolute deviation	Tracking signal
1	16	15.00	1.00	1.00	1.00	1.00
2	13	15.20	−2.20	−1.20	1.60	−0.75
3	18	14.76	3.24	2.04	2.15	0.95
4	14	15.41	−1.41	0.63	1.96	0.32
5	20	15.13	4.87	5.51	2.54	2.16
6	16	16.10	−0.10	5.40	2.14	2.53
7	14	16.08	−2.08	3.32	2.13	1.56
8	18	15.66	2.34	5.66	2.15	2.63
9	22	16.13	5.87	11.53	2.57	4.49
10	30	17.31	12.69	24.22	3.58	6.77
11	41	19.84	21.16	45.38	5.18	8.76
12	48	24.08	23.92	69.30	6.74	10.28
13	59	28.86	30.14	99.44	8.54	11.64
14	67	34.89	32.11	131.55	10.22	12.87
15	75	41.31	33.69	165.24	11.79	14.02
16	80	48.05	31.95	197.19	13.05	15.11
17	—	54.44	—	—	—	—

The forecast works reasonably well for the first half of the data, but the errors increase in the second half. In period 9 the tracking signal rises to 4.49, which shows that the forecast is no longer performing well. Some action is needed, perhaps simply increasing the value of α. If, however, we draw a graph of the demand there is a clear upward trend in the second half (see Figure 3.16). We must conclude that exponential smoothing performs well for relatively stable time series, but does not perform well if there is some other pattern. A way of dealing with these is described in the following section.

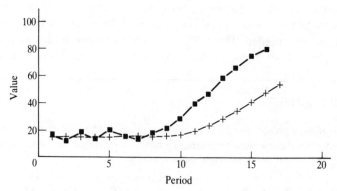

Figure 3.16 Forecasts for Worked Example 3.15: ■ demand; + forecast.

In summary

Exponential smoothing produces forecasts by adding portions of the last forecast and the latest demand. This reduces the weight given to data as its age increases. Sensitivity is adjusted by the value given to the smoothing constant, α. A tracking signal can ensure the forecasts are still reasonable.

3.5.4 Models for seasonality and trend

The methods described so far are reasonably good for constant time series, but need some adjustment for other patterns. In this section we will develop a model that can be used for data that has both seasonality and trend. We will consider trend to be the amount by which demand grows between two consecutive periods. Thus, if two consecutive periods have demands of 100 and 120, the trend is 20. If two consecutive periods have demands of 100 and 80, the trend is -20, and so on. Seasonality is a regular cyclical pattern, which is not necessarily annual. It is measured by seasonal indices, which are defined as the amounts deseasonalized values must be multiplied by to get seasonal values. Then:

$$\text{Seasonal index} = \frac{\text{Seasonal value}}{\text{Deseasonalized value}}$$

Suppose a newspaper has average daily sales of 1000 copies in a particular area, but this rises to 2000 copies on Saturday and falls to 500 copies on Monday and Tuesday. The deseasonalized value is 1000, the seasonal index for Saturday is 2.0, the seasonal indices for Monday and Tuesday are 0.5, and seasonal indices for other days are 1.0.

There are several ways of forecasting demand with seasonality and trend. The easiest of these is to split the demand into separate components, and then forecast each component separately. The final forecast is found by recombining the separate components (see Figure 3.17). To be more specific, we will consider the actual demand to be made up of four components:

- underlying value (which is the basic value of demand);
- adjustment for trend (which is an addition or subtraction to allow for steady increases or decreases);
- seasonal index (which allows for regular cyclical variation);
- random noise (which cannot be forecast).

Then:

$$D(t) = \left(\begin{array}{c}\text{underlying} \\ \text{value}\end{array} + \begin{array}{c}\text{adjustment} \\ \text{for trend}\end{array}\right) * \begin{array}{c}\text{seasonal} \\ \text{index}\end{array} + \text{noise}$$

117

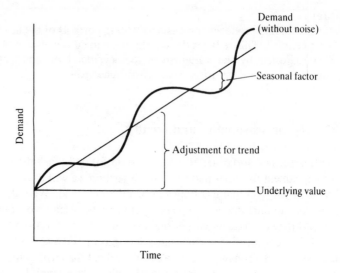

Figure 3.17 Demand with seasonality and trend.

The steps in this procedure are then as follows:

(1) Deseasonalize demand and use exponential smoothing to give the smoothed underlying value.

(2) Use exponential smoothing on the trend to give a smoothed adjustment for trend.

(3) Use exponential smoothing on the seasonal index to give the smoothed index for the period.

(4) Add the underlying value to the trend adjustment and multiply by the seasonal index to give the forecast.

$$F(t + 1) = \begin{bmatrix} \text{smoothed} & \text{smoothed} \\ \text{underlying} + \text{adjustment} \\ \text{value} & \text{for trend} \end{bmatrix} * \begin{matrix} \text{smoothed} \\ \text{seasonal} \\ \text{index} \end{matrix}$$

Thus:

$$F(t + 1) = [U(t) + T(t)] * I(n)$$

where:

$U(t)$ = smoothed underlying value for period t

$T(t)$ = smoothed trend for period t

$I(n)$ = smoothed seasonal index for period t, which is the nth period of a cycle

This may seem a little complex, but is quite straightforward as illustrated by the following example.

WORKED EXAMPLE 3.16

Records show that demand over the past 12 periods has been as follows:

t	1	2	3	4	5	6	7	8	9	10	11	12
$D(t)$	301	310	152	198	399	402	301	315	522	498	432	468

Forecast demand for the next five periods.

SOLUTION

Exponential smoothing is an updating process, so we must have initial values before we can start. We will use the first two-thirds of the data to find reasonable initial values and then do some fine tuning over the last third of the data.

If we take the first eight values we can draw a linear regression line through them, and the usual calculations give $a = 243.46$ and $b = 11.95$. This regression line effectively gives deseasonalized values and therefore allows seasonal indices to be calculated (see Table 3.10 and Figure 3.18).

Table 3.10

t	Deseasonalized value	Seasonal value, $D(t)$	Seasonal index
1	255.41	301	1.18
2	267.36	310	1.16
3	279.31	152	0.54
4	291.26	198	0.68
5	303.21	399	1.32
6	315.16	402	1.28
7	327.11	301	0.92
8	339.06	315	0.93

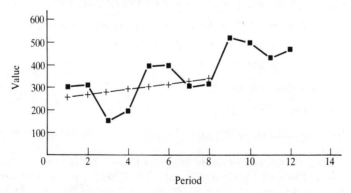

Figure 3.18 Demand and deseasonalized values for Worked Example 3.16: ■ demand; + deseasonalized demand.

The data shows a clear season which is four periods long. The eight periods of data used to find initial values have two complete cycles. The seasonal index for each period in a cycle can be found by averaging values in the two cycles:

- for first period in cycle, $I(1) = (1.18 + 1.32)/2 = 1.25$
- for second period in cycle, $I(2) = (1.16 + 1.28)/2 = 1.22$
- for third period in cycle, $I(3) = (0.54 + 0.92)/2 = 0.73$
- for fourth period in cycle, $I(4) = (0.68 + 0.93)/2 = 0.81$

The trend, $T(8)$, is the value of b in the regression equation, which is 11.95. The initial underlying value is the deseasonalized value at period 8, $U(8)$, which is $243.46 + 8 * 11.95 = 339.06$. The only other value we need is a smoothing constant, α, and we will take this as 0.2. This gives a complete set of initial values, and the next stage is to tune these using the last third of the data.

To start the forecast, we know that:

$$F(t + 1) = \left(\begin{matrix} \text{underlying} \\ \text{value} \end{matrix} + \begin{matrix} \text{adjustment} \\ \text{for trend} \end{matrix}\right) * \begin{matrix} \text{seasonal} \\ \text{index} \end{matrix}$$

Substituting the initial values of $U(8) = 339.06$, $T(8) = 11.95$ and $I(1) = 1.25$ gives:

$$F(9) = [U(8) + T(8)] * I(1)$$
$$= (339.06 + 11.95) * 1.25$$
$$= 438.76$$

This compares with the actual demand of 522.

The forecast for period 10 can now be found by updating values using the procedure described above.

(1) *Deseasonalize the latest demand and use exponential smoothing to find the smoothed underlying value.*
   The last underlying value is $U(8) = 339.06$, but the trend, $T(8)$, has to be added to this to give the underlying value for the next period. The latest demand is $D(9) = 522$ and the seasonal index for the first period of the cycle is $I(1) = 1.25$, so the latest deseasonalized demand is $522/1.25 = 417.6$. Exponential smoothing is used to give the smoothed underlying value.

$$U(9) = \alpha * [D(9)/I(1)] + (1 - \alpha) * [U(8) + T(8)]$$
$$= 0.2 * 417.6 + 0.8 * 351.01$$
$$= 364.33$$

In general this calculation is:

$$U(t) = \alpha * [D(t)/I(n)] + (1 - \alpha) * [U(t - 1) + T(t - 1)]$$

(2) *Use exponential smoothing on the trend to give a smoothed adjustment for trend.*
   The latest value for trend is the difference between the last two underlying values. These are $U(8) = 339.06$ and $U(9) = 364.33$, so the latest trend figure is $364.33 - 339.06 = 25.27$. The last value for trend was 11.95, so a

smoothed value is found using exponential smoothing:

$$T(9) = \alpha * [U(9) - U(8)] + (1 - \alpha) * T(8)$$
$$= 0.2 * 25.27 + 0.8 * 11.95$$
$$= 14.61$$

In general this calculation is:

$$T(t) = \alpha * [U(t) - U(t-1)] + (1 - \alpha) * T(t-1)$$

(3) *Use exponential smoothing on the seasonal index to find the smoothed index for the period.*
The latest figure for the underlying value is $U(9) = 364.33$. The latest actual demand for period 9 is 522, so the latest seasonal index for the first period in the cycle is $522/364.33 = 1.43$. The last value was 1.25, so a smoothed seasonal index is calculated using exponential smoothing:

$$I(1) = \alpha * [D(9)/U(9)] + (1 - \alpha) * \text{last value for } I(1)$$
$$= 0.2 * 1.43 + 0.8 * 1.25$$
$$= 1.29$$

In general this calculation is:

$$I(n) = \alpha * [D(t)/U(t)] + (1 - \alpha) * I'(n)$$

where $I'(n)$ is the previous value of the seasonal index.

(4) *Add the underlying value to the trend adjustment and multiply by the seasonal index to give the forecast.*
We can now substitute values and produce a forecast for the next period, but have to be careful with the seasonal index. Although we have just updated a value for $I(1)$, the next forecast is for period 10, which is the second period in the cycle and the latest value for $I(2)$ must be used.

$$F(t+1) = \begin{pmatrix} \text{underlying} \\ \text{value} \end{pmatrix} + \begin{pmatrix} \text{adjustment} \\ \text{for trend} \end{pmatrix} * \begin{matrix} \text{seasonal} \\ \text{index} \end{matrix}$$
$$= [U(t) + T(t)] * I(n)$$
$$F(10) = [U(9) + T(9)] * I(2)$$
$$= [364.33 + 14.61] * 1.22$$
$$= 462.31$$

This compares with the actual demand of 498.

This tuning procedure can be repeated as follows.

(1) Latest figure for deseasonalized, underlying value:

$$U(t) = \alpha * [D(t)/I(n)] + (1 - \alpha) * [U(t-1) + T(t-1)]$$
$$U(10) = \alpha * [D(10)/I(2)] + (1 - \alpha) * [U(9) + T(9)]$$
$$= 0.2 * [498/1.22] + 0.8 * [364.33 + 14.61]$$
$$= 384.79$$

(2) Latest figure for trend:

$$T(t) = \alpha * [U(t) - U(t - 1)] + (1 - \alpha) * T(t - 1)$$
$$T(10) = \alpha * [U(10) - U(9)] + (1 - \alpha) * T(9)$$
$$= 0.2 * [384.79 - 364.33] + 0.8 * 14.61$$
$$= 15.78$$

(3) Latest figure for seasonal index for the second period of the cycle:

$$I(n) = \alpha * [D(t)/U(t)] + (1 - \alpha) * I'(n)$$
$$I(2) = \alpha * [D(6)/U(6)] + (1 - \alpha) * I'(2)$$
$$= 0.2 * [498/384.79] + 0.8 * 1.22$$
$$= 1.23$$

(4) Next forecast:

$$F(t + 1) = [U(t) + T(t)] * I(n)$$
$$F(11) = [U(10) + T(10)] * I(3)$$
$$= [384.79 + 15.78] * 0.73$$
$$= 292.42$$

We now continue this updating for as long as there are demand figures.

$$U(11) = 0.2 * [432/0.73] + 0.8 * [384.79 + 15.78] = 438.81$$
$$T(11) = 0.2 * [438.81 - 384.79] + 0.8 * 15.78 = 23.43$$
$$I(3) = 0.2 * [432/438.81] + 0.8 * 0.73 = 0.78$$
$$F(12) = [438.81 + 23.43] * 0.81 = 374.41$$

$$U(12) = 0.2 * [468/0.81] + 0.8 * [438.81 + 23.43] = 485.35$$
$$T(12) = 0.2 * [485.35 - 438.81] + 0.8 * 23.43 = 28.05$$
$$I(4) = 0.2 * [468/485.35] + 0.8 * 0.81 = 0.84$$

This finishes the fine tuning of the variables, as there is no more historic data. In this example, the forecasts do not seem particularly good, because actual demand rose faster than expected. We could improve the forecasts either by starting again with different initial values, or by getting more historic data to tune the forecasts. With the data available, however, forecasts can be found for any period in the future (see Figure 3.19).

$$F(13) = [U(12) + T(12)] * I(1) \quad = [485.35 + 28.05] * 1.29 \quad = 662.29$$
$$F(14) = [U(12) + 2 * T(12)] * I(2) \quad = [485.35 + 2 * 28.05] * 1.23 \quad = 665.98$$
$$F(15) = [U(12) + 3 * T(12)] * I(3) \quad = [485.35 + 3 * 28.05] * 0.78 \quad = 444.21$$
$$F(16) = [U(12) + 4 * T(12)] * I(4) \quad = [485.35 + 4 * 28.05] * 0.84 \quad = 501.94$$
$$F(17) = [U(12) + 5 * T(12)] * I(1) \quad = [485.35 + 5 * 28.05] * 1.29 \quad = 807.02$$

and so on.

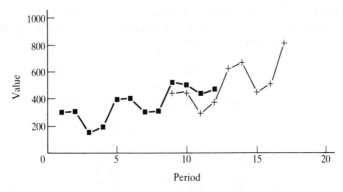

Figure 3.19 Demand and forecasts for Worked Example 3.16: ■ demand;
+ forecasts.

Two problems with this approach are the need to initialize variables and
the selection of smoothing constants. As the exponential smoothing process
reacts to errors, the initial values are not so important, provided the process is
tuned over some period. In the example above, better forecasts could have been
obtained if the method was tuned using more demand figures. The values for α
can be arbitrarily set around 0.15, but these forecasts tend to be sensitive to
values of the smoothing constants. It is worth while putting some effort into their
selection. The most useful way of doing this is to do trial runs with different
values of α on historic data and compare the resulting errors. In the example
above, we used the same value for all components, but there is no need to do
this. The forecast could, for example, be made more responsive to changes in
underlying values than to trend.

WORKED EXAMPLE 3.17

Quarterly demand for a product has been recorded over the past three years as follows:

Quarter	1	2	3	4	5	6	7	8	9	10	11	12
Demand	190	143	101	168	228	184	138	213	270	210	150	255

Use a constant value of $\alpha = 0.2$ to produce forecasts for the next year.

SOLUTION

We will again use the first two-thirds of the data to get initial values and then tune the
forecasts over the last third. The line of best fit through the first eight points has $a =$
146.54 and $b = 5.30$. Then the initial trend, $T(8)$, $= 5.30$ and the underlying value,

$U(8)$, $= 146.54 + 8 * 5.30 = 188.94$. The regression line gives deseasonalized values, so we can use this to calculate seasonal indices for each period in the season. The data has a clear season of four periods (Table 3.11).

Table 3.11

t	$D(t)$	Seasonality removed	Seasonal index
1	190	151.84	1.25
2	143	157.14	0.91
3	101	162.44	0.62
4	168	167.74	1.00
5	228	173.04	1.32
6	184	178.34	1.03
7	138	183.64	0.75
8	213	188.94	1.13

The average seasonal index for the first period in the cycle is $(1.25 + 1.32)/2 = 1.29$. Similarly the average seasonal indices for the other periods are 0.97, 0.69 and 1.07 respectively.

We now have all the initial values needed and the next step is to tune these over the last third of the data using the updating procedure described above. This gives the results in Table 3.12, where the seasonal indices given refer to the following period. Thus the forecast for period 9 is $(188.94 + 5.30) * 1.29 = 250.57$, and so on (see Table 3.12).

Table 3.12

Period	t	8	9	10	11	12
Demand	$D(t)$	213	270	210	150	255
Basic series	$U(t)$	188.94	197.25	205.82	213.29	223.61
Trend	$T(t)$	5.30	5.90	6.44	6.64	7.38
Seasonal index	$I(n)$	1.29	0.97	0.69	1.07	1.31
Forecast	$F(t)$		250.57	197.06	146.46	235.32

The updated seasonal indices are 1.31, 0.98, 0.69 and 1.08 respectively. At the end of this tuning, reasonable values have been found and we can do the actual forecasting for the next year (see Figure 3.20).

period 13 forecast $= (223.61 + 7.38) * 1.31 = 302.60$

period 14 forecast $= (223.61 + 14.76) * 0.98 = 233.60$

period 15 forecast $= (223.61 + 22.14) * 0.69 = 169.57$

period 16 forecast $= (223.61 + 29.52) * 1.08 = 273.38$

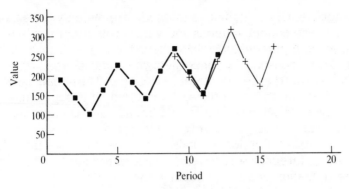

Figure 3.20 Demand and forecasts for Worked Example 3.17: ■ demand; + forecasts.

In summary

Data with seasonality and trend can be split into four components of underlying value, trend, seasonal index and noise. The first three of these can be forecast separately and combined to give overall forecasts. The use of computers for this messy, but straightforward application of exponential smoothing has obvious benefits.

SELF ASSESSMENT QUESTIONS

3.20 Why is the forecasting method called 'exponential smoothing'?

3.21 An exponential smoothing forecast can be made more responsive by:

(a) using a higher value of α
(b) using a higher value of N
(c) using a lower value of α
(d) changing initial values?

3.22 What is a tracking signal?

3.23 How can exponential smoothing be used to forecast demand which has a trend?

3.24 Define all the terms in the equation

$$F(t + 1) = [U(t) + T(t)] * I(n)$$

SUMMARY OF CHAPTER

This chapter has discussed various aspects of forecasting. It started by considering the need to forecast and how this affects various aspects of operations management. Then it looked at ways in which forecasts can be made.

There are three basic approaches to forecasting: judgemental, causal and projective. When there is no relevant quantitative data, judgemental or qualitative methods are the only ones that can be used. These collect opinions and views from groups of 'experts', and range from personal insight to the more formal Delphi method.

Most forecasting is concerned with time series, where demand is measured at regular intervals of time. These can usually be described by an underlying trend, on to which is superimposed a random noise. This noise cannot be forecast, and is the reason why forecasts will almost inevitably contain errors. The larger the amount of noise, the less reliable will be the forecast. Three measures of forecast error were considered: mean error, mean absolute deviation and mean squared error.

If there is valid numerical data, either causal or projective methods can be used. Causal forecasts look for relationships between variables, as illustrated by linear regression. This calculates the line of best fit through a set of data and checks to see if the model is appropriate (using the coefficients of determination and correlation).

Projective methods make forecasts based only on past demand figures. Actual averages, moving averages and exponential smoothing can work well with constant time series. Exponential smoothing is the most widely used method, but it needs some adjustment to deal with patterns, such as seasonality and trend.

PROBLEMS

3.1   The productivity of a factory has been recorded over a 10-month period, together with forecasts made the previous month by the production manager, the foreman and the management services department. Compare the three sets of forecasts in terms of bias and accuracy.

Month	1	2	3	4	5	6	7	8	9	10
Productivity	22	24	28	27	23	24	20	18	20	23
Prodn Manager	23	26	32	28	20	26	24	16	21	23
Foreman	22	28	29	29	24	26	21	21	24	25
Mgmt Services	21	25	26	27	24	23	20	20	19	24

3.2   A local amateur dramatic society is staging a play and wants to know how much to spend on advertising. Its objective is to attract as many people as possible, up to the limit of the hall capacity. For the past 11 productions the spending on advertising (in hundreds of pounds) and subsequent audience is shown in the following table. If the hall capacity is now 300 people, how much should be spent on advertising?

Spending	3	5	1	7	2	4	4	2	6	6	4
Audience	200	250	75	425	125	300	225	200	300	400	275

3.3   Ten experiments were done to assess the effects of bonus rates paid to salespeople on sales, with the following results:

Bonus	0	1	2	3	4	5	6	7	8	9
Sales (100s)	3	4	8	10	15	18	20	22	27	28

What is the line of best fit through this data?

3.4   Sales of a product for the past 10 months are shown below. Use linear regression to forecast sales for the next six months. How reliable are these figures?

Month	1	2	3	4	5	6	7	8	9	10
Sales	6	21	41	75	98	132	153	189	211	243

3.5   Find the two-, three- and four-period moving average for the following time series, and, by calculating the errors, say which gives the best results:

t	1	2	3	4	5	6	7	8
$D(t)$	280	240	360	340	300	220	200	360

3.6   Find deseasonalized forecasts for the following time series and hence identify the underlying trend:

t	1	2	3	4	5	6	7	8	9	10
$D(t)$	75	30	52	88	32	53	90	30	56	96

3.7   Use exponential smoothing with smoothing constant equal to 0.1, 0.2, 0.3 and 0.4 to produce one-period ahead forecasts for the following time series. Use an initial value of $F(1) = 208$ and say which value of α is best.

t	1	2	3	4	5	6	7	8
$D(t)$	212	216	424	486	212	208	208	204

3.8 The following data has seasonality, but no trend. Use values of $\alpha = 0.2$, $U(0) = 90$, $I(1) = 0.7$ and $I(2) = 1.3$ to give forecasts for periods 7 to 10.

t	1	2	3	4	5	6
$D(t)$	100	160	95	140	115	170

3.9 Eight periods of data show a season of two periods. The first half of the data has been used to get initial values of:

- seasonal index for first period in cycle = 1.2
- seasonal index for second period in cycle = 0.8
- initial underlying value = 100
- initial trend = 10

The rest of the data is:

Period	5	6	7
Period in cycle	1	2	1
Values	130	96	160

Forecast demand for the next four periods using a smoothing constant of $\alpha = 0.15$.

CASE STUDY – ELECTROTIME

Electrotime is a major manufacturer of electronic timers. It sells large numbers of these to other companies, which use them in their own products. Electrotime's best selling products are a range of basic timers used in domestic electrical equipment like washing machines and tumble driers. Other timers of this type are used in central heating controls, street lights, radio clocks, and so on. The company also makes more accurate timers, which are typically used at sporting events, and can record times to an accuracy of one-thousandth of a second. At the most expensive end of their range are specialized timers, typically used in scientific instruments, which are accurate to at least one-hundred thousandth of a second. These are usually designed to meet specific orders.

Electrotime is part of a diversified engineering group which has manufacturing plants in 37 countries around the world, and sells in over 120 countries. The parent company controls Electrotime fairly loosely and is content to leave most operating decisions to local managers.

Electrotime employs a large number of specialized engineers who work in a very technical environment. Standard company policy is to fill management jobs by promoting those engineers who have been with the company longest. The parent company has often suggested that this leaves Electrotime with good engineering skills, but lacking in commercial skills. In response to this the Managing Director has recently appointed Susan Walker as a Business Analyst. Susan is a graduate from the City of London School of Business and is the only person in the company, apart from accountants, who has a commercial academic qualification.

When she joined the company, Susan reported to the Production Manager, Jim McGovern. In her first week, after some familiarization with the company, Jim gave her an initial project. He described it as follows:

> I normally put new arrivals to work in the design area for a few weeks so they get a feel for the company products and how they work. In your case, however, you wouldn't understand any of this so it would be a waste of time. I thought you could do a bit of forecasting to start with. Every month head office insist we produce forecasts for the weekly demand for regular products for the next three months. I normally find someone in the office who has a bit of spare time and ask them to do this, but as you are here you can do it. It shouldn't take you very long.

Susan was very keen to make a good impression. She knew about forecasting and felt a good job here would improve her standing in the company. The first thing she did was to find David Hume, who had prepared the forecasts for last month. He told her:

> I did the forecasts last month and about two other times in the past three years. This is the sort of job you are given if you don't look busy at the right time. I don't know what the others do, but I take the last three months sales, plot these on a graph, draw a straight line through this by eye, and say this is the forecast for the next three months. It's a waste of time really, as we send these figures to head office, but never get any information back.

Susan thought she could do something useful here, so she looked for some past records. She soon found the store of past sales records. Every week for the past 10 years a clerk had recorded, by hand, the number of units sold of over 2000 items. These, together with other related figures, now filled eight filing cabinets in the administration area. Susan felt that she could not spend too long analysing these without showing some results, so she decided her best plan was to start with one of the best selling items. She collected the weekly sales for this item over the past six years, as shown in Table 3.13.

Table 3.13

Week	Year 1	Year 2	Year 3	Year 4	Year 5	Year 6
1	5312	6683	6987	6993	8460	8661
2	5247	6620	7009	7003	8413	8708
3	5201	6675	6557	6937	8372	8654
4	5188	6682	6418	6988	8312	8555
5	5151	6678	6374	6990	8290	8539
6	5145	6639	6300	7012	8280	8499
7	5161	6642	6230	6887	8256	8597
8	5098	6601	6228	7003	8227	8530
9	5091	6598	6240	6989	8209	8520
10	5083	6500	6241	7015	8192	8487
11	5080	6513	6128	6821	8210	8519
12	5085	6501	6102	7015	8179	8557
13	5089	6488	6091	6999	8215	8599
14	5093	6498	6024	6822	8317	8607
15	5110	6421	5904	7045	8282	8711
16	5110	6375	5902	6994	8298	8779
17	5115	6311	6002	7092	8428	8778
18	5180	6204	5907	7110	8553	8843
19	5181	6198	6001	7230	8584	8854
20	5190	6103	6021	7251	8623	8927
21	5195	6047	6013	7285	8788	9087
22	5220	6052	5902	7304	8775	9218
23	5230	5995	6022	7566	8923	9197
24	5280	5986	5918	7612	8901	9234
25	5301	5900	6089	7700	9081	9309
26	5367	5880	6111	7822	8954	9298
27	5452	5779	6089	7917	9122	9356
28	5500	5873	6124	8033	9207	9397
29	5497	5921	6299	8122	9246	9441
30	5495	5935	6336	8209	9256	9460
31	5689	6001	6474	8307	9267	9465
32	5760	6039	6591	8440	9271	9483
33	5802	6056	6698	8447	9278	9491
34	5801	6109	6780	8556	9260	9503
35	5991	6147	6887	8601	9217	9398
36	6079	6193	6991	8635	9220	9443
37	6080	6233	6986	8670	9200	9461
38	6150	6243	6995	8745	9217	9503
39	6235	6278	7065	8753	9101	9376
40	6355	6339	7092	8695	9117	9372
41	6354	6375	7088	8690	9091	9370
42	6350	6380	6935	8721	9006	9289
43	6480	6435	7043	8596	8929	9234
44	6520	6478	6988	8700	8933	9202
45	6533	6501	7053	8648	8946	9199

46	6520	6492	6934	8632	8817	9206
47	6580	6487	7000	8712	8901	9124
48	6611	6501	6911	8699	8871	9034
49	6643	6543	7010	8677	8800	8999
50	6692	6720	6900	8553	8789	8970
51	6693	6737	6878	8607	8667	8965
52	6689	6888	6945	8487	8657	8824

Suggested questions

- What is your opinion of the current management of Electrotime?
- What are the problems faced by Susan Walker?
- How should she tackle the forecasting project?
- What can be done with the figures collected?
- What changes should be made in the future?
- What might the parent company do?

SOLUTIONS TO SELF ASSESSMENT QUESTIONS

3.1 All plans and decisions are effective at some point in the future. They need relevant information about prevailing circumstances, and this must be forecast.

3.2 No. Forecasting should be incorporated into the general organization, it is not necessarily mathematical, and it does not necessarily project historic data.

3.3 Judgemental, projective and causal forecasting.

3.4 Relevant factors include: what is to be forecast, why this is being forecast, whether quantitative data is available, how the forecast affects other parts of the organization, how far into the future forecasts are needed, availability of reliable data and how frequently it is updated, what external factors are relevant, how much the forecast will cost and how much errors will cost, how much detail is required, how much time is available, and so on.

3.5 Judgemental forecasts are subjective views based on opinions and intuition rather than quantitative analysis.

3.6 Personal insight, panel consensus, market surveys, historical analogy and Delphi method.

3.7 There are a number of problems, including unreliability, conflicting views from experts, cost of data collection, lack of available expertise, and so on.

3.8 Forecasting methods look at the underlying pattern, but they cannot deal with short-term, random noise. Errors are introduced by noise, incorrectly identifying the underlying pattern and changes in the system being forecast.

3.9 The mean error is defined as:

$$\text{Mean error} = 1/n * \sum_{t=1}^{n} E(t)$$

$$= 1/n * \sum_{t=1}^{n} [D(t) - F(t)]$$

Positive and negative errors cancel each other, so the mean error should have a value around zero unless the forecasts are biased.

131

3.10   Mean absolute deviation

$$= 1/n * \sum_{t=1}^{n} ABS[D(t) - F(t)]$$

Mean squared error

$$= 1/n * \sum_{t=1}^{n} [D(t) - F(t)]^2$$

3.11   Use alternative methods for a typical time series and calculate the mean error, mean absolute deviation and mean squared error for each. All other things being equal, the best method is the one that gives smallest errors.

3.12   Linear regression finds the line of best fit (measured by the sum of squared errors) relating a dependent variable to an independent one.

3.13 $X(i)$ and $Y(i)$ are the ith values of independent and dependent variables respectively; a is the point where the line crosses the Y axis, b is the gradient of the line; $E(i)$ is the error introduced by random noise.

3.14   The proportion of the total sum of squared error which is explained by the regression.

3.15 -1 to $+1$. The coefficient of determination is the square of the coefficient of correlation.

3.16   Multiple linear regression and non-linear regression.

3.17   Because older data tends to swamp more recent (and more relevant) data. Actual averages should only be used if demand is known to be constant.

3.18   (c) Using a lower value of N.

3.19   By using a moving average with N equal to the cycle length.

3.20   Because the weight given to data declines exponentially with the age of the data, and the method smoothes the effects of noise.

3.21   (a) Using a higher value of α.

3.22   A measure that is used to monitor a forecast. When its value increases beyond some point it is a signal that the forecast is performing badly and some remedial action is needed.

3.23   An allowance for trend should be added to the forecasts (which is equivalent to using the model described for seasonality and trend with seasonal indices fixed at 1.0).

3.24 t = time period, $F(t)$ = forecast for time t, $U(t)$ = smoothed underlying value for t, $T(t)$ = smoothed trend for t, $I(n)$ = smoothed seasonal index for period t, which is the nth period of a cycle.

REFERENCES FOR FURTHER READING

Benton W.K. (1972). *Forecasting for Managers* Reading: Addison-Wesley

Bowerman B.L. and O'Connell R.T. (1979). *Forecasting and Time Series* Mass: Duxbury Press

Box G.E.P. and Jenkins G.M. (1976). *Time Series Analysis: Forecasting and Control* rev. edn. San Francisco: Holden Day

Hanke J.E. and Reitsch A.G. (1986). *Business Forecasting* 2nd edn. Boston: Allyn and Bacon

Linstone H.A. and Turoff M. (1975). *The Delphi Method: Techniques and Applications* Reading: Addison-Wesley

Makridakis S., Wheelwright S.C. and McGee V.E. (1983). *Forecasting: Methods and Applications* 2nd edn. New York: John Wiley

Thomopoulos N.T. (1980). *Applied Forecasting Methods* New Jersey: Prentice-Hall

Trigg D.W. and Leach A.G. (1967). Exponential smoothing with an adaptive response rate *Operational Research Quarterly*, **18**, 53−9

Wheelwright S.C. and Makridakis S. (1985). *Forecasting Models for Management* 4th edn. New York: John Wiley

Whybark D.C. (1972). A comparison of adaptive forecasting techniques *Logistics and transportation Review*, **8**, 13−26

Willis R.E. (1987). *A Guide to Forecasting for Planners and Managers* New Jersey: Prentice-Hall

Younger M.S. (1979). *A Handbook for Linear Regression* Mass: Duxbury Press

Chapter 4

Facilities location

SYNOPSIS

Chapter 2 looked at product planning, where the objective is to ensure that an organization makes suitable products to satisfy customer demand. Chapter 3 then described ways of forecasting demand for these products. Now we will move on to the related question of locating facilities for the product. In other words, we have answered the questions, 'What should be made?' and 'How many should be made?' and are now looking at 'Where should things be made?'.

Whenever an organization wants a new factory, warehouse, shop or any other facility it has to make a decision about the best location. This is an important decision which may have ramifications over many years. Location decisions can also be complex and depend on many interacting factors. The organization can take an international view, deciding which country to locate in, or a more local view, deciding which city or even which street to locate in.

There are essentially two approaches to location decisions. The first one compares a limited number of feasible locations and selects the best; the second one uses geometrical arguments to suggest where the best location would be in principle, regardless of site availability.

Ways of comparing feasible locations are considered first, starting with a costing approach which estimates the total cost of operating at each location. Unfortunately, it is difficult to estimate costs accurately, as all costs will vary over time, and there are many factors that cannot be costed. Scoring models can be used as an alternative means of comparison.

A number of geometric models can also be used. These look at the layout of customers and suppliers and suggest locations that will achieve some objective. The most straightforward of these is the centre of gravity method.

The problem of locating a single facility can be extended in several ways. One extension looks at problems of simultaneously opening several facilities to cover an area. An iterative costing algorithm is described for this. Another extension looks at locations on networks. We will illustrate problems of this type by the single median and the set covering problems.

The chapter finishes with a case study to illustrate one type of problem.

OBJECTIVES

After reading this chapter and completing the exercises you should be able to:

- discuss location decisions and appreciate their importance;
- describe a typical physical distribution system;
- discuss factors that affect location decisions internationally;
- compare locations by estimating the total cost of operations;
- describe ways in which location decisions for services differ from those for goods;
- use scoring models to compare locations;
- describe geometric models and use the centre of gravity method;
- use an iterative procedure to find the best combination of several possible locations;
- appreciate problems of locations on networks;
- solve the single median and set covering problems.

4.1 INTRODUCTION

4.1.1 Location as a part of physical distribution

Problems of locations are often considered part of physical distribution. This is the function that is concerned with the physical movement and storage of goods on their journey between original suppliers and final customers.

Typically, the movement of goods through an organization starts with raw materials and components brought from suppliers. These are collected at a processing plant which performs various operations. The finished products are then moved to warehouses, and there may be several types of warehouse before products reach the ultimate customer. During this movement, stocks of raw materials, work in progress and finished goods will be held at several points. There are, of course, many variations on this basic model, one of which is shown in Figure 4.1.

Such distribution systems have evolved because many types of processing can be done best in specialized units which are some distance away from either customers or suppliers. The best locations for power stations, for example, are usually away from cities and may be away from fuel supplies. Coal, or some other fuel, must be moved to the power stations, while electricity is moved away from them. The alternative to such a distribution system would be for every individual electricity user to have their own generator. The purpose of a distribution system, then, is to ensure that all products are moved as efficiently as possible.

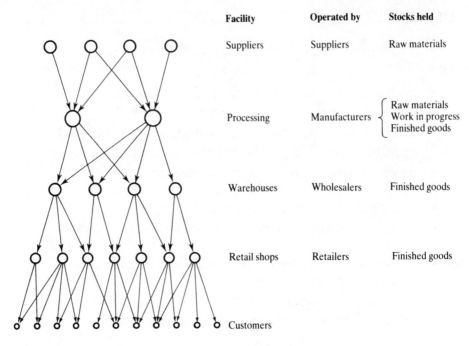

Facility	Operated by	Stocks held
Suppliers	Suppliers	Raw materials
Processing	Manufacturers	Raw materials Work in progress Finished goods
Warehouses	Wholesalers	Finished goods
Retail shops	Retailers	Finished goods

Figure 4.1 A typical distribution system.

There are several advantages to the type of distribution system described in Figure 4.1, including:

- processing is separated from warehousing, retailing, and so on, so that each organization can develop and use its own expertise;
- processing can benefit from economies of scale by concentrating operations away from both customers and suppliers;
- wholesalers keep large stocks from many suppliers, allowing retailers a choice of goods;
- wholesalers are near to retailers and have short lead times;
- manufacturers do not need to carry large stocks of finished goods;
- retailers can carry less stock as wholesalers offer reliable delivery times;
- wholesalers can place large orders and reduce unit prices;
- distribution costs are reduced as large orders are moved between operating plant and wholesalers (rather than small orders moved directly to retailers or customers).

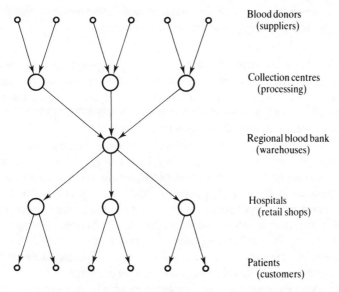

Blood donors
(suppliers)

Collection centres
(processing)

Regional blood bank
(warehouses)

Hospitals
(retail shops)

Patients
(customers)

Figure 4.2 Distribution system for a blood bank.

These benefits have encouraged many organizations to adopt similar structures. Blood banks, for example, commonly have regional centres which act as wholesalers, as shown in Figure 4.2.

Sometimes the term 'physical distribution' is used to describe only the movement of products from a processing plant to customers. Then the movement of raw materials from suppliers to processing plant is called 'materials management' and the whole process is described as 'logistics'. In this chapter we will use the terms logistics and physical distribution to mean the same thing, and assume they are concerned with all aspects of movement and storage.

Now we have a general view of the physical distribution function, and can add some details about specific concerns. In particular, we can list the types of decision that are needed.

- *Location*: where should facilities be built, how many facilities should there be, how big should facilities be, etc.?

- *Transport*: what mode of transport should be used, what routes should be taken, how big should vehicles be, etc.?

- *Warehousing*: how many levels of warehouse should be used, what kind of materials handling equipment should be used, how should warehouses be designed, etc.?

- *Inventory control*: what items should be kept in stock, when should orders be placed, how much should be ordered, etc.?

- *Communications*: how are stock records kept, how can customers check availability, how are invoices processed, etc.?

We could ask many questions about the organization and operation of distribution systems, but in this chapter we will concentrate on the question of facility location. In general, we will assume that suppliers and customers are in fixed positions and try to find the best locations for processing plants, warehouses, retail shops and any other facilities.

Commercial estate agents (perhaps with some prejudice) say, 'The three most important things for a successful business are location, location and location'. Certainly, the decisions about location are of fundamental importance to an organization. On a small scale, we would not expect a discothèque to do well in an area where most people are retired. On a larger scale, a company with production facilities in Japan and major markets in Western Europe would be unwise to locate its warehousing operations outside the European Community. There are many examples of companies which have located in the wrong area and have either closed down or suffered very high costs.

Sometimes companies are tempted to an area by short-term opportunities (perhaps the availability of development grants) and ignore the long-term consequences. Once a location is chosen, however, it usually has to remain fixed for several years. If a manufacturing plant or a power station is located in the wrong place the company may have to live with this decision for years or even decades. Even if warehouse space is rented, it is a major undertaking to close down and move to another area.

As well as being important, location decisions can be very complicated. The decision of where a family should buy a house seems difficult, but this is trivial compared with the interacting factors which influence a decision about where to open a new factory. A wide view would start by looking at the attractions of different countries or geographical regions. Then it would take a more local view and consider alternative towns or cities. Finally it would look at different locations within a preferred town. At each stage it might examine operating costs, wage rates, tax rates, international exchange rates, competition, current locations, exchange regulations, availability of grants, reliability of supplies, and so on. A few less tangible factors are the political situation, international relations, hidden costs, legal considerations, future developments of the economy, and so on.

In summary

Location decisions are often considered as part of physical distribution. Choosing the right location for a facility is an important decision which can have consequences over a long time. Such decisions are complex and involve many factors.

SELF ASSESSMENT QUESTIONS

4.1 What is physical distribution?

4.2 Why are location decisions important?

4.3 A distribution system organizes the movement of goods between suppliers, factories, warehouses, retail shops and customers. Is this statement:

(a) true
(b) false
(c) partly true?

4.1.2 Alternatives to locating new facilities

A company only needs to make location decisions when it expands (or sometimes contracts) and opens new facilities. New facilities are inevitably expensive and many organizations prefer to look for alternatives. If, for example, a company decides to sell its goods in a new market it might set up production facilities there. It need not necessarily do this, however, as there are five distinct options. These are listed below in order of increasing investment:

(1) *Licensing/franchising*: local operators are allowed to make and supply the company's products in return for a share of the profits.

(2) *Exporting*: the company makes the product in its existing facilities and sells it to a distributor operating in the new market.

(3) *Local warehousing and sales*: the company makes the product in its existing facilities, but sets up its own warehouses and sales force to handle distribution in the new market.

(4) *Local assembly/finishing*: the company makes most of the product in existing facilities, but opens limited facilities in the new market to finish or assemble the final product.

(5) *Full local production*: the company opens complete facilities in the new market.

Choice of the best of these options depends on many factors, such as capital available, acceptable risk, target return on investment, existing operations, time-scale, local knowledge, transport costs, tariffs, trade restrictions, available personnel, and so on.

One way of avoiding the problem of locating new facilities is simply to alter existing ones. This is, however, still a location decision with the implication that the current site is the best available. In essence, when an organization wants to change its facilities (either expand, move or contract) it has three alternatives:

- expand, or change, existing facilities at the present site;
- use additional, new facilities at another site (while continuing to operate existing facilities);
- close down existing operations and relocate.

Surveys suggest around 45% of companies choose on-site expansion, a similar number open additional new facilities, and 10% close down existing operations and relocate.

An important factor in such decisions is the economies of scale, which means that larger facilities are usually more efficient than smaller ones. This often encourages expansion of existing facilities rather than opening additional ones. A more detailed analysis, however, shows other complications as a number of costs increase with the size of facilities. We can illustrate this by some costs of warehousing.

- *Operating costs*. Larger warehouses are generally more efficient than smaller ones. The operating cost of warehouses is minimized with a few, large facilities, and rises with increasing numbers of smaller ones.

- *Stock holding costs*. With fewer warehouses there will be little duplication of stock so these costs will be low. As the number of warehouses increases, the amount of stock duplication rises, leading to higher stock holding costs.

- *Local delivery costs*. These are the costs of moving goods from warehouses to customers. If there are many warehouses they will, on average, be close to customers so the local delivery costs are low. Conversely, if there are few warehouses, customers will, on average, be further from warehouses and the costs of local delivery are high.

- *Trunking costs*. These are the costs of delivering from suppliers to warehouses. If there are few warehouses, large deliveries are made to a few locations and costs are low. As the number of warehouses rises smaller deliveries are made to more destinations and the trunking costs rise.

We could include many other factors, such as management costs, communications, fixed costs, employment effects, customer service, data processing, and so on. If we just plot the four costs described, however, we get a graph of the form shown in Figure 4.3. This shows that some optimal number of warehouses can be determined. In practice, analyses of this type give guidelines for the optimal number of facilities, and this can be reviewed in the light of other factors that cannot be quantified.

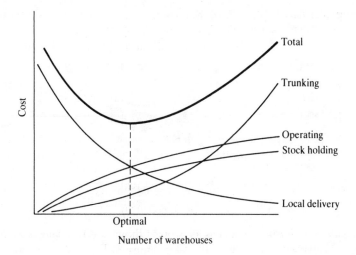

Figure 4.3 Variation of costs with number of warehouses (and hence average size).

WORKED EXAMPLE 4.1

A company is looking at various options for expansion. After a lot of thought it has decided to adopt one of five alternatives. Each of these has total costs which can be classified as either a fixed annual payment (for rent, electricity and other overheads) or a variable cost which depends on throughput (handling, depreciation, staffing, and so on). Estimates of fixed annual cost and variable cost per unit of throughput are shown in Table 4.1.

Table 4.1

Alternative	Fixed cost (£)	Variable cost (£)
A. Open new medium-sized facility	40,000	45
B. Open two new small facilities	120,000	35
C. Expand current facility	450,000	26
D. Build large new facility and close old one	400,000	18
E. Build large new facility and keep old one	600,000	22

Over what range of throughput would each alternative be most attractive?

SOLUTION

This is an extension of the break-even analyses described in Chapter 2. One thing we can see from the figures is that alternatives C and E will never be cheapest, as they are always

141

more expensive than D. The choice is then between alternatives A, B and D. The costs for various throughputs are shown in Figure 4.4.

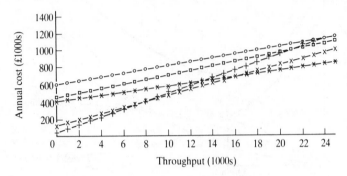

Figure 4.4 Break-even graphs for Worked Example 4.1: + alternative A; × alternative B; □ alternative C; * alternative D; ○ alternative E.

Alternative A is the cheapest until the throughput reaches X, with:

$$40,000 + 45 * X = 120,000 + 35 * X$$
$$10 * X = 80,000$$
$$X = 8000$$

After this point alternative B is cheaper than A. B remains the cheapest alternative until:

$$120,000 + 35 * X = 400,000 + 18 * X$$
$$17 * X = 280,000$$
$$X = 16,471$$

After this point D remains the cheapest.

In summary

There are several alternatives to opening new facilities. Expanding existing facilities can give economies of scale, but a fuller analysis is needed to identify the optimal number of locations.

SELF ASSESSMENT QUESTIONS

4.4 If a company wants to start supplying products to a new market, does it have to open new facilities there?

4.5 What are the three location alternatives if a company wants to expand its facilities?

4.6 Economies of scale mean that it is always cheaper to operate a single large warehouse than a number of smaller ones. Is this statement:

(a) true
(b) false
(c) partly true?

4.2   SELECTING THE GEOGRAPHIC REGION

In the last section we said there were several alternatives to opening new facilities. If, after careful analysis, it is decided that some new facility is needed, we can begin discussing its location. This discussion might start with a wide view and look at the attractions of different countries or geographical regions. After this, more detailed discussions might look at alternative towns and cities, and then sites within cities.

Starting at the top of this hierarchy of decisions, a decision may be needed about the country of operation. The obvious reason for an organization to open facilities in a country is to meet local demand for its products. Licensing and exporting need no local facilities, but they do not allow much control over products. Most companies which forecast long-term demand for their products in a particular region will open some kind of local facilities. This has a number of advantages, including greater control over products, higher profits, avoidance of import tariffs, easier transportation, reduced costs, and so on.

In recent years, many companies have opened manufacturing plants in developing countries to take advantage of lower costs. Low wage rates, for example, encouraged many electronics companies to open factories in the Far East. Similarly, car manufacturers opened plants in Mexico, Brazil and Eastern Europe. Often these facilities have simply provided a convenient base for international trade. A Japanese company, for example, might open a factory in Taiwan to supply goods to Europe. Sometimes the trade has other significance, when, for example, an American company moves one of its plants to Mexico, and then imports the products back to the United States. Although the transport costs are much higher, the reduced operating costs more than compensate for these.

It has now become increasingly clear that low wage rates do not necessarily mean low overall costs. There are many parts of the world where low wage rates are accompanied by very low productivity. Perhaps more importantly, manufacturing processes have changed so that labour costs often form a very small fraction of overall costs. Most organizations will now prefer to locate in areas which are near markets and have reliable suppliers, good infrastructure, high productivity and skilled workforce, even if they also have high labour costs.

Steel production gives an interesting example of such changes. Originally, steel mills were located near to sources of coal and iron ore. Unfortunately, these sites had the disadvantage of being some distance from customers. Later, it was found that operating costs could be reduced by opening large, new mills in countries like Taiwan and South Korea. These relied on imported coal and ore, so they were located near to suitable ports and transport routes. One problem is that transporting steel is very expensive, and when the cost of delivering to customers is added these mills often become uncompetitive. The cheapest supplier of steel is often the one nearest to the customer, regardless of its operating costs.

It is interesting to see how the attractiveness of locations varies over time. By their nature, location decisions are long term in effect, but the circumstances in an area may change dramatically during the lifetime of any facilities. One of the key requirements of a location, then, is some measure of stability. This may be difficult, particularly as opening new facilities may inevitably change an area. If we consider the Far East, for example, much of the region used to combine high productivity with low wage rates. The rapid development of manufacturing has meant that wages and other costs have risen quickly and make the area less attractive for new investment. High transport costs, import tariffs and quotas mean their products are often more expensive than those made in Europe or North America. Japanese car makers now find it more profitable to open plants nearer their main markets than to continue direct exporting from Japan.

The location of sites in international markets depends on a number of factors. Some of these are commercial, but experience suggests that three other factors play an important part in successful developments.

(1) *Cultural factors*. It is easier to expand into an area which has a similar language, culture, laws and costs, than to expand into a completely foreign area. Thus, a company currently operating in Canada would find it easier to expand in the United States than in, say, Korea.

(2) *Organization*. If operations expand overseas, there are essentially two ways in which they can be organized. The company may choose to operate internationally or multinationally. An international organization maintains its headquarters in the 'home' country and runs its worldwide activities from there; a multinational organization opens subsidiary headquarters around the world so that each area is largely independent.

(3) *Operations*. Another concern is whether it is better to use the same operations around the world or to adapt to the local environment. McDonald's hamburger restaurants, for example, use very similar operations in all countries in which they work. Other organizations would try and blend in with the local environment and do things in ways that are more familiar to their host countries.

Before leaving this international view of location it is worth mentioning a few long-term trends. We have mentioned Japan several times, and this country gives a good example of economic changes. In the 1950s Japan was still receiving economic aid from America, but by the 1980s it had become the strongest industrial power in the world. It has now been followed by Singapore, South Korea, Hong Kong, Taiwan, and other countries on the Pacific rim. This development of the Pacific rim as a manufacturing centre is likely to continue for the foreseeable future.

Eastern Europe provides another area where rapid economic development is likely to occur, led by a united Germany. This kind of growth inevitably means that other areas will go into a comparative decline. In the United States, for example, the South and South West coast are developing faster than the North and are becoming relatively more prosperous. In Europe the South (and latterly the East) is developing a lot faster than the North. This does not, of course, mean that the areas which industrialized first are declining in prosperity, only that their rate of growth is slower than newer areas.

Another long-term trend is the decline of urban areas in industrialized countries. City populations are declining as new operations open on green field sites. Conversely, developing countries see a growth in urban areas, where people are moving away from the poverty of subsistence agriculture and towards the more prosperous industrial cities.

Overall, although long-term location decisions depend on economic stability, it may be difficult to guarantee this in any area.

In summary

There is a hierarchy of decisions in location, starting with the 'country or geographical region of operation. There may be several reasons for selecting a particular country, including proximity to markets, low operating costs and a range of other factors. There are several long-term trends in location, including the development of manufacturing in new areas, the growth of international operations and changes in urban area populations.

SELF ASSESSMENT QUESTIONS

4.7 What is the overall approach to location decisions?

4.8 Low wage rates mean a country is an attractive location for industry. Is this statement true or false?

4.9 Name three non-economic factors that play an important part in the success of an international development.

4.10 If jobs are created in one country, they must inevitably be lost in another. Is this statement true or not?

4.3 COSTING ALTERNATIVE LOCATIONS

Once a decision has been made about the country or geographical region of operation, more detailed decisions are needed about towns, cities and individual sites. There are many possible approaches to location decisions, and the best approach depends on specific circumstances. One approach which is *not* recommended is personal preference. In this, the decision maker simply chooses a site he or she likes, perhaps in the town in which he or she grew up, or the area in which holidays were taken. This kind of biased decision making is quite common, but it is not the best way to approach important decisions.

Here we will restrict ourselves to rational analyses based on a number of models. These models follow one of two distinct approaches.

- *Feasible set approach*, where there are only a small number of feasible sites and the best has to be selected.
- *Infinite set approach*, which uses geometric arguments to show where the best site would be if there were no restrictions on availability.

Thus, a feasible set approach would compare sites which are currently vacant and choose the best, while an infinite set approach would find the best location in principle and then look for a site nearby.

The specific models we will consider are:

(1) Feasible set approaches

(a) Costing methods, which find the cost of operating at each potential location and select the location which minimizes the total costs.

(b) Scoring models, which allocate scores to each location and allow comparisons to include non-quantifiable factors (in the same way that products were compared using scoring models in Chapter 2).

(c) Specialized algorithms, which consider specific problems, like the set covering algorithm.

(2) Infinite set approaches

(a) Geometric models, which use some characteristics of the layout of customers and suppliers.

We will start by looking at feasible set approaches. Here comparisons between alternative sites are needed, and an obvious analysis looks at the total cost of alternative locations. There are many costs which could be used in such evaluations, but we will simplify calculations by classifying these according to transport costs (both inwards and outwards) and operating costs.

- *Cost of inward transport*: the cost of moving goods and services into the facility from suppliers. Typically this includes the cost of transporting raw materials and components.
- *Cost of outward transport*: the cost of moving finished goods and services out to customers.
- *Operating cost*: the total cost of running the facility.

These costs will obviously vary with location. In particular, sites near to suppliers will have low costs for inward transport, but high costs of outward transport. Conversely, sites near to customers will have low costs for outward transport, but high costs for inward transport (as shown in Figure 4.5).

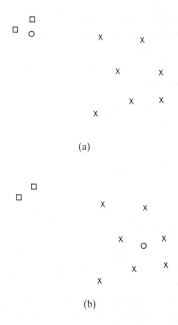

(a)

(b)

Figure 4.5 Transport costs at different locations. (a) Locations near suppliers have high transport-out costs, but low transport-in costs. (b) Locations near customers have high transport-in costs, but low transport-out costs. □ suppliers; × customers; ○ facility.

Operating costs depend on a number of factors such as wage rates, local taxes, reliability of local suppliers, weather conditions, and so on. If we add these three costs for each alternative site we get a direct comparison which will identify the best.

$$
\begin{array}{c}
\text{Total cost} \\
\text{of facility}
\end{array}
=
\begin{array}{c}
\text{Operating} \\
\text{cost}
\end{array}
+
\begin{array}{c}
\text{Cost of} \\
\text{inward} \\
\text{transport}
\end{array}
+
\begin{array}{c}
\text{Cost of} \\
\text{outward} \\
\text{transport}
\end{array}
$$

The obvious problem with this approach is that costs are not known with certainty in advance. How, for example, could accurate costs be assigned to outward transport when the precise demand and set of customers is not known before opening? Even if the costs are known, they are likely to change and the analysis will become dated. Thus, we have to recognize that the costing analyses give measures which can be used to compare locations, but they do not necessarily represent the costs which will actually be incurred. As usual, we can say that costing analyses give one piece of information, but all available facts should be considered before a decision is made.

If the costs are only used to give comparisons of locations, we can make some simplifications to the calculations. The cost of delivering products to a particular customer may be difficult to find exactly, but we can simplify this by assuming transport costs are proportional to the straight line distance from the facility to the customer. We can easily find map coordinates for the customer and the facility, and then take:

$$COST = DISTANCE * FACTOR * QUANTITY * PRICE$$

where:

DISTANCE = straight line map distance between facility and customer

FACTOR = a factor to allow for the actual distance being longer than the straight line distance, and any scaling for the map coordinates used

QUANTITY = the expected weight of goods to be transported between the facility and the customer

COST = the cost of moving unit weight a unit distance

This equation gives the cost of delivering to one customer, so if we do this calculation for all potential customers and add the results we get an overall cost for local deliveries. A similar calculation gives the total cost for deliveries from suppliers.

The cost figures are only valid for comparison, so any consistent convention for costs is acceptable provided it is used in the same way for all locations. Care should, however, be taken when adding these transport costs directly to operating costs. This should only be done if all costs are reasonably accurate and are in consistent units. In practice, there is often little difference in operating costs between nearby locations, so these can actually be removed from the equation.

WORKED EXAMPLE 4.2

A warehouse is located at coordinates (12,16) and delivers to two customers which are located at (15,20) and (6,8). The scale of the map has each unit corresponding to 10 kilometres. Experience suggests that a straight line map distance of 1 kilometre corresponds to 1.6 kilometres of actual road distance. It costs an average of 20 pence per tonne kilometre to move goods. What is the annual cost of outward transport if forecast demands from the customers are 8 tonnes a week and 12 tonnes a week respectively?

SOLUTION

The straight line distances between the warehouse and customers can be found from Pythagoras.

Distance from warehouse to customer 1 is:

$$\sqrt{[(15 - 12)^2 + (20 - 16)^2]} = \sqrt{25}$$
$$= 5$$

Distance from warehouse to customer 2 is:

$$\sqrt{[(12 - 6)^2 + (16 - 8)^2]} = \sqrt{100}$$
$$= 10$$

We also know that FACTOR = 1.6 and PRICE = 0.2.
Then the expected weekly cost of transport to the first customer is:

$$\text{COST} = \text{DISTANCE} * \text{FACTOR} * \text{QUANTITY} * \text{PRICE}$$
$$= 5 * 10 * 1.6 * 8 * 0.2$$
$$= 128$$

Similarly for the second customer:

$$\text{COST} = \text{DISTANCE} * \text{FACTOR} * \text{QUANTITY} * \text{PRICE}$$
$$= 10 * 10 * 1.6 * 12 * 0.2$$
$$= 384$$

Then the total transport cost is the sum of these two, which is £512 a week or £26,624 a year.

In Worked Example 4.2 the cost is only a consistent measure and will not be the actual amount paid for transport. This will vary with vehicles used, frequency of journeys, routes taken, organization of drivers, actual orders placed, and so on. If we were comparing different sites it would have been just as valid to simplify the calculations even further. FACTOR, for example, could be set as 1, and DISTANCE replaced by the simpler rectilinear distance, which is defined as:

$$\text{Rectilinear distance} = \frac{\text{Difference in}}{X \text{ coordinates}} + \frac{\text{Difference in}}{Y \text{ coordinates}}$$

The approach to site selection is then illustrated in the following example.

WORKED EXAMPLE 4.3

A company wants to build a depot to serve five major customers located at coordinates (120,120), (220,120), (180,180), (140,160) and (180,120). Average weekly demands, in vehicle loads, are 20, 5, 8, 12 and 8 respectively. Two alternative locations are available at (140,120) and (180,140). Which of these would be preferable if operating costs and transport inwards costs were the same for each location?

SOLUTION

A map for this problem is shown in Figure 4.6.

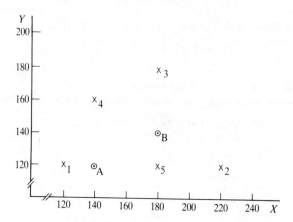

Figure 4.6 Map for Worked Example 4.3.

As operating costs and transport inward costs are the same for both locations all we need is a means of comparing the costs of local deliveries from each location, A and B. We will take DISTANCE as the rectilinear distance, and FACTOR as 1 to give the costs. Then the distance from B to customer 2 is:

difference in X coordinate + difference in Y coordinate
$$= (220 - 180) + (140 - 120)$$
$$= 60$$

and so on.

| Customer | A | | | B | | |
	Dist.	Load	Dist. * Load	Dist.	Load	Dist. * Load
1	20	20	400	80	20	1600
2	80	5	400	60	5	300
3	100	8	800	40	8	320
4	40	12	480	60	12	720
5	40	8	320	20	8	160
Total			2400			3100

It is clear that location A is better. We can confirm this with calculations based on straight line distances. Then the distance from B to customer 2 is:

$$\sqrt{[(\text{difference in X})^2 + (\text{difference in Y})^2]}$$
$$= \sqrt{[(220 - 180)^2 + (140 - 120)^2]}$$
$$= \sqrt{[1600 + 400]}$$
$$= 44.7$$

and so on.

Customer	A			B		
	Dist.	Load	Dist. * Load	Dist.	Load	Dist. * Load
1	20	20	400	63.2	20	1264
2	80	5	400	44.7	5	223.6
3	72.1	8	576.9	40	8	320
4	40	12	480	44.7	12	536.4
5	40	8	320	20	8	160
Total			2176.9			2503.9

Again A is confirmed as the better choice.

As we suggested in Worked Example 4.2, the choice of best location may vary with the throughput. Each location will have operating costs which depend on throughput, and these can be considered as a combination of fixed and variable costs. Then, the total cost rises linearly with throughput, but the rate of increase will be different for each location. This suggests that different locations will be attractive for different throughputs.

In summary

There are essentially two approaches to location problems: feasible set and infinite set. The first of these compares alternative sites and can be illustrated by costing methods. These find the cost of operating a facility at each potential location by adding transport, operating and other costs. Only comparisons are needed, so these costs can be in any consistent units.

SELF ASSESSMENT QUESTIONS

4.11 What is the difference between a feasible set approach and an infinite set approach to facility location?

4.12 What costs might be included in a costing model?

4.13 What is the difference between inward transport and outward transport?

4.4   SCORING MODELS

The last section discussed costing models, but several problems can be identified with these:

- accurate costs are difficult to find;
- data depends on accounting conventions;
- costs will vary over time;
- customer locations may not be known in advance;
- customer demands may not be known exactly;
- there are many factors which cannot be costed;
  and so on.

The exclusion of factors which cannot be costed is particularly import-ant. How, for example, could a cost be attached to an attractive lifestyle in one location? This would certainly be a benefit for employees, reduce employee turnover and assist in recruiting, but it would be very difficult to evaluate as an operating cost. Other factors, which may also be important but which are difficult to quantify, include:

- *Country and region*
  - availability and quality of workforce;
  - climate;
  - local and national government policies;
  - availability of development grants;
  - attractiveness of locations;
  - quality of life (including health, education, welfare and culture);
  - reliability of local suppliers;
  - infrastructure (particularly transport and communications);
  - economic stability of area.

- *City or location*
  - nearness to customers and suppliers;
  - location of competitors;
  - cost of available sites;
  - size of available sites;
  - potential for expansion;
  - local restrictions on operations;
  - community feelings.

One way of considering such non-quantifiable factors is to use a scoring model. We have already described these in Chapter 2 to compare different products. For location decisions the process can be summarized as:

- decide the relevant factors in a decision;
- give each factor a maximum number of points (or weight);
- consider each location in turn and assign a score for each factor;
- add the total score for each alternative and identify the highest;
- discuss the result and make a final decision.

The factors used and relative weights will obviously change with circumstances. Experience suggests that decisions about the location of a new factory are dominated by factors like:

- labour relations in the area;
- environment and quality of life for employees;
- proximity to customers;
- proximity to suppliers and services;
- quality of infrastructure.

For comparison, decisions about the location of a hamburger restaurant would consider factors like:

- population density in the area;
- socio-economic characteristics of the area;
- location of competitors;
- location of retail shops;
- traffic, access and parking;
- visibility of site.

This confirms the obvious point that manufacturers have different location objectives to service industries. In general, manufacturers try to gain economies of scale by building large, centralized facilities which may be near raw materials. Then a factory will look for a location with low costs, a skilled workforce, near to suppliers. Services, however, must be near to their customers. They cannot keep stocks of their services, so they must spontaneously meet any demand. Then a retail shop will look for a location with high revenues, cheap labour, near to customers. These differences are the reason why town centres contain shops, but no factories. An extreme form of such differences occurs in primary industries, where mines and quarries, for example, are located near the raw materials regardless of all other factors.

WORKED EXAMPLE 4.4

A company is considering four alternative locations for a new depot. It decides the most important factors and their relative weights, as shown in Table 4.2.

Table 4.2

Factor	Maximum score
Climate	10
Infrastructure	20
Accessibility	10
Construction cost	5
Community attitude	10
Government views	5
Proximity to suppliers	15
Proximity to customers	20
Availability of workers	5
Total	100

After considerable discussion the scores in Table 4.3 were allocated for each site. What is the relative importance of each factor? Which site should be selected?

Table 4.3

Factor	Location			
	A	B	C	D
Climate	8	6	9	7
Infrastructure	12	16	15	8
Accessibility	6	8	7	9
Construction cost	3	1	4	2
Community attitude	6	8	7	4
Government views	2	2	3	4
Proximity to suppliers	10	10	13	13
Proximity to customers	12	10	15	17
Availability of workers	1	2	4	5

SOLUTION

The most important factors are the available infrastructure and proximity to customers (with up to 20 points each). These are a bit more important than the proximity of suppliers (with up to 15 points), but are twice as important as climate, accessibility and community attitude (with up to 10 points each). Construction cost, government views and availability of workers are least important.

Adding the scores for each location gives:

Location	A	B	C	D
Total scores	60	63	77	69

These scores suggest that location C is the best. Any other information would now have to be analysed before coming to a final decision.

In summary

Many location decisions include subjective factors which cannot be quantified. Scoring models allow such factors to be compared.

SELF ASSESSMENT QUESTIONS

4.14 Scoring models allow both qualitative and quantitative data to be used in a location decision. Is this statement true or false?

4.15 Are the same factors important for locating a factory as locating a retail shop?

4.16 What factors might be important in locating a professional service, such as a doctor's surgery?

4.5   GEOMETRIC MODELS

The last two sections described ways of comparing potential sites, using feasible set approaches. In this section we will move on to describe some infinite set approaches.

Many location models are based on the geographic layout of customers and suppliers. These models generally assume that the operating cost is constant, and the best location can be found from the relationship of a facility with its customers and suppliers. The basic assumption is that facilities should be located near the centre of potential demands and supplies. One way of defining the centre is to calculate the centre of gravity of demand. This uses an analogy from engineering, with the demand at each customer replacing the weight.

The centre of gravity is defined as:

$$X(0) = \frac{\Sigma X(i) * W(i)}{\Sigma W(i)} \qquad Y(0) = \frac{\Sigma Y(i) * W(i)}{\Sigma W(i)}$$

where:

> $X(0)$, $Y(0)$ are coordinates of the centre of gravity (i.e. facility location);
> $X(i)$, $Y(i)$ are coordinates of each customer and supplier, i;
> $W(i)$ is expected demand at customer i, or expected supply from source i.

This gives a reasonably good location, but it should really only be considered a starting point for further investigation. There may, for example, be no site available anywhere near the centre of gravity, or available sites may be too expensive. The centre of gravity might be a long way from roads, in an area with no workforce or even in a river. Perhaps the best use of such approaches is in cutting down the area of search. This suggests a particularly useful approach to locations which would:

- use the centre of gravity to find a reasonable location for facilities;
- search near this location to find a feasible set of locations;
- use a costing method to compare these alternative locations;
- add costs and other information to a scoring model;
- discuss all available information and come to a final decision.

WORKED EXAMPLE 4.5

An assembly plant is planned to take components from three suppliers, and send finished goods to six regional warehouses. The locations of these and the amounts supplied or demanded are shown in Table 4.4. Where would you start looking for a site for the assembly plant?

Table 4.4

Location	X,Y coordinates	Supply/demand
Supplier 1	91,8	40
Supplier 2	93,35	60
Supplier 3	3,86	80
Warehouse 1	83,26	24
Warehouse 2	89,54	16
Warehouse 3	63,87	22
Warehouse 4	11,85	38
Warehouse 5	9,16	52
Warehouse 6	44,48	28

SOLUTION

The calculations for this are done in Table 4.5.

Table 4.5

i	X(i)	Y(i)	W(i)	X(i) * W(i)	Y(i) * W(i)
Supplier 1	91	8	40	3,640	320
Supplier 2	93	35	60	5,580	2,100
Supplier 3	3	86	80	240	6,880
Warehouse 1	83	26	24	1,992	624
Warehouse 2	89	54	16	1,424	864
Warehouse 3	63	87	22	1,386	1,914
Warehouse 4	11	85	38	418	3,230
Warehouse 5	9	16	52	468	832
Warehouse 6	44	48	28	1,232	1,344
Totals			360	16,380	18,108

Then substitution gives the centre of gravity as:

$$X(0) = \frac{\Sigma X(i) * W(i)}{\Sigma W(i)} = \frac{16,380}{360} = 45.5$$

$$Y(0) = \frac{\Sigma Y(i) * W(i)}{\Sigma W(i)} = \frac{18,108}{360} = 50.3$$

A good place to start looking for locations is around (45.5,50.3) as shown in Figure 4.7. As this is very close to warehouse 6 it might be preferable to expand on this site rather than look for an entirely new location.

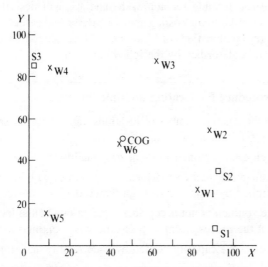

Figure 4.7 Locations for Worked Example 4.5: □ suppliers; × customers; ○ centre of gravity.

In summary

The centre of gravity method is an example of an infinite set approach to facility location. It gives a reasonable starting point for locations, and can be used to cut down the area of search to find a feasible set.

SELF ASSESSMENT QUESTIONS

4.17 How would you define the centre of gravity of customer demand?

4.18 The centre of gravity is an example of a feasible set approach. Is this statement true or false?

4.19 The centre of gravity finds the optimal location for a facility. Is this:

(a) true
(b) false
(c) partly true?

4.6   LOCATING MULTIPLE FACILITIES

So far we have looked at problems of locating a single facility. Suppose, though, that we wanted to locate several facilities to cover a geographical area. We might, for example, have 12 areas in which to make deliveries, but only want to build depots in three of these. How could we select the best three? This is clearly an extension of the feasible set approach, and we will describe an iterative method which is similar to the costing approach described earlier. In essence, we will repeatedly try combinations of locations until we get a satisfactory solution. This method can be described by the following steps.

Iterative procedure for locating multiple facilities

(1)   Find the desired number of locations and arbitrarily select an initial set from those available.

(2)   Assign each customer to its nearest facility.

(3)   Calculate the total cost, which is the sum of weights moved multiplied by distances through which they are moved.

(4)   If the solution is not acceptable, change one of the locations and repeat the process from step 2; otherwise continue with step 5.

(5)   Calculate the capacity needed by each facility and stop.

This can be demonstrated most easily with an example.

WORKED EXAMPLE 4.6

Eight areas are to be served by two depots. Limited access means that only four areas are suitable for depots. The distances between areas and demands in each area, $W(i)$, are given in the following table. The company is willing to pay up to 800 units for distribution, with the condition that no depot should meet a total demand of more than 90 units. Find a suitable combination of two depot locations.

Area	A	B	C	D	$W(i)$
A	0	6	20	7	10
B	6	0	12	15	20
C	20	12	0	4	15
D	7	15	4	0	30
E	12	8	10	11	5
F	22	12	17	27	25
G	30	24	32	6	10
H	6	5	9	11	20

SOLUTION

Following the process described above, step 1 starts by arbitrarily selecting two areas for depots. We will select A and B.

Step 2 then assigns each customer to its nearest depot (asterisked in the table below).

Step 3 finds the cost of this combination by multiplying the weight, $W(i)$, by the shorter, asterisked distance.

Area	$W(i)$	A	B	Cost
A	10	0*	6	0
B	20	6	0*	0
C	15	20	12*	180
D	30	7*	15	210
E	5	12	8*	40
F	25	22	12*	300
G	10	30	24*	240
H	20	6	5*	100
Totals	135			1070

The total cost of this combination is 1070, which is above the allowable limit of 800. We then move to step 4 and change one of the locations. The changes can be selected arbitrarily, but it is preferable to follow some systematic method. Here we will change B to C, return to step 2 and calculate a revised cost.

Area	W(i)	A	C	Cost
A	10	0*	20	0
B	20	6*	12	120
C	15	20	0*	0
D	30	7	4*	120
E	5	12	10*	50
F	25	22	17*	425
G	10	30*	32	300
H	20	6*	9	120
Totals	135			1135

The total cost of this combination is 1135. This is again too high so we change the combination of locations to, say, A and D, and return to step 2.

Area	W(i)	A	D	Cost
A	10	0*	7	0
B	20	6*	15	120
C	15	20	4*	60
D	30	7	0*	0
E	5	12	11*	55
F	25	22*	27	550
G	10	30	6*	60
H	20	6*	11	120
Totals	135			965

The cost of this combination is 965. This is closer to the acceptable figure, but we still need to continue, trying areas B and D.

Area	W(i)	B	D	Cost
A	10	6*	7	60
B	20	0*	15	0
C	15	12	4*	60
D	30	15	0*	0
E	5	8*	11	40
F	25	12*	27	300
G	10	24	6*	60
H	20	5*	11	100
Totals	135			620

This gives a total cost of 620 which is far less than the acceptable figure. This finishes the iterations and we move on to step 5.

Step 5 calculates the capacity required by each depot. Each area is assigned to its nearest depot, so depot B serves areas A, B, E, F and H, with a total demand of 80, while depot D serves areas C, D and G, with a total demand of 55. This satisfies all the conditions and is the final solution. If this solution broke the requirement that no depot would meet a total demand of more than 90 units, the iterative procedure would be continued. Then, iterations would continue until either a satisfactory solution is found, or all combinations have been tried and none of them is found to be satisfactory (in which case the conditions have to be modified).

In summary

Sometimes more than one location is needed. An iterative costing method can be used to find satisfactory solutions to multiple location problems with a feasible set of alternative locations.

SELF ASSESSMENT QUESTIONS

4.20 Why might more than one location be needed?

4.21 The iterative costing procedure described always finds an optimal solution. Is this statement

(a) true
(b) false
(c) partly true?

4.22 The iterative procedure described systematically costs combinations of locations. Describe a systematic sequence for costing two locations from five available.

4.23 What happens if this procedure ends without finding an acceptable solution?

4.7 LOCATION OF FACILITIES ON NETWORKS

4.7.1 Single median problem

So far in this chapter we have described locations by map coordinates. An alternative representation would have locations as the nodes on a network, with roads (or other connections) shown as links or arcs between the nodes. Figure 4.8, for example, shows a region with six locations and connecting links.

The number on the arc could be distance or travel time, the number in each node is an identifier and the number against each node could be population or demand. Thus node 6 has a demand of 10 and is a distance 6 from node 1.

Suppose each node on the network shown in Figure 4.8 represents a town and the arcs are the road network connecting them. A useful question is, 'In which town should a facility be located to give the lowest average distance to

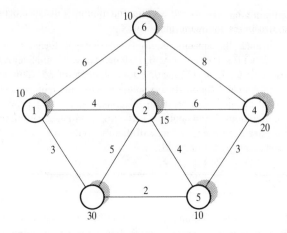

Figure 4.8 Network of six locations and connecting links.

customers?' This is the single median problem, and the procedure for solving it has the following steps.

Procedure for the single median problem

(1) Calculate the minimum distances between nodes and put these in a distance matrix.

(2) Multiply each column, i, of this matrix by the demand in town i.

(3) Add all the terms in each row.

(4) The single median is identified by the row with the smallest sum.

This procedure is illustrated in the following worked example.

WORKED EXAMPLE 4.7

The network in Figure 4.8 shows six towns, their populations (in thousands) and the distances between them. A supermarket is planning to open in one of the towns and wants to find the location which minimizes the average travel distance of customers. Where should it open?

SOLUTION

The problem of finding a town with minimum average travel distance is the single median problem.

By examining the network we can find the minimum distance between each pair of towns, as shown in the following matrix.

		Town 1	2	3	4	5	6
	1	0	4	3	8	5	6
	2	4	0	5	6	4	5
T	3	3	5	0	5	2	9
o	4	8	6	5	0	3	8
w	5	5	4	2	3	0	9
n	6	6	5	9	8	9	0

Step 2 multiplies each column, i, by the demand in town i. We do not know the actual demands, so will approximate this by the population of the towns (in thousands).

Town	1	2	3	4	5	6
Population	10	15	30	20	10	10
1	0	60	90	160	50	60
2	40	0	150	120	40	50
3	30	75	0	100	20	90
4	80	90	150	0	30	80
5	50	60	60	60	0	90
6	60	75	270	160	90	0

Step 3 adds the terms in each row.

		Total
	1	420
T	2	400
o	3	315*
w	4	430
n	5	320
	6	655

Step 4 identifies the single median as town 3, which has the lowest row total. A supermarket here would minimize the average travel distance of the towns' populations.

In summary
Some location problems can be represented by networks. The single median problem finds the location in a network which minimizes the average distance or cost to all customers.

4.7.2 Set covering problem

The single median problem found the location which minimizes the average time for customers to reach a facility. Often we are not so worried by the average time as by the maximum time or distance. Hospital emergency wards, for example, might be placed so that everyone in a region is within 30 minutes' travel time of the nearest. Similarly bus stops, fire stations and police stations are located so that the whole population is within a specified maximum travel time. The problem, then, is to take a network of nodes and arcs, and find the locations which ensure that all nodes are within a specified maximum distance of a facility. A formalized version of this problem is called the 'set covering problem', and the algorithm for solving this has the following steps.

Procedure for the set covering problem

(1) Calculate the minimum distances between nodes and put these in a distance matrix.

(2) Create a coverage matrix. This is made up of zeros and ones with:

    (a) elements = 1 if the distance is less than the specified maximum;

    (b) elements = 0 if the distance is greater than the specified maximum.

(3) If there is one column with all zeros, stop. No feasible solution exists and the maximum allowed distance must be increased or more potential locations added.

(4) If any column has only a single '1' the row containing this '1' must receive a facility. Add the row to the list of facilities and then eliminate the row and all columns with '1' in this row from the matrix.

(5) If any row is dominated by another (i.e. the entry is always ≤ the entries in another row) remove the dominated row.

(6) If any column dominates another column (i.e. the entry is always ≥ the entries in another column) remove the dominating column.

(7) Repeat steps 4 − 6 until:

    (a) the coverage becomes complete − optimal solution is found; or

    (b) no rows or columns are eliminated during a pass − obtain a solution by inspection.

Although this procedure seems rather complicated when formally described, it is really quite straightforward. This is illustrated in the following worked example.

WORKED EXAMPLE 4.8

The following table shows a matrix of travel times between possible locations for ambulance stations and areas in a city. Government policy suggests that ambulance stations must be at most 30 minutes away from all population areas. Find the best locations for achieving this.

					Areas			
		A	B	C	D	E	F	G
	V	5	11	20	33	27	36	33
Possible	W	33	35	17	10	53	41	18
locations	X	18	39	41	12	33	22	37
	Y	13	6	43	25	38	33	20
	Z	35	47	41	44	15	51	43

SOLUTION

Step 1 calculates the minimum distances between areas and puts these in a distance matrix. In this example this has already been done, except that travel time is substituted for distance.

Step 2 creates a coverage matrix. The maximum permissible travel time is 30 minutes, so the coverage matrix is created by replacing all entries in the distance matrix by 1 if the entry is less than 30, and 0 if it is more than 30.

					Areas			
		A	B	C	D	E	F	G
	V	1	1	1	0	1	0	0
Possible	W	0	0	1	1	0	0	1
locations	X	1	0	0	1	0	1	0
	Y	1	1	0	1	0	0	1
	Z	0	0	0	0	1	0	0

Step 3 looks for columns with all zeros. There are none of these, so a feasible solution can be found.

Step 4 looks for columns with only a single '1'. Column F has only a single '1', which means that a station must be built at location X. As well as covering area F, a station at X will also cover areas A and D. Thus row X and columns A, D and F are eliminated from the matrix.

		Areas			
		B	C	E	G
Possible	V	1	1	1	0
locations	W	0	1	0	1
	Y	1	0	0	1
	Z	0	0	1	0

Step 5 shows that row Z is dominated by row V and can be removed from the matrix. The implication here is that we will never choose location Z: location V can reach all towns which location Z can serve, as well as a number of additional ones.

		Areas			
		B	C	E	G
Possible	V	1	1	1	0
locations	W	0	1	0	1
	Y	1	0	0	1

Step 6 shows that column B dominates column E and can be removed from the matrix. The implication here is that if we can reach area E from a location, we can always reach area B from the same location.

		Areas		
		C	E	G
Possible	V	1	1	0
locations	W	1	0	1
	Y	0	0	1

Now the procedure is repeated from step 4. Column E has a single '1' and a station must be located at V. This station will also cover area C, so removing row V and columns C and E gives the final matrix.

		Areas
		G
Possible	W	1
locations	Y	1

This leaves either W or Y to serve area G. The overall solution is then:

Location X serves areas A, D and F.
Location V serves areas B, C and E.
Location W or Y serves area G.

In summary

Sometimes, particularly with emergency services, it is important to locate facilities so that all customers are within some maximum distance. One problem of this type is the set covering problem.

SELF ASSESSMENT QUESTIONS

4.24 In a network, what do the nodes and arcs represent?

4.25 What is the single median of a network?

4.26 What are the entries in a coverage matrix?

4.27 What is the objective of the set covering problem?

4.28 What other objectives might a network location problem have?

SUMMARY OF CHAPTER

Previous chapters considered what products an organization should supply and how to forecast consequent demand. This chapter looked at the location of facilities to meet this demand. This is an important question, as the success of an organization often depends on its location. Moreover, once a location decision is made its effect can be felt for a long time.

Location decisions are often considered as part of the physical distribution function. This organizes the flow of materials from initial suppliers through to final customers.

A location decision is needed whenever an organization expands (or sometimes contracts) its operations by opening new facilities. There are several options to opening new facilities, including licensing, exporting, opening a local warehouse/sales office, using local finishing/assembly, and full local production. If a decision is made to expand, an organization must decide between on-site expansion, opening additional facilities and closing existing facilities to relocate.

Location decisions are complicated and involve a number of interacting factors. The overall process is sequential, determining the number (and hence size) of facilities, the country or geographic region, the town or city and finally the exact location within the town. There are several trends in location at regional and national levels.

More detailed location decisions are based on either a feasible set or infinite set approach. The first of these compares available locations and was illustrated by costing methods and scoring models. The second approach looks at the layout of customers and suppliers and was illustrated by the centre of gravity method. Often these methods can be used together, so that a centre of gravity method can find a starting point for identifying a feasible set of locations.

Two types of more specialized algorithm were then described. The first was an extension to the costing method, but with several locations needed. The second looked at locations on networks, illustrated by the single median and set covering problems.

PROBLEMS

4.1 A company manufactures a total of 60 tonnes of goods a week in factory A and 40 tonnes a week in factory B. The map coordinates of these factories are (8,9) and (52,47) respectively. These goods are delivered to 12 main customers whose average weekly requirements and coordinates are shown in Table 4.6. The company wants to improve its customer service and decides to open a distribution centre. There are four possible locations, each with the same operating costs, located at (20,8), (61,19), (29,32) and (50,22). Which of these locations would be best?

Table 4.6

Customer	Average requirements	Coordinates
1	4	(11,16)
2	11	(30,9)
3	8	(43,27)
4	7	(54,52)
5	17	(29,62)
6	10	(11,51)
7	16	(12,69)
8	2	(27,38)
9	4	(51,6)
10	6	(43,16)
11	3	(54,16)
12	12	(12,60)

4.2 A new electronics factory is planned in an area that is encouraging industrial growth, and there are five alternative sites. A management team is considering these sites, and has suggested important factors and their relative weights as shown in Table 4.7. They also gave scores to each of the sites. What is the relative importance of each factor? Which site appears best?

Table 4.7

Factor	Maximum score	Scores for sites				
		A	B	C	D	E
Government grants	10	2	4	8	8	5
Community attitude	12	8	7	5	10	5
Availability of engineers	15	10	8	8	10	5
Experienced workforce	20	20	15	15	10	15
Nearby suppliers	8	4	3	6	3	2
Education centres	5	5	4	1	1	5
Housing	5	2	3	5	3	2

4.3 Find the centre of gravity of the data in Problem 4.1. What would be the cost of a distribution centre located there?

4.4 An assembly plant is being planned to take components from four suppliers and send finished goods to eight regional warehouses. The locations of these and the amounts supplied or demanded are shown in Table 4.8. Where would you start looking for a site for the assembly plant?

Table 4.8

Location	X,Y coordinates	Supply/demand
Supplier 1	7,80	140
Supplier 2	85,35	80
Supplier 3	9,81	120
Supplier 4	11,62	70
Warehouse 1	12,42	45
Warehouse 2	60,9	65
Warehouse 3	92,94	25
Warehouse 4	8,79	45
Warehouse 5	10,83	60
Warehouse 6	59,91	35
Warehouse 7	83,49	50
Warehouse 8	85,30	85

4.5 Ten geographical areas are to be served by two facilities. There are only sites available in five of these areas. The demands in each area, $W(i)$, and the distances between areas are given in Table 4.9. The company is willing to pay up to 6000 units for distribution, but would prefer the costs to be less than 5500. What combination of locations would you recommend?

Table 4.9

Area	$W(i)$	A	B	C	D	E
A	50	0	12	25	17	50
B	100	12	0	15	20	29
C	70	25	15	0	13	51
D	20	17	20	33	0	32
E	40	50	29	51	32	0
F	20	40	27	41	56	20
G	30	23	19	30	34	15
H	60	10	5	62	19	40
I	20	22	10	4	26	61
J	80	30	22	50	34	35

4.6 Find the single median for the network of towns and roads shown in Figure 4.9.

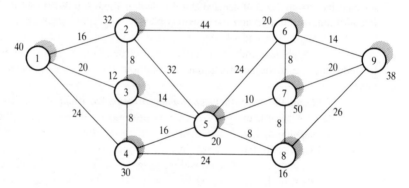

Figure 4.9 Network of towns and roads for Problem 4.6.

4.7 Find the set covering locations for the network shown in Figure 4.9, if the maximum journey length is (a) 10 miles and (b) 40 miles.

CASE STUDY – AUTHWAITE AUTO SALES

Background

Richard Authwaite has lived all his life in the Province of Alberta in Canada. He left school at 18 and took a job as a salesman for a main distributor of General Motors. He was promoted from Salesman to Manager of Fleet Sales, then to General Sales Manager and finally to Director of Marketing and Sales. He stayed with the same company for over 25 years until he reached his mid-forties. He recognized that he had reached the top of the company and had to make an important decision. He could:

- continue with the same job until he retired, recognizing that a move would become increasingly difficult as he got older;

- look for a new job in a bigger company within the next year or so (although this could be difficult as most companies in the trade preferred to promote from within);

- use his experience to set up a company of his own.

As he was considering these possibilities he saw an advertisement from an East European car manufacturer who wanted to start distributing in Alberta. Richard answered the advertisement and spent a year negotiating with the manufacturer. At the end of this he agreed to set up his own company called Authwaite Auto Sales, and the manufacturer agreed to give him exclusive rights to distribute the manufacturer's cars throughout the whole of Alberta for two years.

Although the manufacturer was impressed by Richard and his experience, it had not been keen to entrust all its proposed distribution in Alberta to a new and untried company. Richard argued, however, that sales would inevitably be small to start with and he could give the manufacturer the opportunity of a dynamic new company, with considerable experience in the business, which would grow with the manufacturer's own expected business. In the end a compromise was reached whereby the company offered an exclusive contract which would be reviewed after a year and renegotiated after two years.

Richard invited three other directors who had worked for him in the past to join the company. These provided a range of experience and gave some finance to the company.

- Gordon Mikaluk left school at 16 to become a car mechanic. He continued to work as a mechanic for many years until he was eventually promoted to Service Manager. He is now 50 years old and is looking for an opportunity to make some money for his retirement.

- Sarah Precik has a degree in Mechanical Engineering. When she graduated from the University of Texas she worked for an oil company, but lost her job during a slump in the early 1980s. She decided to move out of the oil industry and initially spent several years as a mining consultant in Eastern Europe. She speaks fluent Czechoslovakian and Polish, with some Russian, and it was during her travels that she became interested in the car industry. On her return to North America she worked on manufacturing and design problems for General Motors.

- The last director is Dennis MacGregor. He worked in banking and insurance where he handled various aspects of car financing. He is now 30 years old and is ambitiously looking for a long-term career which would be both challenging and financially rewarding.

The four directors are now at the stage of setting up their distributorship and their first problem is to find a location for their head office and main showroom.

Location of head office and main showroom

In the long term the company plans to open a series of facilities around Alberta. In the short term, however, the directors have to decide where to open their 'flagship' site. The directors recognize the importance of this decision and realize that their future success depends on how well this first facility operates. Unfortunately, they have spent many hours over a period of weeks discussing the location and have not yet reached agreement.

At one point they decided to pass the problem to a firm of management consultants, but Dennis MacGregor reported the likely costs of this exercise. He found that firms in similar circumstances had paid up to £50,000 for an initial report while a more detailed analysis could cost £125,000. The directors decided they could not afford to spend this amount and they would have to solve the problem themselves.

Summary of discussions

After prolonged discussions the directors could still not agree on the best location for their first centre. A brief summary of their views would be as follows.

- Gordon Mikaluk argues that the location should be in Calgary. The cars could be shipped by sea to Vancouver and then brought to Calgary by train, or they could be shipped to the Great Lakes and again moved by train. There are good handling facilities in Calgary and the transport would be easy and efficient. In addition, Calgary is the largest city in Alberta and, therefore, has the largest potential market. The four directors have all lived in Calgary and they understand local conditions. There are already a number of main dealers located in Calgary, and they would, presumably, choose the best location. He suggested that they should start looking for somewhere to open in Calgary as soon as possible.

- Sarah Precik is critical of Gordon Mikaluk's approach as being old fashioned and relying more on where he feels at home than on any business criterion. She says their aim should be to put the decision making in Authwaite Auto Sales on a sensible footing and not be governed by emotion. As a subjective approach would be unreliable, they should use some formal analysis. The sale of cars is likely to depend on the population so they should look at a map of Alberta, see where the main centres of population are, see how many cars they expect to sell to each of these, and then it would be fairly straightforward to do some analysis which would tell them the best location. This would be more convincing to the manufacturers who will review their operations at the end of the year.

- Dennis MacGregor does not like the idea of opening a single location to see if it works, but suggests they should set up a comprehensive distribution network as quickly as possible. This would include head offices in the down-town area of Calgary or Edmonton, a central receiving area near to a rail terminal, and local sites around Alberta. The fastest way of achieving this would be to take over an existing distributor, or several distributors, to give coverage throughout Alberta.

- Richard Authwaite says that Dennis MacGregor's scheme is too ambitious, while the other two put the convenience of the company above the customers. He says there is only one way to sell cars and that is to provide customers with a product they want in a location they can easily get it from. Thus Sarah Precik's idea is ludicrous as the location of the centre of population could be out in the wilds where nobody can get to it. Richard's idea is to see where other distributors have their showrooms and open up near by. In particular, he would look for a large dominating location which customers would be able to see from a long way off, which they would pass frequently, where they would go to buy cars, and where other distributors have traditionally been able to sell.

The time is now getting short for a decision. The directors are concerned that if they delay any longer the manufacturer will consider them indecisive, and they will not have time to give a good showing at their first year review. To build entirely new premises could take a year. An alternative would be to find existing premises which are empty and could be bought relatively cheaply. Another option, which would be more difficult, would be to find premises which can be rented temporarily until the company finds more suitable, permanent premises.

The manufacturer is anxious to get the distribution network set up and wants to see if the decision to use Authwaite was sensible. Although willing to wait a reasonable time for results, the manufacturer would withdraw support if

Figure 4.10   Sketch of the Province of Alberta, Canada.

things dragged on. A decision must be made now, so Richard Authwaite tells the other three directors they have one week to summarize their views and produce a report. At the end of this week the reports will be distributed. After a further week for examination, comment and discussion they will make a decision. The other directors said that this is rather authoritarian and they do not have enough time to collect relevant information to support their cases, but Richard said that if they do not make a decision soon they could continue arguing forever.

Suggested questions

- What alternatives did the car manufacturer have for distributing cars in Alberta? Why was Richard Authwaite given exclusive distribution rights?
- What are the likely strengths and weaknesses of Authwaite Auto Sales?
- Should the company approach a consultant to help with the location decision?
- What methods might Sarah Precik use to locate their centre?
- What are the characteristics of the site which Richard Authwaite would recommend?
- How would you summarize the reports of the directors? What are the weaknesses and strengths of each of these?
- Would you recommend they open a single location, and if so where should it be?
- Overall, what decisions would be the best for Authwaite Auto Sales?

SOLUTIONS TO SELF ASSESSMENT QUESTIONS

4.1 The management function concerned with the physical movement and storage of goods on their journey between original supplier and final customer.

4.2 They are effective in the long term, have high associated costs, serious consequences for mistakes, difficulty of correcting mistakes, affect all operations in an organization, and so on.

4.3 (c) Partly true. This is one illustration of a distribution system, but there are many different configurations, most of which do not involve factories, retail shops, and so on.

4.4 No. It could license local manufacturers or export its products without opening local facilities.

4.5 Expand on the same site, open additional facilities at new sites, or close down existing facilities and move to a new location.

4.6 (b) False. There are also diseconomies of scale which often allow small warehouses to be cheaper than large ones.

4.7 This is a sequential process which determines the number (and hence size) of facilities, the country or geographic region, the town or city and finally the exact location within the city.

4.8 False. Low wages may be accompanied by low productivity, high costs (operating, transport, etc.), and many other disadvantages.

4.9 There are many factors that may be important, and we considered them under the general headings of culture, organization and type of operation.

4.10 Not necessarily. Entirely new jobs may be created which would otherwise not exist.

4.11 A feasible set approach compares a small number of feasible sites and selects the best, while an infinite set approach uses geometric arguments to show where the best site would be if there were no restrictions on availability.

4.12 All costs of operating a facility should, ideally, be included. The most important ones are transport (inwards and outwards) and operating costs.

4.13 Inward transport (trunking) moves goods from suppliers into the facility. Outward transport (local delivery) moves goods from the facility to customers.

4.14 True.

4.15 No.

4.16 There are many possible factors, including population density, age of population, income distribution, nearest hospitals, locations of other surgeries, access by public transport, roads and parking, security, other local businesses (such as pharmacies and dentists), fee arrangements, and so on.

4.17 The centre of gravity is defined as:

$$X(0) = \frac{\Sigma X(i) * W(i)}{\Sigma W(i)}$$

$$Y(0) = \frac{\Sigma Y(i) * W(i)}{W(i)}$$

where: $(X(0), Y(0))$ is the centre of gravity, $(X(i), Y(i))$ are coordinates of each customer and $W(i)$ is expected demand at customer i.

4.18 False. The centre of gravity is an infinite set approach.

4.19 (b) False. The centre of gravity gives a reasonable starting point to look for available locations, but it certainly does not give an optimal location.

4.20 There are several reasons for this. Perhaps the main one is to maintain customer service over a geographical region.

4.21 (c) Partly true. Usually a satisfactory solution is specified and the procedure stops when this is achieved. If, however, all possible combinations of locations are tested the procedure will give an optimal solution.

4.22 Any systematic sequence will do, but one (with locations A, B, C, D and E) is AB, AC, AD, AE, BC, BD, BE, CD, CE, DE.

4.23 Eventually the procedure will test all combinations of locations, so if it fails to find a satisfactory one, no satisfactory solution can exist. Then the two alternatives are to be less demanding and accept the best solution identified, or increase the number of locations.

4.24 The nodes are locations, typically customers or towns, while the arcs are links between them.

4.25 The location that minimizes average travel distance or time.

4.26 1, if the arc is less than the specified maximum distance, and 0 otherwise.

4.27 To find locations on a network which ensure all nodes are within a specified maximum distance of a facility.

4.28 There are many possible objectives, including finding acceptable values for the maximum journey time, finding multi-medians, finding the location with maximum coverage, minimizing total costs (including operations), and so on.

REFERENCES FOR FURTHER READING

Ballou R.H. (1985). *Business Logistics Management* 2nd edn. Englewood Cliffs: Prentice-Hall

Bowersox D.J., Closs D.J. and Helferich O.K. (1986). *Logistical Management* 3rd edn. New York: Macmillan

Cooper J. (ed.) (1988). *Logistics and Distribution Planning* London: Kogan Page

Coyle J.J., Bardi E.J. and Langley C.J. (1988). *The Management of Business Logistics* 4th edn. St Paul: West Publishing

Fitzsimmons J.A. and Sullivan R.S. (1982). *Service Operations Management* New York: McGraw-Hill

Francis R.L. and White J.A. (1987). *Facilities Layout and Location: An Analytical Approach* Englewood Cliffs: Prentice-Hall

Schmenner R.W. (1982). *Making Business Location Decisions* Englewood Cliffs:Prentice-Hall

Shapiro R.D. and Heskett J.L. (1985). *Logistics Strategy* St Paul: West Publishing

Tompkins J.A. and White J.A. (1984). *Facilities Planning* New York: John Wiley

Voss C., Armistead C., Johnston B. and Morris B. (1985). *Operations Management In Service Industries and the Public Sector* Chichester: John Wiley

Chapter 5

Process planning and design

SYNOPSIS

Previous chapters have discussed a number of strategic questions for organizations. Chapter 2 described aspects of product planning, while Chapters 3 and 4 discussed demand forecasting and location. These chapters tackled the questions of *what* should be made, *how many* should be made and *where* they should be made. This chapter looks at another important question, which concerns the process used, or *how* the product is made.

The chapter starts by reviewing the focus of an organization and discussing the links between the product and the process used to make it. Organizations should use an appropriate process for their products and some factors are described which affect this choice.

The chapter then describes a classification of process types according to project, job shop, batch, mass production and continuous flow. The distinct characteristics of each are described, together with the types of product for which each is most useful.

There are several ways in which the efficiency of a process can be improved. These range from reorganizing equipment operators to increasing the level of automation. In general, higher levels of automation are assumed to be more efficient. Different levels of automation are classified according to manual, mechanized or automated. Characteristics of these are described, together with comments on the selection of the most appropriate. Although much of the discussion is phrased in manufacturing terms, many of the principles can be applied to services.

The next section discusses the ways in which processes can be described and analysed. This concentrates on process charts, including precedence diagrams and multiple activity charts.

The chapter ends with a case study describing a practical process decision.

OBJECTIVES

After reading this chapter and completing the exercises you should be able to:

- appreciate the importance of processes in an organization;
- discuss factors that affect the choice of process;
- describe a classification of processes and the characteristics of each type;
- suggest ways in which the productivity of intermittent processes can be improved;
- outline the characteristics of process technologies (manual, mechanized and automated);
- discuss the various levels of automation that are available;
- use appropriate analyses to select the best level of automation;
- discuss processes within the service sector;
- use different types of process chart, including precedence diagrams and multiple activity charts.

5.1 PROCESS PLANNING

5.1.1 Focus of an organization

Chapter 1 suggested that an important issue for an organization is whether it has a product focus or a process focus. In essence, an organization with a product focus sees itself as making a product; one with a process focus sees itself as using a process. Thus:

- a company which sees itself as running a bottling plant has a process focus, while one which sees itself as making bottled lemonade has a product focus;
- a printer has a process focus, while a newspaper publisher has a product focus (one prints things, the other produces newspapers);
- expensive restaurants have a process focus (they cook food), while hamburger restaurants have a product focus (they supply hamburgers).

This distinction between product and process focus is somewhat artificial as all organizations both make products and use processes. The important point is that organizations view themselves in different ways and emphasize different aspects of their operations.

There is a clear link between the type of product and focus. An organization which makes small batches of highly variable products is more likely to have a process focus; one which makes large batches of a few similar products is likely to have a product focus. Then, the characteristics of an organization with a process focus will include:

- low volumes;
- high variability in products;
- short runs before products are changed;
- products in the growth stage of their life cycle;
- flexible processes;
- closer links with customers;
- higher cost;
- longer delivery times;

and so on.

This is, of course, only a guideline and there are many exceptions.

In Chapter 2 we looked at some aspects of product planning, and in this chapter we are going to look in more detail at the process. The process is the means by which a product is made. In different circumstances a process might change:

- the physical form (when manufacturing a product);
- the owner (by selling);
- location (by transport);
- age (by warehousing until needed);
- condition (by repair);

and so on.

The end result of a process is some form of product (whether goods or services), so process planning and design try to find the best way of making a particular product.

> Process planning and design are concerned with the detailed description of operations needed to make a product, and the connections between these operations. The aim is to design the most efficient means of making a product.

A decision about the process must be made whenever an organization introduces a new product. This is not, however, the only time when process planning is needed. Questions should be asked about the process whenever there is a significant change in operations. This includes:

- when an entirely new product is being introduced;
- when an old product is changed;
- when demand significantly increases or decreases;
- when costs of inputs or operations alter;
- when competitors change their products or there are other changes in the market;
- when the current performance is judged to be unsatisfactory.

In summary

The process describes the way in which a product is made. Process planning and design are needed to ensure that each product is made in the most efficient way.

5.1.2 Factors affecting process design

Decisions about the process can have long-term consequences on profitability, production, costs, flexibility, and so on. When a car manufacturer builds an assembly line it can cost several hundred million pounds to set up. If the company decides later that it should not have used an assembly line, correcting the mistake will be very expensive. This example also shows that there is often no process which is obviously best for a product. Ever since Henry Ford started building cars on assembly lines it has been accepted that this is the best process for mass-produced cars. Recently, however, several companies have come to doubt this, including Volvo whose plant at Uddevalla in Sweden has small groups of people assembling separate cars in workshops.

A number of factors concerning both the product and the organization affect process design. We have already suggested, for example, that level of demand will affect the process. Many other factors may be important, including the following.

Pattern of demand

The most obvious factor for the process is overall demand. It is usually assumed that higher levels of demand are associated with more automated processes. Portraits, for example, can either be painted or photographed. Painters satisfy a very low demand by a manual process, while film processors satisfy a very high demand with completely automated processes.

As well as the absolute demand, the changes in demand can affect the process. A demand which is highly seasonal will need a more flexible process than one where the demand is stable. The process must have enough capacity to meet peak demands and yet still make products efficiently during slacker times.

The choice of process is also affected when the product is at some point in its life cycle where the underlying pattern of demand is likely to change. If, for example, a new product has recently been introduced the process should be capable of making both current demand and expected demand when the product moves into its growth stage.

Flexibility needed

If there is variation in demand the process must be flexible enough to respond to this. This is sometimes called demand flexibility. Another aspect of flexibility is called product flexibility. This relates to how quickly a process can stop making one product and start making another. The combination of these two allows a process to respond quickly to changes in customer needs.

Until quite recently, there was a direct relationship between flexibility and capital intensity. High volume processes meant high levels of automation, and this in turn meant expensive specialized equipment. Conversely, low volume processes meant low automation, and this in turn meant cheaper, general-purpose equipment. In the past few years this has changed, and later in the chapter we will discuss some aspects of flexible automation.

Another aspect of flexibility concerns the workforce. A flexible process relies on operators who are skilled enough to do a variety of different jobs. They must be able to change from making one product to another fairly quickly. This kind of workforce, which is better trained and more skilled, inevitably comes at a higher cost.

Amount of vertical integration

An organization usually gets supplies of raw materials from a number of sources, and distributes its products to a number of destinations. Coordinating this movement of products from initial suppliers to final customer is the function of physical distribution. Vertical integration refers to the amount of the physical distribution function (or supply chain) which is owned by one organization. A manufacturer which buys all its components from suppliers and sells all finished products to wholesalers has little vertical integration. Another manufacturer which makes all its own components and sells to customers through its own distribution system has more vertical integration.

There are two distinct types of vertical integration. Backward integration means an organization takes over its suppliers so that it makes its own components and raw materials. Forward integration means that an organization takes over its customers, so that it controls its own distribution system.

Vertical integration affects the process in a number of ways. More vertical integration is usually associated with higher volumes. The large investments needed also tend to reduce the amount of flexibility in a process. The extra control over suppliers may allow lower stocks of materials, and so on.

One aspect of vertical integration is the 'make or buy' decision. This asks whether it is better for an organization to buy one of its components from suppliers or to make the component itself. There are a number of reasons why an organization may decide to buy a component rather than make it, including:

- it does not have enough free capacity;
- demand may be very variable (suppliers can cope with this because aggregate demand from many sources is likely to be more stable);
- the component may be cheaper to buy than to make;
- it cannot justify the research and development costs;
- it lacks experience in making the component;
- it may not be able to guarantee as high quality as specialist suppliers.

Customer involvement

In most manufacturing processes the customer is not involved at all, but is deliberately kept at a distance. Sometimes, however, particularly with services, customers can play an active part in the process. In petrol stations, self-service restaurants and bank cash machines, customers take over much of the process which was previously done by employees.

Those processes with high customer involvement must generally give some kind of personalized service. This implies that they are more flexible and less capital intensive.

Product quality

There is increasing pressure for organizations to make products of consistently high quality. The traditional means of ensuring high quality was to employ highly skilled craftsmen to make small numbers of a product. This is still appropriate for many products, but there are many others where higher quality can be generated by automated processes. The most reliable computers are not those which are made by hand, but those which come from completely automated assembly lines.

In summary

It may be difficult to say which is the best process in given circumstances, but factors which affect the choice include demand pattern, flexibility needed, vertical integration, customer involvement and product quality.

SELF ASSESSMENT QUESTIONS

5.1 What is meant by 'process'?

5.2 What is process planning and when is it used?

5.3 What factors can be important in process design?

5.4 What factors tend to increase the amount of flexibility in a process?

5.5 What is meant by vertical integration?

5.2 PROCESS DESIGN

5.2.1 Types of process

We have now discussed some factors which affect the choice of process and can move on to give some details of the different types of process which are available. There are several possible classifications, but a useful one looks at the frequency with which products change. At one extreme are continuous flows like an oil refinery which makes the same product without any changes or interruptions for 24 hours a day. At the other extreme are single projects like satellite manufacturers which seldom make the same product twice. These processes differ in two important ways:

- the variety, or number of different products;
- the quantity, or number of units made.

Expanding this idea allows a classification of processes according to:

> **Types of process**
> - project
> - job shop
> - batch
> - mass production
> - continuous flow

Each of these is suited to different product types and quantities, and has a number of distinct characteristics, as outlined below.

(1) *Project*. In this type of process a single unit is made, usually tailored to individual customer specifications. Each product is essentially unique, so the process is characterized by wide variety, with little standardization or specialized equipment. There must be a lot of flexibility in the process to deal with new situations and problems. This implies a skilled workforce who may work in teams to tackle specific parts of the work. The process is controlled by project management methods. Although the number of units made is low, each may involve a considerable amount of work. This kind of process usually has very high unit costs.
Examples: shipbuilding, satellite assembly, general contractors building an office block, authors writing a book, management consultants preparing a report.

(2) *Job shop*. An organization using this type of process makes small quantities of a wide variety of products. This is typical of small engineering works which make products primarily to customer specifications. The range of products made by an organization is narrower than for project processes, but there is still considerable variety. The process uses general-purpose equipment which must be set up and changed every time a new product is started. Each product may go through a different sequence of operations on the equipment. This implies flexibility from equipment and a skilled workforce. As each product may only use a part of the resources available (both human and equipment), utilization can be low. Conversely, depending on the current mix of jobs, there may be bottlenecks as some resources are temporarily overloaded. The mix of diverse products makes scheduling and keeping track of work difficult. Job shop processes usually have high unit cost.

Examples: makers of specialized vehicles, printers, furniture manufacturers, restaurants.

(3) *Batch processing*. This occurs when small batches of similar products are made on the same equipment. In a job shop, every time a new product is started there are a series of costs for setting up the equipment and associated disruptions. These can be reduced by making a number of units in each run. Over time, a series of batches are made, with products held in stock until they are needed to meet customer demand. Essentially, the more units made in each batch, the smaller are the set-up costs per unit. This process is useful for medium volumes of products where customer requirements are known in advance. This means there must be less product variety and little customizing. The equipment used is still fairly general, but there is room for some specialization. The process can have frequent set-ups and changes, so some skilled labour is needed.

Examples: book publishers, pharmaceutical and clothes manufacturers, bottling plants.

(4) *Mass production*. This is typical of an assembly or production line which makes large numbers of identical units of a single product. Cars and washing machines, for example, are typical products from assembly lines. There is very little variety in the product, except small changes to the basic model usually introduced in the finishing. Mass production processes rely on a steady, high demand for a product which is known in advance. Then specialized equipment can be designed and installed to make a specific product. As the product does not change, there are no disruptions to the process and few management problems. There is, for example, no need to schedule individual pieces of equipment or keep detailed progress checks on individual units. Once the system has been set up it needs a small

workforce to keep it functioning, and in extreme cases may be completely automated. Unit costs for such processes are low.
Examples: cars, consumer electronics, washing machines, lemonade bottlers.

(5) *Continuous flow*. These are used for high volumes of a single product or small groups of related products, such as bulk chemicals. The process is different to assembly lines as the product emerges as a continuous flow rather than discrete units. Such processes use highly specialized equipment which can operate for 24 hours a day with virtually no changes or interruptions. The process is capital intensive, but when working it needs a very small workforce, and the high volume leads to low unit costs.
Examples: petrol refineries, breweries, paper mills, sugar refineries.

The types of process listed above are in order of increasing production quantity, and decreasing variety. Another important difference is that projects and job shops are make-to-order systems, which wait to receive an order from a customer, and then make the product requested. Batch, mass production and continuous flow are make-to-stock systems, which make the product according to prescribed plans, and then keep it in stock until customers actually demand it.

These and other characteristics are summarized in Table 5.1 and Figure 5.1.

Table 5.1 Characteristics of different types of process.

Process type	Volume	Product variation	Frequency of changes and set-ups	Equipment	Labour force	Capital cost	Unit cost
Project	one	one-off	not applicable	general	large, highly skilled	low	high
Job shop	low	considerable	frequent	general	large, highly skilled	low	high
Batch processing	medium	some	some	less	smaller, less skilled	medium	medium
Mass production	v. high	little (minor modifications)	none	specialized	small, unskilled	high	low
Continuous flow	continuous	none	none	specialized	small, unskilled	v. high	low

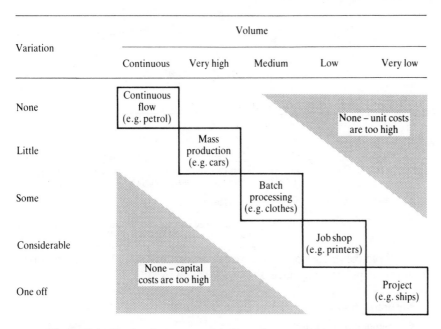

Figure 5.1 Types of process and their product quantities and variation.

Chapter 2 described how the demand for a product changed over its life cycle. There is a clear link here with the process used to make the product. We can illustrate this by the following simplified review.

In the product planning stage, small numbers of a product are made on a project basis. These may be prototypes or samples used to test various aspects of the product. Later, when the product is in the introduction stage, demand is small and several variations may be used to test market reaction. These are made with a job shop process. As the product moves through the introduction and into a growth stage, the variety of products is reduced as those variations which were not well received are removed. The volume of remaining versions increases and batch processing is the most effective. As the product moves into its maturity stage, demand is stable, product variation is reduced and competition increases. Then higher efficiency is needed to produce higher volumes at lower costs. Specialized equipment may be justified and the process moves towards mass production. Finally, as sales of the product begin to decline, emphasis changes from improving the process to reducing production without leaving equipment idle.

This evolution is illustrated in Figure 5.2. It is clear that developments and innovation are needed in both the product and process as they move through the life cycle, and the effort put into such innovation is shown in Figure 5.3. This view is, of course, highly simplified, and many products never achieve the volumes necessary to support batch production, let alone mass production.

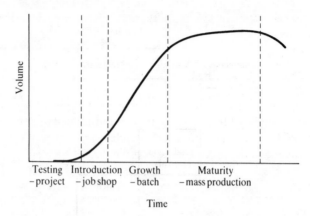

Figure 5.2 Different processes used during the product life cycle.

From the discussion so far, we can suggest that selection of the best type of process depends on a range of factors like:

- production volume
- demand variability
- product variability
- product flexibility
- available capital
- appropriate technology
- workforce skills
- management skills
- materials used
- quality needed
- customer involvement
- vertical integration.

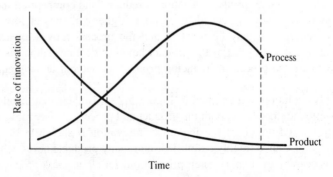

Figure 5.3 Effort put into innovation during the product life cycle.

In later sections we will look at some of these factors in more detail, particularly available technology.

In summary

The main types of process can be classified as project, job shop, batch, mass production and continuous flow. Each of these is most suited to different types of product and production quantities. There is a clear link between the stages in a product life cycle and the process used to make the product.

SELF ASSESSMENT QUESTIONS

5.6 What are the different types of process available?

5.7 Which type of process would be most appropriate for:

(a) washing machines
(b) liquid fertilizer

(c) 'home baked' cakes
(d) specialized limousines
(e) printed T-shirts?

5.8 Which type of process is generally more appropriate for a product at each stage in its life cycle?

5.2.2 Improving the productivity of intermittent processes

Continuous flow and mass production processes use specialized equipment which, once started, needs little supervision by either management or operators. The processes are characterized by high capital costs, but low variable costs, and a utilization which can approach 100%. Conversely, intermittent processes, like projects and job shops, make a variety of products and the mix changes continually. Each job may use a different combination and sequence of equipment and operators. This variability means it is difficult to get high utilization of resources. At some times a lot of resources will be idle, either because of short-term imbalances between capacity and workload or because of set-ups needed between changes of product. At other times there will be bottlenecks as some resources are in heavy demand. The average utilization of resources is low, and a typical job shop is lucky to achieve 25%, and often sinks as low as 5% or 10%. The result is that intermittent processes are characterized by low capital costs, but high variable costs.

The clear implication is that if an organization wants to increase the utilization of resources (to give higher productivity and return on investment) it should move away from intermittent processes like projects and job shops, and towards continuous processes like mass production. This reasoning has led many organizations to use assembly and production lines. Many products, however, never have demands which are either high enough or reliable enough to justify the capital expenditure needed for a mass production process. These products must continue to use intermittent processes, with their higher unit costs. There are, however, several ways of improving the productivity of intermittent processes. Three alternatives are mentioned below.

Reorganize machine operators

A common characteristic of job shops and other intermittent processes is that they have one operator assigned to a piece of equipment. We have already said that the utilization of equipment is low, so this implies that the operator spends a lot of time idle and waiting for something to do. Productivity could obviously be improved by assigning one operator to a number of machines.

This approach is most useful when machines can operate for some time without direct operator involvement. Then an operator might be kept busy loading and unloading several machines which actually work without the operator. It is easiest if an operator can be assigned to identical machines, but sometimes operators must be assigned to different types. The drawbacks with this is the need for a more skilled workforce, and the reliance on machines that can operate for some time without any attention.

Increase batch sizes with group technology

A more imaginative approach to the problem is to use group technology. In this a number of distinct products, which share some characteristic, are grouped together to form a single batch. Several different products may, for example, each need a 5 centimetre hole to be drilled. These products can all be combined into a single batch for the drilling process. The equipment set-up time is then reduced, and more efficient equipment may be justified by the larger batches.

Use flexible automation

Group technology gives larger batches, and may improve efficiency by allowing more automation. Perhaps a more interesting alternative is to use flexible automation. This uses high technology equipment to reduce the set-up time between products. Numerically controlled machines, for example, can be reprogrammed very quickly between batches. Similarly, industrial robots can make a variety of products with very little set-up time. Such systems allow small batches to be made with an efficiency which approaches that of larger batches. They are also the basis of flexible manufacturing systems, which are discussed in the following section.

In this discussion of processes, we are beginning to mention specific equipment, like robots and numerically controlled machines. Before we go much further, it would be appropriate to describe some of the technologies that can be used in processes. This is done in the following section.

WORKED EXAMPLE 5.1

A manufacturing company is planning the process for making a new product. A consultant has suggested that companies making similar products have costs that depend on the type of process as follows.

	Annual fixed cost (£)	Variable cost (£)
Job shop	100,000	50
Batch	250,000	40
Mass production	1,000,000	15

The company has forecast demand for the product at 25,000 units a year. Which process will probably suit it best? Within what ranges is each type of process best?

SOLUTION

This is an example of a break-even analysis, with characteristics shown in Figure 5.4.

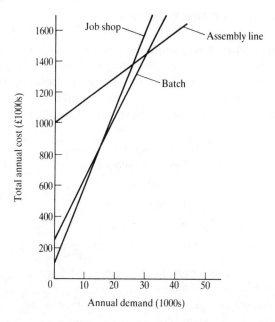

Figure 5.4 Break-even analysis for Worked Example 5.1.

A job shop process is best for demand, D, from zero until:

$$100,000 + 50 * D = 250,000 + 40 * D$$
$$\text{i.e. } D = 15,000$$

A batch process is best for demand from 15,000 until:

$$250,000 + 40 * D = 1,000,000 + 15 * D$$
$$\text{i.e. } D = 30,000$$

After this a mass production process is best.

With a forecast demand of 25,000 a year the company should look at batch processes.

In summary

The productivity of intermittent processes is lower than that of continuous processes. This can, however, be raised by reorganizing operators, group technology or flexible automation.

SELF ASSESSMENT QUESTIONS

5.9 What types of process have highest productivity, and why?

5.10 How might the productivity of intermittent processes be increased?

5.3 PROCESS TECHNOLOGIES

5.3.1 Classification of technologies

We have described one classification of processes based on the volume of throughput. We could have used several other classifications, and a particularly useful one depends on the amount of automation. This describes the technology used in a processes as:

> **Level of technology**
> - manual
> - mechanized
> - automated

This classification refers to the method of controlling equipment. A manual lathe needs an operator to load it and then control the operation; a mechanized lathe might need manual loading, but will then operate without further intervention; an automated lathe can operate without any operator intervention at all. A manual system for sorting letters in a post office needs

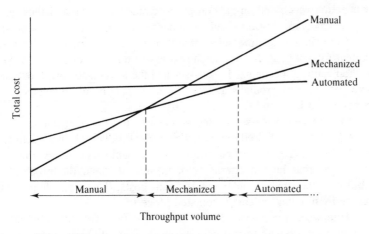

Figure 5.5 The cost of different technologies.

people to put letters in appropriate bags; a mechanized system has operators directing equipment to put letters in appropriate bags; an automated system has scanners to read the post code and automatically move letters to appropriate bags.

This classification is clearly linked to the previous one, with a general assumption that higher levels of automation are used for higher volumes of output. Thus, low volume processes are usually manual, higher volumes move to mechanized processes and very high volumes use automation (as shown in Figure 5.5). We might visualize:

- projects and job shops with manual processes;
- batches made with mechanized processes;
- mass production and continuous flow using automation.

As we shall see later in the chapter this is generally true, but it is a clear simplification. Recent developments, particularly in computing, have aimed at introducing automation to lower volumes of production.

Historically, manual processes were developed first, and gave the foundations for industry. It is interesting that productivity is still phrased in terms of 'output per person' even in high technology industries. Manual processes are still widely used, as they offer considerable flexibility with low capital costs. Their disadvantages are high unit cost, need for a skilled workforce, and variable quality. If the production quantity is to be increased in a manual process, more people and equipment are employed. This gives flexibility with low costs, and consequently low risk. There comes a point, however, when it is cheaper to invest in some mechanized process.

Mechanized processes were developed with the industrial revolution, and were the most advanced technology available until quite recently. Initially, mechanization was based on general-purpose machines such as lathes, grinders and drills. Later, more specialized machines were dedicated to one product, and the reduction in set-up time substantially increased productivity. This step is equivalent to switching from a batch process to mass production. As we have seen, the resulting mechanized processes had the advantages of producing high volumes of uniform products at low unit cost, but the disadvantages of high capital cost and inflexibility.

Mechanized processes still need operators to load the machines, do some of the operations, and help if there are any problems. This allows machines with relatively low levels of sophistication. As available technology improved it became clear that human operators often slowed down the process, added variability to the quality and increased unit costs. These problems could be overcome by moving towards automated processes.

Automated processes have been developed most recently, and have become much more widespread with the availability of cheap computer control systems. Some aspects of these are described in the rest of the chapter.

In summary

The technology used in processes can be used to classify them according to manual, mechanized or automated. In general, there is a link between the technology used and the throughput volume.

5.3.2 Approaches to automation

It is clear that throughput and productivity can often be improved by using automation. This has traditionally meant using equipment which has been specially designed to make a single product. Unfortunately, this kind of automation is capital intensive, and can only be justified for the high volumes of mass production. Systems of this kind have now become known as fixed or hard automation. More recently, there has been considerable progress in using high technology for lower volume processes. In essence, the aim is to use automation for intermittent processes. This is the basis of flexible or programmable automation.

The first step towards automation for intermittent processes was numerically controlled (NC) machines. These were originally simple, general-purpose machines which were designed to run without the immediate control of humans. In other words, they allowed mechanization rather than automation. Initially, paper tapes were used to control the machines, and their functions could be quickly and conveniently reprogrammed by simply replacing the tape. Such systems were based on the early work of Jacquard who used punched cards to control weaving looms in the nineteenth century.

Numerically controlled machines developed into large machine tools which could follow a series of pre-programmed instructions, perhaps drilling, planing, milling, boring and turning products of many different shapes and sizes. Such tools are now the most widely used form of flexible automation. They have the advantages of not needing a human operator except to change the program or load the machine, and give consistently high quality at low unit cost.

The control of NC machines passed from paper tapes to magnetic tapes and more recently to microcomputers. Essentially, each machine is now programmed and controlled by a microcomputer dedicated to its operation. Such computerized numerically controlled machines (CNC) do a series of operations without interruption. Readily available programs allow even low production quantities to be done reliably and at low unit cost. Such systems, where computers assist in the actual manufacturing processes, are called computer-aided manufacturing (CAM). Numerically controlled machines were the early examples of this, but attention has recently moved to industrial robots.

Industrial robots were developed in the 1960s, but their use has only become common since the 1980s. In essence they are stationary machines which have reprogrammable 'manipulators' to move materials through a variety of tasks and perform a limited range of activities. Thus, a robot can move a spray to paint a car, or a welding torch to assemble panels into car bodies. Car assembly lines were the first major users of robots and as technology improved the range of jobs they can do they have increased. Typically, they are used for spot welding, spray painting, testing, automatic inspection and limited assembly. They have obvious uses in reaching places which are difficult for humans to get at, or handling dangerous substances, such as explosives, hot steel ingots or radio-active materials. Industrial robotics is an area where considerable developments can be expected in the future.

The next step in automated production uses flexible manufacturing systems (FMS). In this system, the computers which control each piece of equipment (CNC or robot) are combined, so a number of separate machines are under the control of a central computer. This computer can then coordinate the operations of individual machines and can optimize the overall production schedule. The flow of goods is also computer controlled by an automated transport system, with wire-guided trucks moving between machines. This system carries products, components, materials and tools as needed. The link between the transport system and the manufacturing machines is made with automatic loading and unloading stations at each point of transfer. Thus we can list the essential parts of an FMS as:

- a central computer to schedule, route, load and control operations;
- a number of machines under the control of the central computer;
- a computer-controlled transport system between machines;
- computer-controlled loading and unloading equipment.

Once an FMS is programmed the system can work with very little human intervention. Such systems have the flexibility to make small batches almost as efficiently as large ones. The main drawbacks are obviously the high capital cost and amount of skills needed to set up and run such a process. None the less, many traditional job shops are being replaced by flexible manufacturing systems.

Flexible manufacturing systems are sometimes described as computer-integrated manufacturing (CIM) but terms in this area are often used vaguely and there is some disagreement. A common view is that CIM is a further extension of FMS, so that FMS consists of the actual machines, while CIM includes design and related systems.

There are obvious advantages to flexible manufacturing systems. They allow faster changes between different products and these changes are much cheaper. Labour costs are reduced to a minimum and by allowing the computer to control the scheduling and routing, utilization of machines can be very high. If the computer also controls inventories, stocks of raw materials and work in progress can be reduced. Perhaps the final advantage concerns the quality. If goods are produced automatically, they have a consistently high quality, without the variation found in less automated processes.

Conversely, there are some disadvantages to FMS. The equipment is obviously expensive to buy and set up. Part of the initial cost comes from the considerable effort needed to ensure that a system is suitable for all the products that are planned. Although the machines can be programmed to make many different products, there are limitations and they lack the flexibility of some other processes. The technology is still at a relatively new stage and there are often teething troubles and difficulties in finding technology which is good enough and robust enough to satisfy all requirements.

Another type of computer assistance comes in design. For many years designers have used the graphics capabilities of computers to design products on a VDU. The traditional view of a draughtsman sitting at a drawing board is replaced by someone sitting at a computer terminal and directing changes. This interaction allows designs to be tested and changed very quickly. Initial designing time is also saved by having computers store designs of similar products. Rather than start designing from scratch, similar designs are re-covered and modified as necessary. This process is called computer-aided design (CAD). While a computer is used to show current designs on a screen, it can also do related calculations. Thus CAD can:

- reduce initial design time;
- allow very rapid changes to existing design;
- enhance basic drawings, perhaps showing how the actual product will look, rotating it, showing other perspectives, and so on;
- do calculations about stresses, strengths and any other engineering factors;
- estimate costs for products as they are being designed;

- generate bills of material;
- make links with other computer systems.

This last benefit is particularly significant. In the past, even when designs were drawn with the help of computers, there was a break between the design stage and the manufacturing stage. The suggestion was soon made that if computers were designing the products (CAD) and controlling the machines (CAM) why were the two systems not linked to make a single CAD/CAM system? Such systems are now common. Designs are worked on and finalized in the CAD part of a system and are then automatically transferred to the CAM part which generates the programs needed to control machines, followed by actual manufacture. Such systems can produce even low volumes of goods very efficiently. Prototypes, for example, can be produced quickly and cheaply, or perhaps eliminated. Such systems can also be linked to other management systems to:

- update stock levels and order new materials and parts;
- print invoices and check accounts;
- record operating performances and other statistics.

We have discussed automation in the design and manufacturing process, and there seems little to prevent the development of an 'automated factory'. This would have a product designed with computer assistance, and then computers would take over to do all the following stages automatically. Manufacture would be planned and controlled, parts would be ordered, final products delivered, bank accounts updated, without any human intervention. It would be a gross exaggeration to say such factories exist at the moment, but the principles have been established and the reality is not far away.

In summary
Automated systems can produce consistently high quality at low unit cost. Traditional 'hard' automation was inflexible, but recent developments have aimed at flexible automation. This brings the benefits of mass production processes to smaller volumes. There are several levels of automation available in manufacturing, with numerically controlled machines, robots, flexible manufacturing systems and automated factories. These are assisted by computer-aided design.

5.3.3 Choosing the level of technology

High technology can increase the productivity of a process, but this does not mean that every organization should immediately replace its current processes by high technology alternatives. There are a number of other factors that must be considered. The most obvious of these are the costs. High technology systems have low operating costs but high capital costs. This means that unless high volumes are made the capital costs are spread over too few units and the unit cost is high. Low technology systems have low capital costs but high variable, and hence unit, costs. A balance is needed between these and forecast demand for the product could indicate a preferred level of technology.

There are also other trade-offs. Higher levels of automation usually reduce the flexibility and variability in a system. Sometimes barriers are created between customers and the final product, which may be one reason why bread 'baked on the premises' is popular, and people walk past cash dispensing machines to talk to someone in a bank. Perhaps the major criticism of automated systems, however, is that they ignore the skills which people can bring, including:

- pattern recognition;
- creativity;
- intelligent use of all available information;
- use of subjectivity and judgement;
- flexibility;
- ability to adapt to new and unusual circumstances.

Conversely, the advantages of machines include the fact that they:

- work with consistent precision;
- are very fast and powerful;
- can perform many tasks simultaneously;
- store large amounts of information;
- can work continuously without tiring;
- are reliable.

People and machines are better at different jobs and because automation is better in some circumstances, it should not be assumed that it is better in all circumstances.

WORKED EXAMPLE 5.2

A product can be made by three different processes. The costs vary with annual production, with estimated total unit costs for each type of process as:

Manual process: £20 a unit regardless of quantity
Hard automation: £100 $- 2 * D$
Flexible automation: £80 $- 3.3 * D + 0.036 * D^2$

where D is annual demand in thousands of units.
Over what range would each level of automation give the lowest unit cost?

SOLUTION

If we draw a graph of the unit costs for various annual production quantities we get the results shown in Figure 5.6.

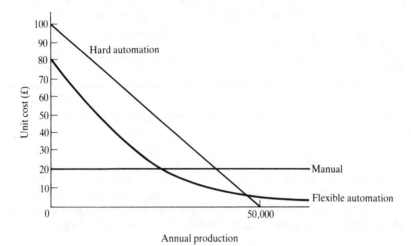

Figure 5.6   Unit costs for Worked Example 5.2.

The manual process has lowest total unit cost from a demand of zero until:

$$80 - 3.3 * D + 0.036 * D^2 = 20$$
$$D = 25 \text{ (taking the appropriate root)}$$

The flexible automation process has the lowest unit cost for demand from 25,000 until:

$$100 - 2 * D = 80 - 3.3 * D + 0.036 * D^2$$
$$D = 47.75 \text{ (taking the positive root)}$$

The hard automation process gives lowest unit cost for demand above 47,750.

WORKED EXAMPLE 5.3

A factory works two eight-hour shifts a day, five days a week for 50 weeks a year. One unpleasant job for a welder is to get into an awkward, enclosed space to spot weld two parts of a product together. For this, welders are paid £7 an hour directly with a further £3 an hour in other costs. It has been suggested that a suitable robot could be bought to do the job for £150,000. This would work virtually non-stop for an expected life of 7 to 10 years, and with operating costs of £2 an hour. Would this be a reasonable investment?

SOLUTION

The present system costs £10 an hour with no capital costs. The robot costs £2 an hour but has a capital cost of £150,000. The robot will recover its costs after $150,000/(10 - 2) =$ 18,750 hours. The factory works $2 * 8 * 5 * 50 = 4000$ hours a year, so the robot will recover its costs in $18,750/4000 = 4.7$ years. This is well within the expected lifetime, so the robot should be considered.

This analysis has not included interest payments, depreciation or opportunity costs. These could easily be added in a more detailed calculation.

WORKED EXAMPLE 5.4

Your company is considering an automated assembly plant which has an initial cost of £12 million, an installation cost of £3 million and maintenance costs of £0.6 million a year. This plant will reduce operating costs by £4 million a year and will have a salvage value of £2 million at the end of five years (its expected life). Use a discounting rate of 10% a year to see if the plant would be a reasonable investment (assuming all savings and maintenance costs occur at the end of a year).

SOLUTION

The plant will cost £15 million to buy and install. Then it will give net savings of £3.4 million a year for five years. Present values for costs and savings can be found by using the discounting rate of 10%. This gives the following values over a five-year period, including £2 million for scrap at the end of year 5. (Figures in Table 5.2 are in millions of pounds working to two places of decimals.)

Table 5.2

Year	Discount factor	Cost	Present value	Savings	Present value
—	1.00	15	15.00	—	—
1	1.10	—	—	3.4	3.09
2	1.21	—	—	3.4	2.81
3	1.33	—	—	3.4	2.56
4	1.46	—	—	3.4	2.33
5	1.61	—	—	5.4	3.35
Total			15.00		14.14

The net present value of the assembly plant is $-£0.86$ million, so it does not seem a good investment.

In summary

Automation can bring advantages, but it does not necessarily provide the best process in all circumstances. The choice of process depends on a number of factors.

SELF ASSESSMENT QUESTIONS

5.11 What classification could be used to describe the technologies available for processes?

5.12 What types of automation might you see in a factory?

5.13 What do the following abbreviations stand for?

(a) NC   (d) CAD
(b) CNC   (e) FMS
(c) CAM   (f) CIM

5.14 What are the main purposes of automating production?

5.15 Rank the following in terms of increasing levels of automation:

CIM   NC   FMS   CAM   CNC

5.16 Automation increases productivity and should be introduced as widely as possible. Is this statement:

(a) true
(b) false
(c) partly true?

5.4   PROCESSES IN THE SERVICE SECTOR

Although much of the previous section has referred to processes used in manufacturing, many of the same principles apply to services. Processes can still be classified according to project, job shop, batch, mass production and continuous flow. Consider, for example, the service provided by a restaurant. Specialized restaurants exist, where customers phone in their orders in advance and the restaurant then prepares the meal requested. This is a project. Expensive restaurants have an extensive menu, so the preparation of any meal is like a job shop. Canteens and cafeterias have set meals, which are produced in batches. Busy hamburger restaurants function like mass production assembly lines. Meals are discrete, so it is difficult to describe a continuous flow process, but perhaps the coffee or beer served with meals approaches a continuous flow.

Again there is the familiar pattern with intermittent processes having more flexibility but higher unit costs, while mass production has less flexibility but lower unit costs. Unfortunately, many services such as those provided by dentists, lawyers, doctors, accountants, hairdressers, taxis, and so on, are produced either singly or in very small batches. In other words, each customer demands a different product from the service. This means that the process is set up for projects, with considerable flexibility, but high costs. At best, the processes for most services could be described as job shops.

In recent years, however, automation has become much more common in services. There are now many types of service which routinely use some form of technology. This technology can again be classified according to manual, mechanized or automated. The only problem is that services are so diverse it is difficult to describe automation in the same general terms we used for manufacturing. The service offered by a lawyer, for example, has little in common with a postal service. Perhaps the principles behind automation in services can best be illustrated by some specific examples.

(1) *Offices*. The operations done in offices include typing, copying, filing and handling messages. Until recently all of these were done manually, with an electric typewriter as the most sophisticated technology available. The clerical jobs have now been transformed by technology. Word processors and desk top publishers have significantly increased the productivity of typists. Copying can be done either by automatic photocopiers or using networked word processors. Filing is done on computerized databases. Messages are handled by electronic mail or FAX machines. Longer term developments aim for the paperless office and the virtual elimination of manual clerical jobs.

(2) *Banks*. Customers in banks used to be served exclusively by tellers. These provided a flexible service, but queues formed at busy times. A way round this was to introduce plastic cards and automated cash dispensing machines. Then, a manual operation was replaced by an automated one, cheques were replaced by machine-readable cards, paperwork was reduced, the customers did some of the work themselves, and banking operations have become less expensive.

(3) *Supermarkets*. Customers in grocery shops used to tell an assistant what they wanted. The assistant would then fetch the goods, weigh and wrap them, and present a bill. Supermarkets introduced a mechanized system, where customers did most of the work, and checkout operators added the costs and presented a bill. The next stage is automated, with computer-readable shopping lists, automatic materials handling equipment to fetch and deliver goods to a customer, and automatic debiting of bank accounts.

(4) *Post office*. Sorting letters was a labour-intensive manual process, but now it is largely automated, with the use of post codes. More recently the need to send letters has been reduced by electronic mail and FAX machines.

(5) *Warehousing*. Traditionally, warehouses had people moving goods to and from racks, with stock movement recorded on cards. Such systems could not cope with high volumes or rapid movements, so mechanized systems were introduced. Later, automated warehouses were developed for high volumes, where computers not only record

stock movements but also control the necessary physical handling of goods.

(6) *Reservation systems*. Airlines started using on-line reservation systems in the 1960s. They are now considered essential, and similar systems are used by buses and trains, theatres, sporting events, taxis, and so on.

There are many examples of service organizations moving to automated processes. As with manufacturing, the aim is to bring the efficiency of mass production processes to smaller batches. As the average productivity of service industries is low, this area has considerable potential for future development.

In summary
The general points raised for manufacturing processes can also be applied to services. Most services use a project process and have high associated costs. An increasing number of services can benefit from automation. This is an area with considerable potential for future development.

SELF ASSESSMENT QUESTIONS

5.17 How could you classify the types of process available to services?

5.18 Services are expensive because the batch size is small and each job is considered as a

project. Is this:

(a) true
(b) false
(c) partly true?

5.5   ANALYSING A PROCESS

5.5.1 Process charts

So far this chapter has described the kinds of process available and the factors that affect the choice of the most appropriate. Later chapters look at how parts of the process can be organized. This means we need some way of describing the details of a process and, in particular, the sequence of individual operations that combine to form the process. The easiest way of doing this uses a process chart.

There are several different types of process chart, but they all rely on breaking down the whole process into a number of distinct operations. Each of these operations must be sufficiently distinct for us to identify a beginning and end. Suppose, for example, we look at the process which a patient goes through

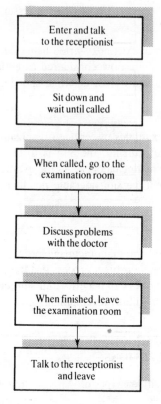

Figure 5.7 Process chart for a visit to a doctor's surgery.

when visiting a doctor at the surgery. The operations might be described as follows:

- Enter and talk to the receptionist.
- Sit down and wait until called.
- When called, go to the examination room.
- Discuss problems with the doctor.
- When finished, leave the examination room.
- Talk to the receptionist and leave.

This can be drawn as the informal process chart shown in Figure 5.7.

A similar chart could be drawn for any product going through a process, so a simple assembly process could be represented as shown in Figure 5.8.

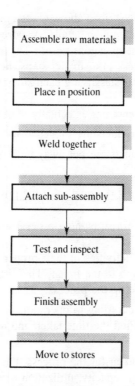

Figure 5.8 Process chart for a simple assembly.

A process chart should be able to answer questions like:

- What operations are done?
- What is the sequence of these?
- Which operation cannot be started until others have finished?
- When is each operation done?
- How long does each take?
- Who is working on the operation?
- Is there any idle time?
- Are there any inspections?
- Are products being moved?
  And so on.

When these questions have been answered, we should have a clear picture of the current process. Then we can start asking about potential changes and improvements. Why are things done in the current way and how might they be done better?

The informal chart described above gives a general view of the steps in a process, but it does not give enough details. A more formal approach is needed to add details and answer the questions raised. This formal approach could start by breaking down the process into smaller steps, noting the time for each step and the distance moved, and classifying each step according to:

- *operation*, where something is actually done;
- *movement*, where products are moved;
- *storage*, where products are put away until they are needed;
- *delay*, where products are held up;
- *inspection*, which tests the quality of the product.

Then the procedure for drawing a process chart is as follows.

(1) List all the steps or activities in their proper sequence from the start of the process through to the finish. This list should include all operations that make up the process.

(2) Classify each step according to operation, movement, inspection, delay and storage. Find the time taken and distance moved in each step.

(3) Add the total time taken for the process, the rate of doing each operation, maximum capacity, utilization of each step, and any other relevant information.

These three stages give a detailed description of a process, and an example of the resulting chart is shown in Figure 5.9. Stages 1 and 2 are probably done by observation, while stage 3 is a calculation. The next part of the analysis is concerned with the efficiency of operations and suggestions for improvement.

(4) The desired rate of output from the process is determined (probably from the forecast demand for products).

(5) For each step in the process, compare the actual output with the desired output. Ensure that the process is appropriate and the sequence of operations is sensible and balanced.

(6) If the process is out of balance or there are bottlenecks or equipment with low utilization, adjustments might be made. In particular, the capacity might be changed or the sequences might be adjusted so that balance is returned to the process.

Figure 5.9 shows a process chart, with the time and distances given. The maximum capacity of each step can now be found. Step 1 takes 2.5 minutes, so the maximum number of units which can be processed is $60/2.5 = 24$ an hour. Step 2 takes 2 minutes, so the capacity is 30 an hour, and so on. The overall

Process chart: Part 421/302									
Step number	Description	Operation	Movement	Inspection	Delay	Storage	Time (min)	Distance (metres)	Comment
1	Fetch components		X				2.5	50	
2	Put components on machine	X					2.0		
3	Start machine	X					1.2		
4	Fetch sub-assembly		X				3.0	40	
5	Wait for machine to stop				X		5.2		
6	Unload machine	X					2.0		
7	Inspect result			X			1.5		
8	Join sub-assembly	X					5.0		
9	Move unit to machine		X				2.5	25	
10	Load machine and start	X					2.0		
11	Wait for machine to stop				X		5.0		
12	Unload machine	X					1.4		
13	Carry unit to inspection area		X				2.0	25	
14	Inspect and test			X			5.2		
15	Carry unit to finish area		X				1.4	20	
16	Finish unit	X					5.5		
17	Final inspection			X			3.5		
18	Carry unit to store		X				5.3	45	

Summary		No.	Time		
	Operations	7	19.1	Time:	56.2 min
	Movements	6	16.7	Distance:	205 metres
	Inspections	3	10.2		
	Delays	2	10.2		
	Storage	0	0		
		18	56.2		

Figure 5.9 Example of a process chart.

capacity of the process must be judged by the step that takes the longest time. Finishing the product takes 5.5 minutes, so this product cannot be made at a rate faster than 60/5.5 = 10.9 units an hour. If forecast demand is higher than this, the process must be changed, perhaps adding more finishers, or changing the way the finishing is done. This, of course, must raise a whole series of questions about quality and flexibility.

The process chart can also be used to suggest areas where improvements might be found. In steps 5 and 11 the operator has to wait a total of 10.2 minutes. This might be reduced by better planning. In steps 1, 4, 9, 13, 15 and 18 the product is moved a total of 205 metres, taking 16.7 minutes. This might be reduced by better layouts. Questions like these are discussed in the following chapters.

WORKED EXAMPLE 5.5

Draw a chart of the process involved when a person goes to a bank and asks for a personal loan.

SOLUTION

Details of the process, and particularly the time, will vary considerably. Figure 5.10 shows an example of a chart.

Process chart:	Personal bank loan								
Step number	Description	Operation	Movement	Inspection	Delay	Storage	Time (min)	Distance (metres)	Comment
1	Customer selects bank and visits		X						
2	Initial screening	X					5		
3	Move to loans office		X				2	15	
4	Wait				X		10		
5	Discuss with loans officer	X					15		
6	Complete application forms	X					15		
7	Carry forms to verifier		X				2	10	
8	Forms are checked			X			2		
9	Wait as credit analysis and verification is done				X		25		
10	Supply further information	X					5		
11	Move back to loans office		X				2	15	
12	Wait				X		20		
13	Forms are checked			X			5		
14	Complete arrangements	X					15		
15	Leave		X						

Summary		No.	Time		
	Operations	5	55	Time:	123 min
	Movements	5	6	Distance:	40 metres
	Inspections	2	7		
	Delays	3	55		
	Storage	0	0		
		15	123		

Figure 5.10 Process chart for Worked Example 5.5.

This describes the process from the customer's point of view. There will be a few variations if written for the bank.

Figure 5.11 Precedence diagram when A must be done before B.

In summary

Process charts describe the details of a process. They break down the whole process into distinct steps and show what is happening at each point. Their purpose is to describe the details of the existing process and highlight areas where improvements might be made.

5.5.2 Precedence diagrams

An alternative form of process chart is a precedence diagram. This uses a network of nodes and arcs to represent the relationship of operations in a process. Suppose, for example, a simple process consists of two operations A and B, and A must be completed before B can start. We can represent the operations by two nodes and the relationship by an arc, as shown in Figure 5.11. The arrow from A to B is a directed arc which shows that B must be done after A. The length and orientation of the arc have no significance.

This approach can be extended to more complex processes, as illustrated in the following example.

WORKED EXAMPLE 5.6

The process in a bottling hall consists of the following six operations:

(1)   Clean and inspect the bottle.
(2)   Fill the bottle.
(3)   Put a cap on the bottle.
(4)   Stick a printed label on the bottle.
(5)   Put the bottle in a box and move it away.

Draw a precedence diagram of this process.

SOLUTION

Some operations must clearly be done before others, so the bottle must be filled before the cap is put on, and so on. We must start by defining all these precedences. Operation 1 (cleaning and inspecting the bottle) can be done right at the beginning. Operation 2 (filling) and 4 (labelling) can both be done immediately after 1. Operation 3 (capping) can be done after 2, while operation 5 (putting in box) must wait until both 3 and 4 are finished. This gives the following list of precedences:

Operation	Must be done after
1	—
2	1
3	2
4	1
5	3,4

Now these relationships can be drawn as a precedence diagram. This starts with the earliest operations and moves systematically through the process. Thus, we start by drawing operation 1 at the left, and then add operations 2 and 4. Operation 3 is added after 2. Finally operation 5 is added, after both 3 and 4 are finished. The complete precedence diagram is shown in Figure 5.12.

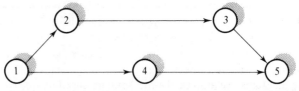

Figure 5.12 Precedence diagram for Worked Example 5.6.

WORKED EXAMPLE 5.7

A product has to go through 11 operations with the precedences shown in the following table. Draw a precedence diagram of the process.

Operation	Must be done after
1	—
2	1
3	1
4	2,3
5	4
6	4
7	4
8	5
9	6,7
10	8,9
11	10

SOLUTION

To draw the precedence diagram we start with the earliest operations and then systematically work through all other operations. Operation 1 can be done right at the start. When 1 is finished both operations 2 and 3 can start. Operation 4 can be done after both 2 and 3, and so on. These precedences are shown in Figure 5.13.

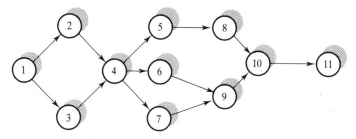

Figure 5.13 Precedence diagram for Worked Example 5.7.

In summary
Precedence diagrams are a form of process chart based on a network representation. Operations are represented by nodes and relationships by directed arcs.

5.5.3 Multiple activity charts

Process charts and precedence diagrams show the relationships between the operations in a process. They are useful in describing and analysing a process, but they do not make clear what each participant in the process is doing at any time. We may, for example, be interested not only in the total time that an operator is busy during a process, but also how this time is distributed. If there are a few long periods when the operator is idle, he or she may be able to do additional tasks, but this would not be possible if the operator is idle for a number of short periods. This kind of analysis can be easily done using a multiple activity chart.

A multiple activity chart has a timescale down the side of the diagram, with all the participants listed across the top. Then, the time each participant works on the process is blocked off. Suppose, for example, two typists work on word processors which are connected to a single high quality printer. The participants in the process are the typists, the word processors and the printer. If each typist has a series of documents to type, each of which takes 15 minutes to type and 5 minutes to print, we could draw a multiple activity chart for their operations during the first hour of a day, as shown in Figure 5.14. This assumes (for simplicity rather than reality) that the two typists start at the same time, that

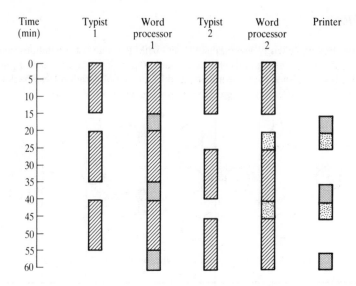

Figure 5.14 Example of a multiple activity chart.

the printer can only print one document at a time, that the word processor cannot be used while a document is being printed, and that each document must be printed before the next one is typed.

This chart shows at a glance what each participant is doing at any time in the process. At the start of the day, both typists use their word processors to type documents. After 15 minutes they both finish. Word processor 1 is connected to the printer, while both typists and word processor 2 wait for the printer to finish. After 20 minutes typist 1 starts a second document, while word processor 2 is connected to the printer, and so on. At the end of the hour, we can see that both typists have been idle for 15 minutes, the word processors are in use all the time (after the initial 5-minute wait), and the printer has been used for 25 minutes.

WORKED EXAMPLE 5.8

One person is currently employed to operate each of three machines. The machines work a cycle with 6 minutes for loading, 6 minutes of operating and 4 minutes for unloading. An operator is required for the loading and unloading, but the machine can operate without any supervision. It is proposed to make savings by using two people to operate the three machines. Draw a multiple activity chart to see if this is feasible. (Start with all people and machines idle and follow the process for a 60-minute period.) What are the resulting utilizations?

SOLUTION

A multiple activity chart for three machines and two operators is shown in Figure 5.15.

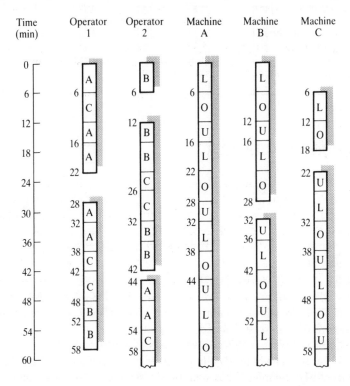

Figure 5.15   Multiple activity chart for Worked Example 5.8.

The process starts with operators 1 and 2 loading machines A and B respectively. These machines start operating, while operator 1 loads machine C. Machines A and B are unloaded as soon as they are finished, and are then reloaded. Machine C has to wait to be unloaded until an operator is free. This process continues for the 60 minutes. At the end of this time operator 1 has been idle for 8 minutes, operator 2 has been idle for 8 minutes, and the three machines have been idle for 0, 4 and 10 minutes. Utilizations are 87% for operators and an average of 92% for machines. Some of this idle time was needed at the start of the day, and if we had run the chart for longer the average utilization of machines would have increased. Overall the new arrangement seems to be feasible.

In summary
Multiple activity charts are a form of process chart which show what each of the participants in a process is doing at any time.

SELF ASSESSMENT QUESTIONS

5.19 What is the purpose of process charts?

5.20 How is the maximum rate at which a product can be made found from a process chart?

5.21 What are precedence diagrams used for?

5.22 What exactly is meant by 'operation A precedes operation B'?

5.23 Multiple activity charts are one type of process chart, and there are many other types. Is this statement true?

SUMMARY OF CHAPTER

This chapter has described some aspects of process design and planning. The chapter started with a classification of processes according to project, job shop, batch, mass production and continuous flow. Each of these has different characteristics and is appropriate for different product types and quantities. Organizations should choose the most appropriate method of making their products. This choice is determined by a number of factors including demand, variation in demand and product mix, capital available, workforce skills, and so on. The choice may also be related to the stage of the product in its life cycle.

Productivity of intermittent processes is lower than that of continuous processes. Their productivity may be improved by reorganizing equipment operators, using group technology, or flexible automation.

The technologies available for processes were classified according to manual, mechanized or automated. Several levels of automation were described, ranging from numerically controlled machines to automated factories. The most appropriate level of automation should be selected for any process, but this is not necessarily the highest level that is technically feasible.

Many ideas in the chapter were introduced by reference to manufacturing. The same principles could be applied to services. Much of the service sector uses project or job shop processes, and these tend to be expensive. There is considerable diversity in the service sector, and many services are now highly automated. This is an area with considerable potential for development.

The last section in the chapter looked at process charts. These describe the details of an existing process and highlight areas where improvements might be made. Several types of chart were described, including process diagrams and multiple activity charts.

PROBLEMS

5.1 A manufacturing company is considering a new product, but has not yet forecast demand. Experience suggests that the costs will depend on the type of process used, as follows.

	Annual fixed cost	Variable cost
Project	100,000	2000
Job shop	150,000	250
Batch	450,000	150
Mass production	1,500,000	100

Within what range is each process best?

5.2 A product can use three different processes whose total unit costs vary with annual production as follows:

- manual process: fixed at £40 a unit
- hard automation: £300 $- 20 * D$
- flexible automation: £160 $- 4 * D + 0.8 * D^2$

where D is the annual demand in hundreds of units. Over what range would each type of process give the lowest unit cost?

5.3 A factory works three eight-hour shifts a day for five days a week. It could save £20 an hour in labour costs by buying an industrial robot for £250,000. If the factory pays 15% interest on a debt with the bank, and the robot has a life expectancy of 7 years, is it a good investment?

5.4 It is suggested that a new machine will generate the following incomes and costs over the next five years. Use a discounting rate of 12% to see if the machine would be a good investment.

Year	Income	Costs
—	—	36,000
1	5,000	—
2	27,000	12,000
3	36,000	—
4	12,000	4,000
5	2,000	—

5.5 Draw two alternative process charts for the process of getting a mortgage from a building society.

5.6 A product has to go through eight operations with the precedences shown in the following table. Draw a precedence diagram of the process.

Operation	Must be done after
1	—
2	1
3	2
4	1
5	4
6	3,5
7	3,6
8	5,6

5.7 A unit of product comes off a production line and a random sample is taken for inspection. The inspection of each unit has three separate elements, each of which uses a different type of machine. There are two machines of each type in the inspection area. Each unit of product takes 3 minutes on each machine for inspection, and then 2 minutes on each machine for final adjustment. There are three inspectors working in the area. Draw a process chart for the inspection area. How many units can be inspected each hour?

CASE STUDY – RETOOLING FOR THE FX100A CAMERA

Jim Wright had just been passed the agenda for next month's meeting of the Board of Directors. He looked quickly at the names of those who would be attending, and loosely classified them as 'Family', 'Names', 'Bankers' and 'Workers'. The company had been founded 80 years ago with the aim of supplying inexpensive cameras to meet the rapidly growing demand. It had been run by the same family until 20 years ago, when the Board of Directors consisted of distant relatives of the original founder. Unfortunately, the family had little interest in the business and was clearly incapable of running an efficient company. Despite falling sales, the family kept drawing large salaries and expenses, but refused to invest any money in the business. The company began to run at a considerable loss and was only saved from bankruptcy by a group of banks and other institutions. They lent enough money for a major restructuring of the company, with the conditions that the family gave up complete control and allowed the banks to appoint a number of directors (the 'Bankers'). At this time two other groups were invited to join the Board:

- a small number of well known business figures, some of whom had considerable experience and others whose name looked impressive on company correspondence (the 'Names');

- executives of the company, including Jim Wright as Production Director (the 'Workers').

At the next Board meeting there would be eight Workers, who usually came up with the ideas and proposals about which the Board had to make decisions. Jim Wright felt that these were reasonably competent people who had been responsible for the turn round of the company. He felt that the growing demand for the company's products and increasing profits were due entirely to the executives' good work. He also felt that the company would be much better run if the other Board members would retire and not interfere.

There would also be five members of the Family at the meeting, and these could be relied on to oppose any expenditure. They consistently suggested that profits should be distributed among shareholders to give them 'realistic' compensation. The six Bankers who would be present were cautions. They would support sensible investment, provided it guaranteed a satisfactory long-term return. Four Names were expected to attend, but these rarely said anything and Jim suspected they were only there for the free lunch.

Jim next looked down the agenda and found 'Item 4. Retooling for FX100A. 15 minute presentation by Jim Wright. 45 minute discussion'. This meant he had 15 minutes to present the case for retooling the assembly line that made the FX100A camera. This was the company's best selling line, and produced 40% of company profit. Before time limits were put on each agenda item, Jim recalled one meeting that had spent two hours discussing the allocation of car parking spaces to senior management.

Jim considered the retooling of the best selling product to be an important project. The current process had really just grown with demand, and there had never been a chance to make fundamental changes. Jim felt that the company should now be moving to a more automated process and had initiated the retooling project. He had hired a firm of consulting engineers to prepare a report on feasible alternatives. This report consisted of a two-page executive summary, 10 pages of recommendations, 100 pages of discussion and 450 pages of detailed appendices. Although copies had been distributed to all the directors, Jim assumed that he would be the only one who had read it. Most of the Bankers and Workers would have read the executive summary, but he suspected that the Family and Names would not even have opened it.

Because Jim was Production Director, had read the consultants' report, and was familiar with developments in the area, he felt that he was in the best position to make a reasoned decision about retooling. His aim was to modernize the assembly process by moving away from the manual system and towards automation. He needed the Board's agreement for this, so his plan was to present some information and guide the discussion at the Board meeting until it agreed with his views. He would, of course, only have time to present selected information. The consultants had, for example, discussed moving the factory to a new site in a development area. Jim liked living where he did and saw no point in raising such irrelevant points at the meeting. The consultants had also suggested that improvements to the present process could increase productivity by 5%. Jim felt sure that if this kind of improvement could be made his staff would have told him. Mentioning this to the Board might put the production team in a bad light, so it was more sensible to ignore it.

Jim enjoyed giving presentations and felt that he would have no problem getting the Board to agree to his proposals with a minimum of discussion. He began to prepare his presentation by extracting information from the consultants' report. He would make a number of slides, and the first of these would have to give some details of the product (Jim suspected that some of the Board had little idea what the company actually made).

The company was only concerned with the process used to make one product, which was the FX100A semi-automatic camera. This is an expensive camera which is noted for its high quality. Its main customers are professional photographers and keen amateurs; 80% of production is exported, primarily to the United States and European Community.

The FX100A was made on three parallel assembly lines in a fairly modern factory. The factory bought raw materials and components from a number of suppliers. These were stored in the old works, which was also used to make some components and sub-assemblies. Twenty years ago the assembly plant had been built on the back of the old works. All assembly was now done here, with requests for parts sent to the old works as needed. Deliveries were guaranteed within half an hour. Stocks of finished goods were kept in the warehouse, which had been built five years ago adjacent to the other buildings.

Jim made a number of notes for the slides in his presentation as follows.

Product

FX100A semi-automatic camera.
The company's best selling product.
Contributes 40% of profit.

Monthly sales over the past two years

	1989 (£)	1990 (£)
January	7,700	8,200
February	4,300	5,100
March	6,800	6,000
April	12,100	11,300
May	14,300	13,700
June	15,000	15,200
July	15,400	15,900
August	13,600	14,400
September	9,500	10,400
October	7,100	6,500
November	11,600	12,800
December	17,200	16,800

Current production

- Raw materials and components stored in the old works, where components and sub-assemblies are made.
- Three parallel assembly lines in the assembly plant, working a single eight-hour shift each day for five days a week. The manual assembly is labour intensive. There are 258 separate operations in the process. If all goes well these take a total of an hour and a half for each camera.
- Finished products are moved to the warehouse. Most of these are exported.

Number, cost and availability of employees

- 168 working on the assembly line, for a standard 38-hour week and an average of five hours a week overtime.
- 12 supervisors working a standard 38-hour week and an average of seven hours a week overtime.
- one floor manager working a standard 38-hour week, with unpaid overtime as necessary.

The company uses a formula for staff costs which takes into account wages, stoppages, subsidized meals, training and a range of other direct costs. This gives guidelines for the total cost of employing one person for an hour, as:

- Assembly line workers: £10 an hour normally and £13 an hour for overtime.
- Supervisors: £14 an hour normally and £17 an hour for overtime
- Floor Manager: £18 an hour (with no overtime payments).

Each employee gets 33 days a year paid holiday. Sickness, training and other absences mean that an average of 12.3 assembly line employees are absent in any particular day.

Quality

The FX100A sells well because of its consistently high quality. During assembly there are 24 separate inspections and last year these detected 4749 faults. Most of these were minor and could be corrected, but about 10% meant the camera had to be scrapped. The company received 511 complaints from customers and replaced the camera under a comprehensive warranty.

Main alternatives for retooling

Alternative 1 − Hard automation

This replaces the manual assembly by machines designed especially to assemble the FX100A automatically.

- Capital costs: planning and design, £1.5 million
  production machines, £6 million
  associated equipment, £1.5 million
  refurbishing plant, £1 million
- Operating costs: maintenance at 6% of cost a year
  depreciation at 17% a year
  capital at 18% a year
- Time: 18 months to complete installation
- Staff: 20 operators equivalent to current supervisors
  six maintenance engineers, each with a total cost of £40,000
  a year
- Savings: all of current assembly line costs
  £250,000 a year in the old works by moving assembly to the
  main plant
- Capacity: 1000 units a day

Alternative 2 – Flexible automation

This replaces the manual assembly by CNC machines and general-purpose robots which could be programmed to automatically assemble the FX100A.

- Capital costs: planning and design, £1 million
  production machines, £5 million
  associated equipment, £1 million
  refurbishing plant, £1 million
- Operating costs: maintenance at 8% of cost a year
  depreciation at 12% a year
  capital at 18% a year
- Time: 1 year to complete installation
- Staff: 30 operators equivalent to current supervisors
  10 maintenance engineers, each with a total cost of £40,000 a
  year
- Savings: all of current assembly line costs
  £250,000 a year in the old works by moving assembly to the
  main plant
- Capacity: 800 units a day

Other points

- Unemployment in the area is generally high, but there are severe shortages of some specific skills.
- Seven trade unions had members within the company.
- The consultants' report had listed a total of six feasible alternatives for tooling, which Jim had reduced to two.
- The company made seven different types of camera, all using a similar process.

- The FX100A camera accounts for 30% of camera sales of the company.
- The company also makes a range of camera accessories.
- Four of the current Board members are close to retirement.
- The 'Family' still owns 35% of the shares in the company.

Suggested questions

- How would you describe the senior management of the company?
- Was Jim Wright adopting a reasonable approach to the retooling?
- What other alternatives could the consultants have proposed?
- What factors have not been considered in the figures presented?
- What are the benefits and disadvantages of each alternative?
- What conclusions can be reached with the data presented?
- What additional information would you need before making a final decision?

SOLUTIONS TO SELF ASSESSMENT QUESTIONS

5.1 The way in which a product is made.

5.2 Process planning ensures that each product is made in the most efficient way. It is needed whenever a new product is introduced, or whenever there is a significant change in operations.

5.3 Many factors can affect process decisions, including demand pattern, flexibility needed, vertical integration, customer involvement and product quality.

5.4 Good design, low volumes, little automation, skilled workforce, general-purpose machines, little vertical integration, and so on.

5.5 The amount of the overall supply chain which is owned by one organization.

5.6 One classification is project, job shop, batch, mass production and continuous flow.

5.7 The choice depends on forecast demand, but typically:

(a) mass production **(b)** continuous flow **(c)** batch **(d)** project **(e)** job shop.

5.8 A simplified view gives: planning uses project, introduction uses job shop, growth uses batch, maturity uses mass production.

5.9 Continuous processes such as continuous flow and mass production. There is no time lost by set-ups and other disruptions, the processes are largely automated so more advanced technology can be used, specialized equipment can be used, the process is designed especially for a single product, and so on.

5.10 There are several possibilities, including reorganization of equipment operators, group technology and flexible automation.

5.11 A useful classification has manual, mechanized and automated.

5.12 Numerically controlled machines, robots, flexible manufacturing systems and automated factories, all with computer-aided design.

5.13 **(a)** Numerically controlled
(b) Computerized numerically controlled
(c) Computer-aided manufacturing **(d)** Computer-aided design **(e)** Flexible manufacturing system
(f) Computer-integrated manufacturing.

5.14 To improve productivity, reduce unit costs and obtain consistent high quality.

5.15 The processes have differences beyond the level of automation used, but a rough guide would be NC, CNC, CAM, FMS and CIM.

5.16 (c) Partly true. Automation can increase productivity, but it is not appropriate for all circumstances.

5.17 The same as manufacturing: project, job shop, batch, mass production and continuous flow.

5.18 (b) False. Many services are not expensive and some have extensive automation.

5.19 They describe the details of a process and highlight those areas where improvements might be made.

5.20 By finding the number of units that each step in the process can handle an hour (say). The maximum overall output is the smallest throughput in any particular step.

5.21 They are a type of process chart which concentrates on the relationships between individual operations. They are used for analysing and describing processes.

5.22 Operation A must be finished before operation B starts, and B can start as soon as A is finished.

5.23 Yes.

REFERENCES FOR FURTHER READING

Amstead B.J., Oswald P.F. and Bregman M.L. (1977). *Manufacturing Processes* 7th edn. New York: John Wiley

Ayres R.U. and Miller S.M. (1983). *Robotics: Applications and Social Implications* Cambridge: Ballinger Publishing

Buffa E.S. and Sarin R.K. (1987). *Modern Production/Operations Management* 8th edn. New York: John Wiley

Chang T.C. and Wysk R.A. (1985). *An Introduction to Automated Process Planning Systems* Englewood Cliffs: Prentice-Hall

Collier D.A. (1986). *Service Management: The Automation of Services* Reston: Reston Publishing

Doyle L.E., Keyser C.A. *et al.* (1985). *Manufacturing Processes and Materials for Engineers* 3rd edn. Englewood Cliffs: Prentice-Hall

Groover M.P. and Zimmers E.W. (1984). *CAD/CAM: Computer Aided Design and Manufacturing* Englewood Cliffs: Prentice-Hall

Hayes R.H. and Wheelwright S.C. (1984). *Restoring Our Competitive Edge* New York: John Wiley

Hill T. (1985). *Manufacturing Strategy* Basingstoke: Macmillan

Susnjara K. (1982). *A Manager's Guide to Industrial Robotics* Shaker Heights: Corinthian Press

Chapter 6

Layout of facilities

SYNOPSIS

In the last chapter we saw how a number of factors, including the type of product and the quantities made, determine the best type of process. We also saw how charts could be used to describe a process and highlight areas that might be improved. One of the areas of concern was the distance travelled in a process, which can be reduced with a good layout of facilities. This chapter describes various aspects of facility layout.

Different types of layout can be classified in a number of ways, but the most useful is based on process, product, hybrid, fixed or specialized. The first two are the most important and are described in more detail. Process layouts group together equipment of similar types, while product layouts group together all equipment needed for a particular product.

The main problem in designing process layouts is minimizing the amount of movement between areas. For small problems this can be done intuitively, but larger problems need more formal procedures. The amount of computation for process designs can become so large that computers must be used.

A product layout is characterized by assembly lines. These consist of a series of work stations, each performing a number of operations in a prescribed sequence. The main problem here is to ensure that each work station in the line has the same throughput, and a smooth flow of units is produced. A simple algorithm is described for this problem.

Many facilities have a mixture of product and process layouts, and these are described as hybrid. Some specific examples of this are described in terms of work cells. There is also a range of layouts that do not fit into either category. Fixed-location layouts, for example, keep the product in a single location where all work is done. The chapter discusses these and other specialized layouts, concentrating on warehouses, offices and retail shops.

Finally the chapter ends with a case study to describe a practical illustration. This study was specially chosen to show an unusual context.

OBJECTIVES

After reading this chapter and completing the exercises you should be able to:

- discuss the meaning and importance of facility layout;
- describe alternative layout strategies;
- discuss the characteristics of process layouts;
- design good process layouts that minimize movement between areas;
- use systematic layout planning for new process layouts;
- discuss the characteristics of product layouts;
- use a line-balancing algorithm for product layouts;
- describe hybrid layouts, particularly work cells;
- discuss the characteristics of fixed layouts;
- describe some factors in specialized layouts such as warehouses, offices and retail shops.

6.1 LAYOUTS FOR TYPES OF PROCESS

6.1.1 Introduction

In Chapter 5 we saw how a number of factors, including the type of product and the quantities made, determine the best type of process. Now we will move to a related question and ask how the separate operations of a process should be laid out.

> The aim of layout design is to organize the physical arrangement of facilities so that a process can be as efficient as possible.

All products move through a series of operations as they are being processed and layout design finds the layout that allows these movements to be done as efficiently as possible. Well laid out facilities are efficient and allow a smooth flow of work; poorly laid out facilities reduce efficiency, effective capacity and utilization. The basic layout raises a number of related questions about how much space should be given to each operation, how the space should be configured, what handling equipment should be used, what services are needed in each area, and so on.

The overall objectives of layout design can be described as:

(1) to arrange the facilities needed by a process so that desired output is achieved with minimum resources; or

(2) to lay out available facilities so that the maximum output is achieved.

These objectives must be met without breaking a number of constraints which result from:

- product design
- planned capacity
- process used
- space available
- constraints of the building
- other site constraints
- appropriate materials handling
- capital investment available
- service areas needed
- communications and information flows
- requirements of employees
- safety·
- quality of environment

and so on.

Layout design is an example of constrained optimization, as it attempts to optimize some measure (perhaps maximizing throughput) subject to a series of constraints. It is sometimes suggested that linear programming can help, but practical difficulties severely limit its use. In this chapter we will describe some other approaches.

We have suggested several times that organizations can have either a product focus (if they consider themselves as primarily making a product) or a process focus (if they consider themselves as primarily using a process). This focus is reflected in several aspects of the organization, particularly its layout of facilities. A manufacturing company with a process focus will cluster all similar machines in a single area. Separate areas are used for drilling, grinding, milling, painting, and so on. A company with a product focus will group together all the machines needed to make a particular product. Separate areas make different products. These are two basic layouts, more details of which are given in the following section.

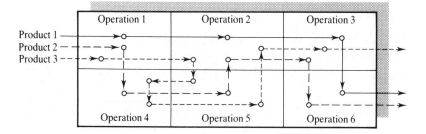

Figure 6.1 Layout with process focus.

In summary

Layout is concerned with the physical arrangement of facilities. The object of layout design is to optimize some function (perhaps maximize throughput) subject to a series of constraints imposed by buildings, management policy, resources availability, and so on.

6.1.2 Alternative layout strategies

An organization with a product focus uses a different layout than one with a process focus. There are a number of different types of layout, and one classification has:

- process layout
- product layout
- hybrid (including group) layout
- fixed layout or fixed-position layout
- specialized layout (such as retail shops and warehouses).

Organizations with a process focus group together all similar pieces of equipment. Thus, drills will be put in one area, grinders will be put in another area, sanding machines in a third area, milling machines in a fourth, and so on. Hospitals put all equipment for emergencies in one ward, surgical patients in another, paediatrics in another, and so on. Each product has a different sequence of operation, so will follow a unique route through the facilities. Each unit must be moved as necessary as it progresses through the process. This type of layout is illustrated in Figure 6.1.

The second kind of layout is product layout, where all the equipment used to process a particular product is put close together. A common form of this lines up equipment in the order it is needed, and passes each unit of a product straight down the line. In manufacturing this is the basis of production or assembly lines, as illustrated in Figure 6.2.

227

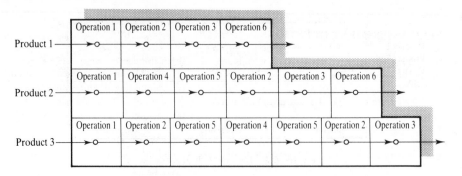

Figure 6.2 Layout with product focus.

In practice many layouts are a combination of product and process, so some operations are laid out with a process focus and others have a product focus. These are called hybrid layouts. A product might, for example, be made from a number of sub-assemblies. Some of these are made by a process with a product layout and some with a process layout. Then the overall layout is a hybrid. Perhaps the most important examples of this are work cells, where most operations use a process layout but a few have a product layout.

The fourth category of layout is fixed or fixed position, where products stay in the same place and all operations are done at this site. This is used for large projects such as shipbuilding, construction or airplane assembly.

The final category of layout includes all others, particularly specialized layouts such as those in warehouses, offices or retail shops.

In summary

There are several different types of layout, and these can be classified according to product, process, hybrid, fixed and specialized (see Table 6.1).

Table 6.1 Classification of layout type.

Layout type	Examples
Process	job shops, hospitals, kitchens
Product	electronic assembly lines, milk bottling
Hybrid	fast-food restaurants, airport passenger terminals
Fixed	shipbuilding, road laying
Specialized	warehouses, offices, retail shops

SELF ASSESSMENT QUESTIONS

6.1 What is meant by 'layout' and why is it important?

6.2 What are the objectives of layout design?

6.3 What constraints might there be on layout?

6.4 What different types of layout are there?

6.5 What type of layout would be used for:

(a) bottling whisky

(b) a library
(c) assembling communication satellites
(d) assembling washing machines
(e) a university campus
(f) making specialized sports cars?

6.6 Which kind of layout is most likely to be found in:

(a) a project
(b) a job shop
(c) mass production?

6.2 PROCESS LAYOUTS

Process layouts collect together in one area all resources that perform a similar function. This layout works best when many different products are to be produced on the same equipment, and is characterized by small batch sizes of diverse items. This has obvious links with intermittent processes, like job shops, so we can infer the following advantages and disadvantages.

Advantages of process layout
(1) It allows a variety of products to be made on the same equipment.
(2) The equipment is general purpose and less expensive than equipment used in product layouts.
(3) The operations can continue if some equipment is unavailable because of breakdown or planned maintenance.
(4) It is suitable for low volumes and variable demand.
(5) Products can be made for specific orders.

Disadvantages of process layout
(1) It is best suited to small batches which give lower utilization of equipment and higher unit costs.
(2) Movement of jobs is complicated, with larger stocks of work in progress.
(3) Scheduling work on equipment is complicated and must be done continuously.
(4) High levels of operator skills are needed.
(5) Control of work is difficult, including supervision, accounting and stock control.
(6) There is extensive materials handling.

6.2.1 Patterns in movements

The quality of process layouts is often judged by the amount of movement between areas. Then the main objective is to design layouts that minimize this movement (or minimize the associated transportation cost). There are several ways of tackling this, but the most widely used are based on simple rules of thumb. Obviously, if there is a lot of movement between two areas these should be placed as close together as possible, while areas with no movement can be placed far apart. This implies that the basic data needed is a list of all movements between areas over some representative time. This can be found by observation over a typical period.

A traditional way of designing layouts is to draw a plan of the available space and add the resulting movements. A system of arrows might be used for this, where the thickness of the arrow corresponds to the number of movements. Humans are very good at recognizing patterns and these maps quickly allow some guidelines for layouts to be developed. More recently, computer software is used to simplify the drawing of plans and allow very rapid comparisons of alternative layouts.

WORKED EXAMPLE 6.1

A museum consists of seven main galleries. These have recently been renovated and attendance has risen considerably. A questionnaire was given to patrons to see how they liked the new arrangements. Most comments were favourable, but some people felt they passed the same exhibits several times before visiting all the galleries. To see if this was true, the routes taken by all people visiting the gallery during a typical morning were recorded. A dominant pattern of movements was recorded on a plan of the museum as shown in Figure 6.3. In this diagram the thickness of the arrows corresponds to the number of people following the path. How might the layout of the galleries be improved?

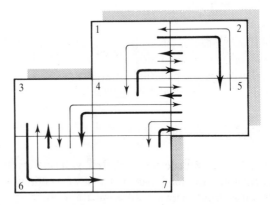

Figure 6.3 Original layout of museum in Worked Example 6.1.

SOLUTION

If we look at the dominant flows in Figure 6.3 we can see that the criticisms are justified. Some systematic improvements to the layout can be made as follows.

- Most people walk through gallery 4 while they try to get between galleries 5 and 6. Conversely, gallery 5 is visited twice (after both galleries 1 and 7) but it does not have a central position. An obvious improvement would be to exchange galleries 4 and 5, so gallery 5 moves to the centre and gallery 4 moves out of the way.
- Most people walk through gallery 3 to get to gallery 6 and then return to gallery 3. These two could also be exchanged.

These simple adjustments give the simpler movements shown in Figure 6.4.

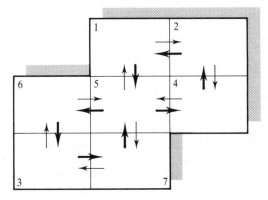

Figure 6.4   Improved layout that reduces movement.

In summary

Process layouts are typical of job shops. A major problem with layout design is to minimize movements between areas. For simple problems, good layouts can be found by recognizing the patterns of movement.

6.2.2 Designing process layouts

Informal approaches to layout design work well with small problems, but a more formal approach is needed for larger ones. If we continue to concentrate on minimizing the movements between different areas, there are three steps in the overall design.

(1) Collect relevant information concerning:
   (a) space required for each area
   (b) quantities moved between areas
   (c) number of trips between areas
   (d) and so on.

(2) Build a general block plan and try to minimize the total movement.

(3) Add details to the block plan to give a final layout (using architects, engineers, consultants and other expertise).

The key step of this process is the second, where a general block plan is produced. This block plan can be designed and evaluated by the following procedure.

(1) List the separate areas or departments to be located and determine the space needed by each one.

(2) Build a 'from−to' matrix. This records the number of trips directly between each pair of areas, and can usually be found by observation over some representative period.

(3) Use logical or sensible arguments to develop an initial schematic diagram for the layout (perhaps based on the current layout).

(4) Determine a cost for this layout. This can be phrased in terms of total metres moved (= Σ movements $*$ distance), kilogram-metres moved (= Σ movements $*$ distance $*$ weight) or some other convenient measure. If this solution is acceptable go to step 6, otherwise continue to step 5.

(5) Improve the initial layout. This may be done by trial and error, some algorithm, or experience. Go back to step 4.

(6) Complete the block plan by including details of cost, additional constraints, preferred features, problems, and so on.

The most obvious difficulty with this approach is finding a suitable improving procedure for step 5. In practice there are several alternatives, often using a computer to evaluate a large number of alternatives. One common procedure is repeatedly to exchange two or three areas, continuing to evaluate solutions until an improvement is found.

The overall approach can be illustrated by an example.

WORKED EXAMPLE 6.2

A simple process consists of six areas of equal size to be fitted into a rectangular building. Data collected from process charts and observation gives the following table of expected movements between areas.

	To					
From	A	B	C	D	E	F
A	—	30	10	0	12	0
B	0	—	10	40	5	0
C	0	5	—	60	0	20
D	0	10	15	—	0	10
E	60	20	0	0	—	10
F	0	0	30	5	10	—

These figures are in appropriate units to include both the number of journeys and the amount of goods carried. (As we are using these figures for comparison the only requirement is that they are consistent.) Draw a block diagram of a good layout for the process.

SOLUTION

Step 1 has already been done, with six areas A to F each needing the same amount of space.

Step 2 builds a from–to matrix. Assuming that a journey from A to B is effectively the same as a journey from B to A, we can combine the top and bottom halves of this matrix to give a revised from–to matrix.

	To					
From	A	B	C	D	E	F
A	—	30	10	0	72	0
B		—	15	50	25	0
C			—	75	0	50
D				—	0	15
E					—	20
F						—

Step 3 uses a logical argument to develop an initial plan. One approach is to rank the links according to the frequency with which they occur. Thus, the busiest link is C–D with a value of 75, next comes A–E with a value of 72, and so on.

Rank	Link	Value
1	C–D	75
2	A–E	72
3	B–D	50
4	C–F	50
5	A–B	30
6	B–E	25
7	E–F	20
8	B–C	15
9	D–F	15
10	A–C	10

Common sense would suggest that areas C and D should be close together as they have most movements, while A and D have no movement and can be far apart. If we concentrate on those areas which should be close together, and move down the ranking above, we could suggest the layout shown in Figure 6.5.

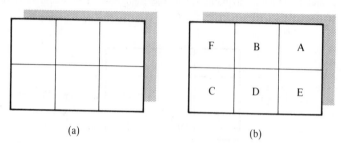

(a)   (b)

Figure 6.5 Layouts for Worked Example 6.2. (a) Rectangular building with six equally sized areas. (b) Proposed original layout.

This layout can be evaluated by multiplying the factors in the from–to table by the distance on each journey. We will simplify calculations by assuming the areas are squares with sides one unit long and use rectilinear distances. Then F is 1 unit from C, 2 units from D, 3 units from E, and so on. The distances are given in the following table. Again we should emphasize that we are only looking at comparisons, so the actual units are unimportant provided they are consistent.

		To					
		A	B	C	D	E	F
	A	—	1	3	2	1	2
	B	—	—	2	1	2	1
From	C	—	—	—	1	2	1
	D	—	—	—	—	1	2
	E	—	—	—	—	—	3
	F	—	—	—	—	—	—

Multiplying the number of movements by the distance gives the cost of movement between areas as follows.

		To					
		A	B	C	D	E	F
	A	—	30 * 1	10 * 3	0	72 * 1	0
	B		—	15 * 2	50 * 1	25 * 2	0
From	C			—	75 * 1	0	50 * 1
	D				—	0	15 * 2
	E					—	20 * 3
	F						—

234

The total cost for this layout is the sum of these elements which is 477. If we had previously decided that the highest acceptable cost is 430, we would now have to adjust the layout and evaluate an alternative.

Step 5 looks for improvements to this layout. One weakness is the distance between E and F which contributes 60 to the total cost. This could be reduced by rearranging the areas as shown in Figure 6.6.

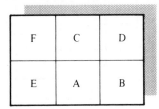

Figure 6.6 Revised layout for Worked Example 6.2.

Using the same evaluation procedure as before gives a total cost of 417. As this is now below the acceptable limit on cost we need not look for further improvement.

		A	B	C	To D	E	F
	A	—	30 * 1	10 * 1	0	72 * 1	0
	B		—	15 * 2	50 * 1	25 * 2	0
From	C			—	75 * 1	0	50 * 1
	D				—	0	15 * 2
	E					—	20 * 1
	F						—

In simple examples like this it would be little effort to look at more layouts and ensure that we have found the optimal one, but in larger problems this could involve a great deal of effort.

Now that we have a block plan, details can be added, starting with the exact size and shape of each area, as well as layout of aisles, stairs, offices and other general-purpose areas. Later, details of individual pieces of equipment, furniture and partitions can be added.

WORKED EXAMPLE 6.3

One floor of a building has six office areas, which are all the same size. The current layout is shown in Figure 6.7. The company feels that a lot of unnecessary movements are made between areas and would like to reduce this by at least 25%. During a random period records were kept of the number of movements between areas as shown in the following table. How might the layout of areas be improved?

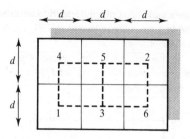

Figure 6.7 Original arrangement of office areas for Worked Example 6.3.

		To				
From	1	2	3	4	5	6
1	—	160	120	100	0	0
2	40	—	0	200	80	0
3	60	0	—	0	80	10
4	20	240	0	—	100	0
5	0	0	100	0	—	120
6	20	40	10	20	140	—

SOLUTION

Assuming there is no difference between a trip from area 1 to area 6 and a trip from area 6 to area 1, the number of such trips can be combined to give the following from–to matrix.

		To				
From	1	2	3	4	5	6
1	—	200	180	120	0	20
2	—	—	0	440	80	40
3	—	—	—	0	180	20
4	—	—	—	—	100	20
5	—	—	—	—	—	260
6	—	—	—	—	—	—

The distance between any two areas can be found from Figure 6.7. These distances can be in any consistent units, so we will assume all movements use the corridor and the areas are rectangles with sides of unit length. The distances between areas are shown in the following table.

		To					
		1	2	3	4	5	6
From	1	—	3	1	1	2	2
	2	—	—	2	2	1	1
	3	—	—	—	2	1	1
	4	—	—	—	—	1	3
	5	—	—	—	—	—	2
	6	—	—	—	—	—	—

Multiplying the number of movements by the distance gives a measure of total cost.

Total cost = Σ movements * distance

		To					
		1	2	3	4	5	6
From	1	—	600	180	120	0	40
	2	—	—	0	880	80	40
	3	—	—	—	0	180	20
	4	—	—	—	—	100	60
	5	—	—	—	—	—	520
	6	—	—	—	—	—	—

Adding all the elements in this matrix gives the cost of the current layout as 2820. A lot of this comes from the frequent movements between areas 2 and 4, and between areas 5 and 6. An improved layout would move these areas closer together. We could try a limited move by exchanging areas 2 and 5. This gives the distance and total cost matrices shown overleaf (see also Figure 6.8).

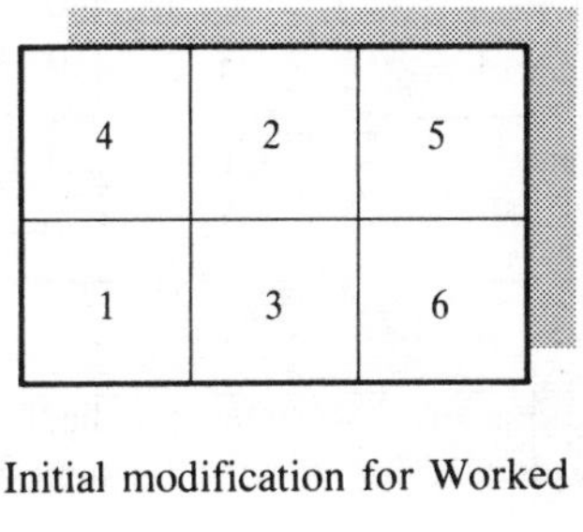

Figure 6.8 Initial modification for Worked Example 6.3.

	To					
From	**1**	**2**	**3**	**4**	**5**	**6**
1	—	2	1	1	3	2
2	—	—	1	1	1	2
3	—	—	—	2	2	1
4	—	—	—	—	2	3
5	—	—	—	—	—	1
6	—	—	—	—	—	—

	To					
From	**1**	**2**	**3**	**4**	**5**	**6**
1	—	400	180	120	0	40
2	—	—	0	440	80	80
3	—	—	—	0	360	20
4	—	—	—	—	200	60
5	—	—	—	—	—	260
6	—	—	—	—	—	—

Adding the elements in this matrix gives a total cost of 2240. This is an improvement of over 20%, but it does not meet the target of 25%. The highest costs now occur between areas 1 and 2, between areas 2 and 4, and between areas 3 and 5. These should be closer together, and a more radical redesign to the layout may be needed. One option is shown in Figure 6.9 with distance and cost matrices shown below.

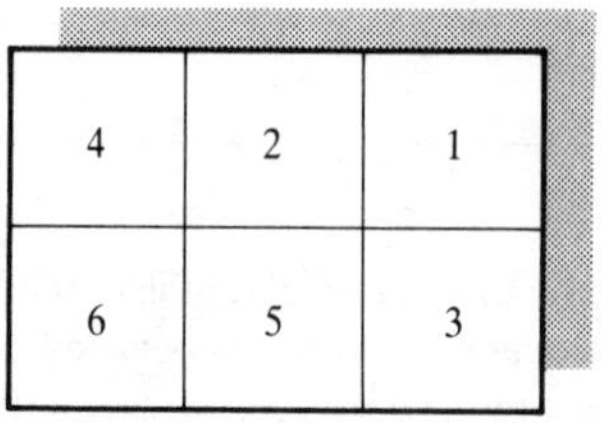

4	2	1
6	5	3

Figure 6.9 Final plan for Worked Example 6.3.

	To					
From	**1**	**2**	**3**	**4**	**5**	**6**
1	—	1	1	2	2	3
2	—	—	2	1	1	2
3	—	—	—	3	1	2
4	—	—	—	—	2	1
5	—	—	—	—	—	1
6	—	—	—	—	—	—

			To			
	1	2	3	4	5	6
1	—	200	180	240	0	60
2	—	—	0	440	80	80
From 3	—	—	—	0	180	40
4	—	—	—	—	200	20
5	—	—	—	—	—	260
6	—	—	—	—	—	—

This has a total cost of 1980, which achieves the desired reduction in movement. The overall search can now be stopped, and other considerations added, such as detailed plans, aesthetic considerations, availability of services, areas that must be in fixed locations (such as loading bays), and so on.

In summary
A more formal process can be used to find good designs for process layouts. This is an improvement procedure which relies on judgement and intuition. This becomes increasingly difficult for larger problems.

6.2.3 Systematic layout planning

The method described above is based on the measurement of work flows between areas. In certain circumstances this may not be possible, when, for example, a layout is to be found for a completely new process. At other times the collection of the data may be particularly onerous, or the patterns of movement may not be the best measure for layout. Whatever the cause, some alternative method must be used.

A commonly used method is called systematic layout planning. This replaces the from—to matrix described above by subjective evaluations of how close areas should be together. Suppose, for example, a large office block has a safety and security group. There may not be many movements between this group and the main reception area, but it may be important for them to be located near by so they can control access to the building whenever necessary. Conversely, a noisy or dangerous piece of machinery should be located as far as possible from quiet office areas. Such subjective evaluations can be formalized into a number of distinct categories. These use letters to signify how important it is that two areas are close together.

> **Importance that two areas be close together**
> - A Absolutely essential
> - E Especially important
> - I Important
> - O Ordinary importance
> - U Unimportant
> - X Undesirable

When judgements are made about closeness, the usual reason for the decision is based on:

(1) sharing the same facilities;

(2) sharing the same staff;

(3) ease of supervision;

(4) ease of communications;

(5) sequence of operations in a process;

(6) customer contact;

(7) safety;

(8) unpleasant conditions;

and so on.

Then we might have a matrix showing the importance that a set of areas are close together, along with the reason, as shown below. This shows that areas B and D must be close together because they share the same facilities, while C and E must not be close together because of unpleasant conditions, and so on.

		Area					
		A	B	C	D	E	...
	A	–	U/–	O/3	O/3	X/8	...
	B	–	–	A/5	E/1	U/–	...
Area	C	–	–	–	U/–	X/8	...
	D	–	–	–	–	I/2	...
	E	–	–	–	–	–	...
	⋮	⋮	⋮	⋮	⋮	⋮	⋮

Designing layouts with this kind of information must inevitably be rather informal. The usual approach is to take connections in the order of importance.

Then all the As and Xs are taken in order with connections made as necessary, then all the Es are taken, then all the Is, and so on. As the connections are less important, they will usually get further apart.

WORKED EXAMPLE 6.4

A new office is about to be opened, with six equally sized areas as shown in Figure 6.10(a). The importance that areas are close together is described by the following matrix.

		Area					
		A	B	C	D	E	F
	A	–	E/2	U/3	U/2	A/1	I/2
	B	–	–	X/8	O/3	U/–	U/–
Area	C	–	–	–	X/8	I/8	U/–
	D	–	–	–	–	O/5	E/2
	E	–	–	–	–	–	E/1
	F	–	–	–	–	–	–

Suggest a layout for the office.

SOLUTION

Starting with the available space shown in Figure 6.10(a) we can put the two X connections (B–C and C–D) as far apart as possible. Then the A connection (A–E) can be added close together. One trial layout for this is shown in Figure 6.10(b).

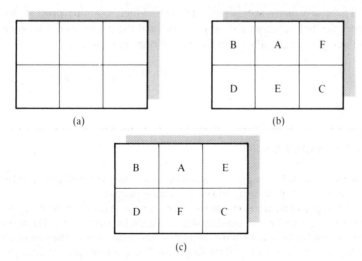

(a)

(b)

(c)

Figure 6.10 Layouts for Worked Example 6.4. (a) Available space.
(b) Trial layout with A and X connections made. (c) Final layout.

When we move on to the E connections (A−B, D−F and E−F), this trial layout only satisfies one of these. An obvious improvement is to exchange E and F, as shown in Figure 6.10(c). This still satisfies the A and X connections, but also satisfies two of the E connections. It also satisfies both of the I connections and one of the O connections. This solution seems satisfactory, but if we were unhappy with it we could continue making adjustments until we found an improvement.

In summary

Sometimes it is not possible to construct a matrix that shows the movements between areas, or else these movements are not important in layout decisions. In these cases systematic layout planning allows subjective views to be used.

6.2.4 Use of computers in designing process layouts

A major failing with the procedure described above is the need to identify improvements to layouts by intuition or common sense. Although this works very well for small problems, it is less reliable for larger problems. Unfortunately, more rigorous approaches use a lot of computation and cannot really be tackled by hand. Typically, they start with a layout, and then make small adjustments to look for improvements. Perhaps two or three areas are moved around at a time until a better result is found. The number of possible adjustments of this kind is large, and the associated calculations are best done on a computer.

There are many specialized packages which examine process layouts. The principles behind these are very simple, and the packages are inexpensive. The following example illustrates the use of one such package.

WORKED EXAMPLE 6.5

A new layout is needed for a process, and a computer program was used to solve this. Data was input, and Figure 6.11 shows the resulting output.

The output summarizes the data starting with the areas of the nine departments (the areas which cannot be used are described as a tenth Department A). The next tables show the current layout and the movements between departments. The cost of moving between departments was set as 1.0 for simplicity. The computer then iteratively checks for improvements to the layout and prints the results when an optimal layout is found.

Figure 6.11

```
                    Input Data -- Performance Criterion

Criterion: Minimize

  Number of departments =  10

  Number of rows in the initial layout =  20

  Number of columns in the initial layout =  25



  Input Data -- Number of Cells in Each Department:

      Department  1 :    27     Not fixed
      Department  2 :    15     Not fixed
      Department  3 :    70     Not fixed
      Department  4 :    42     Not fixed
      Department  5 :    24     Not fixed
      Department  6 :    14     Not fixed
      Department  7 :    48     Not fixed
      Department  8 :    35     Not fixed
      Department  9 :    24     Not fixed
      Department  A :   207     Fixed

      Total            506



  Input Data -- Initial Layout

           1 2 3 4 5 6 7 8 9 0 1 2 3 4 5 6 7 8 9 0 1 2 3 4 5
       1   1 1 1 1 1 1 1 1 1 7 7 7 7 7 7 7 7 7 7 7 7 7 7 7 7
       2   1                 1 7
       3   1 1 1 1 1 1 1 1 1 7 7 7 7 7 7 7 7 7 7 7 7 7 7 7 7
       4   2 2 2 2 2 A A A A A A 8 8 8 8 8 A A A A A A A A
       5   2         2 A           A 8       8 A             A
       6   2 2 2 2 2 A           A 8       8 A             A
       7   3 3 3 3 3 A           A 8       8 A A A A A A A A
       8   3         3 A           A 8       8 9 9 9 9 9 9 9 9
       9   3         3 A A A A A A A 8       8 9             9
      10   3         3 6 6 6 6 6 6 6 8 8 8 8 8 9 9 9 9 9 9 9 9
      11   3         3 6 6 6 6 6 6 6 A A A A A A A A A A A A A
      12   3         3 A 5 5 5 5 5 5 A                       A
      13   3         3 A 5           5 A                     A
      14   3         3 A 5 5 5 5 5 5 A                       A
      15   3         3 4 4 4 4 4 4 4 A                       A
      16   3         3 4           4 A                       A
      17   3         3 4           4 A                       A
      18   3         3 4           4 A                       A
      19   3         3 4           4 A                       A
      20   3 3 3 3 3 4 4 4 4 4 4 4 A A A A A A A A A A A A A
```

```
                Input Data -- Interdepartmental Flows     Page  1

From     To
1        1:     20.00 2:        0 3:        0 4:    35.00 5:    70.00
         6:         0 7:        0 8:    45.00 9:        0 A:        0
2        1:     30.00 2:        0 3:    50.00 4:        0 5:    20.00
         6:         0 7:        0 8:        0 9:    10.00 A:        0
3        1:     10.00 2:    10.00 3:        0 4:        0 5:    35.00
         6:     40.00 7:        0 8:        0 9:    70.00 A:        0
4        1:         0 2:        0 3:        0 4:        0 5:    10.00
         6:     50.00 7:    40.00 8:    80.00 9:        0 A:        0
5        1:     10.00 2:        0 3:    10.00 4:        0 5:        0
         6:         0 7:    25.00 8:    25.00 9:    50.00 A:        0
6        1:     25.00 2:        0 3:    30.00 4:    45.00 5:        0
         6:     25.00 7:    50.00 8:    20.00 9:    15.00 A:        0
7        1:         0 2:        0 3:        0 4:    70.00 5:        0
         6:     60.00 7:        0 8:    80.00 9:        0 A:        0
8        1:         0 2:        0 3:        0 4:        0 5:        0
         6:    120.0 7:        0 8:        0 9:        0 A:        0
9        1:         0 2:    25.00 3:        0 4:    35.00 5:        0
         6:     15.00 7:        0 8:    10.00 9:        0 A:        0
A        1:         0 2:        0 3:        0 4:        0 5:        0
         6:         0 7:        0 8:        0 9:        0 A:        0
```

Continues overleaf

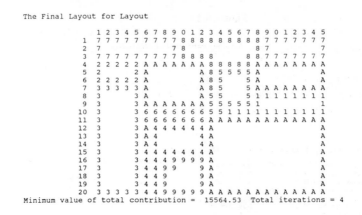

Figure 6.11 Example of computerized layout design.

In summary

Standard programs are readily available for solving the process layout problem. These generally use an iterative procedure for finding the optimal layout.

SELF ASSESSMENT QUESTIONS

6.7 The advantages of product layouts are closely linked to those of intermittent processes like job shops. Is this statement true?

6.8 Good process layouts can often be found by looking at the pattern of movements. Is this statement true?

6.9 What is the main problem with designing process layouts?

6.10 Why might the number of movements between areas not be an appropriate way to judge a layout?

6.11 What do the letters A, E, I O, U and X signify in layout decisions?

6.12 Why are computers used for designing process layouts?

6.3   PRODUCT LAYOUTS

Product layouts cluster together the equipment needed to make a specific product. Then dedicated equipment is laid out so the product can move through it in a steady flow. It may be easiest to picture this as an assembly line. The implication is that product layouts are usually associated with mass production processes. The advantages and disadvantages of product layouts are linked to these processes, and they generally work well with large batches or continuous production of the same product.

Advantages of product layout

(1) A high rate of output can be achieved.

(2) High equipment utilization leads to low unit costs.

(3) Few operators are needed with increased automation.

(4) Materials handling is easy with low stocks of work in progress.

(5) Scheduling facilities is easy.

(6) Control of operations is easy, including supervision, accounting and stock control.

(7) High and consistent quality is obtained.

Disadvantages of product layout

(1) Operations are inflexible, with changes to output rate, product or process being difficult.

(2) Equipment failure and routine maintenance can disrupt the whole process.

(3) Equipment may be specialized and expensive.

(4) Operators find the work dull.

(5) High initial investment.

(6) Cannot deal with variable demand.

6.3.1 Work stations

Product layout is simpler than process layout as it essentially consists of a sequence of equipment through which the product moves. The main problem is to ensure that this movement occurs as smoothly as possible.

Equipment on the line may be divided into a number of distinct work stations. As a product moves down the line a sequence of operations is performed. These operations can be grouped together so that several are done at each work station. Thus, the line consists of discrete work stations, each of which does a number of operations, and products are passed from one work station to the next. The work stations may be separate equipment or people doing specific jobs. A typical product layout is shown in Figure 6.12.

Two key issues in the design of product layouts are the capacity of each station and the rate at which it works. The objective is to have a smooth flow of products down the line, with high utilization of all stations. This means the capacity and speed of working of each station must be about the same. This

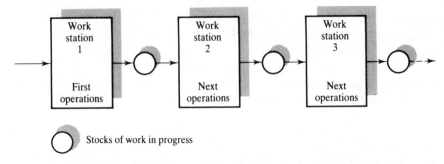

Figure 6.12 Division of a line into discrete work stations.

problem is referred to as line balancing. If a line is unbalanced, some stations will process products quickly and stock of work in progress will build up in front of the next station which is working more slowly. This in turn leads to bottlenecks which cause delays and low utilization of facilities further down the line.

Consider a simple line that has two operations, the first taking one minute and the second three minutes. With the simple layout shown in Figure 6.13(a) the maximum throughput of the line is one unit every three minutes, determined by the second operation. Unfortunately, this leaves the first operation with a utilization of only 33% and the line is unbalanced. An obvious solution is to put three sets of equipment for the second operation in parallel.

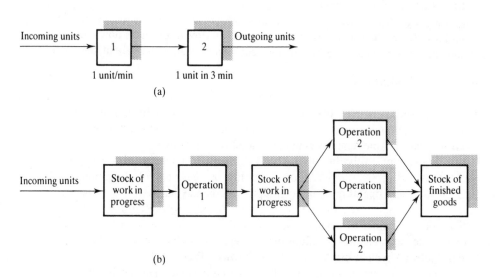

Figure 6.13 Layouts for simple illustration of line balancing.
(a) Layout producing one unit every three minutes. (b) Layout of a perfectly balanced line producing one unit every minute.

This would triple production and achieve full utilization. The line is then perfectly balanced. The aim of line balancing is to achieve the highest possible utilization of all parts of the line.

The maximum output of a line is determined by the station that has lowest output. If this maximum is below forecast demand, additional facilities must be used. Conversely, if the maximum is above forecast demand the equipment is being under-utilized and some savings might be made.

To some extent the flow along the line is buffered by putting stocks of work in progress between each station. This has the advantage of uncoupling adjacent work stations, so that if one breaks down for a short time the other can continue working normally. There are, however, disadvantages of such work in progress, not least of which are the cost of holding stocks and the need to have sufficient storage space near the line. It is preferable to have low stocks of work in progress and a balanced line.

Two basic pieces of information are needed to tackle problems of line balancing:

- times for each operation on the line;
- precedence relationships between operations.

The time taken to complete each operation can be found by observation. The precedence relationship is best described using a precedence diagram of the type described in Chapter 5.

In summary
Product layouts can be visualized as assembly lines, with a sequence of work stations. The main problem is to ensure a smooth flow of products down this line and this is achieved by ensuring that each work station has about the same throughput.

SELF ASSESSMENT QUESTIONS

6.13 Product layouts are generally more capital intensive than process layouts, but give lower unit costs. Is this statement true?

6.14 What is the purpose of stocks of work in progress between work stations?

6.15 What determines the maximum output of a product layout?

6.3.2 Line balancing

In a product layout each operation must be done in a specified sequence, which can be represented on a precedence diagram. Each operation in the process is likely to take a different time, and yet a smooth flow of products down the line is needed, with all equipment used as fully as possible. This smooth flow is achieved by line balancing.

Lines consist of a series of work stations, so the basis of line balancing is to assign operations to each work station so that the line is balanced. The procedure for this is in three parts.

(1) Find the cycle time, which is the maximum time a station can work on each unit. This is calculated by dividing the planned output by the time available. If, for example, planned production is 60 units an hour, then each operation in the line can last at most one minute. If the operations at any work station take longer than this a bottleneck is created and the planned output cannot be achieved.

(2) Calculate the theoretical minimum number of work stations needed for the entire process. This is found by dividing the total time needed for all operations on a unit by the cycle time. If, for example, it takes a total of five minutes to make a product and the cycle time is one minute, the minimum number of work stations along the line is five. In practice, this can almost never be achieved because of fractional values, the unevenness of work times and the constraints of activity precedence.

(3) Do the actual line balancing and allocation of operations to each work station. The total time taken for operations in each work station should be as close as possible to the cycle time. An algorithm for this is described below.

The procedure for the third step, actually balancing the line, is best done using the precedence diagram. The steps are then as follows.

(1) Draw a precedence diagram for the process.

(2) Assign the first operation to the first work station.

(3) Starting with the earliest operations (normally at the left-hand side of the diagram):
    (a) ignore all operations that have already been assigned to work stations;
    (b) ignore all operations whose predecessors have not yet been finished;
    (c) ignore all operations for which there is not enough time left on the current work station.

(4) We now have a set of operations which could be added to the current work station. Use some criterion to rank these for addition to the work station. A common criterion is to select the longest operations first.

(5) Add operations in this order to the work station until:
    (a) there are no more operations in the list identified in step 4. If

there are still operations which have not been allocated go back
to step 3; or

(b)   no more jobs in the list identified in step 4 can be added to the
work station without exceeding the cycle time. If there are any
operations remaining, set up another work station and go back to
step 3; or

(c)   all operations have been allocated, in which case the initial
design has been completed. Go to step 6.

(6)   Calculate the utilization of each work station and make small
adjustments to improve the final balanced assembly line.

WORKED EXAMPLE 6.6

If each operation described in Figure 6.14 takes four minutes, design a line that will
process six units an hour.

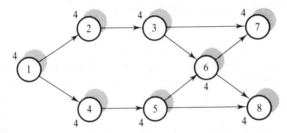

Figure 6.14   Precedence diagram for Worked Example 6.6.

SOLUTION

(1)   The cycle time is found by dividing the time available (say one hour) by the
planned output (six units). Thus, cycle time = 10 minutes.

(2)   Calculate a theoretical minimum number of work stations. The process
consists of eight operations taking four minutes each, so the total time
required for each unit is 32 minutes. The theoretical minimum number of
work stations is this total time divided by the cycle time = 32/10 = 3.2. We
know from this that we will actually need at least four work stations.

(3)   The balancing is done by assigning operations to work stations using the
algorithm described above.

● Step 1 draws the precedence diagram, which is given in Figure 6.14.

● Step 2 assigns operation 1 to work station 1.

● Step 3 finds the set of operations which can be added to work station 1: these
are operations 2 and 4.

● Step 4 ranks these in order. Here there is little to choose, so we will
arbitrarily choose a ranking of 2 then 4.

- Step 5 goes down the ranking and adds operations until the cycle time is reached. This happens when operation 2 has been added. There are still unallocated processes, so an additional work station is needed, and the procedure returns to step 3.

- Step 3 identifies the operations which can be added to work station 2 as 3 and 4.

- Step 4 ranks these, arbitrarily, in the order 3 then 4.

- Step 5 adds both of these to work station 2, then returns to step 3.

- Step 3 identifies the activities which can be added to work station 2 as 5 and 6.

- Step 4 ranks these, arbitrarily, in the order 3 then 4.

- Step 5 adds both of these to work station 2, then returns to step 3. without exceeding the cycle time. Work station 3 is set up and the procedure returns to step 3.

This continues until all operations have been assigned to work stations (see Figure 6.15), when the results in Table 6.2 are given.

Table 6.2

Work station	Operations	Time used	Spare time	Utilization
1	1,2	8	2	80%
2	3,4	8	2	80%
3	5,6	8	2	80%
4	7,8	8	2	80%

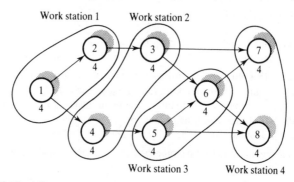

Figure 6.15 Allocation of operations to work stations in Worked Example 6.6.

There are several alternative solutions to this example, each of which is equally attractive. The average utilization can also be found by dividing the theoretical minimum number of work stations (3.2) by the actual number (4).

WORKED EXAMPLE 6.7

The operations in a product layout are shown in Table 6.3.

Table 6.3

Operation	Time (minutes)	Operation must follow
A	5	—
B	10	A
C	4	B
D	6	B
E	4	C,D
F	2	E
G	4	F
H	5	G
I	3	H
J	2	G
K	5	J
L	8	G
M	4	L
N	2	I,K,M
O	6	N
P	1	O
Q	5	P

The line works an eight hour day during which target output is 48 units. Design a balanced layout for the process.

SOLUTION

Start by calculating the cycle time:

$$\text{Cycle time} = \frac{\text{time available}}{\text{number of units to be made}}$$

$$= 480/48$$
$$= 10 \text{ minutes}$$

If a work station spends more than 10 minutes on a unit the output is reduced and the target of 48 units a day cannot be reached.

The theoretical minimum number of work stations is found by dividing the total time to make one unit of the product by the cycle time. The time to complete all operations on a unit is 76 minutes, so:

$$\text{Theoretical minimum} = \frac{\text{total time for a unit}}{\text{cycle time}}$$
$$= 76/10$$
$$= 7.6$$

This theoretical minimum number of work stations is the ideal, where each station is fully occupied all the time and work flows perfectly smoothly through the line. In practice it tells us we need at least eight work stations.

Now the heuristic for assigning operations to work stations can be used. This starts by assigning operation A to work station 1. The only activity which is not eliminated by step 3 is B. This cannot, however, be added to work station 1, as it gives a time greater than the cycle time.

The procedure then returns to step 3 and starts work station 2 with operation B. Step 3 then produces a ranked list of C and D, but neither of these can be added to work station 2 as they give times greater than the cycle time.

Step 3 allocates operation C to work station 3.

This procedure is continued to give the results in Table 6.4 (see also Figure 6.16).

Table 6.4

Work station	Activities	Used time	Spare time
1	A	5	5
2	B	10	—
3	C,D	10	—
4	E,F,G	10	—
5	L,J	10	—
6	H,K	10	—
7	M,I,N	9	1
8	O,P	7	3
9	Q	5	5

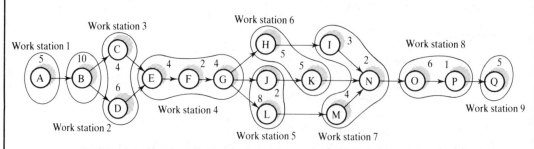

Figure 6.16 Precedence diagram and work stations for Worked Example 6.7.

This configuration has an overall efficiency given by:

$$\text{Efficiency} = \frac{\text{time used in a day}}{\text{number of stations} * \text{time on each}}$$

$$= 76 * 48/9 * 480$$

$$= 84.4\%$$

The heuristic approach described gives good layouts but a number of modifications might improve the results. One of these looks at the ranking used for selecting the next operation to be added to a work station (step 4). A useful criterion for making this ranking is longest activity first. There are several other possible rankings, such as:

- rank operations in order of number of directly following activities;
- rank operations in order of the total processing time of following operations.

A number of improving procedures have also been developed which take the initial solution and systematically exchange operations to find improvements. These are best done with computers.

In summary

The aim of line balancing is to ensure a smooth flow of products through the layout, with all resources used as fully as possible. A simple algorithm can be used to design balanced layouts.

SELF ASSESSMENT QUESTIONS

6.16 What is the aim of line balancing?

6.17 What is a perfectly balanced line, and is this often achieved?

6.18 What is the cycle time and why is it important?

6.19 Does the algorithm described for line balancing always give an optimal answer?

6.4 HYBRID LAYOUTS

Many facilities do not use either a total process layout or a total product one. They use a combination of layouts where some parts are process oriented and other parts are product oriented. This arrangement is called a hybrid layout. Suppose a product is assembled from two types of component, one of which is made in a job shop, and the other is made on a production line. The overall layout would then be a hybrid.

One common hybrid arrangement is a work cell. This is an arrangement with a dominant process layout, but with some operations set aside in a product layout. This layout is perhaps most easily visualized in terms of a manufacturer with most machines laid out in a process layout, but with a certain sequence of operations repeated so frequently that a special area (or work cell) is set aside to

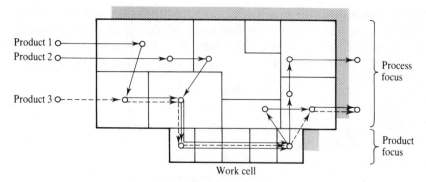

Figure 6.17 Work cell.

deal with these on an assembly line. These cells can be viewed as islands of product layout in a sea of process layout, as shown in Figure 6.17.

The overall purpose of work cells is to obtain the high utilizations and other benefits of product layouts in a process environment. This type of layout has become more popular with the growth of group technology and flexible manufacturing. Group technology combines families of products which have some common characteristics so they can be processed in larger batches. If these batches get big enough it would be useful to do the common operations using a product layout, even though most other operations use a process layout.

We can mention several examples of work cells.

- A job shop which gets an order to make a large number of a particular product. It might then maintain its overall process focus but would set aside a separate work cell as an assembly line to meet the order.

- An airport passenger terminal has a process focus (with ticket purchase area, check-in area, cafeteria, duty free shops, etc.) but there are some product layouts (such as customs clearance).

- A fast-food restaurant has areas of the kitchen set aside for different purposes, but a line which prepares all hamburgers.

- A hospital has wards set aside for different types of illness, but the patient admissions area has a product focus.

Some people suggest that there is an important difference between the first of these examples and the others. The arrangement in the job shop is essentially temporary to meet a specific order, while the others are all designed as permanent arrangements. If this distinction is important, we might use the term 'work cell' to describe a temporary arrangement and 'focused work centre' to describe a permanent arrangement. Then work cells are flexible arrangements which can easily be changed, while focused work centres are more capital intensive and need more dedicated resources. A knitwear manufacturer, for example, might use a process layout. If a long-term contract is obtained to supply one type of garment to a supermarket chain the company may move some machines to a separate area specifically to make this garment on an assembly line. If this arrangement is permanent it would be a focused work centre. Obviously the borderline between work cells and focused work centres is unclear and the distinction is largely artificial.

The idea of a focused work centre can be extended to focused factories. With these, the focused work centre is now moved to another building. Thus a focused factory will use a product layout to make a component or product for use in another facility. A factory which uses an assembly line to make windscreen wiper motors for cars would be an example of a focused factory.

In summary

Hybrid layouts have some operations with a product layout and others with a process layout. Work cells are common examples of this arrangement, where a predominantly process layout has some areas with product layouts. Focused work centres and focused factories extend this idea.

SELF ASSESSMENT QUESTIONS

6.20 What are hybrid layouts?

6.21 What is a work cell and why are they used?

6.22 What is the difference between a work cell, a focused work centre and a focused factory?

6.5   FIXED-POSITION AND SPECIALIZED LAYOUTS

The layouts described above cover many circumstances, but there are a number of other layouts which have different characteristics. Some of these are designed for specialized applications, where 'specialized' means they are for a specific purpose and does not mean they are rare or difficult to find. There is, in fact, an almost limitless variety of specialized layouts. We will illustrate these by four common ones for fixed layouts, warehouses, offices and retail shops.

6.5.1 Fixed-position layouts

We have already mentioned fixed-position layouts, where the product stays still and operations are all done on the same site. This typically occurs when a product is too large or heavy to move around, and standard illustrations of this are shipbuilding, airplane manufacture and construction sites. The approach is also useful when special environments (such as dust-free rooms) are needed.

Such layouts have many disadvantages and they are usually only adopted because moving the product would be either impossible or very difficult. Among the disadvantages are:

- all materials and components must be moved to the site;
- all people involved with operations must be moved to the site;
- there may be limited space at the site;
- a reliable schedule of operations must be maintained;
- disruptions to this schedule might cause delays in completion;
- the intensity of work varies;
- external factors (such as weather conditions) may affect operations; and so on.

One way to partially avoid these disadvantages is to do as much of the work as possible off-site. A road bridge, for example, must be completed on-site, but many of the parts can be pre-cast or assembled off-site and moved for erection.

In summary

Fixed layouts keep the product in the same location and all operations are done on this site. There are several drawbacks with this arrangement, and it should only be used if there is no alternative.

6.5.2 Warehouses

The purpose of a warehouse is to store goods at some point on their journey between suppliers and customers. The essential elements in a warehouse are:

- an arrival bay, where goods coming from suppliers are delivered and checked;
- a storage area, where the goods are kept as stock;
- a departure bay, where customers' orders are assembled and sent out;
- a materials handling system, for moving goods around as necessary;
- an information system, which records the location of all goods, arrivals from suppliers, departures to customers, and all other relevant information.

The object of layout design in warehouses is to minimize the total cost of unit throughput (see Figure 6.18 for a typical layout). Many of the costs are fixed or determined by management policy (Chapter 11, for example, gives a discussion of stock holding policy). The main variable cost which is controlled

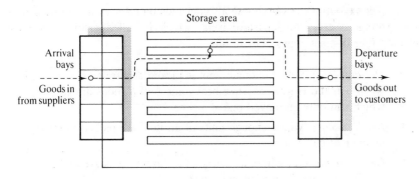

Storage area

Arrival bays

Departure bays

Goods in from suppliers

Goods out to customers

Figure 6.18 Layout of a typical warehouse.

by layout arises from the time spent locating items and either adding them to stock or removing them. Constraints on the layout come from available space, materials handling equipment, total investment in stock, and so on.

The layout will depend to a large extent on the goods being stored and the handling equipment used. If the goods are small and light (such as boxes of pills) materials handling can be done by hand and the warehouse should be made small enough to walk round, with goods stored in easy reach. If the goods stored are large and heavy (such as engines) materials handling will use fork lift trucks and the warehouse should be big enough for these to manoeuvre. These illustrate two approaches to warehousing, which are manual and mechanized. The third level of technology is automated, where materials handling equipment does not need human control. The level of technology used gives warehouses with different characteristics.

(1) *Manual*. Warehouses must store light items which are easy to lift. Storage is in shelves which are close together, but can be no higher than 2 metres. The warehouse must be heated, lit and allow people to work comfortably.

(2) *Mechanized*. Examples are fork lift trucks, conveyors and tow lines. Some equipment needs wide aisles in which to manoeuvre, but goods can be stored higher (perhaps up to 12 metres with a fork lift truck and higher with conveyors). Fork lift trucks have high costs and are best suited to short journeys around loading and unloading bays. Conveyor systems are cheaper for small items and need less space.

(3) *Automated*. These use guided vehicles, robots and automated addition and withdrawal from storage areas. These systems use narrow aisles and can be very high, allowing computer-controlled cranes to reach all items very quickly. As people do not work in the storage areas, money can be saved on heating and lighting.

The layout of the warehouse also depends on the way goods are moved from storage shelves to departure bays (which is called picking). We can mention four distinct approaches to this:

- *Out-and-back*, where a single item is picked at a time. This is used when demand is low, or when heavy and bulky goods are stored which can only be moved one at a time.
- *Batch picking*, where enough units of an item are picked to satisfy a number of customers.
- *Customer picking*, where a variety of different items are picked to satisfy an order from a given customer.
- *Zone picking*, where a picker stays in one area and items are loaded as required on to passing conveyors.

We have only mentioned a few of the factors in warehouse layout, and must appreciate that there are many other considerations. There is an almost limitless range of possible warehouse designs, each of which is best suited to particular types of product.

WORKED EXAMPLE 6.8

A store has a rack with nine colours of paint in litre cans. At one end of the rack is an issue area where the storekeeper works. Weekly demand for the paint is as follows.

Colour	Red	Blue	White	Black	Brown	Green	Yellow	Grey	Pink
Gallons	100	140	860	640	320	120	240	40	60

If all paint is stored in identical sized bins, what would be a reasonable layout for the rack? What would be a reasonable layout if the size of bins varies with the weekly demand?

SOLUTION

An objective here would be to minimize the distance walked by the storekeeper, assuming that each can of paint needs a separate journey. The paint should be laid out so that colours with highest demand are nearest the issue area. The layout then has paint in order white, black, brown, yellow, blue, green, red, pink and grey (see Figure 6.19(a)). If each bin is one unit wide, this has a total travel distance for the storekeeper of:

$$2 * (1 * 860 + 2 * 640 + 3 * 320 + 4 * 240 + 5 * 140 + 6 * 120 + 7 * 100$$
$$+ 8 * 60 + 9 * 40)$$
$$= 2 * 7020$$
$$= 14,040$$

with the factor of two allowing for return journeys.

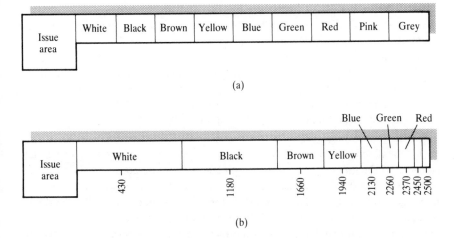

(a)

(b)

Figure 6.19 Layouts for Worked Example 6.8. (a) Initial layout for identically sized bins. (b) Layout with different sized bins.

If the size of the bin is proportional to the weekly demand for paint, and paint is taken from the middle of the bins, it does not matter in which order the paint is put in the rack.

Keeping the same order of paint, and using a unit of distance of 'one litre of storage space' the middle of the white bin is 860/2 = 430 units, the middle of the black bin is 860 + 640/2 = 1180 units, the middle of the brown bin is 860 + 640 + 320/2 = 1660 units, and so on (see Figure 6.19(b)). The total distance travelled is 2 * (860 * 430 + 640 * 1180 + 320 * 1660 . . .) = 6,350,400. Even if the paint were stored in exactly the reverse order the cost would still be the same.

In summary

Warehouses store goods at some point on their journey between suppliers and customers. There is an almost endless variety of warehouse designs, each of which is suited to particular products and materials handling equipment. Some guidelines can be given for good layout.

6.5.3 Offices

Unlike factories and warehouses, which are concerned with the movement of physical goods, offices are concerned with the movement of information. This can be done:

- face to face
- in meetings or groups
- by telephone, intercom or simultaneous computer link
- on paper
- by electronic mail or delayed computer link.

If all communications were indirect (using telephones or some other equipment) the amount of movement in offices could be considerably reduced. In practice, most efficient communications are done face to face, and this requires more planning. Those areas with most personal contacts should clearly be placed near to each other, while those with less personal contact can be separated, even if they have a lot of indirect contact. This is, however, only the beginning of office design.

Despite available technology, most offices rely on substantial numbers of office workers, and so the offices have to have conditions in which the workers are comfortable, and can work efficiently. Some of this work is best done in private offices, while other jobs are best done in open areas. Discussing private financial arrangements with a customer, for example, is best done in a private office, but processing high volumes of routine paperwork is best done in open areas. Alternative layouts for offices can be described as:

- desks arranged in rows in an open area;
- desks arranged less formally in open areas, with filing cabinets, plants and book cases separating areas;
- desks in open areas separated by movable partitions which are typically about 2 metres high;
- areas divided into separate offices by semi-permanent floor to ceiling partitions;
- permanent separate offices.

The choice of which is best depends on the type of work being done and how much this varies.

There are a number of other factors which should be taken into account with office design. These include:

- the amount of face-to-face contact needed will determine the total movements;
- employees within groups usually have a lot of face-to-face contact;
- the type of work determines the best type of office, ranging from formal open plans to separate offices;

- individual offices usually have different facilities, size and location depending on the job and status of the occupant;
- areas to be visited by customers often have different requirements to those kept for work;
- some special facilities may be needed, such as conference or committee rooms, lecture theatres and board rooms;
- there must be specific areas for lounges and rest rooms, cloak rooms, storage areas, cleaning equipment, and so on;
- aisles should allow all areas to be reached quickly, but without too much traffic past people's work places;
- shared facilities, such as photocopiers, files and coffee machines, should be convenient for everyone.

In summary

Offices are concerned with the movement of information. Although this may contain some automation, it relies largely on office staff. The layout should allow these people to work comfortably and efficiently.

6.5.4 Retail shops

The layout of retail shops is related to that of warehouses. They both have goods brought in which are stored and then taken out to satisfy customer demand. There is, however, a fundamental difference. A good warehouse design minimizes the total distance travelled to collect goods, so those with highest demands are kept near the issue area. A supermarket realizes that the longer customers are in the shop the more they will buy. Then a good layout maximizes the purchases by dispersing high demand items of basic food, like bread and milk, around the shop and forcing customers to pass lots of other goods before finding them all.

Several guidelines have been suggested for shop layouts, including:

- Disperse basic goods around the shop, preferably around the outside aisles.
- Do not have crossover aisles as customers should be encouraged to walk the full length of each aisle.
- Use the first and last aisles for high-impulse items which have high profit margins.
- Set the image for the store near the door: if customers see a lot of special sales here they will assume all prices are low.
- Put magazines and chocolates near the checkouts.

- The ends of aisles have high visibility and should be used, perhaps for special promotions.
- Put goods which are attractive to children within their reach.
- Circulate customers clockwise.

And so on.

In summary

Retail shops have similarities with warehouses, but their layout has entirely different objectives.

SELF ASSESSMENT QUESTIONS

6.23 Fixed layouts keep all equipment in fixed locations and move products through these in a specified sequence. Is this statement true?

6.24 What are the disadvantages of fixed layouts?

6.25 What determines the appropriate level of automation in a warehouse?

6.26 Even automated and paperless offices will need staff to work there. Is this true?

6.27 Is it true that offices which customers are likely to visit should be more luxurious than others?

6.28 The layout of supermarkets should allow customers to collect their goods as conveniently as possible. Is this statement true?

SUMMARY OF CHAPTER

Layout is concerned with the way the facilities of a process are physically arranged. The objective of layout design is to optimize some measure (perhaps maximizing throughput) subject to the constraints placed on the process. These constraints may come from a number of sources. A good layout will ensure that an operation is efficient and runs smoothly, while a poor layout will reduce efficiency, effective capacity and utilization.

Layout strategies were classified according to process, product, hybrid, fixed and specialized. Each of these has different characteristics and is best suited to different circumstances.

Process layouts group together similar types of facilities. This is typical of the layout in a job shop, and many of the characteristics of process layouts come from this link. The main problem with designing process layouts is to minimize the amount of movement between areas. For simple problems this can be done by observing the pattern of movement. For larger problems a more formal procedure was described. This can rely on intuition to suggest ways of improving layouts, or more rigorous procedures which involve a lot of computation. The implication is that computers are used for larger problems.

Product layouts group together the facilities needed to make a product. They are characterized by assembly or production lines and many of their characteristics come from this link. The main problem with product layouts is to ensure a smooth flow of goods down the line. This requires all work stations on the line to have about the same throughput, and an algorithm was described for achieving this. Precedence diagrams are useful for this algorithm.

Hybrid layouts were described, emphasizing work cells. The chapter finished by describing some specialized layouts such as fixed layout, warehouses, offices and retail shops.

PROBLEMS

6.1   A process layout has five identically sized areas in a line. Observed movements between these areas during a typical period are as follows.

	A	B	C	D	E
A	—	17	12	42	2
B	12	0	1	22	6
C	0	22	0	17	7
D	47	11	3	0	12
E	53	5	6	25	0

What is the best layout for these areas?

6.2   One floor of a building has six office areas, which are all the same size. The current layout is shown in Figure 6.20, but this seems to have a lot of unnecessary movement between areas.

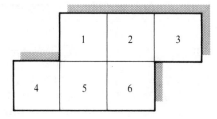

Figure 6.20 Layout for Problem 6.2.

During a random period, records were kept of the number of movements between areas as shown in the following table. How might the layout of areas be improved?

	1	2	3	4	5	6
1	—	—	100	—	35	—
2	120	—	10	20	15	10
3	—	15	—	80	—	75
4	—	55	—	—	75	—
5	—	10	—	125	—	—
6	80	20	—	—	—	—

6.3 Some equipment uses a product layout. The process for making a product consists of a sequence of 15 operations with the following times.

Operation	1	2	3	4	5	6	7	8	9	10	11	12	13	14	15
Time (minutes)	2	6	8	4	10	2	1	15	11	8	2	4	10	7	5

Find the best allocation of operations to work stations for different levels of production.

6.4 An assembly line has seven activities:

Activity	Description
A	Clean bottle
B	Inspect bottle
C	Fill bottle with liquid
D	Put top on filled bottle
E	Put label on bottle
F	Put bottles into boxes
G	Seal boxes and move

The times for each step have been found from observation and the precedence relationships are:

Activity	Time (seconds)	Activity must follow
A	20	—
B	5	A
C	20	B
D	5	C
E	5	B
F	10	D,E
G	5	F

The forecast demand for bottles is 120 an hour. Calculate the cycle time and minimum number of work stations needed. Balance the line by assigning operations to work stations.

6.5 Confirm the results for Worked Example 6.8, that if the storage length of a rack is proportional to demand, and goods are removed from the centre of the area, the order in which goods are arranged does not matter.

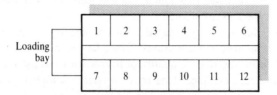

Figure 6.21 Layout for Problems 6.6 and 6.7.

6.6 A warehouse has a single aisle with 12 bins as shown in Figure 6.21. It stores six products with the following characteristics. Design a good layout for the warehouse.

Product	Withdrawals	Bins needed
1	150	1
2	700	3
3	50	1
4	900	3
5	450	2
6	300	2

6.7 If the design in Problem 6.6 referred to a supermarket, how would the design differ?

CASE STUDY – THE JULIAN WILSON ART STUDIO

Julian Wilson left university with a degree in Fine Art. He worked for an international bank for five years, but was often frustrated by his lack of commercial knowledge. With the bank's help, Julian joined an MBA course, feeling that this qualification would help his future career.

For many years Julian had spent a lot of time developing his hobby, which was landscape painting. While he was doing his MBA two of his pictures were selected for exhibition in the prestigious Markum-Lebeau Gallery in Bond Street. This success, together with a growing dissatisfaction with the MBA course, made Julian reconsider his future in banking. By the time he finished the MBA, he had decided to try and make his living as a professional artist.

Julian joined a group of other artists who rented an attic studio in Chelsea. He worked diligently for two years, but found it difficult to make a reasonable living. His paintings were quite well received but his income was only just enough to live on. He knew that if he continued working his reputation would eventually grow, but in the meantime he needed some means of increasing his income. He could have returned to banking, but was reluctant to do this as he was enjoying his new career as an artist.

Julian reasoned that he might increase his income by increasing his production and simply painting more pictures. This, however, was not really feasible. If he painted faster, he felt the quality of his pictures and therefore the price he could charge would decline. If he tried to charge a higher price, he knew that fewer people would be interested in buying and his income would actually decline. He considered a number of schemes such as renting works to businesses in the area, or asking companies to sponsor him as part of their support for the arts. These schemes had some success, and they also showed that the art market was rather more flexible than Julian originally thought.

His next move was to talk with the artists sharing his studio. At the time there were 12 people, who worked independently and shared the costs of rent, rates, heating, lighting, power, and so on. All 12 were in a similar situation, making enough to survive, but not enough to afford anything more than a basic standard of living. Julian himself was 30 years old and his prospects were worse than they had been nine years before when he joined the bank.

Julian's MBA training made him realize that the process they were using for their paintings was inherently inefficient. The idea that artists are independent people creating individual works of art is valid, but their productivity is low. Julian suggested that instead of working separately they should combine their efforts and increase their combined productivity. The way he proposed to do this was to paint communal pictures so that each artist painted a different part of each picture.

Market research among potential buyers and art dealers showed that landscapes were the most popular type of picture. Julian suggested that the production of a standard picture of this type has six elements:

(1) preparation of the canvas;
(2) painting the sky and cloud formations;
(3) painting the background mountains;
(4) painting the river and the foreground;
(5) painting the trees in the middle distance;
(6) varnishing, framing and finishing.

Each individual artist had strengths and weaknesses, so they could paint some things quickly, but were slow at painting other things. By specializing, one artist could concentrate on the mountains and would be able to paint these very quickly; another would specialize on the trees, and so on. By this method the time needed to paint a picture could be reduced by a factor of at least 10. The resulting pictures were less expensive and could be sold to a wide range of customers.

Needless to say, most of the other artists did not like this idea, but several (who were selling fewer paintings than the others) greeted it with some enthusiasm. If they could earn some money in the short term, they could return to their own work later on. The artists effectively split into two, with seven leaving the studio and five agreeing to try Julian's plan for a trial period. Julian had to work out details of the organization, and an early decision was how to lay out the studio. His first thought was to put the paintings on easels around the workshop, with artists moving in turn to add their part. Then one person would paint the sky on one picture, move on to another picture and paint the sky on that, and so on. This arrangement worked fairly well for the person doing the sky, but others began to complain, particularly the person who was doing the framing and had to carry around a variety of tools and materials.

After a month, Julian realized that if it was difficult taking the materials to the paintings, the paintings ought to move to the materials. He then devised a scheme where the artists stayed more or less in their own areas and the paintings were carried from one area to another as necessary. The studio was divided into separate areas, each of which was about 6 metres square (see Figure 6.22). Artists were assigned to an area and allocated a subject to paint. Near the door were the preparers, beyond them were the sky painters, beyond them were the mountain painters, and so on. Several students and craftsmen were recruited to replace the artists who had left, and the total number of people working in the studio rose to 18.

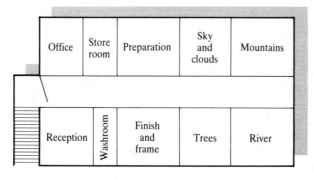

Figure 6.22 Layout of studio.

This scheme was tried for six months with remarkable success. There was a ready market for the cheaper paintings, as each was still considered a signed 'work of art' (the artists used fictitious names for the signatures). The output from the studio rose from 12 a month at an average price of £1500 to 150 a month at an average price of £250. The original artists and new craftsmen were now relatively well off, and they voted to continue the new arrangements.

There were still some operational problems with the studio, as there seemed a lot of movement. People were picking up paintings and carrying them relatively long distances. There were accidents and occasionally people would bump into paintings or spill things so that a half-finished painting would be spoiled. There were complaints that some areas had too little space, some were nearer the coffee in the reception area, some used the washroom too much, and so on. One side of the studio looked out over the river and those who didn't have this view used to complain that they were getting unfairly treated.

Julian decided that they would need yet another reorganization. He could simply reorganize the studio along current lines. He collected some information to help with this, including estimated areas needed for each operation, and typical movements between areas.

		1	2	3	4	5	6	7	8	9	Area
(1)	Preparation	–	45	50	10	4	2	90	5	100	500
(2)	Sky		–	50	40	10	8	80	4	80	300
(3)	Mountains			–	60	30	20	95	3	120	400
(4)	River				–	70	25	45	2	100	400
(5)	Trees					–	80	60	4	120	500
(6)	Finish						–	80	5	115	500
(7)	Reception/store							–	20	20	300
(8)	Office								–	10	200
(9)	Washroom										100

Julian also thought about doing something a little more radical. He thought about installing a production line. This was not as dramatic as it sounds, as such a line would consist of easels with wheels and tracks in the floor to guide them. The easels could then be passed easily from one person on to the next person. Virtually all the movement of people around the studio would be eliminated, with paintings automatically moved between operations.

Julian knew that this step would be unpopular with some of the artists and craftsmen, but as this new process would need fewer people, it would be useful if some left voluntarily. An aim of this system would be to double production, but this raised the question of whether such sales could be maintained, even if the average price was reduced to £150. In addition, any potential bottleneck, caused by different operation times, would have to be removed. Some relevant information for this was estimated as follows.

	Time (minutes) per picture
Preparation	10
Sky	15
Mountains	35
River	30
Trees	40
Finish	10

Having made considerable progress in the past few months, Julian was not sure of what to do now.

Suggested questions

- What were the advantages of moving away from the original scheme with separate artists?
- What were the defects with the fixed-location layout?
- What were the benefits of having separate areas for different operations?
- How might this layout be improved by making relatively minor changes?
- What are the advantages of moving to an assembly line?
- What were the main difficulties Julian had to overcome with each stage of his changes?
- What should Julian do now?

SOLUTIONS TO SELF ASSESSMENT QUESTIONS

6.1 Layout is the physical arrangement of facilities in a process. A well laid out process will be efficient and work smoothly; a badly laid out process will reduce efficiency, effective capacity and utilization.

6.2 To maximize some measure of process performance (perhaps maximizing throughput) subject to the constraints imposed.

6.3 There are many of these, including those imposed by the product design, capacity, process used, materials handling, building, capital available, safety, and so on.

6.4 A useful classification has process, product, hybrid, fixed and specialized.

6.5 The most likely are: **(a)** product **(b)** specialized (maybe process) **(c)** fixed **(d)** product **(e)** process **(f)** hybrid (using some mass-produced parts and some special ones).

6.6 **(a)** Either fixed or process **(b)** process **(c)** product.

6.7 No. It would be true of process layouts.

6.8 Yes.

6.9 The need to recognize intuitively how improvements can be made, or the practicality of using more rigorous methods.

6.10 Because such measures may not be available (particularly for new layouts), the data may be too difficult to collect, or other factors are considered more important.

6.11 They describe the importance that two areas are close together as absolutely essential, especially important, important, ordinarily important, unimportant and undesirable.

6.12 Because the usual procedures for finding improvements to layouts need a lot of computing.

6.13 Yes.

6.14 To separate consecutive work stations so that a short disruption to one does not interfere with the other.

6.15 The smallest output of any work station along the line.

6.16 To ensure a smooth flow of products through the layout, with all resources used as fully as possible.

6.17 A line where all work stations are working to full capacity (so that utilization is 100%). This is very difficult to achieve, because of different operation times, interactions, discrete units, precedence requirements, and so on.

6.18 The maximum amount of time a work station can work on a unit of product. If more than this time is used there will be a bottleneck and the line will not be able to meet its output target.

6.19 No. It is an heuristic approach which gives a good, but not optimal solution.

6.20 A layout which is neither totally process nor product.

6.21 An arrangement with a dominant process layout, but some operations are taken aside in a product layout. They are used to obtain the high utilizations and other advantages of product processes in a process environment.

6.22 Formally, a work cell is a temporary arrangement; a focused work centre is permanent and uses more resources; a focused factory is an entire, separate facility working as an extended focused work centre.

6.23 No. The product is kept in a fixed location, not the equipment.

6.24 All materials, components and people must be moved to the site, there may be limited space, scheduling is difficult, the intensity of work varies, external factors (such as weather conditions) affect operations, and so on.

6.25 The type of goods being stored, demand, capital available, operating costs, space available, and so on.

6.26 Yes − probably. Many transactions are best done face to face, so it seems probable that offices will still need to be staffed.

6.27 No. This often happens, but there is little rationale for treating staff who work in an area all day worse than customers who are only there for a short spell.

6.28 No. Supermarkets can make more profit by keeping customers in the shop as long as possible.

REFERENCES FOR FURTHER READING

Apple J.M. (1977). *Plant Layout and Materials Handling* 3rd edn. New York: Roland Press

Bowersox D.J., Closs D.J. and Helferich O.K. (1986). *Logistical Management* 3rd edn. New York: Macmillan

Francis R.L. and White J.A. (1974). *Facility Layout and Location* Englewood Cliffs: Prentice-Hall

Johnson J.C. and Wood D.F. (1990). *Contemporary Logistics* 4th edn. New York: Macmillan

Mecklenburg J.C. (1973). *Plant Layout: A Guide to the Layout of Process Plants and Sites* New York: John Wiley

Moore J.M. (1962). *Plant Layout and Design* New York: Macmillan

Murdick R.G., Render B. and Russell R.S. (1990). *Service Operations Management* Needham Heights: Allyn and Bacon

Reed R. (1970). *Plant Layout* Homewood: Richard D. Irwin

Steel F.I. (1973). *Physical Settings and Organization Development* Reading: Addison−Wesley

Tompkins J.A. and White J.A. (1984). *Facilities Planning* New York: John Wiley

Chapter 7

Capacity, productivity and utilization

SYNOPSIS

In Chapter 5 we discussed the type of process that is best suited to different levels of demand. Generally, processes for higher demand will have more automation. A major advantage of these automated processes is their ability to give high utilization of resources, and increased efficiency. In this chapter we are going to consider in more detail what such phrases mean.

There are several measures that can be used for assessing the performance of a process or operation. These can describe the level of performance being achieved, how effective the organization is in setting goals, how efficiently it achieves these goals, how high organizational morale is, and so on. This chapter concentrates on the first of these, describing the level of performance achieved. In particular it looks at the capacity of a process, its utilization, productivity and efficiency.

The capacity of a process is the maximum amount of output that can be achieved in a specified time. Sometimes this is easy to measure, but often it needs some calculation or judgement. There is a difference between designed capacity, effective capacity and actual output. The relationships between these allow more precise definitions of efficiency and utilization.

The chapter then moves on to look at productivity. There are several ways in which productivity can be measured, the main ones being total, partial factor and multi-factor productivity.

The chapter then sees how these measures are used for capacity planning. This is essentially a strategic function which matches available capacity to forecast demand. Short-term differences can be overcome by either demand management or capacity management. Some complications with capacity planning are caused by discrete changes in capacity and economies of scale.

The capacity of a process changes over time. Two specific causes of this are learning curves and changing equipment reliability. The effects of learning curves are to reduce the amount of time needed for an operation with increasing repetitions. Conversely, the performance of equipment deteriorates with age, although this may be alleviated by routine maintenance or planned replacement. A related topic is the reliability of a process.

OBJECTIVES

After reading this chapter and completing the exercises you should be able to:

- describe a number of measures for assessing the performance of an organization;
- define capacity and discuss its measurement;
- calculate the designed and effective capacities of a process;
- calculate efficiencies and utilizations;
- define and calculate measures of productivity;
- define and calculate utilization;
- discuss the ways in which capacity and demand can be matched;
- appreciate the effects of discrete changes in capacity and economies of scale;
- give reasons why capacity changes over time;
- use a learning curve;
- find the optimal time between maintenance periods and equipment replacement;
- calculate reliabilities.

7.1   MEASURES OF PERFORMANCE

In Chapter 3 we looked at ways of forecasting demand, and then Chapter 5 showed how this could help to find the best type of process. In particular, higher levels of automation are generally associated with higher demands. One of the reasons for this is that equipment can be used more efficiently and achieve higher productivity. Now we are going to look in more detail at what exactly this means. What, for example, do we mean by 'efficiency', and is high utilization necessarily good?

The basic measure of performance is capacity. This is the total amount of a product that can be processed within a specified time. Determination of the capacity is an important step for all organizations. In effect, we are asking if the capacity to supply products matches the forecast demand. If capacity is too low, some measures should be taken to increase it, or else some demand will remain unsatisfied. Conversely, if there is too much capacity only a portion will actually be used and the spare can either be removed or diverted to another product.

Directly related to the question of capacity are measures of utilization and productivity. Utilization measures the proportion of available capacity that is actually used. Productivity measures the amount of output achieved for each unit of a resource. For example, a facility might have a capacity of 1000 units a week: this is the maximum number of units that can be processed. If the facility is idle half of the time and actually processes 500 units a week its utilization is 50%. If it uses 250 machine-hours of work a week the productivity is two units per machine-hour.

Some of these measures are used very loosely. Efficiency, for example, is a widely used measure, but it often means different things to different people. Here we will define efficiency as the percentage of possible output which is actually achieved. Similarly, utilization is often used mistakenly to describe the proportion of available time a process works. We will use it to describe the proportion of available capacity used.

Some of the terms are often confused. Production, for example, measures the total output from a process, while productivity measures the output achieved for a unit of resource. Thus, 1000 units may be the production while 1000 units per machine-day is the productivity. Similarly, effectiveness measures how well an organization sets its goals, while efficiency measures how well it uses its resources. This is the difference between 'doing the right job' and 'doing the job right'. Opening a walnut with a sledge hammer, for example, would be very effective but it would not be very efficient; building a wall without using cement might be very efficient (as the wall could be built very quickly) but it would not be very effective.

We will discuss these measures in more detail later in the chapter. An important point to make is that there are many alternative measures that could be used. These include:

- effectiveness
- flexibility
- quality
- profitability
- conformance to standards
- morale
- innovation
  and so on.

We can classify these measures according to whether they look at:

- *performance*, with better quality, reduced numbers of breakdowns, fewer accidents, etc.;
- *effectiveness*, with better objectives, decision making, communications, etc.;

- *efficiency*, by using resources better, increasing output, reducing waste, etc.;
- *morale*, improving communications, increasing cooperation, reducing staff turnover, etc.

In the rest of this chapter we will concentrate on measures of performance.

WORKED EXAMPLE 7.1

Two machines are designed to produce 100 units each in a single 10-hour shift. During one shift, the machines were actually used for eight hours, and produced a total of 140 units. What measures can you define for the performance?

SOLUTION

Capacity is the maximum amount that could be produced in a single shift, which is 2 * 100 or 200 units a shift, or 20 units an hour.

Production is the amount actually made, which is 140 units.

Utilization is the proportion of capacity actually used, which is $140/200 = 0.7$ or 70%.

Productivity is the amount produced in relation to resources used, so we can define this as $140/(2 * 8) = 8.75$ units a machine-hour.

Efficiency is the ratio of actual output to possible output, which is $140/(8 * 20) = 0.875$ or 87.5%.

WORKED EXAMPLE 7.2

Ten people make 1000 units of a product each month with direct costs of £125,000. A small reorganization allows 11 people to make 1200 units a month with direct costs of £156,000. How could you measure the performance of the process? Is the reorganization beneficial?

SOLUTION

Two measures can be used here:

- number of units made per person;
- direct costs per unit made.

Calculating these before the reorganization gives:

Number of units per person $= 1000/10 = 100$
Direct costs per unit $= 125,000/1000 = £125$

After the reorganization:

Number of units per person $= 1200/11 = 109$
Direct costs per unit $= 156,000/1200 = £130$

The number of units per person has improved with reorganization, but the direct cost per unit has also risen. It is common for measures of performance to give conflicting views, as they are measuring different things. When we drive a car faster than usual, for example, the time taken for a journey is reduced, but the fuel consumption increases. In this example, whether the reorganization is beneficial depends on the objectives of the organization. If it is aiming to increase output per person it is a success; if the organization is aiming to reduce unit costs it is not a success.

In summary

There are many ways in which the performance of an organization or process can be measured. Here we will concentrate on capacity, productivity, utilization and efficiency. These are defined as follows.

> *Capacity* is the maximum amount of a product that can be processed within a specified time.
> *Utilization* measures the proportion of available capacity which is actually used.
> *Productivity* is the amount produced in relation to one or more of the resources used.
> *Efficiency* is the ratio of actual output to maximum possible output.

SELF ASSESSMENT QUESTIONS

7.1 What measures can be used to see how well a process is working?

7.2 What is the difference between capacity, utilization, productivity and efficiency?

7.3 Is it possible for the utilization of a process to rise while the productivity declines?

7.2 PROCESS CAPACITY

7.2.1 Definition of capacity

The capacity of an operation is the maximum amount that can be processed within a specified time. All operations have some limitation on their capacity: a factory has a maximum output a week; a machine has a maximum throughput an hour; an airplane has a maximum number of seats; a hospital has a maximum number of beds; and so on. The first two of these have clear references to time, but the second two have implicit references. The number of seats on an airplane sets the capacity in terms of a maximum number of passengers per flight; the number of beds in a hospital sets the capacity in terms of a maximum number of in-patients per day. The capacity should always be phrased in terms of maximum output in some specified period.

Sometimes the capacity is obvious (the number of seats in a theatre or rooms in a hotel, for example) but at other times it is less clear and may need some calculation. This is particularly true of services, where the capacity of a grocery store or a warehouse is more difficult to measure. Services often use some surrogate measure to set capacity, such as the number of customers per square metre of floor space. These measures are usually a matter for discussion and agreement rather than calculation. The maximum size of classes in schools, for example, is an agreed number of pupils rather than some limit set by the building. The maximum number of spectators in a football stadium is set by agreed safety regulations rather than physical limitations of space.

Even the capacity of manufacturing operations may be difficult to find. Would it not, for example, be possible to increase the capacity of an assembly line simply by speeding up the flow of goods? Could the capacity of an oil pipeline not be increased by increasing the speed of pumping? An obvious way of increasing capacity is to make the facility work for longer hours, perhaps at weekends or during an extra shift. Is the *normal* capacity then changed, or are we measuring something different? Overall, we have to conclude that the calculation of capacity can be quite difficult, and is based largely on judgement and agreement.

In summary

There are always limits on the capacity of a process, measured as the maximum output in a specified time. Sometimes these limits are obvious, but more often they need some calculation, or agreement.

7.2.2 Calculation of capacity

Suppose a process uses N machines, each working H hours on each of S shifts a day. The total available machine time is $N * H * S$ hours a day. An appropriate measure of capacity may be the number of units the machines can produce in a year. If the machines work for D days a year and each unit of product takes M minutes to process, the total annual capacity of the machines is:

$$\text{Capacity} = \frac{\text{time available in year}}{\text{time to make one unit}}$$
$$= N * H * S * D/(M/60) \text{ units a year}$$

$$\boxed{\text{Capacity} = N * H * S * 60 * D/M \text{ units a year}}$$

where:

N = number of machines
H = hours worked in each shift
S = number of shifts in a day
D = days worked in a year
M = time taken to make one unit (in minutes)

This measure is the maximum output of the machines under ideal conditions. We can call this the *designed capacity*. As operations rarely work under ideal conditions a more realistic measure might be the *effective capacity*. This is the maximum output which could realistically be expected under normal conditions. The difference between designed capacity and effective capacity allows for set-up times, breakdowns, stoppages, maintenance periods, and so on. Most organizations also find that they can get better results when equipment is not stretched to its limit.

We have defined two types of capacity, designed capacity and the lower effective capacity. The actual output will normally be lower than the effective capacity. These measures allow us to define efficiency and utilization more precisely. Efficiency is the ratio of actual output to effective capacity, while utilization is the ratio of actual output to designed capacity.

$$\text{Efficiency} = \frac{\text{Actual output}}{\text{Effective capacity}}$$

$$\text{Utilization} = \frac{\text{Actual output}}{\text{Designed capacity}}$$

WORKED EXAMPLE 7.3

A piece of equipment is designed to work for one eight-hour shift a day, five days a week. When working, the machine can produce 100 units an hour, but 10% of its time is needed for maintenance and set-ups. During one particular week breakdowns, defective output and other problems meant the machine only produced 3000 units. What measures can be found from these figures?

SOLUTION

The designed capacity of the machine is the maximum output which could, ideally, be achieved in a week. This ignores the time needed for maintenance and set-ups.

Designed capacity = $100 * 8 * 5$
= 4000 units a week

The effective capacity is the maximum output which could reasonably be expected. This takes into account the time needed for maintenance and set-ups.

Effective capacity = 100 ∗ 8 ∗ 5 ∗ 0.9
= 3600 units a week

The actual output was 3000 units a week.
Efficiency is the ratio of actual output to effective capacity.

Efficiency = 3000/3600
= 0.833 or 83.3%

Utilization is the ratio of actual output to designed capacity.

Utilization = 3000/4000
= 0.75 or 75%

WORKED EXAMPLE 7.4

A bottling hall has three distinct parts:

- two bottling machines each with a maximum throughput of 100 litres a minute, and average maintenance of one hour a day;
- three labelling machines each with a maximum throughput of 3000 bottles an hour, and planned stoppages averaging 30 minutes a day;
- a packing area with a maximum throughput of 10,000 cases a day.

The hall is set to fill litre bottles and put them in cases of 12 bottles during a 12-hour working day.

(a) What is the designed capacity of the hall?
(b) What is the effective capacity of the hall?
(c) If the bottling hall works at its effective capacity, what is the utilization of each operation?
(d) If the line develops a fault which reduces output to 70,000 bottles, what is the efficiency of each operation?

SOLUTION

The bottling hall can be viewed as the production line shown in Figure 7.1.

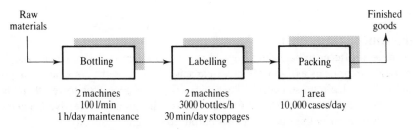

Figure 7.1 Layout of bottling hall in Worked Example 7.4.

(a) All measurements must be in consistent units, and litre bottles a day seems most convenient. The designed capacities of each stage are:

Bottling: 100 litres/min on two machines
= 200 litres a minute
= 200 * 12 * 60 bottles a day
= 144,000 bottles a day

Labelling: 3000 bottles/h on three machines
= 3000 * 3 * 12 bottles a day
= 108,000 bottles a day

Packing: 10,000 cases/day
= 10,000 * 12 bottles a day
= 120,000 bottles a day

The designed capacity of the whole process is set by the smallest capacity of any operation, and this is clearly labelling. The maximum throughput of the bottling hall is 108,000 bottles a day, and this is the designed capacity.

(b) The effective capacity of each stage takes into account planned stoppages, so the effective capacity of each stage is:

Bottling: 144,000 * 11/12 = 132,000 bottles a day
Labelling: 108,000 * 11.5/12 = 103,500 bottles a day
Packing: 120,000 bottles a day

The limiting capacity is still the labelling operation, and overall effective capacity is 103,500 bottles a day.

(c) If the hall works with a throughput of 103,500 bottles a day, the utilizations of each part of the line are:

Bottling: 103,500/144,000 = 0.719 or 71.9%
Labelling: 103,500/108,000 = 0.958 or 95.8%
Packing: 103,500/120,000 = 0.863 or 86.3%

(d) With an actual output of 70,000 bottles the efficiency of each operation is:

Bottling: 70,000/132,000 = 0.530 or 53.0%
Labelling: 70,000/103,500 = 0.676 or 67.6%
Packing: 70,000/120,000 = 0.583 or 58.3%

In summary

There is a difference between designed capacity (which is the maximum output in ideal circumstances) and effective capacity (which is the maximum output under normal circumstances). The actual output is generally lower than the effective capacity. Efficiency is the ratio of actual output to effective capacity, while utilization is the ratio of actual output to designed capacity.

SELF ASSESSMENT QUESTIONS

7.4 Which of the following describes the capacity of a process:

(a) amount of processing actually used during some time period

(b) maximum amount of processing available in some period

(c) proportion of available processing used during some period

(d) minimum amount of processing which covers costs?

7.5 What is the difference between designed capacity and effective capacity?

7.6 What units could you use to measure the capacity of:

(a) a train

(b) a cinema

(c) a squash club

(d) a social work department?

7.7 Which is largest, actual output, designed capacity or effective capacity?

7.8 If six machines work for eight hours a day, 330 days a year, each making one unit of an item every six minutes, what is the designed annual capacity of the machines? If actual output is 100,000 units a year what is the utilization of the machines? Why might this difference arise?

7.3 PRODUCTIVITY

7.3.1 Increasing productivity

In recent years there has been a consistent drive for manufacturing industry and services to improve their productivity. Much of this has been fueled by the observation that some countries, particularly Japan, have found ways of dramatically improving industrial productivity. As a consequence their share of world trade has increased, and Japan now has a higher GDP per capita than any other industrialized country. This trend towards higher productivity is most obvious in manufacturing industries, and while it is less clear in the service sector, there have still been some clear improvements.

It is sometimes argued that improving the productivity of a manufacturing process is relatively straightforward. Technological innovations allow computers and robots to play a larger part in automated processes and, by investing heavily, the productivity can be improved dramatically. Many companies have moved in this direction, but large sales are needed to justify the investment. The result often has production concentrated in a small number of large companies. This is apparent in many industries where a few very large companies dominate the market. There are, for example, three major car manufacturers in the United States and about six in Europe, four major computer suppliers in the United States, two major breweries in Canada, and so on.

Similar effects are less obvious in service industries, which are still labour intensive. There are, however, some notable exceptions. Banks use some automation with cash dispensers and electronic fund transfers; secretaries use word processors rather than typewriters; clerical work is largely done on computers rather than bits of paper, and so on. In some specialized services there is a movement towards a few dominant companies, with two major hamburger chains in the United States, four major banks in Britain, two major airlines in Canada, and so on. Despite these examples, it is generally much more difficult to increase productivity in the service sector. If we go to a restaurant, for example, we are served by waiters. These may have low productivity but there seems no way of increasing it without reducing the service level, and effectively change the product being offered.

In summary

In recent years there has been a dramatic improvement in the productivity of some industries, often encouraged by progress in Japan. It is more difficult to get improved productivity in the service sector.

7.3.2 Definition of productivity

Although we have discussed some aspects of productivity we have not really given a detailed definition. At the beginning of the chapter we said that productivity is the amount produced in relation to one or more of the resources used. We can now expand this definition, by saying *total productivity* is the total output divided by the total input, where some consistent units are used for output and input.

$$\text{Total productivity} = \frac{\text{Total output}}{\text{Total input}}$$

Another useful measure of productivity is partial factor productivity. This measures the total output divided by one kind of input. Thus, the amount produced per machine-hour, or the amount produced per kilowatt-hour of electricity, or the amount produced per pound of investment are examples of partial factor productivity.

$$\text{Partial factor productivity} = \frac{\text{Total output}}{\text{Single input}}$$

A few examples of widely used partial factor productivity measures are:

- *equipment productivity*, units of output per machine-hour, tonnes made per operating hour, units made per breakdown, and so on;
- *labour productivity*, units of output per person-hour, pounds of output per pound of labour, shipment made per pound of labour, and so on;

- *capital productivity*, units made per pound of investment, value of outputs per unit of input, and so on;
- *energy productivity*, units of output per kilowatt-hour, units of output for each pound spent on electricity, value of output per barrel of oil used, and so on.

A third measure of productivity is multi-factor productivity, which measures the total output in relation to some specific subset of the inputs. Thus, the total output divided by the labour and material costs, or the output per unit of operating and material cost, or the output per hour of work done at weekends are examples of multi-factor productivity.

$$\text{Multi-factor productivity} = \frac{\text{Total output}}{\text{Subset of inputs}}$$

The purpose of these productivity measures is to assess the performance of an organization. Ordinarily, if the productivity is increased the organization is performing better.

WORKED EXAMPLE 7.5

During the first quarter of a financial year the following information was collected for a product.

Selling price	£40
Units sold	1,000
Cost of raw materials	£8,000
Cost of labour	£5,000
Cost of energy	£7,000
Other costs	£10,000

How could you describe the productivity of the process?

SOLUTION

The total productivity can be found, using consistent units, from:

$$\text{Total productivity} = \frac{\text{total outputs}}{\text{total inputs}}$$
$$= \frac{40 * 1000}{8000 + 5000 + 7000 + 10,000}$$
$$= 1.33$$

This tells us that on average £1.33 of output was produced for each £1 input.

There are several measures of partial productivity, notably:

Materials: $40 * 1000/8000 = 5$
Labour: $40 * 1000/5000 = 8$
Energy: $40 * 1000/7000 = 5.7$
Other costs: $40 * 1000/10,000 = 4$

These measures tell us that £5 of output was produced for every £1 of materials, £8 of output for every £1 of labour, and so on.

There are also several possible calculations for multi-factor productivity, including:

Materials and labour: $40 * 1000/(8000 + 5000) = 3.1$
Materials and energy: $40 * 1000/(8000 + 7000) = 2.7$
Labour and other costs: $40 * 1000/(5000 + 10,000) = 2.7$

These measures tell us that £3.1 of output was produced for every £1 of materials and labour, £2.7 of output for every £1 of materials and energy, and so on.

WORKED EXAMPLE 7.6

In two consecutive years a process had the following characteristics.

	1989	1990
Number of units made	1,000	1,200
Raw materials used	5,100 kg	5,800 kg
Cost of raw materials	£20,500	£25,500
Hours worked	4,300	4,500
Direct labour costs	£52,000	£58,000
Energy used	10,000 kW.h	14,000 kW.h
Energy cost	£1,000	£1,500

How has the productivity changed?

SOLUTION

There are several measures of productivity we could use. Unfortunately, we cannot measure the total productivity, as there are no consistent units for output and input. There are, however, a number of possible single factor productivities that could be calculated.

Units of output per kg of raw material in 1989 were $1000/5100 = 0.196$. In 1990 this was $1200/5800 = 0.207$. Thus, this measure of productivity has risen and the ratio of 1990 productivity to 1989 productivity is $0.207/0.196 = 1.056$. If this ratio is greater than 1, productivity is improving. If it is less than one, this might be an area we could look to for improvements. Other results are:

	1989	1990	1990/1989
Units/kg of raw material	0.196	0.207	1.056
Units/£ of raw material	0.049	0.047	0.959
Units/hour	0.233	0.267	1.146
Units/£ of labour	0.019	0.021	1.105
Units/kW.h	0.100	0.086	0.860
Units/£ of energy	1.000	0.800	0.800

This table shows that labour productivity has risen, raw materials productivity has stayed about the same, but energy productivity has fallen.

In summary

Productivity measures the output achieved for each unit of input. Total productivity considers all inputs, partial factor productivity considers a single input, and multi-factor productivity considers a subset of inputs.

SELF ASSESSMENT QUESTIONS

7.9 What is the difference between total, partial factor and multi-factor productivity?

7.10 Is it possible for some measures of productivity to rise while others are falling?

7.11 A partial factor productivity was measured for two consecutive years, and the ratio of the second year to the first year was found to be 0.85. Does this show:

(a) this productivity has risen
(b) this productivity has fallen
(c) this productivity has neither risen nor fallen
(d) cannot say what has happened?

7.4 CAPACITY PLANNING

7.4.1 Alternative policies

We have now described how capacity can be measured, and how this is affected by utilization, efficiency and productivity. The next step is to describe some aspects of capacity planning, which tries to match available capacity and forecast demand. This is an important function in all organizations. If there is excess capacity there has been too much investment in facilities (at least in the short term) and this is both wasteful and expensive. Conversely, if there is insufficient capacity some demand will not be met, giving lost sales and other penalties.

Capacity planning is essentially a strategic function. The capacity of an operation might be increased by, for example, building another facility. Conversely, excess capacity can be reduced by closing down facilities, or diverting them to other products. These are clearly strategic decisions. Some aspects of capacity planning are, however, shorter term. Capacity could also be increased by leasing additional space, or working overtime. These are tactical and operational decisions.

We could summarize the objectives of capacity planning as making available capacity to match forecast demand in the long term, while making adjustments to correct short-term mismatches. The exact meaning of short term and long term does, of course, depend on circumstances.

> Capacity planning ensures that available capacity is matched to forecast demand over the long, medium and short terms.

Strategic decisions about capacity generally involve changing the facilities available. Short-term mismatches between supply and demand can be corrected by two alternative approaches:

- adjust demand to match available capacity;
- adjust capacity to match demand.

Demand can be adjusted in a number of ways, the most obvious of which is to vary the price. There are, however, constraints on this as prices must be high enough to cover all costs, and competition limits the amount they can be increased. There are other alternatives for adjusting demand, including:

- vary the price, with increases for products with insufficient capacity and decreases for products with spare capacity;
- change the marketing effort, with increases for products with spare capacity and reductions for products with insufficient capacity;
- offer various incentives, such as free samples of products with spare capacity, or discounts (such as cheap off-peak telephone calls);
- make changes to related products, so that substitution may be possible for products in short supply;
- keep spare output in stock to be used later;
- vary the lead time, making customers wait for products in short supply;
- use a reservation or appointment system.

One implication of such demand management is that business may be actively discouraged at times of high demand. This may seem strange but is really quite common. Professional institutions, for example, put up barriers against newcomers wanting to enter; restaurants have queues outside at busy times which discourage people from going there; expensive cars offer long delivery times; artists produce limited editions of prints, and so on. Some of these options show that demand can be managed by changing the lead times which customers have to wait. Demand is then smoothed by having a continuous queue of customers which gets shorter at times of low demand and longer at times of high demand. A formal version of queues is an appointment system, of the type used to smooth demand in almost all professions.

The alternative to demand management is capacity management, which looks for short-term adjustments to make available capacity meet demand. The obvious way of doing this is to change operating time, by working overtime to increase capacity, or short time to reduce it. Important ways of adjusting capacity are:

- changing the total hours worked in any period, by changing the number of shifts or other work patterns;
- employing part-time staff to cover times of peak demand;
- scheduling work patterns so that the total workforce available at any time varies in line with varying demand;
- adjusting equipment and processes to work faster or slower;
- rescheduling maintenance periods;
- using outside contractors;
- leasing extra space;
- adjusting the process, perhaps using larger batches to reduce set-up times;
- making the customers do some work (like using automatic cash dispensing machines in banks or packing their own bags in supermarkets).

These adjustments cannot be done too frequently or too severely. The workforce schedules, for example, cannot be changed every few days, neither can extra space be rented for a few hours at a time. The implication is that capacity planning should aim for a stable output. Dramatic fluctuations in the output are very disruptive and should be avoided. This theme is discussed again in Chapter 8.

In summary

Capacity planning matches available capacity and forecast demand. This is essentially a strategic function, but some aspects are relevant in the shorter term. Short-term adjustments can be made by either demand management or capacity management. There are several ways of achieving either of these.

7.4.2 Discrete increases in capacity

Utilization is the ratio of actual output to designed capacity. Then for a set of machines:

$$\text{Utilization} = \frac{\text{actual output}}{\text{designed capacity}}$$

$$= \frac{\text{actual output}}{N * H * S * 60 * D/M}$$

where:

N = number of machines
H = hours per shift
S = number of shifts worked in a day
D = days worked in a year
M = time to make one unit (in minutes)

This equation can be turned around to see how many machines would be needed to produce a certain number of parts. If U is the average level of utilization expected, and P is the annual production target, the total machine time available must be greater than, or at least equal to, the total time required. With calculations in minutes, this gives:

time available > time required
$$N * H * S * 60 * D * U > P * M$$

or

$$\text{Number of machines} \quad N > \frac{P * M}{H * S * 60 * D * U}$$

If original plans were to use less than N machines, either production plans must be changed, or utilization increased or more machines used. If there are more than N machines available they will be working at an average utilization of:

$$\text{Utilization} = \frac{P * M}{N * H * S * 60 * D}$$

This approach shows the basis of capacity planning, which consists of:

* examine forecast demand and translate this into a capacity requirement;
* calculate the available capacity of present facilities;
* identify mismatches between capacity requirement and projected availability;

- generate alternative plans for overcoming any mismatch;
- evaluate alternative plans and select the best.

This process is sometimes referred to as resource requirement planning.

WORKED EXAMPLE 7.7

A company wants to make 1000 units of a product a week. The product is made on equipment which has a designed capacity of 10 units an hour. The company currently works a single eight-hour shift during weekdays, but could move to double shifts or work at weekends. If the equipment has an expected utilization of 80%, how much equipment does the company need?

SOLUTION

We know the constants $P = 1000$, $M = 6$, $H = 8$ and $U = 0.8$ and these are substituted into the equation:

$$\text{Number of machines } N > \frac{P * M}{H * S * 60 * D * U} > \frac{6000}{384 * S * D}$$

Working a single shift during weekdays has $S = 1$ and $D = 5$ to give:

$N > 6000/1920 > 3.125$

As equipment comes in discrete quantities, this number must be rounded up and four sets are needed. The utilization of these will be:

$$\text{Utilization} = \frac{P * M}{N * H * S * 60 * D} = \frac{1000 * 6}{4 * 8 * 1 * 60 * 5}$$
$$= 0.625 \text{ or } 62.5\%$$

This low utilization results from the need to buy four sets of equipment when only 3.125 sets are actually needed. The company could increase utilization by buying only three sets of equipment and making short-term adjustments to make up the difference.

If the company moved to a double shift, $S = 2$ and $D = 5$ to give:

$N > 6000/3840 > 1.56$

so the company would need two sets of equipment, but again utilization during the shifts worked would be 62.5%.

If the company stayed with a single shift but worked at weekends, $S = 1$ and $D = 7$ to give:

$N > 6000/2688 > 2.23$

so the company would need three sets of equipment and utilization would be:

$U = 6000/10,080 = 0.595 \text{ or } 59.5\%$

The process of capacity planning would be complete when these alternatives are evaluated, and the best solution implemented.

This worked example shows one of the problems with matching capacity and demand. While demand usually comes in small quantities and can take almost any value, capacity often comes in large discrete amounts. Typically, capacity can be increased by using an additional machine, opening another shop, employing another person, using another vehicle, and so on.

Suppose that demand for a product rises steadily over time. Capacity must be increased at some stage, but the increase will come as a discrete step. It is difficult to match capacity with demand when one is essentially continuous and the other is discrete. This problem cannot be avoided, but there are three basic strategies for dealing with it (illustrated in Figure 7.2):

(1)   Capacity can be more or less matched to demand so that sometimes there is excess capacity and sometimes a shortage.

(2)   Capacity can be made at least equal to demand at all times (which requires more investment in equipment and leads to lower utilization).

(3)   Capacity can be added only when the additional facilities would be fully used (which requires lower investment, gives higher utilization, but constrains output).

Each of these is appropriate in different circumstances, but there is seldom an ideal solution where all resources have 100% utilization.

Factors which generally encourage capacity to be increased early (giving the result in Figure 7.2(b)) are:

- uneven or variable demand;
- high profits (perhaps for a new product);
- high cost of unmet demand (possibly lost sales);
- continuously changing product mix;
- uncertainty in capacity;
- variable efficiency;
- capacity increases which are relatively small;
- low cost of spare capacity (perhaps used for other work).

Conversely, the main factor which encourages delaying an increase in capacity until the last possible moment (giving the result in Figure 7.2(c)) is the capital cost. In practice, these capital costs must be offset against increasing costs of running existing equipment at higher levels of utilization.

A related question concerns the size of an expansion. If a process is going to be disrupted by increasing capacity, would it be better to have a few large increases, or more smaller ones (as shown in Figure 7.3). If a set of offices, for example, is going to be extended it will often have a bigger expansion than it currently needs to avoid further disruptions in the future.

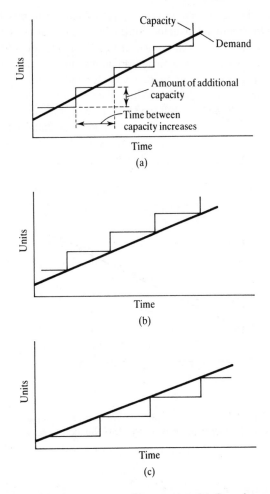

Figure 7.2 Options for increasing capacity. (a) Capacity more or less matches demand. (b) Capacity is always greater than demand. (c) Capacity always lags behind demand.

The benefits of large increases are:

- capacity stays ahead of demand for a long time;
- lost sales are unlikely;
- economies of scale might be found;
- the possibility of an advantage over competitors;
- fewer disruptions;

  and so on.

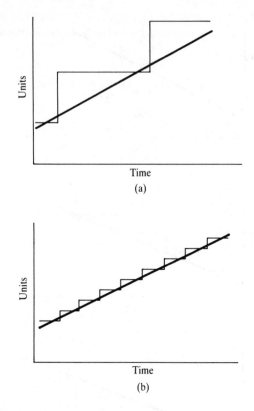

Figure 7.3 Alternative policies for increasing capacity.
(a) A few large increases. (b) More smaller increases.

Conversely the disadvantages are:

- capacity does not match demand very closely;
- disruptions may be serious;
- large capital costs are incurred;
- utilization will be low;
- there is high risk if demand changes;
- the policy is less flexible;
  and so on.

Figure 7.3 shows that capacity is increased after a small shortage has been noticed. It is assumed that small mismatches are overcome by the short-term measures described above. Extra capacity is added when the mismatch becomes longer term. Thus, important questions for capacity planning are:

(1) By how much should facilities be expanded (or contracted)?

(2) When should facilities be expanded (or contracted)?

WORKED EXAMPLE 7.8

A company is reviewing its plans for a product to cover the next three years. The current annual demand is 100 units, and this is rising by 50 units a year. The company can expand capacity now, or at the beginning of next year, but the capacity can only be increased in discrete steps of 50 units. Each unit of spare capacity has notional costs of £400 a year, while each unit of shortage is assigned a cost of £1000 a year. What should the company do about its capacity?

SOLUTION

The company has five alternatives.

Alternative 1. Do not increase capacity, which gives:

Year	Sales	Units of Spare	Shortage
0	100	0	0
1	100	0	50
2	100	0	100

This has total costs of 0 * 400 for spare capacity plus 150 * 1000 for shortages, totalling £150,000 over the three years.

Alternatives 2 and 3. Increase capacity by either 50 or 100 units now, giving:

Year	50 Increase Sales	Spare	Shortage	100 Increase Sales	Spare	Shortage
0	100	50	0	100	100	0
1	150	0	0	150	50	0
2	150	0	50	200	0	0

Increasing capacity by 50 now has total costs of:

50 * 400 + 50 * 1000 = £70,000

293

Increasing capacity by 100 now has costs of:

150 * 400 + 0 * 1000 = £60,000

Alternatives 4 and 5. Increase capacity by 50 units or 100 units next year, giving:

	50 *Increase*			100 *Increase*		
Year	Sales	Spare	Shortage	Sales	Spare	Shortage
0	100	0	0	100	0	0
1	150	0	0	150	50	0
2	150	0	50	200	0	0

Increasing capacity by 50 next year has a total cost of:

0 * 400 + 50 * 1000 = £50,000

Increasing capacity by 100 next year has costs of:

50 * 400 + 0 * 1000 = £20,000

Overall, the best policy is to increase capacity by 100 units next year.

In summary

Capacity planning is made more complicated by the fact that changes in capacity often come in discrete amounts. It is difficult to match this closely to a continuous demand. Important questions ask when capacity should be changed and how big the changes should be.

7.4.3 Economies of scale

We mentioned above that large increases in capacity might lead to economies of scale. This is a common feature that was described briefly in the break-even analyses of Chapter 2. The idea is that bigger operations are able to produce individual units more cheaply than smaller ones. Thus, mass-produced cars are much cheaper to produce than Rolls Royce cars which are made in small numbers; colour supplements to newspapers are cheaper than limited edition prints, and so on.

The cost reductions come from two sources:

- fixed costs are spread over a large number of units;
- more efficient processes can be used, using larger batches and more automation.

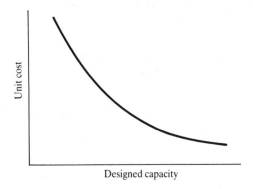

Figure 7.4 Reduction in unit cost with increasing designed capacity.

Figure 7.4 shows how the unit cost may decline with various levels of designed capacity. This figure assumes that the process is fully used. Low utilization obviously increases unit cost, but so does attempting to get excessively high output from resources. Minimum unit cost comes with full utilization, and any divergence from this increases costs. A fuller description of unit costs is given in Figure 7.5.

We have mentioned the economies that come from increasing size, but it is worth pointing out that there are often diseconomies of scale. Eventually the communications, management and organization needed by large facilities tend to get overwhelmingly complex and become less efficient. Some people suggest, for example, that centralized government is inherently inefficient as it involves a large number of interactions between very complex departments.

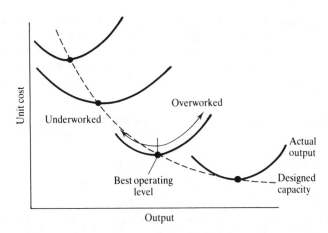

Figure 7.5 Variation in unit cost with designed capacity and actual output.

WORKED EXAMPLE 7.9

The capacity of a service operation depends on the number of staff employed. Total output, measured in some consistent units, is:

Staff	1	2	3	4	5	6	7
Output	25	60	110	150	180	205	220

The fixed cost of the operation is £50,000, and each staff member costs a total of £25,000 to employ. Compare the performance of different numbers of staff.

SOLUTION

We can draw a table of costs as shown in Table 7.1 (values in £1000s).

Table 7.1

Staff	Total output	Additional output per person	Average output per person	Variable cost	Variable cost per unit	Total cost	Total cost per unit
1	25	25	25	25	1.00	75	3.00
2	60	35	30	50	0.83	100	1.67
3	110	50	37	75	0.68	125	1.14
4	150	40	38	100	0.66	150	1.00
5	180	30	36	125	0.69	175	0.97
6	205	25	34	150	0.73	200	0.98
7	220	15	31	175	0.80	225	1.02

The additional output per person is rising for the first three, showing economies of scale, but then declines as diseconomies appear. The highest average output per person is achieved with four staff. The variable cost per unit is also minimum with four staff. The total cost per unit (variable cost plus fixed cost) is minimum with five staff. As the organization is probably most concerned with total cost per unit, the best number of employees should be five.

In summary

Economies of scale need to be considered in capacity planning. These are not inevitable, and sometimes there are diseconomies of scale.

7.12 What are the two alternatives for dealing with short-term mismatches in demand and capacity?

7.13 What are the basic steps in capacity planning?

7.14 Why are discrete increases in capacity a problem?

7.15 What are the two basic questions for capacity expansion?

7.16 Give two reasons for declining unit cost with increasing output.

7.17 Are there always economies of scale with increasing capacity?

7.5 CHANGING CAPACITY OVER TIME

We have described how capacity planning aims to match available capacity and forecast demand as closely as possible. This is made more difficult by factors like discrete capacity and evaluating economies of scale. Another significant problem is that the capacity of an operation changes over time. Even if no changes are made to the process there will be short-term variations due to operator illness, interruptions, breakdowns, and so on. There are also long-term changes in capacity. We will look at two reasons for these, based on learning curves and reducing performance of equipment.

7.5.1 Learning curves

We are all familiar with the idea that the more often something is repeated the easier it becomes. Musicians and sportsmen spend a long time practising so they become more skilful and find it easier to achieve a level of performance. This effect is found in almost all operations, so the efficiency will rise with production numbers. This rise in efficiency is most often found as a decline in the amount of time needed to do an operation, as shown in Figure 7.6. This graph is called a learning curve.

A common shape for learning curves has the time taken to do an operation falling by some fixed proportion every time the number of repetitions is doubled. Typically this proportion is about 10%. Then, if the first time an operation is done it takes some time, T; the second time it takes only 90% of this time; the fourth time it takes 90% of the time needed for the second repetition; the eighth time it takes 90% of the time needed for the fourth repetition; the sixteenth time it takes 90% of the time needed for the eighth repetition, and so on. This is described as a 90% learning curve, or a learning rate of 0.9.

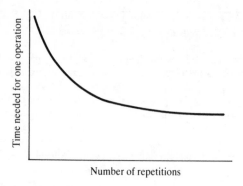

Figure 7.6 A typical learning curve.

The equation for this learning curve is:

$$\text{Learning curve } Y = T * N^b$$

where:

Y = time taken for the Nth repetition
N = number of repetitions
T = time taken for the first unit
b = log R/log 2
R = learning rate

The value of b is fixed for any particular learning rate, so:

- for a 90% learning curve, $R = 0.9$
  b = log 0.9/log 2 = $-0.046/0.301$ = -0.152
- for an 80% learning curve, $R = 0.8$
  b = log 0.8/log 2 = $-0.097/0.301$ = -0.322
- for a 70% learning curve, $R = 0.7$
  b = log 0.7/log 2 = $-0.155/0.301$ = -0.515

WORKED EXAMPLE 7.10

It takes one hour to produce the first unit of a product. How long will it take to make each of the first eight units with a learning rate of 0.8?

SOLUTION

For an 80% learning curve $b = -0.322$, so the time (in minutes) decreases according to:

$$Y = 60 * N^{-0.322}$$

Then substitution of $N = 1$ gives $Y = 60 * 1^{-0.322} = 60.0$
$\qquad\qquad\qquad N = 2$ gives $Y = 60 * 2^{-0.322} = 48.0$
$\qquad\qquad\qquad N = 3$ gives $Y = 60 * 3^{-0.322} = 42.1$

and so on, giving the following results.

Number	1	2	3	4	5	6	7	8
Time for unit	60	48.0	42.1	38.4	35.7	33.7	32.1	30.7

The total time needed to produce eight units is now 320.7 minutes, rather than the simple $8 * 60 = 480$ minutes. The average time for each of the eight units is $320.7/8 = 40.1$ minutes.

WORKED EXAMPLE 7.11

A parts manufacturer found that when it started making a new assembly it took 2000 hours to complete the first one, but this had fallen to 700 hours by the time 200 had been made. What is the rate of learning for the assembly?

SOLUTION

We know that $Y = T * N^b$ and T is 2000. When $N = 200$, $Y = 700$. Substitution gives:

$$Y = T * N^b$$
$$700 = 2000 * 200^b$$

or

$$200^b = 0.35$$

Taking logs gives

$$b * \log 200 = \log 0.35$$

or

$$b = -0.20$$

But

$$b = \log R/\log 2$$

so

$$-0.20 = \log R/0.30$$
$$\log R = -0.06$$
$$R = 10^{-0.06}$$
$$\quad = 0.87$$

Table 7.2 Cumulative learning curves.

N	R = 0.75	R = 0.8	R = 0.85	R = 0.9	R = 0.95
1	1.00	1.00	1.00	1.00	1.00
2	1.75	1.80	1.85	1.90	1.95
3	2.38	2.50	2.62	2.75	2.87
4	2.95	3.14	3.35	3.56	3.77
5	3.46	3.74	4.03	4.34	4.66
6	3.93	4.30	4.69	5.10	5.54
7	4.38	4.83	5.32	5.84	6.40
8	4.80	5.35	5.94	6.57	7.26
9	5.20	5.84	6.53	7.29	8.11
10	5.59	6.32	7.12	7.99	8.95
15	7.32	8.51	9.86	11.38	13.09
20	8.83	10.48	12.40	14.61	17.13
25	10.19	12.31	14.80	17.71	21.10
30	11.45	14.02	17.09	20.73	25.00
40	13.72	17.19	21.43	26.54	32.68
50	15.78	20.12	25.51	32.14	40.22
60	17.67	22.87	29.41	37.57	47.65
70	19.43	25.47	33.17	42.87	54.99
80	21.09	27.96	36.80	48.05	62.25
90	22.67	30.35	40.32	53.14	69.45
100	24.18	32.65	43.75	58.14	76.59
150	30.93	43.23	59.89	82.16	111.57
200	36.80	52.72	74.79	105.00	145.69
250	42.08	61.47	88.83	126.91	179.18
300	46.94	69.66	102.23	148.20	212.18
400	55.75	84.85	127.57	189.27	277.01
500	63.68	98.85	151.45	228.79	340.65

The calculations for a learning curve can be done easily on a spreadsheet, or from tables. Table 7.2 shows the cumulative time to make N units when the time to make the first unit is 1. To find the cumulative time, when the first unit takes T, simply multiply the result in the table by T. So to make eight units with an 80% learning curve and an initial time of 60 takes $60 * 5.35 = 321$, which is the result found in Worked Example 7.10. The total time to make 500 units with a 90% learning curve and initial time of 120 minutes is $120 * 228.79 = 27,455$ minutes.

We can use these cumulative times for doing a number of calculations, perhaps concerning staffing levels needed to satisfy a production plan. Such calculations are illustrated in the following worked example.

WORKED EXAMPLE 7.12

Planned production of a new product in the next eight months is shown below. Trials suggest the first unit will take 40 hours to make and there is a 90% learning curve. How many workers are needed for the product, if each works an average of 200 hours a month?

Month	1	2	3	4	5	6	7	8
Production	4	6	20	30	40	50	100	50

SOLUTION

The calculations for this can be done as in Table 7.3.

Table 7.3

Month	Production	Cumulative production	Cumulative time	Time in month	Workers needed
1	4	4	142.4	142.4	0.71
2	6	10	319.6	177.2	0.89
3	20	30	829.2	509.6	2.55
4	30	60	1502.8	673.6	3.37
5	40	100	2325.6	822.8	4.11
6	50	150	3286.4	960.8	4.80
7	100	250	5076.4	1790.0	8.95
8	50	300	5928.0	851.6	4.26

The cumulative time is found by multiplying the entry in Table 7.2 by 40, so the cumulative time to make 300 with a 90% learning curve is $40 * 148.20 = 5928$ hours. The time needed in the month is the difference between consecutive cumulative times, and when this is divided by 200 it shows the number of workers needed in a month.

In summary

In addition to short-term variations, the capacity of a process will change in the long term. One reason for this is a learning curve, which allows higher efficiency with increasing experience.

7.18 What is meant by an 80% learning curve?

7.19 Is it true that learning rates must be between 0.75 and 1.00?

7.20 Why does the time taken to do an operation decline over time?

7.5.2 Maintenance of equipment

Learning curves make productivity increase over time, but there are also factors that make productivity decrease. The most important of these is caused by the ageing of equipment.

New equipment is expected to work well, but as it gets older it breaks down more often, develops more faults, gives lower quality output, slows down, and generally wears out. If this goes unchecked, the performance of equipment will decline until it becomes unsatisfactory. Sometimes this change is slow (the fuel consumption of a car will rise over a period of seven or eight years) and at other times it is very fast (a bolt, for example, will often fail spontaneously and cause equipment breakdown). A way of avoiding this decline is to introduce policies for routine maintenance and replacement.

The basis of routine maintenance is that equipment is inspected and vulnerable parts are replaced at regular intervals or after a certain number of hours of use. By replacing bits that are worn the equipment is restored to give continuing, satisfactory performance. Optimistically, equipment is restored to almost the same level as a new piece of equipment. A question arises, though, as to how frequently this maintenance should be done. If it is done too frequently, the equipment will run efficiently but the maintenance costs will be very high. If it is done too infrequently, the maintenance cost will be low but the system will still be subject to failures. If these two costs (from maintenance and expected failure) are added together we get some kind of U-shaped curve which has a minimum cost at some optimum maintenance interval (see Figure 7.7).

WORKED EXAMPLE 7.13

If a piece of equipment is kept operating continuously the expected cost of failures rises each week as shown below. Routine maintenance can be done at a cost of £1000 and this brings equipment back up to new condition. What is the optimal time between maintenance periods?

Weeks since maintenance	0	1	2	3	4	5
Cost of breakdowns in week	0	50	150	200	1600	3000

SOLUTION

If the equipment is maintained every week there is no cost for expected breakdowns; if maintenance is done every two weeks the expected cost is £0 in the first week plus £50 in the second week; if maintenance is done every three weeks the expected cost is £0 in the first week, £50 in the second week and £150 in the third week, and so on. Adding the routine maintenance cost of £1000 gives the costs shown in Table 7.4.

Table 7.4

Weeks between maintenance	*Maintenance cost*	*Cost of breakdowns in week*	*Total cost of breakdowns*	*Total cost*	*Cost per week*
1	1000	0	0	1000	1000
2	1000	50	50	1050	525
3	1000	150	200	1200	400
4	1000	200	400	1400	350
5	1000	1600	2000	3000	600
6	1000	3000	5000	6000	1000

Thus, if maintenance is done every four weeks the cumulative cost of breakdowns is £400 and maintenance costs £1000, to give a total cost of £1400. This gives an average of £350 a week. This is the cheapest alternative.

There are, of course, other options than routine maintenance. One of these is simply to replace equipment when its operations decline to some pre-specified level. Another option is to have spare equipment available so that it can take over when there is a breakdown and reduce the effects. These options are discussed in the following sections.

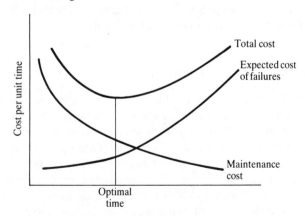

Figure 7.7 Determining the optimal time between maintenance periods.

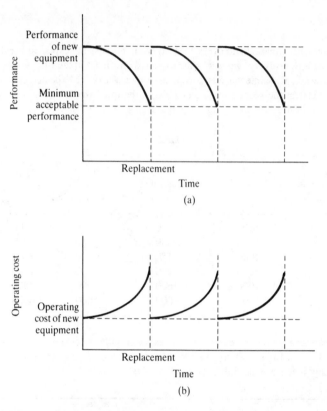

Figure 7.8 Two strategies for replacement. (a) Replacement when performance becomes unacceptable. (b) Replacement to minimize operating costs.

In summary
The performance of almost everything declines with age. Routine maintenance can be performed to keep equipment operating at acceptable levels. Optimal times between maintenance periods can be found.

7.5.3 Replacement of equipment

Routine maintenance can reduce the effects of ageing and keep equipment working efficiently, but a point will come when maintenance and repairs become too expensive and it will be cheaper to buy new equipment. Such replacement decisions can be expensive and need careful planning. Extreme examples of replacement decisions might be power stations, office blocks or ships removed from service. Figure 7.8 shows two approaches to this problem. Firstly, equipment may be replaced when its performance declines to the point where it is no longer acceptable; the output may be too low, quality too poor, breakdowns too frequent, and so on. A drawback of this approach is that its response is too late, as it comes when the equipment is already unsatisfactory. A better alternative would be to analyse costs and keep the equipment operating for the specific time which minimizes total costs.

A useful method of finding the optimal age of replacement is to add the costs of operating equipment over a number of years and divide this by the age to give an average annual cost. Repeating this calculation for several values of lifetime will identify the optimal age of replacement. This approach is similar to the maintenance problem in Worked Example 7.13.

WORKED EXAMPLE 7.14

Every year a company reviews the performance of its production machines so that any replacements can be delivered before the end of the financial year. The cost of replacing each machine is £150,000 and expected resale values at the end of each year are given in the following table. Average annual operating and maintenance costs are also shown in the table. What is the best age to replace the machines?

Age of machine	1	2	3	4	5
Resale value	75,000	45,000	22,500	15,000	7,500
Running cost in previous year	7,500	13,500	22,500	61,500	90,000

SOLUTION

When a machine is sold the total cost of use during its lifetime is in two parts:

- a capital cost equal to the difference between the price of a new machine and the resale value of the old one;
- a running cost which is the cumulative cost of maintenance and operation over the machine's life.

  If a machine is sold after one year of use:

- capital cost is 150,000 − 75,000 = £75,000
- running cost is £7500.

The total cost of using the machine for one year is £82,500.
    If the machine is sold after two years:

- capital cost is 150,000 − 45,000 = £105,000
- running costs are £7500 in the first year plus £13,500 in the second year.

The total cost of using the machine for two years is £126,000, which is an average of £63,000 a year.

Repeating these calculations for other ages of replacement gives the values in Table 7.5.

Table 7.5

Age of replacement	1	2	3	4	5
Capital cost	75,000	105,000	127,500	135,000	142,500
Running cost	7,500	21,000	43,500	105,000	195,000
Total cost	82,500	126,000	171,000	240,000	337,500
Average annual cost	82,500	63,000	57,000	60,000	67,500

Replacement after three years gives the lowest average annual cost.

This analysis has assumed that a new machine will be bought. An alternative would be to buy a second-hand machine. When resale value declines quickly, as it does in this example, second-hand equipment can be bought which is both cheap and relatively new. Care must be taken with such policies, as there are obvious problems with reliability, availability of spare parts, status, use of outdated technology, and so on.

If a machine is bought when it is two years old and used until it is four years old:

- capital cost will be 45,000 − 15,000 = £30,000
- running costs will be £22,500 in the first year plus £61,500 in the second year.

The total cost over two years is £114,000, or an average of £57,000 a year.

If a machine is bought when it is two years old and used until it is five years old:

- capital cost will be 45,000 − 7,500 = £37,500
- running costs will be £22,500 in the first year, £61,500 in the second year and £90,000 in the third year.

The total cost over three years is £211,500, or an average of £70,500 a year.

Repeating this calculation for combinations of ages bought and ages sold gives the following table of average annual costs (entries are in thousands of pounds):

		Age sold 1	2	3	4	5
	0	82.5	63	57	60	64.5
	1	—	43.5	44.3	52.5	63.8
Age bought	2	—	—	45	57	70.5
	3	—	—	—	69	83.3
	4	—	—	—	—	97.5

The cheapest alternative is to buy one-year old machines and sell them a year later.

An obvious flaw in this calculation is the assumption that the value of money is constant. We could now add discounting factors to reduce amounts of money in the future to their discounted present value.

For simplicity we will use a discounting rate of 1% a month, use discrete discounting and assume new machines are bought.

If the machines are replaced after one year of operation:

- capital cost consists of the purchase price minus the resale value, but the resale value has to be discounted by 1.01^{12};

- running costs have to be discounted similarly. As these occur more or less uniformly over the year (i.e. months 1 to 12) we can use an average discounting factor based on the middle of the year (i.e. month 6) equal to 1.01^6.

Total cost then becomes:

- capital cost = $150{,}000 - 75{,}000/1.01^{12}$
       = $150{,}000 - 66{,}558$
       = £83,442

- running cost = $7500/1.01^6$
       = £7,065

- total cost   = $83{,}442 + 7065$
       = £90,507

Similarly, selling the machines after two years of operation has:

- capital cost = $150{,}000 - 45{,}000/1.01^{24}$
       = $150{,}000 - 35{,}441$
       = £114,559

- running cost = $7500/1.01^6 + 13{,}500/1.011^{18}$
       = $7065 + 11{,}286$
       = £18,351

- total cost   = £132,910 or £66,455 a year

Repeating these calculations for other operating periods gives the results shown in Table 7.6.

Table 7.6

Age at replacement	1	2	3	4	5
Capital cost	83,436	114,560	134,274	140,696	145,872
Running cost	7,065	18,351	35,045	75,537	128,126
Net present cost	90,501	132,911	169,319	216,233	273,998
Average cost/year	90,501	66,455	56,439	54,059	54,800

With discounted values the best solution is to replace the machines every four years. This can be compared with the previous solution, without discounts, which recommended replacement every two years.

In summary

Maintenance will reduce the effects of ageing, but eventually equipment must be replaced. The optimal time for this can be found by calculating average annual costs over various lifetimes and selecting the lowest.

7.5.4 Reliability of equipment

A question which is directly related to the maintenance and replacement of equipment concerns its reliability. We have already said that if equipment becomes unreliable and starts to break down, there will come a point when it is better to replace it than continue repairing and maintaining. It is, however, possible to increase the reliability of equipment by having stand-by equipment in reserve, which is only used when there is a breakdown. Some costs are increased (by having unused equipment), but this may be more than offset by the benefits from a more reliable process. This is the principle of the spare wheel in a car.

In this discussion we will define reliability as the probability that a part continues to operate throughout an entire period. Thus, a reliability of 90% means there is a probability of 0.9 that the part will continue to operate normally for the period under investigation. To simplify things we will also phrase the discussion in terms of equipment made up of components, but this is not meant to imply any limit on applications.

The overall reliability of equipment depends on both the reliability of each component and the way they are arranged. If a single component has a reliability of R, putting two identical components in parallel will increase the overall reliability. The assumption is that the second component will only start to operate when the first one fails, and that the system can work adequately with only one of the components operating. Adding more components in parallel increases reliability, as the equipment will only fail when all components fail.

Consider a system of two identical components in parallel with the reliability of each component R, as shown in Figure 7.9. The probability that a component continues normal operations is R, so the probability that it will stop operating during a specified period is $1 - R$. The probability that both components fail is $(1 - R)^2$. The reliability of the system is the probability that at least one of the components is operating which is $1 - (1 - R)^2$. Similarly, the probability that n identical components in parallel will all fail is $(1 - R)^n$, and the reliability of the system is $1 - (1 - R)^n$. It follows that any system of parallel components is more reliable than the individual components.

If components are added in series the reliability of the system is reduced. This is because a system with components in series only works if all separate components are working. Consider two components in series. If the reliability of each is R, the reliability of the two is the probability that both are working, which is R^2. If there are n components in series their reliability is R^n. Thus, a system of components in series is less reliable than the individual components (see Figure 7.10).

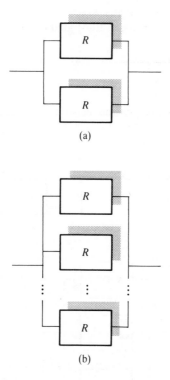

(a)

(b)

Figure 7.9 Reliability of components in parallel. (a) Reliability of two identical components in parallel is $1 - (1 - R)^2$. (b) Reliability of n identical components in parallel is $1 - (1 - R)^n$.

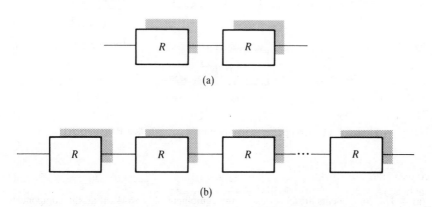

(a)

(b)

Figure 7.10 Reliability of components in series. (a) Reliability of two identical components in series is R^2. (b) Reliability of n identical components in series is R^n.

The reliability of complex systems of components can be found by reducing them to simpler forms, as illustrated in the following worked example.

WORKED EXAMPLE 7.15

Three pieces of equipment can be considered as connected components as shown in Figure 7.11. What is the reliability of each?

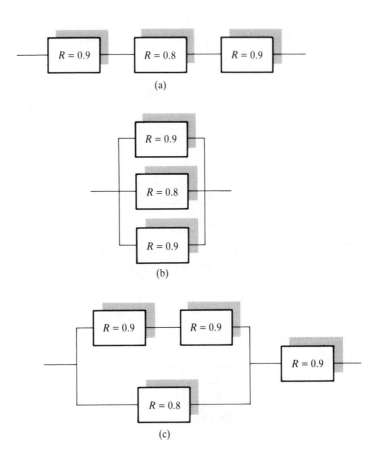

Figure 7.11   Components in equipment for Worked Example 7.15.

SOLUTION

(a)   The components are in series, so the equipment only works if all the components are operating. The probability of this gives the overall reliability of $0.9 * 0.8 * 0.9$ $= 0.648$.

(b)   The components are in parallel, so the equipment fails if all components fail. The probability of this is $(1 - 0.9) * (1 - 0.8) * (1 - 0.9) = 0.002$. Then the overall reliability is the probability that all components do not fail, so that at least one continues to operate, which is $1 - 0.002 = 0.998$.

(c)   The top two components have a combined reliability of $0.9 * 0.9 = 0.81$. This combined component is then in parallel with the bottom component. The probability of both of these failing is $(1 - 0.81) * (1 - 0.8) = 0.038$, so the reliability of these two parts is $1 - 0.038 = 0.962$. This is now in series with the last component, so the overall reliability is $0.962 * 0.9 = 0.866$. The stages in this simplifying process are shown in Figure 7.12.

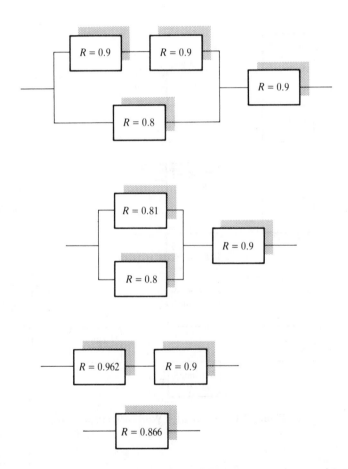

Figure 7.12   Successive stages in simplifying the equipment in Worked Example 7.15.

WORKED EXAMPLE 7.16

Figure 7.13 shows the layout of a shop floor which consists of three parallel production lines A, B and C. When each line is working, their outputs are 10,000, 12,000 and 20,000 units respectively. The diagram shows the reliability of each machine; if a line fails during the week all its production during the week is lost.

(a)   Find the reliability of each line.
(b)   Find the possible outputs from the shop and the probability of each.
(c)   What is the expected average output of the shop?

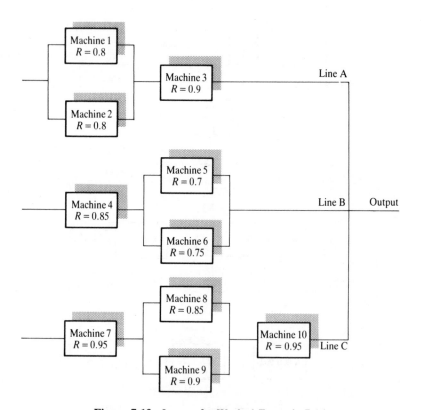

Figure 7.13   Layout for Worked Example 7.16.

SOLUTION

(a)   The first step is to simplify the diagram and find the reliability of each line. If R_i is the probability that machine i continues to function during a week, the reliability of line A is:

$$RA = [1 - (1 - R1) * (1 - R2)] * R3$$
$$= [1 - (0.2 * 0.2)] * 0.9$$
$$= 0.864$$

The reliability of line B is:

$$RB = R4 * [1 - (1 - R5) * (1 - R6)]$$
$$= 0.85 * [1 - (0.3 * 0.25)]$$
$$= 0.786$$

The reliability of line C is:

$$RC = R7 * [1 - (1 - R8) * (1 - R9)] * R10$$
$$= 0.95 * [1 - (0.15 * 0.1)] * 0.95$$
$$= 0.889$$

(b) The total output can be found by taking various combinations of lines failing. If lines A and B fail while line C continues the output will be 20,000. This has a probability of $(1 - RA) * (1 - RB) * RC = 0.136 * 0.214 * 0.889 = 0.026$. Similarly, the other possible values can be calculated as shown in Table 7.7.

Table 7.7

Output	Probability	
0	$(1 - RA) * (1 - RB) * (1 - RC)$	$= 0.003$
10,000	$RA * (1 - RB) * (1 - RC)$	$= 0.021$
12,000	$(1 - RA) * RB * (1 - RC)$	$= 0.012$
20,000	$(1 - RA) * (1 - RB) * RC$	$= 0.026$
22,000	$RA * RB * (1 - RC)$	$= 0.075$
30,000	$RA * (1 - RB) * RC$	$= 0.164$
32,000	$(1 - RA) * RB * RC$	$= 0.095$
42,000	$RA * RB * RC$	$= 0.604$

(c) The average production is from the sum of probabilities times outputs

Expected output $= (0 * 0.003) + (10,000 * 0.021) + (12,000 * 0.012) + \ldots$
$= 35,852$

In summary

The reliability of equipment is the probability that it continues to function normally during the period under investigation. Reliability may be increased by having back-up equipment to take over when there is a breakdown. The overall reliability of a system depends on both the reliability of individual components and the configuration of the system.

SELF ASSESSMENT QUESTIONS

7.21 What is the purpose of routine maintenance?

7.22 Is it likely that maintenance costs for a machine will decline over time?

7.23 When should a machine be replaced:

(a) when it breaks down and can no longer be repaired
(b) when the operating costs rise above the cost of a new machine
(c) when the average annual cost is a minimum
(d) when the operating cost rises above the resale value?

7.24 The optimal age of replacement for a machine has been calculated, with no discounting, to be six years. If future maintenance costs are now raised in line with expected inflation and the calculation is repeated will this:

(a) lower the optimal age of replacement
(b) raise the optimal age of replacement
(c) either lower or raise the optimal age of replacement
(d) have no effect on the optimal age of replacement?

7.25 What is meant by 'reliability'?

7.26 If a number of components are put in parallel is the reliability of a system:

(a) increased
(b) decreased
(c) either increased or decreased?

SUMMARY OF CHAPTER

This chapter looked at ways of describing the performance of a process or operation. There are many measures which can be used, but we concentrated on capacity, productivity, utilization and efficiency.

Capacity measures the maximum output which could be achieved in a specified time. This is sometimes obvious, but generally needs calculating or some agreement. The maximum output of a facility in ideal conditions was defined as the designed capacity, while the maximum output under normal circumstances was the effective capacity. These allowed more precise definitions of efficiency and utilization.

A major aim of organizations is to improve productivity. The chapter mentioned some general trends in productivity. It then gave a detailed definition of productivity, which could be either total, partial factor or multi-factor.

We described how an important objective of capacity planning is to match available capacity to forecast demand. This is essentially a strategic function, but has aspects of both tactical and operational planning. In particular, strategic capacity planning sets the long-term capacity, while shorter term mismatches between capacity and demand can be overcome by either demand management or capacity management. Central questions in capacity planning are when to change capacity and by how much. These decisions should include factors like discrete changes in capacity and economies of scale.

A problem for long-term planning is that capacity changes over time. Two specific reasons for this were described. The effect of learning curves is to reduce the time needed for an operation as the number of repetitions increases. Conversely, equipment declines with age and its efficiency is reduced. This may be offset by routine maintenance or replacement. In either case the best time for action can be calculated. An associated problem calculates the reliability of equipment.

PROBLEMS

7.1   Coffee machines in a works' canteen are designed to serve up to 2000 cups of coffee in a two-hour meal break. During a typical break they were used for 90 minutes and served 1000 cups. How could their performance be measured?

7.2   A family doctor sees patients for an average of 10 minutes each. There is an additional five minutes of paperwork associated with each visit, so appointments are made at 15-minute intervals. Each surgery lasts for five hours a day, but during one surgery the doctor was called away for an emergency which lasted an hour. Four patients who had appointments during this time were told to come back later. How could the doctor's performance in the surgery be measured?

7.3   A ski lift consists of pairs of chairs pulled on a continuous wire from the bottom of a ski run to the top. Ordinarily one pair of chairs arrives at the bottom of the slope every three seconds. If the lift works 10 hours a day for 100 days a year, what is its designed capacity? On a typical day 10% of users need help getting on the lift, and they cause average delays of 10 seconds. A further 25% of people using the lift are alone, and only one chair of the pair is used. What is the utilization of the lift?

7.4   In two consecutive years a process had the following characteristics.

	Year 1	Year 2
Number of units made	5,000	6,500
Raw materials used	15,000 kg	17,500 kg
Cost of raw materials	£40,000	£50,500
Hours worked	1,200	1,500
Direct labour costs	£12,000	£18,000
Energy used	20,000 kW.h	24,000 kW.h
Energy cost	£2,000	£3,000

How has the productivity changed?

7.5 A service organization tries to deal with 100 customers a day. Each person in the organization can see three customers an hour, but has to do associated paperwork which takes an average of 40 minutes a customer. Employees also lose about 20% of their time when they do other things and cannot deal with customers' work. The standard working day in the organization is from 0900 to 1600 five days a week, with an hour off for lunch. How many employees should the organization hire, and what is their utilization? One week the organization only dealt with 90 customers. What were the resulting efficiency and utilization?

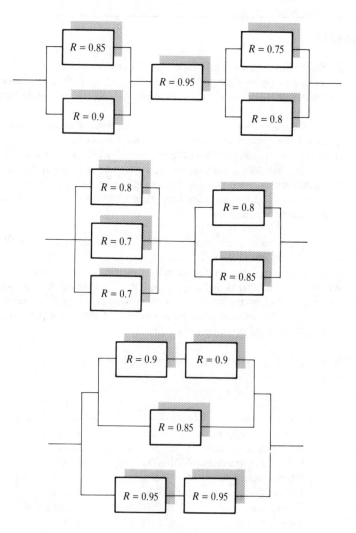

Figure 7.14 Layout of components for Problem 7.10.

7.6 The fixed cost of a process is £110,000, and the capacity can be increased by using more machines at a cost of £55,000 each. The total output of the operation, measured in some consistent units, is:

Machines	1	2	3	4	5	6	7	8
Output	55	125	230	310	375	435	460	470

What number of machines would give lowest unit cost?

7.7 It takes 25 minutes to make the first unit of a product. How long will it take to make each of the next nine units with a learning rate of 0.9?

7.8 New cars cost a company £12,000 each, with resale values and maintenance costs shown below. What is the optimal age of replacement?

Age of car (years)	1	2	3	4	5	6
Resale value	8000	5000	3000	2000	1200	600
Annual maintenance	1000	1200	1500	2000	3000	8750

7.9 What is the optimal age of replacement for the cars in Problem 7.8 if a discounting rate of 1% a month is used?

7.10 What are the reliabilities of the sets of components shown in Figure 7.14?

CASE STUDY – RAVENSTONE HOTEL

The Ravenstone Hotel was built six years ago on the sea front at Scarborough. It has 105 rooms and its guests are a combination of people staying on business and on holiday. During the peak months of June and July, the hotel is fully booked and has to turn away potential customers. Conversely, during quieter months there are a lot of empty rooms and the hotel tries to encourage business.

The hotel has a considerable range of rates, depending on the season, the days, length of stay, number of people sharing a room, whether they use group bookings, conference rates, senior citizens' discounts, weekend specials, and so on. The average number of people in a room is 1.5, and the total income from room bookings in 1990 was £1,290,000. About 60% of this was spent on direct operating costs.

The other main source of income for the hotel is its restaurant. This is open for breakfast, morning coffee, lunch, afternoon tea and dinner. All of these are designed as a service to guests and just cover costs, with the exception of the evening dinner. This is very popular and runs at a profit. A small survey suggested that about half the people who stay in the hotel plan to eat dinner in the restaurant. It is often difficult to get a table at a convenient time and guests change their plans, so only about 40% of guests actually eat dinner there. Throughout the year it is estimated that 30% of people eating in the restaurant are guests, and the remaining 70% are visitors. There is a limit to the number of people who can eat dinner in an evening, and this is currently about 160, depending on the exact composition of parties.

Again, it is difficult to suggest a typical meal cost, but in 1990 the total income from the restaurant was £800,000 from food and £530,000 from the bar service. Rough estimates suggest that 40% of the average bill for food is spent directly on buying and preparing the food, 25% of the average bar bill is spent on buying and preparing drinks, and about 10% of both bills is needed to cover miscellaneous operating costs.

The management of the hotel is now considering expansion, based on the increasing numbers of guests, the number of enquiries being turned away, and the overcrowding of the restaurant. To justify the expansion the following figures have been collected.

Year	Number of guest-nights
1985	10,200
1986	13,100
1987	18,800
1988	24,900
1989	28,800
1990	33,300

Month	Average rooms per night		
	1988	1989	1990
January	31	36	42
February	12	17	25
March	23	29	36
April	41	48	61
May	76	85	92
June	105	105	105
July	98	104	105
August	52	78	103
September	43	59	70
October	12	17	24
November	10	14	23
December	39	39	40

Some figures were also collected for a small sample of days to see how many enquiries had to be turned away. There is no way of saying if these figures are typical or not.

| | Number turned away per day | |
Month	Hotel	Restaurant
January	1	6
May	3	12
July	30	36
August	24	41
November	2	8

Three alternative expansions are possible, each of which is largely independent of the others.

(1) When the hotel was built the top floor was never completed. This could now be finished, making 30 more rooms. The capital cost of these would amount to £375,000, with additional fixed costs of £65,000. Operating costs would rise by about £55,000 a year.

(2) An additional wing could be added to the hotel, adding 60 more rooms. The capital cost of these would be £850,000, with additional fixed costs of £150,000. Operating costs would rise by about £100,000 a year.

(3) An extension to the restaurant. This could either be a major extension to add 160 diners a night, or a smaller extension to add 80 diners a night. The larger expansion has total capital costs of £600,000 and additional operating costs of £250,000 a year. The smaller expansion has total capital costs of £450,000 and additional operating costs of £150,000 a year.

Suggested questions

- What are the current capacities of the hotel and restaurant?
- How might the hotel cope with widely varying demand during the year?
- What are the likely demands for rooms and dinners in the future?
- Which, if any, expansions should the hotel management consider?

SOLUTIONS TO SELF ASSESSMENT QUESTIONS

7.1 There are many possible measures, based on actual performance, effectiveness, efficiency and morale. We concentrated on capacity, productivity, utilization and efficiency to describe actual performance.

7.2 Capacity is the maximum amount of a product that can be processed within a specified time; utilization measures the proportion of available capacity that is actually used; productivity is the amount produced in relation to one or more of the resources used; efficiency is the ratio of actual output to effective capacity.

7.3 Yes, if the efficiency decreases.

7.4 **(b)** Maximum amount of processing available in some period.

7.5 Designed capacity is the maximum output in ideal circumstances, while effective capacity is the maximum output that can be expected under normal circumstances.

7.6 **(a)** Passengers per trip; **(b)** customers per performance; **(c)** games per day; **(d)** cases per week.

7.7 In decreasing order, they are designed capacity, effective capacity and actual output.

7.8 Designed capacity = $6 * 8 * 10 * 330 =$ 158,400 units a year. Utilization = $100,000/158,400 = 0.631$. The difference is due to a combination of planned circumstances (maintenance period, set-ups, etc.) and unplanned ones (breakdowns, shortage of materials, etc.).

7.9 Total productivity measures the ratio of total output to total input, partial factor productivity measures the output for a single input and multi-factor productivity measures the output for a subset of inputs.

7.10 Yes.

7.11 **(b)** This productivity has fallen.

7.12 Demand management and capacity management.

7.13 Examine forecast demand and translate this into a capacity requirement, calculate available capacity, identify mismatches between capacity required and available, generate alternative plans for overcoming any mismatch, evaluate these plans and select the best.

7.14 High utilizations come when capacity and demand are closely matched. This cannot be done when demand is continuous, but capacity is discrete.

7.15 When to expand (or contract) and by how much to expand (or contract)?

7.16 Spread of fixed costs over more units and use of more efficient processes.

7.17 No, there may be no economies or even diseconomies of scale.

7.18 If the first operation takes T, the second takes $0.8 * T$, the fourth takes $0.8^2 * T$, the eighth takes $0.8^3 * T$, and so on.

7.19 No.

7.20 Experience and practice make jobs easier, short cuts are found, skills increase, routines are known, and so on.

7.21 To stop the performance of equipment falling below an acceptable level (with timing to minimize costs).

7.22 No.

7.23 **(c)** When the average cost per year is minimized.

7.24 **(a)** Lower the optimal age.

7.25 The probability that a part continues to operate throughout a period.

7.26 **(a)** Increased.

REFERENCES FOR FURTHER READING

Adam E.E., Hershauer J.G. and Ruch W.A. (1981). *Productivity and Quality: Measurement as a Basis for Improvement* Englewood Cliffs: Prentice-Hall

Chen G.K.C. and McGarrah R.E. (1982). *Productivity Management: Text and Cases* Hinsdale: The Dryden Press

Freidenfelds J. (1981). *Capacity Expansions: Analysis of Simple Models with Applications* New York: Elsevier North-Holland

Griffin J.M. (1971). *Capacity Measurement in Petroleum Refining* Lexington: Heath Lexington Books

Hayes R.H. and Wheelwright S.C. (1984). *Restoring our Competitive Edge: Competing through Manufacturing* New York: John Wiley

Huettner D. (1974). *Plant Size, Technological Change, and Investment Requirements* New York: Praeger

Manne A.S. (ed.) (1967). *Investments for Capacity Expansion: Size, Location and Time Phasing* Cambridge: MIT Press

Morris W.T. (1967). *The Capacity Decision System* Homewood: Richard Irwin

Reed R. (1961). *Plant Layout, Factors, Principles and Techniques* Homewood: Richard Irwin

Sink D.S. (1985). *Productivity Management: Planning, Evaluation, Control and Improvement* New York: John Wiley

Tomkins J.A. and White J.A. (1984). *Facilities Planning* New York: John Wiley

Wild R. (1980). *Operations Management* Oxford: Pergamon Press

Chapter 8

Planning and scheduling

SYNOPSIS

In the last few chapters we have looked at a number of strategic decisions for operations management. In particular, Chapter 7 described one such decision, which was capacity planning. This tries to match available capacity with forecast demand. Although capacity planning is essentially a strategic function, there are tactical and operational aspects. In this chapter we are going to look at some of these.

Once strategic decisions about capacity have been made they set the scene for lower levels of planning. We will describe this planning in terms of aggregate plans, master schedules and short-term schedules. Generating and evaluating such plans can be a complex procedure which needs many iterations before a satisfactory solution is found. In other words an initial plan is designed, evaluated and then repeatedly adjusted until it is acceptable.

Aggregate planning translates the forecast demand and capacity plans into production schedules for families of products for, typically, each of the next few months. An aim is to meet demand while keeping production reasonably constant. Such plans can be designed in a number of ways, but the most useful are based on intuition, graphs of cumulative supply and demand, or a matrix approach. These are convenient and easy to use, but generally rely on the skills of individual planners. Mathematical models can be used (generally based on linear programming formulations) but there are problems incorporating the complexity of real situations.

The next stage of planning is to break down aggregate plans into master schedules. These show more details, particularly a timetable for production of individual products. The methods of designing a master plan are similar in principle to the methods of aggregate planning.

The final step in planning is short-term scheduling, which designs very detailed plans for individual jobs and equipment. There are several methods for this, but the most common rely on simple scheduling rules. Several of these are described to achieve different objectives. The same principles can be applied to scheduling operators.

The chapter ends with some comments on how plans can be maintained and controlled.

OBJECTIVES

After reading this chapter and completing the exercises you should be able to:

- discuss the different levels at which planning occurs;
- define capacity plan, aggregate plan, master schedule and short-term schedules;
- discuss the factors that make planning complicated;
- describe an iterative planning process;
- use updating procedures for schedules;
- appreciate the purpose of aggregate planning;
- use graphical and matrix methods for aggregate planning;
- outline a linear programming formulation for aggregate planning;
- appreciate the purpose of a master schedule;
- design a master schedule from aggregate plans;
- appreciate the purpose of short-term scheduling;
- use a variety of scheduling rules;
- discuss the control of schedules.

8.1 HIERARCHY OF PLANNING DECISIONS

8.1.1 Introduction

In the last chapter we discussed how capacity planning attempts to match available capacity and forecast demand. This match should be as close as possible. If there is spare capacity, resources are not being used as efficiently as possible; if there is a shortage of capacity, some demand is not being met.

Capacity planning is essentially a strategic function with implications in the long term. Capacity might be increased by building more facilities, recruiting more staff, changing the process to use higher technology, increasing capital investment, and so on. Reducing capacity might involve closing facilities, laying off staff, selling equipment, and so on. These are essentially strategic decisions.

Even when the long-term capacity is set at some defined level, it may be necessary to make short-term adjustments. There are a number of ways of doing this, such as rescheduling maintenance periods, working overtime, using subcontractors, using an appointment system, and so on. The implication is that capacity planning is essentially strategic, but there are other aspects that are both tactical and operational. As an illustration, the capacity of a manufacturing process might be increased by building another factory. This is a strategic capacity decision. While this factory is being built, capacity might be increased by leasing additional space. This is a tactical decision. While the leased space is being prepared, overtime may be worked at weekends. This is an operational decision.

Once long-term decisions have been made about capacity, a series of tactical decisions can be made about resources. These in turn allow a set of operational decisions about schedules. In this chapter we will follow this sequence starting with capacity planning and moving down the hierarchy of decisions through to operational scheduling.

In summary

Capacity planning is essentially a strategic function, but there are tactical and operational aspects to it. Strategic capacity plans start a sequence of planning which looks at operations in increasingly more detail.

8.1.2 Definition of planning levels

Strategic capacity plans set the overall capacity of an operation. This is followed by a hierarchy of decisions about how this capacity can best be used and what short-term adjustments are needed. There is some disagreement about the terms used to describe the various stages in this hierarchy of plans, but we will consider the distinct steps as follows.

(1) *Aggregate plans*, which show the overall production planned for families of products, typically by month.

(2) *Master schedules*, which show a detailed timetable of production for individual products, typically by week.

(3) *Short-term schedules*, which show the detailed allocation of jobs to equipment, typically by day.

Then we can summarize the overall planning process as follows.

An organization's mission leads to strategic decisions about what to make, where to make it, how to make it, and so on. These are transformed into capacity plans, which try to match long-term forecast demand with available capacity. These capacity plans lead to medium-term aggregate plans which might, typically, show planned monthly production for families of products over the next year or so. This aggregate plan is broken down to give the master schedule, which shows a timetable for the production of individual products, perhaps by week. In turn, the master schedule is broken down into short-term schedules, which list the jobs to be done on all equipment, probably by day (see Figure 8.1).

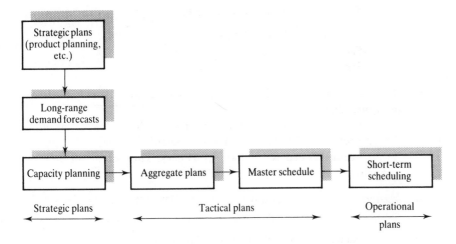

Figure 8.1 Hierarchy of plans.

In a manufacturing context the sequence of decisions might be as follows. A company's mission describes what industry it is in, and then a strategic decision is to make a certain product for the next few years, with long-term forecasts suggesting annual demands. Capacity planning is then needed to see how many of the products can be made in each factory in each year, with necessary adjustments to match capacity with demand. The overall capacity plan is then broken down into an aggregate plan to see how many of the products are to be made each month in each factory, taking into account factors such as current stocks, availability of manpower, machines, and so on. This monthly aggregate plan is then broken down into master schedules to show the number of products of each specific type to be made in each week. The weekly master schedule is then broken down into short-term schedules to show daily timetables of machines, operators and other equipment assigned to each product.

This process can be illustrated by a specific example of a company which makes a series of 'tools' in three factories. Its series of decisions is as follows.

(1) *Strategic plans*: making the fundamental decisions.
   The company plans to make tools for the next few years, with associated decisions about how they are made, and so on. It plans to continue operations in three factories A, B and C.

(2) *Capacity plans*: examine long-term forecasts and make adjustments to match capacity to these.
   Long-term forecasts suggest sales of 5000 tools a year. There is a shortage of capacity of 1000 tools a year. A decision is made to overcome this by increasing the staff in Factory C and working two shifts at Factory B.

327

This allows forecast demand to be met by:

Factory A making 1000 tools a year.
Factory B making 2000 tools a year.
Factory C making 2000 tools a year.

(3)   *Aggregate plan*: breaks down the capacity plans into monthly plans for individual facilities.

Factory A makes 100 tools in January. This needs a staff of 100 and achieves 90% utilization of equipment.

Factory B makes 250 tools in January. This needs 200 staff and achieves 85% utilization of equipment, and so on.

(4)   *Master schedule:* breaks down aggregate plans into weekly plans for individual products.

Factory A. Week 1 of January 10 alpha tools
5 beta tools
10 super tools
Week 2 of January   5 alpha tools
25 super tools
Week 3 of January 10 alpha tools
10 super tools
and so on.

(5)   *Short-term schedules*: breaks down master schedule into daily timetable for individual batches of tools and equipment.

Factory A. Week 1 of January
Monday morning shift
1 alpha tool on machines 1 to 4
1 super tool on machines 5 to 8
then 1 beta tool on machines 1 to 8
Monday afternoon shift
2 beta tools on machines 1 to 8
Tuesday morning shift
1 alpha tool on machines 1 to 4
1 beta tool on machines 5 to 8
then 1 super tool on machines 1 to 8
and so on.

In the rest of this chapter we will look at some specific methods of planning and scheduling. In particular, we will make some general points about the planning process and illustrate these by reference to aggregate planning. Because the design of the master schedule is, at least in principle, similar, we will spend less time on this. Later we will look in more detail at short-term scheduling.

In summary
Capacity planning is one step in a hierarchy of plans, and is followed by the increasingly detailed aggregate plans, master schedule and short-term schedules.

8.1 Capacity planning is a purely strategic function. Is this statement true?

8.2 What is the sequence of steps in planning?

8.3 Which types of plan are likely to refer to:

(a) individual locations
(b) individual products
(c) individual equipment?

8.2 THE PLANNING PROCESS

8.2.1 Overall procedure

In the last chapter we described the stages in capacity planning as:

- examine forecast demand and translate this into a capacity requirement
- calculate the availability of present facilities
- identify mismatches between capacity requirement and projected availability
- generate alternative plans for overcoming any mismatch
- evaluate alternative plans and select the best.

This procedure is sometimes referred to as resource requirement planning. We can illustrate the general procedure by the following example.

WORKED EXAMPLE 8.1

A coach operator plans its capacity in terms of 'coach days'. It classifies its business according to 'full day', which are long distance journeys, or 'half day', which are shorter runs. Forecasts show expected annual demands for the next two years to average 400,000 full-day passengers and 750,000 half-day passengers. The company has 61 coaches, each with an effective capacity of 40 passengers a day for 300 days a year. Breakdowns and other unexpected problems reduce efficiency to 90%. The company employs 86 drivers who work an average of 220 days a year, but illness and other absences reduce their efficiency to 85%. If there is a shortage of coaches the company can buy extra ones for £110,000 or hire them for £100 a day. If there is a shortage of drivers the company can recruit extra ones at a total cost of £20,000 a year, or hire them from an agency for £110 a day. How should the company approach its capacity planning?

SOLUTION

Following the stages listed above, we can start by translating the forecast demand into capacity requirements. 400,000 full-day passengers are equivalent to 400,000/40 = 10,000 coach days a year, or 10,000/300 = 33.33 coaches. 750,000 half-day passengers are equivalent to 750,000/(40 * 300 * 2) = 31.25 coaches. Thus the total demand is 64.58 coaches. Each coach needs 300/220 drivers, so the company needs a total of 88.06 drivers.

The next stage is to calculate the capacity of existing resources. The company has 61 coaches, but the efficiency of 90% makes an availability of 61 * 0.9 = 54.9 coaches. There are 86 drivers, but an efficiency of 85% reduces availability to 86 * 0.85 = 73.1 drivers.

Now we know both requirements and availability, so we can identify any mismatch. Without details of the timing we can only take overall figures, so there is a total shortage of 64.58 − 54.9 = 9.68 coaches and 88.06 − 73.1 = 14.96 drivers.

The next stage is to generate alternative plans for eliminating the mismatch. In this case the alternatives are either to buy or hire coaches, and employ or take temporary drivers. The only information we have to evaluate these alternatives are some costs.

To buy 10 coaches would cost £1,100,000. To hire coaches to make up the shortage would cost 9.68 * 300 * 100 = £290,400 a year. There is, of course, the other alternative of buying some coaches and hiring a smaller number. We do not have enough information to make the final decisions, but a reasonable solution would go along the line of buying eight coaches and making up any shortages by hiring (that is, short-term capacity adjustments).

Similarly, to hire 15 drivers would cost £300,000 a year, while using temporary drivers from an agency would cost 14.96 * 220 * 110 = £362,032 a year. There is also the option of hiring some drivers, say 13, and making up any shortages by hiring (again short-term capacity adjustments).

This approach is typical of the planning process. At each stage the requirements are compared with availability, and any mismatches noted. Then alternative plans are generated to achieve the requirements and overcome any mismatch, these are evaluated and the best is chosen and implemented. This sets the scene for the next stages of planning.

The generation and evaluation of alternative plans can be quite compli-cated. Plans are rarely simple, and there is usually a range of competing objectives and many non-quantifiable factors to consider. A more realistic view of planning would replace the single procedure described by an iterative process, which keeps modifying proposed plans until a satisfactory one is found. The process then becomes:

(1) assess requirements and availability and propose a plan for overcoming mismatches;

(2) assess the plan and identify defects (perhaps broken constraints or unmet objectives);

(3)   revise the plan to overcome these defects;

(4)   repeat stages 2 and 3 until a satisfactory plan is found.

This procedure is illustrated in Figure 8.2. The diagram also shows that the planning process does not end, but is continuous. As plans for each period are finalized and implemented, planning starts for the next period. This allows current plans to form the basis for future plans, ensuring stability and continuity in operations.

This iterative procedure recognizes that a 'satisfactory' solution is difficult to define (often based on experience, compromise between conflicting objectives, subjective evaluation, and so on). This is primarily because of the large number of factors that have to be considered. We have said that these plans are based on a desire to match capacity and demand, but there are many other factors, such as:

- Operations
     machine capacity
     stable production
     new equipment planned
     use of subcontractors
     productivity

- Materials
     availability of raw materials
     inventory policies
     current inventory levels
     constraints on storage

- Finance
     information on costs
     financing arrangements
     exchange rates
     economic climate

- Human resources
     workforce levels
     levels of skills and productivity
     unemployment rates
     hiring and training

- Marketing
     reliability of forecasts
     competition
     new product
     product substitution

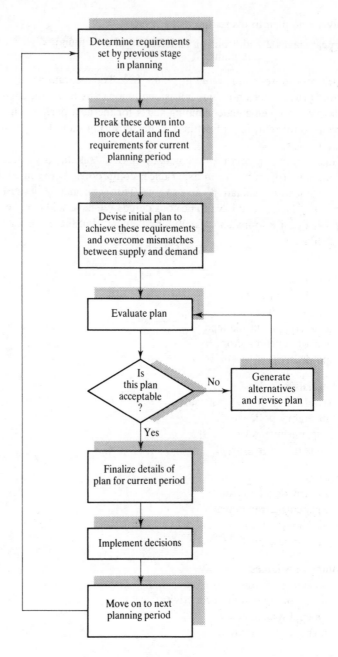

Figure 8.2 Iterative planning process.

Finding a satisfactory balance between such factors is often difficult, and the iterative planning procedure may be repeated many times until a proposed plan gets general agreement.

In summary
An overall planning procedure takes the requirements from the previous stage of planning, devises detailed plans to achieve these, evaluates these plans and selects the best. In practice this is usually an iterative procedure, with plans repeatedly updated to take into account various factors.

8.2.2 Updating procedures

An important point in the matching of supply and demand is the role of stock. Stocks of a product are used to give a buffer, so that production during a period need not exactly match forecast demand in the period. The demand can be met from three internal sources:

- from stocks already held at the beginning of the period;
- from production during the period;
- from future production with late delivery.

If we define $S(T)$ as the stock level at the end of period T, $P(T)$ as the production in period T and $D(T)$ as the demand. Then:

$$\begin{array}{cccc}
\text{Stock at end} & \text{Stock at} & \text{Production} & \text{Demand met} \\
\text{of this} & = \text{end of last} + \text{during this} - & \text{during this} \\
\text{period} & \text{period} & \text{period} & \text{period}
\end{array}$$

$$S(T) = S(T - 1) + P(T) - D(T)$$

This assumes there are no back orders, where some demand in one period is met by production from the following period. If we take this into account we have:

$$S(T) = S(T - 1) + P(T) - D(T) - B(T - 1) + B(T)$$

where $B(T)$ is the number of back orders in period T which are met from production in period $T + 1$.

The process of planning, then, is based on an assessment of existing stock levels, planned production and acceptable late deliveries. The mix adopted should minimize the organization's overall costs, maximize its overall profit, or optimize some other measure of performance.

WORKED EXAMPLE 8.2

Demand for a product over the next eight months has been forecast as follows.

Month	1	2	3	4	5	6	7	8
Demand	15	25	25	30	40	40	25	20

A minimum of 10 units are kept in stock, and no back orders are permitted. There are currently 35 units in stock and production is in batches of 50, with a very short lead time. Devise a production plan to satisfy the demand.

SOLUTION

We can do the calculations for this in Table 8.1.

Table 8.1

Month	1	2	3	4	5	6	7	8	9
Stock at beginning	35	20	45	20	40	50	10	35	15
Demand	15	25	25	30	40	40	25	20	
Production	0	50	0	50	50	0	50	0	
Stock at end	20	45	20	40	50	10	35	15	

At the beginning of the first month there are 35 units in stock and demand during the month is 15. Thus no production is needed and the stock at the end of the month is $35 - 15 = 20$. This stock of 20 is available at the beginning of the next month, when demand is 25. A batch of 50 units is made, so that stock at the end of the month is $20 + 50 - 25 = 45$.

As there must be at least 10 units left in stock, a batch of 50 is made whenever the stock at the beginning of a month minus demand in the month is less than 10. This procedure continues for subsequent months.

The production plan shown is only one alternative. Many others are possible, and they should each be evaluated before a final choice is made.

The procedure illustrated in Worked Example 8.2 can be used for planning other resources. If, for example, we replace stock levels by employees we can do some manpower planning.

$$\begin{array}{c}\text{Number}\\\text{employed}\\\text{in current}\\\text{month}\end{array} = \begin{array}{c}\text{Number}\\\text{employed}\\\text{last}\\\text{month}\end{array} - \begin{array}{c}\text{Dismissals and}\\\text{resignations at}\\\text{end of last}\\\text{month}\end{array} + \begin{array}{c}\text{New hires}\\\text{at beginning}\\\text{of current}\\\text{month}\end{array}$$

Similarly we could find the availability of any other resource.

In summary

The current availability of a resource can be found by updating the availability during the last period. This is particularly useful for products that are kept in stock.

8.4 Where do the initial requirements for a planning period come from?

8.5 A planning process starts off with general plans, and these are looked at in increasing detail at each consecutive stage of planning. Is this statement true?

8.6 How do updating planning procedures work?

8.3 AGGREGATE PLANNING

8.3.1 Introduction

Aggregate plans and master schedules bridge the gap between strategic capacity plans and operational details. This section considers aggregate plans, and the following section looks at master schedules.

Aggregate planning takes the forecast demand and capacity, and translates this into production plans for each family of products for, typically, each of the next few months. The aggregate plan only looks at the production of families of products and is not concerned with individual products. A knitwear manufacturer, for example, may produce many different styles, colours and sizes of jumpers and skirts. The aggregate plan only shows the total production of jumpers and the total production of skirts. It does not look in any more detail at the production of a particular style, colour or size. Aggregate plans will look at the total number of barrels to be produced, or books to be printed, but not the number of barrels of each chemical or the number of volumes of each title.

Aggregate planning assumes the long-term demand has been forecast, and that capacity plans allow this to be met. Now the forecast demand and capacity plan are transformed into an aggregate plan which considers questions like the following:

- Should production be kept at a constant level or changed with demand?
- Should stocks be used to meet changing demand (producing stock during periods of low demand and using stocks during periods of high demand)?
- Should subcontractors be used for peak demands?
- Should the size of the workforce change with demand?
- How can work patterns be changed to meet changing demand?
- Should prices be changed?
- Are shortages allowed (perhaps with late delivery)?
- Can demand be smoothed?

One of the most important questions is how much variation is allowed in the aggregate plan. The usual answer to this is as little as possible. There are distinct advantages in maintaining stable production, including:

- planning is easier;
- flow of products is smoother;
- there are fewer problems with changes;
- larger lot sizes reduce costs;
- stocks can be reduced (as there is less variation);
- throughput can be faster;
- quality is more reliable;
- floor space may be reduced;
- experience with a product reduces problems;
  and so on.

We could suggest, then, that an objective of aggregate planning is to devise medium-term schedules for families of products which:

- allow all demands to be met;
- keep production relatively stable;
- keep within the constraints of the capacity plan;
- meet any other specific objectives and constraints.

The final output for aggregate planning is a schedule of production for each family of products, typically for each of the next few months.

There are four main approaches for achieving this which can be classified as:

- intuitive
- graphical
- matrix
- mathematical model.

These are described below.

In summary

Aggregate planning transforms the forecast demand and capacity plans into medium-term schedules for families of products. It tries to find ways of meeting demands, while maintaining stable production and satisfying any other specific constraints and objectives.

SELF ASSESSMENT QUESTIONS

8.7 What period would a typical aggregate plan cover?

8.8 What are the main inputs for aggregate planning?

8.9 Aggregate plans show detailed production by individual product. Is this statement true?

8.10 What is the main output of aggregate planning?

8.3.2 Intuitive approach

Like most plans, aggregate plans are not usually designed from scratch, but will be variations on previous plans: next month's production will probably be similar to last month's. The simplest approach to aggregate planning, then, is to use an experienced planner to review the current situation and, in the light of experiences with similar plans, produce updated ones. In practice, this is the most widely used approach.

Unfortunately, the intuitive approach can give results which are of variable and uncertain quality, they may take a long time to produce, may include bias, and so on. The benefit of the approach is that it is very convenient and easy to use. The process is well understood, and experts can give credible results which are trusted by the organization. This benefit has been reduced in recent years since the availability of simple computer packages. None the less, a skilled planner (perhaps assisted by a spreadsheet package) can give very good results at low cost.

WORKED EXAMPLE 8.3

The aggregate, monthly demand for a family of products is shown below. If this is the only information available, suggest a monthly production schedule for the products.

	January	February	March	April	May	June	July
Aggregate demand	80	70	60	120	180	150	110

SOLUTION

We should usually aim for a stable production rate. Thus, in the absence of any further information, we could suggest a steady production at a rate equal to the average demand of 110. During the first three months the demand will be less than supply, so stocks will rise, but these will be used during the following months (see Table 8.2).

Table 8.2

	January	February	March	April	May	June	July
Demand	80	70	60	120	180	150	110
Production	110	110	110	110	110	110	110
Stock at month end	30	70	120	110	40	0	0

The stock at the end of each month is equal to the stock at the end of the previous month plus the excess of production over demand in the current month.

$$\text{Stock at month end} = \text{Stock at end of last month} + \text{Production} - \text{Demand}$$

An obvious disadvantage of this plan is the high stock levels. If we had more information about costs, stock holding policies, materials supply, availability of workforce and so on we could probably make some improvements.

In summary

Intuitive approaches to aggregate planning are widely used. They have the advantages of being convenient and easy to use, but have several disadvantages, including variable quality.

8.3.3 Graphical approach

The second approach to aggregate planning is to use a graphical or charting method. The most popular form of this is based on a graph of cumulative demand over some appropriate time period. Then an aggregate plan is drawn as a line of cumulative supply. The usual objective is to get the cumulative supply line nearly straight (implying constant production) and as close as possible to the cumulative demand line. The difference between the two lines shows the level of mismatch:

- if at any point the cumulative demand line is below the cumulative supply line, there has been excess production which is accumulated as stock;

- if the cumulative demand line is above the cumulative supply line, there has been insufficient production and some demand has not been met.

Graphical approaches have the advantages that they are easy to use and understand. Their limitations, though, are that optimal solutions are not guaranteed, sometimes very poor solutions are found, and the planning may take some time. Effectively, the method still relies on the skills of a planner.

WORKED EXAMPLE 8.4

The forecast monthly demand for a family of products is shown below. At the end of each month the performance is evaluated, and a notional holding cost of £10 is assigned to every unit held in stock. Any shortages are satisfied by back orders, but each unit of shortage is assigned a notional cost of £100 for lost profit, goodwill and future sales. Each time the production rate is changed it costs £10,000. The designed capacity for the products is 400 units a month, but maximum utilization is generally around 75% of this. The company wants to spend less than £1900 a month on these activities. Devise an aggregate plan for the products.

Month	1	2	3	4	5	6	7	8	9
Aggregate demand	280	320	260	160	120	100	60	100	130

SOLUTION

The designed capacity is 400 units a month, but utilization is generally around 75%, so we should assume a maximum production of $400 * 0.75 = 300$ a month. The company should aim for stable production, and this is particularly important here as changes are very expensive. A first step, then, would be to suggest constant production equal to the average demand of 170 a month. The cumulative demand and supply are then shown in Figure 8.3.

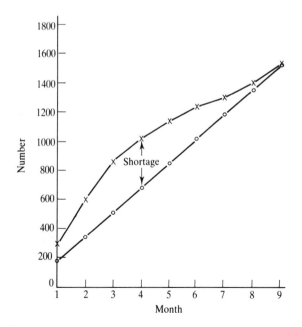

Figure 8.3 Initial aggregate plan for Worked Example 8.4: × demand; ○ supply.

Unfortunately, the cumulative demand line is always above the cumulative supply and there are continuous shortages. We can calculate the total cost of these shortages from Table 8.3.

Table 8.3

Month	1	2	3	4	5	6	7	8	9
Aggregate demand	280	320	260	160	120	100	60	100	130
Cumulative demand	280	600	860	1020	1140	1240	1300	1400	1530
Supply	170	170	170	170	170	170	170	170	170
Cumulative supply	170	340	510	680	850	1020	1190	1360	1530
Shortage in month	90	260	350	340	290	220	110	40	0

Shortage in the month shows the excess of cumulative demand over cumulative supply. The total cost of this plan is due to shortages and is found by adding the total shortages and multiplying this by £100, that is, 1700 * 100 = £170,000. This is considerably above the company target of £1900 a month or a total of £17,100.

Although changing the production rate is expensive, it will be worth while to reduce the shortages found in the initial plan. As demand is heavy in the first three months we might try increasing supply by running the process at its maximum output of 300 units a month. The total demand to be met from production in the remaining months is (1530 − 3 * 300) = 630 for the next six months, averaging 105 a month. Then a reasonable production plan is 300 for the first three months and 105 for the next six months. The cumulative graph of supply and demand is shown in Figure 8.4. There is clearly a close match and we would hope for substantial cost reductions (see Table 8.4).

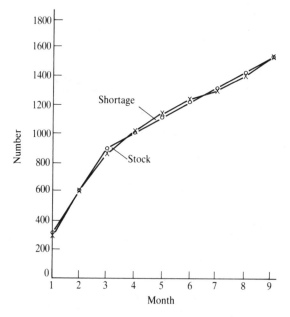

Figure 8.4 Modified aggregate plan for Worked Example 8.4: × demand; ○ supply.

Table 8.4

Month	1	2	3	4	5	6	7	8	9
Aggregate demand	280	320	260	160	120	100	60	100	130
Cumulative demand	280	600	860	1020	1140	1240	1300	1400	1530
Supply	300	300	300	105	105	105	105	105	105
Cumulative supply	300	600	900	1005	1110	1215	1320	1425	1530
Stock at month end	20	0	40	0	0	0	20	25	0
Shortage in month	0	0	0	15	30	25	0	0	0

If cumulative supply is greater than cumulative demand, this shows as a stock at the end of the month. If cumulative demand is greater than cumulative supply, this shows as a shortage in the month. The cost of this plan is found from:

Stock holding	$105 * 10$	$= 1050$
Shortage	$70 * 100$	$= 7000$
Production Change	$1 * 10,000$	$= 10,000$

This gives a total cost of £18,050 or over £2,000 a month. This is certainly an improvement but still does not meet the company target. We must try another iteration with some adjustment to the plan. Shortages still give high costs, so we could try maintaining production at 300 units for another month. Then production in the remaining months is $(1530 - 4 * 300)/5 = 66$ (see Table 8.5).

Table 8.5

Month	1	2	3	4	5	6	7	8	9
Aggregate demand	280	320	260	160	120	100	60	100	130
Cumulative demand	280	600	860	1020	1140	1240	1300	1400	1530
Supply	300	300	300	300	66	66	66	66	66
Cumulative supply	300	600	900	1200	1266	1332	1398	1464	1530
Stock at month end	20	0	40	180	126	92	98	64	0

With this plan there are no shortages, so costs are:

Stock holding	$620 * 10$	$= 6200$
Production change	$1 * 10,000$	$= 10,000$

This total of £16,200 (or £1,800 a month) is within the company target and we could leave this as our final aggregate plan. If necessary, more solutions could be tried, and we could continue making adjustments to the plan until a satisfactory solution is found (see Figure 8.5).

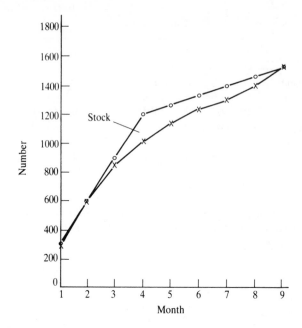

Figure 8.5 Final aggregate plan for Worked Example 8.4: × demand; ○ supply.

The approach described in this example could easily be extended to include a number of other costs. Shortages, for example, could be treated as a combination of lost sales and back orders, while capacity could be examined as a combination of normal capacity, overtime and subcontracted work.

In summary

Aggregate plans can be devised using graphs of cumulative supply and demand. The objective is to match the two lines as closely as possible, while ensuring that there are not too many changes in production level.

8.3.4 Matrix approach

One of the problems with graphs is that they can take a long time to draw and show general patterns rather than details. If we want to evaluate quickly a number of alternatives it is often more convenient to use a matrix representation. The main advantage of this is that it can be drawn on a computer spreadsheet and adjustments made very quickly. In recent years this has become a very popular approach to aggregate planning.

The first step in this procedure is to draw a matrix with the resources available down the left-hand side and the period across the top. Down the right-

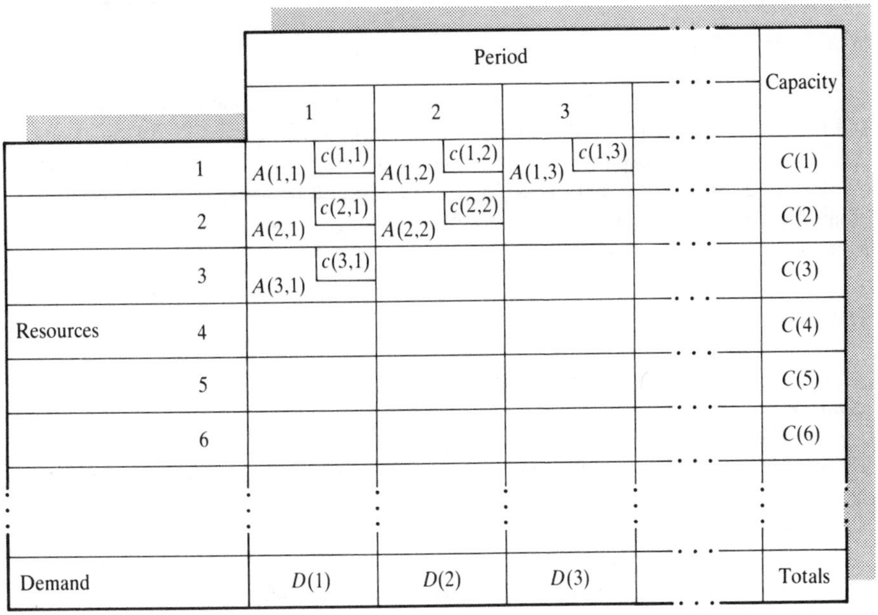

		Period			...	Capacity
		1	2	3	...	
	1	$A(1,1)$ $c(1,1)$	$A(1,2)$ $c(1,2)$	$A(1,3)$ $c(1,3)$	...	$C(1)$
	2	$A(2,1)$ $c(2,1)$	$A(2,2)$ $c(2,2)$		...	$C(2)$
	3	$A(3,1)$ $c(3,1)$			...	$C(3)$
Resources	4				...	$C(4)$
	5				...	$C(5)$
	6				...	$C(6)$
Demand		$D(1)$	$D(2)$	$D(3)$	...	Totals

Figure 8.6 Typical matrix for aggregate planning.

hand side of the matrix is shown the capacity of each resource, and the demand is shown across the bottom. The body of the matrix is used for two values, the cost of using resources and amount of resources used in a period.

In Figure 8.6 $D(i)$ is the total demand for a family of products in period i, $C(i)$ is the capacity of resource i, $c(i,j)$ is the cost of using a unit of resource i in period j and $A(i,j)$ is the amount of resource i actually used in period j.

Typically, the resources are phrased in terms of the number of units that can be made in regular time, overtime and subcontracted in each period. Then $c(i,j)$ becomes the cost of making in one period for supply in another, and might include allowances for keeping in stock or back orders. This leads to a simple method for designing an aggregate plan as follows.

(1) Start with period 1 and find the lowest cost in this column.

(2) Assign as much production to the cell with lowest cost without exceeding either the supply of resources or demand for products.

(3) Subtract the amount assigned from the total capacity to give the spare capacity, and calculate the unmet demand.

(4) If there is unmet demand go to step 1; if all demand has been met, move on to the next period and return to step 1.

(5) Repeat steps 1 to 4 until demand in all periods has been satisfied.

This process can be illustrated by the following example.

343

WORKED EXAMPLE 8.5

The aggregate demand for a family of products for the next four months is 130, 80, 180 and 140. Normal capacity is 100 units a month, overtime has a capacity of 20 a month and subcontractors have a capacity of 60 units a month. The unit cost is £10 for normal capacity, £12 for overtime and £15 from subcontractors. It costs £1 to stock a unit for a month, and no back orders or shortages are allowed. Use a matrix method to devise an aggregate plan for the products.

SOLUTION

The first step is to build a matrix with costs, capacities and demand, as shown in Figure 8.7.

The demands and capacities are given directly in the problem. The costs in each element are a combination of production and stock holding costs. It costs £10 to make a unit in normal work, but if this is used in a later period holding costs are added and its cost rises to $10 + 1 = £11$ in the following period, $10 + 2 * 1 = £12$ in the next period,

		Period				Capacity
		1	2	3	4	
Period 1	Normal work	10	11	12	13	100
	Overtime	12	13	14	15	20
	Subcontract	15	16	17	18	60
Period 2	Normal work		10	11	12	100
	Overtime		12	13	14	20
	Subcontract		15	16	17	60
Period 3	Normal work			10	11	100
	Overtime			12	13	20
	Subcontract			15	16	60
Period 4	Normal work				10	100
	Overtime				12	20
	Subcontract				15	60
	Demand	130	80	180	140	

Figure 8.7 Initial matrix for Worked Example 8.5.

and so on. No back orders are allowed, so the elements for producing in period 2 for demand in period 1, and so on, are crossed out.

Using the procedure described above, the first step is to look down column 1 to find the smallest cost. This is the £10 for normal work done in period 1, so we make as much there as possible. The normal capacity is 100 units, so this leaves a shortage of 30 units. The next lowest cost is £12 for overtime. The capacity of overtime is 20 units, so the shortage is still 10 units, which must be made by subcontracting. These amounts are subtracted from capacities.

Moving to the next period, the lowest cost is the £10 for normal work done in period 2, which can meet all demand.

Moving to period 3, the lowest cost is the £10 for normal work done in period 3, which can meet 100 units of the demand. The next lowest cost is £11 for normal work done in period 2. There is still a capacity of 20 units here, so this leaves a shortage of 60 units. The next lowest cost for which there is spare capacity is £12 for overtime in period 3. This meets 20 units of demand, but there is still a shortage of 40 units. The next lowest cost is £13 for overtime in period 2. This meets 20 units of demand, but there is still a shortage of 20 units, which can best be met from subcontracting in period 3.

This process is repeated for period 4, to give the results shown in Figure 8.8.

		Period 1		Period 2		Period 3		Period 4		Capacity
Period 1	Normal work	100	10	–	11	–	12	–	13	0
	Overtime	20	12	–	13	–	14	–	15	0
	Subcontract	10	15		16		17		18	50
Period 2	Normal work			80	10	20	11	–	12	0
	Overtime				12	20	13	–	14	0
	Subcontract				15		16		17	60
Period 3	Normal work					100	10	–	11	0
	Overtime					20	12	–	13	0
	Subcontract					20	15		16	40
Period 4	Normal work							100	10	0
	Overtime							20	12	0
	Subcontract							20	15	40
	Demand	130		80		180		140		

Figure 8.8 Final solution for Worked Example 8.5.

In summary

A matrix method can be used for aggregate planning. When a computer spreadsheet is used for the calculations, this has become a very popular way of planning.

8.3.5 Mathematical models

All three of the approaches to aggregate planning we have described so far rely, at least to some extent, on the skills of a planner. This is usually reasonable, as planning is a complex process which involves many subjective factors. None the less, we could ask if a more formal mathematical approach might give better answers. A suitable mathematical model of the process could increase the quality and reliability of the plans, but would also reduce the subjective input. Several mathematical models have been proposed, usually based on linear programming. We can illustrate this approach by the following example.

WORKED EXAMPLE 8.6

The major factors for an aggregate plan are inventory levels, changes in production rate and availability of workers. There are costs for:

- supplying a unit of product;
- holding stocks;
- every unit of unmet demand;
- amount of overtime used;
- amount of undertime used (that is, normal working time which is not used);
- increase in production rate;
- decrease in production rate.

The objective is to minimize total costs. Formulate this problem as a linear program.

SOLUTION

We can start by defining the costs mentioned above.
Let:

VC = variable cost of supplying a unit
HC = cost of holding a unit of stock for a unit time
LC = cost per unit of unmet and (therefore lost) demand
OC = additional cost per unit made with overtime
UC = cost per unit of undertime
CI = cost of increasing the production rate
CR = cost of reducing the production rate

There are two other constants:

$D(T)$ = demand in period T
$NC(T)$ = normal capacity in period T

Then we can define the variables:

$P(T)$ = production in period T
$SH(T)$ = stock held at the end of period T
$UD(T)$ = unmet demand in period T
$OT(T)$ = units produced on overtime in period T
$UT(T)$ = units of undertime in period T
$IP(T)$ = increase in production rate during period T
$RP(T)$ = reduction in production rate during period T

Now the objective function can be defined as minimizing the total cost:

$$\text{Minimize } \Sigma_T \; VC * P(T) + HC * SH(T) + LC * UD(T) + OC * OT(T)$$
$$+ \; UC * UT(T) + CI * IP(T) + CR * RP(T)$$

This is subject to a number of constraints which hold for all time periods.
Supply and demand must be balanced:

$$SH(T) = SH(T - 1) + P(T) - D(T) + UD(T)$$

Deviation from normal capacity is either overtime or undertime:

$$P(T) - NC(T) = OT(T) - UT(T)$$

Changes in production rates balance production in each period:

$$P(T) - P(T - 1) = IP(T) - RP(T)$$

Techniques like linear programming have the advantage of finding an optimal solution, in that total costs will be minimized or some other objective achieved, but they have the disadvantages that they are complex, not easy to understand, need a large amount of reliable data and the mathematical formulations may not describe the real situation accurately. Worked Example 8.6 is a considerable simplification of a real problem, but if we consider a 12-month period we would need to find accurate values for seven costs (which could in practice change over time), 24 constants (forecasts and normal capacity which are known to vary and contain some inaccuracies), 84 variables and 36 constraints. Problems of this size are easy to tackle with linear programming packages, but introducing other constraints and variables to make the formulation more realistic soon makes the problem rather cumbersome.

Using a mathematical model for aggregate planning is almost inevitably complex, time consuming, expensive and needs appropriate expertise. There may be difficulties in finding people who are familiar with both the problem and its mathematical formulation. Graphical or matrix approaches can be done quickly and cheaply, so a balance is needed between the costs and benefits of more sophisticated methods. In oil companies and many other organizations, small variations from optimal plans give much higher costs. Then aggregate planning is almost always done by linear programming. In most other organizations slight variations from optimal plans add comparatively little extra cost and aggregate plans rely on graphical or intuitive approaches.

In summary

Mathematical programming can find optimal aggregate plans, but there may be difficulties in accurately representing real situations. A balance is needed between the expected benefit from using mathematical models (rather than simpler methods) and the costs involved.

SELF ASSESSMENT QUESTIONS

8.11 What are the benefits of intuitive aggregate planning?

8.12 How can a good aggregate plan be recognized from a graph?

8.13 When using a graphical method for aggregate planning, what does it mean when the cumulative supply line is above the cumulative demand line?

8.14 What are the benefits of using a matrix method for aggregate planning?

8.15 What is the main benefit of using mathematical programming for aggregate planning?

8.16 When should mathematical programming be used for aggregate planning?

8.4 MASTER SCHEDULE

The aggregate plan shows the overall production by families of products. Once this plan has been accepted it is broken down into more detail to give a master schedule. Thus, the master schedule 'disaggregates' the aggregate plan and specifies the number of individual products to be made in, typically, each week. This gives a detailed timetable of planned output for each product, and is the first time due dates are associated with individual products. An aggregate plan may show 1000 radiators being made next month, while the master schedule gives details for each product, with 50 super radiators, 100 medium radiators and 25 cheaper radiators in week 1, 100 super radiators and 25 medium radiators in week 2, and so on.

The master schedule is constrained by the aggregate plan. In particular, the overall production in the master schedule must equal the production specified in the aggregate plan. There may be some differences to allow for short-term variations, incorrect forecasts, capacity constraints, and so on, but these should be small. Then the overall objective of the master schedule is to devise a detailed timetable for individual products which allows the aggregate plan to be achieved as efficiently as possible.

In principle, design of the master schedule is similar to design of an aggregate plan. In some ways, however, the master schedule is more difficult as it deals with more detail, often down to individual customer orders. The usual methods of designing schedules are based largely on the skills of planners.

The design of a master schedule starts by examining short-term demand as the larger of:

- production specified by the aggregate plan;
- actual customer orders booked for the period.

We know that forecasts are not totally accurate, so this gives the first opportunity to compare actual customer orders with forecast demand. Shortages should usually be avoided, so the demand is set at the larger of these two. Some of this demand can be met from stock, so current stock levels and production capacities are compared and a schedule designed to make up any differences. This schedule must keep within constraints (set by the aggregate plan, the available capacities, and so on), so an iterative approach is used, which is outlined in Figure 8.9.

A variety of inputs may affect the planning process, and an initial schedule is designed in the light of promised delivery times, resources, shortages, costs, raw materials available, and so on. This schedule is assessed and iteratively improved until all requirements are satisfied. If this proves impossible and a feasible schedule cannot be found, the aggregate plan must be changed or availability of some resources changed.

In principle, designing a master schedule is similar to designing an aggregate plan. It is a matter of balancing supply and demand. This is usually done in a matrix, so a computer spreadsheet can be used. We can illustrate the principles by the following example.

WORKED EXAMPLE 8.7

A bicycle manufacturer produces two bicycles, a ladies' and a men's. The aggregate plan has 8000 bicycles made next month, and 6400 the month after. Current stocks are 500 men's and 300 ladies', and the factory has a capacity of 2200 bicycles a week. Men's bicycles usually account for 60% of sales, and actual orders have been received for the following deliveries.

Week	1	2	3	4	5	6
Men's	1400	1200	1000	700	300	—
Ladies'	2000	800	400	100	—	—

Design a master schedule for the next eight weeks.

SOLUTION

A problem here is the unexpectedly high sales for ladies' bicycles in the first two weeks. As there are 300 in stock, 1700 have to be made to meet orders in the first week. This leaves only enough capacity for 500 men's bicycles. These, together with current stocks of 500, still leave a shortage of 400 men's bicycles which must be met by back orders.

In the second week the back orders for 400 men's bicycles can be cleared together with the 1200 actually ordered. This leaves only capacity for 600 ladies' bicycles, so 200 must be back ordered to meet the 800 orders.

The aggregate plan calls for 8000 bicycles the first month. 4400 were made in the first two weeks, so an additional 1800 should be made in each of the last two weeks. In week 3 the back orders for 200 ladies' bicycles could be cleared, plus the 1400 ordered (both men's and ladies'), and an additional 200 for stock (say 100 men's and 100 ladies'). In week 4 dividing the 1800 into 1080 men's and 720 ladies' (to match the expected 60:40 ratio) covers all orders and adds spare units to stock.

In weeks 5 to 8 the planned production of 6400 can be divided into a weekly production of 1600 (960 men's and 640 ladies'). So far there are orders for only 300 units in this period, so the rest are added to stock.

The whole process gives the master schedule shown in Table 8.6.

Table 8.6

Week	1	2	3	4	5	6	7	8
Men's								
Actual orders	1400	1200	1000	700	300	—	—	—
Opening stock	500	−400	0	100	480	1140	2100	3060
Production	500	1600	1100	1080	960	960	960	960
Ladies'								
Actual orders	2000	800	400	100	—	—	—	—
Opening stock	300	0	−200	100	720	1360	2000	2640
Production	1700	600	700	720	640	640	640	640
Total production	2200	2200	1800	1800	1600	1600	1600	1600
Aggregate plan	————— 8000 ———————				———————6400 ——————			

The build-up of stock in later weeks shows that this production has not yet been allocated to customers and reflects stock levels if no more orders are received. In practice, orders will be received and the stock level will be reduced by the amount sold.

This is, of course, only one of many feasible solutions. It has the advantages of meeting the aggregate plan and keeping production at a stable level, but iterative improvements could now be made.

In summary
The master schedule disaggregates the aggregate plan to give a detailed timetable of production for each product in a specified period (usually by week).

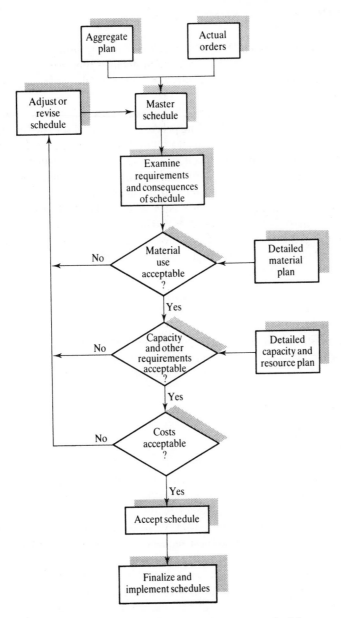

Figure 8.9 Procedure for designing master schedule.

SELF ASSESSMENT QUESTIONS

8.17 What is the main purpose of the master schedule?

8.18 What constraints are set on the master schedule?

8.5 SHORT-TERM SCHEDULES

The master schedule gives a timetable for production of finished items. The final stage in planning is to break this down into detailed timetables for jobs to be done on individual pieces of equipment. This is the role of short-term scheduling.

We will consider two approaches to short-term scheduling. The first of these can be used when the scheduling process is continued for another stage and the master schedule is broken down into yet more detail. This part of the process is called materials requirement planning, or MRP. This is an important topic, especially when extended to methods like manufacturing resource planning and just-in-time systems. These are discussed in Chapter 10. The second approach starts when the planning process has been taken as far as possible (either the master schedule or MRP) and assumes products are in batches to be scheduled on individual pieces of equipment. Producing the timetable for use of equipment is often called job-shop scheduling, and this is described in the following section.

In summary

After the master schedule it may be possible to continue the planning process for another stage (MRP). The final stage in scheduling is to produce timetables for individual pieces of equipment. This is called short-term or job-shop scheduling.

8.5.1 Job shops

Short-term scheduling assumes there are a number of jobs, or batches of products, waiting to be processed on equipment. We want to process these jobs as efficiently as possible, perhaps minimizing the waiting time, minimizing the total processing time, keeping inventories low, reducing the maximum lateness, achieving high utilization of equipment, or some other objective. This problem is effectively one of finding the best sequences of jobs on equipment.

Such sequencing problems seem easy to solve but in practice they are notoriously difficult. Sophisticated methods have been devised for small problems, but these methods can rarely be used for real problems of any size or complexity. Linear programming formulations do work, but the number of variables and constraints limits them to small problems. Some very simple problems can be tackled by queueing theory, but this is not really appropriate for any reasonably complex problem. Despite man-centuries spent searching for solution methods, the most effective way of scheduling remains the use of simple rules. These scheduling rules are heuristic procedures which experience has shown to give generally good results.

Suppose there is a number of jobs waiting to be processed on a single machine. If we assume that the set-up time for each job is constant, regardless of the job that was processed previously, the total time for processing is fixed regardless of the order in which jobs are taken. The sequence of jobs does, however, change other measures, and we can achieve different objectives by taking different sequences.

(1) *First-come-first-served*. This is the most obvious scheduling rule and simply schedules jobs in the order they arrive to be processed. It assumes no priority, no urgency, or any other measure of relative importance. The drawbacks of this rule are that urgent or important jobs may be delayed while less urgent or important ones are being processed. The benefits are simplicity, ease of use and a clear equity. Many queues are based on this system, and when we wait to be served at a supermarket checkout it is reassuring that everybody is treated equally. In some cases, however, the queues have priorities and emergency departments in hospitals, for example, will treat those who are most seriously in need first. This is the basis of a second rule.

(2) *Most urgent job first*. This rule assigns an importance, or urgency, to each job and they are processed in order of decreasing urgency. We mentioned this rule for hospital emergency departments, but it has many other applications. A manufacturer might, for example, calculate when current stocks of parts will run out, and the most urgent job is defined as the one that replenishes those parts that are due to run out first. The benefit of this rule is that jobs that are more important are given higher priority. Unfortunately, those jobs which have low priority may get stuck at the end of a queue for a very long time. Having part finished jobs waiting a long time for processing is generally a symptom of poor planning. It increases stocks of work in progress and causes concerns about the smooth progress of work through the system.

(3) *Shortest job first*. A useful objective would be to minimize the average time spent in the system, where this time is defined as:

$$\text{Time in the system} = \text{processing time} + \text{waiting time}$$

Thus, if a job needs two days of processing, but it waits in the queue for three days:

(a) processing time = 2 days
(b) waiting time = 3 days
(c) time in the system = 5 days

A rule which minimizes the average time spent in the system is to take the jobs in order of increasing duration. The shortest are then processed first. This allows any job which can be done quickly to be processed and moved on through the system, while longer jobs are left until nearer the end. The overall effect is that the average time in the

353

system is minimized. The disadvantage, however, is that long jobs can spend a long time in the system.

(4) *Earliest due date first.* For this rule the queue of jobs is examined and sorted into the order of required delivery date. Those which are expected first are then processed first. This has the obvious benefit of minimizing the maximum lateness of jobs, but again some jobs may have to wait a long time.

Each of these rules is useful in particular circumstances. A student doing coursework, for example, might use such rules, usually without stating them explicitly. One approach is to do work in the order it is set (first-come-first-served). A more common approach is to do coursework in the order in which it is due to be finished (most urgent first, which in this case is the same as earliest due date first). This minimizes the maximum lateness of coursework. If students develop a backlog of coursework they are often tempted to do the shortest first. This will clear their desk quickly, but minimizing the time coursework is in the system may be a questionable objective.

WORKED EXAMPLE 8.8

The following six jobs are to be scheduled on a piece of equipment. Each job fully occupies the equipment for the duration specified.

Job	1	2	3	4	5	6
Duration (days)	6	4	2	8	1	5

(a) How long would it take to finish all jobs if they are scheduled in order of arrival?

(b) What schedule would minimize average time in the system?

(c) Suppose each job makes a batch of products which is put into stock. If the average demand for these products and current stock levels are as follows, what schedule would you suggest? Will stocks of any item run out?

Job	1	2	3	4	5	6
Mean demand	10	15	40	2	5	80
Current stock	260	195	880	20	75	1280

(d) Returning to the basic problem, suppose each job has been promised to customers by the following dates. What schedule of jobs would minimize maximum lateness?

Job	1	2	3	4	5	6
Due date	6	20	22	24	2	10

SOLUTION

(a)   Using the rule first-come-first-served gives the sequence:

Job	Duration	Start	Finish
1	6	0	6
2	4	6	10
3	2	10	12
4	8	12	20
5	1	20	21
6	5	21	26

Then all jobs will be finished by day 26. The sequence of jobs does not change this overall duration, so different sequences do not minimize the 'make span' but try to achieve some other objective.

   The average waiting time is found from the average starting day which is $69/6 = 11.5$ days. The average time in the system is found from the average finishing day which is $95/6 = 15.8$ days.

(b)   The average time in the system is minimized by taking jobs in order of shortest first. This gives the following schedule.

Job	Duration	Start	Finish
5	1	0	1
3	2	1	3
2	4	3	7
6	5	7	12
1	6	12	18
4	8	18	26

The average time in the system is found from the average finishing date, which is $67/6 = 11.2$ (compared with 15.8 days for the first-come-first-served rule).

(c)   If units are made to replenish stocks, it implies that there is a different priority or importance for each job. Then we can use the rule most-urgent-first, where urgency is measured by the number of days of remaining stock (that is, current stock divided by mean demand).

Job	1	2	3	4	5	6
Day's stock remaining	26	13	22	10	15	16
Order of urgency	6	2	5	1	3	4

This gives the following schedule.

Job	Day's stock remaining	Duration	Start	Finish
4	10	8	0	8
2	13	4	8	12
5	15	1	12	13
6	16	5	13	18
3	22	2	18	20
1	26	6	20	26

All jobs are finished before the products are due to run out of stock, except for product 6. Stocks of this will run out two days before the job is finished.

(d) Maximum lateness is minimized by taking jobs in order of due date. This gives the following schedule.

Job	Duration	Start	Finish	Due date	Lateness
5	1	0	1	2	0
1	6	1	7	6	1
6	5	7	12	10	2
2	4	12	16	20	0
3	2	16	18	22	0
4	8	18	26	24	2

This has a maximum lateness of 2 days for jobs 4 and 6, and an average lateness of $5/6 = 0.8$ days. If the first-come-first-served rule is used the maximum lateness is 19 days and average lateness is $35/6 = 5.8$ days.

Job	Duration	Start	Finish	Due date	Lateness
1	6	0	6	6	0
2	4	6	10	20	0
3	2	10	12	22	0
4	8	12	20	24	0
5	1	20	21	2	19
6	5	21	26	10	16

Other scheduling rules

We have illustrated the use of scheduling rules by four specific examples, but there is a wide range of other rules for achieving different objectives. We could, for example, schedule jobs in the order of least work remaining, or fewest operations remaining. We might have a look at the following process and consider combined times for two or three of these. We could look at the slack (which is the time remaining until the job is due minus the time remaining for processing).

One particularly useful rule schedules jobs in order of the critical ratio. The critical ratio is the time remaining until the job is due divided by the time required to complete it. If this ratio is low, the time to complete the job is short compared with the time available and the job becomes urgent. If the ratio is high, there is plenty of time remaining and the job is less urgent. This ratio changes as jobs progress through the operations so that priority changes depend on progress of other jobs within the system.

A large number of alternative rules could be proposed, many of which are designed for particular processes. Although many of these rules are simple, this is not necessarily so, and some are very complicated.

In summary

Job-shop scheduling designs timetables for jobs on individual pieces of equipment. This is a deceptively difficult problem and the best way of getting a solution is to use simple scheduling rules. A number of these are available including the following.

- First-come-first-served — is easy and maintains an obvious equity.
- Most important first — ensures high priority jobs are done first.
- Earliest due date first — minimizes the maximum lateness of jobs.
- Shortest job first — minimizes the average time spent in the system.

SELF ASSESSMENT QUESTIONS

8.19 What is the objective of short-term scheduling?

8.20 What is a scheduling rule?

8.21 Which scheduling rules would you use for:

(a) hospital admission
(b) selling fresh cream cakes
(c) telephone calls
(d) writing reports for consulting clients?

8.22 Are the scheduling rules described the only ones available?

8.5.2 Flow shops

The problems described so far have been concerned with a queue of jobs at a single machine. The scheduling of such jobs is straightforward and we should now expand the scheduling rules to cover more complicated circumstances.

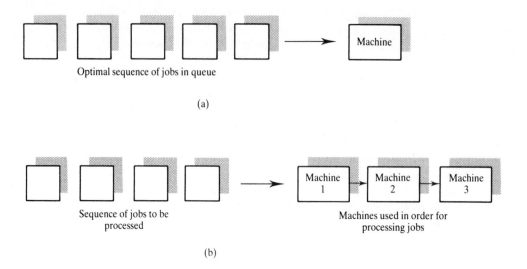

Figure 8.10 (a) Single machine job shop. (b) Flow shop.

Unfortunately, there are very few rules available for this. Scheduling is notoriously difficult and when we get beyond a small number of machines it is almost impossible to find rules that achieve any stated objective. One area where some progress has been made is in flow shops. In a flow shop jobs are processed on the same set of machines in the same order (see Figure 8.10).

A useful rule for scheduling a flow shop with two machines is Johnson's Rule (sometimes called the left−right rule). This assumes that jobs are to be processed on two machines (machine 1 followed by machine 2) and it finds the minimum 'make span'. The make span is defined as the time between starting the first job and finishing the last job.

Johnson's Rule has four steps.

(1) List the jobs and their processing time on each machine.

(2) Find the job with the next shortest processing time on either machine.

(3) If this processing time is on machine 1, schedule the job as early as possible; if the processing time is on machine 2, schedule the job as late as possible.

(4) Do not consider the job just scheduled again, and repeat steps 2 and 3 (working inwards from the ends of the sequence) until all jobs have been scheduled.

This can be most easily demonstrated with an example.

WORKED EXAMPLE 8.9

A series of four jobs is to be processed on machine 1 followed by machine 2. If the times on each machine are as follows, devise a schedule that minimizes the make span.

Job	1	2	3	4
Time on M/C 1	2	3	6	8
Time on M/C 2	4	5	1	7

SOLUTION

The first step of Johnson's Rule has been done, and we now have a list of jobs and their processing times.

Step 2 identifies the shortest processing time as job 3 on machine 2.

Step 3 recognizes that this is on machine 2, so the job is scheduled as late as possible. This gives a sequence which is currently:

... 3

Step 4 removes job 3 from further consideration and returns to step 2. This identifies the shortest remaining processing time (from jobs 1, 2 and 4) as job 1 on machine 1. Step 3 recognizes this is on machine 1, so the job is scheduled as early as possible to give the sequence:

1 ... 3

After deleting job 1 the shortest remaining processing time (for jobs 2 and 4) is job 2 on machine 1. This is scheduled as early as possible to give the sequence:

1   2 ... 3

After deleting job 2 the shortest remaining processing time (for job 4) is job 4 on machine 2. This is scheduled as late as possible to give the final sequence:

1   2   4   3

Then the finished schedule, assuming a notional starting time of 0, is:

Job	Duration M/C 1	Start M/C 1	Finish M/C 1	Duration M/C 2	Start M/C 2	Finish M/C 2
1	2	0	2	4	2	6
2	3	2	5	5	6	11
4	8	5	13	7	13	20
3	6	13	19	1	20	21

Note that jobs can only be started on machine 2 when they have finished on machine 1 and when the previous job on machine 2 has finished. Thus job 2 has to wait until job 1 is finished before it can start, while job 4 is only held up by the time it takes on machine 1.

This solution can be compared with the standard first-come-first-served rule, which has a make span of 26 days.

Job	Duration M/C 1	Start M/C 1	Finish M/C 1	Duration M/C 2	Start M/C 2	Finish M/C 2
1	2	0	2	4	2	6
2	3	2	5	5	6	11
3	6	5	11	1	11	12
4	8	11	19	7	19	26

In summary

It is difficult to find good, general rules for more complicated scheduling problems. One example is Johnson's Rule for a flow shop with two machines.

8.5.3 Scheduling operators

An extension to short-term scheduling looks at manpower requirements. If operators are always assigned to the same piece of equipment, the schedule for this equipment effectively fixes the schedule for the operators. Often, however, this is not the case. When one operator is assigned to several pieces of equipment, or operators are used on different equipment, scheduling them becomes a separate problem. This is particularly relevant when there is a shortage of operators. Then we might use some assignment rule that is similar to a scheduling rule. Perhaps:

- assign operators to the equipment that has the most jobs waiting to be processed;
- assign operators to the equipment that has the job with the earliest due date;
- assign operators to the equipment that has the job that has been waiting longest;
- or some other simple rule.

One simple problem, for which there is an easy rule, is the assignment of operators so that each has two consecutive days off a week. A procedure for this is as follows.

(1) Find the minimum number of operators needed each day of the week.

(2) Identify the two adjacent days with smallest requirements. This means finding the smallest requirement, then the next smallest, then the next smallest, and so on until two adjacent days have been identified.

(3) Assign the next operator these two days off (perhaps giving priority to weekends off if there are ties).

(4) Reduce the requirements by one for those five days when this operator works.

(5) If there are still unmet requirements go to step 2, otherwise a schedule has been found.

This procedure is illustrated by the following example.

WORKED EXAMPLE 8.10

The minimum number of operators needed each day is as follows. What is the minimum number of operators which should be employed, and how are they scheduled?

Day	Mon	Tues	Wed	Thurs	Fri	Sat	Sun
Operators	1	2	3	3	4	4	0

SOLUTION

Step 1 is now complete, and we move to step 2 of identifying the two adjacent days with minimum requirements. Assuming the schedule is continuous, this is Sunday and Monday. Step 3 assigns the first operator to have these two days off and to work Tuesday to Saturday. Step 4 reduces the requirements for Tuesday to Saturday by one, and then we return to step 2.

Day	Mon	Tues	Wed	Thurs	Fri	Sat	Sun
Operators	1	1	2	2	3	3	0

The next repetition again identifies Sunday and Monday as the adjacent days with lowest demand, so the second operator is also assigned to work Tuesday to Saturday, giving the revised requirements:

Day	Mon	Tues	Wed	Thurs	Fri	Sat	Sun
Operators	1	0	1	1	2	2	0

The next repetition has ties for lowest demand, so we arbitrarily give the third operator Tuesday and Wednesday off, and reduce the requirement for other days by one.

Day	Mon	Tues	Wed	Thurs	Fri	Sat	Sun
Operators	0	0	1	0	1	1	0

The next operator is assigned Monday and Tuesday off.

Day	Mon	Tues	Wed	Thurs	Fri	Sat	Sun
Operators	0	0	0	0	0	0	0

This completes the assignment, with all demand met by four operators, and the final schedule is as follows.

	Mon	Tues	Wed	Thurs	Fri	Sat	Sun
Operators required	1	2	3	3	4	4	0
Operators off	3	2	1	0	0	0	2
Operators available	1	2	3	4	4	4	2
Spare operators	0	0	0	1	0	0	2

The spare operators might be used for training, maintenance, or some other function.

In summary

Sometimes scheduling operators becomes a separate problem to scheduling equipment. Then assignment rules can be used which are similar to scheduling rules.

SELF ASSESSMENT QUESTIONS

8.23 What is a flow shop?

8.24 What is the make span?

8.25 When is Johnson's Rule used?

8.26 When might scheduling operators become a problem?

8.6 CONTROL OF SCHEDULES

We have now described the scheduling process from mission down to short-term scheduling. The result is detailed plans which show what each piece of equipment and each person should be doing at any time. The last part of the planning process is to keep these schedules accurate and up to date. In other words, to compare actual performance with plans.

The maintenance of schedules is in two parts. The first part records the progress of jobs and feeds back information. At regular intervals details of the jobs' progress through the operations are added and efficiency, productivity, utilization and other measures reported. This reporting assumes that things are working smoothly and there are no major problems, beyond minor adjustments. The second part of the maintenance occurs when circumstances change or there is some disruption. Then schedules may have to be completely revised.

The ability to do this maintenance relies on an effective control system. The inputs to such a system might include inventory records, bills of materials, routing through the machines, orders for jobs to be done, and so on. The output might include the release of job orders, dispatch of finished jobs, schedule receipts and status reports. Such control systems can be complicated and involve interactions with large numbers of historic and current data files.

Then the main requirements of a control system can be summarized as:

- to schedule orders and jobs in line with agreed plans;
- to warn of problems with resources, delivery dates, and so on;
- to ensure the materials, equipment and operators are available for each job;
- to assign jobs to specific orders and set delivery times;
- to check progress as jobs move through the process;
- to make small adjustments, as necessary, to plans;
- to allow rescheduling if there is a major disruption to plans;
- to give feedback on performance.

Control systems can become complex and yet need decisions quickly. It has been suggested that expert systems might be used for this. The argument says that control systems usually require humans to access many computer files and programs, and then extract information needed to adjust plans. In some circumstances an expert system could be designed to follow a set of rules in a very short time. An expert system has three main parts:

- a knowledge base that stores the information, views and rules that allow decisions to be made;
- an inference engine that determines the rules to be used, the sequence in which they are used, and so on;
- an interface with users.

Despite their considerable potential for the future, expert systems are still at a very early stage of development and their practical use is limited to some specific types of problem.

Before finishing this chapter we should emphasize one final point. Many

363

of the examples we have described have been phrased in terms of 'jobs' being processed on 'machines'. This is purely for convenience. In reality scheduling is one of the most common problems in any organization. All scheduling problems share common features, but they arise in many different guises. Buses and trains work to schedules, delivery vehicles are given drop lists which show when to visit customers, classes are scheduled into rooms, doctors have appointment books, and so on. In essence, we have used one type of process to illustrate an approach to a very widely occurring problem.

In summary

Once schedules have been designed, there must be some control mechanism for comparing actual performance with plans. Such systems may be very complicated.

SUMMARY OF CHAPTER

Some aspects of capacity planning were discussed in Chapter 7. This chapter started by repeating the theme that capacity planning aims to match available capacity with forecast demand. This is essentially a strategic function, but there are both tactical and operational aspects.

Strategic capacity planning is the first step in a hierarchy of planning decisions which look in increasing detail at operations. We described these decisions in terms of aggregate planning, master scheduling and short-term scheduling. Then, capacity plans set the output for each facility over the next few years; aggregate plans looked at the output of families of products in each facility for the next few months; master schedules broke this down by individual products per week; short-term schedules looked at equipment use day to day.

The overall planning process has a number of steps. These start by finding the requirements set by the previous stage of planning. These are broken down into more detail and plans generated to achieve the requirements. The plans are evaluated and the best is selected and implemented. The evaluation of plans can be very complex, and in practice an iterative procedure is used to revise plans repeatedly until an acceptable one is found.

Aggregate planning takes the forecast demand and capacity plans and translates these into schedules for each family of products, typically for each of the next few months. The objectives of aggregate planning are to meet demand while keeping production

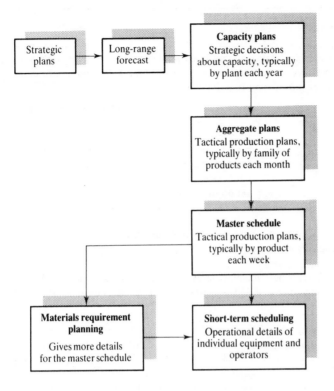

Figure 8.11 Summary of the planning process.

fairly stable, and keeping to any other specific constraints. Several methods were suggested for aggregate planning, based on intuition, a graphical method and a matrix method. More mathematical methods can be used, but it is difficult to incorporate the complexities of real situations.

The next stage in planning is the master schedule. This disaggregates the aggregate plans and shows a detailed timetable for production of individual products.

The master schedule provides an input for short-term scheduling, which produces a detailed timetable for jobs on individual pieces of equipment. Such problems are deceptively difficult to solve, and the most common approach is to use an heuristic scheduling rule. This can also be used for scheduling operators.

The overall planning process is described in Figure 8.11.

The chapter ended with some comments about the control of schedules.

PROBLEMS

8.1 A machine makes two different products A and B. The machine works for 250 days a year, with two eight-hour shifts a day and a utilization of 95%. Other information is as follows.

	A	B
Forecast annual demand	2100	5600
Time to make one unit (h)	2.0	1.5
Batch size	50	100
Set-up time per batch (h)	5	6

If the company currently has three identical machines, how would it start its capacity planning?

8.2 The aggregate, monthly demand for a family of products is shown below. Use intuitive reasoning to suggest a monthly production schedule for the products.

Month	1	2	3	4	5	6	7
Aggregate demand	90	120	100	120	180	270	225

8.3 The forecast monthly demand for a family of products is shown below. At the end of each month the performance is evaluated, and a notional holding cost of £20 is assigned to every unit held in stock. If there are shortages, 20% of orders are lost with a cost of £200 a unit, and the rest are met by back orders, with a cost of £50 a unit. Each time the production rate is changed it costs £15,000. Designed capacity of the system is 400 units a month, but utilization seldom reaches 80%. Use a graphical method to devise an aggregate plan for the products.

Month	1	2	3	4	5	6	7	8
Aggregate demand	310	280	260	300	360	250	160	100

8.4 The aggregate demand for a family of products for the next five months is 190, 120, 270, 200 and 140. Normal capacity is 150 units a month, overtime has a capacity of 10 a month and subcontractors can handle any amount of production. The unit cost is £100 for normal capacity, £125 for overtime and £140 for subcontractors. It costs £15 to stock a unit for a month, while back orders have a penalty cost of £100 a month. Use a matrix method to devise an aggregate plan for the products.

8.5 The aggregate plan of a manufacturer has 12,000, 10,000 and 10,000 units made in the next three months. A master schedule is needed for the two products, A and B. Current stocks are 700 of A and 500 of B, and the factory has a capacity of 3000 units a week. Sales of A are usually twice as large as sales of B, and actual orders have been received for deliveries of:

Week	1	2	3	4	5	6	7
A	2100	1800	1600	1100	800	200	—
B	3000	1400	700	400	100	—	—

Design a master schedule for the next 12 weeks.

8.6 Eight jobs are to be processed on a single machine, with processing times as follows:

Job	A	B	C	D	E	F	G	H
Processing time	2	5	3	8	4	7	2	3

Use a variety of scheduling rules to obtain different results.

8.7 In what order should the jobs in Problem 8.6 be scheduled if they have the following due dates?

Job	A	B	C	D	E	F	G	H
Due date	13	7	8	30	14	20	2	36

8.8 Seven jobs are to be processed on machine 1 followed by machine 2. The time needed by each job on each machine is as follows. What sequence of jobs would maximize the machine's utilization?

Job	A	B	C	D	E	F	G
Machine 1	4	10	20	16	8	24	18
Machine 2	28	14	6	20	10	12	12

8.9 A small museum needs the following numbers of guides.

Day	Mon	Tues	Wed	Thurs	Fri	Sat	Sun
Guides	4	6	8	8	10	14	12

Devise a schedule which gives each guide two consecutive days off.

CASE STUDY – NATURAL HOME BREWERS

Background

In 1932 James Galloway founded Natural Home Brewers in Port Merdoch on the east coast of Scotland. He had brewed beer at home since he was a teenager, and this had become quite well known locally for its high quality. All the local pubs were owned by three national brewers, but there was a small number of clubs that were independent and tried to sell specialized beer. Because there were no local suppliers, other than the national brewers, these clubs imported small quantities of specialized beers, mainly from Scandinavia and Germany.

James Galloway founded Natural Home Brewers to supply quantities of his locally brewed beer to these clubs. Original financial backing came as a grant from the local government anxious to encourage local industry, and a personal loan from the bank. His original objective was to do the bulk of the work himself, with help from his brother and wife. To support the three of them, the company needed to sell about 2000 litres a week.

Natural Home Brewers quickly reached its target production, but after this developed very slowly. There was a clear demand for its beers, but James was more interested in brewing his beer in traditional ways for the local market, than making large profits. By 1945 the company was brewing 6800 litres a week and employing six people.

In the late 1940s there was a dramatic increase in demand for the company's beer. New clubs were opening in the area, and a number of pubs began selling small quantities of Natural Home Brew as a special attraction. By 1955 Natural Home Brewers was employing 120 people. This made it big enough to be noticed by the large national brewers. One of them saw the potential for development, made a generous offer, and bought the company.

The new owners were keen to maintain the image of Natural Home Brewers and kept the name and brands. They started selling the products in their own pubs, as well as maintaining the original markets, and sold the beers over a wider area. By the 1980s Natural Home Brewers employed 1500 people. During various expansions the brewing had been largely automated and although customers thought they were buying from a local brewery, they were buying a standard product which was little different to any other nationally available beer.

Problem with planning

The brewery was now having some trouble with its planning. Several of its most experienced production planners had retired in the same year, and the current planning often seemed to be of variable quality. In particular, there were times when it was difficult to meet demand. Management felt it was time to reconsider the planning process, and introduce some procedure for guaranteeing plans of reasonable quality. The description of this procedure was seen as the first step in computerizing the whole planning process.

A sample of data was collected for an eight-month period, and agreement was reached about a range of variables. Forecast demand for this period was found, in barrels, as follows.

Month	Demand	Month	Demand
January	9,000	May	6,000
February	8,000	June	8,000
March	6,000	July	10,000
April	4,000	August	10,000

Costs and manpower requirements were agreed, with recognition that these could be used for comparing plans, but were not necessarily true figures. These included:

- production cost of £200 a barrel;
- storage cost of 1.5% of production cost a month;
- shortage cost of £10 a barrel a month;
- five man-hours to produce a barrel;
- direct labour force of 225;
- standard wage rate of £8 an hour;
- overtime wage rate of 1.5 times standard rate;
- a standard working week of five days;
- hiring and training cost of £400 a person;
- lay-off cost of £500 a person;
- subcontractors can be used at an additional cost of £5 a barrel;
- opening stock is 2000 barrels;
- a reserve stock is kept of 25% of forecast monthly demand;
- all shortages are back ordered;
- the three main products are lager, bitter and mild which generally account for 50%, 40% and 10% of sales respectively.

Requirements

The management of Natural Home Brewers wanted:

- a set of alternative aggregate plans for the eight-month period;
- a comparison of costs for these plans;
- a recommendation for the best plan;
- a procedure for developing reliable aggregate plans in the future;
- a suggested master schedule;
- a procedure for developing reliable master schedules in the future.

SOLUTIONS TO SELF ASSESSMENT QUESTIONS

8.1 No. It is essentially strategic, but it has both tactical and operational aspects.

8.2 Strategic plans leading to capacity plans, then aggregate plans, master plans and short-term scheduling.

8.3 **(a)** Aggregate plan; **(b)** master schedule; **(c)** short-term schedule.

8.4 A number of sources, including forecasts, plans for last period, decisions at the higher level of planning, and so on.

8.5 Yes.

8.6 They calculate the availability of a resource during the current period, by taking the availability in the last period, adding any new arrivals and subtracting any deletions.

8.7 Typically total production per month.

8.8 Forecast demand, available capacities, objectives for production plans, constraints on production for the next few months, and any other relevant information.

8.9 No. Aggregate plans only show the production of families of products.

8.10 A schedule of production for each product family, by month.

8.11 It is convenient and easy to use; the results may be good, and an experienced planner has credibility in the organization; the process is well understood and trusted.

8.12 The cumulative supply line should be close to the cumulative demand line, and it should not change gradient frequently (to reduce changes in production levels).

8.13 There has been excess production and stocks must have built up.

8.14 The method is easy to understand and use, it is convenient and can easily be transferred to a computer spreadsheet.

8.15 An optimal solution can be found which does not rely on the skill of planners.

8.16 When small deviations from optimal solutions give significant increases in cost.

8.17 To disaggregate the aggregate plan and show a timetable for making individual products.

8.18 These mainly come from the aggregate plan, available capacity, costs and actual customer orders.

8.19 This is the final stage of planning which produces timetables for jobs on individual pieces of equipment.

8.20 A simple heuristic rule which experience has found to give good solutions.

8.21 Useful alternatives would be: **(a)** most urgent first; **(b)** earliest due date first; **(c)** first-come-first-served; **(d)** shortest first.

8.22 No. There are many alternatives, often tailored to circumstances.

8.23 A process where jobs use the same machines in the same order.

8.24 The time between starting the first job and finishing the last.

8.25 To minimize the make span in a flow shop with two machines.

8.26 When operators are not permanently assigned to a piece of equipment, and particularly when they are in short supply.

REFERENCES FOR FURTHER READING

Baker K.R. (1974). *Introduction to Sequencing and Scheduling* New York: John Wiley

Berry W.L., Vollmann T.E. and Whybark D.C. (1979). *Master Production Scheduling: Principles and Practice* Falls Church: American Production and Inventory Control Society

Buffa E.S. and Miller J.G. (1979). *Production – Inventory Systems: Planning and Control* 3rd edn. Homewood: Richard Irwin

Conway R.W., Maxwell W.L. and Miller L.W. (1967). *Theory of Scheduling* Reading: Addison-Wesley

Fitzsimmons J.A. and Sullivan R.S. (1982). *Service Operations Management* New York: McGraw-Hill

Freeland J. and Landel R. (1984). *Aggregate Production Planning: Text and Cases* Reston: Reston Publishing

Glueck W.F. and Jauch L.R. (1984). *Business Policy and Strategic Planning* New York: McGraw-Hill

McLeavey D. and Narasimhan M. (1985). *Production Planning and Inventory Control* Boston: Allyn and Bacon

Salvendy G. (ed.) (1982). *Handbook of Industrial Engineering* New York: John Wiley

Vollman T.E., Berry W.L. and Whybark D.C. (1988). *Manufacturing Planning and Control Systems* 2nd edn. Homewood: Richard Irwin

Waters C.D.J. (1989). *A Practical Introduction to Management Science* Wokingham: Addison-Wesley

Chapter 9

Project network analysis

SYNOPSIS

Chapter 5 described the types of process that can be used to make a product. One distinct type of process was concerned with projects. Projects consist of a set of activities, with a distinct start and finish, which have the aim of making a unique product. Often, this involves heavy capital expenditure. Such projects need detailed planning and this chapter describes the most widely used method of doing this.

The first part of the chapter covers the need for project planning and the information required. This is followed by a description of project network analysis. This starts by identifying the activities that make up a project, and building a dependency table to show their relationships. The dependency table is then transferred to a network of alternating nodes and arcs. The chapter describes activity on arrow networks, rather than the less common activity on node.

Having drawn a network, the next stage is to analyse the timing of individual events and activities, and hence the overall duration of the project. These ideas are introduced by the critical path method which assumes each activity takes a fixed time. The analyses are then extended to the project evaluation and review technique which assumes activity durations follow known distributions.

The timing of the project may need adjusting during either the planning or execution phases. Several calculations relevant to this are described. Any adjustments may need different levels of resources, and give differing costs. A procedure is described to minimize the total cost of a project.

Gantt charts give an alternative view of a project, emphasizing its timing. They also allow the resources used at any time to be calculated, and a procedure for levelling these is described.

OBJECTIVES

After reading this chapter and completing the exercises you should be able to:

- appreciate the need for planning complex projects;
- list the requirements of project management;
- represent projects by networks of connected activities and events;
- calculate early and late times for events, and slack in these;
- calculate earliest and latest start and finish times for activities, and floats in these;
- identify critical paths and hence overall project duration;
- extend these analyses to PERT networks;
- change the times of activities to achieve stated objectives;
- minimize the total cost of a project;
- draw Gantt charts;
- find the resources needed during a project and reschedule activities to smooth these.

9.1 BACKGROUND TO PROJECT NETWORK ANALYSIS

9.1.1 Introduction

Chapter 5 classified the different types of process available to make a product as project, job shop, batch, mass production or continuous flow. Chapter 8 then looked in more detail at the planning needed to maintain these processes. Unfortunately, projects have such distinct characteristics that their planning really needs a different approach. The aim of this chapter is to describe how such planning can be done with the aid of networks.

We can start by defining a project and seeing what distinct characteristics it has. One definition would be:

> A project is a coherent piece of work with a distinct start and finish. It consists of a series of activities that result in a unique product.

Each of us does a number of small projects every day, such as preparing a meal, writing a report, building a fence, or organizing a social function. Such projects need planning, and in particular the identification of:

- the activities that make up the project;
- the order in which these activities must be done;
- timing of each activity;
- resources needed at each stage.

Small projects can be done with almost no formal planning and a little thought is often enough to ensure they run smoothly. Projects can, however, be very large and involve a great deal of money. The installation of a new computer system, building a nuclear power station, organizing the Olympic Games and building a rail tunnel under the English Channel are examples of large projects, and we would expect them to run smoothly only if there had been a considerable amount of planning. Project network analysis is the most widely used technique for helping to organize complex projects.

Project network analysis was developed independently by two groups working in the late 1950s. The first group was concerned with the Polaris missile project for the US Department of Defense. At that time the US government was worried about the slow rate at which its missile systems were being developed, and it gave high priority to the Polaris project. This project involved over 3000 contractors, and to help control it a technique called PERT (project evaluation and review technique) was developed. This reduced the overall length of the project by two years.

The second group worked for Du Pont and developed CPM (critical path method) for planning maintenance programmes in chemical plants. PERT and CPM were always very similar, but any differences in the original ideas have disappeared over time. The one difference which still exists is that PERT stresses probabilistic durations of activities while CPM assumes fixed durations.

In summary

A project is a coherent piece of work which has a distinct start and finish, and an aim of making a unique product. Projects are often very large and rely on detailed planning. Project network analysis is the most widely used technique for doing this planning.

9.1.2 Aspects of project management

A project consists of two phases:

(1) A planning phase, during which the project is defined, its feasibility

tested, goals are set, detailed design work done, resources allocated, times agreed, management and work organized, and so on.

(2) An execution phase, during which materials are purchased and delivered, construction is done, finished work is handed over, initial operations are tested, and so on.

The management of a project is often cited as the key factor in its success. This means that the ultimate success of a project is often determined early in the planning stage, when a project manager and team are assembled. This team looks after the details of the project, and in particular aspects of its design, scheduling and control. To be more specific, they have to analyse available information so they can:

- identify all the activities in the project, together with their interdependence (and hence the order in which activities must be done);
- estimate the duration of each activity, the total length of the project, and the time by which each activity must be finished if this completion time is to be achieved;
- find which activities are most critical to the completion of the project, and the maximum delay in each activity which will not delay the completion time;
- estimate costs, and schedule activities so that overall cost is minimized;
- allocate resources and schedule these so that goals and objectives can be achieved as efficiently as possible;
- monitor the progress of the project, reacting quickly to deviations from plans and making adjustments to schedules as required;
- anticipate problems and take actions necessary to avoid them;
- give regular reports on progress, presenting relevant information in an easily understandable form.

The first five of these points are concerned with scheduling the project and are done in the planning phase. The last three are concerned with control of the project in the execution phase.

Project network analysis can be used for almost any type of project, but it has proved most useful for those that are fairly large (involving a reasonable amount of money so the necessary data collection and analysis is worth while) and complex (so there are enough opportunities for things to go wrong). Such projects will probably be one off, so there is little previous experience that could be used directly. Typical projects include construction (roads, bridges or buildings), organization of large events, launching new products, planning equipment maintenance and manufacture of one-off items.

In summary

Projects consist of planning and execution phases. The management team (headed by a project manager) is concerned with many aspects of the scheduling and control of activities.

SELF ASSESSMENT QUESTIONS

9.1 What is a project?

9.2 What is the purpose of project management?

9.3 Project management is only concerned with

major capital projects. Is this statement true?

9.4 What are the two main phases of a project?

9.5 Where does project network analysis fit into the phases of a project?

9.2 PROJECT NETWORKS

9.2.1 Drawing networks

We used networks to describe processes in Chapter 5. Here we will extend this idea by using them to describe projects. A project network consists of a series of nodes connected by arrows or arcs. We will use the convention that each activity is represented by an arrow and each node represents the point in time at which activities begin and end. The nodes are called 'events' and a network will consist of alternating activities and events. The arrows show relationships between activities and there is no significance in their orientation or length.

Figure 9.1 shows part of a project network. This has two activities A and B, and three events. Event 1 is the start of activity A, event 2 is the finish of activity A and the start of activity B, and event 3 is the finish of activity B.

These networks are called 'activity on arrow' networks. An alternative representation would have nodes representing activities and the arrows showing the relationships. The choice between these is largely a matter of personal preference. Because some of the calculations are easier with activity on arrow networks, we will stick to this notation. We can show how a project network is drawn by a simple example.

Figure 9.1 Part of a project network.

WORKED EXAMPLE 9.1

A greenhouse is to be built from a kit. The instructions make it clear that the project can be considered in three parts:

- A, preparing the base (which will take three days);
- B, building the frame (which will take two days);
- C, fixing the glass (which will take one day).

Draw a network for the project.

SOLUTION

The project is made up of three activities that must be done in a fixed order; building the frame must be done after preparing the base and before fixing the glass. This order can be described by a precedence or dependence table, where each activity is listed along with those activities that immediately precede it (see Table 9.1).

Table 9.1

Activity	Duration (days)	Description	Immediate predecessor
A	3	prepare base	—
B	2	build frame	A
C	1	fix glass	B

Labelling the activities A, B and C is a convenient shorthand and allows us to refer to activity B having activity A as immediate predecessor, which is normally stated as 'B depends on A'. In this table only immediate predecessors are entered, so the fact that activity C (fixing the glass) depends on activity A as well as B need not be separately entered, but can be inferred from other dependencies. Activity A has no immediate predecessors and can be started whenever convenient.

Now we can draw a network from the dependency table, as shown in Figure 9.2.

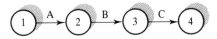

Figure 9.2 Network for Worked Example 9.1.

The directions of the arrows in a project network indicate precedence. Each preceding activity must be finished before the following one is started, and following activities can start as soon as preceding ones are finished. In Worked

Example 9.1, preparing the base must be done first, and as soon as this is finished the frame can be built. The glass can then be fixed as soon as the frame is built.

After drawing the basic network for the project we can consider its timing. It is convenient to assume a notional starting time of 0, and then the start and finish times of each activity can be calculated.

WORKED EXAMPLE 9.2

For the project described in Worked Example 9.1, find the times for each activity. What happens if the base takes more than three days or the glass is delayed, or the frame takes less than two days?

SOLUTION

If we take a starting time of 0, preparing the base can be finished by the end of day 3. Then building the frame can start, and as it takes two days it can be finished by the end of day 5. Then fixing the glass can start, and as it takes one day it can be finished by the end of day 6.

If the concrete of the base takes more than three days to set, or the glass is not delivered by day 5, the project will be delayed. If building the frame takes less than two days the project will be finished early.

We now have a timetable for the project showing when each activity starts and finishes. This timetable allows resources to be scheduled, as we know when each is needed. This quick illustration has shown the major stages of project planning, and we can summarize the steps as follows:

- Define the separate activities.
- Determine the dependence and duration of each activity.
- Draw a network.
- Analyse the timing of the project.
- Schedule resources.

If the timings or resource requirements suggested by the initial plan are not acceptable, the project can be adjusted until a satisfactory solution is found. Finally, when the plan is implemented and the project is running, progress must be monitored to identify deviations from the plan, with adjustments made as necessary.

In summary

Planning is needed for most projects of a reasonable size. Project network analysis helps with this planning. Projects are divided into a number of separate activities, which are represented by arrows in a network of alternating activities and events. After the network is drawn calculations can be done for timing and resource allocation.

9.2.2 Larger networks

The approach to large networks is exactly the same as the approach used in the small illustration in Worked Example 9.1. Drawing networks from dependency tables is a matter of practice, but a useful approach is to start drawing the network on the left-hand side with those activities that do not depend on any other. Then activities that only depend on these first activities can be added, then those that only depend on the latest activities added, and so on. The network is expanded systematically, working generally from left to right, until all activities have been added and the network is complete.

This procedure relies on some implicit rules and before continuing we should state these more formally. The two main rules are:

(1) Before an activity can begin all preceding activities must be finished.
(2) The arrows representing activities imply precedence only and neither the length nor orientation is significant.

There are also, by convention, two other rules:

(3) A network has only one starting and finishing event.
(4) Any two events can only be connected by one activity.

This last rule is only a convenience so we can refer to 'the activity between events i and j' and know exactly which one we are talking about. Using these rules we can draw networks of almost any size. We can illustrate this by the following example.

WORKED EXAMPLE 9.3

A company is opening a new office and identifies the main activities and dependencies as shown in Table 9.2.

Table 9.2

Activity	Description	Depends on
A	find office location	—
B	recruit new staff	—
C	make office alterations	A
D	order equipment needed	A
E	install new equipment	D
F	train staff	B
G	start operations	C,E,F

Draw a network of this project.

SOLUTION

Activities A and B have no predecessors and can be started as soon as convenient. As soon as activity A is finished both C and D can start; E can start as soon as D is finished and F can start as soon as B is finished. G can only start when C, E and F have all finished. This network is shown in Figure 9.3.

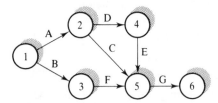

Figure 9.3 Network for Worked Example 9.3.

The network conforms to the rules above, and in particular has a single starting and finishing event, and only one activity between any pair of events.

The network shows that the project can start with activities A and B, but this does not imply that these *must* start at the same time, only that they can start as soon as convenient and must be finished before any following activity can start. Similarly event 2 marks the point at which both C and D can start, but this does not mean they must start at the same time. Conversely event 5 is the point where C, E and F are finished, but this does not mean that they must finish at the same time, only that they must all be finished before G can start.

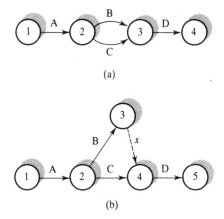

Figure 9.4 Networks illustrating the use of a 'uniqueness dummy'. (a) Incorrect network. (b) Correct network using dummy activity x.

In summary

Networks of almost any size can be drawn from a dependence table. The general approach is to draw the first activities, and then systematically add all following ones.

9.2.3 Dummy activities

There are two circumstances that complicate the networks. The first of these is illustrated by the following dependence table.

Activity	Depends on
A	—
B	A
C	A
D	B,C

We may be tempted to draw this as shown in Figure 9.4(a), but this would break one of the rules above which says, 'any two events can only be connected by one activity'. The conventional way around this is to define a 'dummy activity'. This is not a part of the project, has zero duration and requires no resources, but is simply there to allow a sensible network. In this case the dummy ensures that only one activity goes between two events and is called a 'uniqueness dummy'. In Figure 9.4(b) the dummy activity is shown as the broken line, x.

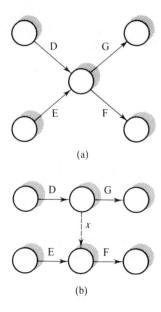

(a)

(b)

Figure 9.5 Networks illustrating the use of a 'logical dummy'. (a) Incorrect part of network. (b) Correct network using dummy activity x.

A second situation, which needs a dummy activity, is illustrated by the part of a dependence table shown below.

Activity	Depends on
D	not given
E	not given
F	D,E
G	D

We may be tempted to draw this part of the network as shown in Figure 9.5(a), but the dependence would clearly be wrong. Activity F is shown as depending on D and E, which is correct, but G is shown as having the same dependence. The dependence table shows that G can start as soon as D is finished but the network shows it as having to wait for E to finish as well. The way to avoid this relies on separating the dependencies by introducing a dummy activity, as shown in Figure 9.5(b). The dependence of F on D is shown through the dummy activity x. In effect the dummy cannot start until D has finished and then F cannot start until the dummy and E are finished: as the dummy activity has zero duration this does not add any time to the project. This type of dummy is called a 'logical dummy'.

These are the only two circumstances (ensuring only one activity goes between any two nodes and ensuring the logic is correct) in which dummies are used.

In the initial example of building a greenhouse, the project was conveniently divided into three activities. It could have been divided into a lot more (such as determine location, clear vegetation, level and prepare ground, dig foundations, lay hardcore, mix concrete, lay concrete base, and so on) but the complexity of the network would increase with the number of activities and the importance of each activity would decline. A balance must be drawn between using too few activities (and reducing its usefulness as a planning aid) and using too many (and needlessly increasing complexity). An activity is defined as a task that consumes both time and resources, but there is no limit on the amounts. The only guidance is the vague statement that a 'convenient' set of activities should be used.

If the number of activities gets above about 30 it is probably best to use a computer package (many of which are available). If the number of activities is very large the network will cover many pages, be complicated and difficult to follow. For large projects a useful approach would be to draw a general, master network showing the major activities of the project, and then for each of these draw a separate, more detailed network. For very large projects it may be useful to go further and break down the more detailed networks into yet smaller parts. This approach would be particularly useful when there are a number of contractors and subcontractors working on a single project. The owner of the project may construct a master network, each contractor could be given a network covering his or her own work, and any major subcontractors could be given separate networks of their parts of the work. At each stage the networks would cover less of the overall project but would show more detail.

WORKED EXAMPLE 9.4

A project is described by the dependency table (Table 9.3). Draw a network of the project.

Table 9.3

Activity	Depends on	Activity	Depends on
A	J	I	J
B	C,G	J	—
C	A	K	B
D	F,K,N	L	I
E	J	M	I
F	B,H,L	N	M
G	A,E,I	O	M
H	G	P	O

SOLUTION

This may seem a difficult network, but the steps are fairly straightforward. Activity J is the only one which does not depend on anything else, so this starts the network. Then activities A, E and I, which only depend on J, can be added. Then activities which depend on A, E and I can be added. Continuing this systematic addition of activities leads to the network shown in Figure 9.6, which includes four dummy activities.

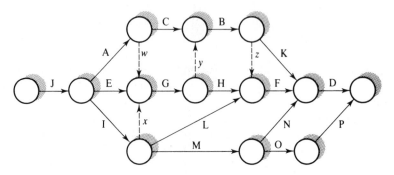

Figure 9.6   Network for Worked Example 9.4.

WORKED EXAMPLE 9.5

The management of a whisky distillery has examined the inventory control system to see how stock levels can be set to meet forecast demand. It has concluded that an expanded computer system is needed which will extrapolate past demand patterns and, based on these, set appropriate stock levels. These stock levels will then be passed to a production control module which varies the quantities bottled.

　　　　The first part of this proposed system is called DFS (Demand Forecasting System) while the second part is ICS (Inventory Control System). The introduction of these is expected to take about 18 months, including linking to the production control module which is already operating. The introduction of DFS and ICS is a self-contained project for which the following activities have been identified. Draw a network for the project.

Activity	Description
A	examine existing system and environment of ICS
B	collect costs and other data relevant to ICS
C	construct and test models for ICS
D	write and test computer programs for ICS models
E	design and print data input forms for ICS data
F	document ICS programs and monitoring procedures
G	examine sources of demand data and its collection
H	construct and test models for DFS
I	organize past demand data

J	write and test computer programs for DFS models
K	design and print data input forms for DFS data
L	document DFS programs and monitoring procedures
M	train staff in the use of DFS and ICS
N	initialize data for ICS programs (ICS staff)
P	initialize data for DFS programs (DFS staff)
Q	create base files for DFS
R	run system for trial period
S	implement final system

SOLUTION

In larger projects there are usually several views on the dependence of activities. These should be sorted out by discussion, preferably in the light of experiences with similar projects. One dependence table for this project is given (Table 9.4) with the associated network shown in Figure 9.7.

Table 9.4

Activity	Depends on	Activity	Depends on
A	—	J	H,K
B	A	K	A,G
C	A	L	J
D	C	M	F,L
E	C	N	B,M
F	D,E	P	I,M
G	—	Q	P
H	A,G	R	N,Q
I	G		

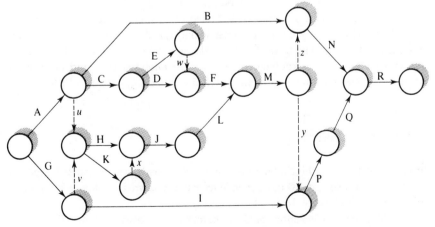

Figure 9.7   Network for Worked Example 9.5.

In summary

Two types of dummy activity may be needed to draw a network. Uniqueness dummies ensure only one activity starts and finishes with the same events and a logical dummy ensures the logic of the network is accurate. Some aspects of networks may need agreement, such as the level of detail used and the precise dependence of activities.

SELF ASSESSMENT QUESTIONS

9.6 In activity on arrow networks, what is represented by:

(a) nodes
(b) arcs?

9.7 What information is needed to draw a project network?

9.8 What are the main rules of drawing a project network?

9.9 When are dummy activities used?

9.10 There is only one network which correctly represents a project. Is this statement true?

9.3 TIMING OF PROJECTS

The timing of events and activities is a major part of project planning. In particular, it is important to find the earliest time an activity can start and the latest time by which it must be finished. It would be difficult to find these intuitively for a project of any reasonable size and a more systematic approach must be used.

At the beginning of the chapter we said that the only real difference between the critical path method (CPM) and the project evaluation and review technique (PERT) is in the timing. In particular, CPM assumes that each activity has a fixed duration which is known exactly, while PERT assumes the duration can vary according to a known distribution. The analyses are identical for each of these, so we will illustrate them by CPM and then move on to PERT.

9.3.1 Event analysis

It is easiest to show the calculations for event times by an example. Suppose a project is represented by the dependence table shown in Table 9.5, where a duration (in weeks) has been added.

This project is represented by the network shown in Figure 9.8, where durations have been noted under the activities.

Table 9.5

Activity	Duration	Depends on
A	3	—
B	2	—
C	2	A
D	4	A
E	1	C
F	3	D
G	3	B
H	4	G
I	5	E,F

The analysis of times starts by finding the earliest possible time for each event, assuming a notional start time of zero for the project as a whole. The earliest time for event 1 is clearly 0. The earliest time for event 2 is when A finishes, which is three weeks after its earliest start at 0. The earliest time for event 4 is when C finishes, which is two weeks after its earliest start at 3 (that is, week 5). Similarly, the earliest time for event 5 is $4 + 3 = 7$, for event 3 is 2 and for event 7 is $2 + 3 = 5$.

When several activities have to finish before an event, the earliest time for the event is the earliest time by which all preceding activities can be finished. The earliest time for event 6 is when both E and F are finished. E can finish one week after its earliest start at 5 (that is, week 6), F can finish three weeks after its earliest start at 7 (that is, week 10). Then the earliest time when both of these can

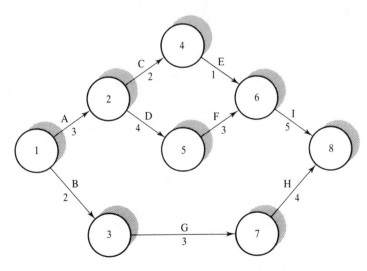

Figure 9.8 Network for illustration of timing.

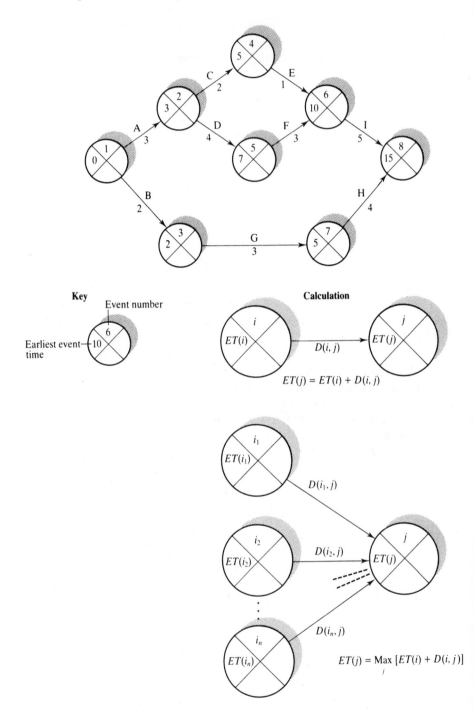

Figure 9.9 Earliest event times added to network.

be finished is week 10. Similarly, event 8 must wait until both activities H and I are finished. Activity H can be finished by week $5 + 4 = 9$ while activity I can be finished by week $10 + 5 = 15$. The earliest time for event 8 is the later of these which is week 15. This gives the overall duration of the project as 15 weeks. Figure 9.9 shows the earliest times for each event added to the network.

The formal statement of the calculations for earliest event time is:

The earliest time of event j is the earliest time by which all preceding activities can be finished.

$$ET(1) = 0$$

and

$$ET(j) = \underset{i}{\text{Max}} \; [\; ET(i) + D(i,j) \;]$$

---

where: $ET(i)$ = the earliest time of event i

$D(i,j)$ = duration of activity linking events i and j

Having gone through the network and found the earliest time for each event we can do a similar analysis to find the latest time for each. This will then identify the events which need strict control and those for which there is some slack.

The procedure for this is almost the reverse of that used to find the earliest times. Starting at the end of the project with event 8, this has a latest time for completion of week 15. To allow activity I to be finished by week 15 it must be started five weeks before this, so the latest time for event 6 is week $15 - 5 = 10$. The latest H can finish is week 15, so the latest time it can start is four weeks before this and the latest time for event 7 is week $15 - 4 = 11$. Similarly the latest time for event 3 is $11 - 3 = 8$, for event 5 is $10 - 3 = 7$ and for event 4 is $10 - 1 = 9$.

For events which have more than one following activity, the latest time must allow all following activities to be completed on time. Event 2 is followed by activities C and D; C must be finished by week 9 so it must be started two weeks before this (that is, week 7), while D must be finished by week 7 so it must be started four weeks before this (that is, week 3). The latest time for event 2 which allows both C and D to start on time is the earlier of these, which is week 3.

Similarly the latest time for event 1 must allow both A and B to finish on time. The latest start time for B is $8 - 2 = 6$ and the latest start time for A is $3 - 3 = 0$. The latest time for event 1 must allow both of these to start on time and this means a latest time of 0. Figure 9.10 shows the network with latest times added for each event.

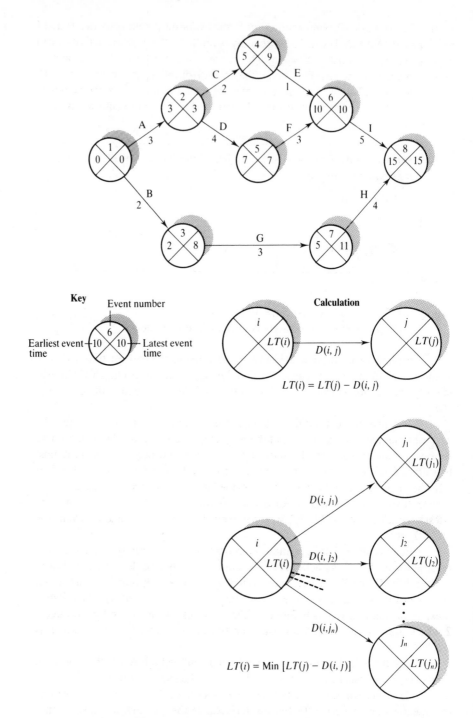

Figure 9.10 Latest times added to network.

The formal statement of the calculation of latest event times is:

The latest time for an event is the latest time which allows all following activities to be started on time.

$$LT(n) = ET(n)$$

and

$$LT(i) = \underset{j}{\text{Min}} [LT(j) - D(i,j)]$$

---

where: $LT(i)$ = latest time of event i
          n = number of events (with the terminal event numbered n)

Some of the events have a certain amount of flexibility in timing (event 3, for example, can occur any time between week 2 and week 8, while event 7 can occur any time between weeks 5 and 11). Other events are fixed without any leeway (events 1, 2 and 5, for example). The amount an event can move is called the 'slack', which is defined as the difference between the latest and earliest times.

$$\frac{\text{Slack for}}{\text{event } i} = \frac{\text{Latest time}}{\text{for } i} - \frac{\text{Earliest time}}{\text{for } i}$$

$$S(i) = LT(i) - ET(i)$$

The more slack an event has the more scope there is for adjustment and less chance of problems. If there is no slack an event must occur at the specified time and any delay will cause the whole project to be delayed. Slack values for this example are shown in Figure 9.11.

In summary
The determination of times for events and activities is an important part of project planning. An earliest and latest time can be found for each event, with slack defined as the difference between these. The slack measures the amount of flexibility in the timing of the event.

9.3.2 Activity analysis

The analysis of project times can be extended to activities, where earliest and latest start times (and corresponding earliest and latest finish times) can be found (see Figure 9.12).

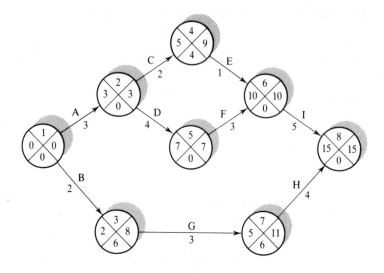

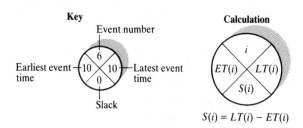

Figure 9.11 Slacks added to the network.

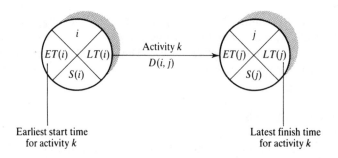

Figure 9.12 Earliest and latest activity times.

Table 9.6

Activity	Duration	Earliest start	Earliest finish	Latest start	Latest finish
A	3	0	3	0	3
B	2	0	2	6	8
C	2	3	5	7	9
D	4	3	7	3	7
E	1	5	6	9	10
F	3	7	10	7	10
G	3	2	5	8	11
H	4	5	9	11	15
I	5	10	15	10	15

The earliest start time for an activity is the earliest time of the preceding event. The earliest finish time is the earliest start time plus the duration.

$$ES(k) = ET(i)$$

and

$$EF(k) = ES(k) + D(i,j)$$

where: $ES(k)$ = earliest start time of activity k which is between events i and j
$EF(k)$ = earliest finish time of activity k

Looking at one specific activity in Figure 9.11, say G, the earliest start time is week 2 and the earliest finish time is, therefore, week $2 + 3 = 5$.

The latest start and finish time for an activity can be found using similar reasoning, but working backwards. The latest finish time for each activity is the latest time of the following event; the latest start time is the latest finish time minus the duration.

$$LF(k) = LT(j)$$

and

$$LS(k) = LF(k) - D(i,j)$$

where: $LF(k)$ = latest finish time of activity k which is between events i and j
$LS(k)$ = latest start time of activity k

For activity G the latest finish is week 11 and the latest start is week $11 - 3 = 8$.

Repeating these calculations for all activities in the project gives the results shown in Table 9.6.

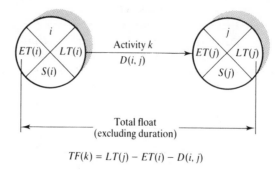

$$TF(k) = LT(j) - ET(i) - D(i, j)$$

Figure 9.13 Calculation of total float.

In this table there are some activities which have flexibility in time: activity G, as we have seen, can start as early as week 2 or as late as week 8, while activity C can start as early as week 3 or as late as week 7. Conversely, there are other activities which have no flexibility at all: activities A, D, F and I have no freedom and their latest start time is the same as their earliest start time. These activities have to be done at a fixed time and if they are late the whole project is delayed. Such activities are called 'critical' and they form a continuous path through the network, called the 'critical path'. The length of this path determines the overall project duration. If one of the critical activities is extended by a certain amount the overall project duration is extended by this amount; if one of the critical activities is delayed by some time the overall project duration is again extended by the time of the delay. Conversely, if one of the critical activities is reduced in duration the overall project duration may be reduced by this amount. A network may have several critical paths in parallel.

Those activities which have some flexibility in timing are the 'non-critical' activities and these may be delayed or extended without necessarily affecting the overall project duration.

In the same way that slack defined the amount of movement available for an event, 'float' defines the amount of movement available for an activity. We will consider three different kinds of float, each of which has a specific purpose. The first is 'total float' which is the difference between the maximum amount of time available for an activity and the time actually used (see Figure 9.13).

Total float $=$ Latest finish $-$ Earliest start $-$ Duration

$TF(k) = LT(j) - ET(i) - D(i,j)$

This is zero for critical activities and will take some positive value for non-critical activities. The total float is the maximum amount the duration of an activity can increase without affecting the completion date of the project.

If all activities start at their earliest times, a 'free float' can be defined.

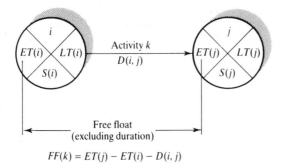

$$FF(k) = ET(j) - ET(i) - D(i, j)$$

Figure 9.14 Calculation of free float.

This is the maximum amount the duration of an activity can increase without affecting any following activity (see Figure 9.14).

> Free float = Earliest time of following event − Earliest time of preceding event − Duration
>
> $FF(k) = ET(j) - ET(i) - D(i,j)$

Finally, if every activity preceding an activity finishes as late as possible and every activity following starts as early as possible, there may still be some 'independent float' which is defined as:

> Independent float = Earliest time of following event − Latest time of preceding event − Duration
>
> $IF(k) = ET(j) - LT(i) - D(i,j)$

This is the maximum amount the duration of an activity can increase without affecting either preceding or following activities (see Figure 9.15).

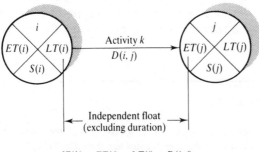

$$IF(k) = ET(j) - LT(i) - D(i, j)$$

Figure 9.15 Calculation of independent float.

Table 9.7

Activity	Duration	ES	EF	LS	LF	Total	Float Free	Indep.	
A	3	0	3	0	3	0	0	0	*
B	2	0	2	6	8	6	0	0	
C	2	3	5	7	9	4	0	0	
D	4	3	7	3	7	0	0	0	*
E	1	5	6	9	10	4	4	0	
F	3	7	10	7	10	0	0	0	*
G	3	2	5	8	11	6	0	0	(−6)
H	4	5	9	11	15	6	6	0	
I	5	10	15	10	15	0	0	0	*

Calculating the floats for activity G in the example above has $ET(i) = 2$, $LT(i) = 8$, $ET(j) = 5$, $LT(j) = 11$ and $D(i,j) = 3$. Then:

$$TF(k) = LT(j) - ET(i) - D(i,j) = 11 - 2 - 3 = 6$$
$$FF(k) = ET(j) - ET(i) - D(i,j) = 5 - 2 - 3 = 0$$
$$IF(k) = ET(j) - LT(i) - D(i,j) = 5 - 8 - 3 = -6 \,(= 0)$$

Activities only have independent float if there is still spare time when preceding activities finish as late as possible and following activities start as early as possible. Many activities which are squeezed for time will have zero independent float and in some cases it will go negative (when it is conventionally recorded as zero).

Repeating the calculations for other activities in the example gives the results shown in Table 9.7.

Critical activities have zero floats, while non-critical activities all have at least some total float. Activity E, for example, could be expanded by up to four weeks without affecting either the overall duration of the project or any following activity. Activity C could also be expanded by up to 4 weeks, but following activities would then start at their latest time. The calculation of floats allows us to identify the critical path, which consists of a chain of activities with zero float and events with zero slack. In this example the critical path is A, D, F and I.

WORKED EXAMPLE 9.6

A small telephone exchange is planned as a project with ten main activities. Estimated durations (in days) and dependencies for this are shown in Table 9.8. Draw the network for this project, find its duration and calculate the floats of each activity.

Table 9.8

Activity	Description	Duration	Depends on
A	design internal equipment	10	—
B	design exchange building	5	A
C	order parts for equipment	3	A
D	order material for building	2	B
E	wait for equipment parts	15	C
F	wait for building material	10	D
G	employ equipment assemblers	5	A
H	employ building workers	4	B
I	install equipment	20	E,G,J
J	complete building	30	F,H

SOLUTION

The network for this is shown in Figure 9.16 and repeating the calculations described above gives the results shown in Table 9.9.

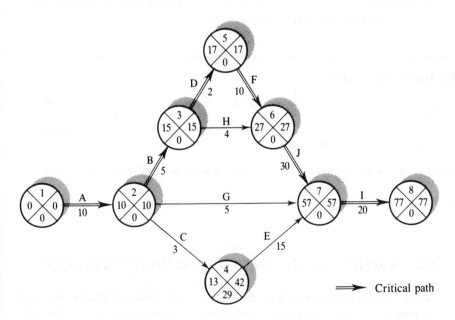

Figure 9.16 Network for Worked Example 9.6.

399

Table 9.9

Activity	Duration	ES	EF	LS	LF	Float Total	Float Free	Float Indep.	
A	10	0	10	0	10	0	0	0	*
B	5	10	15	10	15	0	0	0	*
C	3	10	13	39	42	29	0	0	
D	2	15	17	15	17	0	0	0	*
E	15	13	28	42	57	29	29	0	
F	10	17	27	17	27	0	0	0	*
G	5	10	15	52	57	42	42	42	
H	4	15	19	23	27	8	8	8	
I	20	57	77	57	77	0	0	0	*
J	30	27	57	27	57	0	0	0	*

The duration of the project is 77 days, defined by the critical path A, B, D, F, I and J.

In summary

An earliest and latest start and finish time can be found for each activity. The amount of flexibility which is available can be measured by the floats (total, free and independent). Critical activities have no float and form the critical path(s) which determines the overall project duration.

SELF ASSESSMENT QUESTIONS

9.11 How are the earliest and latest times for an event calculated?

9.12 What is meant by the slack of an event?

9.13 What is meant by the float of an activity?

9.14 What are the different kinds of float?

9.15 How big is the total float of a critical activity?

9.16 What is the significance of the critical path?

9.4 PROJECT EVALUATION AND REVIEW TECHNIQUE

So far we have concentrated on the critical path method (CPM) where each activity is given a single estimate for duration. A useful extension to this adds some uncertainty to activity durations. This extension constitutes the main difference between CPM and PERT (project evaluation and review technique).

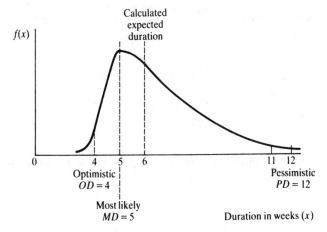

Figure 9.17 Typical Beta distribution of activity duration
(OD = 4, MD = 5, PD = 12).

Experience suggests that activity durations can usually be described by a Beta distribution, which looks something like a skewed Normal distribution. This has one very useful property: the mean and variance can be found from three estimates of duration. The first step is to define for each activity:

- an optimistic duration (OD) which is the shortest time an activity would take if everything goes smoothly and without any difficulties;
- a most likely duration (MD) which is the duration of the activity under normal conditions;
- a pessimistic duration (PD) which is the time needed if there are significant problems and delays.

Expected activity duration and variance are then calculated from the 'rule of sixths':

$$\text{Expected duration} \ = \ \frac{OD + 4 * MD + PD}{6}$$

$$\text{Variance} \ = \ \frac{(OD - PD)^2}{36}$$

Suppose the duration of a particular activity is uncertain but can be assigned an optimistic duration of four days, a most likely duration of five days and a pessimistic duration of 12 days. Figure 9.17 shows a Beta distribution for duration. Assuming this distribution:

401

An introduction to operations management

$$\text{Expected duration} = \frac{OD + 4 * MD + PD}{6}$$
$$= (4 + 4 * 5 + 12)/6$$
$$= 6$$

$$\text{Variance} = \frac{(PD - OD)^2}{36}$$
$$= (12 - 4)^2/36$$
$$= 1.78$$

Expected durations can be used for analysing timing of networks in the same way as the single estimate of CPM.

402

Table 9.11

Activity	Expected duration	Variance
A	4	1.78
B	6	1.78
C	10	0.44
D	4	0
E	7	4.00
F	5	1.00
G	6	0
H	8	2.78
I	8	0.44

The network for this problem is drawn in Figure 9.18.

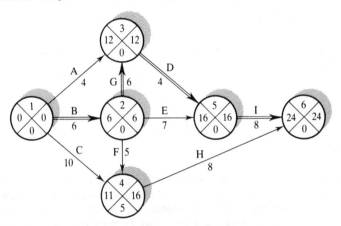

Figure 9.18 Network for Worked Example 9.7.

The critical path for the project is B, G, D and I which has an expected duration of 24. Table 9.12 gives the analysis of activity times.

Table 9.12

Activity	Duration	ES	EF	LS	LF	Float Total	Float Free	Indep.	
A	4	0	4	8	12	8	8	8	
B	6	0	6	0	6	0	0	0	*
C	10	0	10	6	16	6	1	1	
D	4	12	16	12	16	0	0	0	*
E	7	6	13	9	16	3	3	3	
F	5	6	11	11	16	5	0	0	
G	6	6	12	6	12	0	0	0	*
H	8	11	19	16	24	5	5	0	
I	8	16	24	16	24	0	0	0	*

The duration of the critical path is the sum of the durations of activities making up that path. If there is a large number of activities on the path, and if the duration of each activity is independent of the others, the overall duration of the project will follow a Normal distribution. This distribution has:

- a mean equal to the sum of the expected durations of activities on the critical path;
- a variance equal to the sum of the variances of activities on the critical path.

These values can be used to find the probability that a project will be completed by any particular time.

WORKED EXAMPLE 9.8

What are the probabilities that the project described in Worked Example 9.7 will be finished before:

(a) time 26

(b) time 20?

SOLUTION

The critical path has been identified as activities B, G, D and I with expected durations of 6, 6, 4 and 8 respectively and variances of 1.78, 0, 0 and 0.44 respectively. Although the number of activities on the critical path is small, we can reasonably assume the overall duration of the project is Normally distributed (see Figure 9.19). The expected duration then has mean $6 + 6 + 4 + 8 = 24$ and variance $1.78 + 0 + 0 + 0.44 = 2.22$.

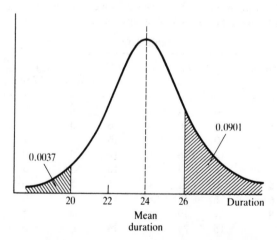

Figure 9.19 Normal distribution of project duration for Worked Example 9.8.

The probability that it will not be finished before 26 can be found using Normal distribution tables with Z as the number of standard deviations the point of interest is away from the mean:

$Z = (26 - 24)/ \sqrt{2.22} = 1.34$ standard deviations

Tables (in Appendix A) show this to correspond to a probability of 0.0901
Similarly the probability it will be finished before 20 is:

$Z = (24 - 20)/ \sqrt{2.22} = 2.68$
Probability $= 0.0037$

In summary

When there is uncertainty in an activity's duration, an expected duration and variance can be found from three estimates using the rule of sixths. The timing analysis is then the same as for CPM networks. The overall project duration is Normally distributed with mean and variance found by adding values for activities on the critical path.

SELF ASSESSMENT QUESTIONS

9.17 What is the difference between CPM and PERT?

9.18 What is the 'rule of sixths' and when is it used?

9.19 How could you calculate the expected duration of a project and its standard deviation?

9.5 RESOURCE PLANNING

9.5.1 Changing project durations

There are two main reasons why project durations may need changing:

(1) When a network is analysed the timing is found to be unacceptable (it may, for example, take longer than the organization has available).

(2) During the execution of a project an activity might take a different time than originally planned.

Reducing the length of a project
Taking the first of these, the initial length of a project may be excessive and need reducing. The first thing we must remember is that the duration of a project is set by the critical path. Then any reductions in the overall duration can only be achieved by reducing the duration of critical activities. Reducing the duration of non-critical activities will have no effect on the overall project duration.

We must also consider what happens when a critical path is shortened. Small reductions may have little effect, but if we keep on reducing the time of the critical path there must come a point when some other path through the network becomes critical. This point can be found from the total float on paths parallel to the critical path. Each activity on a parallel path has the same total float, and when the critical path is reduced by more than this, the parallel path becomes critical.

Another concern is that reductions in the duration of an activity will generally be achieved by using extra resources, and will, therefore, have a higher cost. A decision must be made about the optimal duration which combines reasonable timing and acceptable cost. This is discussed in the following section.

WORKED EXAMPLE 9.9

The project network shown in Figure 9.20 has a duration of 14 weeks with A, B and C as the critical path.

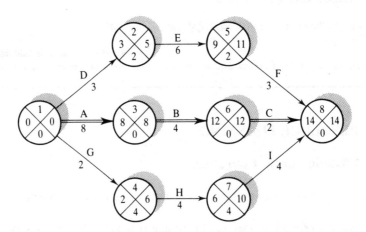

Figure 9.20 Original network for Worked Example 9.9.

If each activity can be reduced by up to 50% of the original duration, how would you reduce the overall duration to:

(a) 13 weeks

(b) 11 weeks

(c) 9 weeks?

If reductions cost an average of £1000 per week what would be the cost of finishing the project by week 9?

SOLUTION

The analysis of activity times for this project is given in Table 9.13.

Table 9.13

Activity	Duration	Earliest		Latest			Float		
		ES	EF	LS	LF	TF	FF	IF	
A	8	0	8	0	8	0	0	0	*
B	4	8	12	8	12	0	0	0	*
C	2	12	14	12	14	0	0	0	*
D	3	0	3	2	5	2	0	0	
E	6	3	9	5	11	2	0	0	
F	3	9	12	11	14	2	2	0	
G	2	0	2	4	6	4	0	0	
H	4	2	6	6	10	4	0	0 (−4)	
I	4	6	10	10	14	4	4	0	

The amount the critical path can be reduced without affecting any parallel path is found from the total float in parallel paths. In this network there are three parallel paths, A−B−C, D−E−F and G−H−I. The total floats of activities on these paths are 0, 2 and 4 respectively. This means that the critical path A−B−C can be reduced by up to 2, but if it is reduced by more than this the path D−E−F becomes critical. If the critical path is reduced by more than 4, the path G−H−I becomes critical.

(a) A reduction of one week is needed in the critical path, so reducing the longest activity (as it is usually easier to find savings in longer activities) would give A a duration of seven weeks and the project could be finished by week 13.

(b) To finish in 11 weeks requires a further reduction of two weeks in the critical path, and this can again be removed from A. Unfortunately the path D−E−F now becomes critical with a duration of 12 weeks and a week must be removed from E (again chosen as the longest activity in the critical path).

(c) To finish in nine weeks would need five weeks removed from the path A−B−C (say four from A and one from B), three weeks removed from the path D−E−F (say from E) and one week removed from the path G−H−I (say from H).

To achieve a five-week reduction in project duration has meant a total reduction of 5 + 3 + 1 = 9 weeks from individual activities, at a total cost of £9000.

In summary

A critical path can only be reduced by a certain amount before another path becomes critical. This limit is the total float of each activity on the parallel path. When reducing project durations a check must be kept on the total floats of parallel paths to see if any are about to become critical.

Delays in projects

The other time a project duration will be changed is during its execution, when activities take a different time than planned. Almost inevitably, this means they take longer than planned. The overall duration of a project is determined by the length of the critical path, so increasing the duration of a critical activity will extend the project by the same amount. The other question we can ask is what happens when a non-critical activity is extended? The answer to this comes from the floats. The total float measures the total amount an activity can expand without affecting the overall project duration. This principle is illustrated by the following example.

WORKED EXAMPLE 9.10

Draw the network for the dependence table (Table 9.14) and calculate the total, free and independent float of each activity. What would happen if activity D is delayed?

Table 9.14

Activity	Duration	Depends on
A	4	—
B	14	—
C	10	A
D	6	A
E	4	C
F	6	D,E
G	12	B

SOLUTION

The network for this is shown in Figure 9.21, with calculated times and floats given in Table 9.15.

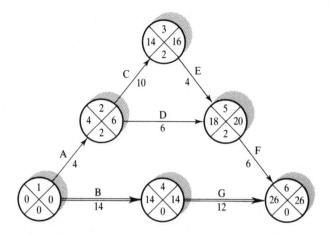

Figure 9.21 Network for Worked Example 9.10.

Table 9.15

Activity	Duration	ES	EF	LS	LF	Float			
						Total	Free	Indep.	
A	4	0	4	2	6	2	0	0	
B	14	0	14	0	14	0	0	0	*
C	10	4	14	6	16	2	0	0	(−2)
D	6	4	10	14	20	10	8	6	
E	4	14	18	16	20	2	0	0	(−2)
F	6	18	24	20	26	2	2	0	
G	12	14	26	14	26	0	0	0	*

The critical path is B and G and the project duration is 26.

Activity D is not critical, so small increases in duration do not affect the duration of the project. D has an independent float of 6 so any extension up to this would have no effect on any other activity in the project. If the duration increases above 6 other activities would be affected.

If the duration of D is increased by 7 (that is, to 13), this makes no difference to the event times on the network, but other activities are now affected. Originally A could finish as late as 6 and F could start as early as 18: this is still true provided only one of them occurs: it is no longer possible for *both* A to finish at 6 and F to start at 18 as D cannot fit in the gap left.

If the duration of D is raised by 9 (that is, to 15) all its free float has been used and following activities are affected. In particular the early start time for F is delayed from 18 to 19.

Finally, if D is expanded by 11 (that is, to 17), all the total float is used and the project will be delayed. Originally there was a total float of 10 and, as the activity has been expanded by 11, the project will be delayed by one. This can be shown in Figure 9.22 where the critical path has switched from B and G to A, D and F.

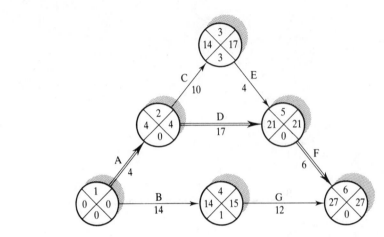

Figure 9.22 Revised network for Worked Example 9.10.

In summary

Whenever an activity expands beyond its independent float it begins to interfere with other activities. When it expands beyond its free float it affects following activities, and when it expands by more than its total float the critical path changes and the project is delayed by an amount:

expansion of activity − total float of activity

SELF ASSESSMENT QUESTIONS

9.20 Which activities must be shortened to reduce the overall duration of a project?

9.21 By how much can a critical path be usefully shortened?

9.22 By how much can a non-critical activity expand:

(a) without affecting any other activity
(b) without affecting any following activity
(c) without affecting the overall project duration?

9.5.2 Minimizing costs

The total cost of a project can be classified according to direct costs (labour, materials, and so on), indirect costs (management, financing, and so on) and penalty costs (if the project is not finished by a specified date).

Total cost = Direct costs + Indirect costs + Penalty costs

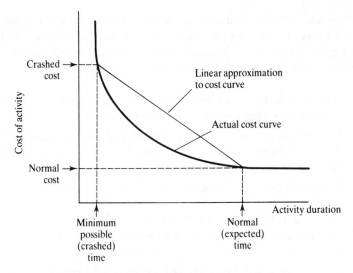

Figure 9.23 Variation of activity cost with duration.

All of these are affected by the duration of the project. Penalty costs are eliminated if the project is finished on time, but this might need more resources and hence increase the direct costs. Sometimes a bonus is paid if a project is finished early, but this may need additional manpower which again increases direct costs. Overall, some kind of balance is needed which either minimizes the total costs, or achieves some stated cost objective.

Cost calculations are based on an implied cost of reducing the duration of an activity (see Figure 9.23). This is calculated from two figures:

(1) *Normal time* is the expected time to complete the activity and this has associated normal costs.

(2) *Crashed time* is the shortest possible time to complete the activity and this has the higher crashed costs.

To simplify the analysis, it is usually assumed that the cost of completing an activity in any particular time is a linear combination of these costs. Then the cost of crashing an activity by a unit of time is:

$$\frac{\text{Cost of crashing}}{\text{by one time unit}} = \frac{\text{Crashed cost} - \text{Normal cost}}{\text{Normal time} - \text{Crashed time}}$$

Now we can suggest an approach to minimize the costs. This starts by analysing a project with all activities done at their normal time and cost. Then the duration of critical activities is systematically reduced. Initially the cost of the project may decline as its duration is reduced, but there comes a point when the cost starts to rise. When this happens the minimum cost has been identified. A more complete statement of the procedure is as follows.

(1) Draw a project network and analyse cost and timings, assuming all activities take their normal, expected times.

(2) Find the critical activity with the lowest cost of crashing per unit time. (If there is more than one critical path they must all be considered at the same time.)

(3) Reduce the time for this activity until one of the following conditions is met:
   (a) it cannot be reduced any further;
   (b) another path becomes critical (when the total float has been used);
   (c) the cost of the project begins to rise.

(4) Repeat steps 2 and 3 until the cost of the project begins to rise.

This procedure is illustrated in the following example.

WORKED EXAMPLE 9.11

A project is described by Table 9.16, where times are in weeks and costs are in thousands of pounds.

Table 9.16

Activity	Depends on	Normal Time	Normal Cost	Crashed Time	Crashed Cost
A	—	3	13	2	15
B	A	7	25	4	28
C	B	5	16	4	19
D	C	5	12	3	24
E	—	8	32	5	38
F	E	6	20	4	30
G	F	8	30	6	35
H	—	12	41	7	45
I	H	6	25	3	30
J	D,G,I	2	7	1	14

There is a penalty cost of £3500 for every week the project finished after week 18. By what time should the project be completed?

SOLUTION

The network for this project is shown in Figure 9.24, with times based on expected durations.

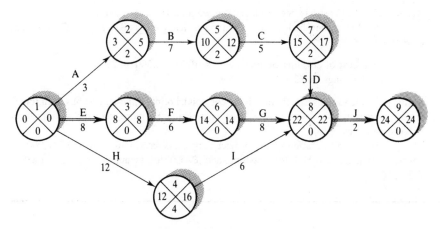

Figure 9.24 Network for Worked Example 9.11.

The critical path is E−F−G−J which has a duration of 24 weeks, and the total cost is found by adding the normal costs of each activity (£221,000) to the six days of penalty costs (£21,000) to give a total of £242,000.

The cost of crashing each activity (in thousands of pounds a week) is as follows.

Activity	A	B	C	D	E	F	G	H	I	J
Reduction in weeks	1	3	1	2	3	2	2	5	3	1
Cost of reduction	2	3	3	12	6	10	5	4	5	7
Cost per week	2	1	3	6	2	5	2.5	0.8	1.7	7

The total float of activities on the parallel path A−B−C−D is 2, so if the critical path is reduced by this amount A−B−C−D becomes critical.

This completes step 1 of the procedure.

Step 2 finds the activity on the critical path (E−F−G−J) with lowest cost of crashing, and this is E at £2000 a week.

Step 3 reduces the time for activity E by two weeks, as beyond this the path A−B−C−D−J becomes critical.

Total cost of crashing by two weeks = 2 ∗ 2000 = £4000
Total savings = 2 ∗ 3500 = £7000

This step has reduced the penalty cost by more than the crashing cost, so we look for more savings.

Step 2 identifies the lowest costs in the critical paths as E in E−F−G−J and B in A−B−C−D−J.

Step 3 reduces the time of these activities by one week, as E is then reduced by the maximum allowed.

Total cost of crashing by one week = 2000 + 1000 = £3000
Total savings = £3500

Again the overall cost has been reduced, so we look for more savings.

Step 2 identifies the lowest costs in the critical paths as B in $A-B-C-D-J$ and G in $(E-)F-G-J$.

Total cost of crashing by one week = 1000 + 2500 = £3500
Total savings = £3500

At this point the savings exactly match the cost, and a minimum total cost has been found. If any more activities were crashed, the cost would be more than the savings from reduced penalties.

The overall duration of the project is now 20 days, with cost of £221,000 for normal activities, £10,500 for crashing and £7000 for penalties to give a total of £238,500.

In summary

The costs of a project can be classified as direct, indirect and penalty. All of these vary with project duration. Project managers should find the duration that minimizes the total cost.

9.5.3 Gantt charts and resource levelling

When a project is being executed, there should be constant monitoring of progress to ensure activities are done at the required times. This is rather difficult if working directly from a network, but a Gantt chart allows progress to be monitored much more easily. A Gantt chart is simply another way of representing a project, which emphasizes the timing of activities. The chart consists of a timescale across the bottom, activities are listed down the left-hand side, and times when activities should be done are blocked off in the body of the chart.

The principles of a Gantt chart are illustrated in the following worked example.

WORKED EXAMPLE 9.12

Draw a Gantt chart for the original data in Worked Example 9.9, assuming each activity starts as early as possible.

SOLUTION

The activity analysis for this example is shown in Table 9.17.

Table 9.17

Activity	Duration	Earliest		Latest			Float		
		ES	EF	LS	LF	TF	FF	IF	
A	8	0	8	0	8	0	0	0	*
B	4	8	12	8	12	0	0	0	*
C	2	12	14	12	14	0	0	0	*
D	3	0	3	2	5	2	0	0	
E	6	3	9	5	11	2	0	0	
F	3	9	12	11	14	2	2	0	
G	2	0	2	4	6	4	0	0	
H	4	2	6	6	10	4	0	0	(−4)
I	4	6	10	10	14	4	4	0	

If each activity starts as early as possible, the time needed is shown by the blocked-off areas in Figure 9.25. The total float of each activity is added afterwards as a broken line. The total float is the maximum expansion that can still allow the project to finish on time, so provided an activity is completed before the end of the broken line there should be no problem keeping to the planned project duration.

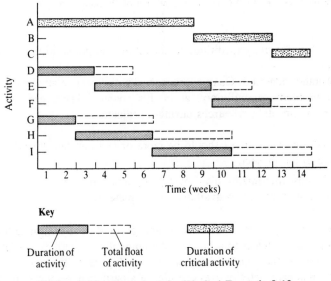

Figure 9.25 Gantt chart for Worked Example 9.12.

The main benefit of Gantt charts is that they show clearly the state of each activity at any point in the project. They show which activities should be in hand, as well as those that should be finished, and those about to start. Any

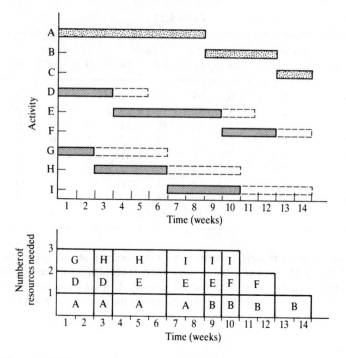

Figure 9.26 Resource use during project of Worked Example 9.12.

delays, with necessary expediting, rescheduling and preparation, can be identified easily.

Another benefit of Gantt charts comes with resource allocation, which is the final problem we will look at in this chapter. There are two specific objectives in allocating resources during a project:

(1) The use of resources should be more or less constant throughout the life of the project.

(2) The cost minimizing plan must be feasible (in other words there must be enough resources available to complete it).

An appropriate objective of resource planning would be to minimize the overall cost of a project, subject to a limit on the amount of resources available.

Consider the Gantt chart shown in Figure 9.25 and assume, for simplicity, that each activity uses one unit of a particular resource (perhaps one team of workers). If all activities start as soon as possible, we could draw a bar chart to show the resources in use at any time. The project starts with activities A, D and G so three teams will be used. At the end of week 2 one team can move from G to H, but three teams will still be needed. Continuing these allocations gives the graph of resources shown in Figure 9.26.

In this example, the use of resources is steady for most of the project and only begins to fall near the end. It is rare to get such a smooth pattern of resource use, and usually there are a series of peaks and troughs which should be levelled. As critical activities are at fixed times this levelling must be done by rescheduling non-critical activities, and in particular by delaying those activities with relatively large total floats. A reasonable approach to resource levelling is:

(1) schedule all activities at their earliest times and find the resources needed throughout the project;

(2) for times when too many resources are needed, delay non-critical activities to times when fewer resources are needed;

(3) if there are conflicts, always give priority to activities with least float.

There are formal methods for scheduling workloads but these tend to need a lot of manipulation and are best done using standard computer software. The simple heuristic approach can be demonstrated in the following example.

WORKED EXAMPLE 9.13

The network shown in Figure 9.27 shows a project consisting of 11 activities over a period of 19 months. If each activity uses one work team, how many teams will be needed at each stage of the project?

Would it be possible to schedule the activities so that a maximum of three work teams are used at any time?

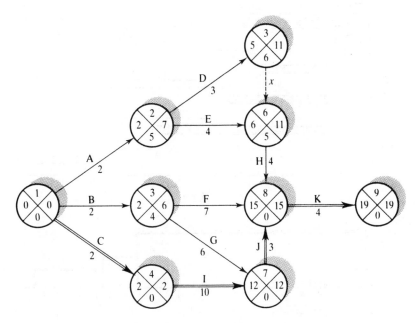

Figure 9.27 Network for Worked Example 9.13.

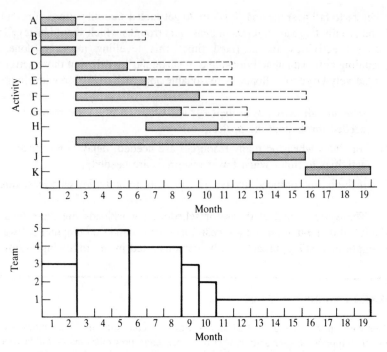

Figure 9.28 Gantt chart and work team requirements assuming that all activities start as early as possible.

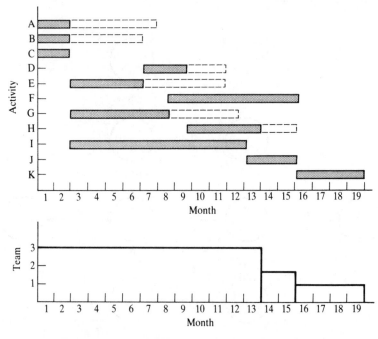

Figure 9.29 Gantt chart and work team requirements with activities rescheduled to smooth load.

SOLUTION

A Gantt chart for this project is shown in Figure 9.28 with the assumption that all activities start as early as possible. This uses a maximum of five work teams during months 3 to 5.

If the number of work teams is to be smoothed, activities with large floats should be delayed. One schedule would delay the start of D until month 7, the start of F until month 9 and the start of H until month 10. This rescheduling reduces the maximum number of work teams required to three and gives a smoother workload, as shown in Figure 9.29.

Rescheduling a project can be done easily if a computer is used for the calculations. Unfortunately, the quality of software for project network analysis is variable. Some programs need details of the network to be specified as input data and simply do the timing calculations. Others do not do the resource levelling. Most programs give results as printed tables, with very few actually drawing the network.

In summary
Gantt charts give another representation of projects, emphasizing the timing. They are used primarily in the planning of resources, and to monitor progress through the execution phase of a project.

SELF ASSESSMENT QUESTIONS

9.23 What is the crashed time of an activity?

9.24 The total cost of a project declines with its duration, as penalty costs, labour costs, financing costs, and so on, are all reduced with shorter times. Is this statement true?

9.25 What are the main benefits of Gantt charts?

9.26 How can the use of resources be smoothed during a project?

SUMMARY OF CHAPTER

A project is a coherent piece of work with a distinct start and finish. It consists of those activities needed to make a unique product. This chapter has described the way in which project network analysis can help with the planning and control of projects.

The relationships between activities in a project can be represented by a dependence table. This can be translated into a network of alternating activities and events. The chapter described 'activity on arrow' diagrams, where nodes represent events.

There are some guidelines for drawing networks. Generally, the first activities are drawn on the left, and later activities are systematically added. Sometimes uniqueness or logical dummy activities must be used.

When the network is complete the timing of the project can be considered. Event analyses find the earliest and latest times for events, with the difference between these measuring slack. Activity analyses find the earliest and latest start and finish times for activities. Associated with these are the total, free and independent floats which measure the amount activities can be expanded or delayed. The critical path identifies those activities which set the duration of the project and need particular attention.

The critical path method (CPM) assumes a fixed duration for each activity, but the chapter described how the project evaluation and review technique (PERT) introduces uncertainty to activity durations. The assumption is that activity durations follow a Beta distribution, allowing expected duration and variance to be calculated from three estimates. The overall project duration is then Normally distributed, with mean and variance calculated from the critical path.

The duration of a project may need adjusting. If reductions are needed the critical activities must be shortened, but if these reductions are large, parallel paths become critical. If non-critical activities are delayed by more than their total float the critical path changes.

The costs of projects can be classified as direct, indirect or penalty. These all change with project duration, and a method was described for minimizing them.

Gantt charts allow the progress of a project to be monitored and can also be used for resource planning.

An overall summary of the process for project network analysis is:

- define the project, agreeing information on activities and events;
- develop a precedence table showing relationships between activities;
- draw a network;
- analyse the timing (event and activity);
- draw a Gantt chart;
- find the resources needed throughout the project;
- make any final adjustments to project timing;
- monitor progress during the execution phase;
- update schedules as necessary.

PROBLEMS

9.1 A project consists of the activities described by the dependence table (Table 9.18). Draw the network for this project.

Table 9.18

Activity	Depends on	Activity	Depends on
A	—	G	B
B	—	H	G
C	A	I	E,F
D	A	J	H,I
E	C	K	E,F
F	B,D	L	K

9.2 (a) An amateur dramatic society is planning its annual production and is interested in using a network to coordinate the various activities. What activities do you think should be included in the network?

(b) If discussions lead to the following activities, what would the network look like?
- (i) Assess resources and select play
- (ii) Prepare scripts
- (iii) Select actors and cast parts
- (iv) Rehearse
- (v) Design and organize advertisements
- (vi) Prepare stage, lights and sound
- (vii) Build scenery
- (viii) Sell tickets
- (ix) Finalize arrangements for opening.

9.3 Draw a network for the dependence table (Table 9.19).

Table 9.19

Activity	Depends on	Activity	Depends on
A	H	I	F
B	H	J	I
C	K	K	L
D	I,M,N	L	F
E	F	M	O
F	—	N	H
G	E,L	O	A,B
H	E	P	N

421

9.4 If each activity in Problem 9.3 has a duration of one week, find the earliest and latest times for each event and the slacks. Calculate the earliest and latest start and finish times for each activity and the corresponding total, free and independent floats.

9.5 Draw the network represented by the dependence table in Table 9.20 and calculate the floats for each activity.

Table 9.20

Activity	Duration (weeks)	Depends on
A	5	—
B	3	—
C	3	B
D	7	A
E	10	B
F	14	A,C
G	7	D,E
H	4	E
I	5	D

If each activity can be reduced by up to two weeks, what is the shortest duration of the project and which activities are reduced?

9.6 A project is represented by Table 9.21 which shows the dependency of activities and three estimates of durations.

- What is the probability that the project will be completed before 17?
- By what time is there a probability of 0.95 that the project will be finished?

Table 9.21

Activity	Depends on	Duration Optimistic	Duration Most likely	Duration Pessimistic
A	—	1	2	3
B	A	1	3	6
C	B	4	6	10
D	A	1	1	1
E	D	1	2	2
F	E	3	4	8
G	F	2	3	5
H	D	7	9	11
I	A	0	1	4
J	I	2	3	4
K	H,J	3	4	7
L	C,G,K	1	2	7

9.7 A project consists of ten activities with estimated durations (in weeks) and dependencies shown in Table 9.22. What are the estimated duration of the project and the earliest and latest times for activities?

Table 9.22

Activity	Depends.	Duration	Activity	Depends.	Duration
A	—	8	F	C,D	10
B	A	6	G	B,E,F	5
C	—	10	H	F	8
D	—	6	I	G,H,J	6
E	C	2	J	A	4

If activity B requires special equipment to be hired, when should this be scheduled? A check on the project at week 12 shows that activity F is running two weeks late, that activity J would now take 6 weeks, and that the equipment for B would not arrive until week 18. What effect will this have on the overall project duration?

9.8 Draw a Gantt chart for the project described in Problem 9.5. If each activity uses one team of people, draw a graph of manpower requirements assuming each activity starts as soon as possible. How might these requirements be smoothed?

9.9 Analyse the times and resource requirements of the project described by the data in Table 9.23.

Table 9.23

Activity	Depends on	Duration	Resources
A	—	4	1
B	A	4	2
C	A	3	4
D	B	5	4
E	C	2	2
F	D,E	6	3
G	—	3	3
H	G	7	1
I	G	6	5
J	H	2	3
K	I	4	4
L	J,K	8	2

9.10 In the project described in Problem 9.6 it costs £1000 to reduce the duration of an activity by 1. If there is £12,000 available to reduce the overall duration of the project how should this be allocated and what is the shortest time in which the project can be completed? What are the minimum resources needed by the revised schedule?

CASE STUDY – MEDITERRANEAN ORANGE

Manhattan Incorporated Softdrinks is a conglomerate company which owns over 350 subsidiaries around the world. One of these subsidiaries is European Softdrinks and Equipment Supply (ESES) which has headquarters in London. This company is expanding its business in Southern Europe and has recently acquired Mediterranean Orange. This should markedly increase its sales in Italy, but the next plan is to open a new warehouse and distribution centre for Mediterranean Orange on the south coast of Spain.

David Peacock is a planner in the headquarters of ESES. Last week he was invited to visit Norman Millar, who is the Associate Director of European Operations. It is very rare for a relatively junior planner to be called to the Director's suite, but Norman Millar soon explained the problem.

> You will probably know that we are expanding operations around the coast of Spain and have recently acquired Mediterranean Orange. You may know about their Villa Marbella distribution centre which is in the late stages of planning. Last month Mr Solstice (President of the Manhattan parent company) contacted Mr Jones (Managing Director of ESES) asking for details of when this centre will be ready. Mr Jones, in turn, asked the managers of Mediterranean Orange, who sent one of their planner's reports. The only problem is the report consists of a table of figures without any explanation. This means absolutely nothing to any of us. We can't go back to Mediterranean Orange, as relations are still forming, and we want to tread carefully. We also need some figures that we can pass on to Mr Solstice fairly quickly. The only thing I know for certain is that we have about 40 weeks to open the centre, and beyond that our costs start rising at 2% a week. Can you look at the table and give us some information before the end of the week?

David Peacock looked at the table (Table 9.24) and said he might manage something within a few days.

Table 9.24

Act	OD	MD	PD	DO	Manning	NC (1000s)	CT	CC (1000s)
AA	3	3	6	BW	14	8	2	10
AB	3	4	7	AG	7	7	3	9
AC	4	4	6	AB,AE,AY	12	12	3	15
AD	2	3	4	AA	3	2	1	4
AE	3	3	3	AD	2	2	3	2
AF	6	8	14	AD	6	12	4	16
AG	2	2	2	BZ	2	1	2	1
AH	6	8	14	AC,AF	10	20	5	35
AI	6	8	14	AF	12	24	6	36
AJ	7	8	11	AH,AK	12	24	5	42
AK	10	14	20	BQ,BY	22	66	6	85
AL	4	5	7	AK	8	10	2	12
AM	3	3	5	AL	4	3	2	4
AN	5	6	9	AJ	6	9	3	13
AO	8	10	12	AZ	24	60	5	72
AP	4	5	6	BQ	8	10	1	12
AQ	8	10	16	BO,BP	9	23	4	25
AR	3	3	3	BE	11	8	3	8
AS	4	5	6	AP,AQ,AR	3	4	3	6
AT	8	10	15	BT,BV	7	18	7	20
AU	5	6	7	AT	15	23	5	25
AV	4	6	8	AS	18	28	4	30
AW	4	5	9	AM,AN,AO	19	24	3	26
AX	4	4	4	BJ	3	3	3	3
AY	1	1	1	BY	2	1	1	2
AZ	4	5	6	AI	8	10	2	14
BA	1	1	1	—	7	2	1	2
BB	4	5	6	BK	21	27	4	30
BC	4	4	4	BJ	23	24	4	24
BD	5	7	9	AX	17	29	4	35
BE	2	2	2	BN	4	2	1	5
BF	3	5	9	BH	9	11	1	14
BG	2	2	2	BH	6	3	2	3
BH	2	4	6	—	7	7	1	9
BI	1	2	3	—	8	4	1	6
BJ	3	3	3	BK	2	2	3	2
BK	2	2	2	BA	10	5	2	5
BL	2	3	4	BA	15	11	2	15
BM	1	1	1	BI,BL	8	2	1	2
BN	2	4	8	BG,BM	12	12	2	14

BO	6	8	10	BG,BM	22	44	4	60
BP	5	7	11	BF	26	44	3	58
BQ	3	3	3	BF	15	11	3	11
BR	3	6	9	BC	15	38	3	48
BS	4	4	4	BD,BR	7	7	4	7
BT	3	4	8	BS	11	11	3	16
BU	2	2	2	BD	13	7	2	7
BV	2	2	2	BU	5	3	2	3
BW	2	3	3	—	6	5	1	12
BX	5	7	7	BW	8	14	3	18
BY	8	10	15	BX	15	38	4	42
BZ	4	5	8	BW	13	16	2	24

Suggested topic

Assume you are David Peacock and write a report for the Directors of the London office.

SOLUTIONS TO SELF ASSESSMENT QUESTIONS

9.1 A coherent piece of work with a distinct start and finish, consisting of a set of activities that make a unique product.

9.2 Project management is concerned with the planning, scheduling and controlling of activities in a project and hence the management of resources. Planning is necessary to ensure that the project runs on time and that resources are used efficiently.

9.3 No. Project management is concerned with all projects including small ones.

9.4 Planning and execution.

9.5 It helps with scheduling during the planning phase and control during the execution phase.

9.6 (a) Events (that is, the start and finish of activities); (b) activities.

9.7 A list of all activities in the project and the immediate predecessors of each activity. Durations, resources needed and other factors can be added but these are not essential for drawing the network.

9.8 The two main rules are:

- before an activity can begin all preceding activities must be finished;
- the arrows representing activities imply precedence only and neither the length nor orientation is significant.

There are also some secondary rules:

- a network has only one starting and finishing event;
- any two events can only be connected by one activity.

9.9 There are two uses of dummy activities:

- uniqueness dummies ensure only one activity is directly between any two events;
- logical dummies ensure the logic of the dependence table is maintained in the network.

9.10 No. For a complex project there are usually many ways of defining the activities, and different views on their dependency. Once a dependency table has been built, there is only one correct network.

9.11 The earliest time of event j is the earliest time by which all preceding activities can be finished.

$$ET(1) = 0$$

$$ET(j) = \text{Max} \big[\, ET(i) + D(i,j) \, \big]$$

The latest time for an event is the latest time which allows all following activities to be started on time.

$$LT(n) = ET(n)$$

$$LT(i) = \text{Min} \big[\, LT(j) - D(i,j) \, \big]$$

9.12 The slack of an event is the amount it can move without affecting the project duration. It is defined as the difference between the latest and earliest event times.

9.13 Float measures the amount of flexibility in an activity's duration (essentially the amount it can expand without affecting other activities).

9.14 Total float is the difference between the maximum amount of time available for an activity and the time actually used.

$$TF(k) = LT(j) - ET(i) - D(i,j)$$

Free float is the maximum expansion without affecting any following activity.

$$FF(k) = ET(j) - ET(i) - D(i,j)$$

Independent float is the maximum expansion without affecting any other activity.

$$IF(k) = ET(j) - LT(i) - D(i,j)$$

9.15 Zero.

9.16 The critical path is the chain of activities that determine the project duration. If any critical activity is extended or delayed the whole project is delayed.

9.17 CPM assumes a fixed activity duration, while PERT assumes that activity durations follow a known distribution.

9.18 The rule of sixths assumes the duration of an activity follows a Beta distribution, in which case:

$$\text{Expected duration} = \frac{OD + 4 * MD + PD}{6}$$

$$\text{Variance} = \frac{(PD - OD)^2}{36}$$

9.19 The project duration is assumed to be Normally distributed with mean equal to the sum of the expected durations of activities on the critical path, and variance equal to the sum of variances of activities on the critical path.

9.20 The critical activities.

9.21 By the amount of total float of activities on a parallel path. Reductions beyond this leave the parallel path as critical.

9.22 **(a)** By its independent float; **(b)** by its free float; **(c)** by its total float.

9.23 The minimum time in which an activity can be completed.

9.24 No. Some costs rise with reduced duration.

9.25 They show what stage each activity in a project should have reached at any time. Any necessary expediting, rescheduling and preparation can be identified quickly.

9.26 By delaying non-critical activities to times when fewer resources are needed.

REFERENCES FOR FURTHER READING

Original reports

Kelley J.E. and Walker M.R. (1959). *Critical Path Planning and Scheduling, Proceedings of the Eastern Joint Computer Conference, Boston*, pp. 160–73

Special Projects Office, Department of the Navy (1958). *PERT, Program Evaluation Research Task* Phase 1 Summary Report, pp. 646–69

Other references

Battersby A. (1970). *Network Analysis for Planning and Scheduling* London: Macmillan

Cleland D.I. and King W.R. (1983). *Project Management Handbook* New York: Van Nostrand Reinhold

Cleland D.I. and Kocaoglu D.F. (1981). *Engineering Management* New York: McGraw-Hill

Goodman L.J. and Love R.N. (1980). *Project Planning and Management: An Integrated Approach* New York: Pergamon Press

Harrison F.L. (1981). *Advanced Project Management* New York: Halstead

Kerzner H.(1984). *Project Management for Executives* New York: Van Nostrand Reinhold

Kerzner H. and Thamhain H. (1984). *Project Management for Small and Medium-Sized Business* New York: Van Nostrand Reinhold

Meredith J.R. and Mantel S.J. (1985). *Project Management* New York: John Wiley

Modder J.J., Phillips C.K. and Davis E.W. (1983). *Project Management with CPM and PERT* 3rd edn. New York: Van Nostrand Reinhold

Waters C.D.J. (1989). *A Practical Introduction to Management Science* Wokingham: Addison-Wesley

Weist J.D. and Levy F.K. (1977). *A Management Guide to PERT/CPM* 2nd edn. Englewood Cliffs: Prentice-Hall

Chapter 10

Material requirements planning and just-in-time systems

SYNOPSIS

Chapter 8 described some aspects of planning, including the development of a master schedule. This master schedule was used to produce short-term schedules for individual equipment and operators. Sometimes it can also be used to schedule the orders of components, parts and other materials. This is the basis of material requirements planning which is described in this chapter.

Material requirements planning (MRP) can be viewed as another stage in planning in which the master schedule is 'exploded', using a bill of material, to give a detailed timetable of requirements for materials and parts.

This approach can only be used when specific conditions are met, but then it can bring a number of advantages. The close matching of material supply to known demand can, for example, significantly reduce stocks of raw materials. One of the main disadvantages is the amount of data manipulation needed, and this inevitably needs a computer.

Sometimes, MRP analyses suggest small, frequent orders. These can be expensive to administer and it would be better to combine several orders into a single larger one. A batching rule is described to give improved ordering policies.

The MRP approach can be extended in several ways. Some extensions are described as MRP II, but the most significant uses just-in-time (JIT) principles. These organize the flow of materials to arrive just as they are needed. This idea has become very popular recently because of the substantial benefits that can be achieved. Kanbans offer a simple way of controlling JIT.

OBJECTIVES

After reading this chapter and doing the associated exercises you should be able to:

- describe MRP;
- list requirements for the use of MRP;
- use MRP to timetable orders and operations;
- discuss the advantages and disadvantages of MRP;
- use a batching rule for variable, discrete demand;
- suggest ways in which basic MRP systems can be extended, including MRP II;
- describe the principles of just-in-time systems;
- describe Kanban systems for controlling JIT;
- discuss the benefits and problems with JIT.

10.1 MATERIAL REQUIREMENTS PLANNING

10.1.1 Introduction

Chapter 8 described some aspects of planning. In particular it described a hierarchy of decisions, with strategic capacity plans being expanded to give aggregate plans, and these in turn being expanded to give a master schedule. The master schedule consists of a timetable for the production of finished products. We described how this master schedule can be used to develop short-term schedules for equipment and operators.

There are, however, other uses of the master schedule, and one of these is to plan the supply of materials needed for operations. This is the basis of MRP which is described in the first part of this chapter (see Figure 10.1).

All operations depend on a reliable supply of materials. These materials may be basic raw materials, components, sub-assemblies, parts or a range of other items. It has traditionally been a function of the procurement or purchasing department to ensure that materials arrive when needed. The function of these departments can be described as:

- identifying possible suppliers;
- selecting suppliers for each material (or order);
- negotiating contracts with suppliers;
- allowing an interface between an organization and its suppliers;
- expediting deliveries when necessary.

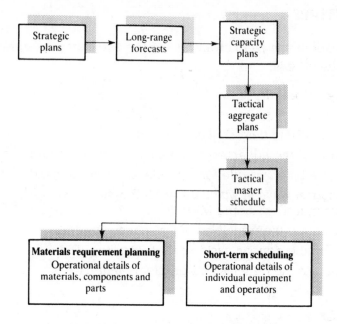

Figure 10.1 Summary of the planning process.

In some organizations procurement includes other functions, such as arranging deliveries, checking the quality of materials delivered, looking for alternative products, recognizing changes in the marketplace, checking financial arrangements, and so on.

In essence, though, the procurement function only arranges the deliveries of materials which are requested by operations. These requests must be based on some formal planning, and MRP offers one way of doing this.

> MRP uses the master schedule to plan the supply of materials so they are available when needed.

The essential characteristic of MRP is that it uses the master schedule for planning material requirements. It starts by seeing what production is planned, and then develops a timetable for orders so the materials arrive in time for their use. The resulting stocks of materials depend directly on the known demand. Such systems are called 'dependent demand inventory systems'. The alternative would be to keep stocks of materials which are high enough to cover any likely demand. These stocks are not directly related to the demand specified in a master schedule and are called 'independent demand inventory systems' (which are described in Chapter 11). An analogy would be the way a chef plans the ingredients needed to cook a week's meals. The MRP approach would look at

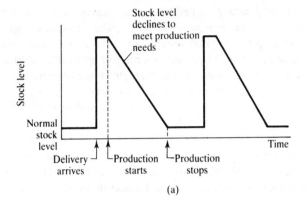

(a)

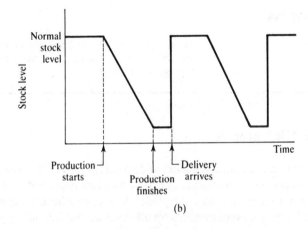

(b)

Figure 10.2 (a) Stock level with MRP. (b) Stock level with independent demand system.

the meals to be cooked each day, use this to determine the ingredients needed, and then ensure these are delivered in time. The alternative 'independent demand' system would see what ingredients have been used in previous weeks and ensure enough of everything is kept in stock to cover likely demand.

An important difference between the two approaches is the resulting pattern of material stocks. With MRP stocks are generally low, but rise just before production starts as orders are delivered. The stock is then used during production and it declines until it returns to its normal, low level. This pattern is shown in Figure 10.2(a). With independent demand systems the stocks are not related to production plans, so higher levels must be maintained. These are reduced during production, but are replenished as soon as possible, to give the pattern shown in Figure 10.2(b).

MRP was originally designed for manufacturing industries. Although the approach has now been extended to many other industries we will, for convenience, stick to the original vocabulary. This talks of components being delivered to make products. The principles are still applicable to some services. Then MRP might talk in terms of, for example, transport arriving to provide part of a service, or staff arriving to help customers.

In summary

Material requirements planning uses the master schedule to organize the delivery of materials. This allows stocks to be matched directly to production plans. The alternative is an independent demand inventory system.

SELF ASSESSMENT QUESTIONS

10.1 What is meant by MRP?

10.2 Is MRP an example of:

(a) a dependent demand inventory system
(b) an independent demand inventory system
(c) neither of these?

10.1.2 The MRP process

MRP is based on an accurate assessment of demand for items. This assessment is not found from projective forecasts, but from the plans described in the master schedule. The important stage is to 'explode' the master schedule using a bill of materials to give detailed requirements for all materials used. A bill of materials, or parts list, is simply an ordered list of all the parts needed to make a particular product. Suppose, for example, a table is made from a top and four legs. The bill of materials is shown in Figure 10.3. In this diagram 'level 0' refers to final products and 'level 1' to the parts, while the figures in brackets show the number needed to make each unit.

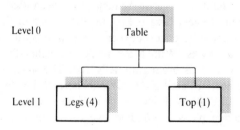

Figure 10.3 Bill of materials for a table.

This is a very simple bill of materials; bills are usually much more complicated, involving many levels and parts. Further details for the table might show that each top is made from a wood kit and hardware, and that the wood kit consists of four oak planks which are 180 centimetres long, 30 centimetres wide and 2.5 centimetres thick, and so on. A partially completed diagram for this is shown in Figure 10.4.

This example of a table can be used to illustrate the overall approach of MRP. Suppose, for example, the master schedule says that 10 tables are to be made in February. We can use this information, together with the bill of materials, to calculate the quantities and times of materials needed. The schedule needs 10 tops and 40 legs to be delivered in time for the tables to be completed in February. If these are bought from suppliers with a lead time of four weeks, we would place orders at the beginning of January. These would arrive by the end of January just before assembly is due to start.

The master schedule shows when items are being produced, and the bill of materials shows what parts are needed for these. Together they can be used to find the gross requirements for parts. Not all of these gross requirements need to be ordered, as there may be some existing stocks. If we subtract the current stocks from the gross stocks, we get a figure for net requirements. There might also be some orders for materials which have already been placed and which will arrive in time to meet the net requirements. If we subtract these from the net requirements we find the amount of materials which are still to be ordered.

$$\text{Materials to be ordered} = \text{gross requirement} - \text{current stock} - \text{stock on order}$$

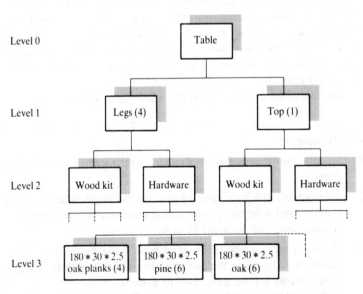

Figure 10.4 Partial bill of materials for a table.

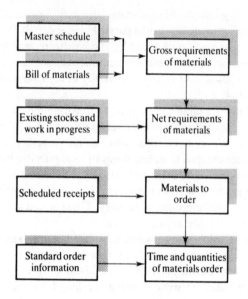

Figure 10.5 The MRP process.

Now we have found the quantities to be ordered, and when these orders should arrive. The next step is to find the time when orders must be placed. This needs information about lead times so that orders can be placed this lead time before the materials are actually needed. The ordering of materials so they arrive in time for use is sometimes called 'time shifting' or 'time phasing'. Finally, there may be some additional information about orders, such as minimum quantities, discounts, and so on. When all this is taken into account we have a detailed timetable for quantities to be ordered. This overall process is summarized in Figure 10.5.

A more detailed view of the MRP process is as follows.

The MRP process

(1) Use the master schedule to find the gross requirements of level 0 items.

(2) Subtract any stock on hand to give the net requirements of level 0 items, and schedule production to start so that these net requirements can be made in time.

(3) If there are any more levels of materials, use the bill of materials to translate the last level of production starts into gross requirements for the next level of material.
If there are no more levels go to step 5.

---

(4) Take each of the materials in turn and:
- (a) subtract the stock on hand and scheduled deliveries to find the quantities of materials to order;
- (b) use the lead time and any other relevant information to find the time of orders.

Go to step 3.

(5) When there are no more levels of materials, finalize the timetable of events.

It is perhaps easier to follow this procedure using a worked example.

WORKED EXAMPLE 10.1

A company assembles dining room tables using bought-in parts of four legs and a top. These have lead times of two and three weeks respectively, and assembly takes a week. The company receives orders for 20 tables to be delivered in week 5 of a production period and 40 tables in week 7, but has current stocks of only two complete tables, 40 legs and 22 tops. When should it order parts?

SOLUTION

It is easiest to follow the calculations in a table, so we will use a standard format, sometimes called 'MRP tables'.

The production schedule for dining room tables is shown in Table 10.1. This gives the gross requirements for level 0 items. Subtracting the stocks of finished tables gives the net requirements. Then allowing a week for assembly gives the start times shown in the assembly plan.

Table 10.1

Level 0 – dining room tables							
Week	1	2	3	4	5	6	7
Gross requirements					20		40
Opening stock	2	2	2	2	2		
Net requirements					18		40
Start assembly				18		40	
Scheduled receipts					18		40

The 'Scheduled receipts' show the number of units which become available in a week, which is the number started the lead time previously.

The bill of materials for this problem has already been shown in Figure 10.3. This can be used in conjunction with the assembly plans to find gross requirements for level 1 items (legs and tops). In week 4, assembly is started on 18 tables, which translates into a gross requirement of 72 legs and 18 tops. Similarly, other gross requirements are:

- legs: $18 * 4 = 72$ in week 4 and $40 * 4 = 160$ in week 6
- tops: 18 in week 4 and 40 in week 6.

Subtracting stock on hand from these gross requirements gives the net requirements. To ensure the parts arrive on time they must be ordered the lead time in advance (that is, two weeks for legs and three weeks for tops). These requirements are shown in Tables 10.2 and 10.3.

Table 10.2

Level 1 − legs Week	1	2	3	4	5	6	7
Gross requirements				72		160	
Opening stock	40	40	40	40			
Net requirements				32		160	
Place order		32		160			
Scheduled receipts				32		160	

Table 10.3

Level 1 − tops Week	1	2	3	4	5	6	7
Gross requirements				18		40	
Opening stock	22	22	22	22	4	4	
Net requirements						36	
Place order			36				
Scheduled receipts						36	

There are no more levels of materials, so we can finalize the timetable of events:

week 2: order 32 legs
week 3: order 36 tops
week 4: order 160 legs and assemble 18 tables
week 6: assemble 40 tables

In this example we have implicitly defined a number of relationships. For example:

$$\text{Scheduled receipts in period } N = \text{Production started or orders placed in period } N - LT$$

where LT is the lead time.

$$\frac{\text{Net requirements}}{\text{in period } N} = \frac{\text{Gross requirements}}{\text{in period } N} - \text{Free opening stock}$$

Here 'Free opening stock' is the amount of stock actually available for use. If, for example, the opening stock is 20 units, but the company always keeps a reserve of 5 units, the free stock is 15 units. Although we have not used the terms in the MRP tables, we might note this definition as:

$$\text{Free opening stock} = \text{Opening stock} - \text{Reserved stock}$$

Sometimes it is easier to ignore any reserved stock, excluding it from all calculations and only showing the free stock in MRP tables. We have not used this convention but have reported all stock on hand.

Perhaps the most important relationship is one we have met before, where:

$$\frac{\text{Opening stock}}{\text{in period } N + 1} = \frac{\text{Opening stock}}{\text{in period } N} + \frac{\text{Scheduled}}{\text{receipts in}} - \frac{\text{Gross}}{\text{requirements}}$$
$$\text{period } N \qquad \text{in period } N$$

These relationships can be illustrated again in a slightly longer example.

WORKED EXAMPLE 10.2

A production schedule requires 45 units of a product to be available in week 12 of a cycle, 60 units in week 13 and 40 units in week 16. There are currently 10 units of the product in stock, but the company always keeps 5 units in reserve to cover emergency orders. Each unit of the product takes two weeks to assemble from 2 units of part B and 3 units of part C. Each unit of part B is made in one week from 1 unit of material D and 3 units of material E. Part C is assembled in two weeks from 2 units of component F. Lead times for D, E and F are one, two and three weeks respectively. Current stocks are 50 units of B, 100 of C, 40 of D, 150 of E and 100 of F. The company keeps minimum stocks of 20 units of D, 100 of E and 50 of F. The minimum order size for E is 300 units, while F can only be ordered in discrete batches of 100 units. An order placed with a subcontractor for 100 units of C is expected to arrive in week 8. Develop a timetable of activities for the company.

SOLUTION

The bill of materials for the product is shown in Figure 10.6, where the lead times are shown under each box.

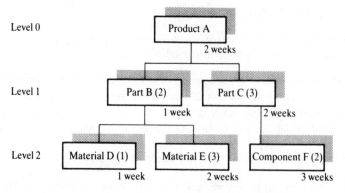

Level 0

Level 1

Level 2

Product A
2 weeks

Part B (2)
1 week

Part C (3)
2 weeks

Material D (1)
1 week

Material E (3)
2 weeks

Component F (2)
3 weeks

Figure 10.6 Bill of materials for Worked Example 10.2.

The analysis then starts at level 0, with production of the final product, A. The company keeps a minimum stock of 5 units of A, so this reserved stock must be remembered when calculating net requirements (see Table 10.4).

Table 10.4

Level 0 − Product A Week	6	7	8	9	10	11	12	13	14	15	16
Gross requirements							45	60			40
Opening stock	10	10	10	10	10	10	10	5	5	5	5
Net requirements							40	60			40
Start assembly					40	60			40		
Scheduled receipts							40	60			40

Now we can move to level 1 materials and expand the assembly plan for A into gross requirements for components B and C. The 40 units of A assembled in week 10 are expanded into gross requirements of 80 units of part B and 120 units of part C. The 60 units of A assembled in week 11 are expanded into gross requirements of 120 units of B and 180 units of C, and so on.

Table 10.5(a)

Level 1 − Part B Week	6	7	8	9	10	11	12	13	14	15	16
Gross requirements					80	120			80		
Opening stock	50	50	50	50	50						
Net requirements					30	120			80		
Start making				30	120			80			
Scheduled receipts					30	120			80		

Table 10.5(b)

Level 1 – Part C											
Week	6	7	8	9	10	11	12	13	14	15	16
Gross requirements					120	180			120		
Opening stock	100	100	100	200	200	80					
Net requirements						100			120		
Start making				100			120				
Scheduled receipts			100			100			120		

Gross requirements for B and C can be partly met from opening stocks, with the shortfall shown in Table 10.5 as net requirements. We must also remember the planned delivery of 100 units of part C in week 8 which moves into stock. This schedule for level 1 parts can now be expanded to give the timetable for level 2 items.

The gross requirements for materials D and E are found from the assembly plans for part B: 30 units of B are started in week 9 and this expands into gross requirements for 30 units of D and 90 units of E, and so on (see Table 10.6). One complication here is the minimum order size of 300 units of E. In week 9 there is a gross requirement of 90 for material E, 50 of which can be met from free stock (keeping the reserve stock of 100). The net requirement is 40, but 300 have to be ordered with the spare 260 added to stock.

Table 10.6(a)

Level 2 – Material D											
Week	6	7	8	9	10	11	12	13	14	15	16
Gross requirements				30	120			80			
Opening stock	40	40	40	40	20	20	20	20	20	20	20
Net requirements				10	120			80			
Place order			10	120			80				
Scheduled receipts				10	120			80			

Table 10.6(b)

Level 2 – Material E											
Week	6	7	8	9	10	11	12	13	14	15	16
Gross requirements				90	360			240			
Opening stock	150	150	150	150	360	300	300	300	360	360	360
Net requirements				40	100			40			
Place order		300	300			300					
Scheduled receipts				300	300			300			

Finally, the gross requirements for component F can be found from the assembly plan for part C: 100 units of C are started in week 9 so this expands into a gross requirement of 200 units of F, and so on (see Table 10.7). Orders must be in discrete batches of 100 units, so they are rounded to the nearest hundred above net requirements.

Table 10.7

Level 2 − Component F *Week*	6	7	8	9	10	11	12	13	14	15	16
Gross requirements				200			240				
Opening stock	100	100	100	100	100	100	100	60	60	60	60
Net requirements				150			190				
Place order	200			200							
Scheduled receipts				200			200				

The timetable of activities now becomes:

week 6: place order for 200 units of F
week 7: place order for 300 units of E
week 8: order for 100 units of C arrives; place orders for 10 units of D and 300 units of E
week 9: start making 30 of B and 100 of C; place orders for 120 units of D and 200 units of F; orders arrive for 10 units of D, 300 units of E and 200 units of F
week 10: start making 40 of A and 120 of B; finish 30 units of B; orders arrive for 120 units of D and 300 units of E
week 11: start making 60 of A; finish 120 units of B and 100 units of C; place order for 300 units of E
week 12: finish making 40 units of A; start making 120 of C; place order for 80 units of D; order arrives for 200 units of F
week 13: finish 60 units of A; start making 80 units of B; orders arrive for 80 units of D and 300 units of E
week 14: start making 40 units of A; finish 80 units of B and 120 units of C
week 16: finish 40 units of A.

In summary

The MRP explodes a master schedule using a bill of materials to allow detailed plans for the ordering of all materials. Accurate information about current stocks, orders outstanding and lead times are then used to schedule orders so that materials arrive in time for use.

10.3 MRP is only relevant for production systems. Is this statement true or false?

10.4 What are the main requirements that allow MRP to be used?

10.5 When building an MRP schedule do you start by considering:

(a) low level items
(b) high level items
(c) any items?

10.6 How is the net requirement for a material found in MRP?

10.1.3 Benefits of MRP

The traditional way of planning orders for materials is 'demand independent'. This uses projective forecasts to find likely demand and then holds stocks that are high enough to cover these. One problem is the unavoidable errors in forecasts. In an effort to overcome these, stocks are increased and associated costs are raised. MRP avoids these costs by relating the supply of materials directly to demand. The result is significantly reduced stocks and associated costs. Other direct benefits include:

- reduced stock levels (with consequent savings in capital, space, warehousing, etc.);
- higher stock turnover;
- increased customer service with fewer delays caused by shortages of materials;
- more reliable and faster quoted delivery times;
- improved utilization of facilities as materials are always available when needed;
- less time spent on expediting and emergency orders.

This ability of MRP to link demand for materials directly to the master schedule is its main advantage, but there are a number of others, such as improved planning. MRP is based on an accurate master schedule, so there is an incentive to produce a reliable plan, and stick to it. Holding large stocks may give more flexibility (by allowing plans to be changed at short notice) but the need to modify plans is often a symptom of poor initial planning, or failure to stick to a plan.

The analyses can give early warning of potential problems and shortages. If necessary, expediting procedures can be used to speed up deliveries, or production plans can be changed. Such planning improves the wider performance of the organization and might be measured in terms of equipment utilization, productivity, customer service, response to market conditions, and so on.

Often, the detailed analysis needed for MRP highlights a number of problems that have previously been hidden. If, for example, a supplier is unreliable this is usually accepted and any potential problems are avoided by keeping higher stocks. This effectively hides the problem, but increases costs. It would be better to recognize the problem and take steps to solve it, either by changing the supplier or discussing ways of improving reliability. This theme is expanded later in the chapter.

In contrast to these advantages, there are also some disadvantages with MRP. The first of these relates to the requirements which must be met before MRP can be used. The MRP process starts with a detailed master schedule which must be known accurately some time in advance. Then we can say that MRP cannot be used if:

- there is no master schedule;
- the master schedule is inaccurate;
- plans are frequently changed;
- plans are not made far enough in advance.

Other requirements, which must be met before MRP can be used, include:

- a parts list or bill of materials which can translate the master schedule into a list of requirements for materials;
- information about current stocks, orders outstanding, supplier reliability, etc.;
- lead times and other information which is needed to allow deliveries of materials to arrive in time for use.

Even when all the requirements are met, the complexity of MRP systems can cause difficulties. The two worked examples described above show very simple situations, yet the amount of data manipulation soon becomes tedious. This in turn implies that MRP can only be used when all related systems are computerized. MRP is not a new idea, but it has only been possible to use it since cheap computing became available in the early 1970s. Since then many standard systems have been developed. The elements of a computerized MRP system are summarized in Figure 10.7.

We have already described the inputs to such a system, but there are several possible outputs. These include the following.

- *A timetable of orders and other operations.*
- *Changes to previous plans.* As the master schedule is revised, or any other changes are made, the MRP schedules are updated. The consequent changes in material requirements and previous orders are reported, including changes to order quantities, cancelled orders or changes of time.

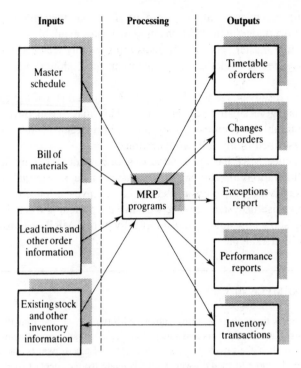

Figure 10.7 A computerized MRP system.

- *Exceptions*. Sometimes the system may note exceptions which cannot be dealt with automatically, and then it should report these. Typically, these include late orders, excessive scrap, requests for non-existent parts, and so on.

- *Performance reports*. These show how well the system is operating and might include measures for investment in stocks, inventory turnover, number of stockouts, and so on.

- *Inventory transactions*. All of these are recorded, so the system maintains accurate records of current stock positions, and reported, so that a check is kept on progress.

Standard software for MRP systems is widely available, but this should be used cautiously. One reason why MRP systems have sometimes failed to bring their potential benefits is the belief that an MRP system can simply be bought and switched on. The introduction of MRP brings about considerable changes to operations and these require commitment from all of the organization. Even if this commitment exists, it should not be assumed that MRP systems are simply an additional tool for planning. They are an integral part of the planning process and should be linked to all other systems.

The prerequisites and substantial data manipulation are the main disadvantage with MRP, but there are others. It might, for example, reduce flexibility

445

in responding to changes. Stocks are expensive, but they allow plans to be changed at short notice: with MRP the only materials available are those needed for the specified master schedule. If plans are suddenly changed the necessary materials may not be available. This might, in turn, slow down responses to market changes.

A final disadvantage which should be mentioned is that the order pattern suggested may give small frequent orders. This may be inconvenient and it might be preferable to combine several orders into larger batches. A procedure for this is described in the following section.

In practice MRP has been found to give considerable benefits and there are many illustrations of companies that have made substantial savings. To produce these savings, the companies have had to invest a lot of time and effort in developing a useful system. Before we leave the topic it is worth beginning an illustration to show how quickly the complexity of real MRP systems rises, even with a simplified example.

WORKED EXAMPLE 10.3

A company makes three sizes of filing cabinet with two, three and four drawers. Each cabinet consists of a case, drawers and a lock. Each case is made from drawer slides and a formed case (which is itself made from a sheet of steel). Each drawer is made from roller supports, a handle and a formed drawer (which is made from a sheet of steel). The bill of materials for the four-drawer cabinet is shown in Figure 10.8, with the figures below the boxes giving lead times in weeks.

There are currently stocks of 50 complete drawers and 100 roller supports, and a delivery of 300 roller supports is expected in week 1. The master schedule for the next 12 weeks is given in Table 10.8.

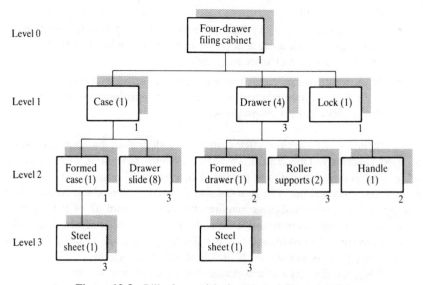

Figure 10.8 Bill of materials for Worked Example 10.3.

Table 10.8

Week	3	4	5	6	7	8	9	10	11
Two-drawer cabinets			100			100		100	50
Three-drawer cabinets			60	120		60			
Four-drawer cabinets		150			150		90		

Devise a plan for ordering and production.

SOLUTION

We are not going to tackle all of this problem, but will make a start on it. The aim is to suggest the large amount of data manipulation in any reasonably sized MRP system. A computer is needed for even small systems.

Starting with two-drawer cabinets, we can draw the table of assembly plans as in Table 10.9.

Table 10.9

Level 0 – Two-drawer cabinets								
Week	4	5	6	7	8	9	10	11
Gross requirements		100			100		100	50
Opening stock								
Net requirements		100			100		100	50
Start assembly	100			100		100	50	
Scheduled receipts		100			100		100	50

Similar tables could be drawn for three- and four-drawer cabinets. From these assembly plans the gross requirements for drawers can be found (150 * 4 in week 4, 100 * 2 + 60 * 3 in week 5, and so on) to give Table 10.10.

Table 10.10

Level 1 – Drawers											
Week	1	2	3	4	5	6	7	8	9	10	11
Gross requirements				600	380	360	600	380	360	200	100
Stock on hand	50	50	50								
Net requirements				550	380	360	600	380	360	200	100
Place orders	550	380	360	600	380	360	200	100			
Scheduled receipts				550	380	360	600	380	360	200	100

The rest of this analysis would continue in the same way, moving progressively up the level of items.

In summary

The main advantage of MRP is its ability to relate demand for materials directly to the master schedule. This reduces stock levels and consequent costs. The main disadvantages are the conditions which must be met before MRP can be used and the amount of data manipulation.

SELF ASSESSMENT QUESTIONS

10.7 What is the main advantage of MRP?

10.8 What is the main problem with using MRP?

10.9 Would it be possible to develop a manual MRP system?

10.10 What are typical outputs from an MRP system?

10.2 BATCHING OF DISCRETE VARIABLE DEMAND

The MRP system we have described may suggest a series of small orders, which are placed every month or even every week. Such frequent orders may be inconvenient and incur high administration and delivery costs. It might be preferable to combine several small orders into fewer, larger batches. In this section we will describe a method of combining orders to ensure that associated costs are kept low. We should, however, start by mentioning that this problem is not unique to MRP, but occurs whenever there is some kind of sporadic demand for an item.

The analysis assumes demand for an item is variable and discrete. In other words the demand varies from one period to the next, and it is assumed to occur at discrete points in time (typically once a week, or once a month). This is typical of the pattern met in MRP systems.

If there are frequent small orders there will be high administration and delivery charges. Conversely, if there are infrequent large orders the administration costs will be lower, but the average stock and consequent holding costs will be higher. We need to find a compromise between these two competing costs. (This theme is expanded in Chapter 11 which looks in more detail at inventory control.)

One way of approaching the problem is based on the assumption that there is some optimal number of periods' demand which should be combined into a single batch. If orders are placed more frequently than this, the administration and delivery charges will rise and give higher costs; if orders are placed less frequently, stock levels will rise and again give higher costs. Thus, we assume a cost curve with a distinct minimum, as shown in Figure 10.9.

We can add all the costs of placing and receiving an order into the single figure RC, the reorder cost. Similarly, all costs associated with holding a unit of

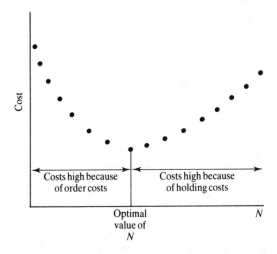

Figure 10.9 Variation in costs with number of periods combined into a single order.

stock for a unit of time can be added to give the single figure HC, the holding cost. Then, if enough stock is bought to cover all orders for the next N periods, we can calculate a total cost. The object is to find the optimal value of N that minimizes this cost.

One way of finding the optimal value for N is to start by considering short stock cycles at the left-hand side of the graph in Figure 10.9. Then increasing N will follow the graph downward until costs start to rise, at which point the optimal has been found. This procedure can be formalized as follows.

(1) First calculate the cost of buying for a single period and compare this with the cost of buying for two periods. If it is cheaper to buy for two periods than for one we are going down the left-hand side of the graph in Figure 10.9 and the cost is reducing as the value of N is increasing.

(2) Next compare the cost of buying for two periods with the cost of buying for three periods. If it is cheaper to buy for three periods we are still on the declining part of the graph and have not yet reached the point of minimum cost.

(3) Continue this procedure, comparing the cost of buying for three periods with the cost of buying for four periods, and so on. In general, we will always compare the cost of buying for the next N periods with the cost of buying for the next $N + 1$ periods.

(4) The procedure is continued until at some point it becomes cheaper to buy for N periods than for $N + 1$ periods. At this point we have reached the bottom of the graph and found the point of minimal cost. Any further increases in N would increase costs as we climb up the right-hand side of the graph.

449

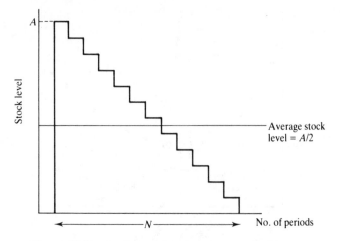

Figure 10.10 Stock level for an order covering N periods.

This procedure finds a good (though not necessarily optimal) length for the next stock cycle. Fortunately, there is a short cut to the arithmetic which removes most of the work and the derivation of this is as follows.

Consider one order for an item, where enough is bought to satisfy demand for the next N periods. We will define the variable demand in period i to be $D(i)$, so that an order to cover all demand in the next N periods will be for

$$A = \sum_{i=1}^{N} D(i)$$

units. We will assume that this arrives in stock at one time, so the highest stock level is A. We will also assume that the item is used steadily for production and the stock will return to zero when production has finished. The average stock level can be approximated by $A/2$ and the cost of holding this is $(A/2) * N * HC$ (see Figure 10.10). Then the cost of stocking the item over the N periods is the sum of:

Reorder cost $= RC$
Holding cost $=$ average stock level $(A/2) *$ time held $(N) *$ holding cost (HC)

$$= \frac{HC * N * \sum_{i=1}^{N} D(i)}{2}$$

If this cost is divided by N, we get an average cost per period, $VC(N)$, of:

$$VC(N) = \frac{RC}{N} + \frac{HC * \sum_{i=1}^{N} D(i)}{2}$$

Now, if instead of combining orders for the next N periods, we combine orders for the next $N + 1$ periods, the cost is found by substituting $N + 1$ for N in this equation.

$$VC(N + 1) = \frac{RC}{N + 1} + \frac{HC * \sum\limits_{i=1}^{N+1} D(i)}{2}$$

We are interested in finding the point at which $VC(N + 1)$ becomes larger than $VC(N)$ so:

$$VC(N + 1) > VC(N)$$

$$\frac{RC}{N + 1} + \frac{HC * \sum\limits_{i=1}^{N+1} D(i)}{2} > \frac{RC}{N} + \frac{HC * \sum\limits_{i=1}^{N} D(i)}{2}$$

which can be simplified to:

$$\boxed{N * (N + 1) * D(N + 1) > \frac{2 * RC}{HC}}$$

This inequality allows us to define a solution procedure. This starts by setting N equal to 1 and comparing the cost of ordering for one period with the cost of ordering for two periods. If the inequality is invalid it is cheaper to order for two periods than for one, so we are moving down the left-hand side of the costs in Figure 10.9. Then we set N equal to 2 and compare the costs of ordering for two and three periods. If the inequality is still invalid, the costs are reducing and we are still coming down the left-hand side of the curve. Then we keep on increasing N, until eventually the inequality will become valid. This means that we are at the bottom of the cost curve and an optimal value for N has been found. The process then stops. A flow diagram of this procedure is shown in Figure 10.11.

There are several available batching rules, but the one described usually gives good results. It does not guarantee optimal ones because of the assumptions made (such as fixed and known costs, fixed demand which occurs at discrete points, an optimal solution which occurs as soon as costs begin to rise, the approximation for average stock level, and so on). Although it seems a little complicated, the procedure is quite straightforward and can be done very conveniently using a spreadsheet. Its working can be illustrated by a simple example.

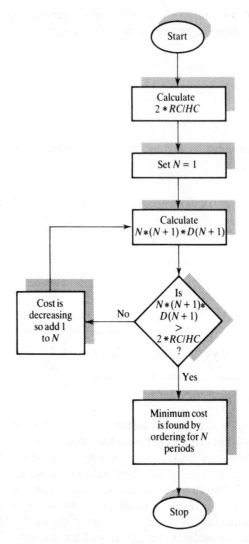

Figure 10.11 Procedure for finding an optimal value for N.

WORKED EXAMPLE 10.4

A supplies manager estimates the total cost associated with placing an order for an item and having it delivered to be £90, while its holding costs amount to £4 a month. If an MRP analysis of demand for the item as given below, find an ordering policy which will give reasonable costs.

Month	1	2	3	4	5	6	7	8	9	10	11	12
Demand	1	3	5	8	8	5	2	1	1	5	7	19

SOLUTION

Following the procedure shown in Figure 10.11, we calculate $2 * RC/HC$, with $RC = 90$ and $HC = 4$:

$$\frac{2 * RC}{HC} = \frac{2 * 90}{4} = 45$$

Then, starting with $N = 1$, $N + 1 = 2$ and $D(2) = 3$ we calculate:

$$N * (N + 1) * D(N + 1) = 1 * 2 * 3 = 6$$

As this is less than 45 the inequality is invalid and we have not reached the minimum.
Next take $N = 2$, $N + 1 = 3$ and $D(3) = 5$ we calculate:

$$N * (N + 1) * D(N + 1) = 2 * 3 * 5 = 30$$

This is less than 45 so the inequality is still invalid and we have not reached the minimum.
Next take $N = 3$, $N + 1 = 4$ and $D(4) = 8$ we calculate:

$$N * (N + 1) * D(N + 1) = 3 * 4 * 8 = 96$$

This is more than 45 so the inequality is valid and we have found the minimum cost with $N = 3$.

This means we order enough at the beginning of month 1 to last for the first three months (that is, $1 + 3 + 5 = 9$) and schedule this to arrive before the beginning of month 1.

It is easier to do these calculations in a table, as shown in Table 10.11.

Table 10.11

Month, i	1	2	3	4
Demand, $D(i)$	1	3	5	8
N	1	2	3	
$N * (N + 1) * D(N + 1)$	6	30	96	
Delivery	9			

We can now continue the analysis for further months. The only thing to remember is that every time a new calculation is started the value of N returns to 1 and the demand figures are updated accordingly (see Table 10.12).

Table 10.12

Month, i	1	2	3	4	5	6	7	8	9	10	11	12
Demand, $D(i)$	1	3	5	8	8	5	2	1	1	5	7	19
N	1	2	3	1	2	3	4	5	6	1	2	1
$N * (N + 1) * D(N + 1)$	6	30	96	16	30	24	20	30	210	14	114	
Delivery	9			25						12		

> A good ordering policy would ensure 9 units arrive by month 1, 25 by month 4 and 12 by month 10. To ensure these deliveries arrive on time, orders must be placed at least the lead time in advance.

In summary

MRP often leads to small frequent orders. The cost of administering these is high, and it might be preferable to combine several orders into a single larger one. A batching rule has been described to find how many orders should be combined to minimize associated costs.

SELF ASSESSMENT QUESTIONS

10.11 Why might several small orders be combined into a single larger one?

10.12 Is it always preferable to place fewer larger orders than more smaller ones?

10.13 What is a batching rule?

10.14 Why does the batching rule described only give a good rather than an optimal solution?

10.3 EXTENSIONS TO MRP

Because of its dependence on computers and the need to link several systems, MRP only really became feasible in the early 1970s. Since then it has been widely adopted in manufacturing industry, and even in some services which can satisfy the requirements for a detailed master schedule. Bearing in mind this proven success, it is not surprising that extensions have been found to the basic system.

The first extensions gave enhanced procedures for dealing with variable supply, supplier reliability, wastage, defective quality, variable demand, variable lead times, and so on. Several different batching rules were also developed to deal with different circumstances. Later, more significant changes were made, primarily to take advantage of increasingly sophisticated computer systems. The first major extension became known as Manufacturing Resources Planning, or MRP II.

By the early 1980s it was recognized that the MRP approach of exploding a master schedule to determine material requirements could be expanded to other functions. Ordering and purchasing were included in MRP, but why not extend the analyses to dispatching, distribution, production processes and even on to marketing and finance? A master schedule could, for example, be used to show the amount of machinery and equipment needed in each period. This, in turn, could be used to determine manning levels, and so on. Eventually the master schedule could be used as the basis for planning most of the resources used in an operation. This was the intention of MRP II.

The original aim of MRP II was to provide an integrated system, with all parts linked back to a production plan. Several computer systems were developed for this, including:

- COPICS (Communications Oriented Production Information and Control System) by IBM, which was later enhanced in MAPICS (Manufacturing Accounting and Production Information Control System);
- Factory Management System by Hewlett-Packard;
- Production Control System by Burroughs;
- MAC-PAC by Arthur Anderson;
- and many other packages.

Sometimes, if not usually, such complete integration proved impractical and parts of the system were adopted, often using different names.

- Distribution Resources Planning scheduled transport and other logistics functions associated with the delivery and storage of raw materials and the distribution of finished goods at the end of the process.
- Capacity Requirements Planning is that part of the system which goes back from the master schedule to ensure the available capacity is large enough to deal with planned production.
- Resource Requirements Planning is sometimes used to mean the same as MRP II, and sometimes used in a wider sense to include all planning decisions.

All such systems rely heavily on computing, and the installation of working systems can be very complicated and expensive. Some extensions to MRP, which are radically different, are just-in-time (JIT) systems. One view of these is that they are so fundamentally different to MRP systems that they are not an extension, but a completely different approach. We will consider these suggestions in more detail in the following section.

In summary
Since MRP systems were introduced in the early 1970s there have been continuous improvements. Some of these extend the functions considered by MRP to give integrated Manufacturing Resources Planning (MRP II).

SELF ASSESSMENT QUESTIONS

10.15 What is meant by MRP II?

10.16 Distribution Resources Planning relies on the availability of computer systems. Is this statement true or false?

10.4 JUST-IN-TIME SYSTEMS

10.4.1 Principles of JIT

In recent years few, if any, topics have received as much attention in high volume manufacturing organizations as 'just-in-time' or 'JIT'. This gives a view of manufacturing which is known by different names, including 'zero inventory', 'stockless production', 'Toyota system', 'Japanese manufacturing', 'world class manufacturing' and 'continuous flow manufacturing'. The main reason for the attention is the unparalleled success of Japanese manufacturing, and the observation that some Japanese companies use just-in-time systems. It follows that if these systems have played even a small part in the success of Japanese industry they should be considered elsewhere.

MRP aims to match the supply of materials with demand and thereby reduce the stocks which would otherwise be necessary. Essentially stocks exist to allow for short-term mismatches between supply and demand. MRP attempts to reduce these mismatches and hence reduce stocks. It follows that the less the mismatch, the less stock will be needed. Obviously, then, if the mismatch can be completely eliminated, so can stocks. This is the basis of just-in-time (JIT) systems. Their aim is to coordinate the flow of materials so that the supply of materials exactly matches demand and that materials arrive for use just as they are needed (see Figure 10.12).

> The aim of just-in-time systems is to coordinate the supply of materials so they arrive just as they are needed.

An analogy for this is someone buying fuel for the lawnmower. If that person has a petrol engine there is a mismatch between supply (bought from a garage) and demand (when the lawn is being mowed), so stocks of fuel have to be kept in the petrol tank and spare can. If the person has an electric motor the supply of electricity is exactly matched to demand and no stocks are needed. The petrol engine uses a conventional material control system, while the electric motor uses a JIT system where fuel arrives just as it is needed.

At one level JIT can be viewed as a system for controlling stocks, but it has a much wider impact than this. JIT really involves a change in the way an

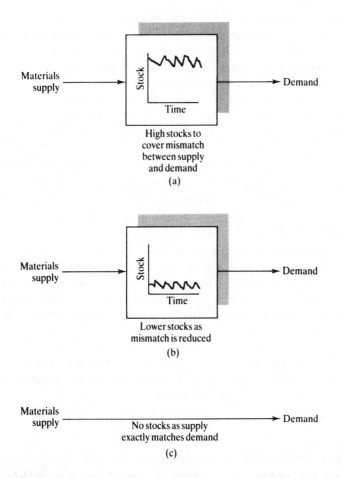

Figure 10.12 Stock levels with different materials planning methods. (a) Conventional system. (b) MRP system. (c) JIT system.

organization views its operations and workforce. The basis of this view is that all wastage of resources, including stock holdings, is unnecessary and should be eliminated, or at least minimized. This in turn leads to the belief that problems in an organization should be identified and solved rather than hidden. We can look at four examples of what this means, starting with one we have already mentioned.

(1) Stocks are held in organizations to cover short-term differences between supply and demand. JIT systems assume these stocks are actually being used to hide problems that will keep on recurring. Organizations should really find the reasons why there are differences between supply and demand, and then take whatever action is necessary to overcome these.

457

(2) When a machine on a production process breaks down the usual practice is to transfer production to another process or start making another product. The JIT approach does not allow this kind of flexibility, as it is based on continuous, uninterrupted production. Management is forced to recognize there is a problem with the reliability of the machine, the reason why it broke down is examined, and action is taken to ensure that it does not break down in the future.

(3) Organizations have traditionally specified acceptable levels of quality for their products. This usually defines some arbitrary figure like 'three defective units or less in 100 means the supply is acceptable'. JIT recognizes that all defects have costs, and it is really cheaper to prevent these from ever happening than to correct them later. In other words, JIT systems aim for perfect quality with no defects and take whatever action is necessary to achieve this.

(4) It is often felt that suppliers and customers are in some sort of conflict, where one can only benefit at the expense of the other. JIT systems rely totally on their suppliers and this kind of division cannot be allowed. Instead it is shown that customers and suppliers are partners with a common objective and they should work closely together.

Now JIT can be seen not just as a means of minimizing inventories, but as a whole way of viewing operations. Its overall aim is to minimize waste by identifying and solving any problems found.

In summary
Just-in-time systems aim to produce a smooth flow of products through operations, with materials arriving just in time for their use. To achieve this, operations must be organized to minimize waste, with problems identified and solved rather than hidden.

10.4.2 Kanban systems

Although JIT appears attractive in principle, it is only useful if there is some way of implementing and controlling the system so that materials do actually arrive just as they are needed. One way of doing this is based on Kanbans. 'Kanban' is the Japanese for visible record, or card, and much of the development of control systems for JIT was done by Toyota. For this reason the method is sometimes called the Toyota or Japanese production system. This starts with a 'pull' system for controlling the movement of work through a process.

The traditional way of moving work through a process is a 'push' system. In this, each work station finishes the work that has been planned for it and 'pushes' the output to the next work station, before starting its next planned job. This ignores what the next station is actually doing. It might be that the next station is working on something completely different or is waiting for a different product to arrive. At best, the second work station must finish its current job before it can start working on the new material just passed to it. The result is delays and increased stocks of work in progress. If there are serious imbalances or disruptions to production these stocks can become very big.

JIT uses a 'pull' approach, where a work station finishes its operations, and then requests materials from the preceding work station. The preceding work station only starts producing the requested materials when it receives this request, so that stocks of work in progress are eliminated. In practice, there must be some lead time, so requests for materials are passed backwards before they are actually needed. Materials will also be delivered in small batches rather than in continuous amounts. This means that some stocks of work in progress are still needed to ensure undisrupted production, but these are much lower than for 'push' systems. It would, then, be fairer to say that JIT minimizes stocks rather than eliminates them.

One obvious problem is that operations must be perfectly balanced, with the output from each work station exactly matching the requirements of following stations. If there is some imbalance, equipment will remain idle until it is called on to start production and utilization will be low. In practice, this problem is met in all operations and is by no means unique to JIT systems. JIT would, however, consider any imbalance to be unacceptable and would find ways of eliminating it.

One of the key differences between JIT and MRP systems is their use of computers. MRP systems rely on heavy use of computers to explode plans, while JIT systems try to simplify procedures and avoid this reliance. JIT would also consider changing the production rate as inherently inefficient, so it relies on stable production. This simplifies planning and control so that a simple manual system can be used. This is where Kanbans appear.

Kanban systems provide a mechanism for coordinating the flow of materials for JIT operations. In essence a system of cards is used to arrange the movement and production of materials. The simplest system is as follows.

- Materials can only be moved in containers. Then a single type of Kanban is used to give permission to move a container of materials.

- When a work station needs more materials (when its stock of materials falls to some predetermined level) a Kanban is attached to an empty container and this is taken to the preceding work station. The Kanban is then attached to a full container, which is returned to the work station.

- The empty container is a signal for the preceding work station to start work on this material, and it produces just enough to refill the container.

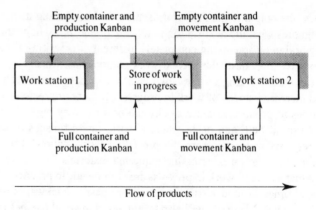

Figure 10.13 Outline of a Kanban system with two work stations.

The main point here is that the message is passed backwards to the preceding work station to start production, and it only makes enough to fill the container. Materials can only be moved in containers, and containers can only be moved when they have a Kanban attached. This gives a rigid means of controlling the amount of materials produced and the time they are moved. This control ensures that stocks of work in progress are minimized and do not accumulate.

A more usual Kanban system is slightly more complicated and uses two distinct types of card: a production Kanban and a movement Kanban. Then the process is:

- When a work station needs more materials a movement Kanban is put on an empty container which gives permission to take it to the area where work in progress is kept.

- A full container is then found, which will have a production Kanban attached.

- The production Kanban is removed and put on a post. This gives permission for the preceding work station to produce enough to replace the container of materials.

- A movement Kanban is put on the full container, giving permission to take it back to the work station.

This process is summarized in Figure 10.13.

JIT operations almost always use a product layout, so that movements of materials are minimized. In particular the small stocks of work in progress are kept as part of the line. As each container has a Kanban attached to it, the number of Kanbans effectively determines the amount of work in progress. When a new JIT system is installed, some flexibility may be kept by having a fairly large number of Kanbans. However, an inherent part of JIT is its continuous solving of problems and searching for improvements. This means that when the system is working properly there will be a continuous search for ways of reducing the number of Kanbans.

One other element of control comes into play when things go wrong. Associated with JIT, there is often a system called Andon. This has three signals, often coloured lights, above each work station.

- A green signal shows that the station is working as planned.
- An amber signal shows the work station is falling a bit behind.
- A red signal shows a serious problem.

This allows everyone to see where problems are growing, and to look for ways of solving these.

In summary
Just-in-time systems need some means of control. Kanbans are one convenient alternative which provide a simple and completely manual system for controlling the production and movement of materials.

10.4.3 Key elements in JIT systems

JIT can bring very substantial benefits, but it can certainly not be used in every organization. The operations within an organization need to have several characteristics before the organization can begin to consider the adoption of JIT principles.

- Any changes in production have associated costs and delays. The basis of JIT is that such changes should be avoided, so it needs a stable environment which allows production to be constant at a fixed level.
- The specified production must allow a smooth and continuous flow of products through the process.
- If deliveries of materials are to be made at just the time they are needed, the materials must come in small lots, as larger lots will increase stocks of work in progress.
- These small lots must have low reorder costs or else the frequent deliveries would become prohibitively expensive. Similarly, lead times (or set-up times) must be short or else the delay in responding to a request for materials will be unacceptably long.
- If materials arrive which are defective, they will disrupt production, as there is no stock to provide cover. Suppliers must, therefore, be totally reliable and provide materials which are free from defects.

- If there is a disruption, the workforce must be able to find out why and then take the action necessary to correct it. This implies a skilled and flexible workforce which is committed to the success of the organization.

If we continued arguing in this way we could draw up a list of the key elements in a JIT system, as follows.

- stable environment
- continuous production at fixed levels
- balanced production
- reliable production equipment
- minimum stocks
- small lot sizes
- short lead times
- low set-up and delivery costs
- efficient materials handling
- reliable suppliers
- consistently high quality of materials
- flexible workforce
- fair treatment and rewards for employees
- ability to solve any problems
- an efficient method of control
  and so on.

Some of these elements lead, in turn, to other characteristics. The need to reduce lead times, for example, means that flexible equipment is needed and this, together with the stable production, usually means high production quantities using sophisticated automation. Similarly, totally reliable quality means that this must be considered at all times, including new designs, definitions of 'acceptable' quality, and quality management programmes. The stable production allows focused factories to be used for parts and materials. Ensuring the commitment of the workforce usually involves profit sharing schemes, quality circles and the belief that the workforce is the single most important factor in the success of an organization.

Although it is a simple idea, the introduction of JIT will have a considerable impact on an organization. It is a step that requires total commitment from all of the workforce and needs a completely different view of many operations.

In summary

Not every organization can use JIT systems. There are many conditions which must be met before JIT becomes possible. When it can be implemented JIT brings fundamental changes to an organization.

10.4.4 Benefits of JIT

We have already mentioned one major advantage of JIT, which is dramatically reduced stocks of raw materials and work in progress. This leads directly to a number of other advantages, such as reductions in space needed, warehousing costs, investment in stocks, and so on.

Other benefits from JIT come from the necessary reorganization. Several of these have already been mentioned, including:

- reduced lead times
- total time to make a product is reduced
- increased productivity
- increased equipment utilization
- simplified planning and scheduling
- reduced paperwork
- improved quality of materials and products
- reduced cost of scrap and wastage
- improved relations with suppliers
- emphasis on solving problems in production
- better participation of workforce
  and so on.

There are, of course, some difficulties with JIT. It can only work in certain types of operation and does not work well when there are irregularly used parts or specially ordered material. Perhaps its inflexibility is another weakness, as it is difficult to change product design, mix or demand levels. Once the system has been set up for a specific number of a product it is difficult to change this, either at short notice or in the longer term.

Some of the benefits may also be seen as disadvantages. Having frequent set-ups and small batches, for example, is essential but this contradicts accepted management practices which have developed over many decades. Similarly, JIT requires decisions to be made on the shop floor. This devolved decision making, with responsibility given to lower levels in the workforce, may be considered an advantage or a disadvantage depending on viewpoint.

Perhaps one major disadvantage of JIT is its deceptively simple appearance. There is a tendency to read a description of it and try to introduce it piecemeal into existing operations. It should be emphasized that JIT requires a complete change of attitudes and operations within an organization. Its successful introduction is likely to take several years of careful planning and controlled implementation.

In summary

Just-in-time systems can offer many advantages. Some of these come directly from the procedures used, while others are indirect results of the reorganization needed. A successful system requires careful planning and implementation.

SELF ASSESSMENT QUESTIONS

10.17 JIT is a system for controlling stocks. Is this statement:

(a) true
(b) false
(c) partly true?

10.18 Is it true to say that JIT systems eliminate stocks of work in progress?

10.19 What is the purpose of Kanban systems?

10.20 What do you think are the three main advantages of JIT?

10.21 Would it be a good idea to introduce JIT in part of a process to see how it works?

SUMMARY OF CHAPTER

In Chapter 8 we described a hierarchical approach to the planning within an organization. Part of this showed how the tactical master schedule could be used to develop operational timetables for equipment and operators. Sometimes it is also possible to extend the use of a master schedule to include plans for the supply of materials. This is the basis of material requirements planning (MRP).

MRP uses a master schedule to find requirements for materials. In this 'dependent demand' system stocks are matched directly to production plans. The alternative is to use an independent demand system in which enough stocks are held to cover likely demand at any time.

MRP 'explodes' a master schedule using a bill of materials to give detailed materials requirements. Orders for materials and operations are then timetabled to allow the master schedule to be achieved. There are a number of requirements before MRP can be used (a reliable master schedule, detailed bill of materials, accurate stock records, supplier information, and so on). These have frequently limited MRP to production systems, but it is becoming more widely used in service operations.

The main benefit of MRP is its ability to match supply of materials to known demands. This reduces stock levels and associated costs. Conversely, its main disadvantages are the need for certain requirements to be met before it becomes feasible, and the amount of data manipulation.

Sometimes the basic approach of MRP gives frequent small orders, which might be difficult and expensive to administer. Costs may be reduced by combining several small orders into a single larger one, and a batching rule for this was described.

The use of MRP only became feasible with the availability of cheap computing in the early 1970s. Since then it has become widely used and several extensions have been devised, notably MRP II.

Just-in-time systems also try to match supply with demand. These organize the flow of materials so that each is delivered just as it is needed. Such systems can be controlled using Kanbans. There are several key elements in JIT, including stable environment, small batches, total quality, and so on. These limit its potential use. Where feasible, JIT systems can bring substantial benefits, but they require an entirely new perspective of operations.

PROBLEMS

10.1 A company which makes a final product, A, receives orders for 40 units for delivery in week 16 of a production cycle, 60 units in week 13 and 50 units in week 12. It takes one unit of component B and two units of component C to make each unit of A, and assembly takes two weeks. Components of B and C are bought from suppliers with lead times of three and two weeks respectively. Current stocks of A, B and C are 5, 10 and 20 units respectively and an order for 40 units of C is due to arrive in week 7. Devise a production and order plan for the company.

10.2 Each unit of product AF43 is made from 12 units of BL19, 10 units of CX23 and 20 units of DY33. Each unit of BL19 is made from two units of EM08, two units of FF87 and two units of GO95. Each unit of both EM08 and DY33 is made from six units of HX22. A master schedule calls for 60 units of AF43 to be ready by week 8 of a planning cycle and 50 units by week 10. There are minimum order sizes of 2000 units for HX22, and 500 units of both FF87 and GO95. Information about stocks and lead times in weeks (either for assembly or orders) is given in Table 10.13.

Table 10.13

Item	Current stocks	Minimum stocks	Lead time (weeks)
AF43	20	10	2
BL19	230	50	3
CX23	340	100	1
DY33	410	100	3
EM08	360	200	2
FF87	620	200	2
GO95	830	200	2
HX22	1200	200	4

Devise an order schedule for the materials.

10.3 It costs £0.125 to store a unit of an item for one month. The total cost of placing an order for the item, including delivery, is £100. An MRP analysis has found the following demands for the item.

Month	1	2	3	4	5	6	7	8	9	10	11	12	13
Demand	100	50	60	60	100	100	80	60	40	70	80	100	140

Determine a good ordering policy for the item.

10.4 It costs £1 to hold one unit of an item in stock for one month, and each order costs a total of £60. There are currently no stocks of the item, but MRP analysis has suggested the following demands. Find a good ordering policy for the item.

Month	1	2	3	4	5	6	7	8	9	10	11	12
Demand	40	39	60	81	238	722	998	1096	921	161	0	40

Do you think this is the best ordering policy available?

CASE STUDY – SCHMIDT MACHINE WORKS

Background

A recent international conference on inventory management was held in Vienna. The local branch of the Austrian Institute for Management took the opportunity to invite one of the speakers to give a talk at its regular lunch time meetings. The speaker was an American who was described as 'an internationally renowned expert in dependent demand inventory systems with experience in over 80 companies'.

In the audience for this talk were Sityuen Feng and Helmut Bayer who worked in the Finance Section of Schmidt Machine Works. Schmidt is a leading manufacturer of parts for knitting and sewing machines, based in Basel, but with manufacturing facilities in Austria and West Germany.

The speaker started his talk by saying, 'Of course, everybody uses MRP these days, so I will describe some of the more interesting mathematical analyses that I have done on extensions to dependent demand inventory systems'. Sityuen and Helmut looked at each other anxiously and settled down for a boring presentation. By the end of the hour most of the audience had left, but Sityuen and Helmut stayed to ask some more questions. The following day they met to discuss the talk.

Sityuen had talked to the speaker and said:

> Our main problem is that we have never heard of MRP let alone use it. The speaker was an American who was obviously not used to talking to European managers. An important point is that he wrote the paragraph about himself being 'an internationally renowned expert' and this is simply not true. He is an academic who has never worked in industry, and has only worked in two American universities. His international experience consists of talking to American companies who have overseas operations. Overall, the speaker was so dishonest in his description of his own credentials that we cannot rely on anything he says. I suggest we forget about it and carry on as usual.

Helmut replied by saying:

> I partially agree. The speaker was dishonest and his talk was irrelevant and boring. None the less, I talked to some people after the meeting and they had some interesting comments. In particular, I found six people who used MRP. I still do not know what this is, but they all said they found it very useful and saved the company a lot of money. Usable systems apparently need a lot of development, but there are

considerable benefits, ranging from better planning to improved communications. Three other people said they used just-in-time systems, but it appeared that two of these were really MRP. I suggest we do a little study to see if MRP could be used in Schmidt.

After a long discussion they decided to do an experiment to see if it was worth considering MRP in more detail. For this they talked to Pieter Keller from the Production Section.

Experiment

Pieter understood the problem and described what he thought would be a suitable experiment. He said:

The principles of MRP are very easy, but it is difficult to implement. I suggest we pick a couple of products at random and see if MRP would give any savings. We currently make around 2500 different products so this experiment would simply lay the foundations for a more detailed study. I have selected two products, and as I couldn't get all the information about these (the stock levels, for example, changed continuously) I just made up some typical figures. Again, the real process is so complicated that I made a number of simplifications. The results are given in the following tables. I think these should allow some useful results.

Pieter also explained the present inventory system. This has stock levels reviewed at the end of each fortnight, with orders placed to bring stocks up to specified target levels. This level is determined by a formula where each item is classified as A, B or C. Then the target stock levels are:

- A: 1.2 times expected demand in lead time plus two weeks;
- B: 1.4 times expected demand in lead time plus three weeks;
- C: 1.6 times expected demand in lead time plus four weeks.

This system seems to work, but there were some concerns about current stocks. There had recently been very high demand for products which had forced production to increase, and stocks of work in progress seemed rather low.

The figures suggested by Pieter related to two products with codes AP4072 and FL7341. The expected production of AP4072 will remain steady at around 100 units a week for the next two years. FL7341 varies a little more, and monthly production is estimated as shown in Table 10.14.

Table 10.14

| | Year 1 | | Year 2 |
Month	Production	Month	Production
1	24	1	60
2	20	2	56
3	18	3	45
4	25	4	65
5	31	5	93
6	45	6	110
7	56	7	132
8	50	8	124
9	46	9	117
10	40	10	110
11	38	11	98
12	56	12	136

Holding costs are taken to be 0.2% of unit cost a week with shortage costs of 10% of unit cost a week. If stocks of an item are about to run out, it is possible to request urgent deliveries, which cost about twice as much as normal deliveries. Much of Schmidt's production is sold to Germany, so it is common to quote prices in Deutschmarks. Times are quoted in weeks and other details are given in Table 10.15.

Table 10.15

Product code	Unit cost	Reorder cost	Category	Current stock	Lead time	Assembly time	Made from: code	(units)
AP4072	—	—	—	6	—	2	LF3281	(4)
							LF3282	(1)
LF3281	—	—	—	10	—	1	SF3822	(25)
							TG4071	(5)
SF3822	4	80	A	200	2	—	—	
TG4071	20	120	B	75	3	—	—	
LF3282	—	—	—	16	—	2	AX0012	(50)
							AX1012	(50)
							LX6734	(4)
AX0012	10	50	A	1000	2	—	—	
AX1012	20	50	A	625	2	—	—	
LX6734	—	—	—	104	—	1	LK0039	(10)
							LK0040	(10)
LK0039	5	120	A	240	3	—	—	
LK0040	6	180	A	360	2	—	—	

Item							Components
FL7341	—	—	—	14	—	3	CD4055 (2), CD5988 (4), CE0993 (1)
CD4055	—	—	—	83	—	2	ML8001 (1), MK0126 (2), MK0288 (4)
CD5988	—	—	—	122	—	3	LY4021 (10), LY4022 (20), LY4023 (10)
CE0993	—	—	—	96	—	2	NY0032 (6), NX9774 (3), NX0312 (12)
ML8001	—	—	—	50	—	1	ML0082 (20), ML0083 (10)
MK0126	—	—	—	122	—	2	FY0017 (6), NP4021 (24), LF7031 (12)
MK0288	—	—	—	124	—	1	ML0082 (40), ML0094 (10)
ML0082	—	—	—	250	—	1	BP0174 (4), BR3051 (1)
ML0083	—	—	—	220	—	1	BQ7441 (4), BQ7442 (8)
FY0017	4	80	B	86	4	—	—
NP4021	2	160	A	450	2	—	—
LF7031	6	120	B	265	3	—	—
ML0094	—	—	—	150	—	1	PX1570 (5), PX1571 (5), PX1572 (1)
LY4021	—	—	—	200	—	3	ML0083 (6), BQ6399 (2)
LY4022	—	—	—	122	—	4	ML0094 (12), LF7031 (12), LF7032 (2), LF7033 (1), LF7034 (12)
LY4023	—	—	—	60	—	1	LF7033 (1), LF7939 (60)
NY0032	—	—	—	24	—	1	ML0083 (10), ML8001 (1)
NX9774	—	—	—	36	—	1	LF7032 (2), LF7034 (12), BQ7742 (8)
NX0312	—	—	—	240	—	1	ML0094 (12), LF7031 (12), AP7031 (1)
BQ6399	43	220	B	33	3	—	—
LF7033	86	380	C	40	1	—	—
LF7939	75	420	A	120	2	—	—

ML8001	118	420	B	22	2	—	—	
LF7032	66	120	B	145	4	—	—	
LF7034	—	—	—	850	—	2	PX4971	(12)
							PX3055	(2)
BP0174	8	40	A	85	2	—	—	
BR3051	6	80	A	155	2	—	—	
BQ7441	—	—	—	360	—	1	FY0017	(6)
							FZ0149	(1)
BQ7442	24	40	B	86	3	—	—	
LF7031	6	120	A	780	4	—	—	
AP7031	—	—	—	66	—	2	PX1571	(10)
							PX1420	(2)
							PX3055	(1)
FZ0149	120	420	C	260	5	—	—	
PX1420	69	120	B	857	3	—	—	
PX1570	12	40	A	1250	2	—	—	
PX1571	8	40	A	2450	3	—	—	
PX1572	86	80	B	475	2	—	—	
PX3055	57	80	B	125	1	—	—	
PX4971	15	80	A	750	2	—	—	

Suggested questions

- What comments can be made about the lunch time presentation?
- Would a trial, like the one suggested, give useful information?
- What other approach might Sityuen and Helmut adopt?
- For the products chosen, how well does the present inventory control system work?
- Would MRP bring any benefits for these products?
- What would be the next stage for considering an MRP system in Schmidt Machine Works?

SOLUTIONS TO SELF ASSESSMENT QUESTIONS

10.1 Material requirements planning is a process in which the master schedule is used to plan the arrival of materials, components, parts, and so on.

10.2 (a) .

10.3 False. MRP was initially developed for production systems, but it has since been applied in a variety of circumstances.

10.4 A master schedule, bill of materials, information about current stocks and lead times.

10.5 (a) Low level items.

10.6 By subtracting free stock from gross requirements.

10.7 It relates demand for materials directly to a master schedule, rather than relying on projective forecasts.

10.8 The requirements that limit its applicability, and the amount of data manipulation.

10.9 It would be possible in principle, but the complexity and amount of data manipulation would make such a system impractical for any but the simplest products.

10.10 Timetable of orders, changes to orders, exceptions report, performance reports and inventory transactions.

10.11 Because small orders have high administration and delivery costs. These are reduced with larger orders.

10.12 No. Larger orders imply higher average stock levels. The cost of holding this might be more than the savings made in administration and delivery.

10.13 A rule to suggest how many separate orders should be combined into a single larger order.

10.14 Because it uses approximations for the average stock level (and probably costs), demands are assumed to be discrete and occurring at fixed points, and we have assumed that an optimal solution occurs as soon as cost begins to rise (but it may fall again later).

10.15 Manufacturing Resources Planning, which extends the MRP approach to a wide range of functions.

10.16 True. All MRP based systems rely heavily on computer systems.

10.17 (c) JIT does control stocks, but this is only one of its functions. It has a wider objective of eliminating all waste by identifying and solving problems.

10.18 No. They minimize stocks of work in progress but do not necessarily eliminate them.

10.19 To control just-in-time systems.

10.20 These are a matter of opinion, but one view might suggest reduced stocks, easier planning and higher quality.

10.21 JIT requires a fundamental change in attitudes, plans, operations and procedures. It is not really the sort of thing which can be tried as a small experiment in part of a process.

REFERENCES FOR FURTHER READING

APICS (1971). *Special Report: Materials Requirement Planning by Computer* American Production and Inventory Control Society, Falls Church, Virginia

Goldratt E. and Cox J. (1986). *The Goal* New York: North River Press

Hall R. (1983). *Zero Inventories* Homewood: Dow Jones-Irwin

Hall R. (1987). *Attaining Manufacturing Excellence* Homewood: Dow Jones-Irwin

Lee S.M. and Schwendiman G. (eds) (1983). *Management by Japanese Systems* New York: Praeger

Love S. (1979). *Inventory Control* New York: McGraw-Hill

Monden Y. (1983). *Toyota Production System: Practical Approach to Production Management* Atlanta: Industrial Engineering and Management Press

Orlicky J. (1975). *Material Requirements Planning* New York: McGraw-Hill

Schonberger R.J. (1982). *Japanese Productivity Techniques: Nine Hidden Lessons in Simplicity* New York: Free Press

Schonberger R.J. (1986). *World Class Manufacturing* New York: Free Press

Smolik D.P. (1983). *Material Requirements of Manufacturing* New York: Van Nostrand Reinhold

Vollmann T.E., Berry W.L. and Whybark D.C. (1988). *Manufacturing Planning and Control Systems* 2nd edn. Homewood: Richard D Irwin

Wight O.W. (1974). *Production and Inventory Management in the Computer Age* Boston: Cahners Publishing

Wight O.W. (1982). *The Executive's Guide to Successful MRP II* Williston, Vermont: Oliver Wight Publications

Chapter 11

Independent demand inventory systems

SYNOPSIS

Chapter 10 described how material requirements planning could be used to control stocks. This is an example of a dependent demand inventory system, where the demand for an item is related directly to a master schedule. The alternative method of inventory control is an independent demand system, where demand for an item is found by projective forecasting. This chapter describes some aspects of independent demand inventory systems.

Stocks are important to almost every aspect of operations. Raw materials are delivered and stored until needed, stocks of work in progress ensure smooth production, and finished goods are stored to meet anticipated customer demand. Very little can be made or sold without stocks being kept somewhere. These stocks are expensive and they need careful control.

In this chapter we introduce some ideas of *scientific inventory control*. In particular, we discuss the reasons why stocks are needed, how much they cost and how these costs can be minimized.

The first analysis is the classic *economic order quantity* which defines a fixed order quantity to minimize the costs of a simple inventory system. Although the analysis is based on a number of assumptions, it gives results which are robust and widely applicable. The analysis is extended by adding lead times and finite production rates.

If demand is highly variable, other approaches must be used. The chapter describes a model where demand is assumed to follow a Normal distribution. Then a policy is defined which allows a specified level of customer service to be achieved. This leads to descriptions of safety stock and periodic review systems. One specific example of variable demand occurs when stocks are held only for a single period before they are scrapped. This is discussed in terms of the newsboy problem.

All inventory control systems need some effort, and sometimes the costs involved do not warrant this. An ABC analysis can show how much attention should be given to each item.

OBJECTIVES

After reading this chapter and completing the exercises you should be able to:

- appreciate the need for stocks of varying types;
- define the costs associated with holding stocks;
- discuss various approaches to inventory control systems, and the questions they answer;
- calculate economic order quantities using the 'classic analysis';
- calculate reorder levels for constant lead times;
- calculate the effect of moving away from the economic order quantity;
- calculate the effects of finite production rates;
- appreciate the need for safety stock when demand varies;
- define 'service level';
- calculate a safety stock when lead time demand is Normally distributed;
- describe periodic review systems and calculate target stock levels;
- find the optimal number of purchases to cover a single period (the newsboy problem);
- do ABC analyses of inventories.

11.1 BACKGROUND TO STOCK HOLDINGS

11.1.1 Reasons for holding stocks

In Chapter 10 we described how material requirements planning could be used to control stocks. This was an example of a dependent demand·system, where the demand for an item is directly related to a master schedule. The alternative approach to stock control is an independent demand system. In essence, these find expected demand for an item from projective forecasts based on historic demand patterns. In this chapter we will describe some aspects of independent demand inventory systems. Before we go into details, however, it would be sensible to look at some of the fundamental questions raised by inventory control. We can start this by asking why organizations actually hold stock.

Almost all organizations hold stocks of various kinds and there are always associated costs (to cover warehouse operations, tied-up capital, deterioration, and so on). An obvious question, then, is, 'Why do organizations hold

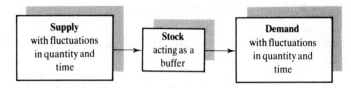

Figure 11.1 Stock as a buffer between variable supply and demand.

stock?'. There are several answers to this, but the dominant one is, 'To allow a buffer between supply and demand'.

In Chapter 10 we described how just-in-time systems view stocks as a waste of resources and attempt to eliminate them completely. In practice, however, small stocks are unavoidable and JIT really aims for stock minimization rather than elimination. We can demonstrate this by considering the stock of work in progress between two work stations. This stock can only be eliminated if each unit of output from the first work station is transferred immediately it is finished to start work on the second work station. If there is any delay in starting on the second, or if several units are transferred across at the same time, there are stocks of work in progress. Usually it is impossible to match supply and demand exactly so some stocks, however small, are inevitable.

Similarly, stocks of raw materials are kept because deliveries tend to be in large quantities, while operations withdraw them in smaller quantities. At the other end of the process, stocks of finished goods are built up until an order is met, or a large enough batch is accumulated to be sent to a distribution centre.

The main purpose of stocks, then, is to act as a buffer between supply and demand, and to allow operations to continue smoothly. The short-term mismatch between supply and demand rates is only one reason for holding stock. We could also argue that unexpected variations in supply are inevitable (caused by delays to delivery vehicles, breakdown of equipment, disruptions to supplier's production, rejections of poor quality materials, and so on). Similarly, demand for finished goods will include random variations which cannot be forecast (see Figure 11.1).

Other reasons for holding stocks include:

- to act as a buffer between different production operations (that is, they 'decouple' operations);
- to allow for demands which are larger than expected, or at unexpected times;
- to allow for deliveries which are delayed or too small;
- to take advantage of price discounts on large orders;
- to buy items when the price is low and expected to rise;
- to buy items which are going out of production or are difficult to find;
- to make full loads and reduce transport costs;
- to provide cover for emergencies;
  and so on.

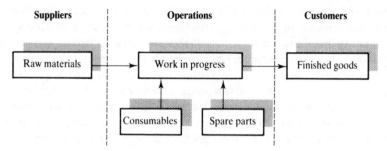

Figure 11.2 Classification of stock holdings.

Just about everything is held as stock somewhere, whether it is raw materials in a factory, finished goods in a shop or tins of baked beans in a pantry. These stocks are generally classified (see Figure 11.2) according to:

- raw materials
- work in progress
- finished goods.

This is a fairly arbitrary classification, as one company's finished goods will be another company's raw materials. Some organizations (notably retailers and wholesalers) can have stocks of finished goods only, while others (manufacturers, say) have all three types in different proportions. On a national scale, around 30% of stocks are raw materials, 40% work in progress and 30% finished goods. Some stock items do not fall easily into these categories, and two additional types can be defined as:

- spare parts (for machinery, equipment, etc.)
- consumables (oil, paper, etc.).

Whatever the reason for holding stocks, there are associated costs and these are often surprisingly high. We will consider these in the following section.

In summary
The main purpose of stocks is to act as a buffer between supply and demand. If smooth operations are to be maintained through variations in supply and demand, the need to carry stock of various kinds is an inevitable consequence. This incurs costs which are often high.

11.1.2 Costs of carrying stock

Typically, the total cost of holding stock is around 25% of its value a year. This is a considerable investment and organizations look for policies that minimize their inventory costs. In some circumstances minimizing costs is analogous to minimizing stocks, but this is not inevitably true. JIT works on the basis that stocks are wasteful and should be eliminated, but independent demand systems work on the basis that stocks are inevitable and the associated costs should be minimized. The two approaches are appropriate for different circumstances. JIT systems are most useful for high volume manufacturing, and at present have only proved beneficial in a narrow range of operations. This means that most operations use other approaches, including independent demand inventory systems. These inventories are typified by wholesalers or retailers who are more concerned with stocks of finished goods than with work in progress or raw materials.

One option for eliminating stocks of finished goods would be to guarantee deliveries within a specified time. This policy works if production lead times are short (so that products can be made to order) or someone else is prepared to hold stocks (perhaps a manufacturer, wholesaler, importer or main distributor). Such systems might reduce stock holding costs, but the service, measured by delivery time, is inevitably reduced. The implication is that a balance is needed between service offered and costs of stock holding.

We have mentioned the aim of minimizing costs, so we need to look at these in a little more detail, and define a number of distinct types.

Unit cost (*UC*)

This is the price of the item charged by the supplier, or the cost to the company of acquiring one unit of the item. It may be fairly easy to find values by looking at quotations or recent invoices from suppliers. Sometimes, however, it is more difficult when there are several suppliers offering alternative products or giving different purchase conditions. If a company makes the item itself, it may be difficult to set a production cost or to calculate a valid transfer price.

Reorder cost (*RC*)

This is the cost of placing a repeat order for an item and might include allowances for drawing up an order (with checking, signing, clearance, distribution and filing), computer time, correspondence and telephone costs, receiving (with unloading, checking and testing), supervision, use of equipment and follow-up. Sometimes costs such as quality control, transport charges, sorting and movement of received goods are included in the reorder cost.

The reorder cost should ideally be for repeat orders and not a first order (which might have additional allowances for searching for suitable suppliers, checking reliability and quality, negotiations with alternative suppliers, and so on). In practice, the best estimate for a reorder cost might be found by dividing the total annual cost of the purchasing department by the number of orders sent out.

A special case of the reorder cost occurs when the company makes the item itself and is concerned with stocks of finished goods. Here the reorder cost is a batch set-up cost and might include production documentation costs, allowance for production lost while resetting machines, idle time of operators, material spoilt in test runs, time of specialist tool setters, and so on.

Holding cost (*HC*)

This is the cost of holding one unit of an item in stock for a unit period of time. The obvious cost is for tied-up money, which is either borrowed (with interest payable) or could be put to other use (in which case there are opportunity costs). Other holding costs are due to storage space (supplying a warehouse, rent, rates, heat, light, etc.), loss (due to damage, deterioration, obsolescence and pilferage), handling (including special packaging, refrigeration, putting on pallets, etc.), administration (stock checks, computer updates, etc.) and insurance. Typical annual values for these, as percentages of unit cost, are:

Item	% of unit cost
cost of money	10 – 20
storage space	2 – 5
loss	4 – 6
handling	1 – 2
administration	1 – 2
insurance	1 – 5
Total	19 – 40

Shortage cost (*SC*)

If an item is needed but cannot be supplied from stock, there is usually a cost associated with this shortage. In the simplest case a retailer may lose direct profit from a sale, but the effects of shortages are usually much more widespread. Goodwill and loss of potential future sales might be added as well as an element for loss of reputation. Shortages of raw materials for a production process could cause disruption and force rescheduling of production, retiming of maintenance periods, laying off employees, and so on. Also included in shortage costs might be allowances for positive action to counteract the shortage, perhaps sending out emergency orders, paying for special deliveries, storing partly finished goods or using alternative, more expensive suppliers.

Shortage costs are almost invariably difficult to find. There is general agreement, however, that they can be very high, particularly if production is stopped by a shortage of raw materials. This allows us to look at the purpose of stocks again and rephrase our earlier statement by saying, 'the cost of shortages can be very high and to avoid these organizations are willing to incur the relatively lower costs of carrying stock'.

Now we have described the separate costs we can combine them with other variables to develop a model of an inventory system.

In summary

Holding stocks is expensive, with typical costs amounting to 25% of unit cost a year. The costs of holding stock can be classified as unit, reorder, holding or shortage.

11.1.3 Approaches to inventory control

Inventory control systems look for answers to three basic questions.

(1) *What items should be stocked?*
No item, however cheap, should be stocked without considering the related benefits and costs. This means that checks are needed to stop new items being introduced unnecessarily, with regular searches to remove obsolete or dead stock.

(2) *When should an order be placed?*
This depends on the inventory control system used, type of demand (high or low, steady or erratic, known exactly or estimated), value of the item, lead time between placing an order and receiving it into stock, supplier reliability, and a number of other factors.

(3) *How much should be ordered?*
If large, infrequent orders are placed average stock levels are high but the costs of placing and administering orders is low; if frequent small orders are placed average stock levels are low but the costs of placing and administering orders is high.

The following analyses assume that the item considered is genuinely needed, and then concentrate on the last two questions of when to order and how much to order. Two different policies are commonly used to answer these.

- *Fixed order quantity* approach, where an order of fixed size is placed whenever stock falls to a certain level. A central heating plant, for example, may order 20,000 litres of oil whenever the amount in the tank falls to 2000 litres. Such systems need continuous monitoring of stock levels and are better suited to low, irregular demand for relatively expensive items.

- *Periodic review* approach, where orders of varying size are placed at regular intervals to raise the stock level to a specified value. Supermarket shelves, for example, may be refilled every evening to replace whatever was sold during the day. The operating cost of this system is generally lower and it is better suited to high, regular demand of low value items.

Variations in the stock levels over time for these two approaches are illustrated in Figure 11.3.
We will start by looking at fixed order quantity systems in the following section and then return to periodic review systems later in the chapter.

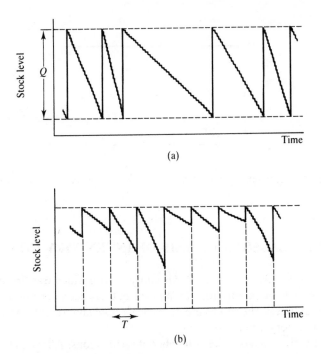

Figure 11.3 Alternative inventory control policies. (a) Fixed-order quantity system. (b) Periodic review system.

In summary

Independent demand inventory systems try to minimize the total costs of carrying stock by determining which items should be stocked, when orders should be placed and how large orders should be. Two alternative policies are periodic review and fixed order quantity.

SELF ASSESSMENT QUESTIONS

11.1 What is the main reason for holding stock?

11.2 How might stock holdings be classified?

11.3 How is demand for an item found in an independent demand inventory system?

11.4 List four types of cost associated with stock holdings.

11.5 What are the fundamental questions for inventory control systems?

11.6 Name two approaches for determining order quantities in independent demand inventory systems.

11.7 Which inventory control system would you use for controlling the stock of nuts and bolts in a company store:

(a) fixed order quantity
(b) periodic review
(c) either
(d) cannot say without more information?

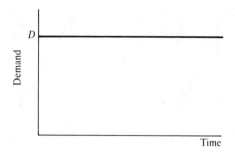

Figure 11.4 Continuous, constant demand known to be fixed at D per unit time.

11.2 THE CLASSIC ANALYSIS OF INVENTORY CONTROL

This is the basic analysis of *scientific inventory control* which was first described in the 1920s. It is often attributed to Wilson, but has been developed independently several times. The results are very widely used and form the basis of most operating inventory control systems.

The basic analysis makes a number of assumptions. Although these make the situation described unrealistically simple, they can easily be relaxed and allow a more realistic analysis.

11.2.1 Assumptions of the analysis

The analysis considers a single item where the demand is known to be continuous and constant at exactly D per unit time. Then a graph of the demand over time is shown in Figure 11.4.

Replenishment of the stock is assumed to be instantaneous, so that when an order arrives it is all available for use immediately. It is also assumed that unit cost (UC), reorder cost (RC) and holding cost (HC) are all known exactly, while the shortage cost (SC) is so large that all demands must be met and no shortages are allowed.

Initially, we will also assume that the lead time between placing an order and its arrival is zero. This means that there is no point in placing orders until existing stock is completely exhausted. We are using a fixed order quantity system, so that orders are always placed for the same quantity, Q. Then, as units are removed from stock to meet the demand, the stock level follows the sawtooth pattern shown in Figure 11.5.

The overall approach of this analysis is to find costs for a single stock cycle, then dividing this result by the cycle length gives a cost per unit time. Minimizing this cost per unit time allows us to find an optimal order quantity. Details of this are described in the following section.

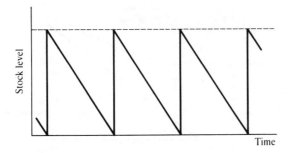

Figure 11.5 Stock level for the classic analysis.

In summary

The assumptions for the classic analysis include:

- a single item is considered;
- demand for this item is known exactly;
- demand is continuous and constant;
- costs are known exactly;
- replenishment is instantaneous;
- no shortages are allowed.

11.2.2 Economic order quantity

Consider one cycle of the saw-tooth pattern shown in Figure 11.5.

At some point an order is placed for a quantity, Q, which arrives instantly. This is used at a constant rate, D, until no stock remains, at which point another order is placed (see Figure 11.6). The resulting stock cycle has

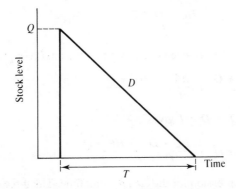

Figure 11.6 A single stock cycle for the classic analysis.

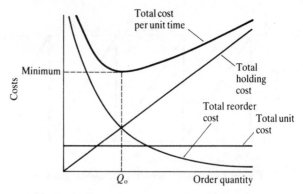

Figure 11.7 Varying costs with order quantity.

length T and we know:

$$\frac{\text{amount entering stock}}{\text{in the cycle}} = \frac{\text{amount leaving stock}}{\text{in the cycle}}$$

$$Q = D * T$$

The total cost for the cycle is found by adding the three components of cost (unit, reorder and holding), remembering there are no shortage costs.

Total cost for cycle:

- total unit cost = number of units ordered (Q) * unit cost (UC)
    = $UC * Q$
- total reorder cost = number of orders (1) * reorder cost (RC)
    = RC
- total holding cost = average stock level ($Q/2$) * time held (T) * holding cost (HC)
    = $\dfrac{HC * Q * T}{2}$

Adding these three gives the total cost per cycle as:

$$UC * Q + RC + \frac{HC * Q * T}{2}$$

If this is divided by the cycle length, T, we find the total cost per unit time, TC.

$$TC = \frac{UC * Q}{T} + \frac{RC}{T} + \frac{HC * Q}{2}$$

Then substituting $Q = D * T$ gives:

$$TC = UC * D + \frac{RC * D}{Q} + \frac{HC * Q}{2}$$

We now have an expression for the cost per unit time. The three elements on the right of this equation can be plotted separately against Q, as shown in Figure 11.7.

The total unit cost ($UC * D$) is independent of Q and can be considered 'fixed'; the total holding cost rises linearly with Q and the total reorder cost falls as Q increases. Clearly, large infrequent orders give high total holding costs and low total reorder costs; small frequent orders give low total holding costs and high total reorder costs. Adding the three contributing costs gives a total cost curve which is an asymmetric 'U' shape with a distinct minimum. This minimum corresponds to the optimal order size which we will call Q_o. To find the value Q_o (which is often called the economic order quantity, EOQ) we differentiate the total cost function with respect to Q, and set this to equal zero.

$$0 = -\frac{RC * D}{Q_o^2} + \frac{HC}{2}$$

or

$$Q_o = \sqrt{\frac{2 * RC * D}{HC}} \qquad \text{Economic order quantity}$$

This result can be substituted back into the equations for stock cycle length ($T = Q/D$) and total cost to give the corresponding optimal values:

$$\text{Optimal cycle length} \quad T_o = \sqrt{\frac{2 * RC}{HC * D}}$$

$$\text{Minimum total cost} \quad TC_o = UC * D + \sqrt{2 * RC * HC * D}$$

The equation for minimum total cost contains a 'fixed' element, $UC * D$, which does not vary with order quantity and a 'variable' element, VC_o, which does, so:

$$TC_o = UC * D + VC_o$$

$$VC_o = \sqrt{2 * RC * HC * D}$$

WORKED EXAMPLE 11.1

The demand for an item is constant at 20 units a month. Unit cost is £50, cost of processing an order and arranging delivery is £60, and holding cost is estimated to be £18 per unit per annum. What is the economic order quantity, corresponding cycle length and costs?

SOLUTION

Listing the values we know in consistent units:

D = 20 * 12 = 240 units a year
UC = £50 per unit
RC = £60 per order
HC = £18 per unit per year

Then substitution gives:

$$Q_o = \sqrt{\frac{2 * RC * D}{HC}} = \sqrt{\frac{2 * 60 * 240}{18}} = 40 \text{ units}$$

$$T_o = \sqrt{\frac{2 * RC}{HC * D}} = \sqrt{\frac{2 * 60}{18 * 240}} = 0.167 \text{ years} = 2 \text{ months}$$

$$VC_o = \sqrt{2 * RC * HC * D} = \sqrt{2 * 60 * 18 * 240} = £720 \text{ a year}$$

$$TC_o = UC * D + VC_o = 50 * 240 + 720 = £12,720 \text{ a year}$$

The optimal policy (with total costs of £12,720 a year) is to order 40 units every 2 months.

The calculations in this example could be done in several ways. The cycle length, for example, could be calculated from:

$$Q_o = D * T_o \text{ so } 40 = 240 * T_o \text{ and } T_o = 0.167 \text{ years or 2 months}$$

An interesting result is found if we look at the total reorder cost and total holding cost when Q_o is ordered.

$$\text{Total holding cost} = \frac{HC * Q_o}{2} = \frac{18 * 40}{2} = £360$$

$$\text{Total reorder cost} = \frac{RC * D}{Q_o} = \frac{60 * 240}{40} = £360$$

It is not coincidence that these two costs are the same. When orders are placed for the economic order quantity, the total reorder cost is always the same as the total holding cost. The variable cost could, therefore, have been found from multiplying either of these by 2.

$$VC_o = HC * Q_o = 18 * 40 = £720$$

or

$$VC_o = 2 * RC * D/Q_o = 2 * 60 * 240/40 = £720$$

Several other methods of calculation could be used, but each should, obviously, give the same answers.

In summary

The classic analysis of inventory control identifies an optimal order quantity of:

$$Q_o = \sqrt{\frac{2 * RC * D}{HC}}$$

This result allows calculation of several related measures.

11.2.3 Reorder levels for fixed lead times

The economic order quantity answers the question of how much to order, but we still need to know when to place an order. This decision is based on the lead time, LT, between placing an order and its arrival in stock. For simplicity, we

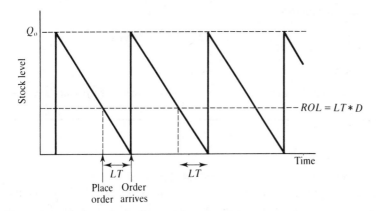

Figure 11.8 Orders are placed when the stock declines to reorder level, *ROL*.

will start by assuming that this is fixed. The stock level follows the saw-tooth pattern shown in Figure 11.5, with stock rising when a delivery is made and falling slowly back to zero. To ensure a delivery arrives just as stock is running out, an order must be placed a time *LT* earlier. The easiest way of finding this point is to look at the current stock and place an order when there is just enough left to last the lead time. With constant demand of *D*, an order is placed when the stock level falls to $LT * D$ and this point is called the reorder level (see Figure 11.8).

> Reorder level = Lead time demand
> $ROL = LT * D$

One way of using such a system in practice is called the 'two-bin system'. In this, stock is kept in two bins, one of which holds an amount equal to the reorder level while the second holds all remaining stock. Demand is met from the second bin until this is empty. At this point the stock level has declined to the reorder level and it is time to place an order.

WORKED EXAMPLE 11.2

Demand for an item is constant at 20 units per week, reorder cost is £125 an order and holding cost is £2 per unit per week. If suppliers guarantee delivery within 2 weeks what would be the best ordering policy for the item?

SOLUTION

Listing the variables in consistent units:

D = 20 units per week
RC = £125 per order
HC = £2 per unit per week
LT = 2 weeks

Then substitution gives:

$$Q_o = \sqrt{\frac{2 * RC * D}{HC}} = \sqrt{\frac{2 * 125 * 20}{2}} = 50 \text{ units}$$

$$ROL = LT * D = 2 * 20 = 40 \text{ units}$$

The optimal policy is to place an order for 50 units whenever stock declines to 40 units.

This approach works well provided the lead time is less than the length of a stock cycle. In Worked Example 11.2 the lead time was 2 weeks and the stock cycle was 2.5 weeks. Suppose the lead time is raised to 3 weeks. The calculation for reorder level then becomes:

$$ROL = LT * D = 3 * 20 = 60 \text{ units}$$

The problem is that the stock level never actually rises to 60 units, but varies between 0 and 50 units. Because the lead time is longer than the stock cycle, there will always be at least one order outstanding, as shown in Figure 11.9.

The way around this is to recognize that the calculated reorder level relates to both stock on hand and stock on order (and arriving shortly). A new order should be placed when stock on hand plus stock on order equals the lead time demand. The reorder level then equals lead time demand minus any stock on order.

$$ROL = \text{Lead time demand} - \text{Stock on order}$$

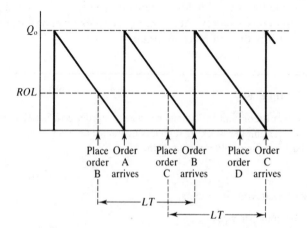

Figure 11.9 Orders when lead time is longer than stock cycle.

In Worked Example 11.2 the order quantity is 50 units, so if the lead time is 3 weeks, there would still be one order of 50 units outstanding when it is time to place another order. Then:

$$ROL = 3 * 20 - 50 = 10 \text{ units}$$

An order for 50 units is placed whenever actual stock declines to 10 units.

When the lead time is very long there may be several orders outstanding at any time. Extending the observations above, we can give the general rule:

When lead time is between $n * T$ and $(n + 1) * T$ order an amount Q_o whenever stock on hand falls to $LT * D - n * Q_o$.

This recognizes the fact that there will always be n orders outstanding when a new order has to be placed. When $n = 0$ this reduces to the first simple rule we described.

In summary

The easiest way of finding the time to place an order is to define a reorder level. For constant lead time and demand the reorder level equals lead time demand minus any stock on order.

11.2.4 Sensitivity analysis

Usually, the economic order quantity gives an awkward order size like 88.39 units. In practice, such order sizes may be awkward or even impossible. Cement may be delivered in 50 kg bags, so an order for 88.39 kg will automatically be rounded to 100 kg. Orders for 88.39 tyres must be rounded to 88 tyres, but it may be more convenient to order 90, or even 100 tyres. The question we should ask, then, is what effect such rounding and movement away from the economic order quantity has on overall costs.

The cost of ordering Q_o can be compared with the cost of ordering any other quantity, Q. As the fixed costs remain unchanged we need only consider the variable costs, and we know that:

for Q_o

$$VC_o = \sqrt{2 * RC * HC * D}$$

for any value of Q

$$VC = \frac{RC * D}{Q} + \frac{HC * Q}{2}$$

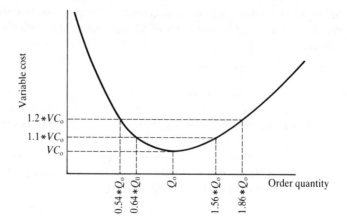

Figure 11.10 Variation in variable cost with order quantity.

The ratio of these is:

$$\frac{VC}{VC_o} = \frac{\dfrac{RC * D}{Q} + \dfrac{HC * Q}{2}}{\sqrt{2 * RC * HC * D}}$$

which can be simplified to:

$$\boxed{\frac{VC}{VC_o} = \frac{1}{2}\left[\frac{Q}{Q_o} + \frac{Q_o}{Q}\right]}$$

As VC must be greater than VC_o, this ratio is always greater than one and shows the proportional rise in variable cost as we move away from Q_o.

If we substitute specific values into the equation we can find the amount of movement away from the optimal order quantity which raises the variable cost by a specific amount, say, 10%.

$$\frac{VC}{VC_o} = \frac{1.1}{1} = \frac{1}{2}\left[\frac{Q}{Q_o} + \frac{Q_o}{Q}\right]$$

Now if we set Q as a proportion of Q_o, so that $Q = f * Q_o$ this gives:

$$2.2 = \frac{f}{1} + \frac{1}{f}$$

or

$$f^2 - 2.2 * f + 1 = 0$$

Solving this quadratic equation gives either $f = 0.64$ or $f = 1.56$. In other words the amount ordered can be increased to 156% of the optimal value or reduced to 64% and only raise variable costs by 10%. A similar analysis shows that the order quantity can be increased to 186% of Q_0 or reduced to 54% and only raise variable costs by 20%. This is one reason why the classic analysis is so widely used; it is recognized that the calculation is based on a series of assumptions and approximations but the total cost rises slowly with small changes around the optimal. The *EOQ* gives a good guideline for order size in many circumstances (see Figure 11.10).

WORKED EXAMPLE 11.3

The economic order quantity for an item has been calculated as 169 units, with associated variable costs of £5700 a year. What would be the cost if orders were rounded to 200 units? What range of order size would keep variable costs within 10% of optimal?

SOLUTION

We know that VC_0 = £5700 with Q_0 = 169, so substituting Q = 200 gives:

$$\frac{VC}{VC_0} = \frac{1}{2}\left[\frac{Q}{Q_0} + \frac{Q_0}{Q}\right]$$

$$\frac{VC}{5700} = \frac{1}{2}\left[\frac{200}{169} + \frac{169}{200}\right]$$

or

VC = £5781, a rise of only 1.4%

To keep the variable cost within 10% of optimal, the order quantity can vary between 64% of Q_0 (0.64 * 169 = 108 units) and 156% of Q_0 (1.56 * 169 = 264 units).

WORKED EXAMPLE 11.4

Demand for an item is constant at 500 units a month. Unit cost is £100 and shortage costs are known to be very high. The purchasing department sends out an average of 3000 orders a year, and total operating costs are £180,000. Any stocks incur capital financing charges of 15%, warehouse charges of 7% and other overheads of 8% a year. The lead time is constant at one week.

- Find an appropriate ordering policy for the item.
- What is the reorder level if the lead time increases to 3 weeks?
- Within what range could orders be placed and keep variable costs within 10% of optimal?
- What would be the variable cost if orders were placed for 200 units at a time?

SOLUTION

Listing the values we know and making sure the units are consistent:

$D = 500 * 12 = 6000$ units a year
$UC = £100$ a unit

$$RC = \frac{\text{annual cost of purchasing department}}{\text{number of orders raised a year}} = \frac{180,000}{3000}$$
$$= £60 \text{ an order}$$

$HC = (15\% + 7\% + 8\%)$ of unit cost a year $= (0.3) * UC$
$= £30$ a unit a year

$LT = 1$ week

- Substitution gives:

$$Q_o = \sqrt{\frac{2 * RC * D}{HC}} = \sqrt{\frac{2 * 60 * 6000}{30}} = 154.9 \text{ units}$$

$$T_0 = \sqrt{\frac{2 * RC}{HC * D}} = \sqrt{\frac{2 * 60}{30 * 6000}} = 0.026 \text{ years} = 1.3 \text{ weeks}$$

$$VC_o = \sqrt{2 * RC * HC * D} = \sqrt{2 * 60 * 30 * 6000} = £4647.58 \text{ a year}$$

$$TC_o = UC * D + VC_o = 100 * 6000 + 4647.58 = £604,647.58 \text{ a year}$$

The lead time is less than the stock cycle, so:

$$ROL = LT * D = 1 * 6000/52 = 115.4 \text{ units}$$

The optimal policy is to order 154.9 units whenever stock declines to 115.4 units.

- If the lead time is increased to 3 weeks, this is between two and three stock cycles, so there will be two orders outstanding when it is time to place another. Then:

$$ROL = LT * D - 2 * Q_o = 3 * 6000/52 - 2 * 154.9 = 36.4 \text{ units}$$

- To keep variable costs within 10% of optimal, order quantities could vary between 64% of Q_o (= 99.1 units) and 156% of Q_o (= 241.6 units).

- If fixed order sizes of 200 units were used the variable costs will be:

$$VC = RC * D/Q + HC * Q/2 = 60 * 6000/200 + 30 * 200/2$$
$$= £4,800 \text{ a year}$$

In summary

The variable cost of holding stock rises slowly around the economic order quantity. Orders may, therefore, be rounded to convenient sizes without incurring high penalties.

SELF ASSESSMENT QUESTIONS

11.8 What are the main assumptions of the 'classic analysis'?

11.9 What is meant by the economic order quantity?

11.10 If small orders are placed frequently (rather than placing large orders infrequently) does this:

(a) reduce total costs
(b) increase total costs

(c) either increase or decrease total costs
(d) have no effect on total costs?

11.11 What is meant by the reorder level?

11.12 How is the reorder level calculated?

11.13 It is important to order exactly the economic order quantity, as even small differences will give much higher costs. Is this statement true or false?

11.3 INVENTORY CONTROL FOR PRODUCTION SYSTEMS

We suggested earlier that independent demand inventory systems are best suited to situations like warehouses and retailers. This does not, of course, mean that they are restricted to such applications. Most inventories of all kinds are controlled by systems based on the economic order quantity. In this section we will consider one extension of the basic analysis which is particularly relevant to production systems. This assumes that replenishment is done at a finite rate rather than instantaneously.

A component which is made in one work station at a rate of 10 an hour will feed this output into stocks of work in progress at the same rate. Then, assuming none is used, the stocks will rise steadily by 10 units an hour. Similarly, if an item is manufactured at some finite rate, it may be moved into stocks of finished goods at this rate rather than arrive in batches. We can extend the classic analysis by removing the assumption of instantaneous replenishment and allow units to be moved into stock at a finite rate, P. This situation is shown in Figure 11.11.

If the rate of production is less than the rate of demand (that is, P is less than D) there is no problem with stock holding. Supply is not keeping up with demand and as soon as a unit is made it is transferred straight out to customers. Inventory problems only arise when the rate of production is higher than the

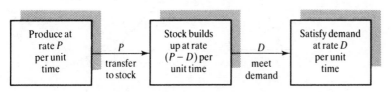

Figure 11.11 Stock movements with a finite production rate.

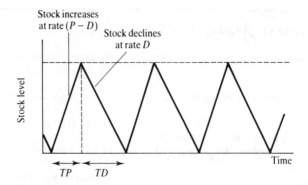

Figure 11.12 Changing stock level with finite production rate.

demand (that is, P is greater than D). Then stock builds up at a rate $(P - D)$ for as long as production continues.

Production is stopped when a large enough batch of the item has been made, so we will say that after some time TP, the work station moves on to process other items. When production is stopped, demand from customers continues at a rate D and is met from the accumulated stock. After some further time, TD, the stock is exhausted and production must restart. The resulting stock level is shown in Figure 11.12.

We want to find an optimal value for the batch size. This is equivalent to the previous analysis which found an optimal order quantity, and the overall approach is the same. In particular, this involves finding the total cost for a single stock cycle, dividing this by the cycle length to give a cost per unit time and then minimizing this cost.

Consider (Figure 11.13) one cycle of the stock pattern shown in Figure 11.12.

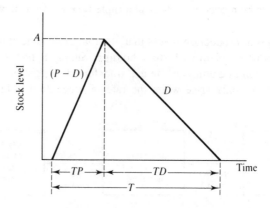

Figure 11.13 A single stock cycle with finite production rate.

Batches of size Q are made, and if replenishment were instantaneous this would be the maximum stock level. As units are actually fed into stock at a finite rate and are continuously being removed to meet demand, the maximum stock level will be lower than Q and will occur at the point where production is stopped. The value for A, the highest actual stock level, can be found in terms of other variables as follows.

Looking at the productive part of the cycle, TP, we have:

$$A = (P - D) * TP$$

We also know that total production during the period is:

$$Q = P * TP \text{ or } TP = Q/P$$

Substituting this value for TP into the equation for A gives:

$$A = Q * \frac{(P - D)}{P}$$

The analysis now continues as before, remembering that in this case RC, the reorder cost, is really a production set-up cost.

Total cost for a cycle:

- total unit cost = number of units ordered (Q) * unit cost (UC)
  = $UC * Q$

- total set-up cost = number of production set-up (1) * set-up cost (RC)
  = RC

- total holding cost = average stock level $(A/2)$ * time held (T) * holding cost (HC)

$$= \frac{HC * A * T}{2} = \frac{HC * Q * T}{2} * \frac{(P - D)}{P}$$

Adding these three gives the total cost per cycle as:

$$UC * Q + RC + \frac{HC * Q * T}{2} * \frac{(P - D)}{P}$$

Dividing this by the cycle length, T, gives a total cost per unit time, TC:

$$TC = \frac{UC * Q}{T} + \frac{RC}{T} + \frac{HC * Q}{2} * \frac{(P - D)}{P}$$

Then substitution of $Q = D * T$ gives:

$$TC = UC * D + \frac{RC * D}{Q} + \frac{HC * Q}{2} * \frac{(P - D)}{P}$$

When this is compared with the result for the classic analysis, the only difference is the factor $(P - D)/P$. The analysis could be continued by plotting this total cost curve against batch size, Q, and finding an asymmetric 'U' shaped curve with a distinct minimum. Differentiating the total cost equation with respect to Q and setting the derivative to equal zero gives the optimal batch quantity, Q_o. We will not repeat the arithmetic, but note the results only differ from the classic analysis by the factor $(P - D)/P$.

Finite production rate	Classic analysis
$Q_o = \sqrt{\dfrac{2 * RC * D}{HC}} * \sqrt{\dfrac{P}{P - D}}$	$Q_o = \sqrt{\dfrac{2 * RC * D}{HC}}$
$T_o = \sqrt{\dfrac{2 * RC}{HC * D}} * \sqrt{\dfrac{P}{P - D}}$	$T_o = \sqrt{\dfrac{2 * RC}{HC * D}}$
$VC_o = \sqrt{2 * RC * HC * D} * \sqrt{\dfrac{P - D}{P}}$	$VC_o = \sqrt{2 * RC * HC * D}$
$TC_o = UC * D + VC_o$	$TC_o = UC * D + VC_o$

Again there is a compromise between large, infrequent batches (with consequent high holding costs but low set-up costs) and small frequent batches (with low holding costs but high set-up costs). With a finite production rate the stock level is somewhat lower than it would be with instantaneous replenishment, so we would expect, all other things being equal, to make larger batches. This is confirmed by the results above where batch size increases by $\sqrt{P/(P - D)}$.

WORKED EXAMPLE 11.5

Demand for an item is 600 units a month and relevant costs have been estimated as:

- production set-up cost of £64 an order;
- shop order preparation of £50 an order;
- scheduling of shop order at £11 an order;
- insurance of 1% of unit cost a year;
- obsolescence, deterioration and depreciation allowance of 2% of unit cost a year;
- capital costs of 20% of unit cost a year;
- storage space at £5 per unit per annum;
- handling costs of £6 per unit per annum.

Shortage costs are so large that no shortages are allowed.
Each unit costs the company £20 and the rate of production is 1200 units a month. Determine the optimal batch quantity and the minimum variable cost a year.
By rescheduling work the company could reduce its effective rate of production to 700 units a month at an additional cost of £200 a month. Would this be worth while?

SOLUTION

Every cost must be classified as unit, reorder or holding (with no shortage costs). Then:

$D = 600 * 12 = 7200$ units a year
$P = 1200 * 12 = 14{,}400$ units a year
$UC = £20$ a unit

Collecting together all costs which arise per order gives:

$RC = 64 + 50 + 11 = £125$ per order

Holding costs are of two types, a percentage (1%, 2% and 20%) of unit costs and a fixed amount (£5 + £6) per unit per year.

$HC = (5 + 6) + (0.01 + 0.02 + 0.2) * 20$
$= £15.60$ a unit a year

Substituting these values gives

$$\sqrt{\frac{P}{P - D}} = \sqrt{\frac{14{,}400}{14{,}400 - 7200}} = 1.414$$

$$Q_o = \sqrt{\frac{2 * RC * D}{HC}} * \sqrt{\frac{P}{P - D}} = \sqrt{\frac{2 * 125 * 7200}{15.60}} * 1.414$$

$= 480$ units

$$VC_o = \sqrt{2 * RC * HC * D} * \sqrt{\frac{P - D}{P}} = \sqrt{2 * 125 * 15.60 * 7200} \,/1.414$$

$= 5299.1/1.414 = £3748$ a year

The last part of the question reinforces the view that stocks are only needed because of mismatches between supply and demand. If supply could be matched exactly to demand, there would be no need to hold stock. It follows that the smaller this mismatch can be made, the smaller will be the total cost of holding stock. By paying to reduce the production rate we might save money by more closely matching supply and demand.
Reducing P to $700 * 12 = 8400$ units a year gives:

$$VC_o = \sqrt{2 * RC * HC * D} * \sqrt{\frac{P - D}{P}} = 5299.1 * \sqrt{\frac{8400 - 7200}{8400}}$$

$= £2003$ a year

The initial saving is $(3748 - 2003) = £1745$, but if we add the additional rescheduling cost of £200 a month the total cost becomes $2003 + 2400 = £4403$ a year and the rescheduling is not worth while.

In summary

The classic analysis can be extended by adding a finite production rate. This makes the analysis more appropriate for production systems, and adds a factor of $\sqrt{(P - D)/P}$ to the standard results.

11.14 When are finite production rates important for stock control:

(a) when production rate is greater than demand
(b) when production rate is less than demand
(c) when production rate equals demand
(d) never?

11.15 When compared with instantaneous replenishment, does a finite production rate lead to:

(a) larger batches
(b) smaller batches
(c) same size batches
(d) could be either larger or smaller batches?

11.4 PROBABILISTIC DEMAND

The analyses we have described so far have all assumed that demand is constant and known exactly. In practice this is rarely true and the demand for almost any item varies over time. In addition, there is usually some uncertainty which is ignored in the classic analysis. Fortunately, these effects are generally small and *EOQ* models can still give useful results. Sometimes, however, the variations are too large and another approach must be used. A range of appropriate models has been developed; we will start by looking at demand which is Normally distributed.

We can easily show why the results from models which assume constant demand are not appropriate for demand which is Normally distributed. Consider what would happen in a typical stock cycle. Calculations would be based on mean demand, but when demand in the lead time is greater than average, or if a delivery arrives late, stock will run out and there will be shortages. The costs of these shortages can be high in terms of lost profit, lost goodwill, interrupted production, and so on. Unfortunately, the lead time demand will be above the mean value in 50% of cycles, giving a clearly unacceptable performance.

Some other approach is needed for variable demand, and this is based on the balance between shortage costs and holding costs. It is difficult to find accurate costs for stockouts, but they are usually high in relation to holding costs. This means that organizations are willing to hold additional stocks, above their perceived needs, to add a margin of safety (Figure 11.14). These 'safety stocks' are available if the normal working stock is exhausted. The question we can now ask is, 'How much safety stock should be held?'

In principle, it should be possible to calculate the cost of stockouts and balance them with the cost of holding stock. In practice this is rarely possible as stockout costs are notoriously difficult to find and are often little more than informed guesses. Analyses based on such shortage costs are often unreliable. An alternative approach relies more directly on the judgement of management and allows a 'service level' to be used. This involves a positive decision to specify the desired probability that a demand is met directly from stock (or, conversely, the maximum acceptable probability that a demand cannot be met

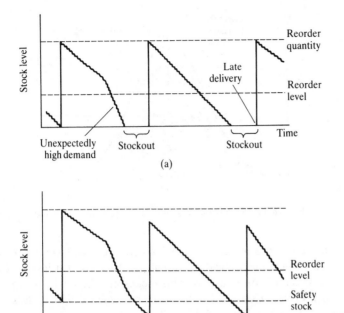

Figure 11.14 Adding a safety stock to avoid stockouts. (a) Unexpectedly high demand or late deliveries leading to stockouts without safety stock. (b) Stockouts are avoided by adding a safety stock.

from stock). Typically a company will specify a service level of 95%, implying a probability of 0.05 that a demand is not met.

There are several different ways of defining service level, including percentage of orders met from stock, percentage of units met from stock, percentage of periods without stockouts, percentage of stock cycles without stockouts, percentage of time there is stock available, and so on. In the remainder of this analysis we will use the probability of not running out of stock in a stock cycle. This is sometimes called the cycle service level.

Consider an item for which demand is known to be Normally distributed with a mean of D per unit time and standard deviation of σ. If the lead time is constant at LT, the lead time demand is Normally distributed with mean of $LT * D$, variance of $\sigma^2 * LT$ and standard deviation of $\sigma * \sqrt{LT}$. This result is derived from the fact that variances can be added but standard deviations cannot.

> If demand in a single period has mean D and variance σ^2,
>> demand in two periods has mean $2 * D$ and variance $2 * \sigma^2$,
>> demand in three periods has mean $3 * D$ and variance $3 * \sigma^2$,
>> and so on, so that
>> demand in LT periods has mean $LT * D$ and variance $LT * \sigma^2$.

499

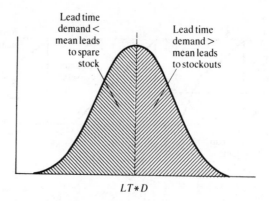

Figure 11.15 Normal distribution of lead time demand.

With constant demand we used lead time demand ($= LT * D$) as a reorder level. If lead time demand is Normally distributed, it will be greater than the mean value on half of occasions. This means that there will be stockouts in 50% of stock cycles. Conversely, the lead time demand will be less than the mean in 50% of stock cycles, and this will give spare stock (as shown in Figure 11.15).

To give a cycle service level which is greater than 0.5 we need to add a safety stock, and the reorder level then becomes:

> Reorder level = Lead time demand + Safety stock

This assumes that the lead time is less than the stock cycle time, so we do not need to consider stock already on order.

The size of the safety stock depends on the service level specified. If a high service level is required the safety stock must also be high. Specifically, when lead time demand is Normally distributed the calculation of safety stock becomes:

> Safety stock $= Z *$ Standard deviation of lead time demand
> $= Z * \sigma * \sqrt{LT}$

where Z is the number of standard deviations away from the mean.

Values for Z are found in standard Normal tables (see Appendix A). To give some examples,

> $Z = 1$ means a stockout will occur in 15.9% of stock cycles,
> $Z = 2$ gives stockouts in 2.3% of stock cycles,
> $Z = 3$ gives stockouts in 0.1% of stock cycles,

and so on.

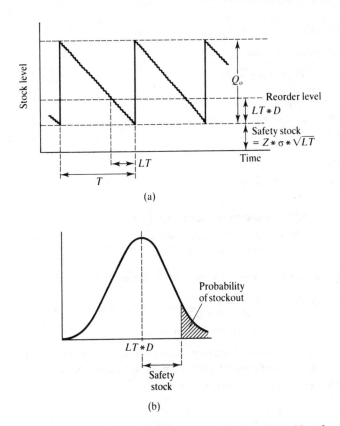

Figure 11.16 Effects of adding a safety stock. (a) Stock cycles with safety stock. (b) Probability of stockout with safety stock.

The effects of safety stocks are shown in Figure 11.16. If demand varies widely, the standard deviation of lead time demand will be high and very high safety stocks would be needed to ensure a service level near to 100%. This may be prohibitively expensive and companies will usually set a lower level, typically around 95%. Sometimes it is convenient to give items different service levels depending on their importance. Very important items may be given levels close to 100%, while less important ones are set around 85%.

WORKED EXAMPLE 11.6

Demand for an item is Normally distributed with a mean of 200 units a week and a standard deviation of 40 units. Reorder cost (including delivery) is £200, holding cost is £6 a unit a year and lead time is fixed at 3 weeks.

- Describe an ordering policy that will give a 95% cycle service level.
- What is the cost of holding the safety stock in this case?
- By how much would the costs rise if the service level is raised to 97%?

SOLUTION

Listing the values we know:

D = 200 units per week
σ = 40 units
RC = £200 per order
HC = £6 per unit per year
LT = 3 weeks

Substitution of these gives:

$$Q_o = \sqrt{2 * RC * D/HC}$$
$$= \sqrt{2 * 200 * 200 * 52/6}$$
$$= 833 \text{ (rounded to the nearest integer)}$$

$$ROL = LT * D + \text{safety stock}$$
$$= 600 + \text{safety stock}$$

For a 95% service level Z = 1.64 standard deviations from the mean. Then:

$$\text{Safety stock} = Z * \sigma * \sqrt{LT}$$
$$= 1.64 * 40 * \sqrt{3}$$
$$= 114 \text{ (to the nearest integer)}$$

The best policy is to order 833 units whenever stock declines to 600 + 114 = 714 units. On average, orders should arrive when there are 114 units remaining.

- The expected cost of the safety stock is:

  = safety stock * holding cost
  = 114 * 6
  = £684 a year

- If the service level is raised to 97%, Z becomes 1.88 and:

  $$\text{Safety stock} = Z * \sigma * \sqrt{LT}$$
  $$= 1.88 * 40 * \sqrt{3}$$
  $$= 130$$

  The cost of holding this is:
  = safety stock * holding cost
  = 130 * 6
  = £780 a year

In summary

The assumption that demand is constant gives reasonable results as long as actual variations are small. If the variations are large a different model must be used. When the lead time demand is Normally distributed, the reorder level is given by:

$$ROL = \text{lead time demand} + \text{safety stock}$$
$$= LT * D + Z * \sigma * \sqrt{LT}$$

where Z determines the cycle service level.

SELF ASSESSMENT QUESTIONS

11.16 What is meant by service level and why is it used?

11.18 How might the service level be improved?

11.17 What is the purpose of safety stock?

11.5 PERIODIC REVIEW SYSTEMS

At the beginning of the chapter we said that two different ordering policies could be used (see Figure 11.17):

- Fixed order quantity system, where an order of fixed size is placed whenever stock falls to a certain level.
- Periodic review system, where orders of varying size are placed at regular intervals to raise the stock to a specified level (the target stock level).

If the demand is constant these two systems are identical, so differences only appear when the demand varies. We can, therefore, extend the last analysis by considering a periodic review system where demand is Normally distributed. Then we look for answers to two basic questions:

- How long should the interval between orders be?
- What should the target stock level be?

The order interval, T, can really be any convenient period. It might, for example, be convenient to place an order at the end of every week, or every morning, or at the end of a month. If there is no obvious cycle we might aim for a certain number of orders a year or some average order size. One approach would be to calculate an economic order quantity, and then find the period which gives orders of about this size. The final decision is largely a matter for management judgement.

Whatever interval is chosen we need to find a suitable target stock level,

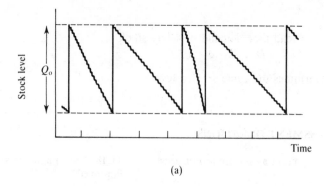

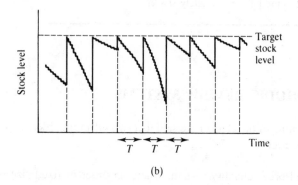

Figure 11.17 Alternative inventory control systems. (a) Fixed-order quantity system. (b) Periodic review system.

TSL. The system then works by examining the amount of stock on hand when an order is placed and ordering the amount that would bring this up to *TSL*.

Order quantity = Target stock level − Stock on hand

Suppose the lead time is constant at *LT*. When an order is placed, the stock on hand plus this order must be enough to last until the next order arrives, which is $T + LT$ away (as shown in Figure 11.18).

The target stock level should be high enough to cover mean demand over this period so *TSL* must be at least $(T + LT) * D$. As demand is Normally distributed, some safety stock is needed to allow for the 50% of cycles when demand is above average. Assuming both the cycle length and lead time are constant, the demand over $T + LT$ is Normally distributed with mean of $(T + LT) * D$, variance of $\sigma^2 * (T + LT)$ and standard deviation of $\sigma * \sqrt{(T + LT)}$. A safety stock can then be defined as:

$$\text{Safety stock} = Z * \text{standard deviation of demand over } T + LT$$
$$= Z * \sigma * \sqrt{(T + LT)}$$

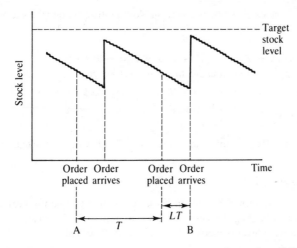

Figure 11.18 Order placed at A must cover demand until B.

Then:

$$\begin{aligned}\text{Target stock level} &= \frac{\text{Demand over}}{T + LT} + \text{Safety stock} \\ &= D * (T + LT) + Z * \sigma * \sqrt{(T + LT)}\end{aligned}$$

This argument has assumed that the lead time is less than the cycle length. If this is not true the order placed must also take into account the stock already on order, so that:

Order quantity = Target level − Stock on hand − Stock on order

---

WORKED EXAMPLE 11.7

Demand for an item has a mean of 200 units a week and standard deviation of 40 units. Stock is checked every four weeks and lead time is constant at two weeks. Describe a policy which will give a 95% service level. If the holding cost is £2 a unit a week, what is the cost of the safety stock with this policy? What would be the effect of a 98% service level?

SOLUTION

The variables are:

$$\begin{aligned}D &= 200 \text{ units} \\ \sigma &= 40 \text{ units} \\ HC &= £2 \text{ a unit a week} \\ T &= 4 \text{ weeks} \\ LT &= 2 \text{ weeks}\end{aligned}$$

For a 95% safety stock Z can be found from Normal distribution tables to be 1.64. Then:

$$\text{Safety stock} = Z * \sigma * \sqrt{(T + LT)} = 1.64 * 40 * \sqrt{6}$$
$$= 161 \text{ (rounded to the nearest integer)}$$
$$\text{Target stock level} = D * (T + LT) + \text{safety stock}$$
$$= 200 * (6) + 161$$
$$= 1361$$

When it is time to place an order, the policy is to find the stock on hand, and place an order for:

$$\text{Order size} = 1361 - \text{stock on hand}$$

If, for example, there were 200 units in stock the order would be for 1161 units.
The cost of holding the safety stock is $161 * 2 = £322$ a week.
If the service level is increased to 98%, $Z = 2.05$ and

$$\text{Safety stock} = 2.05 * 40 * \sqrt{6}$$
$$= 201$$

The target stock level is then 1401 units and the cost of the safety stock is $201 * 2 = £402$ a week.

In summary

A periodic review system places orders of variable size at regular intervals. The quantity ordered is enough to raise stock on hand plus stock on order to a target level, TSL, where:

$$TSL = D * (T + LT) + Z * \sigma * \sqrt{(T + LT)}$$

SELF ASSESSMENT QUESTIONS

11.19 How is the order size calculated for a periodic review system?

11.20 Will the safety stock be higher for:

(a) a fixed order quantity system
(b) a periodic review system
(c) both the same
(d) could be either?

11.6 SINGLE PERIOD MODELS

Sometimes an inventory policy is not concerned with the long term, but with the short term, often as little as a single stock cycle. This is particularly relevant for seasonal goods. A stock of Christmas cards, for example, should satisfy demand in December, but will have very little value in January. Inventory control will, therefore, seek to minimize costs during December. The classic example of this is phrased in terms of a newsboy who sells papers on a street corner. The newsboy has to decide how many papers to buy from his supplier when the customer demand is uncertain. If he buys too many papers he is left with unsold stock, which has no value at the end of the day. If he buys too few papers he has unsatisfied demand, which could have given a higher profit. Because of this example, single period problems of this type are usually referred to as newsboy problems. Although it is a widely occurring problem, we will stick to the original description of a newsboy selling newspapers.

The analysis assumes that customer demand follows a known probability distribution, so we know the probability of selling each number of newspapers. If we also know the profit on each paper sold, PROF, and the loss on each paper bought but not sold, LOSS, we can suggest an optimal policy.

Suppose the newsboy buys n newspapers. His expected profit on the nth is $P(n) * \text{PROF}$, where $P(n)$ is the probability he sells the nth paper. Alternatively, we could say that the expected loss on the nth paper is $(1 - P(n)) * \text{LOSS}$, where $(1 - P(n))$ is the probability he does not sell the nth paper. As $P(n)$ is the probability that the nth paper is sold, it is really the cumulative probability that the demand is greater than or equal to n. The newsboy will only buy n papers if his expected profit is greater than his expected loss. In other words:

$$P(n) * \text{PROF} > (1 - P(n)) * \text{LOSS}$$

or

$$P(n) > \frac{\text{LOSS}}{\text{PROF} + \text{LOSS}}$$

The newsboy's profit continues to rise with n while the inequality remains valid, but at some point the inequality will become invalid and his profit begins to fall. This, then, identifies his best policy. He should buy the largest value of n which will ensure the inequality is still valid.

WORKED EXAMPLE 11.8

In mid-December the owner of a conifer plantation employs a contractor to cut enough trees to meet the expected demand for Christmas trees. He supplies these to a local wholesaler in batches of 100. Over the past few years the demand has been as follows.

Batches	1	2	3	4	5	6	7	8	9
Probability	0.05	0.1	0.15	0.2	0.2	0.15	0.1	0.05	0

If it costs £8 to cut and trim a tree which sells for £12, how many trees should be cut down?

SOLUTION

PROF is the profit on a batch of 100 trees, which is $100 * (12 - 8) = £400$.
LOSS is the loss on a batch of unsold trees, which is $100 * 8 = £800$.
Then we want the highest value of n which ensures the inequality remains valid:

$$P(n) > \text{LOSS}/(\text{PROF} + \text{LOSS})$$
$$> 800/(400 + 800)$$
$$> 0.67$$

The cumulative probabilities of selling at least n trees are:

n	1	2	3	4	5	6	7	8	9
$P(n)$	1.0	0.95	0.85	0.70	0.5	0.3	0.15	0.05	0

Hence the largest value of n for which the inequality is valid is 4. The plantation owner should have 400 trees cut down.

WORKED EXAMPLE 11.9

A tour operator wants to book a number of hotel rooms in anticipation of future bookings for holidays. The number of holidays actually booked is equally likely to be any number between 0 and 99 (for convenience rather than reality). Each hotel room booked costs the operator £150, and he charges holiday makers £250. How many rooms should he book?

SOLUTION

Here LOSS = 150 and PROF = $(250 - 150) = 100$.
We want $P(n) > \text{LOSS}/(\text{PROF} + \text{LOSS}) > 150/(100 + 150) > 0.6$.
As each number of bookings is equally likely, the probability of each number, n, is 0.01 for all values of n from 0 to 99.

n	0	1	2	3	4	...	39	40	41	...
$P(n)$	1.0	0.99	0.98	0.97	0.96	...	0.61	0.60	0.61	...

The largest value of n which ensures the inequality is valid is 40.

In summary

Sometimes stocks have to be controlled over a single period. In such cases expected profit can be maximized by ordering the largest number of units which ensures the inequality $P(n) > \text{LOSS}/(\text{PROF} + \text{LOSS})$ is still valid.

11.21 What is meant by a single period model?

newsboy problem?

11.22 What is the meaning of $P(n)$ in the

11.23 Why must the inequality $P(n) >$ LOSS/(PROF + LOSS) remain valid?

11.7 ABC ANALYSIS OF INVENTORIES

A considerable effort is needed to ensure the control of inventories continues to be smooth and efficient. Most inventory control systems are computerized, but they still need manual effort to input data, check values, update supplier details, confirm orders, and so on. The computer system itself might incur high operating costs. For some items, especially cheap ones, this effort is not worth while. Very few organizations, for example, include routine stationery in their computerized stock system. At the other end of the scale are very expensive items which require special care above the routine calculations.

An ABC analysis is one way of putting items into categories which reflect the amount of effort worth spending on inventory control. This kind of analysis is sometimes called a Pareto analysis or the 'rule of 80/20' (suggesting that 80% of inventory items need 20% of the attention, while the remaining 20% of items need 80% of the attention). ABC analyses define:

- A items as expensive and needing special care;
- B items as ordinary ones needing standard care;
- C items as cheap and needing little care.

Typically an organization might use an automated system to deal with all B items. The computer system might make some suggestions for A items, but final decisions are made by managers after reviewing the circumstances. Some C items might be included in the automatic system, but the very cheap ones may be left out, with any control left to *ad hoc* procedures.

An ABC analysis starts by calculating the total annual use of items in terms of value, by multiplying the number of units used in a year by the unit cost. Usually, a few expensive items account for a lot of use, while many cheap ones account for little use. If we list the items in order of decreasing annual use by value, A items are at the top of the list and C items are at the bottom. We

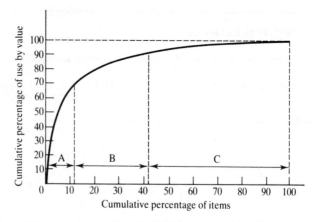

Figure 11.19 Typical ABC analysis for inventories.

might typically find:

Category	% of items	Cumulative % of items	% of use by value	Cumulative % of use by value
A	10	10	70	70
B	30	40	20	90
C	60	100	10	100

Plotting the cumulative percentage of annual use against the cumulative percentage of items gives a graph of the type shown in Figure 11.19.

WORKED EXAMPLE 11.10

A small store consists of ten categories of product with the following costs and annual demands:

Product	P1	P2	P3	P4	P5	P6	P7	P8	P9	P0
Unit cost (£)	20	10	20	50	10	50	5	20	100	1
Annual demand (100s)	2.5	50	20	66	15	6	10	5	1	50

Do an ABC analysis of these items. If resources for inventory control are limited, which items should be given least attention?

SOLUTION

The annual use of P1 in terms of value is $20 * 250 = £5000$. If this calculation is repeated for the other items and they are sorted into order of decreasing annual use by value we get:

Product	P4	P2	P3	P6	P5	P8	P9	P1	P7	P0
Cumulative % of items	10	20	30	40	50	60	70	80	90	100
Annual use (1000s)	330	50	40	30	15	10	10	5	5	5
Cumulative annual use	330	380	420	450	465	475	485	490	495	500
Cumulative % annual use	66	76	84	90	93	95	97	98	99	100
Category	<—A—>	< — B —->	< ——————— C ———————>							

The boundaries between categories of items are sometimes unclear, but in this case P4 is clearly an A item, P2, P3 and P6 are B items and the rest are C items.

The C items account for only 10% of annual use by value and these should be given least attention if resources are limited.

In summary

ABC analyses allow items to be categorized according to importance so that available effort can be shared out appropriately. Typically 20% of items account for 80% of use by value (A items) while the bulk of items accounts for very little use by value (C items).

SELF ASSESSMENT QUESTIONS

11.24 What is the purpose of doing ABC analyses of inventories?

11.25 Which items can best be dealt with by routine, automated control procedures?

SUMMARY OF CHAPTER

This chapter has described some ways of controlling stock holdings. Chapter 10 looked at material requirements planning as an example of dependent demand systems, and in this chapter we examined independent demand systems. These are based on estimates of future demand, which are generally found from projective forecasts.

The main purpose of stocks is to provide a buffer between supply and demand. Both supply and demand are likely to contain variations and uncertainties, and if operations are to continue smoothly, stocks are inevitable. Unfortunately, these have associated costs which can be quite high. The implication is that the cost of not holding stocks would be even higher.

Inventory control systems aim at minimizing costs by answering three fundamental questions about what to stock, when to place orders, and how large orders should be.

The chapter then described a fixed order quantity system, which found an economic order quantity to minimize costs for a simple inventory system. The reorder level shows the times at which orders should be placed. This 'classic analysis' was extended by adding a finite production rate.

The first models described were based on constant demand. If the demand is highly variable or uncertain another approach must be used. Ideally a balance might be found between holding costs and shortage costs. In practice, accurate shortage costs are so difficult to find that a service level is often used instead. Analyses were then described based on cycle service levels and Normally distributed demand. This allowed a safety stock to be calculated.

The next analysis considered periodic review systems which placed regular orders to bring stocks up to a target level. One special analysis with uncertain demand considered stocks of items which are only kept for a single period before being scrapped. An optimal policy for this was described in relation to the newsboy problem.

The final section discussed an ABC analysis which indicates the effort worth spending to control different types of item.

PROBLEMS

11.1 The demand for an item is constant at 100 units a year. Unit cost is £50, cost of processing an order is £20 and holding cost is estimated at £10 per unit per annum. What are the economic order quantity, corresponding cycle length and costs?

11.2 A company works 50 weeks a year and has demand for an item which is constant at 100 units a week. The cost of each unit is £20 and the company aims for a return of 20% on capital invested. Annual warehouse costs are estimated to be 5% of the value of goods stored. The purchasing department of the company costs £45,000 a year and sends out an average of 2000 orders. Determine the optimal order quantity for the item, the optimal time between orders and the minimum cost of stocking the item.

11.3   Demand for an item is steady at 20 units a week and the economic order quantity has been calculated at 50 units. What is the reorder level when the lead time is:

(a) 1 week   **(b)** 3 weeks   **(c)** 5 weeks   **(d)** 7 weeks?

11.4   How would the results for Problem 11.1 change if the item could only be supplied at a finite rate of 10 units a week?

11.5   A manufacturer forecasts its demand for components to average 18 a day over a 200-day working year. If there are any shortages, production will be disrupted with very high costs. The holding cost for the component is £40 a unit a year and the cost of placing an order is estimated to be £80 an order. Determine:

- the economic order quantity;
- the optimal number of orders a year;
- the total annual cost of operating the system (including the cost of purchases) if the real interest rate is 25% a year;
- the effect on the inventory system if the components are made internally and can only be supplied at a finite rate of 80 units a day.

11.6   A company advertises a 95% cycle service level for all stock items. Stock is replenished from a single supplier who guarantees a lead time of 4 weeks. What reorder level should the company adopt for an item which has a Normally distributed demand with mean 1000 units a week and standard deviation of 100 units? What would the reorder level be if a 98% cycle service level is used?

11.7   An item of inventory has a unit cost of £40, reorder cost of £50 and holding cost of £1 per unit per week. Demand for the item has a mean of 100 per week with standard deviation of 10. Lead time is constant at 3 weeks. Devise an inventory policy for the item to give a service level of 95%. How would this be changed to achieve a 90% service level? What are the costs of these two policies?

11.8   Describe a periodic review system with an interval of 2 weeks for the company described in Problem 11.6.

11.9   A small store consists of ten categories of product with the following costs and annual demands:

Product	X1	X2	X3	Y1	Y2	Y3	Z1	Z2	Z3	Z4
Unit cost (£)	20	25	30	1	4	6	10	15	20	22
Annual demand (100s)	3	2	2	10	8	7	30	20	6	4

Do an ABC analysis of these items.

11.10 Annual demand for an item is 2000 units, each order costs £10 to place and the annual holding cost is 40% of the unit cost. The unit cost depends on the quantity ordered as follows:

- for quantities less than 500 unit cost is £1;
- for quantities between 500 and 1000 unit cost is £0.80;
- for quantities of 1000 or more unit cost is £0.60.

What is the optimal ordering policy for the item?

CASE STUDY – CONGLETON LEAD REFINERY

Congleton Lead Refinery is one of several refineries owned by the international group Meridian Metals. The Congleton Refinery imports a silver–lead–zinc ore (mined by other Meridian companies in Australia and southern Africa) and refines it into pure metals. The profitability varies with the market price for refined metals, and recent weaknesses in the price of lead have made the company look for ways of reducing operating costs.

A team of management consultants has been advising the Congleton Refinery on ways to improve productivity. Their study was drawing to a close when the project manager from the consultancy, Nigel Chatterton, was asked to visit Congleton's Vice President of Operations, Beatrix de Witte. Beatrix explained the purpose of the visit.

> Thank you for all your work on improving the productivity of the refinery. Your suggestions for rescheduling operations and resequencing some of the processes will certainly allow us to reduce the amount of plant and equipment, and still meet our expected demands.
>
> Can I ask you to do a small final study? Because we will be working with less back-up equipment it is obviously important that the equipment we have continues to work. This in turn depends on our stocks of spare parts. We keep about 25,000 items in the stores and would like you to make some suggestions for improving the effectiveness of our equipment. If you talk to Laurens van Hooste he can give you some details of the present system.

Nigel Chatterton assured Beatrix that the consultancy had considerable experience with similar inventory systems and would be pleased to do a study for Congleton. He said their final report was suggesting such an investigation, and felt that a modest project would bring substantial benefits. Nigel would talk with Laurens van Hooste who was the Supplies Manager for Congleton and then submit a formal proposal for the investigation.

Laurens van Hooste described the present inventory control system as follows.

We have 25,000 different items which vary from paper clips to 15 tonne buckets for ore movers. It is important to note that there is no such thing as a typical item. Demand ranges from zero to 100,000 units a year. Current stocks range from one (we carry a few spare engines and big things like that) to several hundred thousand (iron balls used in the ore crushers, for example). Lead times vary from 10 minutes (for things bought in a local shop) to almost 2 years (for imported furnace bricks). The unit price ranges from almost nothing to £100,000. The reorder price varies from almost nothing (for things we buy regularly from local suppliers) to very large amounts (when we need a specialized piece of equipment to be designed and delivered). Shortage costs range from almost nothing to very large sums for things which we absolutely must keep in stock.

I am very pleased you are going to help with the inventory control. The present system was installed about ten years ago, and has been constantly updated ever since. I am sure you can make some improvements. We are very keen to improve efficiency, and will help your investigations in any way we can.

Nigel found a description of the current system, which was very well documented. Since the original system was installed it had been completely revised twice and had many smaller adjustments whenever improvements were identified. The system categorized items in a number of ways and dealt with each category differently. Firstly, it considered their importance.

- Essential items had to be kept in stock whatever the cost.
- Important items were given a notional service level of 97%.
- Ordinary items were given a notional service level of 93%.
- Low priority items were given a notional service level of 80%.

About 5% of items were essential, 20% important, 50% normal and 25% low priority.

A second classification of items looked at how long they had been stocked.

- New items had their expected demand suggested either by the department requesting the item or by suppliers.
- When an item had been in stock for four months a short history of demand was developing, and forecasts for future demand were made from average values over these four months.
- After nine months, more historic data was available, and forecasting was switched to exponential smoothing. The parameters used for forecasting were monitored and revised every month.

A third classification of items referred to their use.

- Stocks of heavily used items were reviewed at the end of every working day.

- Stocks of normally used items were reviewed at the end of every week.
- Stocks of lightly used items were reviewed at the end of every month.
- Stocks of sporadically used items were reviewed every time there was a withdrawal.
- Stocks of items which had no recorded movement in the past year are considered for removal from stock.

About 20% of items were in each of these categories.

A large interactive computer system controlled the whole inventory control system. It recorded all transactions and distributed appropriate reports on performance and action to be taken. At the end of every working day, for example, it would list the heavily used items which had fallen to their reorder levels and send suggested purchases to the Procurement Section. These suggested purchases covered quantities to be ordered (as specified by the economic order quantity), preferred supplier, supplier reliability rating, lead time, historic quality of deliveries, alternative suppliers, special conditions, probability of shortages if no action is taken, and so on. The Procurement Section would examine the suggested orders the next day, make any modifications necessary, and confirm arrangements with the computer. The computer would then print orders, arrange payments, make any other arrangements necessary, and update its records.

At the end of every week the computer would monitor the inventory performance. Forecasts, for example, would be compared with actual demand. If there were small differences no action would be taken, but items where differences were larger were listed, together with suggestions for changing parameters in the forecasting models. If the differences were severe a report was made that some more radical action may be needed. All final decisions were under the direct control of the Supplies Department.

Nigel felt that the system appeared to be working rather well. It was based on sound principles and the stocks seemed to give little trouble, considering the complexity of a system containing £15 million worth of stock. His immediate problem was to prepare a proposal for an investigation of the system. This would have to include details of the work to be undertaken and potential benefits. He felt that this report should be finished within a week.

Suggested questions

- Describe, in detail, the current inventory control system.
- What information does this system need?
- Are there any obvious weaknesses in the current system?
- In what areas would you look for improvements to the system?
- What additional information is needed to assess the system?
- How does Congleton view its inventory control system?
- What should Nigel Chatterton suggest in his proposal?

SOLUTIONS TO SELF ASSESSMENT QUESTIONS

11.1 To act as a buffer between supply and demand.

11.2 There are several possible classifications, but a useful one has raw materials, work in progress, finished goods, spare parts and consumables.

11.3 By using projective forecasts of past demand.

11.4 Unit cost (UC), reorder cost (RC), holding cost (HC) and shortage cost (SC).

11.5 What items to stock, when to place orders, how much to order.

11.6 Fixed order quantity and periodic review systems.

11.7 **(d)** Cannot say without further information. We could be tempted by the periodic review system as this is preferable for high regular demand of low value items, but there is really not enough information to form a valid opinion.

11.8 A single item is considered, demand is known exactly, demand is continuous and constant, costs are known exactly, replenishment is instantaneous, no shortages are allowed.

11.9 The order quantity which minimizes costs in the circumstances assumed by the classic analysis.

11.10 **(c)** Either increase or decrease total costs, depending on the economic order quantity.

11.11 The amount of an item which is in stock when an order for replenishment should be made.

11.12 It is the lead time demand minus any stock already on order.

11.13 False. Costs generally rise slowly around the economic order quantity.

11.14 **(a)** When production rate is greater than demand. If production rate is less than demand there is no stock at all and demand is not being met.

11.15 **(a)** Larger batches (all other things being equal).

11.16 The service level gives some measure of the probability that a demand can be satisfied. This chapter has used cycle service level, which is the probability that an item remains in stock during a cycle. It is used because alternative analyses are based on shortage costs which are very difficult to find.

11.17 Without safety stock there would be shortages in 50% of cycles. The safety stock reduces the probability of shortages, and increases service levels.

11.18 By increasing the amount of safety stock.

11.19 Order size is equal to the difference between current stock and target stock level. Target stock level equals expected demand over $T + LT$ plus safety stock. If there are any orders outstanding they should be subtracted from the order size.

11.20 **(b)** All other things being equal, the safety stock will be higher for a periodic review system.

11.21 A model where the item is only held in stock for a single period and is then scrapped.

11.22 It is the probability that at least n papers are sold.

11.23 If n is high enough for the inequality to become invalid each newspaper bought will make an expected loss.

11.24 ABC analyses are a means of determining which items are most important so that appropriate effort can be spent on controlling their stocks.

11.25 B items.

REFERENCES FOR FURTHER READING

Early work

Harris F. (1915). *Operations and Cost* Chicago: A. Shaw & Co.

Raymond F.E. (1931). *Quantity and Economy in Manufacture* Chicago: McGraw-Hill

Wilson R.H. (1934). A scientific routine for stock control *Harvard Business Review* No. XIII

Later work

Fogarty D.W. and Hoffmann T.R. (1983). *Production and Inventory Management* Cincinnati: South-Western Publishing

Hadley G. and Whitin T.M. (1963). *Analysis of Inventory Systems* Englewood Cliffs: Prentice-Hall

Lewis C.D. (1970). *Scientific Inventory Control* London: Butterworths

Lewis C.D. (1975). *Demand Analysis and Inventory Control* London: Saxon-House

Love S.F. (1979). *Inventory Control* New York: McGraw-Hill

Plossl G. and Welch W.E. (1979). *The Role of Top Management in the Control of Inventory* Reston: Reston Publishing

Tersine R.J. (1987). *Principles of Inventory and Materials Management* 3rd edn. New York: Elsevier North-Holland

Silver E.A. and Peterson R. (1985). *Decision Systems for Inventory Management and Production Planning* 2nd edn. New York: John Wiley

Waters C.D.J. (1989). *A Practical Introduction to Management Science* Wokingham: Addison-Wesley

Chapter 12

Quality assurance

SYNOPSIS

In recent years organizations have put much greater emphasis on the quality of their products. This is partly a result of changing manufacturing processes (such as JIT) and partly a response to consumers who are unwilling to accept low quality products. The quality of an organization's products is a major factor in its success: it affects reputation, marketing effort, market share, prices, profits, costs, liability for defects, and almost every other aspect of operations.

The first attempts to increase product quality concentrated on statistical quality control. This emphasized the inspection of finished products as a means of detecting faults. Recent developments have moved towards a wider role for quality assurance which involves all parts of the organization. This aims at preventing defects occurring at any time during the production process.

One problem with discussing quality is the difficulty of finding a general definition. Many alternatives have been proposed, but there is still a feeling that quality is, 'something we recognize when we see it'. In practice, the overall quality of a product is judged by a range of factors, some of which can be measured, while others are subjective judgements.

There is a traditional belief that increasing quality inevitably increases costs. This is not necessarily true, and there is a growing realization that making products of high quality can be cheaper than making low quality ones. It is, for example, cheaper to find a fault before a product is passed on to a customer than to correct it when the customer complains.

Total quality control is based on the idea that everyone in the organization must be concerned with quality. Such schemes may be difficult to implement, but experience suggests they can bring substantial benefits.

Inspections are a key element in quality assurance. In essence, these try to find the characteristics of a whole population by looking at a random sample. Some inspections are designed to ensure products are reaching specified quality standards, while others ensure the process is performing as designed.

Single samples are usually used of test products. These, typically, take a random sample from a batch of products, and test to make sure the number of defects is below a maximum permitted number. Sometimes more complex sampling schemes are used. Control charts are the main method of testing the process.

OBJECTIVES

After reading this chapter and completing the exercises you should
be able to:

- appreciate the importance of product quality and the aims
  of quality assurance;
- discuss ways in which quality can be defined;
- outline the developments leading to total quality control;
- discuss quality assurance in services;
- classify the costs of quality assurance and show how these
  can be minimized;
- say why samples are taken and use sampling distributions;
- calculate sample sizes and maximum numbers of defects for
  acceptance sampling;
- draw an operating characteristic curve;
- use control charts for process control;
- calculate control limits for p-charts with attribute sampling
  and X and R charts for variable sampling.

12.1   BACKGROUND TO QUALITY ASSURANCE

12.1.1 Importance of quality

Chapter 2 described various aspects of product planning, and suggested that a
combination of different factors determines the overall demand for a product.
One suggestion for the most important of these was:

- quality
- availability
- price.

Moreover, a broad view of 'quality' can include both availability and
price. Thus, we can suggest that the quality of a product is of fundamental
importance in determining its demand. People are concerned about the quality of
products whether they are a family buying a new car, an electorate voting for a
government, a patient having an operation, or a company buying a piece of
equipment. Although high quality may not ensure the success of a product, it is
certain that low quality will ensure its failure. This is clearly not a new concern,

so we might assume that:

- quality assurance is an area that organizations have been looking at for a long time;
- all the main problems were solved some time ago.

The first of these is true, but the second is certainly not. Quality assurance is an area which is still evolving. The past few years have seen a whole range of new developments, and some people are even referring to the 'quality revolution'. There are really two reasons for this:

- improved processes can guarantee high quality production (and in the case of JIT systems can only work with perfect quality);
- more demanding consumers who are unwilling to accept low quality products.

The second of these is a consequence of the first, as customers are now aware that products of reliably high quality can be made. The implication is that only those organizations which meet these demands for high quality can expect to survive. Unless organizations make positive efforts to supply goods of the quality demanded by customers they have no chance of long-term success. This introduces the role of the quality assurance function, which is to ensure that products are of high quality.

> Quality assurance is concerned with all those functions in an organization which ensure products reach the consistently high quality demanded by customers.

Organizations supplying high quality products get a good reputation which makes it easier to sell their products. Experience also suggests that customers are willing to pay higher prices for higher quality. This can be viewed in two ways. Firstly, those companies which make good products can add a premium to the price. Alternatively, customers are unwilling to accept low quality, so poor products must sell at low prices (and perhaps not cover production costs).

Another important point for some organizations is that producers are often held responsible for the consequences of defects in their products. A car manufacturer, which makes a car with defective brakes, can be liable for resulting accidents; surgeons can be liable if their negligence during an operation injures a patient; airplane manufacturers can be responsible for deaths caused if one of their planes crashes; and so on.

We can summarize these points by saying that high quality products are important for ensuring an organization's long-term survival (see Figure 12.1).

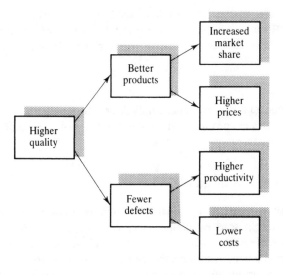

Figure 12.1 Some benefits from higher quality.

In particular they:

- enhance reputation;
- increase competitiveness;
- improve sales and market share;
- increase productivity;
- ensure profitability;
- reduce marketing effort needed;
- reduce liability for defective products;
- reduce costs.

The statement that increasing quality can reduce costs is particularly interesting. This contradicts the traditional view that increasing quality can only be bought at increasing cost: to make a higher quality product takes more time, more careful operations, more skilful workforce, better materials, and so on. This is not necessarily true, and there are many examples where increasing the quality of products actually reduces their cost. If, for example, a washing machine is sold with a faulty part, the manufacturer will send somebody to the customer's home to repair it. It would have been cheaper to find the fault before the machine left the factory. It would have been even cheaper to make a machine that did not have a fault in the first place, rather than spend money on detection and correction.

It is this realization that high quality can actually reduce costs and improve profits which is the most important development in quality assurance in recent years. This idea is considered in more detail in the following sections.

In summary

Quality is important because it has implications for reputation, marketing effort, market share, prices, profits, costs, liability for defects, and almost every other aspect of an organization's operations.

12.1.2 Definitions of quality

One problem with discussing 'quality' is finding a consensus about how it is defined. We might start by taking specific examples and saying that a Rolls Royce car is of very high quality. We could look at a china dinner service and say its quality is much higher than that of a plastic equivalent. But when we try to generalize these observations, we come across serious problems. If the purpose of a car is to provide transport between two points, then a cheap car will do it just as well as a Rolls Royce. If the purpose of a dinner service is to provide a surface to rest food on while we eat, a cheap plastic one works just as well as an expensive china one. The problem is that quality has many dimensions, only some of which can be measured. If we consider, for example, a television set, we may judge its quality by how expensive it is, how attractive the cabinet is, how big it is, how easy it is to operate, how clear the picture is, how accurate the colours are, how often it needs repairing, how long it will last, how many channels it can be tuned to, how good the sound is, what additional features it has, and so on.

Many definitions of quality try to overcome this difficulty. Some are vague and refer to inherent values, such as 'Quality measures innate excellence'. Others are a bit more specific, such as 'Quality measures the fitness of a product for its intended use'. Other suggestions look at the product's design and say 'Quality measures the degree to which a product conforms to designed specifications'. Other definitions balance performance with cost and suggest that quality is related to the ratio of performance to cost. There are many possible definitions of quality, relating to:

- innate excellence;
- reliability;
- durability;
- the degree to which a product conforms to design specifications;
- uniform products with no variability;
- fitness for intended use;
- how closely a product matches consumer demands and preferences;

- attractive appearance and style;
- ratio of performance to cost;
- acceptable performance at reasonable price;
- perception of good quality by customers;
- deliveries on time;
- good after-sales service;

  and so on.

There are many views about quality, but perhaps the most frequent one is 'We don't know how to define quality but we recognize it when we see it'. This is particularly true of services. It would be difficult to measure the quality of a haircut, but people know when they go to a hairdresser and get a bad one.

The problem is that an overall view of quality takes into account many factors. Some of these can be measured (weight, number of breakdowns a year, guaranteed life, and so on) while others cannot (appearance, comfort of facilities, courtesy of staff, and so on). Goods usually have more measurable attributes than services and these allow a better judgement of quality. None the less, the overall quality of all products, whether goods or services, must be judged by a range of factors, some of which are measurable and some of which rely on opinion.

Another difficulty in defining quality is that it depends on the perspective taken. With a car, for example, an engineer might judge it on the basis of its conformance to engineering design, or power generated per cubic centimetre of engine capacity, a salesperson might judge it by how quickly it sells, an insurance company by how frequently and severely it is damaged in accidents, a mechanic by how easy it is to maintain, a banker by how long it will last and how much it depreciates, a customer by the colour of the paint, and so on. Two completely different views might be taken:

(1) An internal view of the producer, which might define quality as the closeness of a product's performance to its designed specifications.

(2) An external view of the customer, which defines quality as how well a product does the job it was bought for.

In the past there was a tendency for organizations to emphasize the internal view, suggesting that a product which meets the standards of the producer should be acceptable to the customers. More recently, the obvious point has been recognized that customer perceptions of a product's quality are more important. This does not mean that customers will demand the highest quality which is attainable, but they demand some balance of attributes which gives them acceptable overall quality. A Rolls Royce car, for example, is a car of the highest quality, but most people include price in their judgement of overall quality and then buy a cheaper car which is more appropriate to their needs. The result is that producers must then make a range of products, each of which gives high quality when judged by different criteria.

In essence we are defining two aspects of quality:

(1)   Designed quality, which determines the quality that a product is designed to have (essentially set by customer demand).

(2)   Quality conformance, which shows how closely a product achieves the designed quality.

These two are combined in the function of quality assurance. Then the function of quality assurance is to determine the quality demanded by customers and ensure the product consistently reaches this quality.

In summary

It is difficult to give a general definition of quality as there are many viewpoints, measures and judgements. Overall quality is judged by a range of these factors. This allows a range of products with different designed quality to meet demands from different customers.

12.1.3 Trends in quality assurance

We have already said that attitudes to quality have changed markedly in recent years. We can describe the background to this by looking at some trends.

Historically it was accepted that the quality of products could not be guaranteed. This often meant that an 'overage' was allowed to cover defective parts or materials. If, for example, a factory needed 100 components it would buy 110 on the assumption that 10 would be defective. This overage was often doubled, as suppliers who were asked for 110 units would send 120. A long standing example of this is a request for 12 loaves which would be satisfied by a 'baker's dozen'.

This custom of allowing routine overage has become less common. An obvious reason is the expense which could typically add 10% to costs. Another, more significant reason is the rejection of the assumption that suppliers cannot avoid sending a certain number of defective products. Customers are now aware that high quality can be guaranteed, and they have put increasing pressure on producers to ensure that defective units are not sold.

The first reaction to demands for increasing quality was to use more rigorous inspections. For many years statistical quality control remained the main tool for ensuring product quality. Within the past few years, however, there has been a significant change. This came with the realization that the best way to improve quality is not to inspect production and discard defective units, but to ensure that no defective units are made in the first place. With careful management, manufacturing processes can make consistently high quality products. This allows the emphasis in quality assurance to change from identifying those defects which are known to be present, to making fewer defects. This change was illustrated by the phrase (which has become something of a cliché) that 'you can't inspect quality into a product'.

The term 'quality control' is now usually applied to sampling and inspection. The broader function for ensuring quality is known by terms like 'quality assurance', 'quality management' and 'quality engineering'. These are based on the idea that quality assurance cannot be treated in isolation, but must have a role in every part of an organization. A formalized view of this is given by 'total quality control' (TQC). This is an approach where the whole organization systematically looks for ways of improving product quality. More details of this are given later in the chapter.

TQC is largely a Japanese development, and it is worth noting the influence of Japanese industry on quality assurance. Chapter 10 looked at just-in-time systems which have materials delivered just as they are needed. No stocks are kept to provide cover for defective materials, so such systems rely on the perfect quality of all deliveries. JIT systems were developed in Japanese manufacturing industries, which not surprisingly took a leading role in quality assurance.

In the 1940s Japanese manufacturing industry had been disrupted by wars, plant and equipment were out of date, productivity was low, and products suitable for the wartime economy were no longer needed. To start the regeneration of its industries, Japan made cheap, low quality imitations of products from other countries. As industry developed, living standards rose and operating costs became higher. It became increasingly difficult to make cheap products, so Japanese manufacturers began to concentrate on more expensive ones. The key element in their success was the recognition that they could compete by offering consistently high quality.

The Japanese emphasis on quality was illustrated by studies in the early 1980s which found that air conditioners manufactured in America had 70 times as many defects on the assembly line as those made in Japan, and had 17 times as many breakdowns in the first year of operation. An American manufacturer of television sets had more than 150 defects per 100 completed sets, and was trying to compete with Japanese companies which averaged 0.5 defects per 100 completed sets.

In summary

Improved manufacturing processes and more demanding customers have led organizations to look for ways of improving quality. Their first attempts relied on inspections specified by statistical quality control. Later, quality assurance expanded to a wider role which ensures high quality products are made in the first place. Japanese industry has played a leading role in the development of quality assurance.

12.1 If the price is right people will buy a product regardless of its quality. Is this statement true or false?

12.2 Why is quality assurance important to an organization?

12.3 The best way to ensure the quality of a product is to have a lot of inspections to find faults. Is this statement true?

12.4 Why is it difficult to define 'quality'?

12.5 Name two functions of quality assurance.

12.6 What is the difference between quality control and quality assurance?

12.2 MANAGEMENT OF QUALITY

12.2.1 Total quality control

Traditionally, organizations have used a separate quality control department to inspect the work of production departments. These two functions had different objectives, with production trying to make products as quickly as possible while quality control ensured that products met specifications, possibly by slowing down production. This inevitably introduced some conflict, with one department seen as benefiting only at the expense of the other. Sometimes this conflict became so intense that it was forgotten that the two departments were aiming for the same end, which was satisfied customers.

There have been two significant changes in recent years. The first comes with the realization that quality can be maintained during the production process. Thus the important time for quality assurance is not during inspections at the end of production, but during the process itself, or even before in the planning stages. In essence, quality assurance is not seen as a separate function but as an integral part of the process leading to a product. Production departments are more responsible for their own quality. The second change is associated with the first, and concerns the role of the quality assurance department. This has changed from inspecting to facilitating. Its job is now to work with customers, production, engineers, and other involved functions, and to enable products to be made of the appropriate quality. They can advise production about the best means and procedures to meet the quality specified by customers.

The transfer of some quality assurance from a separate department to part of the production function does not simply mean that different people do the same inspections. It is part of a fundamental change in an organization's attitude towards quality. This is the basis of total quality control (TQC), which recognizes that quality must be a part of every function in an organization. Everybody in the organization must be working for quality, from top management down through every layer.

We can see the effect of this by looking at the people working directly on the production process. Here, each person becomes responsible for passing on to following operations only products of perfect quality. This is often called 'quality at source', with 'job enlargement' for each person who is now responsible for both his or her previous job and an inherent quality assurance function. Part of the different attitude now emerges with people being rewarded for achieving high quality, when they have traditionally been rewarded for high volumes, often regardless of quality.

The effects of quality at source are:

- responsibility for quality is put on each person in the production process;
- quality assurance people have time to do work other than routine inspections;
- an area of potential conflict has been removed.

Quality at source has a range of other features. Each work station checks the quality of its own product, so the operators must be capable of doing and understanding statistical analyses. These analyses need not be complicated, but typically include checklists, histograms and Pareto analyses. The results are displayed so that everyone knows how well each work station is working, with any problems identified and solved.

As each person is responsible for passing on products of perfect quality, if a fault is found it shows that something has gone wrong. Quality at source programmes give anyone authority to stop the production process and investigate a fault. The reason for the fault is found and suggestions made for avoiding further faults in the future. This compares with traditional practices which only stop the production process as a last resort, and the cause of the fault may then go unnoticed until the problem becomes severe.

Quality at source relies on a responsible workforce who want to improve the quality of products. Their ideas for improvements can be discussed in regular meetings like quality circles. These are informal, voluntary groups of about 10 people involved at all levels in a part of the process. A quality circle meets for an hour once or twice a month to discuss ways in which the operation might be improved. The participants might identify a problem which is affecting the quality of their product, discuss alternatives for improvements, examine comments put into a suggestions box, suggest modifications to designs, and so on. Their aim is simply to discuss the operation and try to find improvements.

Quality circles have proved useful in companies adopting them, but they can only be used when a number of conditions are met. These include:

- a well educated workforce capable of recognizing, analysing and solving problems;
- people who are able and willing to exchange ideas;

- people who see themselves as working for the good of the organization;
- a management team that is willing to share information on costs and operations.

These conditions suggest a list of other factors which are needed for a successful quality assurance programme. W. E. Deming has been a leading proponent of quality assurance for the past 40 years or so, and he identifies several important factors, including the following.

- Top management must be committed to achieving high quality.
- The organization must adopt a long-term approach to improving quality.
- Management must persist despite short-term problems.
- Managers must clearly state their quality objectives and what must be done to achieve these.
- Do not accept the view that some defects are inevitable.
- Ensure materials are of high quality.
- Do not emphasize output at the expense of quality.
- Use statistical methods to identify sources of poor quality.
- Encourage discussion of ways to improve quality (including quality circles).
- Make sure everyone is properly trained to do his or her job.
- Improve supervision.
- Encourage quality at source and a 'do it right first time' approach.
- Be open to suggestions for improvement (including suggestion boxes).

Some of these are particularly interesting. The fact that people should be properly trained for their jobs, including training in quality assurance, has led to some major training programmes. Ford in America, for example, is reported to have sent over 6000 people to training courses in two years. The quality of the company's products depends to a large extent on the bought-in materials, so Ford also trained over 1000 suppliers. There was a clear statement that Ford would only consider suppliers whose feelings towards quality matched its own. It has now become common for large companies to use only those suppliers who can work with their TQC system. In essence, they have a list of potential suppliers who meet the requirements set by their TQC system, and anyone who is unwilling or unable to do this is not even considered. This approach is an obvious extension of the close links between suppliers and customers demanded by JIT systems.

Another interesting point is the commitment needed by top management. There is often a tendency to blame workers for poor quality, but Deming suggests this is unfair. A production process can be divided into two parts:

(1) The system over which management has control and which contributes 85% of the variation in quality.

(2) The workers who are under their own control and contribute 15% to variation in quality.

Major improvements in quality can only come from managers improving the system rather than workers improving their own performance. This is exactly analogous to the productivity measures described in Chapter 7. There it was suggested that the best way to improve productivity was not to make people work harder, but to improve the design of the process. A person digging a hole with a spade, for example, can work very hard but still have a lower productivity than a lazy person with a mechanical digger. Similarly, a person working very conscientiously to get good quality in a poor system will get worse results than a less conscientious person in a better system.

Specific ways in which the system might be at fault include poor maintenance and therefore reliability, use of poor materials, poor work environment, putting too much pressure on operators, and so on. Specific ways in which workers might be at fault include poor training and lack of understanding of the system. These might also be considered faults of management, so we can reiterate the belief that quality depends on the active participation of all levels in the organization.

The quality of a product is usually set at the design stage. Thus, the best way to ensure a product is of high quality is not by monitoring the production process, but by designing a good product. One aspect of this design is that a product should be robust enough to maintain high quality despite any small fluctuations in the production process. Taguchi is another leading figure in quality assurance, and he has suggested statistical methods for conducting experiments to find the best values for all variables in the production process. This work is rather specialized, so details are left to the references at the end of this chapter.

Although we have concentrated on the benefits of TQC, there are disadvantages. The most important of these is the time and commitment needed by everyone in the organization. Although it seems that this might limit the use of TQC systems to larger companies, the principles are generally applicable. A wide range of organizations have found the benefits of high quality far outweigh the costs of attaining it. Some explanations of the costs involved are given later in the chapter.

In summary

Total quality control is based on the principle that everyone in the organization must be involved with quality assurance. They should work continually to improve quality, taking appropriate measures, such as quality management, quality at source and quality circles.

12.2.2 Quality of services

Many products have some specific attribute that can be measured to assess the quality. Thus we can measure the weight of a sack of coal, or the volume in a bottle of detergent. It is then relatively simple to make sure that each unit reaches this measure of quality, but the overall quality of the product still relies on subjective judgements. How clean, for example, is the coal or how good does the detergent smell.

The problem with judging the quality of services is that they do not have as many measurable attributes as goods, and judgements about quality are largely a matter of opinion. There are, of course, usually some measurable attributes. The quality of service offered by a bank, for example, will include measures (such as ratio of loans to deposits, interest rates, charges, total deposits, and so on) and attributes that cannot be measured (such as how secure any investment is, how courteously customers are treated, how competently transactions are processed, whether there is a pleasant environment, and so on).

Generally, the attributes that cannot be measured refer to customer expectations about:

- reliability
- availability
- competence
- courtesy
- understanding customer
- credibility
- security
- comfort of surroundings

and so on.

We suggested earlier that it is difficult to measure the quality of a haircut, but people know when they go to a hairdresser and get a bad one. Similarly, restaurants rely on their reputation to attract customers, but it is impossible to measure the quality of their products. How, for example, can we measure the taste of a meal or compare the quality of a waiter who smiles as we approach with one who scowls?

The simple answer is that we cannot measure these attributes directly, so must look for indirect measures. In particular, we can suggest that the overall quality of a service must be measured by the extent to which it matches customer expectations. Then, the measurement of service quality depends on the quality assurance function to:

- identify customer expectations;
- help in the design of services to meet these expectations;
- assess actual performance of service, by finding how closely customers perceive their demands have been met.

The standard way to assess customers' reactions is to question them after they have received the service. This sort of evaluation is done frequently by airlines and fast-food restaurants. Customers are usually asked to evaluate a series of features of the service by, for example, giving each a score between 1 (for excellent) through 3 (for average) to 5 (for very poor). The response to these questionnaires shows how closely customer expectations are being met, and what areas need improvement.

This approach, does, of course, have the usual problems with questionnaires, relating to sample size and selection, phrasing of fair and relevant questions, appropriate analysis of results, and so on.

WORKED EXAMPLE 12.1

A university is trying to measure the quality of teaching in one of its faculties. How can it do this?

SOLUTION

Some aspects of teaching can be measured, so data can be collected on the number of students taught, lectures, tutorials, seminars, and so on given by each faculty member.

Most judgements about the quality of teaching must, however, be made by the customers who are attending classes. The obvious way of assessing this is to give each student a questionnaire to complete at the end of courses. This might ask questions about:

- course content (how relevant it was, how useful, how it fitted in with other courses, etc.);
- how good the teaching was (how interesting classes were, how well the teachers explained things, how they answered questions, etc.);
- teachers' attitudes (how enthusiastic they were, how they encouraged discussion, how they marked exercises, etc.);
- how teachers got on with students (how interested they were, how courteous, how good a sense of humour, etc.);
- how the course matched expectations (whether the course contents were as expected, whether the approach to the subject was useful, and whether any important material was missing, etc.).

By asking for answers on a five-point scale, the responses of the entire class can be averaged, and used as a measure of quality. Areas which score consistently badly can be identified and improved.

Customers are particularly sensitive to the quality of services. Many services are tailored to individual needs, and this means they are expensive. The high cost raises customer expectation, but this is often not met. There is a feeling that the inability to define a good service is used as an excuse for providing a poor one. Unfortunately, we can examine goods before buying them, but services can only be judged after they have been purchased. To be fair, there are a number of reasons why the quality of services may be lower than that of goods. These include the following:

(1) Services are intangible. This means it is inherently difficult to define and measure satisfactory quality.

(2) Services depend on personal contact between customer and supplier. This gives more opportunity for disagreements and perceptions of poor service.

(3) People working in services often see them as short-term jobs. This leads to poor training and lack of dedication.

(4) Customer expectation is lower for services than goods (based largely on experience).

(5) Each product is largely customized to individual requirements. This gives more opportunity for errors.

(6) The spontaneous supply of products means there is less chance to practise and correct mistakes.

In summary

It is particularly difficult to measure service quality as services depend so much on opinions. Surrogate measures can find the extent to which customer expectations are satisfied.

SELF ASSESSMENT QUESTIONS

12.7 TQC means that quality is totally controlled by production departments. Is this statement true?

12.8 What is meant by 'quality at source'?

12.9 What is a 'quality circle'?

12.10 Measuring the quality of services is totally different from measuring the quality of goods. Is this statement:

(a) true
(b) false
(c) partly true?

12.11 How might you measure the quality of a hairdresser?

12.3 COSTS OF QUALITY ASSURANCE

We have already suggested that costs might be reduced by increasing the quality of a product. We can demonstrate this by a simple example. Suppose a manufacturer inspects its products before sending them to a wholesaler and finds defects in 5% of units. The remaining 95% of good units have to cover the cost of producing 5% of scrapped units. If the defects could be eliminated, productivity would improve by 5%, while unit costs would be reduced. In addition, the cost of dealing with defective units returned by customers would be eliminated. Thus the direct savings are:

* increased productivity;
* reduced unit cost;
* reduced administration costs for dealing with customer complaints;
* elimination of procedures for correcting defects;
* reduced warranty costs.

These, and a range of indirect benefits such as increased customer goodwill and improved reputation, should more than compensate for any increased costs. The general view is:

> The additional costs of making better quality products are more than offset by expected savings.

The costs associated with quality assurance can be categorized as:

* design costs
* appraisal costs
* internal failure costs
* external failure costs.

Design costs

These costs refer to the quality that is designed into a product. They include direct design features, such as whether to include certain features, what materials to use, how much time to spend on each operation, how skilled a workforce to use, and so on. They also include indirect factors like how easily a product can be made, how much manufacturing can be done automatically, how well the process is designed, how well procurement is done, and so on. In essence, these are the costs associated with designing the product and process to ensure they are capable of achieving high product quality. Design costs are sometimes referred to as prevention costs, implying they are concerned with the work done to prevent any defect occurring in the final product.

All other things being equal, design costs rise with the quality of the product. Customers will not, however, pay limitless amounts to get products of the highest possible quality. There is a ceiling on the price beyond which they will not pass, regardless of product quality. The difference between price and design cost is a direct contribution to the profit. Identifying the point where this

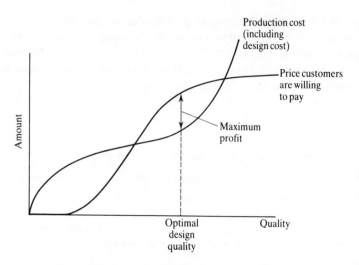

Figure 12.2 Optimal value for design quality.

is greatest allows an optimal design quality to be found. Typical graphs of costs and prices are shown in Figure 12.2.

Appraisal costs

These are the costs of ensuring the designed specifications are actually being achieved. As products move through their process, inspections are made to ensure they are actually achieving the quality specified in the design. These inspections include statistical sampling and testing, which form part of quality control. (We will give some details of these later in the chapter.) Generally speaking, the more effort that is put into quality control, the higher will be the end quality of the product and the higher will be the costs needed to achieve this.

Internal failure costs

As a product goes through its various operations, it may be inspected several times. Any units which do not meet the specified quality are scrapped, returned to an earlier point in the line, repaired, or allowed to continue in the hope that the defect is not important enough to affect the product's value. With the exception of the last, these alternatives involve additional work to bring a unit up to a satisfactory quality. There is also the implication that some work already done has been wasted. The cost of this work forms part of the internal failure cost, which is the total cost of making defective products which are detected somewhere within the process.

Internal failure costs arise directly from the loss of material, wasted labour effort, wasted machine time in making the defective item, and so on. There are also indirect costs such as the need for higher stock levels, longer lead times, and additional capacity to allow for scrap and rejections.

The further a product goes through the process, the larger will be the amount spent on it and the more expensive it will be to scrap or rework. Ideally, then, defects should be found as early in the process as possible. We can also see that the option mentioned above of allowing a defective unit to continue in the process is misguided. It involves spending more money on a unit which is known to be defective, and subsequent detection and scrapping will increase the total waste.

External failure costs

Suppose a product has gone through the entire production process, is delivered to a customer and is then found to be defective. The producer will usually give some kind of performance guarantee or warranty and will be responsible for correcting any faults. The product must be brought back from the customer, and replaced, reworked or repaired as necessary. The cost of this work forms part of the external failure cost, which is the total cost of making defective products which are not detected within the process, but are recognized as faulty by customers.

External failure faults are often the highest costs of quality assurance and are the ones that should generally be avoided. When a car manufacturer, for example, finds a fault in some of its cars it may have to recall the whole production. In 1982 General Motors had to recall 2.1 million cars at a cost of over $100 million (since then GM has become one of the leaders in quality management). These costs can be even higher if product failure causes other problems. A defective part in an airplane, for example, might cause a crash which leaves the manufacturer facing very high penalties.

Both internal and external failure costs will decline with increasing quality.

In summary

Quality assurance costs can be classified as design, appraisal, internal failure or external failure. The first two of these rise with increasing quality, while the last two decline. Overall, there are usually lower costs associated with higher quality.

When to start quality control

Traditionally, companies have put most effort into quality control, often at quite a late stage in the process. The longer a unit is in its process, the higher is the investment that has been made in it. The major effort in quality assurance should, therefore, be put at the beginning of the process, starting in the development and design stages. Similarly, inspections should be started as early as possible. Materials sent by suppliers should be routinely tested on arrival, but there is a strong case for inspections to start before this in suppliers' factories.

Inspections should be continued all the way from the production of materials through to the completion of the final product and its transmission to

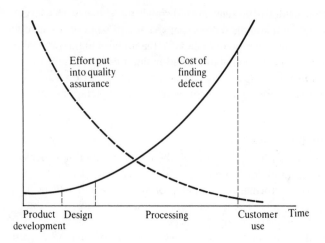

Figure 12.3   Cost of finding defects and effort put into quality assurance.

customers. If the main part of the inspection is done early enough this should ensure that the further a product moves through its process the fewer defects will be found. Certainly by the time the product gets to the customer it should be as nearly free of defects as possible (see Figure 12.3).

A more formal statement of when inspections are most useful includes:

- at material suppliers' plants during their processing;
- on arrival at the plant (including all materials from suppliers);
- at regular intervals during the process;
- before high cost operations;
- before irreversible operations (like firing pottery);
- before operations which might hide defects (like painting);
- when production is complete;
- before shipping from the plant.

Suppliers of computer systems give an interesting example of developments in quality assurance. Early computer systems were moved from production facilities to staging centres, where they were assembled and tested before delivery to customers. When everything was working properly, the system was dismantled, shipped to the customer and then reassembled. There it went through a process of testing and checking to make sure everything was working as well as possible. For some time after this, the equipment was run in and teething troubles were overcome. The interesting point is that despite all the checks during the manufacturing process, the major quality assurance effort was made at the end of production and even after delivery to the customer. Clearly, any faults found at this stage would be very expensive to correct. Nowadays, quality assurance is done before and during production of computer systems, and when they arrive at customers they are simply plugged in and start working.

WORKED EXAMPLE 12.2

A company keeps records of estimated costs (in thousands of pounds a year) for two years immediately prior to revising its quality assurance programme and two years immediately following. How effective has this programme been?

Year	1	2	3	4
Sales value	1247	1186	1456	1775
Costs				
Design	8	9	30	32
Appraisal	17	20	64	65
Internal failure	72	75	24	20
External failure	60	66	23	17

SOLUTION

The easiest way to assess the quality assurance programme is to calculate the total cost as a proportion of sales. The most convenient unit for this is pounds spent per thousand pounds of sales.

Year	1	2	3	4
Costs				
Design	6.4	7.6	20.6	18.0
Appraisal	13.6	16.9	44.0	36.6
Internal failure	57.7	63.2	16.5	11.3
External failure	48.1	55.6	15.8	9.6
Total	125.8	143.3	96.9	75.5

The new quality assurance programme has put more emphasis on design and appraisal, with consequent savings in failures. The overall results are a decline in costs and an increase in sales. The programme can, therefore, be judged a success.

In summary
Total costs of operations might be reduced by producing goods of a higher quality. Quality assurance should be started as early in the process as possible.

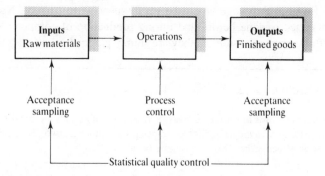

Figure 12.4   Elements in statistical quality control.

SELF ASSESSMENT QUESTIONS

12.12   Higher quality inevitably comes at a higher price. Is this statement true or false?

12.13   Why will internal failure costs decline with increasing quality?

12.14   How can the costs involved in quality assurance be classified?

12.15   When should checks for quality be started in a process?

12.4   STATISTICAL QUALITY CONTROL

12.4.1 Statistical sampling

Even when each work station in a process takes responsibility for passing on only products of perfect quality, independent checks are still needed to ensure products are achieving their designed quality. Sometimes, for example, the tests necessary are too long or complicated to be done during production. Although the approach to quality control has changed, sampling and inspection still form a key element in quality assurance. Ideally, its role has changed from finding how many defects are present, to ensuring that all products remain free of defects.

There are two types of statistical quality control, one of which tests the quality of products while the other tests the performance of the process (see Figure 12.4):

(1)   Acceptance sampling is done at the beginning and end of an operation. It takes a random sample of products to see whether the whole batch of input or output should be accepted.

(2)   Process control is done during the process. It takes a random sample to see if the process is working within acceptable limits or if it needs adjusting.

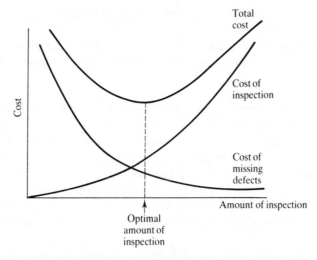

Figure 12.5 Finding an optimal amount of inspection.

The rest of this chapter describes these tests in more detail. We will start by discussing some general points about statistical sampling.

The approach to both acceptance sampling and process control is essentially the same. A random sample of units is taken from a batch and tested to see how many of the sample conform to designed specifications. If a predetermined number of the sample reach an acceptable standard the whole batch is accepted or the process is said to be working satisfactorily. If fewer than the predetermined number reach an acceptable standard the batch is rejected or the process is adjusted.

An obvious question is why use a sample and why not test all the products. There are three reasons for this:

(1) *Expense*. The cost of testing each unit may be high. If the proportion of defects is low it would be very expensive to test each unit to find the few defects. We can also mention that no inspection is completely reliable, as inspectors become tired and bored and make mistakes, automatic tests develop faults, and so on.

The cost of inspection rises with the number of units tested, but the number of defective units found will also rise. There must be a point when the total cost of inspections and missing defective units is minimized, as shown in Figure 12.5.

(2) *Destructive testing*. Sometimes tests are destructive. If we want to find out how long light bulbs last we could test all the production to find the average life, but there would be no bulbs left to sell. Similarly, if we fill bottles of milk or whisky the only way of guaranteeing every bottle contains the right quantity is to empty them into a measuring can.

(3) *Feasibility*. In some cases there is an infinite number of tests that could be done. To test completely the effectiveness of a medicine it would have to be given to everybody who might take it, in all possible circumstances. This would give an almost infinite number of possible combinations.

In some circumstances the entire output of products is tested, but usually a compromise is used with a random sample. If this sample performs well it is assumed that the whole batch is of satisfactory quality; if the sample performs badly, it is assumed that the whole batch is unsatisfactory. Although we talk about 'batches' being accepted, this does not imply that we are only concerned with batch production. The output during a particular period may be arbitrarily considered as a batch, or in projects and job shops a batch may be one or two units. The principles of quality control apply whatever the production quality or process used.

Unfortunately, sampling is not entirely accurate. A good batch might be rejected because the sample has an unusually large number of defects in it. Conversely, we may accept a bad batch because our sample had an unusually small number of good ones in it. Suppose, for example, a batch of 1000 units has 100 defective ones. Most samples of 100 units would have about 10 defective ones, but there will be some random variations. Sometimes these random variations will be wider, and in the extremes we could have a sample with either 100 defective units or zero. It is these wider variations which introduce errors to the sampling. Statistical sampling looks for a way of reducing the effects of these errors, as described in the following sections.

In summary

Inspections and testing are an important part of quality assurance. Inspections are designed to test either the products or the process. A sample of products is usually tested as it is infeasible to test the entire production.

WORKED EXAMPLE 12.3

Light fittings are made on an assembly line. At one point the electric wiring is fitted, and experience suggests that faults are introduced to 4% of units. An inspection at this point would find 80% of faults and would cost £0.30 to inspect each light and £0.50 to correct faults. Any fault not found will continue through the line and will be detected and corrected later. This later test costs £0.20 a unit and each fault corrected costs £5. Is it worth inspecting all light fittings when the wiring is fitted?

SOLUTION

The answer to this is found by calculating the expected costs of doing a 100% inspection and not doing one.

With 100% inspection the expected costs per unit are:

- inspection = £0.30
- faults detected and corrected = 0.04 * 0.8 * 0.5 = £0.016
- later inspection = £0.20
- faults not found until later = 0.04 * (1 − 0.8) * 5 = £0.04

to give a total of £0.556.

Without inspection, costs per unit are:

- later inspection = £0.20
- faults left from earlier = 0.04 * 5 = £0.20

to give a total of £0.40 a unit.

It is clearly cheaper not to do a 100% inspection when the wire is fitted.

12.4.2 Sampling distributions

Larger samples will inevitably have higher testing costs than smaller ones. On the other hand, they will give more reliable results. A compromise is needed so that the sample is large enough to be representative of all units in the batch and yet small enough to be reasonable and cost effective.

In statistical terms all of the production is termed the population, so we are concerned with taking representative samples from a population. Because of random variations, we would expect there to be some variation from sample to sample. If, for example, boxes of fruit are being packed with an average weight of 25 kg we would not be surprised to find a series of four samples with average weights of 25.2 kg, 24.8 kg, 25.1 kg and 25.0 kg. If we took a longer series of samples, the mean weight would follow a distribution. This is called the sampling distribution of the mean. The sampling distribution of the mean has three useful properties:

(1) If the population is Normally distributed, or if a sample of more than about 30 is used, the sampling distribution of the mean is Normally distributed.

(2) The mean of the sampling distribution of the mean equals the mean of the population.

(3) The variance of the sampling distribution of the mean is calculated from $SD/\sqrt{n}$, where SD is the standard deviation of the population and n is the sample size.

The second property confirms the observation that larger samples give more reliable results (see Figure 12.6).

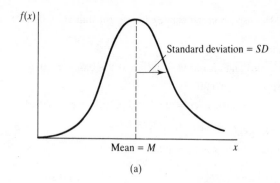

Mean = *M*

(a)

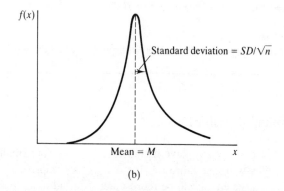

Mean = *M*

(b)

Figure 12.6 Comparison of the population distribution with the sampling distribution of the mean. (a) Distribution of population. (b) Sampling distribution of the mean.

In summary

If samples of size *n* are taken from a population the mean value taken by variables is described by the sampling distribution of the mean which is Normally distributed (for large samples), has the same mean as the population and a smaller standard deviation.

WORKED EXAMPLE 12.4

A production line makes units with a mean length of 100 cm and a standard deviation of 1 cm. What is the probability that a random sample of 35 units has a mean length of less than 99.6 cm?

SOLUTION

With a sample size of 35 the sampling distribution of the mean is Normally distributed with a mean of 100 cm and a standard deviation of $1/\sqrt{35} = 0.169$ cm.
The number of standard deviations 99.6 cm from the mean is:

$$Z = (100 - 99.6)/0.169 = 2.37$$

Normal tables show that this corresponds to a probability of 0.0089, as shown in Figure 12.7.

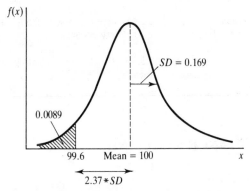

Figure 12.7 Sampling distribution of the mean for Worked Example 12.4.

Hence, 0.89% of samples will have a mean length of less than 99.6 cm.

WORKED EXAMPLE 12.5

A machine produces parts which have a standard deviation in weight of 1 g. A sample of 100 parts was taken and found to have a mean weight of 2 kg. What is the 95% confidence interval for the true weight of the parts?

SOLUTION

A sample of 100 units has a mean of 2 kg and standard deviation of $1/\sqrt{100} = 0.1$ g. The confidence interval defines the range in which 95% of observations will lie, and this is 1.96 standard deviations from the mean. Although we do not know the true mean of the population we can approximate it to the population mean of 2 kg.

Then the 95% confidence interval is $2000 +/- 1.96 * 0.1$ which is 1999.804 to 2000.196 g, as shown in Figure 12.8.

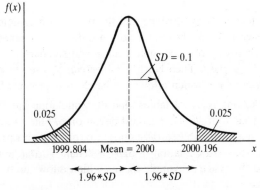

Figure 12.8 Sampling distribution of the mean for Worked Example 12.5.

12.16 What is the difference between acceptance sampling and process control?

12.17 Why are samples used?

12.18 Are the results from statistical sampling completely accurate?

12.19 What is the sampling distribution of the mean?

12.5 ACCEPTANCE SAMPLING

12.5.1 Introduction

Acceptance sampling uses a number of units taken from a batch of products to test whether the whole batch meets designed quality. This testing needs some criterion of quality which allows us to describe a unit as either 'acceptable' or 'defective'. Sometimes this criterion is obvious. If, for example, bottles have to be filled with a minimum of one litre we could define 'defective' as containing less than a litre and 'acceptable' as containing a litre or more. Sometimes the criterion relies less on measurement and more on judgement. A piece of furniture with polished wood, for example, may be rejected because its finish does not look good to an experienced inspector.

This kind of testing in which a unit is described as either acceptable or defective is called sampling by attributes. The alternative is sampling by variables. This involves measuring some continuous property, such as the weight, length or power output of an engine. The average performance of the variable is then compared with some specified acceptable level to see if the batch should be accepted.

We can illustrate these two approaches by referring to a batch of delivered materials. This is inspected to see if the whole batch meets quality standards.

- If the testing is by attribute and the proportion of defective units is known to be p, the proportion of defects in samples of size n is Normally distributed with mean p and standard deviation $\sqrt{p * (1 - p)/n}$. Then Normal tables can be used to find the range of defect numbers which allows the batch to be accepted.

- If the testing is by variables, and the population has mean value for this variable of M and standard deviation SD the mean of the sample is Normally distributed (assuming a large enough sample) with mean M and standard deviation of $SD/\sqrt{n}$. Then Normal tables can be used to find the range of sample means which allow the batch to be accepted.

The approaches are illustrated in the following worked examples.

WORKED EXAMPLE 12.6

A company has specified that materials it receives should contain at most 4% defective units. It receives a large shipment and takes a sample of 200 units. What criterion should the company use to reject a batch if it wants to be 95% sure of not making a mistake?

SOLUTION

The proportion of defective units, p, is 0.04. In samples of size n the proportion of defective units is Normally distributed with mean 0.04 and standard deviation

$$= \sqrt{p * (1 - p)/n} = \sqrt{0.04 * 0.96/200} = 0.014$$

95% of sample proportions are within 1.96 standard deviations of the mean, so 95% of samples will have proportions of defectives between:

$$0.04 + 1.96 * 0.014 = 0.067 \text{ and } 0.04 - 1.96 * 0.014 = 0.013$$

With a sample of 200 this means that 95% of batches will have between $200 * 0.067 = 13.4$ and $200 * 0.013 = 2.6$ defective units.

WORKED EXAMPLE 12.7

Batches of raw materials are delivered with a guaranteed average weight of 25 kg a unit and standard deviation of 1 kg. A sample of 20 units is taken to test each delivery, and the company want to be 95% sure that its rejected batches are in fact defective. What range of mean weights is acceptable in the sample?

SOLUTION

The mean weight of samples will be Normally distributed with mean 25 kg and standard deviation $1/\sqrt{20} = 0.224$ kg.

95% of samples will be within 1.96 standard deviations of the mean, so the range of acceptable sample means is:

$$25 + 1.96 * 0.224 = 25.44 \text{ kg and } 25 - 1.96 * 0.224 = 24.56 \text{ kg}$$

In summary

Acceptance sampling can use sampling by attributes or sampling by variables. In either case ranges of acceptable values can be found for batches.

12.5.2 Single sample acceptance sampling

In this section we will describe some more details of single sample acceptance sampling, concentrating on the more common sampling by attribute.

The general procedure for single sample acceptance sampling is as follows:

- Specify a sample size.
- Take a sample of this size from a batch.
- Specify a maximum allowed number of defects in the sample.
- Test the sample to find the number which are actually defective.
- If the number of defects is greater than an allowed maximum number, reject the batch.
- If the number of defects is less than the allowed maximum number, accept the batch.

To begin this kind of analysis we need some means of saying when a unit is acceptable. This must be a policy decision that is part of the designed quality. When this decision has been made we can design a sampling plan to ensure the designed quality is achieved. This specifies two values, which are a sample size, n, and a maximum number of defective units acceptable in a sample, c.

Decisions about designed quality are complex, but four important factors are the following:

(1) *Acceptance quality level (AQL)*. This is the overall percentage of defects which is considered acceptable. Figures around 2% are often quoted for this, but recent developments suggest that the real target should be zero.

(2) *Lot tolerance per cent defective (LTPD)*. This is the upper limit on the percentage of defective units that customers are willing to accept in a batch. Any batches with more than this percentage of defects are unacceptable.

(3) *Producer's risk (α)*. This is the probability of rejecting a good batch (type I error).

(4) *Consumer's risk (β)*. This is the probability of accepting a bad batch (type II error).

These definitions are based on the idea that customers are willing to accept an overall level of quality equal to AQL. As customers are demanding higher quality this figure is inevitably approaching zero. Figures of 2%, which are often

Table 12.1

LTPD/AQL	c	n * AQL
44.89	0	0.05
10.95	1	0.36
6.51	2	0.82
4.89	3	1.37
4.06	4	1.97
3.55	5	2.61
3.21	6	3.29
2.96	7	3.98
2.77	8	4.70
2.62	9	5.43
2.50	10	6.17

quoted, might be considered temporary measures used until an organization can achieve a lower level.

Although customers are willing to accept an overall proportion of defects given by *AQL*, they may be willing to accept an occasional batch which is as poor as the *LTPD*. They will not, however, accept any batches with a higher proportion of defects.

The other two factors are measures of risk, and a producer will clearly want to minimize α, while consumers will want them to minimize β. Typical sampling plans call for values of α equal to 0.05 and β equal to 0.1.

These four factors allow calculation of appropriate values for n and c. As each unit is either acceptable or defective a Binomial process can be used to describe the number of defective units in each sample. Then the probability of exactly c defects in any sample of n is:

$$P(c) = \frac{n!}{r! (n - c)!} * p^c * (1 - p)^{n-c}$$

where p is the proportion of defective units, or the probability that a random unit is defective.

In practice, however, the easiest way of finding values for n and c is to use standard tables (such as those in Dodge and Romig listed in the references at the end of this chapter). An excerpt from such tables is given in Table 12.1.

The procedure is to calculate the ratio of *LTPD/AQL* and find the entry in the table which is equal to, or just greater than, this value. The next column shows an appropriate value for the acceptance level, c, and the implied sample size is given in the final column.

WORKED EXAMPLE 12.8

A company buys components in batches from a supplier. The supplier uses an acceptance quality level of 2% defectives and a 5% risk of rejecting good batches at inspections. The company accepts batches with a maximum of 6% defective, and wants the probability of accepting a bad batch to be no more than 8%. What would be appropriate values of n and c?

SOLUTION

The values given are:

$$AQL = 0.02$$
$$LTPD = 0.06$$
$$\alpha = 0.05$$
$$\beta = 0.08$$

Then $LTPD/AQL = 3$. The value in Table 12.1 which is equal to or slightly larger than this is 3.21, which corresponds to $c = 6$. The associated ratio of $n * AQL$ is 3.29. As we know $AQL = 0.02$, $n = 3.29/0.02 = 164.5$.

The sampling plan is now:

- take samples of 165 units;
- if six or fewer units are defective accept the batch;
- if more than six units are defective reject the batch.

In summary

Values for acceptable quality level, lot tolerance per cent defective, producer's risk and consumer's risk can be used to find appropriate sample size and acceptable proportion of defects. The easiest way of calculating these is to use standard tables.

12.5.3 Operating characteristics

Values for n and c define an acceptance sampling plan. The overall purpose of such plans is to differentiate acceptable batches from those which should be rejected. How well a sampling plan actually discriminates between these is described by its operating characteristic (OC) curve. An OC curve shows the probability that a sampling plan will accept batches with different proportions of defects. Each combination of n and c has a distinct curve of the general form shown in Figure 12.9. We have already suggested the position of two points on the curve, the first being defined by AQL and $(1 - \alpha)$, and the second by $LTPD$ and β.

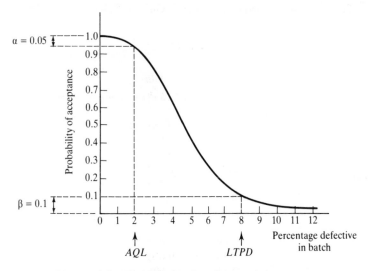

Figure 12.9 Typical operating characteristic curve.

An operating characteristic curve is drawn by taking the specified values of c and n, and then finding the probability of rejecting different batches. This procedure is illustrated in the following worked example.

WORKED EXAMPLE 12.9

Draw the operating characteristic curve for a sampling plan with $n = 100$ and $c = 3$.

SOLUTION

The probability that a unit is defective is p, and the probability that a batch of 100 units has r defective ones is given by the Binomial distribution. In this case n is reasonably large and p is reasonably small, so we can approximate the Binomial distribution by a Poisson distribution. Then:

$$P(r) = \frac{e^{-M} * M^r}{r!}$$

where M is the mean number of defects in a batch.

We can start drawing the OC curve by taking an arbitrary value of p, say 0.05. The mean number of faults in a batch, M, is then 5 and the probability a batch is accepted is:

$$P(0) + P(1) + P(2) + P(3)$$

These values can either be calculated or found in tables (Appendix C) to be:

$$0.0067 + 0.0337 + 0.0842 + 0.1404 = 0.265$$

Similarly, we can find other values as shown in Table 12.2.

Table 12.2

p	Probability of acceptance
0.01	0.981
0.02	0.857
0.03	0.647
0.04	0.433
0.05	0.265
0.06	0.151
0.07	0.082
0.08	0.042
0.09	0.021
0.10	0.010
0.11	0.005
0.12	0.002

When these values are plotted they give the operating characteristic curve shown in Figure 12.10.

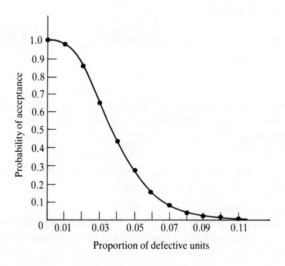

Figure 12.10 Operating characteristic curve with $n = 100$ and $c = 3$.

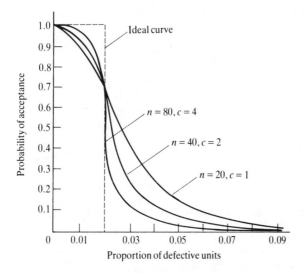

Figure 12.11 Operating characteristic curves with increasing sample size.

If we are looking for a clearer distinction between good and bad lots the OC curve should be as steep as possible, and would ideally be vertical. A vertical OC curve would differentiate perfectly between an acceptable batch (which would have a probability of acceptance equal to 1) and an unacceptable batch (with a probability of acceptance of 0). The way to get a steep curve is to take large samples. Even if the proportion of defectives remains the same, taking a larger sample will give more reliable results, as illustrated in Figure 12.11. Unfortunately, larger samples are more expensive and a balance is needed between the costs and benefits. Some benefits from small sample sizes are reduced costs, samples can be analysed quickly to allow faster responses, and smaller samples might increase sensitivity to small changes.

Operating characteristic curves show how the probability that a batch is accepted is reduced as the proportion of defective units in it increases. Poor batches are, therefore, more likely to be rejected while good batches are more likely to be accepted. This improves the overall quality of products by selectively rejecting low quality batches. We can now ask how good the average quality of remaining products is, and the answer is found from:

Average outgoing quality $(AOQ) = p *$ probability of accepting a batch

Thus a low value for AOQ means there are few defects. When the proportion of defective units, p, is small, most batches are accepted and AOQ remains low. As p increases the AOQ also rises. As p continues to increase further, more batches start to be rejected and the AOQ begins to decline. With high values of p, most

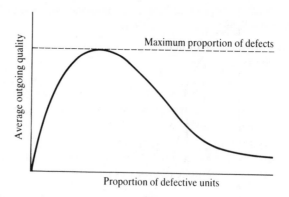

Figure 12.12   Variation of *AOQ* with proportion of defective units.

batches are rejected and the *AOQ* is again low. This pattern is illustrated in Figure 12.12.

In summary

The operating characteristic curve is distinct for every combination of *n* and *c* and shows the probability that a batch with differing numbers of defects will be accepted. This can be used to find the average outgoing quality.

12.5.4 Sequential sampling plans

Single sampling plans are by far the most common, but more complicated sequential ones can be developed. Double sampling plans, for example, specify two numbers for defects: a maximum number of defects which is acceptable in a sample, and a minimum number. A sample is taken and if the number of defects is above the maximum, the batch is rejected. If the number of defects is below the minimum the batch is accepted. If the number of defects is between the maximum and minimum a second sample is drawn from the same batch and tested. The results of both tests are combined to allow a final decision about the batch.

A typical double sampling plan is as follows:

- Take a sample of 50.
- If less than two units are defective, accept the batch.
- If more than four units are defective, reject the batch.
- If two, three or four units are defective, take another sample of 50 from the same batch.

- If the total number of defects in the two samples is less than five, accept the batch.

- If the total number of defects in the two samples is five or more, reject the batch.

The benefit of this approach is that fewer samples are needed to get the same reliability as in single tests. It is sometimes suggested that double sampling plans can halve the amount of testing needed to get a certain level of reliability, but this is rather a simplification.

More complicated sequential plans can be developed, taking a series of samples, but the added complications can rarely be justified.

In summary

Double or more complicated sampling plans can be used instead of single sampling. These use reduced amounts of sampling to get the same reliability.

SELF ASSESSMENT QUESTIONS

12.20 What is the difference between sampling by attribute and sampling by variable?

12.21 What is meant by *AQL*, *LTPD*, *AOQ*?

12.22 Why would an ideal operating characteristic curve be vertical?

12.23 Average outgoing quality must increase as average product quality increases. Is this statement true or false?

12.24 What is the benefit of a double sampling plan over a single plan?

12.6 PROCESS CONTROL

12.6.1 Control charts for attributes

There are two objectives in taking samples: acceptance sampling checks the quality of products, and process control checks that the process is working as planned. There must inevitably be some small random variations in the performance of a process, so process control checks that it is working within an acceptable range. The way of doing this is to take samples over time to see if there are any noticeable trends. If there is a clear trend the process might need adjusting. The main analysis of such results uses process control charts.

We will start by describing process control charts for attributes, so we are again considering outcomes which are either acceptable or defective. Process control charts plot a series of observations for the performance of the process over time. Typically, a series of samples is taken and the proportion of defective

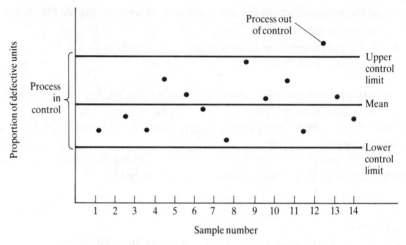

Figure 12.13 Typical process control chart.

units in each is plotted. This is sometimes called a *p*-chart. Although we will use the proportion of defective units to illustrate control charts, any suitable measure could be used.

The proportion of defective units in a sample will usually be around the mean value. Provided it does not vary far from the mean, the process is said to be in control. If there is a trend the proportion of defective units moves away from the mean. When it reaches some specified limit, the process is said to be out of control and corrective action is needed. The important decision in *p*-charts is to define what is meant by out of control. For this, two control limits are set, an upper limit (*UCL*) and a lower limit (*LCL*). Provided the output remains between these two limits the process is in control, but if it moves outside the limits it is out of control (as shown in Figure 12.13).

The problem is to define the control limits. This relies on the result quoted earlier, that the proportion of defective units in a large sample of size n is Normally distributed with mean, M, and standard deviation, SD, with:

$$SD = \sqrt{\frac{M * (1 - M)}{n}}$$

This is a standard result which we will not prove, but it allows us to calculate control limits as:

Upper control limit $= UCL = M + Z * SD$
Lower control limit $= LCL = M - Z * SD$

Z is the number of standard deviations corresponding to the specified confidence limit. This confidence limit is chosen as part of the designed quality. It specifies the proportion of samples which would normally be within a range if the process is in control. Thus a 95% confidence interval (corresponding to $Z = 1.96$) would find the range within which 95% of samples would lie if the process is in control. If the process is changing, the proportion of samples outside the control limits will change and some investigation and adjustment is needed.

In summary

Process control takes periodic samples of the product and uses these to check that a process is still operating as planned. This ensures the output is between two specified control limits.

WORKED EXAMPLE 12.10

A sample of 500 units of the output was collected from a process for each of 30 working days when it was known to be operating normally. The number of defective units was recorded each day as shown in Table 12.3.

Table 12.3

Day	Number of defects	Day	Number of defects	Day	Number of defects
1	70	11	45	21	61
2	48	12	40	22	57
3	66	13	53	23	65
4	55	14	51	24	48
5	50	15	60	25	42
6	42	16	57	26	40
7	64	17	55	27	67
8	47	18	62	28	70
9	51	19	45	29	63
10	68	20	48	30	60

Draw a control chart with 99% confidence limits.

SOLUTION

The average proportion of defects a day is:

$$M = \frac{\text{total number of defects}}{\text{number of observations}} = \frac{1650}{30 * 500} = 0.11$$

$$SD = \sqrt{\frac{M * (1 - M)}{n}} = \sqrt{\frac{0.11 * 0.89}{500}} = 0.014$$

The 99% confidence limit with a two-tail test has $Z = 2.58$, so:

$$UCL = M + Z * SD = 0.11 + 2.58 * 0.014 = 0.146$$
$$LCL = M - Z * SD = 0.11 - 2.58 * 0.014 = 0.074$$

If the proportion of defects is between 0.074 and 0.146 the process is under control and differences are simply random variations. If the proportion of defects is outside this range the process is out of control and adjustments are needed (see Figure 12.14). With samples of 500 the process is under control when the number of defects is between 0.074 * 500 = 37 and 0.146 * 500 = 73.

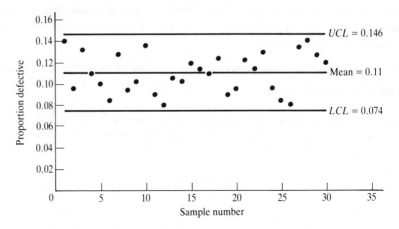

Figure 12.14 Control chart for Worked Example 12.10.

Process control charts will have some observations that lie outside the control limits purely by chance. With a 95% confidence interval 5% of samples will lie outside the control limits purely by chance. This means that each observation suggesting the process is out of control should be investigated to see if the process really is out of control or whether it is actually operating normally. The charts also show other signals that should be investigated. If, for example, there is a trend, even though the process is in control, it is a sign for further investigation. Symptoms for investigation are, then:

- a single reading outside the control limits;
- a clear trend;
- several consecutive readings near to a control limit;
- several consecutive readings on the same side of the mean;
- a sudden change in apparent mean levels;
- very erratic observations.

In summary
Any unexpected observations in a control chart should be investigated carefully before any conclusions are drawn.

12.6.2 Control charts for variables

Control charts can also be used with variable, rather than attribute, sampling. The approach is essentially the same, with upper and lower control limits specified by a number of standard deviations away from the mean. We again use the sampling distribution of the mean which is Normally distributed with the mean the same as the process mean and standard deviation equal to $SD/\sqrt{n}$, where SD is the process standard deviation.

WORKED EXAMPLE 12.11

A process makes packaged food with a mean weight of 1 kg and standard deviation of 0.05 kg. Samples of 10 are taken to ensure the process is still in control. Find the control limits which will include 99% of sample means if the process is functioning normally.

SOLUTION

The means of samples will be distributed Normally with mean = 1 kg and standard deviation = $0.05/\sqrt{10}$.

A confidence interval of 99% corresponds to a 2.58 standard deviation. Then:

$$LCL = M - Z * SD = 1 - 2.58 * 0.05/\sqrt{10} = 0.959$$
$$UCL = M + Z * SD = 1 + 2.58 * 0.05/\sqrt{10} = 1.041$$

Provided the mean of samples stays within this range the process is in control. If it moves outside the range it is out of control and needs investigation.

The approach used in Worked Example 12.11 relies on the mean and standard deviation of all the output being known. As sampling removes the need for testing all output, these values may not be known. Then there are two alternatives. Firstly, we could use the values from samples to approximate the mean and standard deviation of the whole process. This needs reliable data. A classic mistake is to take a sample, use data from this to approximate the mean value for the process, and then test the sample to see if it conforms to the process mean!

A more satisfactory alternative is to add a measure for the range of observations. This gives two charts which are generally called X and R charts, X being the sample mean and R the sample range. The range of a sample is simply defined as the difference between the largest observation and the smallest. Suppose, for example, a manufacturer takes samples to monitor the weight of a product. An X chart monitors the mean weight in the samples and an R chart monitors the ranges found within the samples.

X and R charts are drawn in exactly the same way as p-charts for

Table 12.4

Sample size	Factor for X chart A	Factors for R chart	
		D1	D2
2	1.88	0	3.27
3	1.02	0	2.57
4	0.73	0	2.28
5	0.58	0	2.11
6	0.48	0	2.00
7	0.42	0.08	1.92
8	0.37	0.14	1.86
9	0.34	0.18	1.82
10	0.31	0.22	1.78
12	0.27	0.28	1.72
15	0.22	0.35	1.65
17	0.20	0.38	1.62
20	0.18	0.41	1.59
25	0.15	0.50	1.54

attributes. To help find the control limits we will also define:

X = mean value of a sample
MX = overall mean of the sample means
R = range of a sample
MR = overall mean of the sample ranges

With m samples this gives:

$$MX = \frac{\sum^{m} X}{m} \qquad MR = \frac{\sum^{m} R}{m}$$

Now we need to find the upper and lower control limits. These are fairly straightforward to calculate, but standard tables are readily available (see, for example, Grant and Leavenworth listed in the references at the end of the chapter). To save unnecessary calculation we will simply refer to these tables and state the control limits.

For means:
$LCL = MX - A * MR \qquad UCL = MX + A * MR$

For ranges:
$LCL = D1 * MR \qquad UCL = D2 * MR$

Values for A, $D1$ and $D2$ are given in the tables, an extract of which is given in Table 12.4. These values relate to 99.7% confidence intervals and are sometimes known as three-sigma control limit factors.

WORKED EXAMPLE 12.12

Samples of ten units have been taken from the output of a process in each of the past 20 days. Each unit in the sample was weighed. The mean weight in each sample and the range were as shown in Table 12.5.

Table 12.5

Sample	Mean	Range	Sample	Mean	Range
1	12.2	4.2	11	12.5	3.3
2	13.1	4.6	12	12.3	4.0
3	12.5	3.0	13	12.5	2.9
4	13.3	5.1	14	12.6	2.7
5	12.7	2.9	15	12.8	3.9
6	12.6	3.1	16	12.1	4.2
7	12.5	3.2	17	13.2	4.8
8	13.0	4.6	18	13.0	4.6
9	12.2	4.3	19	13.2	5.0
10	12.0	5.0	20	12.6	3.8

Draw X and R charts for the process.

SOLUTION

The overall mean values for weight and ranges are:

$$MX = 252.9/20 = 12.65 \qquad MR = 79.2/20 = 3.96$$

Then we look up the factors for samples of size 10 and find:

$$A = 0.31 \quad D1 = 0.22 \text{ and } D2 = 1.78$$

Then for means:

$$LCL = MX - A * MR \qquad UCL = MX + A * MR$$
$$= 12.65 - 0.31 * 3.96 \qquad = 12.65 + 0.31 * 3.96$$
$$= 11.42 \qquad\qquad = 13.88$$

and for ranges:

$$LCL = D1 * MR \qquad UCL = D2 * MR$$
$$= 0.22 * 3.96 \qquad = 1.78 * 3.96$$
$$= 0.87 \qquad\qquad = 7.05$$

Provided future samples keep within these ranges the process is in control, but if they move outside these ranges the samples are out of control (see Figure 12.15).

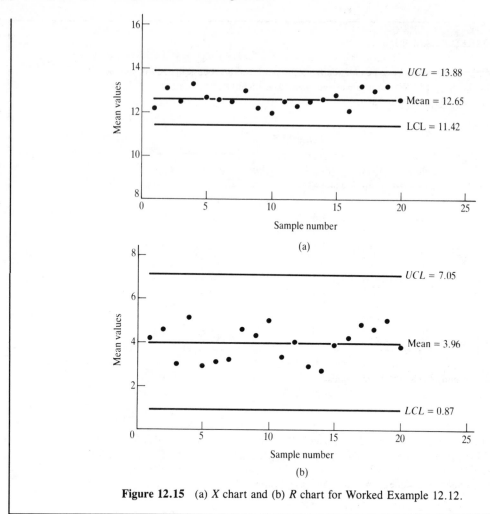

Figure 12.15 (a) X chart and (b) R chart for Worked Example 12.12.

In summary

If population values are known, process sampling by variables is very similar to sampling by attributes. If the population values are not known X and R charts can be used.

SELF ASSESSMENT QUESTIONS

12.25 With p-charts, would a larger confidence interval be nearer or further away from the mean than a smaller one?

12.26 What does it mean if an observation is outside the control limits in a process control chart?

12.27 What patterns should be investigated in a control chart?

12.28 Why are R charts used?

SUMMARY OF CHAPTER

This chapter described some aspects of quality assurance. In recent years organizations have recognized the importance of product quality, and have put more effort into all aspects of quality management. A major incentive for this is the observation that customers are demanding high quality, and that meeting this demand can bring a number of advantages to an organization. Among these advantages are higher sales, increased profits and lower costs.

It is almost impossible to propose a general definition of quality which takes into account all the different dimensions and viewpoints. This often leads to general statements like, 'we cannot define high quality, but we recognize it when we see it'. Overall quality is usually judged by a number of factors, some of which can be measured and some of which rely on opinion. This means that a key element in a product's success is the customer's perception of its quality.

In recent years organizations have realized that quality affects every part of an organization. This realization has led quality assurance away from its traditional role of quality control (doing the inspections specified by statistical quality control) to a wider role encompassing all aspects of quality. Total quality control gives a formalized programme for quality assurance throughout an organization. This encourages features like quality at source and quality circles.

There is a traditional belief that high quality can only be achieved by high costs. This is not true, and there is considerable evidence that the costs of ensuring high quality are more than offset by the savings. In particular, increasing costs of design and appraisal are more than covered by savings in internal and external failures.

Statistical sampling is an important part of quality assurance. This uses random samples to test either the quality of products (acceptance sampling) or the performance of the process (process control).

Single samples are the most common form of acceptance sampling. With sampling by attributes, two important questions are the sample size and the maximum number of defects in a sample which is acceptable. Tables of appropriate values can be used, based on acceptable quality level, lot tolerance per cent defective, producer's risk and consumer's risk. Related calculations allow an operating characteristic curve to show the probability of accepting a batch containing different numbers of defects. Sometimes more complex sampling plans might be used, such as double or sequential plans.

The other purpose of sampling is process control. The most

effective analysis for this uses process control charts which plot the performance of a series of samples. The process is in control when the output remains between two control limits. p-charts plot the progress of attributes, whose variables can be checked using X and R charts.

PROBLEMS

12.1 A company estimates costs (in thousands of pounds) over the past six years to be as shown in Table 12.6. Describe what has been happening.

Table 12.6

Year	1	2	3	4	5	6
Sales value	623	625	626	635	677	810
Costs						
Design	6	8	18	24	37	43
Appraisal	15	17	22	37	45	64
Internal failure	91	77	32	36	17	10
External failure	105	101	83	51	27	16

12.2 A part is made on an assembly line. At one point an average of 2% of units are defective. It costs £0.50 to inspect each unit at this point, and the inspection would only find 70% of faults. If the faults are left, all parts will be found and corrected further down the line at a cost of £4. Would it be worth while inspecting all units at this point in the line?

12.3 A machine produces parts with a standard deviation in length of 2 cm. A sample of 40 units is taken and found to have a mean length of 148.7 cm. What are the 95% and 99% confidence intervals for the true length of the parts?

12.4 Soft drinks are put into cans which hold a nominal 200 ml, but the filling machines introduce a standard deviation of 10 ml. The cans are put into cartons of 25 and exported to a market which requires the mean weight of cartons to be at least the quantity specified by the manufacturer. To ensure this happens, the canner set the machines to fill cans to 205 ml. What is the probability that a carton chosen at random will not pass the quantity test?

12.5 A company says that its suppliers should send at most 2% defective units. It receives a large shipment and takes a sample of 100 units. The company wants to be 95% sure that a rejected batch is really unsatisfactory. What criteria should it use to reject a batch?

12.6 Batches of raw materials are delivered with a guaranteed average length of 100 cm and standard deviation of 1 cm. A sample of 100 units is taken to test each delivery, and the company want to be 95% sure that its rejected batches are in fact defective. What range of mean weights is acceptable in the sample?

12.7 A component is made in batches and transferred from one part of a plant to another. When it is made an acceptance quality level of 1% of defectives is used, but transferred batches are allowed to have a maximum of 4% defective. Limits are imposed to accept a 5% risk of rejecting good batches, and a 10% risk of accepting bad batches. What would be a suitable sampling plan for the component?

12.8 Draw the operating characteristic curve for a sampling plan with $n = 50$ and $c = 5$.

12.9 Twenty-four samples of 200 units were collected from a process which was known to be operating properly. The number of defective units was as shown in Table 12.7.

Table 12.7

Day	Number of defects	Day	Number of defects	Day	Number of defects
1	21	9	15	17	20
2	32	10	13	18	19
3	22	11	16	19	25
4	17	12	17	20	16
5	16	13	20	21	15
6	14	14	19	22	13
7	21	15	17	23	24
8	17	16	22	24	25

Draw control charts with 95% and 99% confidence limits on the process.

12.10 A process makes products with a mean length of 75.42 cm and standard deviation of 2.01 cm. Samples of eight are taken to ensure the process is still in control. Find the control limits which will include 99% of sample means if the process is working normally.

12.11 Thirty samples of size 15 have been taken from a process. The average sample range for the 30 samples is 1.025 kg and the average mean is 19.872 kg. Draw X and R control charts for the process.

CASE STUDY – WEST MIDLAND ELECTRONIC CAR COMPONENT COMPANY

David Brown is the Quality Control Manager of West Midland Electronic Car Component Company. As its name suggests, the company makes a range of electronic components for cars. Last year enough components were produced to equip almost 2 million cars. Just over 30% of these were used on the domestic market, while the remainder were exported, mainly to Germany, France, Italy, Spain and Sweden.

David arrived at work at 7.30 one Tuesday morning to find a message asking him to report immediately to the General Manager. When he arrived at the 'executive suite' it was obvious that the General Manager was not in a good mood. As David approached, the General Manager threw him a letter that had obviously come in the morning mail. David glimpsed down the letter and saw two sections which the General Manager had circled in red ink.

> We have looked at recent figures for the quality of one of the components you supply, AM74021-74222, and find there has been some inconsistency of late. As you will recall, we have an agreement that requires 99.5% of delivered units of this product to be within 5% of target output ratings (as specified in our Technical Report 32/AB/12). While your recent supplies have been achieving this, we are concerned that there has been some inconsistency. We had hoped that quality would be improving so that when we renegotiate the contract at the end of this year we would be able to specify higher quality levels. At the moment this would seem difficult for you to meet.
>
> As you know we put considerable emphasis on the quality of our own products and, therefore, think it reasonable to ask suppliers to reach the same standards. We appreciate that you may not have the same resources or expertise as we have, and would appreciate the opportunity to discuss ways of working together to share ideas.

The General Manager waited for a few minutes and said;

> I find it incredible that we are sending poor quality goods to one of our biggest customers. You are paid to control quality around here, and the job is obviously not being done. We have a major complaint, and an offer from complete strangers to discuss the quality of our products. They are suggesting that we can't do the job properly so they will come and show us how to do it. This is clearly your problem, and if you don't come up with some suggestions in the near future we should start looking for someone who can.

David looked uncomfortable. He was in his early fifties and had no intention of taking early retirement or being moved out to another job. On the contrary, he was hoping to become a Director of the company within the next few years. The General Manager was clearly in an aggressive mood and this made David rather defensive. His reply to the letter was, therefore, less constructive than normal.

There is absolutely nothing wrong with the quality of the AM74021-74222 unit. We agreed measures for quality and are consistently achieving that. We haven't improved quality because we did not agree to improve it, and any improvement would increase our own costs. In any case, we are making 995 units in a 1000 at higher quality than requested, and the remaining 0.5% are only just below it. To me, this seems a level of quality that almost anyone would be proud of. We have to accept that some defects will get through even the most rigorous quality control schemes. I think it would be impossible to make any further improvements. As to the fluctuations in quality, these are just normal random fluctuations which are inherent in any process. There is certainly no sign of problems of any kind.

The process for making AM74021-74222 can be considered in five stages, each of which is followed by an inspection. The units then have a final inspection before being sent to customers. The manufacturing process is largely automated. Two of the six inspections are 100% inspections which are done automatically. The remaining four inspections rely on random sampling. The reason for this is the very small number of defective units which would make 100% inspections unacceptably expensive.

David Brown saved all historic figures for quality control. He remembered in past years when they were struggling to achieve a defect rate of 2%, and he felt disappointed that now he was being blamed for achieving better than 0.5%. The AM74021-74222 had been in production for 18 months, and this was the second complaint he had ever received about its quality. The first had been a batch of 500 units shortly after the product had been introduced. By unhappy chance this batch had seven faulty units in it, and the customers had sent back the whole batch. Sorting this out had taken a lot of time and the company had spent about £5000 repairing customer relations and ensuring similar problems did not happen again.

David checked the specifications and felt sure that they were doing as much as could be expected. He considered more 100% inspections, but each manual inspection would cost about £0.60 and the selling price of the unit was only £24.75. There was also the problem that manual inspections were only about 80% accurate. Automatic inspections cost only £0.30 and were almost completely reliable, but they could not cover all aspects of quality. At least three inspections had to remain manual. He looked at reports for the past 18 months and again could find nothing wrong. He decided to produce a six-month summary of weekly figures to show that things really had not changed in this period. During this period there had been few changes in production, and the company continued to work five days a week with two eight-hour shifts a day. The figures and notes he collected are given in Table 12.8.

Table 12.8

Week	A		B		C		D		E		F	
	Ins.	Rej.	Ins.	Rej.	Ins.	Rej.	Ins.	Rej.	Ins.	Rej.	Ins.	Rej.
1	4125	125	350	56	287	0	101	53	3910	46	286	0
2	4086	136	361	0	309	0	180	0	3854	26	258	0
3	4833	92	459	60	320	0	194	0	4651	33	264	0
4	3297	43	208	0	186	0	201	0	3243	59	246	0
5	4501	83	378	0	359	64	224	65	4321	56	291	0
6	4772	157	455	124	401	0	250	72	4410	42	289	0
7	4309	152	420	87	422	0	266	123	3998	27	287	64
8	4654	101	461	0	432	0	278	45	4505	57	310	0
9	4901	92	486	0	457	0	287	0	4822	73	294	0
10	5122	80	512	0	488	0	301	0	5019	85	332	0
11	5143	167	524	132	465	48	290	61	4659	65	287	0
12	5119	191	518	0	435	0	256	54	4879	54	329	0
13	4990	203	522	83	450	0	264	112	4610	55	297	0
14	5231	164	535	63	475	0	276	0	5002	32	267	0
15	3900	90	425	56	288	0	198	0	3820	37	290	58
16	4277	86	485	109	320	0	229	0	4109	38	328	0
17	4433	113	435	0	331	0	265	67	4259	29	313	0
18	5009	112	496	0	387	0	198	62	4821	52	269	0
19	5266	135	501	65	410	0	299	58	5007	51	275	64
20	5197	142	488	0	420	72	301	73	4912	48	267	0
21	4932	95	461	0	413	0	266	0	4856	45	286	0
22	5557	94	510	0	456	0	160	64	5400	39	298	61
23	5106	101	488	74	488	0	204	131	4795	36	326	0
24	5220	122	472	0	532	0	277	125	4989	29	340	56
25	5191	111	465	0	420	0	245	185	4927	42	321	0
26	5620	87	512	45	375	0	223	134	5357	48	332	0

Ins. = Number of units inspected.
Rej. = Number of units rejected (in complete batches).

Summary of inspections

For sampling inspections, all production is considered in notional batches of one hour's production. Random samples are taken from each batch and if the quality is too low the whole batch is rejected, checked and reworked as necessary.

- A, automatic inspection of all units: rejects all defects.
- B, manual inspection of 10% of output: rejects batch if more than 1% of batch is defective.
- C, manual inspection of 10% of output: rejects batch if more than 1% of batch is defective.
- D, manual inspection of 5% of output: rejects batch if more than 2% of batch is defective.

- E, automatic inspection of all units: rejects all defects.
- F, manual inspection of 5% of output: rejects batch if more than 1% of batch is defective.

Suggested questions

- Describe in detail the current quality control system.
- How good is this system?
- Is the General Manager's reaction fair?
- Is David Brown's approach reasonable?
- What can be deduced from the data collected by David Brown?
- How might the present system be improved?
- What other information is needed before making any final decisions?

SOLUTIONS TO SELF ASSESSMENT QUESTIONS

12.1 Generally false.

12.2 Because it has implications for reputation, marketing effort needed, market share, prices charged, profits, costs, liability for defects, and almost every other aspect of an organization's operations.

12.3 No. The best way to ensure high quality is to make the product without faults in the first place.

12.4 Because there are so many opinions, viewpoints, judgements and possible measures.

12.5 Designed quality and quality conformance.

12.6 Quality control inspects products to ensure they conform to designed quality, but quality assurance is a wider function which is involved with all aspects of product quality.

12.7 No. TQC (total quality control) means that product quality is considered in all parts of the organization.

12.8 A scheme where everyone is responsible for passing on products of perfect quality to following operations.

12.9 A small group working in an area which meets informally to discuss ways of improving quality and efficiency.

12.10 (c) Partly true. Services usually rely on more subjective judgement, but there are many similarities.

12.11 By asking customers how satisfied they were with the service.

12.12 False.

12.13 Because fewer defectives will be produced and these should be detected earlier.

12.14 One classification has costs of design, appraisal, internal failure and external failure.

12.15 As early as possible, preferably at the product design stage.

12.16 Acceptance sampling determines if products are conforming to design quality, while process control determines if the process is working properly.

12.17 Because inspecting all the products may be expensive, destructive or infeasible.

12.18 No. There are always random variations.

12.19 The distribution of means found in samples from the population.

12.20 Sampling by attribute classifies units as either acceptable or defective, while sampling by variable measures some continuous value.

12.21 *AQL* is the acceptance quality level, *LTPD* is lot tolerance per cent defective, *AOQ* is average outgoing quality.

12.22 Because this would indicate perfect differentiation between good batches (where the probability of acceptance is 1) and bad batches (where the probability of acceptance is 0).

12.23 False (different numbers of defects may be identified and rejected).

12.24 It uses fewer samples to achieve the same reliability.

12.25 Further away.

12.26 The process is out of control and needs adjusting (but check for random fluctuations before doing this).

12.27 A single reading outside the control limits, a clear trend, several consecutive readings near to a control limit, several consecutive readings on the same side of the mean, a sudden change in apparent mean levels, very erratic observations.

12.28 Because X charts give mean values but they give no indication of variation from these means.

REFERENCES FOR FURTHER READING

Besterfield D.H. (1986). *Quality Control* 2nd edn. Englewood Cliffs: Prentice-Hall

Buffa E.S. (1984). *Meeting the Competitive Challenge* Homewood: Dow Jones-Irwin

Crosby P.B. (1979). *Quality is Free* New York: New American Library

Dehnad K. (1989). *Quality Control, Robust Design and the Taguchi Method* Pacific Grove: Wadsworth & Brooks/Cole

Deming W.E. (1986). *Out of the Crisis* Cambridge: MIT Press

Dodge H.F. and Romig H.G. (1959). *Sampling Inspection Tables − Single and Double Sampling* New York: Wiley

Enrick N.L. (1985). *Quality, Reliability and Process Improvement* 8th edn. New York: Industrial Press

Feigenbaum A.V. (1986). *Total Quality Control* 3rd edn. New York: McGraw-Hill

Gitlow H.S. and Gitlow S. (1987). *The Deming Guide to Achieving Quality and Competitive Position* Englewood Cliffs: Prentice-Hall

Gitlow H.S., Gitlow S., Oppenheim A. and Oppenheim R. (1989). *Tools and Methods for the Improvement of Quality* Homewood: Richard Irwin

Grant E.L. and Leavenworth R.S. (1980). *Statistical Quality Control* 5th edn. New York: McGraw-Hill

Ingle S. (1985). *In Search of Perfection: How to Create, Maintain, Improve Quality* Englewood Cliffs: Prentice-Hall

Ishikawa K. (1985). *What is Total Quality Control?* Englewood Cliffs: Prentice-Hall

Juran J.M. and Gryma F.M. (1980). *Quality Planning and Analysis* New York: McGraw-Hill

Townsend P.L. (1986). *Commit to Quality* New York: Wiley

Chapter 13

Review

SYNOPSIS

This chapter reviews some aspects of operations management. It starts by emphasizing how important the subject is and why it has been receiving more attention in recent years.

Operations management deals with a wide range of circumstances. Although organizations appear to have great variety, they are often faced by similar types of problem. The chapter reviews how some of the problem areas have been tackled in this book.

13.1 BACKGROUND TO OPERATIONS MANAGEMENT

In recent years many industrialized countries have become concerned by their declining share of world trade. Although some redistribution of trade is inevitable, there has been a growing concern that Western countries are failing to compete effectively against countries in, say, the Far East. Japan became a leading manufacturing country in the 1960s and has now been followed by Singapore, South Korea, Taiwan, Hong Kong, and others. For some time there was a feeling that conditions in the Far East were 'different' to Western countries, and this made competition inherently difficult. Unfortunately, evidence is suggesting that this is not true. Consider, for example, the evidence that Japanese companies can open plants in Europe and America and still operate more efficiently than local companies. It has become clear that many of these companies are succeeding because they are better organized and managed.

In the United States this has led to a greater emphasis on manufacturing and production and a renewed interest in competing in international markets. Management education is now seen as a priority, with up to a quarter of all graduates in management or business subjects. Whether or not this effort is working is open to debate. Japan still has a huge balance of trade surplus, while the United States has an equally huge balance of trade deficit.

The growing interest in operations management is not solely a consequence of increasing competition. Technological developments have had a major impact on the processes by which products are made. Computers are the obvious example of a major technological change, but they are usually seen as information processors. Their role in controlling operations is only just beginning to be exploited. Developments in CNC machines, CAD/CAM, robots, computer integrated manufacturing and automated factories are dramatically changing many production processes. Traditional management practices are often inappropriate for new technologies, and organizations need managers who can deal with the changing circumstances.

Another reason for operations management to grow in importance is the realization that an organization's survival depends on the goods and services it produces. Although this may seem obvious, there have been times in the past when 'advertising was king'. In other words, there was a widespread feeling that it did not matter what an organization did; provided it spent enough on advertising it could sell anything it made. This view did not last long, but there has been a string of similar diversions away from basic operations. One view, which became prevalent more recently, was that the way to make money was to keep 'making deals'. This led to speculators buying and selling companies, investing in international currency markets, looking for attractive lawsuits against other organizations, and so on. Thankfully, there is a growing realization that the real way to make money is to make a product for which there is a demand. This is the main function of all organizations, and it is one reason why operations management is of central importance.

Initial work in operations management was done in manufacturing industries. This became known as production management. It was soon realized that the manufacturing sector only accounts for 20% of the GNP of industrialized countries, while services account for almost 80%. Moreover, the problems faced by service industries often had a lot in common with those faced by manufacturers. Opinions evolved to consider the efficient organization and management of 'operations' in general. This became the basis of operations management.

One assumption of operations management is that we can learn lessons from operations in, say, a car assembly plant and apply them in, say, a hospital. Although this may seem strange at first, there are considerable similarities. Plans have to be developed in both, capacities calculated, demands forecast, utilizations found, stock of materials controlled, and so on.

WORKED EXAMPLE 13.1

Discuss the similarities between the operations in a hotel and in a factory.

SOLUTION

Superficially, the operations in a hotel may seem totally different from those in a factory. There are, however, many similarities. Their operations both turn a number of inputs into useful outputs. In more detail, they are both faced by decisions about location, design of facilities, capacity, inventories, demand forecasting, scheduling, quality assurance, and so on. In reality, the management of both organizations is faced by similar problems, and this is why they can both be included in 'operations management'.

There are several other subjects that are closely related to operations management.

(1) Production management is mainly concerned with manufacturing operations.

(2) Management science applies the 'scientific method' to the management of organizations.

(3) Industrial engineering is more concerned with the engineering aspects of processes.

(4) Operational research is becoming more mathematical.

In summary

Operations management is relevant and of central importance to a wide range of organizations faced by many similar problems. This realization has been growing recently and the subject is receiving more attention.

13.2 BRIEF REVIEW OF CHAPTERS

Operations are the central part of all organizations, and operations management must, therefore, be of fundamental importance. The decisions made in operations management give the foundations on which all other management decisions are based.

The subject is so wide that a particular viewpoint was adopted for this book. In particular, we looked at the operations concerned with making a product, and the analyses available for this. These analyses were often quantitative, but this is certainly not a book about applied mathematics. Operations management is a practical subject which looks for ways of solving real problems.

Each chapter in the book has covered a different aspect of operations management. Chapter 1 started by defining the subject and discussing its role in the decision making of an organization. Decisions were classified as strategic, tactical and operational. The next few chapters looked at some strategic decisions. In particular, they looked at what is made, how much is made, where it is made, and how it is made.

- *What* to make was covered in Chapter 2, which discussed aspects of product planning.
- *How many* to make was covered in Chapter 3, which discussed demand forecasting.
- *Where* to make it was covered in Chapter 4, which discussed the location of facilities.
- *How* to make it was covered in Chapter 5, which discussed process design.

Chapters 2 to 4 clearly described strategic issues, while Chapter 5 moved into tactical decisions with a discussion of process planning and design. The next type of tactical decision follows process design and concerns the layout of facilities, which was described in Chapter 6. The process must have enough capacity to meet demand, while the efficiency with which capacity is used can be measured by utilization and productivity. These related topics were discussed in Chapter 7.

One way of ensuring high productivity is by careful planning and scheduling of work. Aspects of this were discussed in Chapter 8. Some planning is relevant to projects, and methods for this were described in Chapter 9. One possible output from planning is a timetable for materials needed. This is the basis for material requirements planning which was discussed in Chapter 10. An alternative just-in-time system was also described. Most stocks are not linked to MRP or JIT systems and they need a different kind of management. This was discussed in Chapter 11 on independent demand inventory systems.

A key requirement in all organizations is reliably high quality. This has increased the emphasis on quality assurance, which was discussed in Chapter 12.

In summary

A number of different decision areas have been discussed. These were taken in a logical sequence, starting with strategic decisions about product design.

13.3 USE OF COMPUTERS

The availability of cheap computers in recent years has had a profound effect on operations management. Some of the developments have included:

- efficient collection of reliable data;
- fast analysis of this data;
- use of more sophisticated quantitative models;
- control of processes;
- construction of databases;
- networking of systems to improve communications;
  and so on.

Some of the methods described in this book use a lot of arithmetic manipulation. This must be done on a computer for problems of any realistic size. Material requirements planning, for example, would be almost impossible to do by hand. There are essentially three ways of getting suitable software:

(1) Buy specialist software. This is usually written by software houses and provides a sophisticated system for a particular purpose. It might, for example, provide a complete MRP system. The software developers usually have considerable experience and expertise in the area and can give very high quality systems. The software can be very sophisticated and is usually quite expensive, particularly if a lot of tailoring is needed to fit specific circumstances.

(2) Write appropriate software in-house. This depends on the availability of skilled analysts and programmers within the organization. If these are available the results can be very good, but the development of a one-off system will inevitably be expensive. If the necessary skills are not available in the organization, using this approach can give poor results.

(3) Buy general-purpose software. A lot of cheap general-purpose software is available which can do a variety of jobs. Perhaps the most obvious examples of this are spreadsheets, which have many applications in operations management. Some general-purpose software has routines for tackling standard problems, such as forecasting and discounting. These packages have the advantage of being cheap and easy to use, but are really only appropriate for simple applications.

The following worked examples illustrate the output from a cheap general-purpose package. This tackles several types of operations management problems, so we will arbitrarily look at three of these for forecasting, MRP and network analysis.

In summary
Developments in computing have had a profound effect on operations management. There are several sources of appropriate software.

WORKED EXAMPLE 13.2

Describe the computer printout shown in Figure 13.1.

```
                          FORECASTING

                Smoothing with Trend & Seasonal Factoring


                          Data Entered


        Number of Years              :       3
        Data Smoothing Coefficient   :      0.2
        Initial Data Value           :      60
        Trend Smoothing Coefficient  :      0.2
        Estimate of Trend            :       5
        Index Smoothing Coefficient  :      0.2
        Index for prior Quarter 1    :      1.2
        Index for prior Quarter 2    :       1
        Index for prior Quarter 3    :      0.8
        Index for prior Quarter 4    :       1


             Sales

        year1    q1     76
          ..     q2     68
          ..     q3     61
          ..     q4     80
        year2    q1    101
          ..     q2     92
          ..     q3     88
          ..     q4    103
        year3    q1    121
          ..     q2    111
          ..     q3    108
          ..     q4    124


                          Solution


    Period  Sales  Smoothed  Trend Est.  Index  Computed  Difference

    y1q1     76     64.67      4.93       1.20     60        16
    ..q2     68     69.28      4.87       1.00     60         8
    ..q3     61     74.57      4.95       0.80     60         1
```

Figure 13.1 Printout for Worked Example 13.2.

577

..q4	80	79.62	4.97	1.00	60	20
y2q1	101	84.58	4.97	1.19	101.09	-0.09
..q2	92	90.10	5.08	1.00	89.21	2.79
..q3	88	98.05	5.65	0.82	76.49	11.51
..q4	103	103.54	5.62	1.00	103.80	-0.80
y3q1	121	107.59	5.31	1.18	130.44	-9.44
..q2	111	112.49	5.22	1.00	113.03	-2.03
..q3	108	120.43	5.77	0.84	96.80	11.20
..q4	124	125.77	5.68	1.00	126.17	-2.17

```
Average Sales              :      91.77
Mean Square Error          :      90.43
Mean Absolute Deviation    :       7.09
```

Forecast

Year 4

```
q1   152.10
q2   133.17
q3   120.16
q4   148.05
```

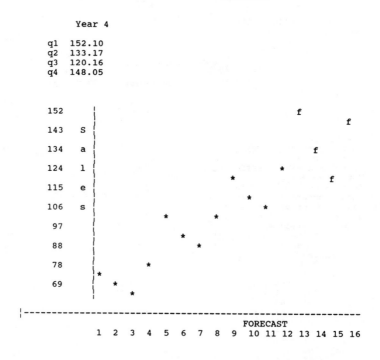

Figure 13.1 (cont.)

SOLUTION

This printout shows a forecast for a single product, where demand has seasonality and trend. The first part of the printout shows the data entered, while the second part does analysis, forecasts demand for the next year and sketches the results.

WORKED EXAMPLE 13.3

Describe the computer printout shown in Figure 13.2.

Project Planning & Control

Three Time Estimates

Data Entered

activity	times		# pred	predecessor numbers	
1-A	Optimistic Modal Pessimistic	2 2 4	0		
2-B	Optimistic Modal Pessimistic	1 2 4	0		
3-C	Optimistic Modal Pessimistic	3 3 3	1	1-A	
4-D	Optimistic Modal Pessimistic	4 5 6	1	1-A	
5-E	Optimistic Modal Pessimistic	5 7 8	2	3-C	4-D
6-F	Optimistic Modal Pessimistic	3 5 9	2	5-E	8-H
7-G	Optimistic Modal Pessimistic	8 11 15	1	2-B	
8-H	Optimistic Modal Pessimistic	6 7 8	1	7-G	
9-I	Optimistic Modal Pessimistic	3 3 3	1	7-G	
10-J	Optimistic Modal Pessimistic	8 11 16	1	6-F	
11-K	Optimistic Modal Pessimistic	7 9 12	1	9-I	
12-L	Optimistic Modal Pessimistic	3 4 5	1	2-B	
13-M	Optimistic Modal Pessimistic	2 3 4	1	12-L	

Figure 13.2 Printout for Worked Example 13.3.

```
14-N    Optimistic        6        1    12-L
        Modal             7
        Pessimistic      10

15-O    Optimistic        4        1    14-N
        Modal             5
        Pessimistic       8

16-P    Optimistic        6        1    14-N
        Modal             8
        Pessimistic      10

17-Q    Optimistic        4        1    15-O
        Modal             5
        Pessimistic       7

18-R    Optimistic        5        3    10-J    11-K    17-Q
        Modal             5
        Pessimistic       5

19-S    Optimistic        4        1    12-L
        Modal             6
        Pessimistic       8

20-T    Optimistic        2        1    19-S
        Modal             3
        Pessimistic       6
```

Solution

Expected

Activity		Start	Finish	Time	Slack	Critical Path
1-A	Earliest:	0	2.33	2.33	6.17	no
	Latest:	6.17	8.50			
2-B	Earliest:	0	2.17	2.17	0	yes
	Latest:	0	2.17			
3-C	Earliest:	2.33	5.33	3	8.17	no
	Latest:	10.50	13.50			
4-D	Earliest:	2.33	7.33	5	6.17	no
	Latest:	8.50	13.50			
5-E	Earliest:	7.33	14.17	6.83	6.17	no
	Latest:	13.50	20.33			
6-F	Earliest:	20.33	25.67	5.33	0	yes
	Latest:	20.33	25.67			
8-H	Earliest:	13.33	20.33	7	0	yes
	Latest:	13.33	20.33			
7-G	Earliest:	2.17	13.33	11.17	0	yes
	Latest:	2.17	13.33			
9-I	Earliest:	13.33	16.33	3	11.50	no
	Latest:	24.83	27.83			
10-J	Earliest:	25.67	37	11.33	0	yes
	Latest:	25.67	37			
11-K	Earliest:	16.33	25.50	9.17	11.50	no
	Latest:	27.83	37			
12-L	Earliest:	2.17	6.17	4	13	no
	Latest:	15.17	19.17			
13-M	Earliest:	6.17	9.17	3	32.83	no
	Latest:	39	42			

Figure 13.2   (cont.)

14-N	Earliest: Latest:	6.17 19.17	13.50 26.50	7.33	13.00	no
15-O	Earliest: Latest:	13.50 26.50	18.83 31.83	5.33	13	no
16-P	Earliest: Latest:	13.50 34	21.50 42	8	20.50	no
17-Q	Earliest: Latest:	18.83 31.83	24 37	5.17	13	no
18-R	Earliest: Latest:	37 37	42 42	5	0	yes
19-S	Earliest: Latest:	6.17 32.67	12.17 38.67	6	26.50	no
20-T	Earliest: Latest:	12.17 38.67	15.50 42	3.33	26.50	no

Project Summary

```
Expected Completion Time :      42
Variance on Critical Path:       4.500
Standard Deviation       :       2.121

Critical Path  =     2-B     6-F     8-H     7-G     10-J
18-R
```

Figure 13.2 (cont.)

SOLUTION

This describes a PERT network with 20 activities (A to T). The first part of the printout shows the data given. This describes the network shown in Figure 13.3.

The second part of the printout gives the earliest and latest start and finish times for activities. This package defines the slack of an activity as the difference between the earliest and latest start times.

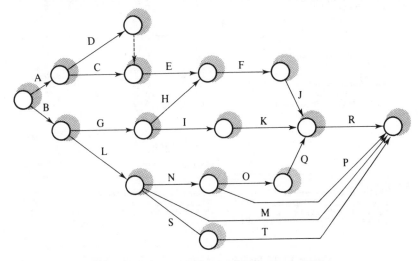

Figure 13.3 Network for Worked Example 13.3.

581

WORKED EXAMPLE 13.4

Describe the computer printout shown in Figure 13.4.

Material Requirements Planning

Data Entered

Number of Time Periods :   10

End Item

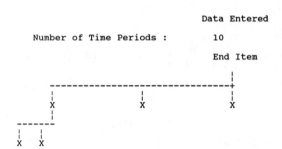

Solution

Level 0 - End Item

Item Number: Part-0   Beginning Inventory: 5
Description: ProductA   Lead Time: 1
Safety Stock: 2
Lot Size: 10

	Period1	Period2	Period3	Period4	Period5
Gross Requirements :	0	0	0	0	0
Scheduled Receipts :	10	0	0	0	0
Available :	15	15	15	15	15
Net Requirements :	0	0	0	0	0
P.O. Receipts :	0	0	0	0	0
P.O. Requests :	0	0	0	0	0

	Period6	Period7	Period8	Period9	Period10
Gross Requirements :	0	0	20	10	40
Scheduled Receipts :	0	0	0	0	0
Available :	15	15	5	5	5
Net Requirements :	0	0	7	7	37
P.O. Receipts :	0	0	10	10	40
P.O. Requests :	0	10	10	40	0

Solution

Level 1 - Comp 1

Item Number: Part-1   Beginning Inventory: 10
Description: ComponentB   Lead Time: 2
Bill of Materials: 2   Safety Stock: 4
Lot Size: 20

Figure 13.4   Printout for Worked Example 13.4.

	Period1	Period2	Period3	Period4	Period5
Gross Requirements :	0	0	0	0	0
Scheduled Receipts :	0	20	0	0	0
Available :	10	30	30	30	30
Net Requirements :	0	0	0	0	0
P.O. Receipts :	0	0	0	0	0
P.O. Requests :	0	0	0	0	0

	Period6	Period7	Period8	Period9	Period10
Gross Requirements :	0	20	20	80	0
Scheduled Receipts :	0	0	0	0	0
Available :	30	10	10	10	10
Net Requirements :	0	0	14	74	0
P.O. Receipts :	0	0	20	80	0
P.O. Requests :	20	80	0	0	0

Level 2 - Comp 1-1

Item Number: MaterialE	Beginning Inventory:	12
Description: Comp-C	Lead Time:	1
Bill of Materials: 5	Safety Stock:	6
	Lot Size:	10

	Period1	Period2	Period3	Period4	Period5
Gross Requirements :	0	0	0	0	0
Scheduled Receipts :	0	20	0	0	0
Available :	12	32	32	32	32
Net Requirements :	0	0	0	0	0
P.O. Receipts :	0	0	0	0	0
P.O. Requests :	0	0	0	0	80

Figure 13.4 (cont.)

SOLUTION

This describes an MRP problem with one end product (Product A), which is made from three components (Component B, Component E and Component F). Component B is assembled from Material C and Material D. The program explodes the bill of materials to give a timetable for planned order requests for the next 10 weeks.

13.4 CONCLUSIONS

Operations management is a central function in all organizations: it provides the foundations on which all other decisions are based. Without efficient operations an organization cannot hope to survive. The purpose of this book is to encourage good practices in operations management.

REFERENCES FOR FURTHER READING

Books on operations management

Adam E.E. and Ebert R.J. (1989). *Production and Operations Management* 4th edn. Englewood Cliffs: Prentice-Hall

Buffa E.S. and Sarin R.K. (1987). *Modern Production/Operations Management* 8th edn. New York: Wiley

Chase R.B. and Aquilano N.J. (1989). *Production and Operations Management* Homewood: Irwin

Dillworth J.B. (1988). *Production and Operations Management* 4th edn. New York: Random House

Evans J.R., Anderson D.R., Sweeney D.J. and Williams T.A. (1990). *Applied Production and Operations Management* 3rd edn. St Paul: West Publishing

Gaither N. (1990). *Production and Operations Management* 4th edn. Chicago: The Dryden Press

Heizer J. and Render B. (1988). *Production and Operations Management* Boston: Allyn and Bacon

Hendrick T.E. and Moore F.G. (1985). *Production/Operations Management* 9th edn. Homewood: Irwin

Krajewski L.J. and Ritzman L.P. (1990). *Operations Management* 2nd edn. Reading: Addison-Wesley

Nahmias S. (1989). *Production and Operations Analysis* Homewood: Irwin

Schmenner R.W. (1990). *Production/Operations Management* 4th edn. New York: Macmillan

Schroeder R.G. (1989). *Operations Management* 3rd edn. New York: McGraw-Hill

Stevenson W.J. (1990). *Production/Operations Management* 3rd edn. Homewood: Irwin

Vonderembse M.A. and White G.P. (1988). *Operations Management* St Paul: West Publishing

Waters C.D.J. (1989). *A Practical Introduction to Management Science* Wokingham: Addison-Wesley

Weis H.J. and Gershon M.E. (1989). *Production and Operations Management* Boston: Allyn and Bacon

Wild R. (1980). *Operations Management* Oxford: Pergamon Press

Books on computing for operations management

Chang Y.L. (1989). *Quantitative Systems for Operations Management* Englewood Cliffs: Prentice-Hall

Chang Y.L. and Sullivan R.S. (1986). *Quantitative Systems for Business* Englewood Cliffs: Prentice-Hall

Dennis T.L. and Dennis T.L. (1988). *Microcomputer Models for Management Decision-Making* St Paul: West Publishing

Erikson R. (1980). *Computer Models for Management Science* 3rd edn. Wokingham: Addison-Wesley

Hall O.P. (1989). *Computer Models for Operations Management* Reading: Addison-Wesley

Nathan J. and Cicilioni R.Y. (1987). *A Spreadsheet Approach to Production and Operations Management* St Paul: West Publishing

Whitaker D. (1984). *OR on the Micro* Chichester: Wiley

Zimmerman S.M. and Zimmerman S.M. (1988). *Operations Management Problems* St Paul: West Publishing

Appendix A

Probabilities for the Normal distribution

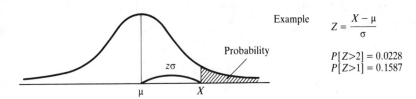

Example $Z = \dfrac{X - \mu}{\sigma}$

$P[Z>2] = 0.0228$
$P[Z>1] = 0.1587$

Normal Deviate z	.00	.01	.02	.03	.04	.05	.06	.07	.08	.09
0.0	.5000	.4960	.4920	.4880	.4840	.4801	.4761	.4721	.4681	.4641
0.1	.4602	.4562	.4522	.4483	.4443	.4404	.4364	.4325	.4286	.4247
0.2	.4207	.4168	.4129	.4090	.4052	.4013	.3974	.3936	.3897	.3859
0.3	.3821	.3783	.3745	.3707	.3669	.3632	.3594	.3557	.3520	.3483
0.4	.3446	.3409	.3372	.3336	.3300	.3264	.3228	.3192	.3156	.3121
0.5	.3085	.3050	.3015	.2981	.2946	.2912	.2877	.2843	.2810	.2776
0.6	.2743	.2709	.2676	.2643	.2611	.2578	.2546	.2514	.2483	.2451
0.7	.2420	.2389	.2358	.2327	.2296	.2266	.2236	.2206	.2177	.2148
0.8	.2119	.2090	.2061	.2033	.2005	.1977	.1949	.1922	.1894	.1867
0.9	.1841	.1814	.1788	.1762	.1736	.1711	.1685	.1660	.1635	.1611
1.0	.1587	.1562	.1539	.1515	.1492	.1469	.1446	.1423	.1401	.1379
1.1	.1357	.1335	.1314	.1292	.1271	.1251	.1230	.1210	.1190	.1170
1.2	.1151	.1131	.1112	.1093	.1075	.1056	.1038	.1020	.1003	.0985
1.3	.0968	.0951	.0934	.0918	.0901	.0885	.0869	.0853	.0838	.0823
1.4	.0808	.0793	.0778	.0764	.0749	.0735	.0721	.0708	.0694	.0681
1.5	.0668	.0655	.0643	.0630	.0618	.0606	.0594	.0582	.0571	.0559
1.6	.0548	.0537	.0526	.0516	.0505	.0495	.0485	.0475	.0465	.0455
1.7	.0446	.0436	.0427	.0418	.0409	.0401	.0392	.0384	.0375	.0367
1.8	.0359	.0351	.0344	.0336	.0329	.0322	.0314	.0307	.0301	.0294
1.9	.0287	.0281	.0274	.0268	.0262	.0256	.0250	.0244	.0239	.0233

Normal Deviate z	.00	.01	.02	.03	.04	.05	.06	.07	.08	.09
2.0	.0228	.0222	.0217	.0212	.0207	.0202	.0197	.0192	.0188	.0183
2.1	.0179	.0174	.0170	.0166	.0162	.0158	.0154	.0150	.0146	.0143
2.2	.0139	.0136	.0132	.0129	.0125	.0122	.0119	.0116	.0113	.0110
2.3	.0107	.0104	.0102	.0099	.0096	.0094	.0091	.0089	.0087	.0084
2.4	.0082	.0080	.0078	.0075	.0073	.0071	.0069	.0068	.0066	.0064
2.5	.0062	.0060	.0059	.0057	.0055	.0054	.0052	.0051	.0049	.0048
2.6	.0047	.0045	.0044	.0043	.0041	.0040	.0039	.0038	.0037	.0036
2.7	.0035	.0034	.0033	.0032	.0031	.0030	.0029	.0028	.0027	.0026
2.8	.0026	.0025	.0024	.0023	.0023	.0022	.0021	.0021	.0020	.0019
2.9	.0019	.0018	.0018	.0017	.0016	.0016	.0015	.0015	.0014	.0014
3.0	.0013	.0013	.0013	.0012	.0012	.0011	.0011	.0011	.0010	.0010

Appendix B

Probabilities for the Student's *t* distribution (two-tail)

Degree of freedom	Student's t distribution												
	Level of significance (α)												
	.9	.8	.7	.6	.5	.4	.3	.2	.1	.05	.02	.01	.001
1	.158	.325	.510	.727	1.000	1.376	1.963	3.078	6.314	12.706	31.821	63.657	636.619
2	.142	.289	.445	.617	.816	1.061	1.386	1.886	2.910	4.303	6.965	9.925	31.598
3	.137	.277	.424	.584	.765	.978	1.250	1.638	2.353	3.182	4.541	5.841	12.941
4	.134	.271	.414	.569	.741	.941	1.190	1.533	2.132	2.776	3.747	4.604	8.610
5	.132	.267	.408	.559	.727	.920	1.156	1.476	2.015	2.571	3.365	4.032	6.859
6	.131	.265	.404	.553	.718	.906	1.134	1.440	1.943	2.447	3.143	3.707	5.959
7	.130	.263	.402	.549	.711	.896	1.119	1.415	1.895	2.365	2.998	3.499	5.405
8	.130	.262	.399	.546	.706	.889	1.108	1.397	1.860	2.306	2.896	3.355	5.041
9	.129	.261	.398	.543	.703	.883	1.100	1.383	1.833	2.262	2.821	3.250	4.781
10	.129	.260	.397	.542	.700	.879	1.093	1.372	1.812	2.228	2.764	3.169	4.587
11	.129	.260	.396	.540	.697	.876	1.088	1.363	1.796	2.201	2.718	3.106	4.437
12	.128	.259	.395	.539	.695	.873	1.083	1.356	1.782	2.179	2.681	3.055	4.318
13	.128	.259	.394	.538	.694	.870	1.079	1.350	1.771	2.160	2.650	3.012	4.221
14	.128	.258	.393	.537	.692	.868	1.076	1.345	1.761	2.145	2.624	2.977	4.140
15	.128	.258	.393	.536	.691	.866	1.074	1.341	1.753	2.131	2.602	2.947	4.073
16	.128	.258	.392	.535	.690	.865	1.071	1.337	1.746	2.120	2.583	2.921	4.015
17	.128	.257	.392	.534	.689	.863	1.069	1.333	1.740	2.110	2.567	2.898	3.965
18	.127	.257	.392	.534	.688	.862	1.067	1.330	1.734	2.101	2.552	2.878	3.922
19	.127	.257	.391	.533	.688	.861	1.066	1.328	1.729	2.093	2.539	2.861	3.883
20	.127	.257	.391	.533	.687	.860	1.064	1.325	1.725	2.086	2.528	2.845	3.850
21	.127	.257	.391	.532	.686	.859	1.063	1.323	1.721	2.080	2.518	2.831	3.819
22	.127	.256	.390	.532	.686	.858	1.061	1.321	1.717	2.074	2.508	2.819	3.792
23	.127	.256	.390	.532	.685	.858	1.060	1.319	1.714	2.069	2.500	2.807	3.767
24	.127	.256	.390	.531	.685	.857	1.059	1.318	1.711	2.064	2.492	2.797	3.745
25	.127	.256	.390	.531	.684	.856	1.058	1.316	1.708	2.060	2.485	2.787	3.725

Appendix B

Degree of freedom	Student's t distribution												
	Level of significance (α)												
	.9	.8	.7	.6	.5	.4	.3	.2	.1	.05	.02	.01	.001
26	.127	.256	.390	.531	.684	.856	1.058	1.315	1.706	2.056	2.479	2.779	3.707
27	.127	.256	.389	.531	.684	.855	1.057	1.314	1.703	2.052	2.473	2.771	3.690
28	.127	.256	.389	.530	.683	.855	1.056	1.313	1.701	2.048	2.467	2.763	3.674
29	.127	.256	.389	.530	.683	.854	1.055	1.311	1.699	2.045	2.462	2.756	3.659
30	.127	.256	.389	.530	.683	.854	1.055	1.310	1.697	2.042	2.457	2.750	3.646
40	.126	.255	.388	.529	.681	.851	1.050	1.303	1.684	2.021	2.423	2.704	3.551
60	.126	.254	.387	.527	.679	.848	1.046	1.296	1.671	2.000	2.390	2.660	3.460
120	.126	.254	.386	.526	.677	.845	1.041	1.289	1.658	1.980	2.358	2.617	3.373
∞	.126	.253	.385	.524	.674	.842	1.036	1.282	1.645	1.960	2.326	2.576	3.291

Appendix C

Probabilities for the Poisson distribution

r	.005	.01	.02	.03	μ .04	.05	.06	.07	.08	.09
0	.9950	.9900	.9802	.9704	.9608	.9512	.9418	.9324	.9231	.9139
1	.0050	.0099	.0192	.0291	.0384	.0476	.0565	.0653	.0738	.0823
2	.0000	.0000	.0002	.0004	.0008	.0012	.0017	.0023	.0030	.0037
3	.0000	.0000	.0000	.0000	.0000	.0000	.0000	.0001	.0001	.0001

r	0.1	0.2	0.3	0.4	μ 0.5	0.6	0.7	0.8	0.9	1.0
0	.9048	.8187	.7408	.6703	.6065	.5488	.4966	.4493	.4066	.3679
1	.0905	.1637	.2222	.2681	.3033	.3293	.3476	.3595	.3659	.3679
2	.0045	.0164	.0333	.0536	.0758	.0988	.1217	.1438	.1647	.1839
3	.0002	.0011	.0033	.0072	.0126	.0198	.0284	.0383	.0494	.0613
4	.0000	.0001	.0002	.0007	.0016	.0030	.0050	.0077	.0111	.0153
5	.0000	.0000	.0000	.0001	.0002	.0004	.0007	.0012	.0020	.0031
6	.0000	.0000	.0000	.0000	.0000	.0000	.0001	.0002	.0003	.0005
7	.0000	.0000	.0000	.0000	.0000	.0000	.0000	.0000	.0000	.0001

r	1.1	1.2	1.3	1.4	μ 1.5	1.6	1.7	1.8	1.9	2.0
0	.3329	.3012	.2725	.2466	.2231	.2019	.1827	.1653	.1496	.1353
1	.3662	.3614	.3543	.3452	.3347	.3230	.3106	.2975	.2842	.2707
2	.2014	.2169	.2303	.2417	.2510	.2584	.2640	.2678	.2700	.2707
3	.0738	.0867	.0998	.1128	.1255	.1378	.1496	.1607	.1710	.1804
4	.0203	.0260	.0324	.0395	.0471	.0551	.0636	.0723	.0812	.0902
5	.0045	.0062	.0084	.0111	.0141	.0176	.0216	.0260	.0309	.0361
6	.0008	.0012	.0018	.0026	.0035	.0047	.0061	.0078	.0098	.0120
7	.0001	.0002	.0003	.0005	.0008	.0011	.0015	.0020	.0027	.0034
8	.0000	.0000	.0001	.0001	.0001	.0002	.0003	.0005	.0006	.0009
9	.0000	.0000	.0000	.0000	.0000	.0000	.0001	.0001	.0001	.0002

r	2.1	2.2	2.3	2.4	μ 2.5	2.6	2.7	2.8	2.9	3.0
0	.1225	.1108	.1003	.0907	.0821	.0743	.0672	.0608	.0550	.0498
1	.2572	.2438	.2306	.2177	.2052	.1931	.1815	.1703	.1596	.1494
2	.2700	.2681	.2652	.2613	.2565	.2510	.2450	.2384	.2314	.2240
3	.1890	.1966	.2033	.2090	.2138	.2176	.2205	.2225	.2237	.2240
4	.0992	.1082	.1169	.1254	.1336	.1414	.1488	.1557	.1622	.1680

Appendix C

r	2.1	2.2	2.3	2.4	μ 2.5	2.6	2.7	2.8	2.9	3.0
5	.0417	.0476	.0538	.0602	.0668	.0735	.0804	.0872	.0940	.1008
6	.0146	.0174	.0206	.0241	.0278	.0319	.0362	.0407	.0455	.0504
7	.0044	.0055	.0068	.0083	.0099	.0118	.0139	.0163	.0188	.0216
8	.0011	.0015	.0019	.0025	.0031	.0038	.0047	.0057	.0068	.0081
9	.0003	.0004	.0005	.0007	.0009	.0011	.0014	.0018	.0022	.0027
10	.0001	.0001	.0001	.0002	.0002	.0003	.0004	.0005	.0006	.0008
11	.0000	.0000	.0000	.0000	.0000	.0001	.0001	.0001	.0002	.0002
12	.0000	.0000	.0000	.0000	.0000	.0000	.0000	.0000	.0000	.0001

r	3.1	3.2	3.3	3.4	μ 3.5	3.6	3.7	3.8	3.9	4.0
0	.0450	.0408	.0369	.0334	.0302	.0273	.0247	.0224	.0202	.0183
1	.1397	.1304	.1217	.1135	.1057	.0984	.0915	.0850	.0789	.0733
2	.2165	.2087	.2008	.1929	.1850	.1771	.1692	.1615	.1539	.1465
3	.2237	.2226	.2209	.2186	.2158	.2125	.2087	.2046	.2001	.1954
4	.1734	.1781	.1823	.1858	.1888	.1912	.1931	.1944	.1951	.1954
5	.1075	.1140	.1203	.1264	.1322	.1377	.1429	.1477	.1522	.1563
6	.0555	.0608	.0662	.0716	.0771	.0826	.0881	.0936	.0989	.1042
7	.0246	.0278	.0312	.0348	.0385	.0425	.0466	.0508	.0551	.0595
8	.0095	.0111	.0129	.0148	.0169	.0191	.0215	.0241	.0269	.0298
9	.0033	.0040	.0047	.0056	.0066	.0076	.0089	.0102	.0116	.0132
10	.0010	.0013	.0016	.0019	.0023	.0028	.0033	.0039	.0045	.0053
11	.0003	.0004	.0005	.0006	.0007	.0009	.0011	.0013	.0016	.0019
12	.0001	.0001	.0001	.0002	.0002	.0003	.0003	.0004	.0005	.0006
13	.0000	.0000	.0000	.0000	.0001	.0001	.0001	.0001	.0002	.0002
14	.0000	.0000	.0000	.0000	.0000	.0000	.0000	.0000	.0000	.0001

r	4.1	4.2	4.3	4.4	μ 4.5	4.6	4.7	4.8	4.9	5.0
0	.0166	.0150	.0136	.0123	.0111	.0101	.0091	.0082	.0074	.0067
1	.0679	.0630	.0583	.0540	.0500	.0462	.0427	.0395	.0365	.0337
2	.1393	.1323	.1254	.1188	.1125	.1063	.1005	.0948	.0894	.0842
3	.1904	.1852	.1798	.1743	.1687	.1631	.1574	.1517	.1460	.1404
4	.1951	.1944	.1933	.1917	.1898	.1875	.1849	.1820	.1789	.1755
5	.1600	.1633	.1662	.1687	.1708	.1725	.1738	.1747	.1753	.1755
6	.1093	.1143	.1191	.1237	.1281	.1323	.1362	.1398	.1432	.1462
7	.0640	.0686	.0732	.0778	.0824	.0869	.0914	.0959	.1002	.1044
8	.0328	.0360	.0393	.0428	.0463	.0500	.0537	.0575	.0614	.0653
9	.0150	.0168	.0188	.0209	.0232	.0255	.0280	.0307	.0334	.0363
10	.0061	.0071	.0081	.0092	.0104	.0118	.0132	.0147	.0164	.0181
11	.0023	.0027	.0032	.0037	.0043	.0049	.0056	.0064	.0073	.0082
12	.0008	.0009	.0011	.0014	.0016	.0019	.0022	.0026	.0030	.0034
13	.0002	.0003	.0004	.0005	.0006	.0007	.0008	.0009	.0011	.0013
14	.0001	.0001	.0001	.0001	.0002	.0002	.0003	.0003	.0004	.0005
15	.0000	.0000	.0000	.0000	.0001	.0001	.0001	.0001	.0001	.0002

r	5.1	5.2	5.3	5.4	μ 5.5	5.6	5.7	5.8	5.9	6.0
0	.0061	.0055	.0050	.0045	.0041	.0037	.0033	.0030	.0027	.0025
1	.0311	.0287	.0265	.0244	.0225	.0207	.0191	.0176	.0162	.0149
2	.0793	.0746	.0701	.0659	.0618	.0580	.0544	.0509	.0477	.0446
3	.1348	.1293	.1239	.1185	.1133	.1082	.1033	.0985	.0938	.0892
4	.1719	.1681	.1641	.1600	.1558	.1515	.1472	.1428	.1383	.1339
5	.1753	.1748	.1740	.1728	.1714	.1697	.1678	.1656	.1632	.1606
6	.1490	.1515	.1537	.1555	.1571	.1584	.1594	.1601	.1605	.1606
7	.1086	.1125	.1163	.1200	.1234	.1267	.1298	.1326	.1353	.1377
8	.0692	.0731	.0771	.0810	.0849	.0887	.0925	.0962	.0998	.1033
9	.0392	.0423	.0454	.0486	.0519	.0552	.0586	.0620	.0654	.0688
10	.0200	.0220	.0241	.0262	.0285	.0309	.0334	.0359	.0386	.0413
11	.0093	.0104	.0116	.0129	.0143	.0157	.0173	.0190	.0207	.0225
12	.0039	.0045	.0051	.0058	.0065	.0073	.0082	.0092	.0102	.0113
13	.0015	.0018	.0021	.0024	.0028	.0032	.0036	.0041	.0046	.0052
14	.0006	.0007	.0008	.0009	.0011	.0013	.0015	.0017	.0019	.0022
15	.0002	.0002	.0003	.0003	.0004	.0005	.0006	.0007	.0008	.0009
16	.0001	.0001	.0001	.0001	.0001	.0002	.0002	.0002	.0003	.0003
17	.0000	.0000	.0000	.0000	.0000	.0001	.0001	.0001	.0001	.0001

r	6.1	6.2	6.3	6.4	μ 6.5	6.6	6.7	6.8	6.9	7.0
0	.0022	.0020	.0018	.0017	.0015	.0014	.0012	.0011	.0010	.0009
1	.0137	.0126	.0116	.0106	.0098	.0090	.0082	.0076	.0070	.0064
2	.0417	.0390	.0364	.0340	.0318	.0296	.0276	.0258	.0240	.0223
3	.0848	.0806	.0765	.0726	.0688	.0652	.0617	.0584	.0552	.0521
4	.1294	.1249	.1205	.1162	.1118	.1076	.1034	.0992	.0952	.0912
5	.1579	.1549	.1519	.1487	.1454	.1420	.1385	.1349	.1314	.1277
6	.1605	.1601	.1595	.1586	.1575	.1562	.1546	.1529	.1511	.1490
7	.1399	.1418	.1435	.1450	.1462	.1472	.1480	.1486	.1489	.1490
8	.1066	.1099	.1130	.1160	.1188	.1215	.1240	.1263	.1284	.1304
9	.0723	.0757	.0791	.0825	.0858	.0891	.0923	.0954	.0985	.1014
10	.0441	.0469	.0498	.0528	.0558	.0588	.0618	.0649	.0679	.0710
11	.0245	.0265	.0285	.0307	.0330	.0353	.0377	.0401	.0426	.0452
12	.0124	.0137	.0150	.0164	.0179	.0194	.0210	.0227	.0245	.0264
13	.0058	.0065	.0073	.0081	.0089	.0098	.0108	.0119	.0130	.0142
14	.0025	.0029	.0033	.0037	.0041	.0046	.0052	.0058	.0064	.0071
15	.0010	.0012	.0014	.0016	.0018	.0020	.0023	.0026	.0029	.0033
16	.0004	.0005	.0005	.0006	.0007	.0008	.0010	.0011	.0013	.0014
17	.0001	.0002	.0002	.0002	.0003	.0003	.0004	.0004	.0005	.0006
18	.0000	.0001	.0001	.0001	.0001	.0001	.0001	.0002	.0002	.0002
19	.0000	.0000	.0000	.0000	.0000	.0000	.0000	.0001	.0001	.0001

Index

Index

Index